# JEWS IN THE MEDITERRANEAN DIASPORA

THE S. MARK TAPER FOUNDATION

IMPRINT IN JEWISH STUDIES

BY THIS ENDOWMENT
THE S. MARK TAPER FOUNDATION SUPPORTS
THE APPRECIATION AND UNDERSTANDING
OF THE RICHNESS AND DIVERSITY OF
JEWISH LIFE AND CULTURE

# JEWS IN THE MEDITERRANEAN DIASPORA

## FROM ALEXANDER TO TRAJAN
### (323 BCE – 117 CE)

JOHN M. G. BARCLAY

University of California Press
Berkeley        Los Angeles        London

*The publisher gratefully acknowledges the
generous contribution to this book provided by
The S. Mark Taper Foundation.*

University of California Press
Berkeley and Los Angeles, California

University of California Press Ltd
London, England

Published by arrangement with T&T Clark Ltd
59 George Street, Edinburgh EH2 2LQ, Scotland

First published 1996

9  8  7  6  5  4  3  2  1

ISBN 0–520–21843–4

Typesetting by Trinity Typesetting, Edinburgh
Printed and bound in Great Britain by Bell & Bain Ltd, Glasgow

092399–21964H6

*For Diana*

# HELLENISTIC CULTURE AND SOCIETY

*General Editors:*
Anthony W. Bulloch, Erich S. Gruen, A. A. Long, and Andrew F. Stewart

I. *Alexander to Actium: The Historical Evolution of the Hellenistic Age,*
by Peter Green

IV. *Antigonos the One-Eyed and the Creation of the Hellenistic State,*
by Richard A. Billows

VII. *The Vanished Library: A Wonder of the Ancient World,*
by Luciano Canfora

X. *The Best of the Argonauts: The Redefinition of the Epic Hero in
Book One of Apollonius' Argonautica,*
by James J. Clauss

XII. *Images and Ideologies: Self-definition in the Hellenistic World,*
edited by A. W. Bulloch, E. S. Gruen, A. A. Long, and A. Stewart

XV. *Hegemony to Empire: The Development of the Roman Imperium
in the East from 148 to 62 B.C.,*
by Robert Kallet-Marx

XVIII. *Interstate Arbitrations in the Greek World, 337–90 B.C.,*
by Sheila L. Ager

XXI. *Pseudo-Hecataeus, "On the Jews": Legitimizing the Jewish Diaspora,*
by Bezalel Bar-Kochva

XXIV. *The Politics of Plunder: Aitolians and Their* Koinon
*in the Early Hellenistic Era, 279–217 B.C.,*
by Joseph B. Scholten

XXVII. *Josephus' Interpretation of the Bible,* by Louis H. Feldman

XXX. *Heritage and Hellenism: The Reinvention of Jewish Tradition,*
by Erich S. Gruen

XXXIII. *Jews in the Mediterranean Diaspora from Alexander to Trajan
(323 BCE–117 CE),*
by John M. G. Barclay

# Contents

Preface     xi

Abbreviations     xiii

Chapter 1: *Introduction*     1
1.1   A Distinguished People     1
1.2   Current Study of the Diaspora     4
1.3   The Scope, Plan and Spirit of This Study     9

## PART ONE: THE DIASPORA IN EGYPT

Chapter 2: *Jews in Ptolemaic Egypt*     19
2.1   Immigration and Settlement: From Alexander to
    Ptolemy V Epiphanes (323–180 BCE)     20
      2.1.1 Immigration     20
      2.1.2 Settlement in the *chora*     23
      2.1.3 Settlement in Alexandria     27

2.2   Prominence and Exposure: From Ptolemy VI
    Philometor to Cleopatra VII (180–30 BCE)     35
      2.2.1 Political Developments     35
      2.2.2 Social Developments     41

Chapter 3: *Jews in Roman Egypt: From Augustus to Trajan
    (30 BCE – 117 CE)*     48
3.1   The Alexandrian Pogrom and Its Aftermath     48
      3.1.1 The Alexandrian Pogrom     51
      3.1.2 The Embassies and Claudius' Response     55
    Excursus: The Legal Status of Alexandrian Jews     60

3.2    Jewish Alienation                                              72
3.3    Jewish Revolt                                                  78


Chapter 4: *Jews in a Diaspora Environment: Some Analytical Tools*  82
4.1    Introduction                                                   82
4.2    'Orthodoxy' and 'Deviation'                                    83
4.3    Jews and Hellenization                                         88
4.4    Assimilation, Acculturation and Accommodation                 92
4.5    Analysing the Evidence                                         98


Chapter 5: *Levels of Assimilation among Egyptian Jews*            103
5.1    High Assimilation                                             103
5.2    Medium Assimilation                                           112
5.3    Low Assimilation                                              117
5.4    Unknown Assimilation                                          119


Chapter 6: *Cultural Convergence*                                  125
6.1    Artapanus                                                     127
6.2    Ezekiel                                                       132
6.3    The Letter of Aristeas                                        138
6.4    Aristobulus                                                   150
6.5    Philo                                                         158
          6.5.1 Philo's Social Context                               158
          6.5.2 Mosaic Philosophy                                    163
          6.5.3 Allegory                                             165
          6.5.4 Israel and the Human Race                            170
          6.5.5 Philo and the Jewish Community                       176


Chapter 7: *Cultural Antagonism*                                   181
7.1    The Wisdom of Solomon                                         181
7.2    3 Maccabees                                                   192
7.3    Joseph and Aseneth                                            204
7.4    The Egyptian Sibylline Oracles                                216

PART TWO: THE DIASPORA IN OTHER MEDITERRANEAN SITES

Chapter 8: *Cyrenaica and Syria*                     231
8.1   Cyrenaica                                      232
8.2   Syria                                          242
       8.2.1 The Hellenistic Era                     244
       8.2.2 The Roman Era                           249


Chapter 9: *The Province of Asia*                    259


Chapter 10: *Rome*                                   282
10.1  Republican Rome                                285
10.2  The Augustan Era                               292
10.3  From Tiberius to Claudius                      298
10.4  From Nero to Trajan                            306


Chapter 11: *Levels of Assimilation among Diaspora Jews
       Outside Egypt*                                320
11.1  High Assimilation                              321
11.2  Medium Assimilation                            326
11.3  Low Assimilation                               331
11.4  Unknown Assimilation                           332


Chapter 12: *Cultural Convergence and Cultural Antagonism
       Outside Egypt*                                336
12.1  Pseudo-Phocylides                              336
12.2  Josephus                                       346
       12.2.1 Josephus' Social Context               346
       12.2.2 *Bellum Iudaicum*                      351
       12.2.3 *Antiquitates Iudaicae*                356
       12.2.4 *Contra Apionem*                       361
12.3  4 Maccabees                                    369


Chapter 13: *Paul: an Anomalous Diaspora Jew*        381

PART THREE: JEWISH IDENTITY IN THE MEDITERRANEAN
    DIASPORA

Chapter 14: *Jewish Identity in the Diaspora: A Sketch*          399
14.1  The Ethnic Bond                                            402
14.2  Social and Symbolic Resources                              413
        14.2.1 The Local Community                               414
        14.2.2 Links with Jerusalem, the 'Homeland'
              and other Diaspora Communities                     418
        14.2.3 The Law/Jewish Scriptures                         424
        14.2.4 The Figure of Moses                               426
14.3  Practical Distinctions                                     428
        14.3.1 Rejection of Alien, Pluralist and Iconic Cult     429
        14.3.2 Separatism at Meals                               434
        14.3.3 Male Circumcision                                 438
        14.3.4 Sabbath Observance                                440
14.4  Conclusion                                                 442


Appendix on Sources                                              445


Bibliography                                                     453


Index of Main Subjects and Places                                491


Index of References                                              496


Index of Modern Authors                                          518

# Preface

This book constitutes the result of a voyage of discovery which has occupied me (in whatever research time I could seize) for more than six years, the most demanding and the most exciting research project I have yet undertaken. I began with the aim of comparing Diaspora Jewish communities with early Christian (especially Pauline) churches, but the first half of the project became so absorbing as to grow to its present size. (I hope to return to its second half, the Pauline churches, in due course.) There have been moments when the sheer scale of the project threatened to overwhelm me – not least when midway through Philo! – but the opportunity to engage continually with primary sources has been my greatest stimulus and pleasure throughout. The further I got into the project, the more I recognized the need for a comprehensive and multi-faceted survey of the Mediterranean Diaspora, which could combine historical and literary studies while approaching the material with sensitivity to the social issues faced by minority ethnic groups. I hope here to have provided such a survey in a form which is useful both to scholars and to students in the field. I have drawn on contemporary scholarship in each specialized sphere of study, but I have also attempted to offer new readings of Jewish history and of the main Diaspora literature arising out of my own fresh engagement with the sources.

The foundations of the project were laid during a period of sabbatical leave in 1990, which was spent in Princeton Theological Seminary. I am grateful to the University of Glasgow for granting me that leave, to the Leverhulme Trust for a Research Award enabling me to travel to Princeton, and to the Seminary for enabling me to live and work on the campus for six months. A special feature of that time was the warmth of welcome I and my family received from Joel Marcus and Martin de Boer and their families. Subsequently, Joel Marcus came to work alongside me in Glasgow and I owe a huge debt to him for so willingly reading drafts of most of this book and for commenting on them with extraordinary acumen. More than that, his good humour and continual encouragement have seen me through many a period when I despaired of ever finishing this project.

Other scholars who have kindly read and commented on parts of this book include William Horbury, Paul Trebilco, Steve Mason, Lester Grabbe, Margaret Williams, Folker Siegert and Alexander Broadie. They have each helped me to clarify and improve my work, although remaining errors of judgment remain, of course, my own responsibility. My colleagues John Riches and Robert Carroll have encouraged and aided me along the way, while my Glasgow students have shown exemplary tolerance towards me as a member of the English Diaspora still assimilating to Glaswegian ways. At the final stages of the work Eddie Adams provided invaluable assistance in checking primary references in most chapters, funded by a small grant from the University of Glasgow.

In many respects the roots of this project go back to my initial introduction to Greek and Latin at University College School, London. There my interest in ancient literature and history was kindled by Dr H. J. K. Usher, a remarkable scholar and teacher. I am greatly indebted to him and to my subsequent classics mentors at Queens' College, Cambridge, for opening up a world which continues to fascinate me.

However, my greatest personal debt is to my wife, Diana, to whom I dedicate this book with great affection. She has had to endure much in the interests of this project, not least its continual absorption of my evenings and weekends. For her tolerance and loving support, and for that shown by Robert, David and Frances for their sometimes distracted father, I am deeply grateful.

4 July 1995

# Abbreviations

All items of bibliography have been cited by author and date (with full details in the final Bibliography), with the exception of the following, which are cited by author only (full details in Bibliography):

Goodenough = E. R. Goodenough, *Jewish Symbols in the Graeco-Roman Period* (cited by volume and page number)

Horbury & Noy = W. Horbury and D. Noy, *Jewish Inscriptions of Graeco-Roman Egypt* (number indicates the number of the inscription)

Lüderitz = G. Lüderitz (with Appendix by J. Reynolds), *Corpus jüdischer Zeugnisse aus der Cyrenaika* (number indicates the number of the inscription)

Noy = D. Noy, *Jewish Inscriptions of Western Europe, Volume 1* (number indicates the number of the inscription)

Schürer = the revised edition of E. Schürer, *The History of the Jewish People in the Age of Jesus Christ* (cited by volume and page number)

Stern = *Greek and Latin Authors on Jews and Judaism* (number alone [e.g. Stern 363] indicates number of the document in this collection; otherwise cited by volume and page number [e.g. Stern 2.125 = volume 2, page 125])

Primary sources are either unabbreviated or follow standard abbrevations.

Thus Josephus,  *Ant = Antiquitates Iudaicae*
  *Bell = Bellum Iudaicum*
  *C Ap = Contra Apionem*

Philo tractates are cited as follows:
*Abr*  *De Abrahamo*
*Aet*  *De Aeternitate Mundi*

| | |
|---|---|
| *Agr* | *De Agricultura* |
| *Anim* | *De Animalibus* |
| *Cher* | *De Cherubim* |
| *Conf* | *De Confusione Linguarum* |
| *Cong* | *De Congressu quaerendae Eruditionis gratia* |
| *Decal* | *De Decalogo* |
| *Det* | *Quod Deterius Potiori insidiari soleat* |
| *Deus* | *Quod Deus Immutabilis sit* |
| *Ebr* | *De Ebrietate* |
| *Flacc* | *In Flaccum* |
| *Fug* | *De Fuga et Inventione* |
| *Gig* | *De Gigantibus* |
| *Heres* | *Quis Rerum Divinarum Heres* |
| *Hyp* | *Hypothetica (Apologia pro Iudaeis)* |
| *Jos* | *De Iosepho* |
| *Leg All* | *Legum Allegoriae* |
| *Legatio* | *De Legatione ad Gaium* |
| *Mig Abr* | *De Migratione Abrahami* |
| *Mos* | *De Vita Mosis* |
| *Mut* | *De Mutatione Nominum* |
| *Op Mund* | *De Opificio Mundi* |
| *Plant* | *De Plantatione* |
| *Post* | *De Posteritate Caini* |
| *Praem* | *De Praemiis et Poenis* |
| *Probus* | *Quod Omnis Probus Liber sit* |
| *Prov* | *De Providentia* |
| *Quaest Gen* | *Quaestiones et Solutiones in Genesin* |
| *Quaest Exod* | *Quaestiones et Solutiones in Exodum* |
| *Sacr* | *De Sacrificiis Abelis et Caini* |
| *Sobr* | *De Sobrietate* |
| *Somn* | *De Somniis* |
| *Spec Leg* | *De Specialibus Legibus* |
| *Virt* | *De Virtutibus* |
| *Vit Cont* | *De Vita Contemplativa* |

## Other Abbrevations:

| | |
|---|---|
| *AJPh* | *American Journal of Philology* |
| *ANRW* | *Aufstieg und Niedergang der römischen Welt*, ed. H. Temporini and W. Haase, Berlin: de Gruyter, 1972– |

| | |
|---|---|
| *BGU* | *Aegyptische Urkunden aus den Staatlichen Museen zu Berlin, Griechische Urkunden* |
| *BJRL* | *Bulletin of the John Rylands Library* |
| *CAP* | A. E. Cowley, *Aramaic Papyri of the Fifth Century B.C.* (see Bibliography; cited by papyrus number) |
| *CBQ* | *Catholic Biblical Quarterly* |
| *CIG* | *Corpus Inscriptionum Graecarum* |
| *CIJ* | J.-B. Frey, *Corpus Inscriptionum Iudaicarum* (see Bibliography; number alone indicates inscription number; otherwise cited by volume and page number) |
| *CP* | *Classical Philology* |
| *CPJ* | V. Tcherikover and A. Fuks, *Corpus Papyrorum Judaicarum* (see Bibliography; number alone indicates papyrus number in this collection; otherwise cited by volume and page number [e.g. 1.13]) |
| *CQ* | *Classical Quarterly* |
| *HTR* | *Harvard Theological Review* |
| *HUCA* | *Hebrew Union College Annual* |
| *IGRR* | R. Cagnat et al., *Inscriptiones Graecae ad Res Romanas Pertinentes* |
| *JAC* | *Jahrbuch für Antike und Christentum* |
| *JBL* | *Journal of Biblical Literature* |
| *JJS* | *Journal of Jewish Studies* |
| *JQR* | *Jewish Quarterly Review* |
| *JRS* | *Journal of Roman Studies* |
| *JSHRZ* | W. Kümmel (ed.), *Jüdische Schriften aus hellenistisch-römischer Zeit*, Gütersloh: Gerd Mohn, 1973- |
| *JSJ* | *Journal for the Study of Judaism* |
| *JSNT* | *Journal for the Study of the New Testament* |
| *JSP* | *Journal for the Study of the Pseudepigrapha* |
| *JSS* | *Jewish Social Studies* |
| *JTS* | *Journal of Theological Studies* |
| LXX | The Septuagint |
| *MAMA* | *Monumenta Asiae Minoris Antiqua* |
| *OGIS* | W. Dittenberger, *Orientis Graeci Inscriptiones Selectae*, 2 vols., Leipzig 1903, 1905 |
| *OTP* | J. Charlesworth (ed.), *Old Testament Pseudepigrapha*, 2 vols., London: Darton, Longman & Todd, 1983, 1985 |
| *PEQ* | *Palestine Exploration Quarterly* |

| | |
|---|---|
| *PGM* | K. Preisendanz, *Papyri Graecae Magicae*, 2 vols., Berlin/Leipzig: Teubner, 1928, 1931 |
| *PW* | *Paulys Real-Encyclopädie der classischen Altertumswissenschaft,* Stuttgart/München, 1894–1972 |
| *NovT* | *Novum Testamentum* |
| *NTS* | *New Testament Studies* |
| *RB* | *Revue Biblique* |
| *REJ* | *Revue des Etudes Juives* |
| *SEG* | *Supplementum Epigraphicum Graecum* |
| *VC* | *Vigiliae Christianae* |
| *VT* | *Vetus Testamentum* |
| *ZNW* | *Zeitschrift für die neutestamentliche Wissenschaft* |
| *ZPE* | *Zeitschrift für Papyrologie und Epigraphik* |

THE MEDITERRANEAN DIASPORA:
main sites mentioned in the text

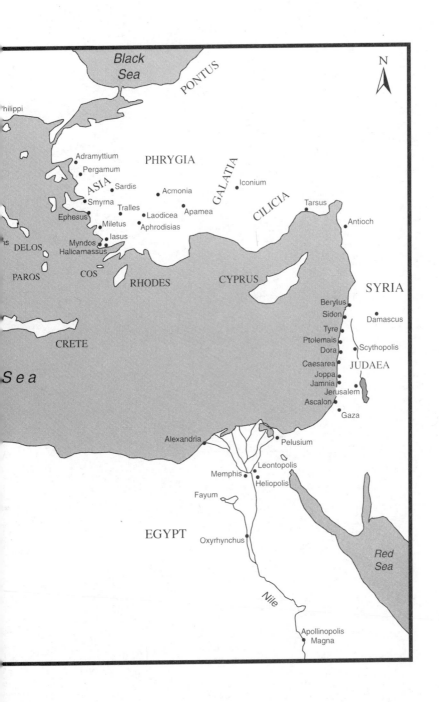

# 1

## Introduction

Behold, a people who will dwell alone,
And will not be reckoned among the nations.
(Numbers 23.9)

### 1.1 A Distinguished People

Balaam's oracle, cited above, encapsulates the sense of distinction which lies at the heart of the Jewish tradition. When, in the third century BCE, the Septuagint translators rendered this prophecy into Greek, they did not alter its sense, although they 'modernized' much else in the accompanying oracles. Their conservatism is striking: they were translating for a Jewish community not at all geographically segregated, but already well established in the cosmopolitan city of Alexandria. What did it mean for Jews in Alexandria, or in other Diaspora locations, to consider themselves 'a people who will dwell alone'? In what sense, if any, were they distinguished in their local environments? And, if Jewish distinction was preserved, how was it expressed, maintained and validated?

Two Jews from the Mediterranean Diaspora suggest answers to such questions in their exegesis of Balaam's oracle. The first is Philo, an Alexandrian Jewish philosopher of the early first century CE, a man steeped in Hellenistic culture but also resolutely faithful to the Jewish community. In recounting the story of Balaam, Philo has the seer add an important interpretative gloss to his blessing of this 'people who will dwell alone'. According to Philo's Balaam, their separation will not be territorial ('by the demarcation of land') but will be effected by

> the particularity of their exceptional customs, not mixing with others to alter the ancestral ways. (*Mos* 1.278)

1

For Philo, Jewish distinction could not be a matter of geography.
By his time Jews had lived in Alexandria alongside Greeks and
Egyptians for centuries, and he had no reason to doubt that they
would remain there for centuries to come. But even in continual
social interaction with non-Jews it was possible, and necessary, to
retain frontiers, social boundaries constituted by the Jews'
'exceptional customs'. It was through such customs that Jews 'lived
alone', not in isolation from 'other nations' but in a careful
regulation of social intercourse designed to maintain the sense of
'otherness'. Such customs constituted the 'ancestral ways' (τὰ
πάτρια), that precious heritage which represented the ethnic
continuity of this distinguished people. Difference was an
inheritance, a legacy from one's forebears to be bequeathed to
generations to come.

Philo's interpretation of Balaam thus focuses on the Jews' social
distinction. But it invites a host of questions. What were the
'exceptional customs' which functioned as social boundaries in
Alexandria or elsewhere in the Diaspora, and how did they serve
to demarcate Jewish social space? What sort of communities were
created to mark out and police these boundaries? Were all Diaspora
Jews as committed as Philo to such 'ancestral ways', and did no
one 'mix with' others to the extent of altering their inheritance?
In general, how did Diaspora Jews adapt to their local environments
and what sorts of assimilation took place? How did local political
and social conditions affect Jewish communities, and how did these
vary through history and from place to place? To the extent that
'the ancestral ways' were preserved in the Diaspora, what effect
did their preservation have on other groups in the complex social
interactions of the Graeco-Roman world?

A second interpretation of Balaam's oracle is offered by Josephus,
a Palestinian aristocrat required to take up residence in the
Diaspora (Rome) at the end of the first century CE. Josephus'
paraphrase of Balaam's oracles (*Ant* 4.114–17) suggests another
sense of 'distinction'. Here Balaam pronounces the happiness of
this people,

> to whom God gives possession of myriad blessings and has
> granted his own providence as perpetual ally and guide. For
> there is no human race which you will not be adjudged to
> excel in virtue and in the pursuit of the most excellent
> customs, pure from evil; and such things you will bequeath
> to children better than yourselves, God watching over you

alone among humankind and providing you with the means
by which you may become the happiest of all people under
the sun. (*Ant* 4.114)

Although Josephus also highlights Jewish customs, he interprets
the singularity of 'the people who will dwell alone' not simply as
social difference but also as moral pre-eminence and historical
privilege. For Josephus, Jews are a distinguished nation, 'not
reckoned among other nations', because they are morally on a
different plane: they 'excel in virtue', their 'excellent customs'
marking not just a social but also an ethical differentiation.
Moreover, they have a unique relationship with God and a special
claim on his providence by which they are assured a glorious
destiny.

   Josephus' view of Jewish distinction invites us to pay attention
to the ways in which Jews in the Diaspora situated themselves in
their social and cultural contexts. Did all Diaspora Jews share
Josephus' sense of the Jews' moral superiority? In what respects
could they understand themselves to 'excel in virtue', and wherein
lay their critique of their host environments? How did other
Diaspora Jews depict the relationship between their people and
God, and how did they view other ethnic groups? Josephus' key
terms, 'virtue' (ἀρετή) and 'providence' (πρόνοια), are in fact
derived not from his Scriptural but from his Hellenistic education.
What sort of acculturation did he and other Diaspora Jews
undergo? In what respects, and to what degree, did they merge
Jewish and non-Jewish cultural traditions, and how did they employ
such cultural syntheses? If, despite this acculturation, Josephus and
others maintained their Jewish distinction, how did they
appropriate and re-employ the Hellenism they absorbed?

   Balaam's oracle, with its divergent interpretations in Philo and
Josephus, thus poses some key questions about the social and
cultural strategies of Jews in the Mediterranean Diaspora. In fact
the difference at this point between Philo and Josephus suggests
that another dimension of 'distinction' must also be explored: the
distinctions *between* Diaspora Jews. Jews lived in many different
geographical locations, in social conditions which varied over time,
and at differing social levels. We can expect to find an almost
infinite variety in the ways they reacted to their variant milieux. In
fact, if we canvassed Philo's and Josephus' works as a whole, the
differences we have noted would not prove to be symptoms of a
wholly divergent outlook: Philo also thinks that Jews are morally

and providentially distinguished (e.g. *Spec Leg* 4.179–80; *Legatio* 3–4), while Josephus, like Philo, regards the ancestral customs as crucial for maintaining social difference (e.g. *Ant* 1.192). But in other respects Philo and Josephus differ markedly, and we cannot assume that either is necessarily representative of others. Jews were spread in very large numbers over the Mediterranean world,[1] in diverse and ever changing social contexts, ranging in status from the impoverished field-hand to the millionaire imperial favourite. Clearly no single piece of evidence can be taken to represent Diaspora Judaism as a whole.

## 1.2 Current Study of the Diaspora

Our reluctance to generalize about such a complex and variegated phenomenon as the Mediterranean Diaspora reflects an important characteristic of current scholarship on post-biblical Judaism. Jonathan Smith captures the present mood when he advocates abandoning the notion of an 'essence' of early Judaism and proposes 'a dismantling of the old theological and imperialistic impulse toward totalization, unification, and integration'. 'The cartography appears far messier. We need to map the variety of Judaisms, each a shifting cluster of characteristics which vary over time' (1980:19–20). This emphasis on plurality ('Judaisms') derives partly from greater attention to detail in recent studies of Judaism, partly also from our contemporary environment, with its multiple expressions of Judaism. Whether or not we use the plural 'Judaisms' in relation to the Diaspora, the range and diversity of the historical evidence certainly indicate that no normative unity can be assumed. In fact, the present generation has seen a flowering of innovative study of Diaspora Jews and Judaism, making research in this field immensely rewarding. In order to gain a longer perspective on

---

[1] Probably several million by the first century CE, but it is impossible to give even approximate figures. Harnack (1908:4–9) and Juster (1914:1.209–12) were probably right to suggest that vastly more Jews lived in the Diaspora than in the homeland, though their calculations of the total number of Jews in the Roman empire differed (Harnack: 4 to 4.5 million; Juster: 6 to 7 million). They are necessarily dependent on Philo's unreliable figure of 1 million Egyptian Jews (*Flacc* 43) and Josephus' notoriously wayward statistics (cf. *Bell* 2.561 and 7.368). Suitable caution on this matter is expressed by Tcherikover in *CPJ* 1.4 and Stern 1974:119, 122.

our work, it will be helpful to survey some of the achievements of the last century of Diaspora scholarship.[2] The decades either side of the turn of the twentieth century were characterized by a new rigour in historical and literary studies, culminating in the extraordinary achievements of the History of Religions School. In this period texts long known were newly edited or subjected to historical and philological analysis of a wholly new order: Jacob Bernays' study of Pseudo-Phocylides (1885, originally published in 1856) and J. Geffcken's edition of the Sibylline Oracles (1902b) may serve as two outstanding examples in our field. The massive industry of historical scholarship in these years is symbolized by Emil Schürer's *Geschichte des jüdischen Volkes im Zeitalter Jesu Christi* (evolving through successive editions from 1874 to 1909) and Jean Juster's *Les Juifs dans l'Empire Romain* (1914). To this day scholars such as Hugo Willrich and Isaac Heinemann (see Bibliography) remain unsurpassed in their acquaintance with the primary sources and the acuteness of their historical perceptions, even if their conceptual frameworks sometimes now appear dated or even distorted.

But those decades also witnessed the discovery of new data which greatly stimulated Diaspora scholarship. In particular, newly discovered papyri from Egypt opened up fresh perspectives on Jewish existence there, and archaeological discoveries, most notably of the synagogue at Dura Europos and the catacombs in Rome, revealed hitherto unknown facets of Diaspora life. Inevitably it took time for such discoveries to become fully absorbed into the discipline, and they may be said to have had their first definitive treatments in three works produced either side of the Second World War. First, Jean-Baptiste Frey edited the *Corpus Inscriptionum Iudaicarum* (=*CIJ*, vol. 1, 1936, updated by Lifshitz 1975; vol. 2, 1952), gathering inscriptions old and new for the first time in a comprehensive (though not entirely adequate) collection. Secondly, Victor Tcherikover and Alexander Fuks presented the *Corpus Papyrorum Judaicarum* in three magnificent volumes, full of significant comment on each text (=*CPJ*, 1957–1964, the last two volumes published after Tcherikover's death in 1958). Thirdly, Erwin Goodenough produced his *Jewish Symbols in the Graeco-Roman Period* (13 volumes, 1953–68), a massive, and in some respects

---

[2]   For an assessment of recent trends in the study of Judaism in general see Kraft and Nickelsburg 1986.

maverick, attempt to prove the presence in the Diaspora of a Hellenized, non-rabbinic and mystical Judaism.

The generation after the Second World War was in some respects a quiet period for Diaspora studies, not least because the discovery of the Dead Sea Scrolls absorbed attention and focused scholarly interest on Palestinian Judaism. In one respect, however, this was a crucial transitional period, for it brought about the collapse of the old scholarly schema in which the 'Hellenistic Judaism' of the Diaspora had been sharply distinguished from the 'rabbinic' or 'normative' Judaism of Palestine. Goodenough's study was conducted largely within the old framework, and in conflict with those, like Wolfson (1948), who had attempted to squeeze Diaspora evidence into a 'rabbinic' mould. The schema was decisively shattered, however, by Martin Hengel's *Judaism and Hellenism* (1974, first German edition 1968), which indicated that Palestine was 'Hellenized' to some degree from a very early period, and that one cannot draw simple geographical frontiers around a cultural phenomenon like 'Hellenization'. Also in this generation many old stereotypes were demolished, like the notion that Philo's Hellenized Judaism was in some sense debased (see Sandmel 1956), or that Diaspora Judaism failed to exert any social or religious attraction after the rise of Christianity (Simon 1986, first published in 1948). Moreover, with the contribution of noted classicists such as Elias Bickerman and Arnaldo Momigliano (see Bibliography), it was possible to view Jewish existence in the Graeco-Roman world in a wider historical perspective. Mary Smallwood's classic, *The Jews under Roman Rule from Pompey to Diocletian* (1981, first edition 1976), synthesized much of the historical work to date, providing a valuable conspectus of political realities both in Palestine and in the Diaspora.

In the last twenty-five years the momentum of research on Judaism in the Hellenistic-Roman period has gathered pace to an extraordinary degree, and has borne much fruit in Diaspora studies. The re-edition of Schürer, updated by a team of Jewish and Christian scholars (1973–87), and the publishing of the multi-confessional *Compendia Rerum Iudaicarum ad Novum Testamentum* (1974– ), indicate the collaborative work being undertaken in this field. The sprouting of new monograph series, journals and academic centres, and the creation of the electronic bulletin-board IOUDAIOS, also demonstrate the new surge of energy. Although some textbooks largely limit their treatment of 'Judaism' to its history and literature in Palestine (e.g. Sanders 1992; Grabbe 1992;

Wright 1992:145–338), very important advances have been made specifically in the study of Diaspora Judaism, on which this book is heavily dependent. We may divide these into four categories:

1. In the first instance, the *non-literary sources* have gained new prominence either through new editions of old material or through the discovery and publication of new finds. The Jewish inscriptions from Egypt have been magnificiently re-edited by William Horbury and David Noy (1992), and the latter has also produced an equivalent volume of material from Western Europe (1993). These have now eclipsed the relevant parts of Frey's *CIJ*, while Gert Lüderitz has published a definitive edition of old and new inscriptional material from Cyrenaica (1983). Not suprisingly, such evidence is beginning to play a prominent part in new studies of the Diaspora (van der Horst 1991; van Henten and van der Horst 1994). But there have also taken place new archaeological discoveries which have given enormous stimulus to scholarship, notably the synagogue at Sardis (see Seager and Kraabel 1983) and the *stele* listing Jews and 'God-fearers' at Aphrodisias (Reynolds and Tannenbaum 1987). These, together with occasional new papyri, have helped to re-open old questions and have required scholars to revise many former assumptions about relations between Jews and Gentiles in the Diaspora.

2. The past twenty-five years have also seen a flurry of *editions and translations of Diaspora literature* bringing it better into the scholarly mainstream. Carl Holladay's editions of fragmentary texts (1983, 1989), Pieter van der Horst's edition of Pseudo-Phocylides (1978), and Howard Jacobson's of the *Exagōgē* by Ezekiel (1983) are just three examples of many in this field, while the scholarly industry on Josephus and Philo has witnessed phenomenal growth. Previously inaccessible texts have also been made more widely available by the appearance of large-scale collections in translation, such as *The Old Testament Pseudepigrapha* (Charlesworth 1983, 1985) and the series *Jüdische Schriften aus hellenistisch-römischer Zeit* (ed. Kümmel et al., 1973– ). Meanwhile, Menahem Stern's monumental *Greek and Latin Authors on Jews and Judaism* (3 volumes, 1974–84) has provided an invaluable resource for the study of attitudes towards Jews in the Graeco-Roman world (replacing Reinach 1895).

3. There have also begun to appear new *full-length investigations of Jews in particular Diaspora locations*. Shimon Applebaum's study of

Jews in Cyrene (1979) was the first in this series, though it is soon to be supplemented or replaced by a volume promised from Gert Lüderitz (announced in Lüderitz 1994:212 n.74). Egyptian Jews were the subject of a full-length, though problematic, study by Aryeh Kasher (1985), and their history has been surveyed in an engaging manner by Joseph Mélèze Modrzejewski (1991). Paul Trebilco has published a fine study of Jewish communities in Asia Minor (1991), on which topic more is due to appear by Irina Levinskaya (1996). Finally the older work on Roman Jews by Harry Leon (1960) has been updated in relation to the third and fourth centuries CE by Leonard Rutgers (1995).

4. Alongside such foundational work in the study of texts and local conditions, the present scholarly climate is characterized by a refreshing *willingness to reopen old questions* and a strong resistance to patterns of consensus inherited from the past. Several important trends have emerged which have helped to refocus scholarly activity. We may mention just four:

(i) A new critical spirit abounds which resists the temptation to fill the gaps in our evidence, and questions the adequacy and accuracy of the evidence we possess. Scholars are now unwilling to take sources on trust, or to transfer conclusions drawn from one Diaspora site to another. The new scholarly mood rightly demands humility in the face of our ignorance, even when new evidence fills in parts of hitherto enormous gaps.

(ii) As we have already noted, there is a corresponding resistance to hidden assumptions of a unitary or univocal Judaism. The Diaspora cannot be assumed to be congruent with the thought and practice of Jews in Palestine, nor can Philo be taken to represent the views of all 'Hellenistic Jews'. John Collins' survey of Diaspora literature, *Between Athens and Jerusalem* (1986), nicely reflects this mood, suggesting that Diaspora Jews defined their identity in many different ways, some national and political, some ethical, philosophical or even mystical. The wide range of literature canvassed, and the determination to let the texts define their own understanding of Judaism, signify important developments in this area. To ask how Diaspora Jews related to their social and cultural environments is now a genuinely open question, with no (or at least fewer) preconceived answers.

(iii) Particular attention has been devoted to the question of the social roles of Jews in their Diaspora environments. Old notions of 'orthodoxy' have been challenged, as well as the assumption that faithful Jews lived largely in social isolation (Kraabel 1982). In fact, new evidence (e.g. from Sardis and Aphrodisias), together with new assessment of the old, suggests that Jews were by no means universally despised or isolated, and the mixture of philo-Jewish and anti-Jewish attitudes in the Graeco-Roman world has had to be reassessed (Gager 1983). In this connection, the existence and significance of the so-called 'God-fearers' has been re-examined (Kraabel 1981; Cohen 1989), as has the notion of an organized Jewish mission to Gentiles (McKnight 1991 and Goodman 1994). Louis Feldman's massive *Jews and Gentiles in the Ancient World* (1993) has surveyed such questions afresh, though not to the satisfaction of all.

(iv) Finally, the Jewish Diaspora is increasingly studied in relation to the wider context of Graeco-Roman society and religion. Diaspora Jews can be usefully compared with other ethnic 'Diasporas', and their conditions better appreciated through a deeper understanding of society, religion and culture in their particular localities (Goudriaan 1992; Cohen and Frerichs 1993). From this perspective Judaism and Christianity may also be viewed alongside each other as ambiguously related minority cults in a vast religious mosaic (Lieu, North and Rajak 1992). Indeed, precisely where to place early Christians alongside Diaspora Jews is an intriguing problem, and there are grounds for studying figures such as Paul alongside other representatives of first century CE Judaism (Tomson 1990; Segal 1990; cf. Boccaccini 1991).

These aspects of the current study of the Diaspora represent its present vitality and indicate the potential for much fresh research. They will all be seen to contribute in important ways to the present volume, whose aims and scope must now be explained.

## 1.3 The Scope, Plan and Spirit of This Study

My aim in this study is to provide a *comprehensive* and *multi-faceted* survey of Jews in the Mediterranean Diaspora from 323 BCE to 117 CE. While individual studies of Diaspora texts or Diaspora locations abound, scholars and students lack at present a comprehensive survey of the field and in particular one which combines *study of the history of Jewish communities in the Diaspora* with *analysis of the main Diaspora literature*. My goal is to examine how Jews reacted to their political, social and cultural environments in the Diaspora, and for this purpose we need to view both their social and political experiences and the varied modes of accommodation or resistance which they adopted in their lives and literature. Thus in this study I will provide a new and detailed analysis of Jewish experience in the Mediterranean Diaspora in all its well-documented locations. I will also examine afresh a range of Diaspora literature in order to illuminate the fascinating range of socio-cultural stances adopted by Diaspora Jews. In the process I have aimed not simply to gather well-established opinions, but to examine all the primary evidence anew; as a result, I will propose at several points new readings of Diaspora history and literature.

Though broad in scope, this study has to operate within certain limits. As the title indicates, my object of study is the *Mediterranean Diaspora*, that is, Jews outside their homeland in the territories bordering the Mediterranean Sea (thus not the eastern, Babylonian Diaspora, nor that situated on the Euxine [Black] Sea). Though this brief might still appear impossibly large, in practice the nature of the evidence available from our period of interest limits our study to a few geographical areas. There are, in fact, only *five locations* in the Mediterranean Diaspora in this period where our literary and/or archaeological evidence is sufficient for us to describe the Jewish Diaspora in any depth: Egypt, Cyrenaica, the province of Syria, the province of Asia and the city of Rome. Only in these locations can we provide a coherent account of the history of the Jewish communities over an extended period of time, and only here does our literary and non-literary evidence combine to give us a moderately full view of Diaspora life.

Even in these five locations, there are, as we shall see, large gaps in our knowledge, leaving huge questions unanswerable; only Egypt, in fact, gives us anything like sufficient material to describe a Diaspora community 'in the round'. But all five stand in a clearly different category from any other Mediterranean location. As Jewish and non-Jewish sources attest, by the turn of the era Jews had spread into very many cities and islands around the Mediterranean basin.[3] Besides the five locations we will study, we know that by the end of our period of study there were Jews in other provinces of Asia Minor (including Cilicia, Lycia, Pamphylia, Pisidia and Pontus), in Macedonia and Greece, in the islands of

---

[3]   The claims of Philo in *Legatio* 281–82 are more or less matched by Strabo *apud* Josephus, *Ant* 14.115 and Luke in Acts 2.9–11, though an element of hyperbole may infect them all.

Cyprus, Crete, Rhodes, Delos, Euboea and Cos, in Illyricum and in many sites in Italy; from the second century CE onwards, we know of Jews in the North African provinces of Africa proconsularis, Numidia and Mauretania, and in Spain and southern Gaul (see Schürer 3.1–86). But in most of these places we have only tiny fragments of information – a small number of inscriptions or the odd literary reference. Valuable as is every item of evidence for the full composite picture, only in the five places named can anything approaching a satisfactory portrait be drawn. In fact, the five which we will study will prove to be sufficiently diverse to indicate how variable were the experiences and responses of Diaspora Jews.

In studying the Mediterranean Diaspora, I have chosen to impose certain *chronological limits* which make sense in relation to the historical evidence available. The starting-point is unproblematic. Although Jews undoubtedly lived outside their homeland for centuries before Alexander the Great, we know almost nothing about them. Alexander's conquests redrew the Mediterranean map so drastically, and brought so many Jews into Egypt in particular, that his death in 323 BCE may sensibly mark the start of our investigation. In fact, as we shall see, it is only in Egypt that we can trace the history of Diaspora Jews for the two centuries after that point. But those two centuries produced such a flowering in Egyptian Jewish life and literature as to give us our best insights into the Hellenization of Diaspora Jews.

The end-point of our survey is rather harder to fix. In Rome there has been no 'end' to the Jewish Diaspora from its foundation to the present day, so that any choice of closure in a historical survey will seem somewhat arbitrary. I have chosen to finish my survey with the death of Trajan (117 CE) for two reasons: i) In this year, as we shall see, the Diaspora communities in Egypt and Cyrenaica were almost totally destroyed in the Diaspora Revolt, so that it is natural to finish the account of their history at this point. In the other Diaspora locations there was no such moment of rupture; indeed, our inscriptional evidence from Rome and Asia Minor only becomes full rather later, in the third and fourth centuries CE. But to take the story so far on would have extended this book excessively. ii) The beginning of the second century CE also happens to be the point after which our literary evidence about Diaspora Jews becomes greatly reduced. The last extant literature from the Mediterranean Diaspora is by Josephus, whose final work (*Contra Apionem*) dates from the very end of the first century CE. With no subsequent narrative comparable to Josephus', our knowledge of later Diaspora history is largely restricted to occasional comments in Christian works, besides the inscriptions and buildings unearthed by archaeology. Meanwhile, the last Roman author to give more than cursory attention to the Jews is Tacitus, who died in 120 CE. Thus the literary evidence conspires with the occasion of the Revolt in Egypt and Cyrene to suggest 117 CE as an appropriate point at which to conclude our study.

As indicated above, this survey of the Mediterranean Diaspora will combine study of the historical experiences of Diaspora Jews with analysis of the main *Diaspora literature*. I have had to make some choices among that literature, and will include here the products of thirteen authors, which are both important in themselves and extant in suffcent quantity to be worth thorough analysis. Josephus and Philo will of course take their place in this canon, but I will endeavour to prevent their massive literary output from dominating the rest. Of the fragmentary works, I will study only those which survive in substantial quantity, namely Artapanus, Aristobulus and Ezekiel. From other Jewish literature which definitely originates in the Diaspora I have chosen to discuss *The Letter of Aristeas, Wisdom of Solomon,* 3 and 4 Maccabees, Pseudo-Phocylides, *Joseph and Aseneth,* and Books 3 and 5 of *The Sibylline Oracles*. I will take Paul as one further example in the spectrum of Diaspora Jews, although he will prove to be a fascinatingly anomalous figure.

Much other Jewish literature from our period cannot be sited for certain in the Diaspora. Nonetheless, of the works which almost certainly do belong to the Diaspora I have had to omit Demetrius, the Pseudo-Philo sermons, the poetic forgeries, the Testament of Abraham and some other Sibylline Oracles[4]. Other literature was translated into Greek in or for the Greek-speaking Diaspora, such as Esther, Sirach and, of course, the Septuagint. The latter would certainly repay close attention as a work of Diaspora literature and theology in its own right, but the scale and complexity of such an analysis prohibits its inclusion here. I hope that what follows will stimulate others to pursue comparable studies of other Diaspora literature, and I would excuse my omissions with Voltaire's dictum that 'the surest way to be boring is in striving to be exhaustive!'

---

[4]   Other works which *might* originate in the Diaspora include: The Testament of Job, Philo the Epic Poet, Pseudo-Eupolemus, Pseudo-Hecataeus, Cleodemus (Malchus) and Theodotus. See the discussion of each in Schürer vol. 3.

The *structure of this book* reflects my aim to combine historical study of Diaspora communities with analysis of Jews' varied responses to their environments. Ideally, one would study each location separately, comparing history, literature and non-literary local evidence; but in practice that is only possible with regard to Egypt. Elsewhere in the Diaspora our evidence is simply too patchy, and the extant literature can rarely be assigned with certainty to any single location. Thus the nature and variable scale of the evidence requires the division of this book into two uneven parts, Part One focusing on the Diaspora in Egypt, and Part Two on the Diaspora in other Mediterranean sites.

Part One will begin with a fresh study of the history of Egyptian Jews from 323 BCE to 117 CE, divided into the Ptolemaic and the Roman eras (chapters 2 and 3 respectively). Before embarking on an analysis of Jews' reactions to their Egyptian milieu, it will be necessary to discuss and define our analytical tools for this task (chapter 4), in particular indicating some heuristic distinctions between assimilation, acculturation and accommodation (chapter 4.4). On this basis we may then survey the spectrum in the assimilation of Egyptian Jews (chapter 5) and offer new readings of their most important surviving literature (chapters 6 and 7). The literature here investigated will be divided into two categories, cultural convergence (chapter 6) and cultural antagonism (chapter 7), reflecting the variety of stances adopted by Jews in their Graeco-Egyptian environment.

Part Two (The Diaspora in Other Mediterranean Sites) will follow the same pattern as Part One, though now covering more than one location. First we will consider afresh the history of the Jewish communities in our four other locations, Cyrenaica and Syria (chapter 8), the province of Asia (chapter 9) and the city of Rome (chapter 10). We will then gather together the limited material from these and other sites to investigate, first, the levels of assimilation among Diaspora Jews outwith Egypt (chapter 11) and, secondly, the selected literature which is not definitely, or which is definitely not, of Egyptian provenance (chapters 12 and 13).

Thus Parts One and Two of this volume correspond in shape, moving from historical survey through the assessment of levels of assimilation to analysis of the relevant literature. The final section (Part Three) adds another facet to our survey of the Mediterranean Diaspora, here drawing on the sources previously discussed to offer a sketch of Jewish identity in the Diaspora. Although there are some topics which cannot be treated here (such as community organization and the attraction of sympathizers and proselytes), I will delineate in outline what I consider the features of Jewish life which helped define and preserve Jewish communities over the period we are studying. At several points in our study special problems could merit more detailed investigation, but I will employ an Excursus only once, in chapter 3, where space is required to discuss the legal status of Alexandrian Jews. To avoid cluttering our discussions with argumentation about the dating of texts, I will include that and other technical material in an Appendix on Sources.

Finally, it remains to say something about *the spirit* in which this project has been conducted. I have made it my priority to become familiar with primary sources, whose reading and analysis has been my greatest pleasure. I have endeavoured to familiarize myself with the chief scholarly literature, but cannot claim comprehensive coverage of this vast field of scholarship. Experts in particular specialisms (e.g. Philo and Josephus) will no doubt find omissions in the secondary literature cited, though I trust they will also share my aim to stimulate readers to explore the primary sources for themselves. I have given my own translations in all cases.

I am not so naive as to imagine that historiography can be a wholly disinterested occupation. Historians inevitably, and properly, work within the framework of the social and cultural issues of their day, and as those issues change so do perspectives on the historical sources. If it is accompanied by critical self-awareness, that hermeneutical reality by no means invalidates historical research, but rather gives it inspiration and direction. This volume is influenced by many factors in the contemporary social scene, but none so important as the need to foster respect and tolerance for minority ethnic groups, in the face of the complex problems created by modern social pluralism. I have gained from a number of studies of minority groups in both ancient and modern history, though not all have been referred to here. My focus on the Jewish Diaspora stems from a combination of three motivating factors. In the first place, the Jewish Diaspora has proved throughout history a 'paradigm case' of minority endurance in an alien context and still today provides resources for reflection on ethnic identity and the preservation of particularity (see e.g. Boyarin 1994:228–60). Secondly, my previous work on early Christianity indicated the importance of the Mediterranean Diaspora in understanding the social and theological development of the early Christian movement; indeed, I remain convinced that a proper appreciation of the Diaspora is vital for comprehending much about the first Christians and the fateful split between Christianity and Judaism. I thus hope that this volume will be of value to students of both Judaism and early Christianity, and hope to follow it myself with a comparative study of Pauline churches. Thirdly, the labour devoted to this study is undoubtedly influenced by the terrible experiences of Jews in the European Diaspora in this century: we all live and work under the shadow of the Holocaust.

The concern for tolerance cuts in many directions and is reflected in my unwillingness to use the pejorative term 'pagan' with respect to non-Jews.[5] Readers may also notice my decision to capitalize the word 'God' in all contexts, whether in reference to the God of Jews or the God/Gods of Gentiles. While the linguistic arguments on this matter are indecisive (is 'God' a proper name or a title?),[6] I have felt it better to equalize all parties in this matter, rather than succumb to the Jewish and Christian presumption that only their Deity is truly 'God', while the rest are merely 'gods' (or worse). As we shall see, Jewish theology and religious practice were often as offensive to Gentiles as the other way around. Of course no stance here is truly 'objective', since 'tolerance' and 'respect' are just as value-laden as is any more particularized commitment. But I think I know which is more conducive to that 'civilized behaviour' (καλοκαγαθία) which Josephus identified as the only basis on which a pluralist society can survive (*Ant* 16.177–78).

---

[5] 'Pagan' was employed in a pejorative sense by the early Christians and retains, in popular usage, derogatory connotations of primitive or even godless religion. Ironically, Jews and Christians learned their most sophisticated theology from 'pagans'!

[6] The presence of the article does not decide the matter in Greek, since θεός and ὁ θεός can be used interchangeably in our sources. Nor can we usefully distinguish between singular 'God' and plural 'gods', since Greek and Roman authors can vary their usage when referring to the same entity. In the Jewish and Christian tradition 'God' has become, in practice, a proper name, in default of the real (unpronounceable) name of the Deity; but the term originated as a title. It would be possible to standardize usage by employing the lower case 'god' or 'gods' throughout, but I prefer to use the upper case since it customarily conveys respect for the beliefs and practices of the relevant worshippers.

# PART ONE

# THE DIASPORA IN EGYPT

# 2

## Jews in Ptolemaic Egypt

Our investigation begins in Egypt, because of all the sites of the Mediterranean Diaspora the Egyptian Diaspora provides by far the fullest body of evidence. This is so for two reasons. In the first place, the Jewish community in Alexandria became extremely large during our period and contained an intellectual élite whose literature (all of it in Greek) became known and treasured to a far greater degree than the literary products of other Jewish centres. The volume and quality of this literature has made Alexandrian Judaism synonymous with 'Diaspora Judaism' to an exaggerated degree, but it remains true that our evidence allows us a profile of the varied socio-cultural reactions of Jews nowhere more fully than in this capital of the Hellenistic world. The second reason for the evidential significance of Egypt lies in the qualities of its sand. The discovery of papyri in such remarkable quantities has constituted the greatest imaginable treasure for ancient historians, not least because the range of papyrus material has illustrated the social realities of ordinary life which are typically ignored in the literature of the time. That these papyri originate mostly from the countryside of Egypt (the χώρα, *chora*) only renders them all the more valuable; and that they contain occasional references to Jews makes them a precious supplement to our largely Alexandrian literature.[1] A valuable body of inscriptional material enhances still further our ability to give a rounded description of Egyptian Jews.[2]

---

[1] Scholarship is greatly indebted to Tcherikover and Fuks for their collection of these papyri in the three meticulously prepared volumes of *CPJ*. Tcherikover's 'Prolegomena' (1.1–111) also remains the best survey of the Egyptian Diaspora, though it has now been supplemented by Modrzejewski 1991.

[2] The Jewish inscriptions from Egypt have been magnificently re-edited by Horbury & Noy 1992.

The chronological limits of this volume correspond to the significant *termini* of the Egyptian Disapora. At one end, the conquest of Egypt by Alexander the Great (d. 323 BCE) brought about its political transformation and the influx of numerous immigrants, including a very considerable contingent of Jews. At the other, the full-scale uprising of Egyptian Jews in 116–117 CE practically obliterated the Jewish population of Egypt. Our task in this and the subsequent chapter is to survey the social and political vicissitudes experienced by Jews in Egypt during this 440-year period.

## 2.1 Immigration and Settlement: From Alexander to Ptolemy V Epiphanes (323–180 BCE)

### 2.1.1 Immigration

At least since the sixth century BCE and the Babylonian capture of Jerusalem, Egypt had been a popular asylum for Judaean refugees, although some, like Jeremiah, disapproved of such an expedient (Jer 44). In some cases Jews had served in Egypt in military garrisons; one unit, of which we receive a fascinating glimpse in the Elephantine papyri, helped to guard the southern boundary of Egypt at Syene.[3] However, Alexander's conquest of Egypt in 332 BCE, and the subsequent establishment of a Macedonian dynasty by Ptolemy I, marked a watershed in the history of Egypt and in the experience of Jews in Egypt. Alexander's army itself brought new settlers in its wake, but it was the immigration policy of Ptolemy I Soter (declared king in 305 BCE) which especially encouraged a massive influx of foreigners. These settled both in the new city of Alexandria, which quickly acquired international fame, and in the *chora*, where there was new land to be cultivated and a burgeoning administrative system to be staffed.

While these immigrants arrived from all parts of the Mediterranean world and the Near East, neighbouring Syria provided a good percentage of this rapid inflow. After a series of wars to settle the ownership of this important territory, Syria came under Ptolemaic rule from 301 to 198 BCE, a century of unified administrative control which made migration far easier. Within this 'Syrian' district

---

[3] For a recent analysis and bibliography see Porten 1984 and Modrzejewski 1991:21–41.

(officially, 'Syria and Phoenicia') was the city of Jerusalem and its attached territory, whose inhabitants were known as Ἰουδαῖοι (*Ioudaioi*). It is important to remember that, though I will usually translate this term as 'Jews', that should not be understood purely, or even primarily, as a *religious* signifier. Ἰουδαῖοι were an ethnic group originally from Judaea, just as Ἰδουμαῖοι (Idumaeans) were natives of Idumaea and Σαμαρῖται (Samaritans) of Samaria. When an individual is labelled in our papyri as 'Pasis the Ἰουδαῖος' ('Pasis the Jew' or 'Pasis the Judaean', *CPJ* 9), that is to distinguish him by ethnicity from others with the same name. In time, the geographical connotations of the term might weaken,[4] and its core ethnic sense might be supplemented by the notion that others could 'become Jews' (by adopting the Jewish way of life). But in the Hellenistic era that extension was rare indeed and, as we shall find, throughout our period the bond of ethnicity constituted the core of the Jews' distinctive identity (see below, chapter 14.1). Even so, in the early Ptolemaic era, when an onlooker surveyed the ethnic mosaic of incomers, the 'Judaeans' were often indistinguishable from their Semitic neighbours and were labelled simply 'Syrians'.[5]

Jewish immigration in this period seems to have been of many types. *The Letter of Aristeas* 12–27 claims that Ptolemy I (305–282 BCE) moved 'up to 100,000' from 'the land of the Jews' into Egypt, enslaving all who were not capable of fighting in his army; but his son, Ptolemy II Philadelphus (282–246 BCE), issued a decree freeing all Jewish slaves, issuing payment to their owners. Much in this account is wholly fantastic, not least the figures and the notion that a Ptolemaic king gave hundreds of talents to his subjects![6] Yet

---

[4] For this reason I am reluctant to follow the practice of some scholars in this field (e.g. S. Mason) is translating consistently 'Judaean'. That translation makes the geographical connotations *primary*, when in fact in later generations appellations which originally signified geographical origin could be reduced to merely ethnic reference.

[5] On the wave of Syrian immigration and the frequent impossibility of distinguishing between Jewish and non-Jewish Syrians see Tcherikover in *CPJ* 1.4–5.

[6] Josephus, *Ant* 12.11–33 follows *Aristeas* but makes the story even less plausible by increasing the compensation to slave-owners from 20 to 120 drachmae! In form and vocabulary the decree in *Aristeas* 22–25 is close enough to authentic official records to suggest to some that it is based on a genuine Ptolemaic decree (Westermann 1938) or even wholly authentic. But Abel 1968a rightly dismisses its content as spurious; cf. Modrzejewski 1991:73–75.

it is likely that many Jews entered Egypt as prisoners of war, caught in the complex ebb and flow of the 'Syrian Wars' which followed the dismemberment of Alexander's empire. The papyri give evidence of a flourishing slave-trade between Egypt and Syria (including Palestine), and there is no reason to doubt that at least some Jews were taken into Egypt on these terms.[7]

In one detail at least the account in *Aristeas* is trustworthy: there is reference here (13) to the employment of numbers of Jews (the figure of 30,000 is probably exaggerated) in the Ptolemaic army, settled throughout the kingdom in forts and garrisons. It was the policy of the early Ptolemies to build a standing army entirely from non-natives, granting immigrant soldiers varied quantities of land (according to their status) to provide them with a regular income. Such 'cleruchs' are amply attested in the papyri, among them a number identifiable as Judaeans/Jews. There is no reason to think that the Ptolemies treated able-bodied Jews of military age any differently than the supply of soldiers from Cyprus, Crete, Asia Minor or any other source. If they could fight and could learn to communicate in the language of the army (Greek), they were a useful resource for a vulnerable dynasty.

But slaves and soldiers were not the only type of Jewish immigrant. We must reckon with a large influx of economic migrants at this time, attracted by the fabled wealth of Egypt and the economic expansion created by Ptolemaic rule.[8] The new city of Alexandria and the huge financial bureaucracy of Egypt afforded much greater opportunities for social advancement than the backwater conditions of Judaea. The ease of travel to Egypt must have reinforced the magnetic attraction of this 'new world' for socially adventurous Jews.

---

[7]    Of the two thousand Zeno papyri, some forty relate to Syria or Palestine, where Zeno travelled on behalf of Apollonius, the Ptolemaic minister (*dioiketes*). One (*CPJ* 7) refers to a Johanna, probably a Jewish slave-girl in Apollonius' household. On the slave-trade between Syria and Egypt see Tcherikover 1961a:68-69. The story of Ptolemy's capture of Jerusalem, which Josephus cites from Agatharchides (*Ant* 12.3–7), is of doubtful value; but Jews probably fought against Ptolemy, at least at Gaza (312 BCE), after which 8000 prisoners were sent to Egypt (Diodorus 19.85.3–4). Tcherikover gives a speculative reconstruction of these events in 1961a:50–58.

[8]    In Josephus' terms, 'drawn by the excellence of the country and the prodigality of Ptolemy', *Ant* 12.9. His citation from Hecataeus in *C Ap* 1.186 refers to Ptolemy's well-known 'kindness'.

## 2.1.2 Settlement in the *chora*

In the social map of Egypt, two entities stood in the sharpest contrast to one another: the *chora* (countryside) and the *polis* (city). In fact there were only three *poleis* in Ptolemaic Egypt: Naucratis, Ptolemais and Alexandria. Of these Alexandria stood in a category all of its own: its official title, 'Alexandria by Egypt', indicates its special status as a semi-independent entity on the edge of its vast hinterland. Thus to understand the conditions of Jewish settlement it is necessary to discuss their two principal environments – the *chora* and Alexandria – quite separately.

The Jewish soldiers who settled in the *chora* – especially in the Fayûm, but also elsewhere in Egypt – are particularly well-documented. We have evidence of Jews at many levels of the military hierarchy, including members of the cavalry élite, a paymaster and various officers.[9] The papyri indicate that many such soldiers acquired wealth, both as 'cleruchs' with their allotted land (which they often leased to tenants) and through financial deals which netted due interest (e.g. *CPJ* 24). Over time, the royal land allocated to these soldiers was recognized as their hereditary possession and thus many Jewish families became established as land-owners. Since, like other cleruchs, they payed reduced taxes and had privileged access to officialdom, they clearly enjoyed significant advantages over native Egyptian farmers.[10]

Although these military personnel were scattered over the Egyptian countryside, they were less exposed to Egyptian influence than one might imagine. The general pattern of life in the early Ptolemaic period suggests a wide gulf between Egyptians and the Greek-speaking classes; those Jews who entered Egypt in a privileged capacity were likely to retain a social distance from the natives. To what extent Jewish soldiers were deployed in specifically Judaean units is unclear: there is no unambiguous evidence for such units, while there are many examples of Jews enlisted in other military groups under 'pseudo-ethnic' titles ('Persians', 'Macedonians' etc.).[11] While the Jewish soldiers we find in the

---

[9] *CPJ* 18–32; Horbury & Noy 115 (=*CIJ* 1531): Eleazar the officer; Llewelyn 1992:164–68.

[10] Bickerman 1988:84–85 notes that the smallest cleruch allotments (24 arourae) were three times larger than the holdings of 94% of Egyptian peasants in 1947.

[11] Tcherikover's cautious conclusion on the question of 'Jewish units' (*CPJ* 1.147–48) is preferable to Kasher's suppositional line of reasoning, 1985:40–48.

papyri sometimes lent to one another or acted as witnesses for fellow Jews, there is also evidence of considerable social interaction with 'Hellenes' of all nationalities (see further, chapter 5.2).

Other Jews were employed in agriculture without the privilege of cleruch status. The farmers Alexander and Ismaelos who tilled tiny plots of parched land (*CPJ* 13) can only be classed as peasants. Others are to be found as tenants in a vineyard (*CPJ* 14) or as shepherds selling the wool of their flock (*CPJ* 9, 38), while at the bottom of the social pyramid are hired field-hands (*CPJ* 36?, 133).[12] We can only guess their social conditions and allegiances, but it is interesting to find one Jewish shepherd in the employment of a temple of Pan (*CPJ* 39).

Since the Ptolemies preferred to staff their tightly controlled bureaucracy with non-natives, it is no surprise to find Jews in the *chora* filling a range of administrative jobs. We have a poignant complaint from an underpaid Jewish guard (*CPJ* 12), and reference to others in the police (*CPJ* 25), even perhaps a chief of police (Horbury & Noy 27 = *CIJ* 1443).[13] A large collection of ostraka from Upper Egypt show Jews engaged in tax-collecting or tax-farming, signalling in some cases considerable wealth.[14] There are also examples of Jews in artisan occupations. It is particularly interesting to find a contract for the use of a pottery in a Fayûm village to be shared between a Jewish and an Egyptian family (*CPJ* 46). Of the four named members of the Jewish family (Horos, Sabbataios, Dosas and Paous), the first and last bear Egyptian names, and none can write Greek (even the scribe's Greek is hair-raising!). Through their occupational and social links they appear to be deeply enmeshed in native Egyptian society.

The wide range in social status among Jews in the *chora* makes it impossible to generalize about their social and cultural affiliations. Our potters and low-grade agricultural workers appear to be those most integrated into their Egyptian context. It is possible that they spoke Greek even if they did not write it; but it is also possible that

[12] Honigman 1993:110–14 casts doubt on the Jewish identity of the individuals mentioned in *CPJ* 36 and 37. Bickerman 1988:85–86 suggests that Jews were particularly valuable to the Ptolemies for their willingness to participate in forms of agricultural production, like viticulture, not traditional in Egypt.

[13] Here one Ptolemaios, chief of police, dedicates a *proseuche* (prayer-house) at Athribis together with the Jews in Athribis. But is not absolutely certain that Ptolemaios is himself a Jew.

[14] *CPJ* 1 section V with a fine introduction by Tcherikover (1.194–203; cf. 1.17–18).

they adopted the native language in its demotic form, which flourished throughout our period.[15] Those whose social position ranked them among the Greek ruling class will have inhabited a very different world. The near-apartheid conditions which determined the non-relations between Greeks and Egyptians will have inclined them more towards Hellenization than Egyptianization. If the evidence of nomenclature is significant, it is noteworthy how many better-off Jewish families began to use Greek names, and our papyrus contracts show Jews fully conversant with Hellenistic legal conventions.[16]

To what extent were Jews in the *chora* able to form and maintain ethnic communities? It was common for national groups to stick together, creating 'Idumaean' or 'Carian' districts, for instance, in towns and villages.[17] In some cases they appear to have developed their own social and political institutions, though their various shapes are now largely invisible.[18] We know of Jewish districts or quarters in various towns – Memphis at least in the Ptolemaic era, and elsewhere at a later date[19] – which indicate the desire of

---

[15] On the probability of Jews speaking demotic see Tcherikover in *CPJ* 1.44; Griffiths 1987:9. On the continuance of Aramaic among Jews in Egypt see below n. 32.

[16] Tcherikover in *CPJ* 1.27–36; Modrzejewski 1991:91–101. We will return to a fuller discussion of assimilation among Egyptian Jews in chapter 5.

[17] See Bickerman 1988:37–38, and the special survey of Memphis by Thompson 1988:82–105.

[18] A still dominant consensus holds that such ethnic groups typically formed a *politeuma*, which Smallwood defines (1981:225) as 'a recognized, formally constituted corporation of aliens enjoying the right of domicile in a foreign city and forming a separate, semi-autonomous civic body, a city within the city'. Cf. Tcherikover in *CPJ* 1.6; Kasher 1985:35 n. 26; Lewis 1986:30–31 (the latter emphasizing their social rather than political roles). In fact no Jewish *politeuma* is attested outside Alexandria (*The Letter of Aristeas* 310) and the meaning of this term there is uncertain (see below, n. 73). Lüderitz 1994 puts the consensus in doubt by insisting on the many different senses of the term *politeuma*. He collects the examples of its use for ethnic associations (1994:196–99), but considers that these were private rather than public institutions.

[19] Thompson 1988:91–92 discusses the Caiaphas stele from the 3rd century BCE which indicates a Jewish district in Memphis (together with a demotic text which refers to 'the commander of the Jews', 99). References to Jewish quarters or streets (?) are found in papyri from the Roman period, from Oxyrhynchos (*CPJ* 423, 454) and Hermoupolis (*CPJ* 468), and in ostraka from Apollinopolis Magna (see Fuks and Lewis in *CPJ* 2.108ff.). The Ptolemaic evidence often indicates concentrations of Judaeans (e.g. at Samareia, *CPJ* 28; at Psenyris, *CPJ* 33). For a list of place-names associated with Jews see *CPJ* vol. 3, Appendix III. Kasher discusses some of these in 1985:106–67.

incoming Judaeans to associate with those who shared their ethnic roots and national customs. Indeed, since Jewish immigration continued right through the Ptolemaic and early Roman periods, such communities were continually refreshed with reminders of their nationality.

Moreover, we have striking evidence of the religious dimensions of that national identity in inscriptions which record the dedication of Jewish 'prayer-houses' (προσευχαί, *proseuchai*). The earliest of these are from the third century BCE,[20] while scattered evidence in the *chora* from later centuries indicates the continuing significance of this institution for Jewish communities.[21] These prayer-houses are our earliest evidence for the 'synagogue' institution which became such an important focus of Jewish life in the Diaspora.[22] That they were *not* named 'temples' indicates that, unlike the earlier garrison at Elephantine and apart from the special case of Leontopolis (see below), the Jews in Ptolemaic Egypt refrained from erecting altars or offering sacrifices. That restraint must indicate their continued orientation to the temple in Jerusalem, an enduring link with the Judaean territory from which their name derived.

While in their rationale and even in their architecture these prayer-houses may owe something to their Egyptian environment,[23] as special Jewish buildings they were a physical token of the distinct character of the Jewish community. Their construction and maintenance, and the acquisition of offices within them, would

---

[20] Horbury & Noy 22 (=*CIJ* 1440) from Schedia, near Alexandria; Horbury & Noy 117 (=*CIJ* 1532a) from Crokodilopolis.

[21] See Tcherikover's list of synagogues in *CPJ* 1.8; the relevant inscriptions are to be found conveniently in *CPJ* vol. 3, and now re-edited by Horbury & Noy 9, 13, 22, 24–25, 27–28, 117, 125–127.

[22] The dedicatory inscriptions and papyri use the term *proseuche* ([house of] prayer) rather than *synagoge* (assembly). The latter could refer to any kind of assembly (it is found in relation to associations of Idumaeans and other social groups). συναγωγή is used for a Jewish association in Egypt in *CPJ* 138 and perhaps in Horbury & Noy 20 (=*CIJ* 1447, though the editors doubt that a Jewish association is here in view). Philo is our first source to use the term in relation to a meeting-*place* (*Probus* 81, with reference to Essenes); cf. the use of συναγώγια (assemblies or assembly-halls?) in *Somn* 2.127 and *Legatio* 311. συναγωγή is used for both the assembly and the assembly-hall in Berenice (Lüderitz 72, 56 CE). The fullest survey of the evidence remains Hengel 1971.

[23] Griffiths 1987 notes the combination of worship and education which has some parallels in Egyptian temples, and, architecturally, the 'pylon' in the *proseuche* at Xenephyris (Horbury & Noy 24 = *CIJ* 1441).

solidify the commitment of better-off Jews to the community they served,[24] while this physical space, and the meetings of the community within it, could provide a focus of loyalty for all Jewish residents in the locality.[25] Thus even if the linguistic component of Jewish ethnicity was lost, as immigrant Jews learnt to speak Greek or demotic, national identity could still be maintained in strength through the social and religious bonds of a community supporting its communal buildings. To what extent the community governed the lives of individual Jews is unclear and we may detect among them varying degrees of assimilation (see below, chapter 5); but it is likely that even a rudimentary communal organization loyal to its national traditions served as a counterweight to the tendency of individuals to submerge their ethnic difference in the interests of social success.[26]

### 2.1.3 Settlement in Alexandria

The city of Alexandria was founded by Alexander himself and established as the capital of Egypt by Ptolemy I Soter. Its unique social position was enhanced by its role as the seat of Ptolemaic power, the attending social and cultural privileges being balanced by obvious political restrictions. In political and cultural affairs, the course of events in Alexandria determined the fate of the whole of Egypt. Thus the fortunes of the Jewish community in Alexandria – although governed by different conditions than those which prevailed in the *chora* – were greatly to influence the whole of the Egyptian Diaspora.

---

[24] Note the private sponsorship in the dedication of buildings in Horbury & Noy 28 (=*CIJ* 1444) and 126 (in which the building is erected 'on behalf of' [ὑπέρ] the donor's family!). There is evidence for the office of *prostates* in Horbury & Noy 24 (=*CIJ* 1441) and 20 (=*CIJ* 1447).

[25] The presence of a room termed *exedra* adjoining the prayer-house (Horbury & Noy 28 = *CIJ* 1444) may suggest the use of the complex for discussion and teaching, so Horbury & Noy ad loc. The use of the epithet 'holy' in relation to the buildings (Horbury & Noy 9 = *CIJ* 1433; 127? = *CIJ* 1435) suggests their special social significance. On the synagogue as locus of community loyalty, and the importance of the Sabbath in this regard, see Tcherikover in *CPJ* 1.29, 94ff. and below, chapter 14.2.1.

[26] Tcherikover suggests there were 'two contradictory tendencies in Egyptian Jewry: the desire to follow old national and religious tradition, and the desire to participate vigorously in all aspects of Hellenistic life. We may assume that when a Jewish community, as a whole, was affected, the first tendency was predominant; but individual Jews, when faced with the innumerable petty problems of everyday life, were more disposed to follow the second' (*CPJ* 1.36).

Alexandria's damp conditions leave us without local papyri, and our knowledge of the Jewish community in the city is largely dependent on literary sources (with a smattering of inscriptions). The fullest material comes from the early Roman period (especially from Philo), and it is difficult to know how much we may extrapolate, from a later era, conditions in Ptolemaic Alexandria.[27] In Philo, and even more in Josephus, apologetic interests clearly colour the presentation of affairs, but to an extent which it is difficult to measure. Most suspicious are the efforts of Josephus to magnify the importance of the Alexandrian Jews in refuting the slanders of Apion (*C Ap* 2.33–64). Here, as elsewhere, Josephus claims that they were settled in Alexandria by Alexander himself on the most favourable terms, being given equal civic rights with 'the Macedonians'.[28] The propaganda element here is now generally acknowledged, and it is likely that Josephus has 'mistaken' the inclusion of some Jews in a 'Macedonian' military unit as a grant of superior political rights for the whole Jewish community.[29]

Nonetheless, there is some evidence that Jews were among the early inhabitants of Alexandria. Josephus preserves a fragment of Hecataeus concerning a Jewish priest, Ezechias, who encouraged fellow-Jews to emigrate to Egypt, citing the terms of their 'constitution' (πολιτεία, *C Ap* 1.186–89). This may not be historically

---

[27] Fraser 1972 provides a comprehensive study of Alexandria in this period.

[28] In *C Ap* 2.33–44 Josephus claims that Alexander settled a colony of Jews in their own quarter, in reward for their valour and faithfulness, giving them equal privilege (ἴση τιμή, 2.35) with the Macedonians. The vague appeal to the letters of Alexander and Ptolemy I, and to the papers of later kings, does not inspire confidence. Only the reference to the *stele* set up by 'Caesar the Great' (2.37) is of any value, and even here Josephus probably confuses Augustus and Julius Caesar. The claim in *Ant* 14.188 that this *stele* pronounced Jews to be citizens of Alexandria is undoubtedly exaggerated and toned down to talk of their 'rights' in *C Ap* 2.37. *Ant* 12.8 attributes to Ptolemy I the establishment of Alexandrian Jews as citizens of equal privilege (ἰσοπολῖται) with the Macedonians. *Bell* 2.487–88 asserts that Alexander, in return for the support of the Jews, gave them permission to reside in Alexandria on equal terms (ἐξ ἰσομοιρίας [?] – the text is uncertain) with the Greeks, while his successors granted them a separate quarter. *Ant* 19.281 gives a dubious version of Claudius' edict, which asserts that the Jews were colonizers of Alexandria from the very earliest times and received equal civic rights (ἴση πολιτεία) from the kings.

[29] See Tcherikover 1961a:318–25 and Fraser 1972:53. We will reserve further discussion of the Jews' status in Alexandria until the Excursus in chapter 3.

reliable,[30] but it would fit the typical Ptolemaic policy of enabling ethnic groups to live 'according to their ancestral laws'.[31] Certainly, individual Jews, probably military settlers, are well attested in early Ptolemaic inscriptions found in an Alexandrian necropolis, written in both Aramaic and Greek.[32]

The evidence for the development of the Alexandrian community is exiguous. By the time of the pogrom (38 CE), the Jews had spread over many parts of the city, but were particularly concentrated in the Δ (Delta) quarter and one other of the five quarters of the city.[33] The spread of synagogue inscriptions bears out the diffusion of the Jewish population in the Ptolemaic era,[34] but the concentration of Jews in certain quarters of the city was probably an early phenomenon, and one of very great significance. The social networks created by common residence in a segment of a large city are of the utmost social importance – as any analysis of minority communities in modern cities will testify. It would be anachronistic to term the Jewish quarter in Alexandria a 'ghetto' (before 38 CE no one confined them to this area), but the desire to stay near their fellow-countrymen indicates the social conservatism of the mass of Alexandrian Jews. Josephus states that the Ptolemies granted the Jews a quarter 'that they might observe a purer way of life, mixing less with people of other races' (*Bell* 2.488). Whatever the purpose of the kings, that certainly represents the social function of this arrangement. In practical terms, the residential concentration of Jews meant a greater chance of

[30] It is often questioned whether Josephus' citations from Hecataeus of Abdera are genuine, though they are defended by Schürer 3.671–77 and Stern 1.21–25. The latter, however, renders this passage very differently (1.38), following a conjectural emendation.

[31] Tcherikover 1961a:300–1.

[32] Horbury & Noy 1–8 (=*CIJ* 1424–31), discussed by the editors, pp. xiii–xvi. Although this cemetery is not wholly Jewish, the concentration of Jewish tombs suggests some communal identity. On the continuance of Aramaic in Ptolemaic Egypt see Horbury 1994:12–17. Thompson 1988:98 notes the difficulty of identifying Jewish cemeteries.

[33] Philo, *Flacc* 55; Josephus, *Bell* 2.495. Josephus, *C Ap* 2.33–36 indicates that the Delta quarter bordered on the sea and was near the palace; see Fraser 1972:34–35.

[34] Horbury & Noy 9 (=*CIJ* 1433, Hadra, Alexandria) and 13 (=*CIJ* 1432, on the other side of the city from Quarter Δ). Philo claims there were many *proseuchai* in every section of the city (*Legatio* 132). The 'great synagogue' referred to by Philo (*Legatio* 134) and in the Talmud (e.g., b Sukkah 51b) has left no traceable remains.

endogamy (marriage within the race), easier access to kosher food, simpler practice of Sabbaths and festivals, and easier avoidance of alien religious cult. In fact the enduring ethnic loyalty of Alexandrian Jews probably owes much to this crucial aspect of their settlement.

There is reason to believe that Alexandrian Jews in the early Ptolemaic period were strongly attracted towards Hellenistic culture. Alexandria was fast becoming the cultural capital of the civilized world, sustained by the vast wealth which it sucked into itself from Egypt, the Mediterranean and further afield. The world-famous Museion and Library represented the ambition of Ptolemy Soter and his son Philadelphus to make Alexandria the hub of Hellenism.[35] The famous scholars who were drawn there (Callimachus, Theocritus, Euclid, Apollonius of Rhodes – to name only the most illustrious) were the academic vanguard of a large-scale project to create what was later recognized as 'the first city of the civilized world, certainly far ahead of all the rest in elegance, size, riches and luxury' (Diodorus 17.52.5). With all its opportunities for social and financial advancement, we can easily imagine successful Jews attracted by the cultural dynamism of this new city. The glittering fortunes of the Tobiad family, who operated as Ptolemaic officials in Palestine, may well have had their counterparts in Alexandria: indeed, according to Josephus, it was in Alexandria among Jews of high social rank that Joseph the Tobiad came to find a suitable son-in-law (*Ant* 12.186–89).

The early Hellenization of Alexandrian Jews is exemplified in the translation of the Jewish Scriptures into Greek. According to *The Letter of Aristeas*, the initiative for the translation came from Ptolemy Philadelphus (282–246 BCE) on the advice of his librarian, Demetrius of Phalerum. There may be some historical core in this tale,[36] but the origins of the Septuagint lie at least as much with the needs of Alexandrian Jews, whose Hebrew Scriptures looked disappointingly 'barbaric' from their Hellenizing perspective. How long they remained bilingual (or, with Aramaic, trilingual) we cannot tell. But it is clear that once the Scriptures were available in Greek, there was much less incentive to learn a foreign and

---

[35] Theocritus *Idyll* 17 is an eloquent commentary on the ambitions of Philadelphus – and the enormous financial resources with which he fulfilled them. According to Philo (*Mos* 2.29), even in the first century CE particularly generous patronage was known proverbially as 'Philadelphian'.

[36] See Bickerman 1988:101–4; Modrzejewski 1991:84–91.

otherwise valueless tongue.[37] 'Thus Alexandrian Jewry discarded one of the most important cultural legacies of ancient Israel, its national language' (Tcherikover).[38] Reading and hearing their Scriptures in Greek, the Alexandrian Jews no longer encountered any linguistic token of their cultural difference. Indeed, the Scriptures themselves now gave religious sanction for the use of the Greek language – and the educational opportunities to which it was the key. In time they came to celebrate the translation as a communal triumph, with elaborate legends and an annual festival on the island of Pharos (Philo, *Mos* 2.41–43). The way this significant token of acculturation became a cause of celebration is deeply suggestive of the dominant trends in Alexandrian Judaism.

It is impossible to recover the historical facts concerning the early political relations between the Jews and the Ptolemaic court, smothered as they are with apologetic overlay. Privileged grants of citizenship and payments for mass emancipation are probably to be dismissed as fancies born of national pride, and even the translation of the Septuagint need not signify any special favour. This is not to suggest that there were ugly facts to be masked, only that the truth was rather more prosaic, with the Judaean immigrants barely distinguished from other similarly useful settlers. The century of Ptolemaic rule over Palestine (301–198 BCE) appears to have been peaceful, even popular,[39] and as far as we know the Judaean immigrants gave no cause for the kings to distrust them. The synagogue inscriptions pay due respect to the reigning monarchs, typically in the form: 'in honour of (ὑπέρ) King Ptolemy and Queen Berenice (or whoever) … the Jews dedicated this prayer-house.' It is significant that none of these inscriptions refers to the monarchs by their full divine titles, and the buildings are dedicated *in honour of* the royals, not *to* them; where indicated it is clear that the object of worship is 'the Most High God' (θεῶι

---

[37] A few papyrus fragments contain Hebrew words or prayers. Their dating is uncertain, but possibly of the Roman period; see Horbury 1994:17–18 and Fraser 1972:284 and n. 777. However, the Nash papyrus (containing the Decalogue and *Shema'* in Hebrew) may be Hellenistic (Albright 1937). On the survival of Aramaic among Jews, see above, n. 32. It is clear that the Scriptures referred to in *Aristeas* are the five books of the Torah, and the use of Genesis and Exodus by Demetrius (in the reign of Ptolemy Philopator, 220–205 BCE) confirms the date of the translation in the third century BCE.

[38] *CPJ* 1.31. By contrast, the Idumaean cult of Kos, fostered by national associations, was continued in the native tongue; see Fraser 1972:280–81.

[39] Polybius 5.86.10; see the account in Tcherikover 1961a:59–75.

ὑψίστωι).[40] Presumably this form of dedication must have been acceptable to the Ptolemies, and there is even evidence that they granted to one prayer-house the status of a place of asylum – a privilege sometimes accorded to Egyptian temples.[41] The Jews' acceptance of such a privilege suggests their support of the legal and political authority of the Ptolemaic regime.

In the early Ptolemaic period (323–180 BCE) there is only one story which suggests serious tension between the court and the Jews. 3 Maccabees relates a tale concerning Ptolemy IV Philopator (222–205 BCE), in which, when prevented by God from entering the Jerusalem temple, the king decreed punishment on all Jews who would not enrol in the worship of Dionysus. When the majority refused, he gathered them in Alexandria and marshalled elephants to trample them to death – a fate from which they were miraculously saved. It is generally recognized that this story is hopelessly garbled, reflecting the fears of Egyptian Jews at a period much later than the time of Philopator.[42] The temple incident is modelled on the story of Heliodorus in 2 Maccabees 3, and the elephant story belongs, if anywhere, to the time of Euergetes II (see below, pp. 37–38). Only the Dionysus reference may belong to the time of Philopator himself: we know he was especially devoted to that God and a papyrus records his decree regulating the Dionysiac cult.[43] The notion that this should be imposed on all Jews is fantastic. It could, however, reflect the situation where Jews who rose to prominence in court circles were faced with the requirement to participate in the religious practices of the palace. 3 Maccabees mentions an 'apostate' Jew, Dositheos, son of Drimylos, in the entourage of the king (1.3). As it happens, papyri record a figure called Dositheos, son of Drimylos (probably the

---

[40] Horbury & Noy 9 (=*CIJ* 1433) and 27 (1443). Onias also dedicated his temple 'to the greatest God' on behalf of the royal family (Josephus, *Ant* 13.67). Fraser 1972:226–27, 282–83 emphasizes the distinction between dedication 'to' and dedication 'on behalf of' a ruler.

[41] Horbury & Noy 125 (= *CIJ* 1449); the inscription probably dates from the first century BCE but refers to a previous grant of 'asylum' status by Ptolemy Euergetes, either Euergetes I (246–222 BCE) or Euergetes II (145–116 BCE). On the right of asylum see Rostovtzeff 1941:2.899–903.

[42] On the date and setting of 3 Maccabees, see below chapter 7.2 and Appendix on Sources. Modrzejewski 1991:121–27 offers a fresh attempt to establish the historicity of 3 Maccabees in relation to the reign of Philopator.

[43] BGU 1211, cited in Walbank 1981:211–12. On the close association of the Ptolemaic dynasty with the Dionysiac cult see Fraser 1972:201–7.

same) as a priest in the royal cult during the reign of Philopator (*CPJ* 127; see below chapter 5.1). Thus it appears that some Jews became highly assimilated during this period in the interests of a political career. 3 Maccabees may contain a memory of such trends, and of the difficulties encountered by Jews who sought advancement while remaining faithful to their exclusive cult.

While in general Judaean immigrants settled peacefully and with every prospect of success, it is here, in relation to their religious peculiarity, that the seeds of later conflict were sown. At the beginning of the Ptolemaic era, Hecataeus of Abdera noted the peculiar aniconic style of Jewish worship and remarked, in a rare negative tone, on their somewhat unsociable and inhospitable style of life' (ἀπάνθρωπός τις καὶ μισόξενος βίος, *apud* Diodorus 40.3.4). More ominous, and more immediately directed against the Jews in Egypt, were the narratives of the Egyptian priest Manetho, who was influential in the court of Philadelphus (282–246 BCE).[44] In one of these, the tyrannical Hyksos regime, a foreign dynasty which devastated Egyptian culture, was associated with the inhabitants of Judaea (*apud* Josephus, *C Ap* 1.73–91). In another, Manetho drew on popular legends to recount the segregation of a crowd of lepers and other polluted persons, led by a priest named Osarseph. This priest was identified as Moses, and the narrative recounts that, in alliance with the 'Shepherds' from Jerusalem, he refused to worship the Gods, sacrificed and consumed the sacred animals, and advocated social isolation (Josephus, *C Ap* 1.228–52). From such passages it appears that Egyptian priests developed a number of stories to rival Jewish accounts of Joseph's rule in Egypt and Jewish versions of the Exodus, in line with a traditional pattern in which dominant

---

[44] These are preserved chiefly in Josephus, *C Ap* 1, where they are both used and rebutted by the Jewish apologist. The most explicit anti-Jewish statements have been attributed to a later editor of Manetho's work ('pseudo-Manetho'); see Gager 1972:113–18 and Gabba 1989:630–35, following Jacoby. This complex and controversial matter cannot be settled here, but it is possible that some of these judgments have been influenced by the doctrinaire conviction that such anti-Jewish statements could not have arisen this early; see the discussion and bibliography in Tcherikover 1961a:361–64, Schürer 3.595–97 and Pucci ben Ze'ev 1993:224–34. Even if Manetho's latent anti-Jewish sentiments were made explicit by a later editor, there is no reason to date that editor long after the Septuagint made the Jewish version of the Exodus available to the Greek-reading public in Egypt.

foreigners were feared and resented as a threat to Egyptian culture.[45] Since religion constituted the core of that culture, the Jews' disdain of the animal-cults was bound to inflame relationships (on Artapanus as an exception, see chapter 6.1). Manetho's narrative shows that such religious tensions, which had already caused difficulties to the garrison at Elephantine,[46] were a potential source of trouble in the early Ptolemaic period.[47]

In the 3rd century BCE, when the Ptolemaic regime was strong and the dominant Greek culture was little influenced by Egyptians, such bones of contention between native Egyptians and immigrant Jews were perhaps of limited political significance. But Manetho's work transmitted native cultural hostilities into Greek and thereby made possible their transference into a wider cultural domain.[48] Later, as Ptolemaic rule weakened under the strain of its dynastic strife, and as it came to depend more on the goodwill of the native population (Egyptian soldiers were first enlisted for the battle of Raphia, 217 BCE), the tolerance and security which Jews enjoyed in the early period could no longer be taken for granted.

---

[45] Osarseph may be a version of the name Joseph, Tcherikover 1961a:363. Jewish tales of the Exodus were deeply offensive to Egyptians, and the annual celebration of the Passover a cause of some irritation (Porten 1984:389). The stories of the diseased people under Moses' leadership look like a response to the Jewish accounts of the plagues (or *vice versa?*). On Egyptian accusations against foreign rulers see Braun 1938:19–23.

[46] *CAP* 30–31, on which see Cowley 1923.

[47] Since Manetho's account is based on popular tales (*C Ap* 1.229), it appears to represent a broad current of Egyptian feeling. The similar tales of expelled lepers found in Lysimachus and Chaeremon indicate the many different versions current among the Egyptian populace (Aziza 1987). Manetho's reference to a law of Osarseph/Moses that 'they should not associate with any except those of their own confederacy' perhaps reflects the social cohesion of the Jews which was already noticeable in this early period. The Egyptian dislike of Jews is reflected in the text of the Torah, where the Egyptians consider it 'abomination' to eat or live with the Hebrews (Gen 43.32; 46.34, since they are 'shepherds', cf. Manetho's term!), and Jewish sacrifices are described as an abomination to Egyptians (Exod 8.22), perhaps because some of the animals sacrificed (e.g. bulls and rams) were sacred to Egyptians. Note also Exod 1.12, where the LXX translation (ἐβδελύσσοντο) may reflect Egyptian attitudes to Jews in the third century BCE.

[48] See Fraser 1972:505–10.

## 2.2 Prominence and Exposure: From Ptolemy VI Philometor to Cleopatra VII (180–30 BCE)

### 2.2.1 Political Developments

Although Judaea passed out of Ptolemaic control at the beginning of the second century BCE, events in their 'homeland' were to exert an important influence on Egyptian Jews in this later Ptolemaic period. In particular, the Hellenizing movement, the desecration of the temple and the Maccabean revolt (175–167 BCE) opened a highly turbulent period in Judaean history in which competing interpretations of Judaism combined with political power-struggles to destabilize the nation. As the nearest safe refuge, it was inevitable that Egypt should receive the overflow from this disturbed pool, both refugees and political exiles (in some eyes, 'pestilential people', 1 Macc 15.15–21).

It is difficult to gauge the effect of this Judaean influx on the Jews already settled in Egypt, but it is unlikely that those who retained their ethnic identity could observe the Jerusalem saga dispassionately. The trauma of these years and the fresh waves of immigration must have done much to heighten the national and political consciousness of Egyptian Jews even if they differed in their judgments on the figures currently in power in Judaea. The letters from Jerusalem to the Jews in Egypt, preserved at the beginning of 2 Maccabees (1.1–2.18), suggest close contacts during the latter half of the second century. They also indicate that at least one segment of the Egyptian Diaspora supported the Hasmonean dynasty and adopted the feast of Hannukah which marked the rededication of the temple. Since Hasmonean ideology fostered a distrust of non-Jews, we may surmise that this attitude, nourished by popular stories of the heroic Maccabeans, may have heightened the ethnic consciousness of the Jewish inhabitants of Egypt.[49]

One particular group of immigrants proved to be of considerable long-term significance. Josephus records that a priest named Onias,

---

[49] See Tcherikover in *CPJ* 1.46–47. (As a modern analogy, one may compare the upsurge of Jewish consciousness among Diaspora Jews after the Six Day War.) Subsequently, the introduction of the book of Esther, and the feast of Purim, suggest a similar atmosphere (Bickerman 1976:225–74). Heinemann 1931:8 suggests that the Hasmonean campaigns against Greek cities created widespread Gentile resentment against Jews, some of which spilled over into Egypt through Greek emigration from Palestine.

thwarted of the high-priesthood in Jerusalem, fled to Egypt and was warmly received in the Ptolemaic court.[50] It appears that there gathered around him a community of Jews who in time came to constitute an important military force. Josephus reports (and archaeology confirms) that this community was settled at a strategic site near Heliopolis, known to Josephus as Leontopolis, but also simply as 'the district of Onias'.[51] It has attracted much interest that Onias constructed here a temple, a sacrificial centre with a full priestly establishment which lasted for more than two centuries before its destruction in 73 CE at the end of the Jewish War. It is likely that this acted as a cultic centre only for the community who lived in its immediate vicinity – much as the Jewish garrison at Elephantine had built their own temple to 'Yaho' centuries before. Certainly extant Jewish literature from Alexandria is silent about this temple, recognizing only the Jerusalem temple as the locale of sacrifice and the object of pilgrimage. Perhaps Onias never intended to attract the whole Egyptian Diaspora: his ambitions could be fulfilled in his priestly leadership of his own community.[52]

In fact Philometor's settlement of Jews in this location seems to have been a shrewd political move. At a time when Egypt still hoped to regain Palestine from Seleucid control, it suited Ptolemaic purposes to harbour a significant anti-Seleucid faction from Judaea, and to encourage their military formation. Moreover, they were granted a site vital for the protection of Egypt's most vulnerable, eastern border. After the invasions and near-annexation of Egypt by Antiochus IV in 170–168 BCE, no Ptolemy could afford to neglect

---

[50] Despite *Bell* 7.423, Josephus makes clear in *Ant* 12.387 that he means Onias IV, and scholars generally accept this latter account. The *Ant* passage suggests a date c. 162–160 BCE; the Ptolemy is therefore Philometor (180–145 BCE). Onias' settlement and temple are described most fully in Josephus, *Ant* 13.62–73 and *Bell* 7.421–36. One papyrus, *CPJ* 132, could throw the question of chronology into confusion, but the reading 'Onias' is not entirely certain – or he may be another of the same name. Modrzejewski 1991:103–8 supports a different chronology.

[51] See e.g. *Ant* 13.65; 14.131; *Bell* 1.190. The 'camp of the Jews' mentioned in the same context seems to have been a separate establishment (Schürer 3.48–49). For an archaeological survey see Kasher 1985:119–35; the inscriptions are collected in Horbury & Noy 29–105 (=*CIJ* 1451–1530).

[52] On Onias' motivation see Tcherikover in *CPJ* 1.44–46. *Ant* 13.62–73 refers to his desire for glory and also his appeal to Isaiah 19.19. The letters of Onias and Ptolemy cited in this passage are clearly spurious – attributing to the king greater concern for Jewish piety than was shown by Onias!

the defences of his country, and the presence of a strong and loyal community at this strategic location fitted royal needs exactly.[53] Thus there emerged in Ptolemaic Egypt a powerful military unit of Judaeans, under the leadership of a general who enjoyed the special confidence of the king. This community of soldiers was to play an important role in Ptolemaic politics and thus to thrust the Jews into the limelight in an unprecedented manner, not always to their advantage.

Philometor's favourable treatment of Onias is matched by other evidence of the prosperity of Jews during his reign (180–145 BCE), though whether he is rightly dubbed by some scholars 'philo-Jewish' is a moot point. Josephus claims (probably with exaggeration) that Philometor placed the whole army under the command of Onias and Dositheos (another Jewish general, *C Ap* 2.49), and reports the king's support of Judaeans in their dispute with Samaritans on the relative merits of their temples (*Ant* 13.74–79). No doubt his decisions were made on the basis of political expediency, but it is intriguing also to find associated with Philometor a Jewish philosopher, Aristobulus.[54] Thus in military and intellectual spheres Jews rose to remarkable prominence at this pivotal moment of the Ptolemaic era.

Whatever favours the Jews received from Philometor were amply repaid by the loyalty of the troops under Onias' command. Philometor struggled throughout his reign to rebuff the claims of his brother (popularly known as Physcon, 'pot-bellied'), who had the support of important segments of the Alexandrian population. At Philometor's death (145 BCE), civil war broke out between Physcon and those loyal to Philometor's widow, Cleopatra II, and at this point Onias made a decision whose implications were to reach far into the future. According to Apion (whose story is endorsed by Josephus, *C Ap* 2.49–56), Onias marched on Alexandria with a considerable force to support the beleaguered queen and her young sons. It seems that this Jewish army was able to call on the support of the Jewish population in the city and thus fatefully committed the Alexandrian Jews to one side of a dynastic

---

[53] On the military significance of the settlement see Tcherikover 1961a:276–81 and Kasher 1985:7–8.

[54] See below, chapter 6.4; his description in 2 Macc 1.10 as 'teacher' of Ptolemy probably inflates his significance.

contest.[55] Militarily the decision was ill-judged: Physcon was too popular to be dislodged and soon gained the throne (as Euergetes II, 145–116 BCE). Fortunately for the Jews, he then married his brother's widow, Cleopatra, and thus diffused the crisis.[56]

For the social and political fortunes of the Jews, Onias' intervention was disastrous. In the short term it exposed the Jews of Alexandria to the wrath of the new king. Josephus (*C Ap* 2.49–56) records a legend in which the king rounded them up ready to be trampled to death by drunken elephants – clearly a variant of the story told in lurid detail in 3 Maccabees and wrongly attributed there to the reign of Philopator (see above, p. 32). It is hard to tell what truth lies behind the legend, but the annual celebration of a miraculous escape from death is probably based on a genuine crisis, unexpectedly resolved.[57] In the long term Onias' intervention established a precedent for future Jewish involvement in political affairs. But it also poisoned the relationships between Jews and non-Jews in Alexandria. More than two centuries later Apion still cast this episode up against the Alexandrian Jews, using it to fuel his charge that they were disloyal to the city. Although they might claim to have supported the legitimate Ptolemaic line, the Jews could now be maliciously portrayed as an alien element in the country, powerful enough to influence events but suspect in their loyalties. It was a reputation which the Jewish community in Egypt was never able to shake off. Tragically, in the Revolt of 116–117 CE, they were to adopt precisely that subversive role with which they had been unfairly charged since the days of Onias.

[55] Only this can explain the subsequent revenge of the king on the Alexandrian Jews. It is striking that Onias could command this loyalty from fellow Jews. Could such generals as the Aetolian Scopas (commander of the army of Ptolemy Epiphanes, Polybius 13.2.1) have called on Aetolian communities to support his cause had a similar situation arisen in his day? The political loyalties of the Jews suggest a strong sense of ethnic identity, even across the social divide between *chora* and *polis*.

[56] Bevan 1927:306–7 notes that most of the Ptolemaic army was in Syria at the time. That Onias failed even in this situation suggests the strength of popular support for Physcon.

[57] Tcherikover (*CPJ* 1.21–23) suggests the king's marriage to his rival brought a sudden amnesty for the Alexandrian Jews. Willrich 1904 argued that the historical kernel of the story in Josephus and 3 Maccabees relates neither to Philometor nor to Euergetes II but to Lathyrus and a crisis for Jews in 88–87 BCE (see below). But the presence of the name Onias in both Apion's and Josephus' account renders his otherwise impressive case problematic.

This is not to suggest that there was any sudden deterioration in the fortunes of Jews after Physcon's coup and Onias' futile march on Alexandria. In their annual festival the Jews celebrated the fact that disaster had been averted, and where prayer-houses were built during Physcon's reign they were dedicated, as before, in honour of the reigning monarch.[58] In fact, the continuing military power of the Jews is demonstrated in their role as river-guards,[59] and especially in the significant part played by Onias' sons in a further dynastic dispute at the end of the second century. After reigning for nine years (116–107 BCE), Ptolemy IX Lathyrus (Soter II) was ousted by his mother, Cleopatra III, in a division of the dynasty which led to continuing hostility and the gradual dissolution of the Ptolemaic empire over the next half century. Both Josephus (*Ant* 13.349) and Strabo (cited by Josephus, *Ant* 13.287) suggest that a crucial component of Cleopatra's power-base was the military force commanded by Chelkias and Ananias, sons of Onias, who now led the military colony in the district of Onias.[60] Strabo's account suggests that Cleopatra's reign was not favoured by the majority of Alexandrians – a fact which could again count to the Jews' discredit when it was remembered that they had given support to an unpopular regime. Prominence inevitably brought exposure, and the Jews were once again dangerously exposed in these years of civil war.

Chelkias and Ananias could be viewed by their contemporaries not just as commanders of a certain military unit, but as representatives of a whole ethnic community with allegiances beyond the boundaries of Egypt. After helping Cleopatra rebuff Lathyrus' attempt to annex Judaea, Ananias is found (Josephus, *Ant* 13.352–55) countering those who advised the queen to occupy Judaea: that would be ungrateful treatment of an ally (Alexander Jannaeus) 'and one moreover who is our kinsman. For you should not be unaware that an injury to him will make all us Jews/Judaeans your enemies' (*Ant* 13.354). If this piece of blackmail has any historical basis it is extraordinarily revealing. It suggests that Jews in Egypt were identified by their leaders with the national interests

---

[58] Horbury & Noy 24 (=*CIJ* 1441) and 25 (=*CIJ* 1442).
[59] Josephus, *C Ap* 2.64, a task which seems to have been broader than merely controlling the crossing at Pelusium, *Bell* 1.175.
[60] A fragmentary inscription mentioning 'Chelkias' has been associated with the son of Onias, but the connection is most uncertain; see Horbury & Noy 129.

of Judaea, and were able to influence a vulnerable Egyptian monarch to the benefit of their homeland. We cannot be surprised that questions would arise as to where the loyalties of Egyptian Judaeans really lay.[61] Ananias' threat suggested that the interests of Judaea would always command higher loyalty than the interests of the country in which he had risen to such prominence. We hear echoes (though they are somewhat uncertain) of an outbreak of violence against Jews in Alexandria in 88 BCE, the date when Lathyrus finally regained power.[62] It represented perhaps not only the king's revenge on his former opponents but also mounting hostility to the influence of Jews in public affairs.

As the Ptolemaic dynasty crumbled it was inevitable that Rome should take an increasing interest in Egyptian affairs. Roman influence had once saved Egypt from a Seleucid conquest (168 BCE), and by the mid first-century BCE the tentacles of Roman power surrounded Egypt, embracing Cyrene, Cyprus and Palestine. Alexandria, however, was deeply suspicious of Rome, and its population fiercely independent. The reign of the Roman puppet, Ptolemy XII Auletes (80–51 BCE), was bitterly resented in Alexandria, a city increasingly wracked by violence and divided by political factions. It can only have added to the ill repute of the Jews when Auletes, once expelled from Egypt by popular revolt, was aided back into the country by Roman power, with the support of Hyrcanus and Antipater in Judaea and the compliance of the Jewish guard at Pelusium.[63] The same pattern of Jewish loyalties – support for Roman power in opposition to the Alexandrian populace – was to be repeated on a further critical occasion in 48/47 BCE. Then the Jews from Onias' district aided Mithridates' relief of Julius Caesar in Alexandria;[64] Alexandrian Jews also gave

---

[61] This is, of course, a classic question for all Diaspora communities. It has been termed in England 'the cricket test': do Pakistanis settled in England support the English or the Pakistani cricket team?

[62] Our only evidence here is Jordanes, *Romana* 81, on which see Tcherikover in *CPJ* 1.25 n63. For an alternative interpretation see Levy 1950–51 and Willrich 1904.

[63] Josephus, *Bell* 1.175; *Ant* 14.98–99. The date of the incident is 55 BCE, three years after Auletes' expulsion from Egypt. See Fraser 1972:124–26.

[64] *Bell* 1.187–92; *Ant* 14.127–32. The latter passage records Antipater's appeal to the Jews in the Onias colony on the grounds of their common nationality and by showing them a letter from Hyrcanus; if this last detail is correct it suggests that even those who worshipped in the temple at Leontopolis recognized the authority of the Jerusalem high-priest.

direct aid to Caesar, despite the opposition of the mass of Alexandrians who considered his presence a step towards Roman annexation.[65]

When Cleopatra VII established her reign (51–30 BCE), her charisma and ambition revived hopes of Ptolemaic glory and the independent power of Egypt. If, in a time of famine, she refused to allow rations of corn to be given to Jews in Alexandria (Josephus, *C Ap* 2.60), that measure must have been politically charged. By now the Jews had become too closely associated with the interests of Rome and too strongly distrusted as an alien element in a city proud of its civic traditions. At Cleopatra's death in 30 BCE, the Jews' allegiance to Rome was to be vindicated by Augustus' annexation of Egypt. But their political alienation had left them vulnerable and was to bear bitter fruit in the following generations.

## 2.2.2 Social Developments

Can we supplement this sketch of the political and military prominence of Jews with broader evidence of their social progress during this second Ptolemaic period? Unfortunately here again our evidence is fragmentary, and almost non-existent for the first century BCE. We will have to rely in part on the fuller evidence of the Roman period, from which some cautious extrapolations can be made. In general, we can confirm the portrait of this period which has begun to emerge, of a community rising in social prominence but simultaneously becoming isolated to a dangerous degree.

Philo's claim (*Flacc* 43) that the Jews in Egypt in the early Roman period numbered 1 million has to be taken with a pinch of salt: no census of Jews could be conducted and exaggeration was in his interests. Nonetheless, the prominence of Jews in the politics of Alexandria around the turn of the era suggests a community which had grown to impressive proportions. Natural increase must be one factor in this growth (it is striking how often Philo refers to the Jewish people as 'populous' [πολυάνθρωπος][66]), but continual

---

[65] See the full discussion of this period in Kasher 1985:13–17.

[66] E.g. *Mos* 1.149; 2.159; *Spec Leg* 1.7, 78, 133; *Praem* 66; *Legatio* 214, 226. Philo also recognizes the populousness of the Egyptians (*Spec Leg* 1.2), a fact which may be attributed to their common disinclination to expose unwanted children (Philo attributes it to the common practice of circumcision and the better diffusion of sperm!).

immigration from Judaea may also have refreshed the Jewish population to a greater degree than that experienced by other ethnic groups. Alongside numerical growth there was a significant advance in social prestige for some Alexandrian Jews. From the second century BCE we know of a number of Jews whose writings suggest their advance to the highest social and educational levels. Aristobulus, the so-called 'teacher' of Ptolemy VI Philometor (2 Macc 1.10), appears to have moved in court circles and to have gained a profound understanding of the Greek philosophical tradition. The author of *The Letter to Aristeas* is also familiar with royal protocol and contributes to a cultured debate on the duties of kings. Alongside these two luminaries we may place Ezekiel the tragedian, the author of *The Wisdom of Solomon* and others, whose works not only display a wide cultural awareness but also presuppose a Jewish audience culturally equipped to appreciate their efforts. We will have more to say about the socio-cultural stance of these authors in chapters 6 and 7, but we note them here to illustrate the social and cultural progress achieved by some Jews during the late Ptolemaic period.[67]

Of course such Jews may represent only a tiny apex at the peak of a large social pyramid. Nonetheless, their cultural sophistication indicates that at least some Jews could pass through the gymnasia of Alexandria – those prized organs of Greek culture whose training was the prerequisite for social success in the life of the city. It is possible that some of these Jews attained full citizenship rights in Alexandria, and not necessarily (as 3 Maccabees would have it) at the expense of their faithfulness to Judaism.[68] In the last century of Ptolemaic rule, Alexandria suffered many periods of political chaos and had its citizenship rules tampered with by several manipulative kings.[69] It is possible to imagine favoured Jews gaining entry to the citizen body by royal nomination as well as through the normal channel of graduation as ephebes.

The economic fortunes of Jews in the later Ptolemaic period are not easy to trace. Commenting on the sufferings of Jews in the pogrom of 38 CE, Philo notes the deprivations of money-lenders,

---

[67] Note also in this connection the metrical Greek epitaphs found especially at Leontopolis, which display in some cases considerable artistic skill: see Horbury & Noy 23, 29–40, 114 and pp. xx–xxiv, and van der Horst 1994.

[68] Tcherikover in *CPJ* 1.37–41. On the vexed question of Jewish political status in Alexandria see the Excursus in chapter 3.

[69] The precedent was set by Physcon (Euergetes II), on whom see Fraser 1972:121–22 and Tcherikover in *CPJ* 1.23 n. 58.

merchants, ship-owners and artisans, some of whom clearly had considerable property worth pillaging.[70] Philo himself came from a family of fantastic wealth (see below, chapter 5.1), probably partly inherited from previous generations. Thus, while we may assume that the bulk of the Jewish residents in Alexandria were of limited means, it is important that the data confirm what we have found in other spheres of life: in their military, political, cultural and economic achievements, some Alexandrian Jews rose to such prominence in the late Ptolemaic period as to exercise a considerable influence on the social life of the city.

At the same time, the Jewish community in Alexandria appears to have achieved a rare degree of political and legal autonomy. In the early Roman period, the community had magistrates (ἄρχοντες), who formed a senate (γερουσία) of elders (πρεσβῦται, *Flacc* 73–85). But previously there had been an ethnarch (ἐθνάρχης) who had either presided over this senate or had performed the tasks later assigned to it.[71] Strabo, who visited Alexandria before this change, was struck by the power of this individual: 'he governs the people (ἔθνος), judges law-suits and supervises contracts and decrees, as if he were the head of an independent state (πολιτεία αὐτοτελής)' (*apud* Josephus, *Ant* 14.117). This suggests a considerable measure of autonomy for a Jewish community confident in its legal and political powers, distinguished as an ethnic unity and large enough to warrant a leader with a rare and impressive title. There is also evidence for a Jewish notary office (*CPJ* 143) and later references to Jewish courts in Alexandria, whose legal competence must have been recognized by the Ptolemaic state.[72] Here was a community with powerful mechanisms of self-regulation and a strong sense of its own identity, almost a state within the state.[73] The fact that members of this distinct community

---

[70] *Flacc* 57; *Legatio* 129; cf. 3 Macc 3.10. Tcherikover analyses these texts in *CPJ* 1.48–50.

[71] Josephus, *Ant* 14.117; Philo, *Flacc* 74. It is often assumed that Augustus created the senate, but Philo's words leave open the possibility that he merely delegated to it the supreme powers previously vested in the ethnarch (Philo calls him a γενάρχης); on *Flacc* 74, see Box 1939 ad loc. and Smallwood 1970:6.

[72] See T. Kethuboth 3.1 and the discussion in Goodenough 1929, whose attempts to trace in Philo indications of Alexandrian Jewish law are not, however, entirely convincing.

[73] The term *politeuma* is associated with the Alexandrian Jews in *The Letter of Aristeas* 310, but it is unclear to whom it refers. The context indicates that it is distinguishable from 'the masses' (who had their own leaders), so it may

also exercised a strong influence on wider social and political affairs carried obvious potential for conflict.

Thus the social and economic success of Jews in their Graeco-Egyptian environment could have ambiguous effects. Moreover, there were important cultural trends in the later Ptolemaic period which acted to their disadvantage. In Egypt's complex mosaic of ethnicity Jews had originally constituted just one immigrant community among many, and both Jewish cleruchs and Alexandrian Jews had been classed with other 'Greeks' in social and cultural distinction from native Egyptians. In time, however, the social barriers between Greeks and Egyptians were partially eroded, while the hostility between Jews and Greeks left the Jews increasingly isolated. To be sure, scholars have often over-estimated the degree of coalescence between Greek and Egyptian cultures, and recent voices have rightly insisted that, in general and certainly at the higher social levels, Greek society kept itself culturally aloof from the civilization it had conquered.[74] Nonetheless, some interpenetration did occur, chiefly as more ambitious Egyptians became Hellenized in 'a slow, uneven and ambiguous process.'[75] Having gained entry into the Ptolemaic army in 217 BCE, Egyptian soldiers came to enjoy the status of cleruch land-holders (though they were given smaller plots), and over time a few penetrated into the upper military echelons. Others who learned Greek gained employment in the local administrative structure. It was from the daughters of such Hellenizing Egyptians that some Greeks took wives (the intermarriage was nearly always this way round); their offspring often bore both Greek and Egyptian names and naturally

represent a smaller propertied group who exercised some administrative functions. Lüderitz 1994:204–8 thinks that it could refer to the *politeuma* of the city of Alexandria and thus not be Jewish at all. It is certainly precarious to base on this one reference far-reaching theories about the 'politeuma' rights of Jews in Alexandria.

[74] Note especially Samuel 1983 and 1989 and Lewis 1986, who maintains that 'the cleavage between the two ethnic groups, and the consciousness of their separateness, remained the dominant fact of socio-political life in Ptolemaic Egypt' (p. 29). A key factor here was the cultural conservatism of the ruling class and their reluctance to learn the native language (Cleopatra VII was the first monarch to do so). The linguistic distinctions, which determined also the legal systems applied to parties at law, were fostered by the Greek pride in education, with the gymnasia as bastions of Hellenistic culture; see also Walbank 1981:115–20 and Bowman 1990:61–63. Goudriaan 1988 rightly insists that ethnicity was determined by social labelling and not simply by descent.

[75] Bowman 1990:61.

sought the privileges of their Greek fathers.[76] The efforts of the Roman authorities to exclude such people from the gymnasia (see below, chapter 3.1) suggest that in the later Ptolemaic era such Hellenized Egyptians were able to break through some of the established ethnic barriers.

In one respect, moreover, the dominant Greeks had always shown a measure of regard for the culture of the country they ruled. Although Egyptian language and literature were disdained, Egyptian religion could not be ignored by people who had long since learned to honour the local Gods in whatever land they found themselves. To be sure, they tended to give Egyptian deities Greek personae, and showed most interest in the Hellenized Egyptian cults of Isis and Serapis; Greeks are rarely found as priests in the traditional cults of the Egyptian deities, not least for linguistic reasons. But there is no mistaking their general respect for the ancient religious traditions of Egypt and their concern not to offend the deities who had been worshipped so successfully by time-honoured customs in hugely impressive temples.[77]

Inasmuch as they maintained their ethnic and cultural distinctiveness, the Jews of Egypt were bound to come under social pressure in this context. When many in their environment were entering a cultural melting-pot, the Jews, it appears, remained largely aloof, preserving their separate identity.[78] At a time when Egyptian nationalism was gaining strength and the Egyptian temples reasserting their social influence,[79] old grievances against the Jews were bound to re-emerge. In the late Ptolemaic period Lysimachus indicates the currency of popular versions of history in which the Jews were once expelled from Egypt as lepers and were characterized by their hatred of religion: these were the sort of people who showed no good will, who maliciously gave bad advice, and who destroyed all temples and altars (*apud* Josephus,

---

[76] Lewis 1986:26–30; Walbank 1981:117–20.

[77] See Samuel 1983:75–101 and Bowman 1990:166–79. While some Greeks found the Egyptian animal cults peculiar, Herodotus (book 2) and Diodorus (book 1) were influential in their attitudes of curious respect.

[78] As Fraser notes: 'only the almost unadulterated survival of Jewish racial integrity and Jewish customs into the Roman period will explain the rapid growth of anti-Semitism in Roman Alexandria. If Jews, like Egyptians, had largely blended with Greeks in the Ptolemaic period, anti-Semitism would be difficult to explain' (1972:57).

[79] See Bowman 1990:30–31 on the native revolts (there were ten between 245 and 50 BCE) and the nationalistic *Oracle of the Potter*.

*C Ap* 1.309). The bone of contention was what Josephus rightly calls the incompatibility of religious customs (*C Ap* 1.224). On the one side is an ancient and sophisticated Egyptian culture, focused in a religious tradition whose animal cults attracted immense popular devotion.[80] On the other, a community of Jews who (with rare exceptions) scorned the animal cults as absurd, and delighted to describe their adherents as sharing the characteristics of the beasts they worshipped.[81] We have only to put ourselves into the shoes of a devout Egyptian to appreciate the animosity that could be directed against an influential Jewish community who maintained the superiority of their foreign customs. It is not entirely surprising to find from the first century BCE a papyrus letter indicating the dangers felt by Jews in Memphis, since 'you know that they loathe the Jews' (*CPJ* 141).[82]

Thus after a period of increasing social and political significance, the Jews of Egypt were to be found at the end of the Ptolemaic era in a precarious position. While their military interventions had displayed the power at their disposal, they had also alienated important sections of the Alexandrian populace, whose discontent was to be compounded by the Roman annexation of Egypt. Numerically and in social organization they had made impressive progress, but in a manner whereby their ethnic distinction had become prominent and their political loyalties suspect. Under the surface of their success lurked animosities which had already broken out in isolated ugly incidents. No doubt the Jewish community welcomed the advent of Roman rule in Egypt (30 BCE),

---

[80] Diodorus recounts (1.83.8) the lynching of a Roman who had killed a sacred cat.

[81] See e.g. Josephus, *C Ap* 1.224–25; 2.66, 85–86; and from Egypt itself, *Aristeas* 138, *Wisdom of Solomon* 15.18–16.14. Most of the animals which were the object of Egyptian worship were classified by Jews as unclean! There may also have been local political rivalries involved, as Bohak 1995 suggests in relation to Onias' settlement.

[82] This papyrus has been further analysed by Rémondon 1960, who notes the religious roots of this anti-Jewish feeling and its particular strength in a religious centre like Memphis. Note however the cautious handling of this text by Modrzejewski 1991:128–30, indicating how the text echoes LXX Exod 1.12. Tacitus, *Hist* 5.4.2, no doubt influenced by Egyptian anti-Jewish literature, suggests that Jews sacrificed rams 'apparently in derision of Ammon. They likewise offer the ox, because the Egyptians worship Apis.' The papyri BGU 1764.12–13 (c. 57 BCE) record disturbances in the Herakleopolite nome involving 'those who do not practise the same religion', possibly Jews.

since they and their compatriots in Judaea had invested much in Rome. Unfortunately, their success was to turn to utter disaster in the course of the next 150 years.

# 3

# *Jews in Roman Egypt: From Augustus to Trajan (30 BCE – 117 CE)*

## 3.1 The Alexandrian Pogrom and Its Aftermath

The annexation of Egypt by Octavian in 30 BCE constituted a devastating blow to Egyptian pride. After Cleopatra's revival of Ptolemaic glory, the demise of the dynasty was a crushing disappointment, and the new regime was inevitably viewed with special resentment. The terms under which the Romans organized their new province were particularly galling: the Ptolemaic army was disbanded and replaced by Roman legions, while the magnificent Ptolemaic palace was taken over by a succession of governors answerable only to the distant emperor. Anti-Roman sentiments were strongest in Alexandria – once indisputably the cultural and financial capital of the Mediterranean world, and now overshadowed by its Western rival. Thus a city already well known for its volatile moods became radically disaffected. Populist leaders easily whipped up emotions in the over-crowded streets, but Alexandrians were seldom able to express their frustration except in petty invective against the governors.[1]

In this context it is easy to see how the Alexandrian Jews could become scapegoats. We have already noted their role in support of Roman troops in the dying years of the Ptolemaic era (p. 40, above). Augustus publicly acknowledged their services in a *stele* (monument) inscribed with his thanks and a clear confirmation

---

[1] Philo's portrayal of Isodorus (*Flacc* 135–39) is matched by Seneca, *Dial* 12.19.6. The contemporary mood in the city is well illustrated by the exuberant acclaim of Euripidean verses in praise of freedom (Philo, *Probus* 141), while at the beginning of the second century CE Dio Chrysostom chides the Alexandrians for their volatility (*Orat* 32). See the discussion of Alexandrian 'nationalism' in Box 1939:xiii–xviii and Willrich 1903:397–400.

of their ethnic and political rights (*C Ap* 2.37, 61).[2] For the first 40 years of the Roman era the Jews in Alexandria enjoyed the leadership of an 'ethnarch' while the Greeks had no king; and although Augustus intervened in c. 11 CE to prevent a further appointment to this Jewish office, the relative Jewish autonomy, which had astonished Strabo (*apud* Josephus, *Ant* 14.117) may still have irked the Greek citizens, who were frustrated in their inability to appoint a βουλή (council).[3] Although they no longer played a military role in Egyptian affairs, the Jews in Egypt could be regarded as a privileged group at a time when privileges were scarce.[4]

One issue in particular seems to have focused grievances against the Jews. In their reorganization of the social and economic structures of Egypt, the Romans attempted to make clear distinctions between native Egyptians and those of genuinely 'Greek' descent. A key aspect of this distinction was the right to enter children for the *ephebeia*, that gymnasium training in which young men were groomed for citizenship and future political participation. This attempt to define the social map involved a complex and controversial investigation of lineage, and this task was given particular urgency by its link with the taxation system. The Romans created a poll tax (*laographia*), applied differentially according to the three recognized classes: Romans, citizens of Greek cities and *peregrini* ('foreigners'). The first two classes were exempt from the tax (or paid it at a reduced rate), while the vast majority of the inhabitants of Egypt fell into the last category. Clearly those who were, or felt they had a right to be considered, citizens had good financial reasons to establish their status, besides the other legal privileges and the social prestige which citizenship entailed.

While the Jews in Alexandria enjoyed certain privileges of self-regulation and freedom to practise their 'ancestral customs', very

---

[2] The ascription of the *stele* to Julius Caesar in the former passage and in *Ant* 14.188 is probably a mistake by Josephus.

[3] Augustus' decision is recorded in Philo, *Flacc* 74 (where he is still described as 'our saviour and benefactor'); the wording of Claudius' decree in *Ant* 19.283 is not easy to square with Philo's account and may be corrupt (but cf. Smallwood 1970:6). Repeated requests by the Alexandrians for permission to appoint a council are attested in *CPJ* 150 (20–19 BCE) and 153 (41 CE); see Tcherikover in *CPJ* 1.55–57.

[4] Cf. Smallwood 1970:11–12 and eadem 1981:233–35. As Bickerman notes in this connection, 'No one likes a privileged alien' (1988:90).

few had the hereditary status of Alexandrian citizenship. Some, however, could lay claim to that status, their ancestors having benefited from the cultural openness of the Jewish community and special grants of citizenship by Ptolemaic kings (see below, Excursus on The Legal Status of Alexandrian Jews). The introduction of the poll tax made the definition of status urgent, and provided a stimulus for as many Jews as possible to claim exemption. The same hope appears to have stimulated others whose status was ambiguous, and already in c. 20 BCE there was concern in Alexandria that the citizen body (*politeuma*) of Alexandrians was being corrupted with 'uncultured and uneducated people' who were putting forward spurious claims in order to evade the tax (*CPJ* 150).[5]

The legal battles faced by Jews are displayed in a petition to the governor dated fifteen years later (c. 5 BCE) from a Jew named Helenos, son of Tryphon (*CPJ* 151). The petition, although badly damaged, appears to concern liability to the poll tax and includes a range of arguments for exemption on the basis of parentage, education and age. It may be significant that his description in the papyrus as an 'Alexandrian' has been scored out by a scribe and replaced by the words 'a Jew from Alexandria'. That correction may be only a technical clarification of his status, but it may also signify the legal and political struggles which faced Jews of a higher social level over the following decades.[6] It was a struggle in which both sides were apt to feel aggrieved. Those Jews whose citizen status was not upheld would complain of discrimination. But there were many Greeks in the citizen body who might feel that 'the Jews' (i.e. those who successfully claimed eligibility) were sneaking their way into privileges to which they had no right.

Such political and legal disputes did not affect all Jews equally. The majority in Alexandria – small-scale artisans, shop-keepers,

---

[5]   On the dating of this document see Tcherikover in *CPJ* 2.26–27. Kasher's doubts about its date and authenticity (1985:311–13) are adequately met by Delia 1991:117–20. Tcherikover 1961a:311–14 gives a valuable summary of the tax-issue and the struggles concerning citizenship.

[6]   It is tempting to read the scribal correction as a hostile act, which it may indeed have been. But given the ambiguity of the label 'Alexandrian' (see Excursus, below), it is possible that the scribe was rightly correcting a title which implied greater rights than those to which Helenos was entitled (Tcherikover in *CPJ* 2.32), or was simply clarifying an ambiguity (Delia 1991:26; Kasher 1985:200–7). There are in fact many other corrections in this papyrus, and some uncertainties in the reading of key terms.

manual workers and the like – had no claims on citizen status and were no doubt more concerned with the pressing needs of daily life. We have fascinating glimpses of the lives of such Jews in contracts for the repayment of small loans, or the conditions laid on Jewish wet-nurses working for 8 *drachmae* a month.[7] But for those higher up the social pyramid, any challenge to their status was a matter of serious concern. There is good evidence for Jewish ship-owners, merchants and even money-lenders in Alexandria, the sort of people with whom Philo felt particular kinship, coming, as he did, from one of the richest families in the city.[8] Such people had the most to lose if the anti-Roman mood were to become diverted into hostility against Jews.

For as long as they remained under the benevolent eye of the Roman authorities, the Jewish community was reasonably secure. But it soon became clear that such benevolence could not be taken for granted, whatever Augustus' *stele* might declare. When Germanicus visited Alexandria in 19 CE he favoured the Alexandrian citizens to the detriment of the Jews – a portent of the policy of his son, Gaius (Caligula). In distributing corn to the citizens, he pointedly displayed the less privileged status of most Jewish residents by excluding them from the benefit (Josephus, *C Ap* 2.63–64). Further, Philo records an uneasy moment (unfortunately undatable) when the Roman governor threatened to disallow the Jewish observance of the Sabbath in affairs of state (*Somn* 2.123–32). Such episodes demonstrated the vulnerability of the Jewish community if future political configurations were to create, even temporarily, a unification of Roman and Alexandrian political interests.

### 3.1.1 The Alexandrian Pogrom

The appointment of A. Avillius Flaccus as governor of Egypt in 32/33 CE initially posed no threat to the Jews. In fact he appears to have acted resolutely to suppress the Alexandrian 'patriotism' which threatened the Jews, disbanding the clubs which were the

---

[7] *CPJ* 146–49; cf. Tcherikover's comments in *CPJ* 1.50–52.

[8] Philo, *Flacc* 57; *Legatio* 129. On Philo's family see below, chapter 5.1. In his account of the pogrom of 38 CE, it is the indignities suffered by people of this social class which Philo feels most keenly, *Flacc* 57, 64, 78–80. Their prominence may have given rise to a perception that the Jews were doing well out of life in Alexandria – a perception echoed in Claudius' comment on their possession of 'an abundance of good things' (*CPJ* 153, line 95).

seed-bed of disaffection and exiling 'trouble-makers' such as Isodorus.[9] However, the death of the emperor Tiberius in 37 CE and the acquisition of power by Gaius radically altered Flaccus' position. His previous political alliances gave him reason to fear Gaius, and he did not relish the prospect of recall to face accusations by his Alexandrian enemies before an unsympathetic emperor, who had a special affection for Alexandria. The Greek leaders in the city (Philo names Dionysius, Lampo and the returned Isodorus) were quick to exploit Flaccus' insecurity, finding him now too weak to resist their demands.[10] Thus, when matters got out of hand in the summer of 38 CE, the governor no longer had the political strength to stamp out disorder with the usual Roman efficiency.

The spark which lit the Alexandrian tinder-box was the visit of the Jewish king, Agrippa, en route from Rome to take possession of his new kingdom (the northern territories in Palestine, previously ruled by the tetrarchs Philip and Lysanias). Although Philo emphasizes the secrecy of his arrival in Alexandria, it is clear that his presence was a matter of jubilation in the Jewish community and was marked by notable public display.[11] Such behaviour was not calculated to make Flaccus' position comfortable, outshone as he was by this new king and imperial protégé. Still less would it please the Alexandrian populace, deprived of their own royalty and confronted by a large community in their midst who fêted a king alien to the interests of the city.[12] Agrippa's previous career

---

[9]  Philo, *Flacc* 1–5, 135–45. Philo's approval of the first five years of Flaccus' rule naturally reflects, like everything else in his account, his partisan Jewish perspective. Although Greek clubs were banned, Jewish meetings in prayer-houses appear to have remained legal; cf. *Legatio* 311–16.

[10]  Philo shows some awareness of the political realities in *Flacc* 6–24, although his notion of a plot hatched between Flaccus and the Alexandrian leaders to 'sacrifice the Jews' (23) is rhetorically exaggerated; cf. Smallwood 1970:14–17.

[11]  Contrast *Flacc* 27–28 with 30 (reference to Agrippa's bodyguard equipped with gold- and silver-plated armour!). The delight of the Jewish community is evident in their negotiations with Agrippa concerning their decree honouring Gaius' accession, which had so far failed to get through to Rome (*Flacc* 103). Willrich's fine analysis of the Alexandrian crisis (1903) rightly discerns the significance of Agrippa's visit, which Philo attempts to play down.

[12]  The annoyance to Flaccus is hinted at in Philo, *Flacc* 30–32, and the insult to Alexandrian pride (*Flacc* 29) is correctly observed by most commentators. One should add the likely resentment against the Jewish community, whose leaders welcomed this foreign king while also benefiting from Alexandrian privileges!

had been so unscrupulous, and his rise to power so sudden, that it was not difficult to mock the pretensions of this new monarch.[13] Someone hit on the idea of a mock royal parade: a well-known lunatic, Carabas (the name means 'Cabbage'), was dressed up in a purple rug, equipped with a paper sceptre, accompanied by a spoof bodyguard and hailed with cries of 'Marin' ('Lord') in the Aramaic language used by Agrippa's subjects.

It was one of those pranks calculated to cause maximum offence with minimum danger. Unfortunately, however, it aroused enough emotion to spill over into a riot, a gathering momentum of street violence which was soon wholly out of control. Stones began to fly, and the crowds, naturally seeking soft targets, concentrated their attack on the more isolated homes and businesses of Jews – that is, those outside the most concentrated Jewish quarter of the city. According to Philo, a terrible succession of atrocities then followed. Over 400 homes and shops were pillaged and Jewish families evicted; most were forced to retreat into the Delta quarter which thus became the first 'ghetto' in history. Outside this quarter individual Jews were set upon, some burned to death, others dragged through the cobbled streets until their bodies were dismembered. Even women were victimized, their Jewish identity tested by a demand to eat pork. Those who refused suffered what Philo records only as 'desperate ill-usage' (*Flacc* 96).

In the midst of this orgy of violence,[14] some of the crowd devised a subtle assault on the Jewish community. It was well-known that the Jewish synagogues were the focus of their religious devotion and that the Jews, peculiarly, allowed there no statue or artistic figure, either of God or of human benefactors. Wherever they could gain entry, the Alexandrian crowds now forced their way into Jewish synagogues and set up statues or busts of the emperor Gaius.

---

The memory of the bitter enmity between Agrippa's grandfather, Herod, and Cleopatra VII may have been another factor in the reaction of the Alexandrian crowds.

[13] Josephus, *Ant* 18.143–239 recounts Aprippa's life-story, including his previous and ignominious visit to Alexandria while on the run from his creditors (151–60); 18.238–39 indicates the surprise at his sudden transition from prison to kingship at Gaius' accession.

[14] It is impossible to establish the precise order of events, not least because Philo's two accounts, in *In Flaccum* and *Legatio ad Gaium*, are inconsistent in their chronology. Some commentators take the attack on the synagogues as the immediate sequel to the mockery of Agrippa, designed to avert Gaius' wrath after this insult to his friend.

Although this took place before Gaius came to insist on his 'divine' status, it was nonetheless a highly effective stratagem.[15] With those figures in place, the buildings were unusable for worship; but to remove them would constitute the gravest offence against the most powerful man in the world. The psychological blow was devastating: with images of Gaius desecrating their synagogues, the Jews were faced with an insult they could do nothing to remove.

That vulnerability was further heightened by the governor Flaccus. Too insecure to prosecute the crimes committed by the crowds, he issued a decree stripping Jews of their most important political rights. According to *Flacc* 54 (cf. 172), Flaccus declared all Jews in Alexandria 'foreigners and aliens' (ξένοι καὶ ἐπήλυδες), thus annulling at a stroke the constitution of the community. At the same time, he allowed himself to be persuaded that the trouble in the city was caused as much by the Jews as by their opponents. Although Philo goes out of his way to insist that the Jews were wholly passive in this crisis, he leaves several clues that the matter was not wholly one-sided – and, indeed, we should not be surprised if some Jews vigorously defended both their persons and their property.[16] In any case, whether his grounds were real or imagined, Flaccus accused the Jews of trouble-making. He had thirty-eight of their elders scourged in the theatre, and condemned others to the outlandish deaths with which he entertained the crowds on Gaius' birthday (August 31st).[17]

One month later, while attempting to celebrate the Feast of Tabernacles, the Jews were treated to the news of Flaccus' arrest. The governor was taken into custody on Gaius' orders and escorted back to Rome to stand trial; ironically, his accusers were not Jews but the Greek leaders of the city who had never forgiven his earlier

---

[15] On the date of Gaius' self-deification and Philo's manipulation of chronology in *Legatio* see Smallwood 1970:206–7.

[16] Philo, *Flacc* 86–94 recounts a search of Jewish houses for arms, which he maintains recovered nothing, not even kitchen knives! The search suggests some grounds for suspicion and it is clear that the Greeks portrayed themselves as victims in these events (*Flacc* 72). The defence of some synagogues (*Legatio* 134) suggests successful Jewish resistance; and Philo himself admits that the Jews 'could not be expected to remain quiet whatever happened' (*Flacc* 48). Nonetheless, there is no reason to think that the Jews were as well armed and organized as they became three years later in 41 CE (*pace* Willrich 1903:407–9); see Box 1939:lix–lxii and Smallwood 1970:47.

[17] Philo, *Flacc* 73–85. Philo does not record the charges, perhaps to avoid leaving any suspicion of Jewish guilt; cf. Balsdon 1934:133.

repression of their activities (*Flacc* 125–27). With the replacement of Flaccus the immediate crisis passed and the riots appear to have abated. But for the Jews many questions had still to be resolved. While the synagogues remained desecrated with images of the emperor, doubts surrounded their right to practise aniconic worship with exemption from the imperial cult.[18] Moreover, while Flaccus' decree remained in force – that the Jews were aliens (ξένοι), not privileged residents (ἐπίτιμοι κάτοικοι, *Flacc* 172) – their communal rights were annulled.[19] Such rights constituted the moorings by which the safety of the Jews was secured (*Flacc* 53). For the Romans the question was not just whether they could restore order in a volatile city; it was also whether the rights of this significant ethnic minority could be accommodated.

### 3.1.2 The Embassies and Claudius' Response

With the permission of the new governor (C. Vitrasius Pollio), both the Jewish and the Greek communities in Alexandria sent delegations to Gaius for his decision on such matters, sailing in the winter of 38 or 39 CE.[20] Philo headed the Jewish five-man delegation and Apion (a famous Homeric scholar) the Greek, and it is to Philo that we owe our knowledge of their fate.[21] For the Jews it was a perilous mission. Gaius was not renowned for his commitment to justice; he was much influenced by Helicon, an Alexandrian and anti-Jewish influence in his household; and his recent obsession with his own divinity was hardly likely to ease relations with Jews who considered such claims blasphemous. In fact, during the months in which they waited for an audience with the emperor, the Jews' crisis was considerably deepened by his decision to endow the Jerusalem temple with an image of himself

---

[18] It appears that the synagogues were not cleared before the decision awaited from Gaius, and eventually given by Claudius (*pace* Smallwood 1970:23). Gaius' anger at the destruction of an imperial altar in Jamnia (*Legatio* 199–206) indicates what his reaction would have been to the dismantling of similar honours in the Alexandrian synagogues. Moreover, Philo shows that aniconic worship and the emperor cult were issues of central importance to his embassy (*Legatio* 118, 132–54, 191, 353–57).

[19] For the question of the political rights on the agenda of the embassy see the Excursus below.

[20] For discussion of the date see Smallwood 1970:47–50.

[21] The information in Josephus, *Ant* 18.257–60 is of secondary value; it is certainly incorrect on the number of delegates.

as Neos Zeus Epiphanes (*Legatio* 346). Philo vividly portrays the sense of looming catastrophe which engulfed the Jewish delegates on hearing this news, the sense that Alexandrian issues, large as they were, had been dwarfed by an imperial death-threat to the whole Jewish people (*Legatio* 184ff.).

Fortunately, thanks to Agrippa's dramatic appeal, the masterful procrastination of Petronius (the legate of Syria) and Gaius' own vacillation, the threat to the temple was averted. The Alexandrian delegates, having waited so long, persisted until their issues could be heard. However, even now they found the emperor less than fully attendant to their claims. Philo's account, which has the Jews tagging along behind an emperor distracted by building operations, no doubt suffers from exaggeration; but it suggests that Gaius had neither the patience nor the sympathy to settle the Jewish case. But for the emperor's assassination in January 41, it might have run on indefinitely.[22]

The news of Gaius' death and the accession of Claudius had a dramatic effect on Jews throughout the empire. In Alexandria, with the hopes of the Alexandrian Greeks suddenly crushed, the Jews no doubt took the opportunity to cleanse their prayer-houses. Moreover, a section of the Jewish community, probably those with least stake in the peace of the city, initiated revenge on their Greek opponents (Josephus, *Ant* 19.278–79). We have no Alexandrian narrator to indicate what form these counter-attacks took, but Josephus admits that weapons were involved and it appears that reinforcements were gathered from the countryside and even from Judaea.[23] It was a fateful move, and no doubt one deeply regretted by the more assimilated members of the community. This aggression of Jews against Alexandrians, however justified by their appalling experiences three years earlier, gave the anti-Jewish leaders in Alexandria just what they were looking for: positive evidence that the Jews were hostile to the interests of the city and trouble-makers in their midst.

---

[22] Josephus' account (*Ant* 18.257–60) suggests that Apion and his delegation had much the better of the argument before Gaius. He also informs us that Alexander the Alabarch, Philo's brother and perhaps one of Philo's delegation, was imprisoned in Rome by Gaius (*Ant* 19.276).

[23] Josephus, *Ant* 19.278; Claudius' *Letter* (*CPJ* 153) lines 96–97. Note also *CPJ* 152, a letter from the summer of 41 CE, where a Greek dealer warns his agent to beware of the Jews.

Although the Roman governor this time successfully restored order, it was clear that this dispute, together with the unresolved issues from Gaius' reign, would have to come before Claudius. Thus new delegations were dispatched from Alexandria. The Greeks seem to have enabled their impressive new ambassadors to take over the issues from the earlier delegation, but the Jews appeared before Claudius in *two* delegations, much to the emperor's annoyance (*CPJ* 153, lines 90–92). It appears that these two Jewish groups – probably the old delegation of Philo and a new one dispatched after the recent violence – signify a split in the Jewish community. Philo's party represented the interests of the higher-status Jews, who sought to restore the *status quo* by diplomatic placation and were anxious to press their claims to citizen status. In all likelihood, the other delegation represented the militant stance of important segments of the Jewish community in Alexandria, which had become radicalized during Philo's absence and willing to resort to violence.[24] Standing before Claudius with their different aims and tactics, they seemed to the emperor as if they lived in 'two different cities' (*CPJ* 153, line 90). Whatever else they had failed to achieve, the Alexandrians' hostility and Gaius' procrastination had divided Jewish opinion and discredited the leadership of socially embedded Jews like Philo. The Jewish instigation of violence and the second Jewish delegation were tokens of the new aggressive mood which had taken hold of the Alexandrian Jewish community.

A number of hearings appear to have taken place before Claudius, with Agrippa playing some mediatorial role on behalf of the Jews. The results emerge in two forms: i) Josephus' version of an edict from Claudius concerning the religious rights of the Alexandrian Jews (*Ant* 19.280–85);[25] and ii) a papyrus copy of a

---

24  This hypothesis of a division in the Jewish community was first mooted by Willrich 1925 and has been widely supported since, though with varying nuances. Willrich suggested that the new delegation was more 'orthodox' than Philo (he pointed to the narrow viewpoint of 3 Maccabees) and hence suspicious of the Hellenizing tendencies of Philo's class. Momigliano 1961:96–97 argued that 'the two embassies came respectively from Jews with and Jews without Alexandrian citizenship', naturally divided by rivalries and jealousies. The fullest and most illuminating treatment of the question is by Tcherikover in *CPJ* 1.66–69 and 2.50–53. Philo's disdain of political militants is clear in *Somn* 2.82–84.

25  For discussion of this edict see Tcherikover 1961a:409–15 and a summary of his views on the interpolations in *CPJ* 1.70–71 n. 45. Cf. Feldman's note in the

letter sent from Claudius to the city of Alexandria, perhaps the most precious of all the papyri concerning Jews in Egypt (P Lond 1912 = *CPJ* 153). Since there are doubts concerning the authenticity of some clauses in Josephus' edict, it is the papyrus letter which provides our best, as well as our fullest, evidence for the decisions of Claudius. And these were to determine the fortunes of Jews in Alexandria for generations to come.

At the request of the Greek delegates, Claudius in his letter accepts various honours bestowed on him by the city and settles some details in its administration; he confirms the right of all current ephebes (except those of slave-descent) to enter the citizen body, but procrastinates on the renewed Alexandrian request to be allowed a *boule*. Concerning the civic unrest in relation to the Jews, Claudius resists the pressure from both sides to put the blame on the other, though he indicates his anger with the whole course of events, especially those who renewed the conflict (meaning, presumably, the Jews). He insists that the Alexandrians behave in a friendly manner towards the Jews and, in particular, that they do not outrage any of their religious customs but allow them to observe their own customs as had Augustus (lines 83–88; cf. the edict in *Ant* 19.283–85).

The Jews, however, are instructed not to be concerned about more than they previously had (μηδὲν πλήωι ὧν πρότερον ἔσχον περιεργάζεσθαι) – a phrase whose meaning depends on what Claudius and the Alexandrian authorities considered to have been the *status quo ante* as far as Jewish political rights were concerned. There is reason to believe that, despite the justified protests of enfranchised Jews, the phrase was meant to suggest that Jews were constitutionally barred from Alexandrian citizenship and that some had been worming their way illegitimately into this category.[26] Certainly Claudius goes on to instruct Jews not to take part in the contests organized by *gymnasiarchoi* and *kosmetae* – officials who regulated the activities of ephebes in the gymnasium.[27] He thus

Loeb edition ad loc.; Bell 1924:15–16; Kasher 1985:262–89 (with further bibliography).

[26] On the validity of this interpretation, against those who consider that all Jews, or none, were seeking Alexandrian citizenship, see the Excursus below.

[27] It is unfortunate that this phrase (lines 92–93) contains difficulties both in text and in translation. It is not entirely clear if the text reads ἐπισπαίρειν or ἐπισπαίειν, and given the copyist's imperfect skills it could be that either of these is a misspelling. Taking the text as ἐπισπαίειν (a corrupt form of ἐπεισπαίειν) would suggest that Claudius prohibits Jews from 'forcing their

appears to ban Jews from future gymnasium education and so from all the opportunities and privileges (including Alexandrian citizenship) which the gymnasia provided.[28] And this impression is confirmed by the following phrase, which urges the Jews to be content with the good things they enjoy *in a city not their own* (ἐν ἀλλοτρίᾳ πόλει, line 95). Despite recognition that the Jews had lived in Alexandria from of old (line 84), Claudius here suggests that it will be illegitimate for Jews to claim 'Alexandrian' status in its full legal sense.[29] His final comments indicate his suspicion of their revolutionary tendencies and threaten drastic action against any disobedience as against 'a common plague for the whole world'.[30] His treatment of 'the Jewish question' thus finishes in a tone calculated to warn Jews neither to question nor to subvert these imperial decisions.

In some respects Claudius' ruling, with its concern not to label either side as the guilty party, constitutes an effective solution to the cycle of violence in Alexandria. But the result was by no means wholly advantageous to the Jews. On the one hand, their communal right to observe their 'ancestral customs' had been vindicated, and further desecration of their synagogues now rendered illegal. On

way into' the games organized by (or, less likely, the elections of) the *gymnasiarchoi* and *kosmetae*. If we keep to the reading ἐπισπαίρειν (which is probably safer), we are left with a verb only once attested in Greek literature, with the sense 'to be in alarm'. Kasher 1985:314–21 (following Radin 1925 and others) has given this verb the sense 'harass', and implausibly suggests that the Jews were causing trouble in the crowds of spectators at the theatre. It is much more likely that the meaning is 'to struggle in' (i.e. take part in) the gymnasium games. See the discussion by Tcherikover in *CPJ* 2.53, Davis 1951:106 and Harris 1976:92.

[28] The ruling on ephebes in lines 53–57 suggests an amnesty for all registered in the *ephebeia* to date (except those of slave-descent). This might suggest that Jews currently registered as ephebes or citizens were not to be struck off the register, but no more were to be admitted in future; so Jones 1926:30.

[29] Claudius may have followed here Apion's reasoning (Josephus, *C Ap* 2.65) that the Jews' religious distinctiveness was evidence against their claim to be Alexandrian citizens. How Philo and his friends responded to this we do not know, and it was perhaps their inability to do so effectively which proved fatal to their cause. Josephus' only response is to say that Jews are being faithful to their own customs, as people who came to Alexandria from outside (*C Ap* 2.67). It is striking how clumsily that plays into the hands of his opponents and how closely its matches Claudius' judgment!

[30] It is possible that this sharp tone is influenced by the simultaneous trouble in the Jewish community in Rome; see Momigliano 1961:29–34 and below, chapter 10.3.

the other hand, those Hellenized Jews who had legitimately gained Alexandrian citizenship must have been deeply dismayed by this verdict. In that little phrase, 'in a city not their own', was sounded the death knell to their long and successful attempts to integrate into the social and political life of the city. Although guaranteed religious freedom, they were now denied permission to give their children the educational and social advancement they had themselves enjoyed.[31] To Philo and those of his social class it was a disaster. In effect Claudius had halted the social and cultural integration of such Jews – at least as long as they identified themselves as Jews. As far as we know, Philo's philosophical enterprise, and all that it represented in cultural accommodation with Hellenism, was taken no further in the next generation. The leadership of the Jewish community passed into the hands of men whose horizons were narrower and whose social ambitions were necessarily restricted. The violent events of 66 CE and the total war of 116–117 CE demonstrate the tragedy of this fatal change of conditions in the Alexandrian community.

## Excursus: The Legal Status of Alexandrian Jews

Any interpretation of the experiences of Alexandrian Jews during these turbulent years has to address a complex range of questions concerning their political and legal rights. An immense body of scholarly literature has been devoted to these controversial matters, only a fraction of which can be referred to here. However, the outlines of the debate may be usefully sketched, and some justification offered for the interpretation given above. After noting the problems of our topic (I) and sketching the main scholarly options (II), I will describe what I consider to have been the *two*

---

[31] It is instructive to contrast the assessment of this solution by Smallwood and Tcherikover. Smallwood views Claudius' decision as 'a statesmanlike and impartial solution, aimed both at rectifying the harm done to the Jews during Gaius' principate and at pacifying the Greeks' (1970:31); cf. Box 1939:lv. She had earlier described the desire of Jews to obtain Greek citizenship, with exemption from its religious obligations, as an 'attempt to make the best of both worlds. It was a selfish aspiration and one which the Greeks justifiably opposed' (1970:14). Tcherikover, however, regrets that Claudius blocked the Jews' opportunities to acquire civic rights. His settlement did not favour the Jews but in fact 'led to very unfavourable results as regards the cultural development of the Jewish community' (in *CPJ* 1.73–74).

legal issues involved in the Alexandrian crisis: the communal rights of the whole Jewish community (III) and the citizen rights of a minority (IV). This double aspect of the crisis can then be shown to explain the varied, and initially confusing, statements offered by our sources (V).

## I. The Problems for Interpretation

A number of interlocking difficulties make it problematic even to see, let alone to interpret, the issues at stake for Alexandrian Jews. We may mention here just four:

1. Problems arise in the first instance from the fact that the Jews' legal rights were already an ambiguous and controversial matter in the period we are investigating. We are fortunate to be able to hear voices from many sides: from the Greeks, in the form of Apion (but only as cited by Josephus in *Contra Apionem*) and the corrector of Helenos' petition (*CPJ* 151); from the Jews, in the form of Philo and Josephus; and from Claudius, in the form of the letter to the Alexandrians (*CPJ* 153) and the decree (but only as cited by Josephus, *Ant* 19.280–85). These make clear that there were many different perceptions of the Jews' rights and that almost every claim was controversial. Thus, for instance, when Claudius rebukes 'the Jews' for being concerned about 'more than they previously had' (*CPJ* 153 lines 89–90) we are hearing only one, inevitably prejudiced, understanding of the situation. This phrase perhaps charges all Jews with the aspirations of a few (we are familiar enough today with generalizing slurs against minority groups) and may well depict as 'more than they previously had' what the Jews concerned thought were their long-established rights! In a controversial matter like this, hardly any statement can be taken at face value.

2. Besides their prejudices, our sources are also woefully inadequate. As already noted, we hear Apion's charges and read Claudius' decree only through Josephus, who has a well-founded reputation for selectivity and adaptation in handling his sources. Our papyrus sources give us more immediate access to the crisis, but they are imperfectly preserved and sometimes ambiguous at crucial points: we have noted the difficulty in discerning the intent in the correction of Helenos' petition (above n. 6) and the problems in interpreting one obscure, and possibly corrupt, term in Claudius' letter (above n. 27). Moreover, we are only imperfectly informed about the terms

under which the Jews were settled in Alexandria, and the rules and conditions of Alexandrian citizenship (Delia 1991). Only the foolhardy would make more than a tentative claim to understand what the Jews and their opponents were really at odds about.

3. Our problems are compounded by the fact that all the central terms in the debate are ambiguous and could be used in more or less technical senses. Πολίτης is the least ambiguous, since it generally has the limited sense of 'enfranchised citizen' of a πόλις (Delia 1991:11–13); but even this term can be used loosely, meaning simply a 'resident' (perhaps, for instance, in Philo, *Flacc* 47). Πολιτεία (with its associate ἴση πολιτεία) is an exceptionally slippery term, since its meaning can range from 'citizenship' through 'constitution' and 'civic rights' to simply 'way of life'.[32] Philo's statement that his embassy to Rome was contending for their πολιτεία (*Legatio* 349) is thus less than helpful in our quest! In the same work he says they were trying to prove that they were Ἀλεξανδρεῖς (*Legatio* 194), but that term also has a range of uses, some legally defined (= an Alexandrian citizen, as is usually clear from the literary or social context), and some reflecting common parlance (= a resident of Alexandria; see Delia 1991:23–28). Discerning in which sense our authors use such terms, or how they exploit their ambiguity, is a peculiarly difficult operation.

4. To complicate matters yet further, scholars' interpretations of the Alexandrian crisis and the Jews' legal ambitions are not uninfluenced by the models they employ and their own political commitments. Those who understand Alexandrian Jews as enjoying (or attempting to gain) citizenship may be unduly influenced by the movement for Jewish 'emancipation' in the West over the last two centuries (though they may evaluate the Jews' ambitions very differently, above n. 31). Conversely, those who consider the Jews could have entertained no such desire, since it constituted a compromise of their 'orthodoxy', may be working with assumptions derived from their own contemporary Jewish contexts.[33] In general,

[32] Some, and perhaps all, of this range is evident in Philo's usage: *Flacc* 53; *Legatio* 157, 193, 349, 363. Colson, in the Loeb translation, renders this term 'citizenship' (except in *Legatio* 193: 'body politic'). Smallwood, in her edition of the *Legatio* (1970), translates 'civic position' or 'political rights'.

[33] Kasher 1985:261 n. 35 accuses Tcherikover of employing false analogies from recent 'emancipation', but is himself accused of political bias ('Israeli Zionism') by Cohen 1982.

it is dangerous to assume that Alexandrian Jews employed simple or unified definitions of 'orthodoxy'; that way we might exclude important evidence on the basis of false assumptions.[34]

## II. The Main Scholarly Options

Although some viewpoints defy simple classification, we may divide the main interpretative options into three categories, which have each in turn represented a consensus view:

1. The older view, now universally abandoned, was that *all Jews in Alexandria were fully enfranchised Alexandrian citizens*. It was Josephus' sweeping and exaggerated statements (listed above, chapter 2 n28) which were chiefly responsible for this opinion. Besides the implausibility of the notion that even the lowliest members of this large community were included in the élite citizen body, the discovery of Claudius' letter (*CPJ* 153) rendered this construction of the situation quite impossible.[35]

2. After the publication of Claudius' letter and other relevant papyri, a number of scholars suggested that *the Jewish community was pressing for the grant of Alexandrian status to all its members*. Thus Bell suggested that 'the Jews were agitating for the full citizenship' and Box wrote of a 'Jewish attempt to gain recognition of a claim to Alexandrine citizenship'.[36] Again there are problems in conceiving of the whole community gaining citizen status (a carefully guarded privilege), though, if moderated to apply only to a minority, this interpretation could make practical sense. Its

---

[34] Kasher 1985 is a particularly glaring example of this Procrustean methodology. Assuming the viewpoint of the author of 3 Maccabees, he writes: 'While some individual Jews may have been interested in the gymnasium in order to gain Alexandrian citizenship, they were most probably apostates, and their small number could not have created a problem great enough to bring to the attention of the emperor' (312–13; cf. pp. 206, 211–32, 312–13, 335–36). Although he notes the existence of Jewish citizens in Cyrene, he does not modify this opinion, whose question-begging assumptions are revealed in the comment that 'they could not have been orthodox Jews in the Palestinian sense' (336). On the problems of categories like 'orthodoxy' and 'deviation' see below, chapter 4.2.

[35] Although supported by Schürer and Juster, this view had already attracted weighty opposition (Willrich, Wilcken, Engers et al.) before the publication of the decisive letter. This early stage of the debate is well summarized by Bell 1924:10–16.

[36] Bell 1924:16; Box 1939:xxxviii; cf. Smallwood 1970:12–13, 16–17, 25; 1981:234.

strength lies in connecting the Alexandrian worries about the purity of their citizen body (*CPJ* 150; 153, lines 52–57) with Claudius' warning to Jews not to seek 'more than they had before' (*CPJ* 153, lines 89–90). However, as we have just seen, that phrase should be treated with caution before it is taken as a straightforward description of reality.

3. A number of influential scholars now argue that *the political rights for which the Alexandrian Jews fought were not citizen rights at all but the 'politeuma' rights of the Jewish community*. According to this viewpoint, the πολιτεία which Flaccus questioned, and which Philo's delegation tried to regain, was the Jewish 'constitution', the civic rights of independence and self-government enjoyed by the Jewish *politeuma* in Alexandria. Thus Smallwood suggested that the Jewish *politeuma* enjoyed an intermediate status between the native Egyptians and the Greek citizens and that it was this status which Flaccus abolished with his decree that Jews were not κάτοικοι but ξένοι (*Flacc* 172).[37] Developing this line of interpretation, and in the fullest recent survey of the question, Kasher 1985 argues that the point at issue between Jews and Greeks was the *politeuma* of the Jews. This was independent of the Greek *polis*, with its rights guaranteed by Roman (earlier Ptolemaic) authority; it thus irked the Greeks in Alexandria who tried to get it abolished and the Jews designated 'foreigners'. The Jews were 'citizens' of their *politeuma* but not of the city, and had no desire to become so either openly or fraudulently. Claudius therefore did not frustrate the Jews' ambitions but vindicated them completely.

This last viewpoint may be said to represent the current consensus, though not all share Kasher's doubts that any loyal Jew would want Alexandrian citizenship, and many consider it likely that at least some Alexandrian Jews were also enfranchised citizens of the *polis*. After wrestling with the sources, and taking into account some recent work on the *politeuma*,[38] I would suggest a picture rather more complex than that currently offered. In particular I believe that the disputes in Alexandria concerned two distinct, though not unrelated, issues: i) the legal status of the Jewish

---

[37] Smallwood 1970:6–11; 1981:227–30. For earlier suggestions along these lines cf. e.g. Davis 1951:93–112.

[38] The sources are best presented by Tcherikover 1961a:309–28 and in *CPJ* 1.36–43, 57–74. Recent studies of the *politeuma* include Zuckerman 1988 and Lüderitz 1994.

community as a whole, and ii) the citizen rights of a minority of Alexandrian Jews. We may examine each in turn.

### III. The Legal Status of the Alexandrian Jewish Community

The immediate cause of Philo's embassy, and the legal issue which had been raised by Flaccus' declaration, was the set of 'rights' (δίκαια) which had been enjoyed by the Jewish community and sanctioned by the supreme authority in Egypt (first the Ptolemies, then the Roman governors). When Flaccus declared that the Jews were ξένοι and not ἐπίτιμοι κάτοικοι (Philo, *Flacc* 54, 172: does Philo reproduce the terms correctly?), he seems to have annulled the guarantees on which the Jewish community relied for the governance of its communal life and the preservation of its ancestral customs.

Unfortunately it is not clear precisely what legal privileges are here in view. It is almost universally assumed that the Jews in Alexandria constituted a πολίτευμα. In fact, as we noted in the previous chapter (above p. 43 n. 73), the only use of this term in relation to Alexandrian Jews is in *The Letter of Aristeas* 310; it is not used either by Philo or by Josephus (except in the latter case in paraphrasing *Aristeas*, *Ant* 12.108). There the 'leaders of the *politeuma*' seem to be distinguished from 'the leaders of the mob' and it is not clear to what sort of institution the former term refers.[39] Even if it does designate some general ethnic association, Lüderitz has demonstrated, against the *communis opinio*, that one would not use the term πολίτης to designate a member of a πολίτευμα; in all cases where the two terms appear together, πολίτης bears reference to the *cities* in which the members of the πολίτευμα had their citizenship (i.e. their cities of origin), not the *politeuma* in which they are currently incorporated.[40]

As we have seen, Josephus' global claims for Alexandrian rights (above, chapter 2 n. 28) are to be treated with some suspicion; in any case they are mostly too vague to aid our enquiry. It seems likely that the rights accorded to the community by the Ptolemies,

---

[39] For the interpretation of this difficult text (which Josephus tried to simplify, *Ant* 12.108), see Tcherikover in *CPJ* 1.9 n. 24; Smallwood 1970:5 n. 5; Kasher 1985:208–11; Zuckerman 1988:181–84; Lüderitz 1994:204–8. Lüderitz 1994 sets out the many possible meanings of *politeuma*.

[40] Lüderitz 1994:194–95: 'that πολίτης was a term for the members of an association (or a politeuma) is nowhere attested and seems improbable' (195); *contra* e.g. Schürer 3.89 n. 4; Kasher 1985:198.

and at least partly sustained by Augustus (inscribed on his *stele*, Josephus, *C Ap* 2.37), concerned two interrelated matters: the right to some measure of self-government and the right to practise their 'ancestral laws'. The first probably included the appointment of a governing body (initially headed by an ἐθνάρχης, then by a γερουσία: see chapter 2, p. 43), the establishment of law courts and archives, and the control of some internal fiscal affairs (e.g. the collections for Jerusalem). The second may have been vaguely expressed, but may also have specified the inviolability of the 'ancestral religion' (the phrase is used twice in Claudius' decree, *Ant* 19.283–84).

Such rights amounted to the recognition that the Jews in Alexandria were not just 'foreigners' whose temporary domicile was in Alexandria, but 'privileged residents' (ἐπίτιμοι κάτοικοι) entitled to call themselves (in the broad sense) 'Alexandrians'. Their special rights set Jews in Alexandria well above ordinary Egyptians and even above most other non-citizen residents in the city; certainly Strabo (*apud* Josephus, *Ant* 14.117) considered that the Jewish community was particularly well developed in its structures and privileges. When Flaccus suddenly dissolved these privileges in the midst of the pogrom of 38 CE he destroyed a long-standing tradition of enormous social value to Alexandrian Jews. He also cut away their ground of appeal against the desecration of the synagogues, which constituted an infringement of their 'ancestral religion'. Since they were unable now to use the synagogues, and had reduced chances of redress for the damage suffered in the pogrom, it was a matter of general concern that Philo's delegation present the case for the πολιτεία-rights of the whole community as urgently and effectively as possible.

## IV. The Citizen Rights of a Minority of Alexandrian Jews

Although the legal status of the whole community was at stake in the Alexandrian crisis, and was perhaps the central brief of Philo's delegation, I would contend that some Alexandrian Jews also had full citizen status, that this had been a long-standing subject of controversy and that it was one of the matters fought over by the competing delegations which appeared before Gaius and Claudius.

Alexandrian citizenship was a prized possession carrying important legal and financial privileges, as well as considerable social prestige. Diodorus informs us that in his day (c. 60 BCE), there were about 300,000 Alexandrian citizens, not all, of course, resident in Alexandria (17.52.6). The status was acquired primarily by inheritance (if both parents were citizens), though it was also sometimes granted to individuals by Ptolemaic kings or by the citizen body (Delia 1991:28–30, 55–56). Whereas the communal rights of the Alexandrian Jews were a matter for the central political authority (the Ptolemaic kings and later the Roman emperors or governors), citizenship was, at least in theory, regulated by the citizen body itself: an important aspect of their request for a Council (*CPJ* 150) was the desire to supervise more effectively the entry of individuals onto the citizen roll.

There is sufficient evidence that at the peak of the Jewish social pyramid were a minority of families, mostly still loyal to the Jewish community, who had attained citizen status, or at least considered they were entitled to it. Because of the ambiguity of the key terms, some of the evidence cited in this regard is of dubious value. We may doubt, for instance, that the Helenos who petitioned the governor (*CPJ* 151) as an 'Alexandrian' was using that term in the narrow legal sense (when he would surely have cited his deme and tribe).[41] We may also treat with suspicion Josephus' claims that Augustus declared the Jews in Alexandria to be 'citizens of Alexandria' (*Ant* 14.188), given his notorious unreliability on these matters (e.g. in his slippery response to Apion, *C Ap* 2.37–72).[42] However, several pieces of evidence suggest clearly enough that a few Alexandrian Jews enjoyed citizen status:

1. It is apparent from a deed of divorce (*CPJ* 144, 13 BCE) that Hermogenes, the husband of the Jewess Apollonia, was an Alexandrian citizen; he was probably also a Jew. Apollonia was not, apparently, of the citizen class (her father Sambathion has no deme indicated). Since future offspring could only be citizens if both parents were of that status, why would this citizen, Hermogenes, marry a non-citizen wife? The most probable answer is that he, like she, was a member of the Jewish community and endogamy had been for him the most important criterion in his marriage.

---

[41] Dositheos, son of Cleopatrides, 'the Alexandrian' is a similarly uncertain case (Josephus, *Ant* 14.236); we have already noted the difficulty in interpreting Philo's assertion that his delegation went to Rome 'to show that we are Alexandrians' (*Legatio* 194).

[42] I also leave out of account Philo, *Probus* 6, appealed to by both Box and Smallwood, but not obviously relevant to Jews at all. *Mos* 1.35 is regarded as revealing by some (e.g. Wolfson 1944 and Tcherikover in *CPJ* 1.63, though they interpret it differently); but it is not clearly related to the contemporary Jewish struggle and its use of terms is inexact (see Barraclough 1984:426).

2. Philo's brother, Alexander, and later a Jew named Demetrius, held the high office of 'Alabarch' (Josephus, *Ant* 18.259; 20.147). Although the meaning of this title is not entirely clear,[43] the possession of this municipal office and, in Alexander's case, his close relations with the imperial court, suggest the highest social prestige.[44] It is rightly assumed by most scholars that such figures must have had Alexandrian citizenship. This would suggest that the same was the case for Philo himself, as indeed Philo's social and educational advantages would themselves suggest.[45]

3. At an earlier period, figures like Ezekiel, Aristobulus and the author of *The Letter of Aristeas* had apparently acquired the most advanced Hellenistic education through the gymnasia (there is no evidence for Jewish schools providing this sort of education). The court profile of the latter two also suggests high status. We have no reason to doubt that there continued to be Jews of this social and cultural level who properly enjoyed the privileges of Alexandrian citizenship in the early years of the first century CE, some perhaps through personal grants of citizenship.[46]

4. In his response to pure allegorists (see below, chapter 5.1), Philo insists that certain tasks are not permissible for Jews on the Sabbath; he includes instituting proceedings in court and acting as a juror (*Mig Abr* 91). Since there was presumably no danger of Jewish courts meeting on the Sabbath, he must have in mind Greek juries, on which only citizens could serve. He would hardly mention this subject unless there was a real possibility that some Jews would break the Sabbath in this matter.

---

[43] It is perhaps connected with customs-collection on the Nile; see the discussion by Tcherikover, *CPJ* 1.49 n. 4, Schürer 3.136 n. 43, and Smallwood 1970:4 n. 4, who considers that these Alabarchs 'must have had Greek citizenship'.

[44] Alexander was 'overseer' of the Egyptian property of Antonia, the mother of Claudius (Josephus, *Ant* 19.276–77).

[45] On Philo's acculturation see below, chapter 6.5. Philo praises those who give their children gymnasium education (*Spec Leg* 2.229–30; cf. *Prov* 2.44–46) and talks of Moses himself having Greek teachers (*Mos* 1.21). It is likely that his family was granted Roman citizenship in Augustus' time (so Fuks in *CPJ* 2.197), and this was normally dependent on citizenship of a Greek *polis* (Delia 1991:39–45).

[46] See especially Tcherikover in *CPJ* 1.37–43, 61–62. Josephus indicates that Apion had received citizenship through a personal grant, and his response indicates that the same may have been the case for some Alexandrian Jews (*C Ap* 2.41).

5. In a well-known passage (*Flacc* 78–80), Philo recounts, among the cruelties of the pogrom, the scourging of leaders of the Jewish community who would normally have been beaten with flat blades, like Alexandrian citizens. Close examination of this passage suggests that this 'privilege' was not normally accorded to all Alexandrian Jews but specifically to the γερουσία, who probably merited this superior form of punishment because they were themselves citizens.[47]

These five pieces of evidence indicate that there were at least some Alexandrian citizens in the Jewish community. Moreover, Josephus indicates that Apion contested specifically the citizen status of such Jews and he counters Apion's arguments on this score throughout *C Ap* 2.38–72. Apion's incredulity that Jews could be called 'Alexandrians' (2.38) is ambiguous (in view of the varied meanings of this term). But when Josephus cites him as asking: *quomodo ergo, si sunt cives, eosdem deos quos Alexandrini non colunt?* ('how then, if they are citizens, do they not worship the same Gods as the Alexandrians?', 2.65; we have to rely here on a Latin version of Josephus' text), it is most probable that behind the Latin *cives* stands an original πολῖται and that this term was being used by Apion in its proper technical sense of 'Alexandrian citizen'. Thus it is very likely that alongside the question of the communal rights of all Alexandrian Jews, Apion's delegation challenged the privileges of Alexandrian Jewish citizens, in line with the long-standing uneasiness in Alexandria about the 'infiltration' of unworthy individuals into the citizen body which we can trace as far back as 20 BCE (*CPJ* 150).

Moreover, it is not necessary to hold that all such Jewish citizens had, by definition, abandoned their loyalties to the Jewish community.[48] If we are right about Philo's family, that was clearly not the case for him (though it became so for his nephew, see chapter 5.1). Moreover, it is hard to see how Apion and his

---

[47] The passage is often read as if it indicated that *all* the Jews in Alexandria had previously been treated like citizens (e.g. Box 1939:lxiv, lxvii; Tcherikover in *CPJ* 1.41, 66). But the 'custom' which was 'also observed in the case of our people' (*Flacc* 79) probably refers to the *differentiation* in treatment of 'nobles' and 'commoners'. What horrifies Philo is the overturning of social status, the honorific punishment of Jewish commoners and the humiliating treatment of their elders (80).

[48] *Pace* the assumption of 3 Maccabees, shared by Kasher 1985 and in large part by Smallwood 1970:13–14 (slightly modified in 1981:234–35).

delegation could have complained about Jewish citizens if they had lost their Jewish identity in becoming citizens: Apion's complaint is precisely that those who claim to be citizens *do not* worship the Alexandrian Gods. Thus, although citizenship normally involved participation in religious activities, it appears that some Alexandrian Jews were exercising citizen rights while declining to take part in the civic cults. Whatever exemptions or compromises were worked out here were clearly resented by Alexandrians who denied that one could uphold Judaean ethnic customs while also enjoying the status of Alexandrian citizenship.[49]

Thus I would contend that the legal crisis facing the Jews in 38–41 CE concerned *both* the immediate and general loss of their communal privileges in Alexandria *and* the long-standing dispute about Jews entering the citizen class, the latter perhaps conducted with special venom in the aftermath of the pogrom.

## V. The Statement of the Issues in the Sources

It is possible that in some cases the ambiguous, and often confusing, statements about the Alexandrian issues in our sources may be best explained by the fact that both the issues outlined above were involved in the dispute. In particular, this may explain certain aspects of the presentation of the controversy by Josephus, Philo and Claudius.

*Josephus*, as we have seen, makes frequent vague appeals to the ἴση πολιτεία of the Jews in Alexandria (chapter 2 n. 28). In part this may be a suitable expression for the high measure of autonomy enjoyed by the Alexandrian community, but when Josephus attempts to suggest that all Alexandrian Jews were also citizens (*Ant* 14.188; *C Ap* 2.38–42, 61–67) he is, perhaps wilfully, confusing citizenship with privileged residence in Alexandria. If this is not simply deceit, it may reflect the fact that Josephus knew that citizenship was one issue in the debate, but from his historical distance was unable to unravel the disparate legal elements of this controversy.

---

[49] For possible compromises one may compare the treatment of the Jewish ambassadors in *The Letter of Aristeas* 181–85. We have good evidence for Jews as citizens in Teucheira, Cyrene, Iasus and Hypaepa – the latter an association of Jewish youths who had graduated as ephebes but apparently retained their Jewish identity (see below, chapter 11.2). Paul may have been a citizen of Tarsus (unless Luke is mistaken, or uses πολίτης loosely, in Acts 21.39). Trebilco 1991:173–85 explores the options for Jews as citizens or civic officials.

*Philo*'s ambiguities in discussing the Jews' πολιτεία in Alexandria can also be explained from this angle. As we have seen, the immediate cause of his delegation was to appeal against Flaccus' sudden removal of their communal rights; but in facing Apion it became clear that the Greek delegation was using this opportunity also to question the citizen rights of the minority of Jews (in Philo's social bracket) who enjoyed such status. Thus there was a double sense in which he was trying to prove that Jews were legitimately 'Alexandrian' (*Legatio* 194): both that all Jews in the community could claim that 'ethnic' label as residents, and that some Jews (like himself) could claim it as a juridical designation of their citizenship. His vagueness on this point may not be unrelated to the fact that his delegation seems to have lost the confidence of others in the community, who sent a second embassy. Does this second delegation suggest a perception that Philo and his fellow ambassadors were overly concerned to defend their narrow interests as citizens, and were neglecting the general concerns of the Jewish community?

Finally, the doubleness of the controversy may shed light on the varying accounts of *Claudius*' verdict. Josephus, anxious to portray Claudius as a supporter of Jewish rights, cites only Claudius' general decree (*Ant* 19.280–85, perhaps with some modifications), which upheld the social and ancestral rights of the community, particularly with regard to religion. The text of the Letter (*CPJ* 153), on the other hand, while urging the Alexandrians not to be intolerant towards the Jews, suggests that Jews cannot in future claim Alexandrian citizenship or enter their sons for ephebe education ('the games'). Thus Claudius effectively dealt with *both* aspects of the matter, the latter being omitted by Josephus as it was a serious setback for the Jews concerned.[50] Thus the result of the controversy was neither total victory nor utter defeat for the Jews: their vital ancestral customs (and perhaps limited autonomy) were indeed restored to them, but the door to citizenship was slammed firmly in the faces of the few who had achieved, or aspired to, this status.

---

[50] Since he denies that citizenship is at issue, Kasher 1985:310–26 has to give a somewhat strained interpretation of the Letter. In fact his analysis reduces the whole debate before Claudius to a terminological squabble as to whether Jews had the right to apply to themselves the label 'citizen' (of their *politeuma*) and 'Alexandrian' (as legal residents, 1985:274–78).

## 3.2 Jewish Alienation

Although Claudius' decisions in 41 CE put paid to the ambitions of assimilated Jews in Alexandria, the grievances of the Alexandrians were by no means settled. After the bright hopes of Gaius' pro-Alexandrian policies, Claudius' return to the Augustan principles of government were to them a bitter disappointment. Perhaps in the very first months of Claudius' rule (or, in any case, within a few years), Isodorus and Lampon, two of the most prominent Alexandrian leaders, were involved in a law-suit against Agrippa before the emperor and found to their cost that the mood of the imperial court had swung decisively against them.[51] By Claudius' order they were executed in Rome, and their deaths reignited Alexandrian hostility to Rome which found expression in an flurry of propaganda, whose papyrus remains are now known as 'The Acts of the Alexandrian [or Pagan] Martyrs'.[52] These repeatedly portray Roman emperors as prejudiced in their judgment against heroic representatives of Alexandria – a bias often attributed to the untoward influence of Jews. This literature thus provides a mirror image of Philo's complaint about *Alexandrian* influence on Gaius: in both cases local hostilities are transferred to the Roman court. It is clear that both in personal attacks on Agrippa (a 'three-obol worth Jew') and in caricatures of Jews (as 'impious') such literature gives vent to deep animosity against Alexandrian Jews.[53]

It is in this period following the riots and counter-riots of 38–41 CE that we see the full effects of that anti-Judaism which had first been injected into the Alexandrian bloodstream by Manetho. The name which towers above all others in this connection is Apion, the leader of the Alexandrian delegation which opposed Philo

---

[51] Scholars continue to dispute whether this trial, of which we have a fragmentary record in the *Acta Isodori* (*CPJ* 156), is to be set in 41 CE (in which case the Agrippa in question is Agrippa I) or 53 (Agrippa II); see Tcherikover in *CPJ* 2.67–70; Musurillo 1954:118–24; Modrzejewski 1991:143–46. Earlier bibliography may be found in Stern 1974:129 n6.

[52] The papyri are collected and discussed in Musurillo 1954 and in *CPJ* 154–59; cf. Modrzejewski 1991:143–46, 156–61.

[53] On Agrippa, *CPJ* 156b; on the impious Jews, *CPJ* 157 and 158. They are also accused of wishing to stir up the whole world, and castigated as living on the same level as despised Egyptians (*CPJ* 156c). On the efforts of both sides in this dispute to label their opponents 'Egyptians' (cf. below, n55), see Goudriaan 1992:86–94.

(Josephus, *Ant* 18.257–59) and the author of a five-volume work on Egypt which included a sizeable section of polemic against Jews.[54] The calumnies which Apion directs at Jews, inasmuch as they can be reconstructed from Josephus' reply, amount to a devastating catalogue:

– On the Exodus, Apion repeated the popular legends of the expulsion of the lepers, the blind and the lame under Moses' leadership, but embellished them with a vicious joke on the Jewish Sabbath – linking it with the Egyptian word for a groin disease which supposedly stopped the Jews marching on the seventh day! He also knew the biblical account of Moses' 40 days on Sinai, which he probably interpreted as a ruse to convince the Jews of the divine origin of his laws (*C Ap* 2.8–32).

– On the Jewish residents of Alexandria, Apion emphasized their foreign origin and their separate residence, and questioned the right of any to be called Alexandrians. Through a history of their activities in the Ptolemaic period he portrayed the Jews as unpatriotic and anti-Alexandrian, disloyal to their rulers and properly excluded from political privileges. Their refusal to honour Alexandrian Gods and their responsibility for recent disturbances made absurd the claim of some to be Alexandrian citizens; and their failure to pay typical honours to the emperor made them all politically suspect to the Empire (*C Ap* 2.33–78; cf. *Ant* 18.257–59).

– On the Jewish religion, besides the general complaint of its peculiarity, Apion rehearsed the extraordinary myths that the Jews worshipped the head of an ass and annually sacrificed a kidnapped Greek with an oath of hostility to all Greeks. He denounced Jews for sacrificing bulls (sacred in Egypt) and for their refusal to eat pork, and derided their practice of circumcision. Finally, as a general critique, he ridiculed Jews for their political weakness and cultural backwardness (*C Ap* 2.79–144).

Reading such polemic even in outline one has the impression of a man who not only disdained but actually loathed the Jews.

---

[54] See Schürer 3.604–7 and Stern 1.389–416. Apion's younger contemporary, the Stoic philosopher Chaeremon, was clearly in the same mould; see van der Horst 1984. The influence of both these figures in Rome ensured that anti-Jewish opinions gained wide currency there.

Moreover he, and others like him, held positions of considerable authority within Alexandria, where they could turn such loathing into social discrimination and rekindle memories of the violence of 38 and 41 CE. Although cultured Jews might claim that their quarrel was only with 'Egyptians', not proper 'Greeks', social and political reality set them in opposition to all non-Jewish residents of Alexandria;[55] and however much they might insist on their continued loyalty to Rome, their reputation as trouble-makers had now become firmly entrenched.[56] Perhaps with two or three generations of peaceable relations, passions might have cooled and the Jewish community might have regained lost ground. But it was not to be. According to Josephus, there were continual clashes with Greeks in which each new crackdown by the authorities further exacerbated the quarrel between the two sides (*Bell* 2.489). And as early as 66 CE the Alexandrian Jews were caught up in another civil war of horrific proportions.

It appears that the troubles which broke out in Alexandria in this year were copy-cat riots, imitations of the violent clashes between Jews and non-Jews which traumatized many of the Greek cities in and around Palestine at the outbreak of the Jewish War.[57] When the citizen body in Alexandria met to send a delegation to Rome (perhaps with complaints about the Jews), some Jews were identified in the crowd. With cries of 'enemies' and 'spies' (testimony to the total breakdown of community relations), they

---

[55] Josephus continually vilifies the Egyptians, but insists that Jews neither hate nor envy Greeks (e.g. *CAp* 2.28–32, 65–67, 121–24). Compare Philo's rhetorical tactic, putting the blame for the troubles on Egyptians (*Flacc* 17, 29; *Legatio* 166) or 'the rabble' (*Flacc* 33–34, 41; *Legatio* 120, 132, 170) with their long-standing hatred of the Jews.

[56] Note especially Philo's efforts to portray the Jews as peaceable subjects (*Flacc* 86–94; *Legatio* 230, 312), who were eager to accord to the emperors all the honours which their laws permitted (*Flacc* 48–49, 97–98; *Legatio* 133, 231–32, 279–80, 355–56). As one of these φιλοκαίσαρες (*Legatio* 280), Philo heaps praise on the Roman empire, and on Augustus and Tiberius in particular (*Legatio* 141–154), and thus assures himself and his readers that the Jews' difficulties under Gaius' were the result of the latter's aberrant behaviour (*Legatio* 14–25). The sentence in Claudius' letter on the Jews as a potential worldwide 'plague' (*CPJ* 153, lines 99–100) must have dismayed Philo particularly.

[57] So at least Josephus' chronology suggests, his account of violence in Alexandria (*Bell* 2.487–98) immediately following the list of uprisings in Greek cities (*Bell* 2.457–86). See further below, chapter 8.2.2. Josephus is our only source for these events in Alexandria; see the critical discussion by Tcherikover in *CPJ* 1.78–79.

were set upon by the crowd and three burned to death (Josephus, *Bell* 2.490–91). This was the trigger for a violent reaction among the Jews, the more volatile of whom set about stoning Greeks, or gathered material to set the amphitheatre on fire. On this occasion the Roman governor was no weak-minded Flaccus, but a highly able and decisive figure called Tiberius Julius Alexander, ironically Philo's nephew and a highly assimilated Jew (see below, chapter 5.1). When his appeals and those of the Jewish 'notables' fell on deaf ears, he unleashed the full might of the Roman legions. Fighting their way through the crowded streets of the Jewish quarter, Alexander's troops met stiff resistance and responded with indiscriminate slaughter. Josephus puts the tally of Jewish casualties at 50,000, and ends his account with gruesome images of Alexandrian citizens having to be torn from the corpses of their Jewish enemies (*Bell* 2.494–98).

Thus once again the Jewish community covered itself with shame in the eyes of the Romans. Philo's hopes of a community secure under Roman protection were now decisively ruined, with the *coup de grace* administered by his own nephew. With their compatriots in Judaea engaged in a revolt against Rome, there was little chance of saving their reputation. And in such memories of Roman soldiers ransacking their homes and butchering their children were sown the seeds of a violent hatred of Rome, which would make Alexandria fertile ground for future uprisings.

In the aftermath of the Jewish War, the Alexandrian citizens appealed to Titus to strip the Jews of their remaining rights. It was a token of his magnanimity that (according to Josephus) he refused to do so (*Ant* 12.121–24), though the decision was probably based on political factors and the calculation that the leaders of the Jewish community were sufficiently powerful to prevent further violence by their more radicalized members. If so, it was a calculation swiftly proved correct by the reaction of the Jewish *gerousia* when 'Sicarii' fled to Egypt at the collapse of the revolt (*Bell* 7.409–20). Their revolutionary propaganda, with its refusal to accord to the emperor the title 'Lord' (δεσπότης), clearly won some support from embittered Jews. But the elders appear to have retained sufficient influence to have them arrested and turned over to the Romans. The divisions in the Jewish community, first apparent in the two delegations dispatched to Claudius, are here again evident. At this stage the propertied classes still had the upper hand; forty years later it was to be a different story.

The destruction of the temple in Jerusalem must have had a devastating effect on the Jews in Egypt, as on their compatriots in Judaea. The literature of Egyptian Jews suggests that the temple was held in the highest regard by Jews of all social classes. Pride in the magnificence of the temple is as evident in *The Letter of Aristeas* as in 3 Maccabees, works of otherwise very different outlooks (see chapters 6.3 and 7.2). That Alexander the Alabarch donated huge plates of gold and silver for the gates of the temple (Josephus, *Bell* 5.205) demonstrates the investment of wealthier Jews, while Philo indicates that poorer Jews understood their annual contributions to provide magical protection from danger or ill health (*Spec Leg* 1.77–78).[58] For all such Jews the Roman destruction of the temple must have constituted an appalling disaster.[59] If we may judge by the alarm expressed thirty years earlier at Gaius' threat to desecrate the temple, it was the greatest imaginable blow to Jewish morale. The presence of Judaean captives, brought to Egypt either permanently or on their way to Rome, can hardly have helped to heal the wound.

In fact this sore was only irritated by Vespasian's decision to confiscate the annual temple tax previously paid to Jerusalem, redirecting it to the temple of Jupiter Capitolinus, which had burnt down in 69 CE.[60] Not only was this a religious affront to Jews, it also constituted a significant social stigma, since this tax now associated all Jews with the rebellion in Judaea and distinguished them from their neighbours as owing extra dues to Rome. In the Egyptian context, as Tcherikover comments (*CPJ* 1.82), 'the Jews were now put to shame not only in the eyes of the Greeks but in the eyes of the Egyptian villagers as well.' Special tax collectors were appointed to collect this revenue and Jews underwent the humiliation of registering themselves – men, women, children and slaves – for an annual payment which they resented and which many could ill afford. The basic rate for the tax was the same as the old temple

---

[58] On Diaspora attitudes to the temple see further chapter 14.2.2.

[59] Even those who worshipped at the temple at Leontopolis were not spared calamity: it was destroyed by the Roman governor in 73 CE (Josephus, *Bell* 7.420–35). Titus may have feared lest it become a focus of political resistance in place of the Jerusalem temple.

[60] Josephus, *Bell* 7.218; Dio Cassius 66.7.2. Josephus carefully omits to mention that the money was used for the temple of Jupiter. As Smallwood comments, Vespasian made Jews 'in effect purchase the right to worship Jahweh by a subscription to Jupiter' (1956:3).

contribution (2 denarii = 2 Attic drachmae = 8 Egyptian drachmae), with slight additions (1 drachma 'first-fruits' and 2 obols currency charge). But it was now levied not just on adult males between the age of 20 and 50 but on *all* members of the family, from the age of 3 to 62! Thus a family with two children would face an annual bill of over 37 drachmae – increasing by 60% the taxes typically paid by farmers in the *chora*.[61] Many, it seems, struggled to pay, and in the struggle no doubt built up stores of hatred for the government which had inflicted so cruel a punishment upon them.

The imposition of this tax on the Jewish population also served to define their identity more clearly: it was now necessary to clarify for official purposes who was (and who was not) a Jew. Tax-collectors perhaps relied on lists of members supplied by synagogues, and they no doubt made sure that even those who had been lax in their payments to the Jerusalem temple were punctilious with regard to 'the Jewish tax'.[62] Some whose Jewish loyalties had become uncertain may have been tempted to cut their ties with the Jewish community: there is certainly evidence in Rome of Jews covering up their racial origins in order to avoid the tax.[63] Conversely, those who were registered for the tax were made all the more conscious of their Jewish identity. After this date there is an apparent increase in the use of Hebrew names in Jewish families, and some evidence of Jewish communities in the *chora* congregating more solidly in separate quarters. Whereas Jews in the *chora* had escaped the bitter experiences of their compatriots in Alexandria, now all Jews, in town and country, found themselves stigmatized

---

[61] The best discussion remains that by Tcherikover in *CPJ* 1.80–82 and 2.204–5 (on *CPJ* 421, a tax list from Arsinoe) and by Lewis and Fuks in *CPJ* 2.108–118 (introducing the tax-receipt ostraka from Apollinopolis Magna). Many of the ostraka indicate payment of the tax in instalments. On the typical income and expenditure of farmers see Johnson 1936:301–22; and on the common problem of debt in the *chora* see Lewis 1983:159–76.

[62] Note the bureaucratic attention to detail in *CPJ* 421; Thompson 1982:333 suggests that the leaders of the Jewish communities may have provided lists of those who paid the old temple dues.

[63] When Domitian administered the tax 'very harshly', he took care to catch 'persons who were either living a Jewish life in secrecy or concealing their Jewish origins in order to avoid the tax that had been imposed on the Jewish people', Suetonius, *Domitian* 12.2. (See further chapter 10.4.) For discussion of this passage and the increased likelihood of 'apostasy' see Smallwood 1956b, Thompson 1982 and Goodman 1989.

by a tax which both heightened their ethnic identity and deepened their political resentments.[64]

## 3.3 Jewish Revolt

It is only on the assumption of prolonged and profound social alienation between Jews and non-Jews that we can explain the ferocity of the Jewish uprising in 116–117 CE and its equally ferocious suppression. During these years the Diaspora communities in Egypt, Cyrenaica, Cyprus and Mesopotamia were involved in the most serious disturbances of their history, a chain of revolutions which left hundreds of thousands dead. This 'Diaspora Revolt' is less well-known than the Palestinian uprisings in 66–73 and 132–135 CE, but was far more significant for the relevant Diaspora communities. For Jews in Egypt, and for those in Cyrenaica and Cyprus, it became a desperate struggle for survival whose result radically altered the course of their history.[65]

In 115 CE some incidents in Alexandria, whose details are now obscure, revived the communal strife between Jews and Greeks; as in 66 CE, Roman troops were called in to settle the matter in a 'battle' (μάχη) between Jews and Romans.[66] The paranoia in the city is indicated by the Greeks' concern lest the 'impious Jews' be well placed to attack the city (*CPJ* 158a, Col VI). At this moment of high tension, the Jews in Cyrenaica began to revolt, and some of their number, led by their 'king' Loukuas, crossed the border into

---

[64] On the increase in the use of Hebrew names and heavier concentration in Jewish quarters see Tcherikover in *CPJ* 1.82–85 and 2.108–9. Our knowledge of Jews in the *chora* in the early Roman period is limited to isolated papyri (*CPJ* 409–34) and the large collection of ostraka (*CPJ* 160–408) which, however, only occasionally betray the social location of the tax-payer. Alongside the peasants, transport operators and craftsmen, note the tax-collector in *CPJ* 240 and the *sitologoi* (corn collectors) in *CPJ* 428. However, the social estrangement of some Jews in the *chora* is indicated already in 41 CE by the support they gave to the Alexandrian Jews (as Claudius complains, *CPJ* 153, lines 96–97).

[65] We will treat here only the revolt in Egypt, though it was closely related to that in Cyrenaica (on which see Applebaum 1979 and below, chapter 8.1). The course of events in these and the other main locations is detailed by Smallwood 1981:389–427 and freshly analysed by Horbury (forthcoming); cf. Pucci 1981. For the dating see Barnes 1989.

[66] See the fragmentary report by the Roman governor, *CPJ* 435. An Alexandrian representation of these events seems to be offered in *CPJ* 158a and 158b (Smallwood 1981:389–96; Pucci ben Ze'ev 1989; Barnes 1989:153–54).

Egypt.[67] Refugees from this invasion appear to have fled to Alexandria, where, in a cruel re-run of the pogrom of 38 CE, Loukuas' 'kingly' pretensions were mocked and the Jewish population viciously set upon.[68] In the civil war that ensued, the magnificent Serapeum was destroyed by the Jews, who nonetheless suffered terrible casualties and the loss of their greatest synagogue (j Sukkah 5.1). Indeed in this climactic Alexandrian struggle, the Greeks appear to have gained so decisive a victory as to reduce the once enormous Jewish community to a rump.

However, the revolt in the *chora* (from the summer of 116 CE) was not so easily contained. Our scattered literary sources, with their lurid descriptions of atrocities, are in places rhetorically overblown, but contemporary papyri and inscriptions confirm the scale and ferocity of the Jewish violence.[69] These make clear that the Jews engaged in widespread destruction of property, tearing up roads and pulling down public buildings, with particular attention to the temples, statues and sacred precincts of the Gods. The scale of this iconoclasm earned the Jews the epithet 'impious' (ἀνόσιοι), and confirmed the accusations of sacrilege which had been levelled against them since the days of Manetho. But there was also slaughter on a terrifying scale. When a frightened mother prays to 'the invincible Hermes' lest the Jews roast her son (*CPJ* 437) one senses the hysteria which gripped the Egyptian countryside as communities were plunged into the horrors of internecine war.[70]

---

67 It is commonly assumed that Eusebius' 'Loukuas' (*Hist Eccles* 4.2) is the same as Dio Cassius' 'Andreas' (68.32); but it is possible that they are two different figures, the former leading Cyrenaean Jews into Egypt, the latter remaining in Cyrenaica (so Horbury [forthcoming]).

68 Eusebius, *Hist Eccles* 4.2–3; *CPJ* 158a, Col I.

69 The chief literary sources are Appian, *Civil Wars* 2.90 (an eye-witness); Historia Augusta, *Vita Hadriani* 5; Dio Cassius 68.32 and 69.8; Eusebius, *Hist Eccles* 4.2–3; and Orosius 7.12. The latter, however, is wholly dependent on Eusebius (only with more colourful exaggeration), while Dio Cassius is extant only in a twelfth century epitome (by Xiphilinus) which may be distorted by anti-Semitism. See the discussion of sources by Tcherikover in *CPJ* 1.86–93 and Horbury (forthcoming). The relevant papyri are collected in *CPJ* 435–50; the inscriptions, mostly from Cyrenaica, are discussed by Fuks 1961 and Applebaum 1979:272–94.

70 Fuks 1961:101–2 notes: 'even if Dio-Xiphilinus' story is stripped of its more terrible details and the notoriously exaggerated numbers discounted, the fact of cruel and severe fighting would seem to remain.'

Our varied evidence suggests that the revolt spread through most regions of Egypt, with the Jews sufficiently organized to pose significant military problems to their opponents. As they rampaged through Egyptian villages, the Jewish forces easily overcame the resistance of the peasants (*CPJ* 438).[71] Greek civilians, even high-ranking officials, were mustered to stem the tide, and in the end it took the combined forces of villagers, Greeks, regular Roman troops and a special expeditionary force under Marcius Turbo to crush the uprising.[72] Egyptian resistance, rooted in religious hatred of the Jews, appears to have become practically a 'holy war' against impiety.[73] Never before in the Roman era had Egypt faced such a military crisis.

How were the Jewish communities in Egypt caught up in this bold and ultimately disastrous revolt? In Alexandria only a history of violence, long-nursed resentments and radical social disaffection can explain how the once integrated Jewish community ended up in total war against it Alexandrian neighbours. The outbreak of the Cyrenaean revolt in the West and news of the Mesopotamian revolt in the East must have encouraged Egyptian Jews to believe that the Roman empire was vulnerable. But it is likely that their most powerful motivation came from the appearance of a 'messianic' figure, Loukuas, who channelled the hopes of divine intervention on behalf of the Jews which we see so powerfully expressed in *The Sibylline Oracles*.[74] It is possible to detect here also the influence of the hope of an ultimate return from the Diaspora, which had been nurtured above all in Egypt and Mesopotamia (Horbury [forthcoming]). Of course, Philo and those of his social and intellectual ilk would have treated such notions with the greatest caution and would never have condoned the violent mood which gripped the Jewish communities. But by 116 CE his class of Jew was neither numerous nor influential enough to prevent such populist fervour from sweeping Egyptian Judaism to its ruin.

---

[71] See further Kasher 1976, noting the evidence for economic crisis in the *chora* at this time.

[72] A collection of papyri (*CPJ* 436–44) indicate the draft of a high-ranking official, Apollonius, into the war against the Jews. Eusebius (*Hist Eccles* 4.2) says that Marcius Turbio was engaged in 'many battles over an extended period' in his efforts to defeat the Jews.

[73] See Frankfurter 1992, suggesting the leadership of the priests in mobilizing Egyptian peasants.

[74] See Hengel 1983 and below, chapter 7.4; *Sib Or* 5 is of particular relevance here. Barnes 1989 unnecessarily plays down the messianic element in the revolt.

We have no means of calculating the physical toll on the Jews in ieir eventual defeat, but we have to imagine the destruction of hole communities. Roman soldiers were renowned for their ithless treatment of revolutionaries, and this time their stern prisals had the full support of both Greeks and Egyptians. As e violence subsided, Jewish property was re-allocated and the ·wish presence in the *chora* all but obliterated.[75] More than 80 ·ars later the inhabitants of Oxyrhynchos still held an annual ·lebration of their victory over the Jews (*CPJ* 450).[76] It was to be ·ell into the third century before Jews were able to re-establish ieir communities in Egypt and never again with the influence iey enjoyed at the height of their prosperity. Thus the most orious centre of Jewish life in the Diaspora, which had produced ie finest literary and intellectual products of Hellenized Judaism, id which had once wielded such military, economic and political fluence, was all but snuffed out in a frenzy of intercommunal ·olence.[77]

Eusebius says many tens of thousands of Jews died (*Hist Eccles* 4.2) and the papyri afford examples of the confiscation of Jewish property (*CPJ* 445 and 448). *CPJ* 460 (145/6 or 167/8 CE) indicates that only one Jew remained in a large village in the Arsinoite nome. The ostraka from Apollinopolis Magna indicate only one Jewish family (with Egyptian names) in the age of Marcus Aurelius, although the Jews previously constituted a whole district (*CPJ* 375–403).
See Modrzejewski 1991:180–81; Frankfurter 1992:213–15.
On the subsequent history of the Egyptian Diaspora see Tcherikover in *CPJ* 1.93–111. His conclusion is apposite: 'The strength of Egyptian Jewry had been broken for ever, and the gathering of new forces was a slow and tedious process, which took a considerable time and indeed was never fully achieved' (93).

# 4

## Jews in a Diaspora Environment: Some Analytical Tools

### 4.1 Introduction

In our historical survey of the Egyptian Diaspora we have observed Jews in many social and political contexts. We have noted the presence of Jews in the Egyptian countryside and in Alexandria, in the Ptolemaic era and in the new conditions created by the Romans – and their presence not as some disengaged body of observers but as actors in the drama of Egyptian history. As has become clear, there was no predictable Jewish role in this drama, no scripted response to such changeable events and conditions. In the turbulent years of the mid-first century CE we find Philo striving to minimize tensions between Jews and Greeks in Alexandria and to maintain the social and cultural harmony from which he and similar Jews had much to gain. But we also find Jewish street-fighters, eager to exact revenge on their Alexandrian enemies, caring little for the delicate political compromises which Philo sought to win. And then Philo's nephew, Alexander, comes on the scene as governor of Egypt – a Jew so successfully integrated into the Roman hierarchy that he has the responsibility for quelling the insurrection of his fellow Jews!

Thus it is evident that preconceptions or generalizations about the response of Jews to their Diaspora environments will serve us poorly. Even in the same country we must distinguish between different social environments, between, for instance, Egyptian villages, Greek towns, the special conditions in Alexandria and the unique environment of the Ptolemaic court – all of which underwent change over time and especially in the transition from Ptolemaic to Roman rule. In response to the complex factors which made up each environment Jews pursued varying types of integration, assimilation, adaptation and acculturation, combining absorption and rejection of their ambient culture(s) in multiple forms. If we bear in mind the complexities and ambiguities of real life, we will resist imagining that Diaspora Jews bought cultural 'package deals' or grouped themselves neatly into the categories which scholars create.

How can we analyse such complexity? We need to employ some analytical categories if we are to describe this reality at all, but we run the risk of over-simplifying or even distorting the evidence. Before offering some constructive proposals, I wish to examine some traditional categories which have been used in this connection, and to suggest their inadequacy for our task (4.2). We can then examine what is meant by 'Hellenization' (4.3), before exploring a way out of our current analytical difficulties (4.4 and 4.5).

## 4.2 'Orthodoxy' and 'Deviation'

Earlier generations of scholars discussed Judaism in our period with the aid of categories such as 'normative', 'classical' or 'native' Judaism. The last epithet makes clear what was implicit in all three, that the 'purest' Judaism was what was dominant in Palestine; and by a quirk of historical short-sightedness Palestinian Judaism was taken to be synonymous with 'Pharisaic' or 'rabbinic' Judaism. If this old consensus has now collapsed, that is largely due to a greater awareness of the plurality in Judaism, at least before the destruction of the temple in 70 CE. Two scholars have been particularly influential in the demolition of the older categories. Erwin Goodenough, in his analysis of Philo and in pioneering studies of archaeological evidence, demonstrated clearly enough, if in somewhat exaggerated form, that there was no universal template of 'normative' Judaism, at least none that could be applied to the Hellenized Diaspora.[1] If this finding could be taken to support a simplistic contrast between 'Palestinian' and 'Hellenistic' Judaism, Martin Hengel has shown in numerous studies that Jews in Palestine were by no means immune from Hellenization.[2] It is thus no longer

---

[1]  Goodenough 1962 and 1969 on Philo. His 13-volume work on *Jewish Symbols* 1953–1968 represents his greatest, and most controversial, achievement in this area; for a critical review see Smith 1967.

[2]  Most famously in Hengel 1974; subsequently in, e.g., Hengel 1980 and 1989. See the fuller survey of scholarship above, chapter 1.2.

possible to analyse Diaspora Judaism by simple measurements against Palestinian Judaism.

The difficulty in finding appropriate criteria for the analysis of Diaspora Judaism is illustrated by the work of Louis Feldman. In an important article on 'The Orthodoxy of the Jews in Hellenistic Egypt' (1960), Feldman surveyed a wide range of Jewish material from Egypt, literary and non-literary, in order to illustrate 'deviations from orthodoxy' among Egyptian Jews. Although he estimated that the number of apostates was not large, he still concluded that the range of 'deviations' on the part of Egyptian Jews 'sapped the religious vitality of the community' (237). Much of the material from this article has been incorporated in a chapter of Feldman's magisterial *Jew and Gentile in the Ancient World* (1993), where, however, the emphasis is somewhat changed. With the addition of evidence from other Diaspora locations, Feldman now interprets the Egyptian data to demonstrate 'the strength of Judaism in the Diaspora' (the chapter heading).[3] My object here is not to assess the social effect of the 'deviations' which Feldman catalogues (and thus adjudicate which of his conclusions is correct) but simply to highlight the difficulties inherent in the categories he employs.[4] These difficulties may be subsumed under two heads:

1. *The use of the category 'deviation'.* Both in the earlier and in the later form of his argument Feldman speaks repeatedly of 'deviations' among Egyptian Jews. In the early version of this material he spoke of 'deviations from orthodoxy' (once with a capital, 'Orthodoxy'); the recent version uses this latter term less frequently and speaks rather of 'deviations from Jewish tradition' (1993:67, 83) or 'deviation … from the traditional norms of Judaism' (1993:74). However, there are some fundamental problems in utilizing such a concept.

[3] Note his conclusion to the chapter: 'Hence, the net effect of the assimilation of the Greek language and culture by the Jews was not defection from Judaism but rather, on the contrary, the creation of a common bond of communication with Gentiles, through which at least some non-Jews were won over to Judaism', 1993:83. The last phrase indicates the thesis of the book as a whole; but the tensions created by using material about 'deviations from Jewish tradition' to support such a thesis are evident throughout the chapter.

[4] My criticisms here should not mask my admiration for Feldman's comprehensive grasp of the evidence and for his refusal to squeeze Egyptian material into a rabbinic mould. He thus rightly takes issue with 'rabbinic' interpretations of Philo, as in Wolfson 1948.

In the first place we must ask by what standard such 'deviation' is measured. 'Deviation' presupposes that there are norms to deviate from, but what norms should be applied? At several points Feldman appeals to a rabbinic norm, citing rabbinic rules, for instance, against attendance at the theatre, spectating at athletics or taking Jews to law in a Gentile court (1993:59 [with n. 68], 61, 77). The problem here is obvious: do we have evidence that such rabbinic rules were applicable to Jews in the Egyptian Diaspora? Even when appeal is made to a biblical norm (e.g. on charging interest, 1993:76),[5] we need to know how such texts were interpreted in the times and circumstances of the Jews involved. Current awareness of the diversity in pre-70 CE Judaism has indicated how hazardous it is to assume a universal norm against which we can simply measure 'deviations'. This does not mean that Jewish communities in particular times and places had no common mind on the limits of acceptable behaviour, but that we need to be attuned to standards of measurement that were *local, contemporary* and *commonly accepted*. Feldman himself recognizes that Philo, while attending theatres and athletic competitions, was 'a devoted and observant Jew' (1993:78, cf. 60–61), held in the highest regard by the leaders of the Alexandrian Jewish community. But he did not allow this recognition to dispel the phantom of a universalizable (rabbinic) norm from which Philo supposedly 'deviated'.

At base our difficulty here is that 'deviation' is not a neutral or objective criterion, but a *label* resulting from a particular judgment. In the sociology of deviance an important contribution has been made by 'the interactionist perspective', which rightly insists that 'deviance' is not a quality inherent in certain acts or persons or indeed an objectively definable entity: rather, the identification of 'deviance' is radically dependent on societal reaction.[6] 'Deviance',

---

[5]   Some papyri, e.g. *CPJ* 23 and 24, show Jews lending to fellow Jews at interest; see the full discussion in Modrzejewski 1991:94–101.

[6]   I have explored this topic and its application to our subject in Barclay 1995. Here I may simply cite a statement which helped to create this new perspective: 'Social groups create deviance by making the rules whose infraction constitutes deviance, and by applying those rules to particular people and labeling them as outsiders. From this point of view, deviance is not a quality of the act the person commits, but rather a consequence of the application by others of rules and sanctions to an "offender." The deviant is one to whom that label has been successfully applied; deviant behavior is behavior that people so label' (Becker 1963:9).

in other words, is in the eye of the beholder: it is not a neutral category with objective status but depends as much on the viewpoint of the labeller as on the activity so labelled. Since those who create and apply the rules differ in their judgments from one society to another, and differ within the same society at different times and in differing circumstances, our first question when encountering charges of 'deviance' should be, 'Whose definitions of deviance are operative here?' (and our second, 'Whose interests do they serve?'). The element of relativism here renders 'deviance' and 'orthodoxy' highly questionable as analytical tools.[7]

The same problems beset the use of the terms 'apostate' and 'apostasy'. Feldman in fact operates with an unusually narrow definition of these terms, refusing to accept that when our sources refer to Jews who 'abandoned the ancestral practices' they mean that they were actually 'apostate': for him, such failure to observe the commandments is something less than becoming 'completely severed from the body of Israel' (his definition of 'apostasy', 1993:79–83). Whether or not this reflects the viewpoint of our sources, it illustrates the fact that 'apostasy', like 'deviance', is a label which can be differentially employed: a Jew may be considered an 'apostate' by some Jews, while others do not consider him/her in such a light.[8] Here too we are confronted with relative judgments. 'Apostasy' is not an objective category in which we may place individuals (or groups) at one end of a spectrum. Rather, it is a judgmental label which Jews used of those they considered to have assimilated too much; but they might disagree as to what constituted 'too much' in this regard. We should be wary, therefore, of apparently objective remarks that 'X was an apostate'. All we can say is that he or she was *considered* an 'apostate' (if some source so indicates); we may then ask how typical was this assessment in that time and place.[9]

---

[7] There is a further danger in the term 'orthodoxy' if it is employed with Christian presuppositions, which give more weight to 'ideas' than practices. See the debate on this matter between McEleney 1973 and Aune 1976; Grabbe 1977 rightly recognized that 'orthodoxy is in the eye of the beholder' and that this term belongs 'within confessional belief rather than historical investigation' (152–53).

[8] See the full discussion of this matter in Barclay forthcoming.

[9] In discussing Palestinian Jews, Feldman notes that 'one man's apostasy may be another's orthodoxy' (1993:38), but he follows this recognition with the statement that 'the question is not what the Sadducees or the Essenes, whose literature is lost, thought, because history's verdict is that they are not the

2. *The undifferentiated treatment of 'Hellenization'.* A further assumption
underlying Feldman's treatment of Diaspora Judaism (and not only
his!) is that any assimilation, Hellenization or 'synthesis of Judaism
and Hellenism' (1993:55–56) constituted a dilution or diminution
of Judaism. Thus Feldman contrasts 'the more assimilated' with
'the more religious' Jews (e.g. 1993:54) and takes the literary
sources to suggest that the majority 'were pious and only
superficially Hellenized' (1960:230). He discusses Hellenization
under such headings as 'Greek language and thought', 'secular
education', 'athletics', 'the theatre' and 'intermarriage', but he
then lumps together a range of phenomena as evidence of
'syncretism' (1993:65–69). This term is here used in the sense of
'admixture with pagan cults' (66), and under this heading is listed:
1) the remark in *The Letter of Aristeas* 16 that Jews worship the God
whom Greeks call Zeus; 2) Artapanus' identification of Moses with
Musaeus and Hermes; 3) Aristobulus' citation of an Orphic poem;
4) Philo's use of 'mystery' language in relation to Moses; 5) the
use of 'Hades' and 'Lethe' in some Jewish inscriptions (indicating
'pagan infiltration', 67); 6) 'pagan' elements in Jewish magical
charms; 7) 'pagan' influence on Jewish art.

These diverse items all indicate some interaction with non-Jewish
culture, but to assign them all to the category 'syncretistic' does
not seem of much analytical value. What is lacking here is an
attempt to *weigh the significance* of such phenomena – an assessment
which involves observing their social contexts and the perceptions
of those who practised or witnessed such activities. Was it as serious
for a woman to have an amulet around her neck as if she failed to
have her sons circumcised?[10] Does Philo's use of 'mystery' language
indicate his approval of mystery cults or merely his appropriation
of their language for the greater glory of Judaism? What, if
anything, is signalled by the use of 'Hades' in a Jewish epitaph? To
answer such questions requires that we *differentiate* between forms
of Hellenization and break away from the neat but misleading

---

mainstream of Judaism' (ibid.). Such reliance on hindsight can only obscure
historical reality: the appeal to 'history's verdict' masks ideological
commitments.

[10] Feldman hints at an answer to this question when he comments that the
syncretism in Jewish amulets 'was all at the level of folklore and hardly
diminished the loyalty to Judaism of the Jewish possessors of these amulets'
(1993:69). But what is required here (though not easy to obtain) is some
measure of the local and contemporary standards of 'loyalty to Judaism'.

construct of the Maccabean literature that 'Judaism' and 'Hellenism' stood against one another as unitary phenomena in mutual antagonism.[11] The illusion that any aspect of Hellenization necessarily undermined Jewish loyalty must be dispelled if we are to make a realistic assessment of Diaspora Judaism. It is to this problematic that we now turn.

## 4.3 Jews and Hellenization[12]

Despite many treatments of the topic, it is not easy to define what is meant by the cultural complex we call 'Hellenism'.[13] From one perspective Hellenism may be viewed as the product of cultural fusion, as the 'Greek' culture carried by Alexander's troops encountered and influenced the variegated eastern cultures. Never static or fixed, the Hellenistic tradition developed over time, boosted as well as modified by the emergence of the Roman empire. It was an urban culture which rarely penetrated into the countryside and was neither missionary in intent nor intolerant of indigenous cultures. The Jews were not the only eastern nation successfully to preserve their native traditions, although their special religious sensitivities created some exceptional problems.

By 'Hellenism', then, we mean the common urban culture in the eastern Mediterranean, founded on the Greek language (the verb *hellenizein* originally meant 'to speak Greek'), typically expressed in certain political and educational institutions and largely maintained by the social élite. Like any cultural complex, its ingredients were multiple, and when treating the topic of 'Hellenization' (that is, cultural engagement with 'Hellenism'), it

[11] 2 Macc 4.12–13 contrasts the Jewish way of life with 'Hellenism' (a term here first coined) and 'the culture of other nations' (ἀλλοφυλισμός); cf. the praise of Razis for his stand for 'Judaism' in the heroic days when there had been no 'mingling' with Gentiles (2 Macc 14.38) and other uses of these terms in 2 Macc 2.21; 8.1; 4 Macc 4.26. On the term 'Judaism' see Amir 1984; and on its 'narrow, prejudicial' definition in the Maccabean literature see Grabbe 1992:169–70.

[12] Although only Hellenization will be discussed here, much of what is said could be applied *mutatis mutandis* to the interface between Jews and, for instance, native Egyptian or Roman culture.

[13] Standard bibliography includes Tarn and Griffith 1959; Walbank 1981; Kuhrt and Sherwin-White 1987; see the overview of the subject in Grabbe 1992:147–70.

is valuable to recall the many different aspects involved.[14] Its principal components may be listed as follows, together with some questions pertinent to Jewish Hellenization:[15]

1. *Political*: the structures of city government and relations with political authorities. What was the political status of Jewish communities in the Diaspora and what were their relations with the Hellenistic kings? To what extent did Jews acquire citizen rights and what was entailed in the enjoyment of those rights? What involvement did Jews have in civic or other political administration? Also to what extent did Jews borrow Hellenistic terms and copy Hellenistic institutions in the administration of their own communities?

2. *Social*: the social patterns of interaction in the Hellenistic (and Roman) cities. To what extent were Jews (as a community or as individuals) part of the mainstream of urban life and to what degree were they socially distinct? What kind and what quality of social contacts did they make and in what spheres of life? What were their economic relations with non-Jews and to what extent did they participate in (or spectate at) athletic and theatrical events? How did they relate to the legal institutions of their host cities? To what extent was Jewish family life conformed to Hellenistic norms?

3. *Linguistic*: the use of the Greek language. Did Greek become the dominant or even the sole language of Diaspora Jews, even in religious matters? How far did Greek influence their choice of nomenclature? How well did individual Jews know Greek, to speak and/or to write?

4. *Educational*: the acquisition of Greek *paideia* (training/ education).[16] Did Jews gain a Greek-medium education? If so, to what level and in what contexts? Did this extend beyond the basic grammatical and literary studies to knowledge of philosophy, rhetoric and the practice of literary criticism? How much were Jews

---

[14] Hengel 1980:60 rightly insists that 'when analysing the concept of "Hellenization", we have to distinguish between very different components.' He distinguishes in broad terms between political, social, literary, philosophical, linguistic and religious aspects of the culture.

[15] See also the discussion in Smith 1987:43–61; Cohen 1987b:34–45; Goldstein 1981; Tcherikover 1961a:344–57.

[16] The importance of this is indicated by the famous remark of Isocrates, *Panegyricus* 50: 'he who shares in our *paideia* is a Greek in a higher sense than he who simply shares in our descent.'

conversant with the scientific, geographical, medical and other aspects of Hellenistic learning? What literary and rhetorical forms did they adopt? Also, and crucially, how did Diaspora Jews utilize the Greek education they acquired?

5. *Ideological*: commitment to cultural norms and values. To what extent did Diaspora Jews absorb the individualistic and virtue-orientated ideals of the Hellenistic world? To what extent were their views about God, the world and humanity (including themselves) moulded by the currents of thought in their cultural environments?

6. *Religious*: adherence to the forms, rites and formulae of Hellenistic religions. To what degree did Jews absorb, imitate or participate in the religious language and practice of the Hellenistic world?

7. *Material*: sharing or borrowing the physical features of Hellenistic culture, e.g. in relation to food, dress, coinage, art and architecture. In what respects did Jews conform to their material environment and in what matters was their material culture distinctive?

This list is not exhaustive (it could easily be expanded) nor are the categories neatly defined (they overlap and interlace in many ways). But the range of activities and spheres of life which are typically grouped under the heading of 'Hellenization' is clearly very diverse, and it is evident that significant Hellenization in one aspect did not necessarily encompass all the other features as well. Moreover, Jewish engagement with 'Hellenism' could operate in each of these spheres to differing degrees. Thus, to take religious Hellenization (6), one may distinguish variant depths of involvement. At one end of the spectrum would be frequent and personal participation in sacrifice to non-Jewish Gods, but lesser levels of involvement might include:

–     observing other people sacrifice
–     non-sacrificial prayer
–     invocation of Greek Deities in magical or legal formulae
–     using Greek divine names in poetry
–     handling coins whose inscriptions bore divine titles
–     incorporating Greek divine names in Jewish nomenclature.
It is clear that these do not represent what Feldman calls 'pagan infiltration' to the same degree.

Thus it is helpful to distinguish between different *kinds* and between different *degrees* of Hellenization. Moreover, in order to weigh its significance, we need to know how contemporary Jews reacted to the Hellenization of their fellows. In most of our period, and in most areas of the Diaspora, it mattered a thousand times more if a Jewish man was Hellenized in respect of his genitals than if he was Hellenized in respect of his speech. Why was this so?[17] The presence or absence of the foreskin was, in physical terms, a wholly superficial phenomenon, but Philo knew that it counted for a lot more in the eyes of the Jewish community in Alexandria than a profound knowledge of Greek philosophy (*Mig Abr* 89–93). Conversely, when we hear that Aristotle met a Diaspora Jew who was truly 'Greek in his soul',[18] that need not indicate any weakening of his social identity and commitments as Jew. It would be difficult to dispute that Philo's 'soul' was considerably more Hellenized than Paul's; but Philo's Jewishness was never doubted by his contemporaries in the way that Paul's was.

Indeed Philo's example indicates that a Diaspora Jew could be, in certain respects, Jewish to the core and Hellenized to the same core.[19] Philo's faith in God as Creator was strengthened by his reading of Plato, not diluted by such Hellenistic education. His conviction that God exercised providential care for humanity was supported and explained by his Stoic theology. As we shall see (chapter 6.5), Philo's Jewish identity was built on his devotion to Scripture, but through allegory he found Scripture fully congruent with such Hellenistic *paideia*, which he took to be not distinctively 'Greek' but simply rational and 'philosophical'. That does not make his Judaism less 'pure' than that of Palestinian Pharisees. As Sandmel rightly insisted (1956:198), Philo's place remains firmly 'in Judaism' even if 'his hellenization is so thorough and so complete that undoubtedly he himself was unaware of how Greek his Judaism is.' Yet Philo was scandalized by the notion that a Jew might be so Hellenized as to cease to observe the Sabbath or to respect the Jerusalem temple (*Mig Abr* 89–93). Once again, then, undifferentiated comments about Jewish Hellenization are of little analytical use.

---

[17] We should note that this difference has nothing to do with *origins*: circumcision was not in fact of Jewish origin, and Egyptian Jews knew that it was not practised only by Jews (Philo, *Spec Leg* 1.2). On the other hand, the Hebrew which they, or their forefathers, abandoned, was originally and uniquely Jewish!

[18] Reported by Clearchus, *apud* Josephus, *C Ap* 1.180.

[19] Cf. Geertz 1979:164 on certain Moroccan Jews: 'Moroccan to the core and Jewish to the same core, they were heritors of a tradition double and indivisible.'

## 4.4 Assimilation, Acculturation and Accommodation

The need to distinguish between different *kinds* and different *degrees* of Hellenization indicates that it might be fruitful to establish scales depicting different kinds of Hellenization.[20] As a first step, it might be helpful to make a distinction between *assimilation* and *acculturation*. 'Assimilation' may be taken to refer to *social integration* (becoming 'similar' to one's neighbours): it concerns social contacts, social interaction and social practices. By contrast, 'acculturation' is here used to refer to the *linguistic, educational and ideological* aspects of a given cultural matrix. Of course, these two phenomena frequently stand in a positive relationship to each other: assimilation is often a means or a consequence of acculturation. Yet they may still be distinguished since they are not by any means necessarily symmetrical. Jewish slaves in Greek households might be, perforce, assimilated to a high degree even if they acquired very limited acculturation; conversely, Jews might acquire considerable expertise in Hellenistic *paideia* while exercising great caution in their social contacts with non-Jews. In general, a minority ethnic group is far more threatened by assimilation than acculturation, since the former subverts the basis of its existence. As the sociologist Sharot notes:

> while substantial or even total acculturation of a subordinate ethnic group need not necessarily involve substantial assimilation, substantial assimilation will always involve substantial acculturation. An ethnic group may retain its cohesiveness and social boundaries despite its adoption of cultural patterns of the majority or core group, but an ethnic culture is almost bound to disappear if the ethnic population is absorbed by the majority. (1976:3)[21]

[20] My reflections on this topic have been aided by some reading in the anthropology of 'acculturation'; see, for instance, the survey of older American research in Siegel 1955. Unfortunately there is as yet no standardized vocabulary: anthropologists and sociologists use common terms in different ways. In what follows I shall attempt to clarify what I mean by the terms and categories I propose, without claiming more than their utility for this particular exercise.

[21] See also Barth 1969, who notes that ethnic boundaries may be preserved despite much cultural interplay across them. Goudriaan's distinction between culture and ethnic identity (1988 and 1992) corresponds to my differentiation between acculturation and assimilation.

1. In measuring *assimilation*, then, we are assessing the degree to which Diaspora Jews were integrated into, or socially aloof from, their social environments. It is important here to pay regard to the 'contact conditions' of their relationships with non-Jews. Sociologists rightly insist that social contacts can vary greatly in their power of influence. A small number of 'primary' relationships (with family, close friends, patrons and mentors) can be of far greater significance than numerous 'secondary' relationships (with acquaintances, customers and others whose connection is distant or formal). Thus, to measure the assimilation of Diaspora Jews we require to know not just how *frequent* were their contacts with Gentiles but also what *quality* of contact was involved. We may take this scale to embrace most of the political, social and material aspects of Hellenization listed above, as well as the sphere of religious practice, and we may mark some representative points on this assimilation scale as in *Figure 1*.

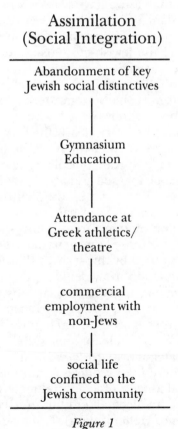

Assimilation
(Social Integration)

Abandonment of key
Jewish social distinctives

Gymnasium
Education

Attendance at
Greek athletics/
theatre

commercial
employment with
non-Jews

social life
confined to the
Jewish community

*Figure 1*

At the top of the scale I have placed those whose social integration involved abandoning the social distinctives fundamental to Jewish identity. As both Jews and non-Jews recognized, the Jewish tradition contained a number of taboos which impeded the assimilation of Jews. Although there were some local and chronological variations, in most cases we may specify fairly easily what these taboos were (see chapter 14): they included the refusal to worship non-Jewish Gods, restrictions on Jewish diet, the observance of the Sabbath and the practice of circumcision (on whose social function see chapter 14.1 and 14.3.3). Thus where we find Jews abandoning such cultural distinctives we may fairly place them among those most assimilated: their failure to observe those 'ancestral customs' which most clearly distinguished them as Jews eased (or resulted from) their integration into non-Jewish society. (That, of course, is not to say that they were, or should be, labelled 'apostate': that, as we have seen, is a matter of judgment depending on the stance of the labeller.) Further down the scale we have placed gymnasium education, which may or may not have involved abandoning the Jewish customs we have named. Lower down is attendance at civic entertainments and commercial employment with non-Jews, neither of which required forming primary relationships. At the bottom we may place those whose social life was confined entirely to the Jewish community, either by choice or by necessity: they were clearly the least assimilated of all.

It may be questioned whether the multiple factors mentioned under the headings of 'political', 'social', 'religious' and 'material' Hellenization should be merged and aggregated on a single scale. Since individuals exercised personal choice in differing circumstances, detailed analysis of particular cases might indeed require differentiation among variant kinds of assimilation. My purpose here is not to impose some generalized model, but simply to use the questions posed by this scale to sharpen our analysis of the evidence. 'Assimilation' represents a conglomeration of such questions, which belong together but are distinguishable from other types of Hellenization; it thus gives us a particular perspective from which to interrogate the variegated and sometimes idiosyncratic evidence available for analysis.

2. Our second category is *acculturation*. The narrow sense in which this term is here used requires confining our attention to certain non-material aspects of a cultural matrix, in particular its language, values and intellectual traditions (cf. categories 3, 4 and 5 in our list of types of Hellenization). Language is, of course, an

integral aspect of social relations, but it also grants access to the non-material aspects of a culture. In acquiring Greek *paideia* (to whatever level), Jews gained access not only to certain literary resources but also to a system of values which constituted, in Greek eyes, the very essence of civilization. Inasmuch as they acquired this common discourse of cultural ideals and recognized virtues, Diaspora Jews may be said to have become acculturated. Thus we may again plot some representative placements on this scale as in *Figure 2.*

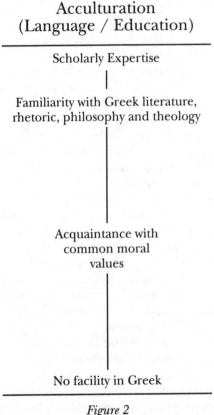

## Acculturation
## (Language / Education)

Scholarly Expertise

Familiarity with Greek literature,
rhetoric, philosophy and theology

Acquaintance with
common moral
values

No facility in Greek

*Figure 2*

At the top of this scale I have placed those expert in the critical traditions of Hellenistic scholarship, the acme of scholarly attainment. Not far below may be placed familiarity in Greek literature, rhetoric, philosophy and theology. Familiarity, of course, is not easily quantified, but it is often evident, for instance, if a

Jewish author really knows the philosophy he purports to discuss or has only a passing acquaintance with its most well-known tenets. Somewhere below this educational summit we may place acquaintance with the common moral values of the Hellenistic world (e.g. the cardinal virtues). For obvious reasons, we may place at the bottom of the scale those who had no facility in Greek.

This scale is in some respects the least precise of the three I am here describing (for a third is to follow). It is clear enough that those at the top and bottom of the scale stand in contrast to one another; the vagueness arises most around the centre. As in the case of assimilation, aggregate assessments could sometimes be broken down in individual cases. Nonetheless, the heuristic value of this scale lies in signalling both that 'acculturation' in this sense can be usefully distinguished from 'assimilation', and that we can expect to find variations among Diaspora Jews in their levels of Hellenistic acculturation: the mere ability to speak Greek, for instance, need not signify much at all.

3. However, we cannot rest content with the simple two-fold distinction so far advanced. There follows another crucial step in distinguishing between acculturation and what I wish to label *accommodation*.[22] Accommodation, in the sense here employed, concerns the *use to which acculturation is put*, in particular the degree to which Jewish and Hellenistic cultural traditions are merged, or alternatively, polarized. Even when Diaspora Jews became familiar with the Greek cultural heritage, it was another matter how they employed what they had learned. Into what framework was their acculturation placed? To what extent was it subordinated to their native Jewish convictions? Or what sort of juxtapositions, modifications and reinterpretations were effected? Highly educated Jews could use their training either to defend or to attack Judaism, either to justify or to undermine its peculiar customs. Studies of the 'colonized' indicate such variant uses of the colonizers' culture – in some cases to modify or even obliterate their native cultural traditions, in others to equip them to resist the colonizers' cultural imperialism. In general one may distinguish between *integrative* and *oppositional* trends in these variant forms of accommodation. Integrative trends would include the imitation of Hellenistic

---

[22] The three categories here described are employed in the title of Mor 1992, but not utilized in the same manner.

culture, its internalization and its employment in reinterpreting the Jewish tradition. Oppositional trends may be manifest in the adoption of a defensive or resistant stance and, at the extreme, the use of Hellenistic weapons to engage in polemic against Hellenism itself. Thus we may establish a spectrum of accommodation as in *Figure 3*.

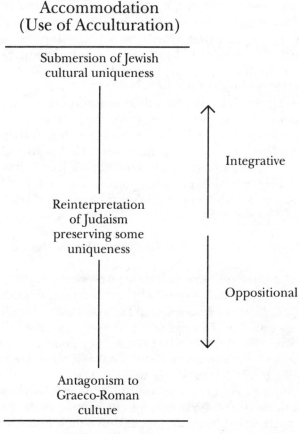

## Accommodation
## (Use of Acculturation)

Submersion of Jewish
cultural uniqueness

Integrative

Reinterpretation
of Judaism
preserving some
uniqueness

Oppositional

Antagonism to
Graeco-Roman
culture

*Figure 3*

It is important to note at once that this scale is intended to measure *how*, not *how much*, Jews used their acculturation. Unlike in the other two cases, the bottom of this scale does not represent a 'zero' point so much as an extreme in one direction in the use of acculturation (hence the arrows on the side). What is measured here is the sort of cultural engagement to which Diaspora Jews devoted their acculturation. At the top would be those whose accommodation entailed the loss of Jewish cultural uniqueness, those, that is, who merged Judaism with the Hellenistic tradition so far as to submerge it altogether. In the middle we may place those who propounded some Hellenistic intepretation of Judaism but preserved its difference or uniqueness in certain respects. At the other end of the spectrum are those whose employment of acculturation is purely oppositional, giving vent to perhaps well-educated but nonetheless virulent antagonism to Graeco-Roman culture. In other words, this scale depicts one of the many paradoxes of our topic: that acculturation could be used to construct either bridges or fences between Jews and their surrounding cultures.[23]

Once again, the middle position on this scale is the least well-defined, since many forms of integration and opposition might coexist in any particular case. Cultural forms can be employed while altering their typical content, and Hellenistic values may acquire new meanings when placed within a Jewish framework. We may expect to find some of the most creative intellectual achievements of Diaspora Jews precisely in this middle ground.

### 4.5 Analysing the Evidence

The three scales outlined above represent an attempt to order and simplify the mass of otherwise confusing material which typically befuddles the discussion of Hellenization. Simplifications are both necessary and dangerous: necessary if we are to make sense of an otherwise uncontrollable mass of evidence, dangerous if they lead us to misconstrue or distort that evidence. We will need to resist the tendency to straightjacket the evidence, recognizing the complexity of real-life conditions in which the categories we have distinguished did not always correspond to the subtle, variable and interrelated facets of life, and in which individuals might live on

---

[23] This paradox suggests, among other things, the importance of rhetorical factors. Writers who purport to condemn all things Greek (using Greek linguistic and rhetorical tools) are generally reacting to some particular political or social ingredient in Hellenism under the mask of a global polemic. I am grateful to Professor Grabbe for clarifying this point for me. The rhetoric of the Hellenized Hasmonean literature is a good case in point (see Bickerman 1962).

the interface of several different cultures. Nonetheless, these scales may be of some heuristic value: they provide us with a starting point for analysis, without which it is hard to grasp the significance of the evidence.

Of course, our most serious problem remains the inadequacy of our evidence. It would be nice to be able to plot all known Diaspora Jews on these three scales. In a very few cases this is almost possible, but in most we lack the depth and breadth of evidence even to attempt such a feat. In general the papyri and the inscriptional evidence afford us mere glimpses of the lives of Diaspora Jews, and what information they (and other notices in literature) provide relates only, and in piecemeal fashion, to our first scale, assimilation. They provide clues about occupations, social practices and social involvements, indicating degrees and kinds of assimilation, but they rarely enable us to assess the acculturation and accommodation of individual Jews. On the other hand, the literature written by Diaspora Jews enables us to make some assessment of the authors' acculturation and accommodation, even if we have only samples of their work and those often influenced by rhetorical considerations.

Because of this variable quality and quantity of evidence, the analyses to be conducted in the rest of this study fall into one of two kinds: assessment of levels of assimilation (chapters 5 and 11) and analysis of the socio-cultural stance of Diaspora literature (chapters 6–7, 12–13). Some further words of explanation about these two exercises will suffice to complete this chapter.

1. *Levels of Assimilation.* In relation to each geographical area – Egypt (chapter 5) and the rest of the Mediterranean (chapter 11) – we will gather what evidence is available concerning the assimilation of Diaspora Jews. Inevitably those that stand out most are the Jews towards the top of the scale whose high level of social integration is, in many cases, the reason for their appearance in our sources. As already indicated, our assessment here is not intended to identify 'apostasy'; different degrees of assimilation could be variously assessed depending on the viewpoint of the assessor.

Our efforts to assess assimilation can only be tentative, given that the evidence is so often fragmentary, obscure or ambiguous. Let one example suffice to illustrate our difficulties. Archaeologists have found a number of inscriptions in the precincts of the temple of Pan Euodus (Pan, Guarantor of Safe Journeys) at El-Kanais in Egypt, on the desert road to the Red Sea. Among these inscriptions are two whose dedicants identify themselves as Jews: one, Ptolemaios son of Dionysius, the Jew (Ἰουδαῖος), simply gives praise to God; the other, Theodotus son of Dorion, the Jew, praises God for a safe sea-crossing.[24] Why, we may ask, do Ptolemaios and Theodotus publicly profess themselves to be Jews (or Judaeans), yet dedicate these inscriptions in the temple of Pan? Since the Deity is referred to only as God (θεός), without specific reference to Pan, do they imagine they are offering thanks to the God of the Jews even in this non-Jewish temple? Or do they consider that Pan (πᾶν = everything) is a proper name for the true God? Or again do they think it is legitimate to worship God in any available context, at least while far from a synagogue and in the relief of safety after a perilous journey?[25] Further, if Ptolemaios and Theodotus wrote an inscription, did they also offer prayer in the temple, or even sacrifice? In other words, do these inscriptions indicate social integration into non-Jewish worship or not? How did these individuals behave when they returned to their own communities? How should we interpret the fact that they identified themselves as 'Jews'/'Judaeans', a unique feature among Egyptian inscriptions? We simply cannot answer such questions, and intriguing as this case may be, it is difficult to make any judgment at all concerning the assimilation of these Egyptian Jews. Here and often elsewhere the evidence leaves us almost entirely at a loss.

2. *The Socio-Cultural Stance of Diaspora Literature.* As noted above, it is only in the case of the literature from the Diaspora that we can attempt to measure levels of acculturation and types of accommodation among Diaspora Jews. While it is valuable to note variations in levels of acculturation, it is particularly interesting to observe the patterns of accommodation by which these authors relate their Jewish traditions to their social and cultural contexts in the Hellenistic world. In most cases this involved complex reactions to Hellenistic culture, but our authors may be roughly

---

[24] Horbury & Noy 121, 122 (= *CIJ* 1537, 1538). The reference to the sea is slightly uncertain, but might refer to shipwreck (see Horsley 1987:113–17); the lettering indicates a date in the late Ptolemaic period. There are also two inscriptions which refer to a certain Lazarus, who visited the temple three times (Horbury & Noy 123, 124).

[25] See the variant possibilites mooted by Frey in *CIJ* ad loc. and Kraemer 1989:46; Horbury & Noy ad loc. think that the framing of the inscriptions is intended to distinguish them from adjacent texts, which refer explicitly to Pan.

divided into two categories according to the *dominant* ethos of their work. In some the emphasis lies on cultural convergence (those in the 'integrative', upper half of the Accommodation scale); in others the dominant mood is one of cultural antagonism (those in the 'oppositional', lower half of that scale). In fact, most authors combined elements of both strategies in weaving their own patterns of Hellenized Judaism, but there are appreciable differences between the mood of, for instance, *The Letter of Aristeas* and 3 Maccabees. In some cases a small difference of judgment could result in a different categorization, but the distinction is still of some heuristic value.

The selection of documents submitted to this sort of analysis, and their allocation to our two geographical spheres, has been explained in chapter 1.3. Here I may add that nothing is to be read into the order in which the documents are discussed (i.e. those discussed first are not 'higher' up a scale than others). Where it is possible to assign dates, I have followed what I consider the most likely historical sequence: thus, in relation to Egypt, I have chosen to discuss Ezekiel, Aristeas and Aristobulus before Philo in the category of 'cultural convergence' (chapter 6). But in many cases no clear chronological sequence can be established and the works discussed in chapter 7 are in no particular historical order. In the case of writings from other Mediterranean sites (that is, those which can be confidently placed elsewhere, or cannot be confidently placed in Egypt), Pseudo-Phocylides and Josephus might be assigned to the category of cultural convergence and 4 Maccabees to that of 'cultural antagonism' (chapter 12). My other example in this field, the apostle Paul, will prove sufficiently anomalous to require treatment in a chapter of his own (chapter 13)!

This chapter has been heavy with theory, discarding unhelpful tools and defining those which will be employed in this book. In order to clarify where we have got to, let me summarize my conclusions:

1. Diaspora Judaism is not helpfully measured against Palestinian Judaism. Categories such as 'orthodoxy' and 'deviation' are misleading and mask ideological judgments which may not reflect the local and contemporary conditions of the evidence we discuss.

2. We need to acquire some means of distinguishing between

different kinds of Hellenization and different degrees of social or cultural engagement. There were many facets to Hellenization, not all of which were equally threatening to Jewish identity.

3. A positive proposal has been mounted, distinguishing Assimilation, Acculturation and Accommodation, each measured on an appropriate scale.

4. Given the character of our evidence, only tentative observations can be made concerning differing 'Levels of Assimilation' (chapter 5 for Egypt, chapter 11 for the rest of the Mediterranean Diaspora). Analysis of literary sources will focus on their forms of accommodation, some inclining more to 'cultural convergence', others to 'cultural antagonism' (chapters 6 and 7 for Egypt; chapters 12 and 13 for the rest of the Diaspora).

Thus we now return to Egypt to continue our large but enthralling investigation of the Egyptian Diaspora.

# 5

## Levels of Assimilation among Egyptian Jews

Our first task is to assess the levels of assimilation to be found among Egyptian Jews. Assimilation, it will be recalled, is here defined as social integration into non-Jewish society, and we have set out above (chapter 4.3 and 4.4) some of the factors which enter into the measurement of such a phenomenon. Thanks to the range and richness of our sources, we know about a great variety of Egyptian Jews and possess evidence which suggests that they were assimilated to very different degrees. As always, however, we are limited by our partial knowledge of the persons concerned. While we can describe the total life-commitments of a few individuals and some groups, in many cases we encounter Egyptian Jews in single and isolated references which give us clues to their social relationships, but leave hidden other aspects of their lives. To use these single visible features to categorize their total social posture is obviously a precarious procedure. Our categorizations must therefore remain somewhat crude and tentative, and I will divide our material no more exactly than into the categories of 'high', 'medium' and 'low' assimilation. We will reserve for a fourth category, 'unknown', those cases where our evidence for Jewish assimilation is intriguing enough to discuss but too uncertain to allow us to reach even tentative conclusions.

### 5.1 High Assimilation

We know of a number of Egyptian Jews who were highly assimilated, though their assimilation took many different forms. It is natural that we should know of so many cases in this category since Jews who assimilated to the degree of losing their Jewish distinctiveness were resented by other Jews, whose comments have in some cases been preserved. They were also figures whose assimilation enabled them to become fully involved in Egyptian social affairs, and in a few cases we encounter them in significant political roles. There were, perhaps, many other Jews whose high assimilation is invisible to us precisely because they have integrated successfully into their social environment. By losing their Jewish identity – by dropping the use of Hebrew names, for instance, and by declining to refer to themselves as 'Jews' – such Jews over generations were absorbed into the general population and became indistinguishable from the Greeks or Egyptians among whom they lived. Many an Alexander or Diophanes or Seos, who feature in our sources without sign of ethnic identity, could be Jews who have lost all indications of their ethnic origin. How many such Jews thereby escape our notice we shall never know.

We may divide our examples of high assimilation into a number of sub-categories, representing different forms of assimilation.

1. *Jews fully integrated into the political/religious affairs of state.* One of the best-known examples of this form of high assimilation is Dositheos, son of Drimylos, whom we have had occasion to mention already (see p. 32). Dositheos appears in a number of papyri (*CPJ* 127) both as the memorandum-writer of Ptolemy Euergetes I (in 240 BCE) and, more significantly, as 'priest of Alexander and the Gods Adelphoi and the Gods Euergetai' (in 222 BCE). His particular theophoric name is so common among Jews as to suggest that he was of Jewish origin, and that supposition is confirmed by the reference to this same figure in 3 Maccabees 1.3. Here he is described as 'of Jewish origin' (τὸ γένος Ἰουδαῖος) although, in the author's view, he had 'altered his customs and abandoned his ancestral beliefs'. The extent of his assimilation is clear both from his political position and from his complete identification with Ptolemaic religion. Our contemporary synagogue inscriptions indicate the care of Jewish communities in Egypt to avoid giving recognition to the claimed divinity of the Ptolemaic kings (see above, p. 31). Thus Dositheos' elevated service in the royal cult must indicate a rejection of his compatriots' religious traditions. The same may be true of Kineas, son of Dositheos (the same Dositheos?), who was priest to Ptolemy Philopator and his mother Cleopatra from 177/6 to 170/69 BCE, and his daughter Berenice who was priestess to Arsinoe Philopator in 169 BCE.[1]

---

[1]   Morkholm 1961:39–40. But note the doubts on the Jewish identity of these individuals in Modrzejewski 1993:85 n. 65.

Similar forms of assimilation may lie behind the story in 3 Maccabees 2.25–33, where, in recounting Philopator's encouragement of the Dionysiac cult, the author refers to some Jews who gladly participated in the cult 'in order to share some of the glory that would come from their association with the king' (2.31). As we shall see (chapter 7.2), 3 Maccabees is not a reliable historical witness and it is hard to assess what lies behind his story at this point. But if this is not purely rhetorical invention, it may be a garbled account of the compromises practised by some Jews whose advancement in the court was eased by their abandonment of the exclusive Jewish religion (see above, chapter 2.1.3).

In the Roman era the most famous case of this form of assimilation is Philo's nephew, Tiberius Julius Alexander. Born c. 15 CE, Alexander was brought up in conditions of exceptional wealth and in a family extremely well connected to the imperial family in Rome.[2] He reached maturity at a time when Jews in Alexandria were becoming socially disgraced and when the Jewish élite had to choose between Jewish loyalty and social prestige. He appears in three of Philo's philosophical tractates (*De Providentia* 1 and 2; *De Animalibus*) as a young man expressing objections to the notion of divine providence and justice.[3] To what extent these treatises represent the real opinions of Alexander is difficult to determine,[4] but the fact that he was associated with such theological scepticism may reflect some historical reality.

More significant, however, than such intellectual questions was the course of Alexander's career in the Roman administration. In 42 CE, probably under Claudius' patronage, he was made *epistrategos* of the Thebaid, and in 46–48 CE appointed the Roman procurator of Judaea (Josephus, *Ant* 20.100–3). Beyond that point his stages of ascent up the ladder of equestrian office are not known, but he emerges again in 63 CE as a high-ranking officer in the Eastern

---

[2]    His father, Alexander the Alabarch, was rich enough to grant a loan of 200,000 drachmae (Josephus, *Ant* 18.159–60). His political connections included his role as 'overseer' of the Egyptian property of Antonia, the mother of the future emperor Claudius (*Ant* 19.276–77).

[3]    For *De Providentia* see Hadas-Lebel 1973 (with Latin translation of the Armenian; Philo Loeb vol. 9 contains only the Greek fragments preserved by Eusebius). For *De Animalibus*, where Alexander's views are discussed in his absence, see Terian 1981.

[4]    See Colson in Loeb vol. 9:449 and the caution of Hadas-Lebel 1973:23–46. Burr 1955:18–21 may give too much credence to the treatises as representing Alexander's views.

army (Tacitus, *Ann* 15.28), and in 66–69 CE with the highest equestrian office of governor of Egypt (Josephus, *Bell* 2.309). As we have seen (chapter 3.2), in the course of his governorship he was obliged to suppress a Jewish uprising in Alexandria, and he spent the final year of the Jewish War as Titus' second-in-command at the siege of Jerusalem (*Bell* 5.45–46, 510; 6.237–42). Thereafter, he may have become prefect of the praetorian guard in Rome.[5]

This extraordinarily successful career appears to have necessitated the abandonment of many Jewish customs. His military advancement itself made Jewish observance well nigh impossible, but the clearest indication of his assimilation is his fulfilment of the religious duties which attended his high office: several inscriptions demonstrate his necessary commitment to Romano-Egyptian polytheism.[6] It is telling that Roman historians mention Alexander without reference to his Jewish origins.[7] Although Josephus says nothing about Alexander's relationship to Judaism in his *Bellum*, in *Ant* 20.100 he states that Alexander 'did not remain faithful to his ancestral customs'.[8] It appears that his assimilation required him to discard most if not all of the practices by which Jewish identity was distinguished.

2. *Social Climbers.* Closely related to the political figures described above are those Jews whose social ambitions led them to abandon key aspects of their Jewish heritage. Philo comments in general terms on those who 'sell their freedom' for the pleasures of food, drink and sex (*Virt* 182), but he notes particularly the lure of social success in this regard. Commenting on Moses' loyalty to Judaism in the Pharaonic palace, Philo remarks that some, puffed up by success, look down on their friends and relations, 'transgressing the laws according to which they were born and bred, and

---

[5]    See the full analysis of his career in Turner 1954 and Burr 1955.

[6]    *OGIS* 663 shows Alexander's role in setting up a relief of Claudius offering worship to the Egyptian Deities Khonsou and Seb. *OGIS* 669 contains his own reference to the providence of the Gods (despite his scepticism in Philo's treatises!) and to the deity of the emperors. See also Fuks' discussion of relevant papyri in *CPJ* 418.

[7]    E.g. Tacitus, *Ann* 15.28; *Hist* 1.1; 2.74, 79; Suetonius, *Vespasian* 6.3.

[8]    As Turner 1954:63 points out, at the time of the publication of the *Bellum* (late 70s CE), Alexander may have been too powerful in Rome for such an offensive reference to his 'apostasy' to be safely made. See my further reflections on this case in Barclay 1995.

subverting the ancestral customs, to which no blame can rightly be attached, by changing their mode of life' (*Mos* 1.31). The reference to 'blame' suggests a conscious repudiation of customs no doubt regarded as restrictive, even 'barbarian', in the elevated circles to which such assimilated Jews aspired.[9]

Josephus gives a vivid illustration of this tendency in the story of Joseph the Tobiad who associated with high society in Alexandria, ate and drank to excess and fell in love with a palace dancing-girl (*Ant* 12.186–89). It is possible that this form of assimilation became more common in Alexandria at the end of our period when the Jewish community there became socially marginalized and disgraced. As we have seen (chapter 3), in the early Roman era social and political pressure began to mount against the Jews. Those whose Jewish identity counted against their admission into gymnasia must have been sorely tempted to abandon their Jewish loyalties for the sake of their social advancement. The violence of the middle years of the first century CE and the imposition of the Jewish tax after 70 CE may have increased this tendency, at least for those who were already somewhat on the edge of the Jewish community. The vehemence of the attack on 'apostates' in 3 Maccabees (probably written in the early Roman era) and Philo's comments noted above may well reflect this situation, where some Jews prized their social and political privileges more than their loyalty to the Jewish tradition. It is also possible that Egyptian Christianity and the development of Gnosticism in Egypt owed something to assimilated Jews who became dissociated from the Jewish community through the political upheavals of the first century and the Diaspora Revolt.[10]

3. *Jews who married Gentiles and failed to raise their children as Jews.* Again Philo is our chief source of information concerning another form of assimilation. In a comment on the Pentateuchal prohibition of marriage to Canaanite women, he highlights the

---

[9] Bassler 1982:95–99 considers Philo's depiction of Joseph in *Somn* 2 to be directed against upwardly mobile and socially pretentious Jews. Cf. the analysis of the evidence in Philo concerning 'apostates' by Wolfson 1948:1.73–86.

[10] The origins of Christianity in Egypt and the roots of Gnosticism are obscure (see Griggs 1990, Pearson 1980 and Green 1985). But some explanation must be given for the Christian use of Philonic tradition and for the presence of Jewish motifs (independently of Christian influence) in Nag Hammadi documents which express anti-Jewish sentiments. For speculations along the lines suggested here see Pearson 1986:132–59 and Amir 1983:50–51.

danger of being 'conquered by conflicting customs', which will result in turning aside from the true path of piety. Even if the Jewish spouse remains firm, he declares, 'there is much to be feared for your sons and daughters', lest they neglect their monotheism, enticed by 'spurious customs' (*Spec Leg* 3.29). He gives a specific biblical example of this phenomenon elsewhere (*Mos* 2.193). He also makes repeated comments on the incident in Numbers 25 when Jewish men were led into idolatry by Moabite/Midianite women (*Mos* 1.295–305; *Spec Leg* 1.54–58; *Virt* 34–44), and highlights the influence of 'foreign women' in introducing their menfolk to 'idolatrous' sacrifices. It is clear that for Philo the Jewish family was crucial in imparting and safeguarding the Jewish tradition, and there is no good reason to doubt the validity of his perspective on this matter. It is natural that the primary relationships created through marriage should in cases of exogamy sometimes work to dilute or even destroy the commitment of Jewish partners to their ancestral traditions.[11]

4. *Jewish Critics and Opponents of Judaism.* Philo defends the Scriptures against many forms of criticism, and the vehemence of his polemical retorts makes it difficult in many cases to establish the target of his attack. Sometimes he lambasts the 'uneducated' who find the text absurd or theologically dubious.[12] But these are probably loyal Jews who simply find sophisticated allegories unconvincing. More dangerous are those who find in the Scriptures nothing superior to the religious legends of the Greeks: those who consider Abraham's offering of Isaac (Gen 22) no more significant than the stories of kings who sacrificed their children (*Abr* 178–93), or the story of Babel (Gen 9) no different from familiar Greek myths (*Conf* 2–13). Although such criticism could have been launched by knowledgeable non-Jews, it is more likely to have arisen from Jews who had come to doubt the value of their own Scriptures. When Philo describes such people as 'rejecting the sacred writings'

---

[11] Exogamy may also be in view in Philo's reference to those who 'corrupt the coinage of noble lineage' (*Praem* 152): they will be dragged down into Tartarus. Cf. also *Spec Leg* 1.315–18, which, in commenting on Deut 13, notes the potential of family relationships to corrupt true piety.

[12] E.g. *Heres* 81 and *Quaest Gen* 4.168; cf. their ridicule of the significance accorded to Sarah's and Abraham's change of names, *Quaest Gen* 3.43, 53. For theological questions about the text see *Plant* 69–72; *Leg All* 3.204–6; see further the discussion of Philo and allegory below (chapter 6.5.3).

(*Quaest Gen* 3.3), as filled with malice and bitterness (*Abr* 184) and as discontented with the ancestral constitution (*Conf* 2), we are probably to detect Jews whose education had contributed to their disenchantment with their own religious traditions, and who now sniped at the Jewish community from the outside.[13]

Those who left the Jewish community through assimilation were clearly well placed to damage their former associates if they chose to align themselves with the opponents of the Jews. It is possible that there are allusions to such hostile former Jews in the invective of *Wisdom of Solomon*. In chapters 2–5 of this work, which probably dates from the early Roman period (see Appendix), there is an extended complaint about the persecution which the righteous have received at the hands of the 'ungodly'. Some of the terms used of these persecutors could suggest that they are assimilated Jews who have repudiated their Jewish upbringing: for instance, they are reproached for 'sins against the law' (ἁμαρτήματα νόμου, 2.12) and described as rebels against the Lord (τοῦ κυρίου ἀποστάντες, 3.10). Scholars continue to debate the identity of these shadowy figures, and it may be that the distortions inherent in the author's polemic make their identification impossible.[14] Nonetheless, it is possible that these passages refer to highly assimilated Jews who have not just abandoned, but now actively oppose, the Jewish community.

5. *Allegorists who abandoned key Jewish practices.* In a famous passage, *Mig Abr* 89–93, Philo criticizes some fellow Jews whose allegorical interpretation of the law caused them to be lax in their observance of distinctive Jewish practices. Philo refers to those who take the literal sense of the laws as a symbol of intellectual truths, in his view overdoing their investigation of the latter while 'carelessly taking no heed of the former' (*Mig Abr* 89). Although Philo does

---

[13] Note how the critics in *Conf* 2–3 now refer to the Scriptures as '*your* so-called holy-books'. For a discussion of these 'hommes savants' who 'assimilent les institutions juives aux coutumes païennes et perdent ainsi de vue leur transcendance', see Daniélou 1958:107–9.

[14] See the discussion of this difficult issue by Grimm 1860:27–30; Focke 1913; Weisengoff 1949; and Larcher 1983:115–17. Apart from this passage there is no evidence (even in Philo) for the persecution of Jews in Egypt by assimilated Jews. Thus it is possible that the author has described non-Jewish opponents with the stereotyped vocabulary of his Jewish tradition; alternatively, he may be reflecting events in Palestine in the turbulent years of Hasmonean rule (so Focke and Larcher).

not rebuke such people as vehemently as, for instance, the social climbers noted above, he does criticize them for their 'recklessness' (*ibid.*). Running through a list of laws – Sabbath, festivals and circumcision – Philo agrees with such allegorists on the spiritual meaning of these rules, but insists on the preservation of their literal observance.[15]

Who were these pure allegorists?[16] Although they have sometimes been regarded as an antinomian sect (and a precursor to Pauline Christianity),[17] Philo's comments might suggest isolated intellectuals whose attachment to the Jewish community was growing weak.[18] Philo refers to such people as those who, 'as though they lived on their own in the desert, or had become disembodied souls, and knew no city or village or home or any company of people at all, overlook the opinions of the masses and search out truth in its naked abstraction' (*Migr Abr* 90). Despite what he says here about 'living alone', this intellectual stance may have been accompanied by a desire to assimilate more to non-Jewish company: their social withdrawal is here described only in relation to Jewish society (the 'masses' are the Jewish populace). If their behaviour resulted in a gradual disengagement from the Jewish community, this may have been compensated for by the development of alternative social connections. In disregarding the opinions of the Jewish majority, such intellectuals placed themselves on the periphery of the Alexandrian Jewish community, whose censure of such behaviour is eloquent testimony to its general conservatism. By neglecting the literal practice of the law they were on the road to its 'abrogation', and such uncertain attachment to the law and the community represented for Philo a worrying strain on the boundaries of Judaism.[19]

---

[15] On Philo's argumentation here, which reveals so much of the tensions within his own thought, see below chapter 6.5.5.

[16] Many scholars describe them as 'extreme allegorists', but the epithet suggests a presumption that Philo's position was self-evidently more reasonable. I use the term 'pure' to indicate the logical consistency of their position, without prejudging the value of such consistency.

[17] E.g. Friedländer 1905:282–86, who refers to them as a 'Religionspartei', while recognizing their individualism.

[18] So rightly Wolfson 1948:1.66–70; Hay 1979–80:47–49.

[19] Philo's reference to the 'censure' of the masses and the 'charges' they might bring (*Migr Abr* 93) suggests that the majority of the Jewish community would be harsher in their judgment of such allegorists than Philo himself. Philo is at least of their intellectual ilk and fully in sympathy with their allegorical interpretation of the law.

6. *Isolated Jews.* A final category of highly assimilated Jews is constituted by those whose circumstances resulted in their isolation from other Jews, with the consequent difficulty of maintaining Jewish customs. Philo seems to reflect the dangers of such isolation when he describes Jacob's fears for his son Joseph:

> for he knew how natural it is for young people to lose their footing and how easy it is for strangers in a land to sin, especially in Egypt which is blind towards the true God because of its deification of created and mortal things; moreover, he knew how wealth and glory could attack minds of little sense and that, left to himself, without an accompanying monitor from his father's house, alone and bereft of good teachers, he would be liable to change to alien ways. (*Jos* 254)

This acute collection of observations encapsulates the cultural pressures on Jews in Egypt, especially young Jews with social and economic ambitions. It also highlights the importance of social networks and, in particular, the primary network of the family. We may imagine the difficulties for Jewish slaves in Egypt who served in non-Jewish households. The slave girl Johanna who worked in the household of Apollonius in the mid-third century BCE (*CPJ* 7) can hardly have found it easy to maintain her Jewish customs; she would certainly have had no choice in the allocation of a mate.[20] The Jewess Martha whom we meet as a freedwoman of one Protarchus, and inheritor of half his estate (*CPJ* 148), must have greatly satisfied her (probably Gentile) owner: one can only speculate at what cost to her loyalty to her Jewish heritage. Similarly, Jewish soldiers who served in predominantly non-Jewish units in the Ptolemaic army may have had little opportunity to practise their 'ancestral customs': it is not altogether surprising to find some, in association with their Gentile comrades, supporting the dedication of religious monuments to Greek or Egyptian Gods (Horbury & Noy 154–156).

More generally, Jewish peasants and artisans in the Egyptian countryside may not always have clung faithfully to Jewish customs. Our papyri indicate that some Jews in the *chora* adopted Egyptian names (Seos, Pasis etc.), spoke demotic and worked alongside Egyptian field-hands and artisans (e.g. *CPJ* 46, 133). That Jews could

---

[20] Cf. also Jonathas, a debt-bondsman in the household of a Cyrenaean (*CPJ* 126).

and did live on the boundary of Jewish and Egyptian cultures is indicated by the work of Artapanus, who presents Moses as the founder of the Egyptian animal cults (see below, chapter 6.1). It is also what we would expect from historical precedent. Jeremiah 44 reflects a belief that Egyptian Jews (in the Persian period) combined worship of Yahweh with the cult of the 'Queen of Heaven', and the Elephantine papyri show that the Jewish garrison on the Nile offered sacrifice both to 'Yahu' and to the Goddess 'Ishumbethel' or 'Anathbethel' (*CAP* 22; cf. 44). Artapanus' positive appreciation of Egyptian religion may not have been unique, and our papyri show Jews not only working in close association with Egyptians (*CPJ* 46) but employed by a local temple (*CPJ* 39). Temples in Egypt were the site of many kinds of industry, with traders setting up stalls in the precincts and paying due worship (and tax) to the relevant God.[21] The social and economic pressures on Jews to 'compromise' their religious exclusiveness must have been great.

## 5.2 Medium Assimilation

Although this category is inevitably somewhat inexact, it is intended to encompass those Jews who had significant social ties with the non-Jewish world but who were also careful to preserve their distinct Jewish identity. This double commitment distinguishes them both from the category above, where Jewish identity is either lost or under strain, and from the category below, where contacts with the non-Jewish world were minimal. Within this rather broad category several types of assimilation can be distinguished.

1. *Jews prominent in court but distinguishably Jewish.* We noted above (pp. 104–6) some cases of Jews who were so fully integrated in the political and religious affairs of state as to lose their commitment to the Jewish tradition. Here we may note that there were some Jews, at least in the Ptolemaic era, who played significant roles in Ptolemaic affairs, while maintaining their Jewish commitments. We have already had occasion to note the figure of Aristobulus, who is

---

[21] Bowman 1990:107, 143 discusses the temple of Serapis at Oxyrhynchus, while noting that 'village temples are known to have been centres of small-scale industry such as weaving and brewing' (172); cf. Thompson 1988:75–78.

referred to in 2 Maccabees 1.10 as 'the teacher of Ptolemy the king' (p. 42). In fact, the historical value of this notice is somewhat doubtful, and the address to the king in two of the fragments may be merely literary convention (see below, chapter 6.4). Thus it is not possible to place Aristobulus securely in the Ptolemaic court; but he may be counted among the Alexandrian scholars whose commitment to his Judaism was just as strong as his commitment to the Greek philosophical tradition. More plausibly within the court itself is the author of *The Letter of Aristeas*, whose knowledge of royal protocol suggests a figure well placed in the administration of the realm. As we shall see (below, chapter 6.3), 'Aristeas' holds firmly to the significance (indeed, superiority) of the Jewish tradition, while valuing much that Hellenistic culture had to offer. When he presents Jews as dining with the king (on their own terms) and yet defends the 'iron walls' of Jewish distinction, he neatly encapsulates the social position on our scale we are describing as 'medium' assimilation.

We may also place in this category the Jewish military commanders, Onias, Chelkias and Ananias, whose role in political and dynastic affairs we have noted above (chapter 2.2.1). Their Jewish commitments are clear in their leadership of the Jewish community at Leontopolis, and also in Ananias' identification of his troops with their 'kinsman', Alexander Jannaeus (Josephus, *Ant* 13.352–55). Yet their role in supporting various branches of the Ptolemaic dynasty signifies their social involvement in the world of Alexandrian politics.

2. *Well-educated Jews who participated in the social and cultural life of Alexandria.* We may take first, as examples of this form of assimilation, the two brothers, Alexander the Alabarch and Philo. Alexander's title indicates an important administrative role, probably connected with customs-collection on the Nile, though its precise remit is unclear.[22] In any case, he was obviously very well connected in Alexandrian society, and indeed beyond Alexandria to the court in Rome (see above n. 2). Nonetheless, in contrast to his son Tiberius Julius Alexander, whom we have discussed above, Alexander the Alabarch appears to have remained faithful to his Jewish tradition. A man who was willing to donate massive plates of silver and gold for the nine gates of the temple in Jerusalem

---

[22]  See Tcherikover in *CPJ* 1.49 n. 4 and Smallwood 1970:4 n. 4.

(Josephus, *Bell* 5.205) was clearly deeply committed to the Jewish religion. Philo also combined involvement in Alexandrian civic life with whole-hearted support of the Jewish community. The depth of Philo's education suggests that he received a thorough training in a gymnasium context (see further below, chapter 6.5.1). Moreover, his familiarity with theatrical and sporting events (chariot races, boxing, wrestling and pancratist contests) indicates that he enjoyed the regular entertainments of Alexandrian citizens.[23] Yet Philo's commitment to the Jewish community is unimpeachable, and illustrated most clearly by his willingness to lead the dangerous embassy to the emperor Gaius (chapter 3.1.2). He thus exemplifies the *modus vivendi* by which some wealthy Alexandrian Jews enjoyed partial assimilation in Alexandrian society while preserving their Jewish loyalties.

It is likely that there were other Alexandrian Jews in this category. As we have seen (chapter 3, Excursus), there were almost certainly other Alexandrian Jews who had passed through the educational and athletic training of the gymnasium and gained Alexandrian citizenship. Yet their Jewish commitments are indicated by the resentment they caused: Apion's complaint that, if they are citizens, they should worship the same Gods as the Alexandrians (Josephus, *C Ap* 2.65) suggests that they generally refused to assimilate to the extent of abandoning their religious exclusiveness.

3. *Jews in various forms of employment with or for non-Jews.* As we noted in the previous chapter (4.4), employment associations are generally of lesser social significance than the primary relationships formed in the family and among close friends. It is thus appropriate to discuss examples of Jews employed with non-Jews in this category of 'medium' assimilation. Yet employment concerns only one segment of an individual's life, and if we knew more about some of the individuals discussed here, we might have placed them higher up our scale; for all we know, a Jewish farm-hand working alongside Egyptians might also have been married to an Egyptian or have started to worship Egyptian Gods.

In many cases we know only the names of the people concerned and cannot tell how to interpret their nomenclature. Even when we can identify Jewish individuals in our sources, we are often

---

[23] The evidence here is discussed by Mendelson 1982 and Feldman 1993:58–63; cf. further, chapter 6.5.1. *Ebr* 20 indicates that he approved of joining clubs, but it is unclear whether these are Jewish or Alexandrian; cf. Borgen 1994:45–46.

uncertain whether the persons associated with them, who bear standard Greek or Egyptian names, are also Jews or not. Also, in some cases the only factor identifying an individual as a Jew is a name of Hebrew origin: yet if that signals commitment to the Jewish tradition at all, it tells us more about the parents who named that individual than about the person who bears the name. It is only in those cases where the relevant individual is identified as Ἰουδαῖος that we can assume some current identification with the Jewish community, though what that identification meant in practice we cannot tell. Generally such a specific ethnic label is to be found only in legal documents; whether other individuals in different contexts would have accepted this identification we cannot tell. Thus all the following material has to be treated with some caution: in most cases the evidence is too limited to be more than merely suggestive.

Among the occupations in which we find Egyptian Jews we may note first their roles in the Ptolemaic *army*. Here, as we have already noted (above, chapter 2.1.2), Jews served in all ranks in infantry and cavalry, from humble footmen to officers and paymasters.[24] In most cases they served in military units of mixed ethnicity (alongside, for instance, 'Macedonians', *CPJ* 31); indeed there is no good evidence of specifically Jewish units before the establishment of the Leontopolis community. Our papyri show Jewish soldiers and cleruchs in a range of legal and financial contracts with both Jews and non-Jews. We cannot tell what this signifies in wider social relations, but it is important that in many of the cases known to us they are specifically identified as 'Jews' or 'Jews of the epigone' (*CPJ* 18–24, 31). Such a label indicates at least that those who drew up the relevant contracts associated these Jewish soldiers with a particular ethnicity; the practical effects of such identification we cannot now trace.

Besides these military cleruchs, Jews were to be found in employment in *agriculture* in a variety of contexts. The shepherd 'Pasis the Jew' who worked on Zenon's estate (*CPJ* 9) was at least recognized as of Judaean descent, as was also 'Seos the Jew' who owed wool to a Gentile wool-trader (*CPJ* 38). Jewish shepherds are to be found alongside non-Jews in a list from the Oxyrhynchite nome (*CPJ* 412), and one Idellas (apparently a Jew, though only his name might indicate this) tended a flock for a temple of Pan

---

[24] See the collection of papyri, *CPJ* 18–32 and Tcherikover's introduction in *CPJ* 1.147–48.

(*CPJ* 39). The same social intermingling is found among other sorts of agricultural workers. Jewish farmers (*CPJ* 13, 29, 42, 44), field-hands (*CPJ* 133) and vineyard workers (*CPJ* 14, 15) are all to be found in normal social intercourse with non-Jews, though in all these cases only their names indicate their probable Jewish origins.

Egyptian Jews are to be found employed also as *artisans*, engaged, for instance, in weaving (*CPJ* 405). In one particularly intriguing case (*CPJ* 10), it appears that a Jewish builder (or overseer of works) on the estate of Apollonius was allowed to keep the Sabbath; he thus retained a key feature of his Jewish identity even while working for a Greek. We also have evidence for Jewish *guards* and policemen, one Samoelis, for instance, working on the estate of the Greek magnate, Zenon (*CPJ* 12; cf. 25). Their employment in the sphere of *transport*, as donkey-owners (*CPJ* 282, 362) or as boatmen on the Nile (*CPJ* 404, 422; Philo, *Legatio* 129), involved constant commercial interaction with non-Jews.

Some Egyptian Jews are to be found in *business relationships* with non-Jews. 3 Macc 3.10 suggests that some Alexandrian Jews were 'engaged in business' with non-Jews, and Philo refers to 'tradesmen', merchants and ship-owners who doubtless had Gentile clients (*Flacc* 57). In the papyri we find Jews in a range of financial relationships, as tax-payers, of course, but also as tax-gatherers (*CPJ* 90, 100–102, 240),[25] both lending money to non-Jews (*CPJ* 152, 413, 414) and taking loans from them (*CPJ* 142, 411, 417). To what extent these relationships were more than merely financial it is impossible to say.

4. *Legal Associations*. Finally we may note forms of association which arose in the legal sphere. Our papyri indicate Jews acting as witnesses for non-Jews (*CPJ* 25), and *vice versa* (*CPJ* 18). They also show Jews coming for trial before non-Jews, most interestingly in two cases (both concerning assault!) where both parties to the dispute appear to have been Jewish (*CPJ* 19, 133). In general it seems that Jews made use of the normal legal institutions and formulae current in Egypt (Modrzejewski 1991:94–101). Jews are to be found undergoing divorce in accordance with the normal rules of Hellenistic law (*CPJ* 144); they also charged normal rates of interest (*CPJ* 20) and made appeals, agreements and depositions according to the formulae then operative (e.g. *CPJ* 18, 37, 43, 142–

---

[25]  See Tcherikover in *CPJ* 1.18–19.

149). If such legal documents and contracts made reference to the Ptolemaic kings as 'Gods' (e.g. *CPJ* 18, 19, 22–24) or to the divinity of an emperor (*CPJ* 411), that was of only formal significance. In a legal context one Soteles son of Josepos made an oath in the name of a Roman emperor (*CPJ* 427), but such formal polytheism need not have signified much by way of social assimilation.

## 5.3 Low Assimilation

Our third category embraces those whose social contact with non-Jews was minimal. Once again, since we can so rarely view life-patterns as a whole, our judgments here have to be made on partial evidence; and it is particularly precarious to say what did not occur on the basis of limited information. However, we may point to two factors which encouraged comparatively low assimilation in some circumstances, before noting a particular Jewish community which seems to have been socially isolated to an unusual degree.

1. *Jewish Residential Districts.* We have observed (chapter 2, n. 19; pp. 29–30) the concentration of Jews in certain streets of Egyptian towns in the *chora*, and their residence in the Delta quarter of Alexandria. Not all Egyptian Jews resided in such predominantly Jewish districts, but for those who did, the social networks formed among Jewish neighbours may have shaped their lives to a significant degree. In this regard, the significance of the 'prayer-house' as a focus of both religious and social identity has already been noted (pp. 26–27), and we may add here some fragmentary evidence for Jewish burial associations (? *CPJ* 138) and dining clubs (? *CPJ* 139).

The establishment of largely Jewish areas of residence may have been particularly significant for Jewish women. One should treat with suspicion Philo's assertion that men's roles are public, suited to social gathering and discourse, while a woman's place is in the home (*Spec Leg* 3.169): he is describing his ideal, which his subsequent polemic indicates is not reflected in the reality of Alexandrian street life. Nonetheless, social expectation probably did restrict women's contacts more to their families and immediate neighbours than was the case for their menfolk, and, despite his rhetorical exaggeration, there is some plausibility in Philo's description of the shock when Roman soldiers ransacked Jewish homes, violently disturbing the comparative seclusion of Jewish women (*Flacc* 89). We may therefore estimate that among the least assimilated Egyptian Jews were Jewish women who lived in wholly or largely Jewish districts.

2. *The Effects of Social Conflict.* Here again we can speak only in general terms of the likely effect of social conditions. The rising tension in community relations in Alexandria in the early Roman period hardly fostered associations between the ethnic communities, and the outbreak of violence in 38 CE must have severed many social links in the city. The Jewish artisans whose workshops were pillaged and the Jewish residents whose houses were ransacked (Philo, *Flacc* 56) can hardly have continued friendly relations with their former customers and neighbours. Indeed, the crowding of Jews even closer in the Delta quarter of the city, and their common plight during the pogrom, probably had a significant effect on the social dynamics of Jewish life in Alexandria. As we noted in chapter 3, a growing trend of social estrangement is evident in the street fighting of 41 CE and in the recurrent violence thereafter, culminating in the uprising of 116 CE. We may surely place among the least assimilated Egyptian Jews those who initiated such street violence in 41 CE, those who were attracted to the call to arms issued by Judaean refugees in 70 CE, and those who fought, with terrible ferocity, in the Diaspora Revolt of 116–117 CE.

3. *The Therapeutae.* A particularly isolated community of Jews was that known as 'the Therapeutae', though unfortunately our only source of information about them is Philo's idealistic *De Vita Contemplativa*. The origins of this community and their relationship to the Essenes in the Jewish homeland are matters of some debate,[26] but for our purposes it is only necessary to consider their social conditions. The community which Philo describes was settled on a hill near the Mareotic Lake, just outside Alexandria, surrounded by farm buildings and villages (*Vit Cont* 21–23). Philo is silent about the economic basis of this community, and it may be that they were not as socially isolated as might appear. But his description of their way of life suggests a 'monastic' community whose members (male and female) had deliberately withdrawn from normal social

---

[26] See the survey of scholarship in Schürer 2.591–97 and Riaud 1986.

intercourse in order to devote themselves to contemplation, worship and biblical exegesis. Whatever the balance in this community between individual solitude and communal celebration, its common ethos provided an alternative society, with its own unusual social norms (*Vit Cont* 72–74). We cannot tell whether the inspiration for this social withdrawal was as exclusively 'philosophical' as Philo suggests, but it seems to have embodied the least assimilated pattern of life to be found among Egyptian Jews.

## 5.4 Unknown Assimilation

The spectrum we have constructed, ranging from Tiberius Julius Alexander to the Therapeutae, indicates the enormous range in the assimilation of Diaspora Jews. There are no doubt many other points on this spectrum which we are unable to detect or describe, but it is clear enough that generalizations in this matter are of little value. We may conclude our survey with material which both intrigues and puzzles the interpreter. In these cases, as in the inscriptions in the temple of Pan described above (chapter 4.5), we simply cannot tell what our evidence signifies, not least here because we cannot be certain that it concerns Jews at all. In particular, two kinds of material require our attention: the possible use by Jews of magical formulae and amulets, and the possible presence of Jews among those named 'Sambathion' who otherwise appear completely Egyptianized.

1. *Jewish Syncretistic Magic?* It is now generally acknowledged that there was a flourishing tradition of magic in Jewish circles in the Graeco-Roman era.[27] During the last century archaeology has brought to light new papyri and new artifacts – amulets, tablets, incantation bowls, etc. – which reveal the extent of Jewish interest in magic and confirm the evidence from contemporary observers that Jews were particularly renowned as magicians and exorcists.[28]

---

[27] The fundamental text remains Blau 1914; cf. Trachtenberg 1939 and the recent survey of the field, with bibliography, by Alexander in Schürer 3.342–79. Although most of the magical papyri come from the third or fourth centuries CE, there are good reasons to regard their traditional formulae as originating much earlier, in many cases from the first century; see Hull 1974:20–27.

[28] For the magical papyri see Preisendanz 1928–1931 and Betz 1986. The continuation of the Jewish magical tradition has been illustrated by Margalioth's publication of *Sepher Ha-Razim* (of Byzantine date), now translated by Morgan

The reasons for Jewish expertise are not hard to find. Jewish magicians could claim access to a mysterious tradition with vocabulary (in Hebrew) all the more potent for being in an unintelligible tongue. The unnamed Jewish God exercised particular fascination since the revelation of his secret name(s) was held to unleash awesome power: among the Artapanus legends discussed below (chapter 6.1) is a story of an Egyptian king who swooned at the sound of this secret name and a priest who was struck down for disparaging it (27.25–26). Moreover, there were certain figures in the Jewish tradition, notably Moses and Solomon, who were famous even among non-Jews for their magical powers,[29] while the development of angelology and demonology in Judaism provided precise explanations of misfortune. Those concerned to ward off evil influences or to gain healing, those anxious to secure success in financial, legal or amatory affairs, those eager to gain advantage over their opponents or premonitions of the future – that is, the majority of the population much of the time – were attracted to magic as a form of access to invincible power. And in the cookbooks of magical charms Jewish recipes enjoyed particular renown.

It is important to observe that magic is not necessarily threatening to the Jewish tradition. Despite many attempts to distinguish 'magic' from 'religion', it is perhaps impossible to divide transactions with the divine in the ancient world into neatly contrasting spheres, either phenomenologically or in terms of the practitioner's intent.[30] The most useful distinction here – and one which explains the disapproval of 'magic' by those in authority – is that 'magic' constitutes a recourse to divine power generally considered unauthorized or anomalous. The secrecy necessary for magical charms, the manipulation of divine forces by means

---

1983. The Jewish reputation in this area is evident in remarks by Juvenal, *Satire* 6.542–48 and Celsus, *apud* Origen, *Contra Celsum* 1.26. The prominence of Jewish exorcism in the New Testament, as practised by Jesus, Jewish Christians and other Jews, is striking; cf. also Josephus, *Ant* 8.45–48.

[29] For Moses' reputation as a magician in the Graeco-Roman world see Gager 1972:134–161 The biblical account of the plagues and the special revelation of the divine name to Moses contributed greatly to his fame in this regard. The special aptitude of Jews in the magic arts is well described by Simon 1986:339–68.

[30] At least, any theoretical distinction typically breaks down in practice (note, for instance, Kee 1986). Well-nuanced discussions of this problem are available in Nock 1972:313–18; Goodenough 2.155–61; Aune 1980:1510–16; and Lane Fox 1986:36–38.

outwith the normal cultic mechanisms, and the effects of 'sorcery' in incongruous events – these all gave to the practice of magic a subterranean quality which was feared by those in positions of power.[31]

Thus it is no surprise to find Philo expanding Pentateuchal texts (Exod 22.18; Deut 18.9–14) into blanket denunciations of 'magicians' and 'sorcerers' (μάγοι καὶ φαρμακευταί), who delude the common people with their 'evil art' (*Spec Leg* 3.93–103).[32] As a representative of the Jewish governing class, whose education made him wary of 'superstition', Philo distrusts the 'charlatans', the 'vulgar women and slaves', who peddle their dubious wares among the gullible masses (*Spec Leg* 3.101–3). But it is significant that he does not condemn their customers outright, but merely considers them hindered from safe arrival at the haven of piety (*Spec Leg* 1.61; 4.50). It appears that this species of 'folk-Judaism' played too significant a role in the lives of ordinary Jews to be eradicated. And since recourse to the expertise of a magician did not necessarily challenge the 'ancestral customs' it could be seen as a relatively harmless activity.[33]

Only one aspect of magic made it potentially dangerous to Jews, and that was its tendency to syncretism. In the world of magic it was important to buy comprehensive insurance. One could not afford to ignore any potential source of influence, either good or evil, and incantations tended towards long lists of names and symbols, some recognizable, some mere gobbledygook. Deities and 'daimons' of all varieties make their appearance in such formulae, and the familiar syncretistic combinations of Egyptian religion are everywhere evident. In fact it is peculiarly hard to determine from this evidence the extent of Jewish participation in the concoction and use of such formulae. Although Egyptian Jews were undoubtedly involved in magical practices, it is impossible to determine their relationship to the precise texts and amulets which we now possess. Both the papyri and the amulets show unmistakable signs of Jewish *influence* – not least in the use of the divine names Iao, Adonai and Sabaoth, in the appearance of Hebrew angels and in references to Moses and the patriarchs. But it is another matter to discern whether such texts had their *origins* among Jews and to what extent they were *used* by Jews in their present syncretistic form.

---

[31] See MacMullen 1966:95–127 and Brown 1972:119–46.

[32] Cf. Philo's views on divination and related practices, *Spec Leg* 1.59–65; 4.48–52.

[33] For the ambivalence of the rabbis on this subject see Urbach 1975:97–102.

The magical papyri which have been preserved nearly all originate from non-Jewish collections. When we find, in a charm heavily influenced by Jewish tradition (even Jewish Scripture), reference to Ammon, Thoth or Ptah, are we to ascribe this to Jewish syncretism or to the expansion and supplementation of a Jewish original by non-Jews?[34]

In most cases, firm conclusions are impossible, but two factors at least should make us open to the possibility of Jewish syncretism. First, even in those texts which are wholly Jewish in origin, prayers are addressed to Helios (the sun), and incantations employ the name of Aphrodite.[35] One therefore cannot rule out the possibility that other, fully polytheistic texts, were also created and utilized by Jews.[36] Second, the religious combinations which we will note in Artapanus provide evidence that at the popular level 'Judaism was sometimes capable of compromises that doubtless increased its prestige and its appeal with the vulgar masses' (Simon 1986:351). We cannot regard it as impossible that Jews used spells addressed to 'the Headless One' in the name of Moses (*PGM* V, 96–172), or that they wore amulets with the images and names of Egyptian Gods alongside inscriptions to Iao Sabaoth.[37]

---

[34] A section of the Great Paris Papyrus, *PGM* IV, 3009–3085 is a case in point. The extent of Jewish material, with detailed reference to biblical events, has persuaded most commentators of the Jewish origin of the core of this text (e.g. Blau 1914:112–17, Deissmann 1927:255–63 and Simon 1986:349–51; but not Bonner 1950:27). But are its attribution to Pibechis, its inclusion of non-Jewish Deities and its reference to 'Jesus, God of the Hebrews' (3020–21) forms of Jewish syncretism or later additions by non-Jews? The name of Jesus does not necessarily indicate direct Christian influence (cf. Acts 19.13).

[35] *Sepher Ha-Razim* 4.60ff.; 1.125ff. Note also the incense offered to angels (1.28ff.) and the spell for necromancy (1.176ff.).

[36] The argument for this position was developed by Goodenough 2.153–295, who maintained that the more the text is centred in Jewish themes and vocabulary, the more likely that its origin is Jewish (see especially 2.190–97, 206–7). While there has been general agreement with this methodology, many of Goodenough's individual judgments have been questioned. In particular, given the wide currency of the divine names Iao, Adonai and Sabaoth, it is precarious to base conclusions of Jewish origin or use on the presence of such names alone. See the review by Nock 1955:568–70.

[37] See Goodenough 2.291–94. For other probably Jewish spells in the *PGM* see e.g. IV, 1169–1226; XIII, 335–40; XXIIa, 17–27; XXIIb, 1–26; XXV, 1–42; cf. the list by Alexander in Schürer 3:359. Since amulets rarely show more than names or common symbols, it is perhaps impossible to judge which were made or used by Jews. Goodenough's discussion 2.208–95 may be over-confident, but proof, on either side, is unobtainable; see also Bonner 1927:28–32, 101–2, 208–10 and Feldman 1993:67–69.

How significant were such forms of syncretism in practice? In particular, what social commitments did such magical charms represent? It is possible that a cure effected through a Serapis charm might lead a Jewish user to offer worship in the appropriate temple. Every merger of Jewish and non-Jewish religion could contribute to a drift from Jewish distinctiveness, and such may indeed lie behind Philo's fears lest the simple folk suffer shipwreck (*Spec Leg* 4.50). But since magic was generally a secret phenomenon, and the possession of amulets a largely private affair, we should perhaps not overrate their practical significance. In a revealing glimpse of ordinary Jewish piety, 2 Macc 12.39–45 tells of the aftermath of a battle in the Maccabean wars when Judas discovered on the bodies of his fallen soldiers amulets dedicated to the Gods of Jamnia. Yet they had fought for Judas in the cause of 'Judaism'! For practical purposes, public commitment to the Jewish community and its traditions was much more significant than 'idolatrous' amulets round a Jewish soldier's neck or the polytheistic love-philtres of a Jewish youth. As Goodenough rightly suggested, it mattered less whether Jews were in this regard purely monotheistic than whether they were 'propagating Jews', that is 'Jews who considered themselves still to belong to the People, Jews bringing up their children in the same feeling' (2.290).

2. *Jewish Egyptianized Sambathions?* In the magical material just considered the mixture of Jewish and non-Jewish influences could be taken to indicate either Jewish 'paganizing' or pagan 'Judaizing'; and, given that no religious traditions could operate in sealed social compartments, either interpretation is possible. In this connection a number of individuals named 'Sambathion' pose a particularly difficult interpretive problem, to which Tcherikover devoted a section of his *CPJ* volume 3, prefaced by a full discussion (*CPJ* 3.43–56). In some cases this name, derived from the Hebrew 'Sabbath', is found alongside other Hebrew or clearly Jewish names, so that the individual concerned may reasonably be regarded as a Jew. But in other cases it is the only Hebrew name in families whose nomenclature is otherwise wholly Egyptian. In such cases Tcherikover took it as 'quite out of the question that the bearers of this name should be Jews, since all their kinsmen are obviously Egyptian' (*CPJ* 3.43). He noted futher the case of one Sambathion who paid tax as an owner of swine (*CPJ* 489), and another where the mummy of a female Sambathion was adorned with traditional Egyptian designs depicting the Goddesses Isis and Nephtys.

Tcherikover commented: 'it can hardly be assumed that a Jewish family adorned the coffin of its deceased kinswoman with scenes borrowed from pagan mythology' (*CPJ* 3.43). He concluded that the Sambathions who are found in such contexts were not Jews but Egyptians whose names reflected widespread respect for the Jewish Sabbath.

In fact, the question is whether *anything* can be assumed here in either direction. It is certainly possible that non-Jews adopted this originally Jewish name, impressed by the practice of the Jewish Sabbath. But that Jewish families might bear almost exclusively Egyptian names should not be ruled impossible, in the light of many known individual cases (e.g. *CPJ* 9, 38, 46). And if some Jews used syncretistic magical formulae and others admired Egyptian animal cults (see below on Artapanus, chapter 6.1), can we rule out the possibility that they buried their dead in Egyptian style?[38] In such tantalizing cases we can only remain agnostic. Given the enormous range of assimilation which we have found among Jews in Egypt, we can afford no preconceptions about what is possible or likely in such cases.

---

[38] For an example of the Jewish use of mummification see Horbury & Noy 133 (= *CIJ* 1536). Tcherikover's questionable assumptions are indicated by his comments on some parallel Roman inscriptions. Junia Sabatis' mortal remains were not buried ('as required by Jewish custom') but burnt (*CIJ* 68), while the tombstones of Aurelia Sabbatia and Claudia Sabbathis were adorned with 'D.M.' (= Dis Manibus, *CIJ* 63, 71): 'it is hard to believe that Jews used these heathen formulae' (*CPJ* 3.45). To describe such persons as 'not Jews, at any rate not orthodox Jews' (*ibid.*) begs all the questions raised above (chapter 4.2).

# 6

## *Cultural Convergence*

It is time now to examine some of the literature produced by Egyptian Jews, in order to assess in greater depth their engagement with their social and cultural environments. In the terms employed above (chapter 4), we wish to examine what sort of accommodation was effected by these Diaspora Jews with their ambient culture(s), conscious that many types of integration or polarization could characterize this cultural interaction.

What sort of questions would help to clarify the socio-cultural stance of the literature we analyse? It will be fruitful to observe, in the first place, how our Jewish authors describe themselves and their fellow Jews: in what ethnic, political or social frameworks do they locate themselves? Similarly significant will be the terms in which they describe non-Jews. What kinds of relationship are depicted between Jews and non-Jews and where do our authors place themselves on the social map of Egypt? Where do they find common ground with others and where do they depict difference? Where difference occurs, how much emphasis is it given and how is it explained? In relation to their theology, how is God described in this literature and what conceptual frameworks are employed in depicting the relationship between God and Jews, and God and non-Jews? What theological and philosophical resources do our authors draw on and what claims do they make for their native traditions? What cultural syntheses are effected and to what end are they employed? Is the Jewish tradition reinterpreted in this encounter and is it thereby strengthened or subverted? In general, can we detect a cultural strategy in our literature and can we relate that strategy to the social and political condition of Jews in Egypt?

These and related questions underlie the investigations which follow. As indicated at the end of chapter 4, I have found it helpful to distinguish in general between those sources which embrace some form of cultural convergence (though they normally still retain some sense of Jewish distinction) and those whose emphasis is better characterized as cultural antagonism. In this chapter we will examine five authors from the Egyptian Diaspora whose works fall into the former category, who integrated their Jewish Scriptures and distinctive practices with the norms and values of their cultural contexts.

Since the production and preservation of literature took place for the most part within a Hellenistic environment, most of our sources bear witness to the interface between Jewish and specifically Hellenistic traditions; moreover, as we have seen, Ptolemaic Alexandria in particular provided ideal conditions for such a cultural interaction. As we noted above (p. 30), the Greek translation of the Pentateuch in the third century BCE was the harbinger of this cultural encounter. The translators' approach to their task was, in the main, extremely cautious, and in linguistic terms the Greek of the Septuagint is extraordinarily servile to the Hebrew original.[1] Nonetheless, there are indications of their sensitivity to their political and cultural environment in the interpretation of the Hebrew text. Particularly striking are the linguistic distinctions they created between Jewish and non-Jewish cult and, conversely, their small steps towards a Hellenizing interpretation of Israel's God. When the God of the burning bush introduces himself in Greek as ἐγώ εἰμι ὁ ὤν ('I am the one who is', Exod 3.14), the potential for a Jewish Platonizing theology is already clear.[2]

The fragments of Demetrius represent the first known attempt to develop this Hellenizing potential, in his case by clarifying the Scriptural chronology and providing an historiographical precision essential for the reputation of the Jewish tradition.[3] Here, however,

[1] See especially Bickerman 1976:167–200 on the Septuagint as a translation; he rightly notes that, despite its syntactical correctness, 'the language of the Greek Torah is foreign and clumsy' (177). Assessment of this matter is, however, hampered by our uncertainty whether our Septuagint texts represent what the translators produced in the third century BCE, and what Hebrew text they were translating.

[2] Political sensitivity is displayed by the avoidance of the term λαγός (hare) in the list of unclean animals (Lev 11.6; Deut 14.7), since the Ptolemaic kings were descended from a man so named! Place names are also sometimes updated (e.g. Heliopolis in Gen 41.45 and Exod 1.11). Bickerman 1988:113–15 notes the careful differentiation in the terminology used for Jewish and Gentile cult. On the possible Hellenizing adaptations of theology in the Septuagint see Freudenthal 1890; Marcus 1945.

[3] Demetrius probably wrote in the reign of Philopator (222–205 BCE). The fragments, preserved in Eusebius, *Praep Evang* 9, have been helpfully discussed by Bickerman 1975, Collins 1986:27–30 and Sterling 1992:153–66.

we shall examine some more extensive examples of cultural convergence which indicate the ability of Egyptian Jews to place their national traditions within Hellenistic moral, historical, philosophical and theological frameworks. The different genres of the material we will examine – drama (Ezekiel), narrative (Artapanus, Aristeas) and philosophical exegesis (Aristobulus, Philo) – indicate the breadth and versatility of this cultural engagement, and our analyses will reveal an extraordinary diversity in the forms of cultural integration attempted. In most cases, our literature represents a convergence of Jewish and specifically Greek traditions. First, however, we must consider the more complex phenonemon of a Jew who reads his Jewish story from the standpoint of a Hellenized Egyptian.

## 6.1 Artapanus

Artapanus is one of the most fascinating figures in Egyptian Judaism. His racy narratives, which freely embellished the biblical story, are known to us, sadly, in no more than three fragments, of which only one is extensive. He is among a number of Jewish writers preserved by the Hellenistic historian Alexander ('Polyhistor'), whose invaluable miscellany was subsequently available to Eusebius, and hence to us.[4] When selecting his material, Alexander greatly abbreviated his sources, sometimes reducing apparently dramatic vignettes in Artapanus' narrative to obscure asides. Nonetheless, he preserved enough of Artapanus' story to reveal an intriguing character whose romanticized life of Moses fosters Jewish loyalty while simultaneously justifying Egyptian religion! 

Artapanus lived in the Ptolemaic era (he can be placed anywhere between 250 and 100 BCE; see Appendix), in a social context in which miraculous tales were apparently more effective than sober history or philosophy. These and other features of his work suggest a 'popular' market, and there are indications that he represents the Hellenized milieu of a country town (perhaps Heliopolis)

---

[4] See the standard work on Alexander by Freudenthal 1875. His important discussion of Artapanus, 143–74, 215–18 effectively demolished earlier doubts about the Jewish identity of Artapanus. For the text here used and an explanation of my citation system, see the Appendix on Sources.

rather than the educated élite of Alexandria.[5] As we shall see, Artapanus was both self-consciously Jewish and supportive of the Hellenized Egyptian culture in which he thrived. It is this synthesis, and in particular its religious dimensions, which make him such an interesting object of study.

Artapanus' Jewish commitments are unmistakably clear. His work, probably titled 'On the Jews' (23.1; 27.1), describes three Jewish heroes, Abraham, Joseph and Moses, focusing on their achievements in Egypt. His narrative is in many cases dependent on the LXX, even in vocabulary, indicating clearly the author's respect for these Jewish Scriptures.[6] Numerous embellishments and alterations are made, all to increase the stature of these heroic characters. Abraham was responsible for introducing astrology to Egypt (18.1). Joseph's outstanding administration included the proper allocation and irrigation of the land (23.2). Moses, the subject of the most eulogistic treatment, 'transmitted many benefits to mankind' (27.4), including the invention of boats, weaponry and various machines (philosophy comes at the end of the list, for good measure). This redescription of biblical characters as the bearers of culture represents an ambitious claim to national superiority. Egypt was widely regarded as the source of Greek civilization, so to claim the Jewish origins of Egyptian lore was no trivial matter. In fact the lengths to which Artapanus is willing to go in this respect are revealed in his assertion that Moses is the figure whom the Greeks know as Musaeus (27.3–4); and Musaeus is here described as the teacher of Orpheus, widely regarded as the founder of Greek culture[7] The pro-Egyptian tone of this

---

[5]  It is striking how often Heliopolis features in Artapanus' story: 23.3, 4 derive from tradition (LXX Gen 41.45, 50), but in both 27.8 and 27.35 he explicitly follows Heliopolite tradition (in the latter case in preference to that of the Memphites). Fraser 1972:1.706; 2.985 n. 199 thus seems right to conjecture a location outside Alexandria, though his choice of Memphis is strange. The majority opinion still favours Alexandria (e.g. Walter 1980a:124–25) largely on the grounds that Artapanus seems to draw on traditions from Hecataeus. In fact the similarities with Hecataeus need not suggest literary dependence, and, even if they do, we need not assume that he was read only in Alexandria. See further Collins 1985a:891 and Sterling 1992:169, 181.

[6]  See the table in Sterling 1992:173–74.

[7]  Commentators rightly point out that Musaeus is usually known as the pupil, not the teacher, of Orpheus; Artapanus has inverted their roles for the greater glory of Moses. On the *topos* of the culture-bringer see Holladay 1977:220–27. Droge 1989:1–35 compares Artapanus with Eupolemus and the Samaritan

apologetic is evident throughout, but nowhere more so than in the notice that when Moses struck the Nile with his rod he established its annual flooding (27.28): the first plague (Exod 7.20–24) is thus reinterpreted as the cause of the natural cycle on which all Egyptian life depends!

In an age when ethnic groups bolstered their pride with tales of national heroes, Artapanus portrayed Moses as the greatest hero of them all.[8] Scholars have noted extensive parallels with the legends of the Egyptian hero, Sesostris, and it is possible that Artapanus' account of Moses' campaign in Ethiopia (27.7–10) was intended to cap stories of similar exploits by Sesostris and others.[9] Embarrassing episodes in the biblical story of Moses are here creatively reworked,[10] while his miraculous powers are highlighted not only in the account of the plagues but also with the addition of new magic tales (27.22–37).[11] What is more, Moses is here described as properly held in divine honour: his rod is revered in Egyptian temples (27.32) and his patronage of the animal cults and priests (see below) is reciprocated by his being named Hermes (27.6). Such an appellation represents an impressive claim (Mussies 1982): Hellenized Egyptians associated Hermes with Thoth-mosis, the scribe of the Gods and supervisor of good order. The multiple associations in Artapanus between Moses and Thoth-mosis (no doubt aided by the similarity of names) suggest that Moses is here elevated to an exceptional status.

The significance for Jews of this Moses-encomium may be appreciated if we recall the derogatory stories in popular circulation, summarized in Manetho's anti-Judaic history (see above, chapter 2.1.3). Where Manetho described Moses as

---

Pseudo-Eupolemus in the claims each makes for Jewish figures as founders of world civilization.

8   See Braun 1938:1–31 and Sterling 1992:175–78. Collins 1985a:892 coins the phrase 'competitive historiography' in this connection.

9   The description of Sesostris by Diodorus 1.53–58 is mirrored exactly by some details in Artapanus' account of Moses. For other expeditions into Ethiopia see Diodorus 1.17–18 (Osiris), 1.55 (Sesostris) and 2.14 (Semiramis), and Herodotus 3.17–25 (Cambyses); cf. Tiede 1972:153–60. The similarities between Artapanus' and Josephus' account (*Ant* 2.238–53) of Moses' Ethiopian campaign are intriguing, but open to many explanations; see Rajak 1978.

10  For one example, the story of Moses' murder of an Egyptian (Exod 2.12), see Barclay 1992a:31–34.

11  Tiede 1972:146–71. For the popular association of Moses with magic, see above, chapter 5.4.

instigating an invasion of Egypt, terrorizing the land, persecuting the priests and destroying the animal cults (Josephus, *C Ap* 1.237–50), Artapanus paints a figure who strengthens the ruling regime, donates land to the priests and founds animal cults, becoming universally loved in the process (27.4–6).[12] What is more, Moses is here the representative of the Jewish people, who are indeed specifically designated his compatriots (ὁμόφυλοι, 27.19).[13] Although never designated their lawgiver (indeed without any reference to law or covenant), Moses clearly bears the destiny of the Jews, and in his personal, cultural and military splendour brings credit to the whole Jewish people (Collins 1986:32–38).

But then we encounter the great enigma of this text. Precisely in order to boost the glory of Moses and the reputation of his people, Artapanus gives the most positive evaluation of Egypt and of Egyptian religion that we have from the pen of any Egyptian Jew. Despite the biblical accounts, the experiences of Abraham and Joseph in Egypt are described in entirely positive terms: many who came down with Abraham 'remained there because of the prosperity of the land' (18.1). The eulogies of Egyptian culture suggest a writer fully 'at home' in his Egyptian environment,[14] and this includes its temples, priests and cults. Even in our short excerpts of Artapanus' work we have several references to the construction of temples (23.4; 27.2, 11, 12) and to the numerous benefits given by Joseph or Moses to the priests (23.2; 27.4, 6), not least the interpretation of hieroglyphics (27.6)![15] Moses is accorded divine honour by the priests and hailed as Hermes (27.6), a cult is instituted for his mother (27.16) and Isis is named in a positive tone (27.16, 32). This clear support for Egyptian religion is further enhanced by reference to Moses' appointment for each nome of

---

[12] See further Braun 1938:26–31 and Sterling 1992:182–83.

[13] The special status of the Jews may also be indicated by the death of Chenephres, explained as divine vengeance for his unjust treatment of the Jewish people (27.20).

[14] There is a reference to Judaea as the 'ancient homeland' (ἀρχαία πατρίς, 27.21), yet Artapanus attempts to define the name Ἰουδαῖοι without reference to the land Judaea (18.1): Abraham's place of origin is known only as 'Syria'. Collins' reference to Artapanus' 'situation of exile' (1986:37) thus seems wide of the mark.

[15] It is puzzling that the final plague involves the collapse of temples (27.33). In general Artapanus modifies the anti-Egyptian character of the plague-stories by claiming that Moses' rod is now dedicated in every Isis temple (27.32); he may be referring to a phallic symbol (Holladay 1977:228 n. 178)!

the God to be worshipped, including cats, dogs and ibises (27.4) – a notion later confirmed by mention of the consecration of the ibis (27.9) and by general reference to 'the animals which Moses had made sacred' (27.12).[16] In other words, our Jewish author hails Moses as the founder of Egypt's animal cults!

The startling nature of these statements has induced some scholars to attempt to reduce Artapanus' claims. To be sure, the foundation of animal cults is not always attributed directly to Moses: 27.9 refers to 'those around Moses' consecrating the ibis, and in 27.12 the temple of the bull Apis is established by Chenephres (Holladay 1977:229–31). Yet at least two texts (27.4, 12) describe Moses' direct patronage of this aspect of Egyptian religion. The animal cults are sometimes given rational explanations: the ibis is acclaimed for its benefits to humankind (27.9), and Moses recommends oxen 'because the land is ploughed by them' (27.12). But such rationalistic explication of the cult by no means undermines its practice. These are precisely the ways in which Hellenized Egyptians (or Egyptianized Greeks) made sense of their devotion to the sacred animals, not means to lessen their significance.[17] And even if the identification of Moses with Hermes has elements of 'euhemerism' (the theory of Euhemerus that the 'Gods' are really mighty men of old, honoured for their achievements), its effect is to justify and promote the worship of Hermes, which thus is taken to glorify Moses.[18] Artapanus' views should not, then, be watered down nor interpreted to represent a demotion of Egyptian religion. While he held that 'the master of

---

[16] The one possibly negative reference to animal cults is in 27.35, which may refer to the destruction of sacred animals in the Red Sea. But without the conjectural addition ἅμα it is possible to read the text as an abbreviated reference to the Jews' acquisition of the sacred animals; see Walter 1980a:135 n. 35b.

[17] I cannot agree with Collins' assertion (1986:35, 37) that, in 'demythologizing' these cultic deities, Artapanus 'undermines their divinity' (cf. Walter 1980a:123–24; Schürer 3.523). Divinity in the ancient world was a function of worship, and if (as Collins admits) Artapanus presents a positive evaluation of these cults he must approve of the divine status thereby accorded to, for example, cats and dogs.

[18] It is sometimes suggested (e.g. Tiede 1972:174) that Isis is subordinated to Moses, since she is identified with the earth which Moses struck with his rod (27.32). But it is not clear that a negative point is intended here, since the incident indicates only the co-operation of the Goddess. When he notes that Isis temples contain dedications of Moses' rod (27.32), Artapanus can hardly intend to repudiate the Isis cult.

the universe' required Egypt to release the Jews (27.22), this does not elevate 'monotheism' over 'polytheism', or 'the God of the Jews' (Collins) over the Gods of Egypt. Like many of his contemporaries, Artapanus can refer interchangeably to God (singular) and Gods (plural): even as a Jew he is both a monotheist and a polytheist.

It is important to face such Jewish syncretism with candour. Artapanus' work cannot be explained away either as a literary deceit or as an over-enthusiastic piece of apologetic.[19] He writes as a Jew and to boost Jewish pride, with the glory of Moses and the miracles of the Exodus as the means of his propaganda. While other Egyptian Jews may have choked at his enthusiasm for the animal cults (see below on *The Letter of Aristeas, The Wisdom of Solomon* and Philo), he shows no sign of embarrassment in this confident cultural synthesis. Perhaps his generous attitude towards Egyptian religion was more common than we realize, and it is possible that, within his own time and community, he represented a popular Egyptianized Judaism.[20] Ironically, the text which Artapanus embellishes (the LXX) contains warnings against foreign religious cults and lists the ibis among the unclean birds (Lev 11.17). Further, Manetho's depiction of Moses suggests that the majority of Jews were known for their rejection, not for their cheerful acceptance, of the animal cults. Yet Artapanus indicates that some Jews effected an important measure of synthesis with Egyptian culture, even Egyptian religion. He indicates the possibility of being both a proud Egyptian and a self-conscious Jew.

## 6.2 Ezekiel

If Artapanus demonstrates the possibilities of cultural convergence between the Jewish tradition and Hellenized Egyptian religion,

---

[19] *Pace* Freudenthal 1875:143–53 (considering the author to have merely adopted the *persona* of an Egyptian priest) and Vermes 1955:73 (reckoning apologetic concerns to have got the better of him). Note Heinemann's penetrating discussion of Artapanus, 1933:367–69.

[20] Holladay 1983:193 wonders whether Artapanus was 'typical of a large segment of Diaspora Jews who did not find pagan traditions threatening or compromising to fidelity to their religious traditions'. If his work was preserved by Jews it was presumably because they found his story valuable. The suggested links between Artapanus and the Jewish community at Leontopolis (in the Heliopolite nome; cf. Josephus, *Ant* 13.62–68) are intriguing but too tenuous to be persuasive (Silver 1973–74; Hengel 1972:239).

Ezekiel represents a different form of synthesis, this time with the Greek literary tradition. Reading the narrative of the Exodus in the LXX, Ezekiel saw the potential to present its dramatic story-line in the form of a Greek tragedy, and was sufficiently well acquainted with the metre, style and form of the classical tragedians to produce a play called *Exagoge* ('Evacuation').[21] Sadly we possess only 269 lines of this play, excerpts preserved by that admirable collector, Alexander Polyhistor, and subsequently used by Eusebius. These probably constitute no more than a quarter of the play, yet they seem to have been chosen from disparate sections and thus enable us to gain a reasonably clear picture of its character and intent. What emerges is a fascinating sample of acculturation, in which Jewish history is reconceived within a specifically Greek framework.

The play begins with a monologue, in fine Euripidean style: Moses recounts the sufferings of the Hebrews in Egypt, his own eventful early life, and his departure from Egypt following his violent intervention in a fight (1–59).[22] The dramatic action then begins with his encounter with Sepphora at the Midianite (here Libyan) well. After some interval, Moses recounts a dream concerning his heavenly enthronement, which is interpreted by his father-in-law, Raguel (=Jethro) (68–89). This quite unbiblical incident is followed by an account of the Burning Bush and of Moses' commissioning, which is strongly coloured by Septuagintal phraseology (90–131). God then predicts the course of the plagues and issues instructions for the Passover, which Moses apparently hands on to the elders of the people (132–192). The crossing of the Red Sea is treated, in acccordance with the conventions of tragedy, by means of a messenger speech, here a solitary Egyptian survivor (193–242). Finally, in a scene which greatly embellishes the biblical account, Ezekiel portrays the arrival of the Israelites at Elim, with a scout recounting an extraordinary sighting of the phoenix (243–60).[23]

---

[21] For details of text and date, see Appendix on Sources. There are indications that this was not the only play Ezekiel wrote, Eusebius, *Praep Evang* 9.28.1.

[22] On the Euripidean character of the prologue see Jacobson 1983:69–70; his first-rate commentary has contributed greatly to my interpretation of the text.

[23] On the significance of the phoenix bird and the possible reasons for its inclusion, see Jacobson 1983:157–64. A verbal link with the oasis at Elim is supplied by the presence there of palm-trees (LXX: φοῖνιξ).

Close study of these fragments reveals Ezekiel's mastery of the metre and vocabulary of the fifth-century tragedians, and indicates, in every scene, his acquaintance with the Greek poetic and historical tradition. In other words, Ezekiel had not only received a thorough gymnasium education, but had responded to it with enthusiastic appreciation. Moreover, it is likely that his play was designed not only to be read but actually to be staged.[24] If so, the presentation of this Jewish drama in the public domain is striking testimony to the confidence of this Alexandrian Jew in his artistic competence. The response of his audience – probably both Jews and Greeks – can only be guessed, but the preservation of the material suggests that it was not entirely unsuccessful.[25]

From a Hellenistic point of view the most striking thing about this drama is its thoroughly Jewish character. In most of the fragments the influence of the LXX is easily observed, and in many of those details in which Ezekiel digresses from his text-base there is good reason to believe that he is following contemporary Jewish exegesis.[26] But the drama is also very significantly focused on the Jewish people. For while Moses is the obvious hero of the piece, Ezekiel seems to go out of his way to place his heroism at the service of his people. The Hebrews (they are consistently called such, not 'Jews' or 'sons of Israel') are early identified as a 'race' (γέννα/ γένος four times in the prologue: 7, 12, 35, 43), and the central elements in Moses' early instruction were his 'ancestral lineage and the gifts of God' (γένος πατρῷον καὶ θεοῦ δωρήματα, 35). This last phrase is repeated in God's commission to Moses where, echoing several passages from Exodus, he declares:

---

[24] So Jacobson 1981, arguing that the structure of the play shows signs of accommodating the biblical narrative to the exigencies of stage-production.

[25] The Alexandrian provenance of Ezekiel has occasionally been questioned – Cyrene, Palestine and Samaria have been suggested as alternatives – but it remains the most likely hypothesis: both in general theme and in some details (see below) Ezekiel reflects Egyptian concerns, and his high level of Hellenistic acculturation makes excellent sense in Alexandria during the second century BCE. See the full discussion by Jacobson 1983:13–17, 85–87 (rebutting Kuiper's claim [1903:174–77] that the confusion of Midian with Libya and the presence there of 'Ethiopians' was an impossible mistake for an inhabitant of Egypt). Although opinions differ on the subject of his intended audience (some suggest only Jews are in view), the apologetic motifs which we shall discuss suggest the work may also be designed for Greeks; see Jacobson 1983:17–18, 80, 100.

[26] Jacobson 1983 *passim*, also arguing that Ezekiel did not use a Hebrew text of the Bible (40–47, 81–84).

I am the God of your 'patriarchs' (γεννητόρων), as you call them,
Abraham and Isaac and Jacob, the third.
I have remembered them, and my gifts (ἐμῶν δωρημάτων),
And I have come to save my people, the Hebrews,
Seeing the ill-treatment and toil endured by my servants (104–8).

This accumulation of election-language is remarkable, though not
unique: elsewhere, too, the Hebrews are declared to be God's
people (112; cf. God as the 'ancestral God', θεὸν πατρῷον, 213)
and God's promises to the Hebrew patriarchs are recalled (155).
The interpretation of the covenant promises as 'gifts' (δωρήματα,
35, 106) fits Hellenistic concepts of God as supreme benefactor,[27]
but there is no attempt to mute the concept of the 'special
relationship' between God and his people which is central to the
Exodus narrative. Indeed, the Egyptian survivor from the Red Sea
not only recognizes in that event 'the hand of the Most High' (239)
but twice declares his conviction that God was the 'helper' (ἀρωγός,
236, 240) of the Hebrews. The term is Homeric, but the concept
is thoroughly biblical.

Yet it is the achievement of Ezekiel to present this particularistic
theme of national election in a linguistic form and conceptual
framework comprehensible and even attractive to Greeks. As
Jacobson notes (1983), the play throughout evokes parallels
between the biblical story of the Exodus and the Greek tales of
liberation from the Persian threat. By defining the Hebrews as the
victims of unjust power (4–13), Ezekiel presents their release as
God's deliverance of the weak (204–13; cf. 50), with divine
judgment visited on that classic sin, pride (ὕβρις, 148). In particular,
the messenger-speech echoes the vocabulary of Aeschylus' *Persae*
(in both cases messengers report decisive events at sea), and the
whole work evokes central themes in Herodotus' account of the
Persian Wars. Any educated reader/spectator would appreciate the
comparison. Here puny Israel parallels the vulnerable Greeks, saved
by divine intervention from the overweening ambition of the
barbarous Egyptians/Persians. Israel's victory at the Red Sea is her
battle of Salamis![28]

---

[27] Cogently argued by Horbury 1986, rendering Jacobson's puzzle and his
alternative interpretation (or emended text) superfluous (1983:109–12).

[28] So Jacobson 1983:24–25, 136–40, with the convincing suggestion that 'Ezekiel's
interest in the *Persae* stemmed from his perception that Greek-Persian history
could be seen as an analogue to Jewish-Egyptian' (138).

Although located in Egypt, Ezekiel's Greek audience would hardly be offended by his venom against the Egyptians; the cultured élite who appreciated dramas of this pedigree were not inclined to consider themselves 'Egyptian'. Thus Ezekiel can give free rein to the biblical animus against Pharaoh and the Egyptian oppressors (1–13), explaining the plagues as just punishment of arrogant and evil men (132–51). At the same time, he is careful to omit those aspects of the story which portrayed the Jews in a poor light (e.g. their disbelief of Moses and their complaints against him) and to alter any details which could be (or had been) used in Egyptian polemic against the Jews. Thus he passes over Joseph's period of rule in Egypt (1–6), conscious of Egyptian associations between Jewish rulers and the hated Hyksos regime. Following the LXX, he has Moses' hand turn only white, not leprous (130), in the light of Egyptian tales of Jewish lepers. And he handles the notorious incident of the 'spoiling of the Egyptians' with especial care, insisting that the Egyptians freely handed over vessels, clothes and jewelry to render due payment for the work performed by the Jews (162–66)![29]

Such details, and the persistent allusions to Greek literature and history, suggest a conscious attempt to align Jews with Greeks in their common Egyptian environment. Jacobson, perceiving echoes of the Greek myth of Danaus (who left Egypt to found the Greek nation), suggests that Ezekiel aimed 'to elicit sympathy and respect for the Jews from his Greek audience, showing that both Greeks and Jews have similar ancestral stories of persecution, escape and return to a homeland' (1983:25). There is certainly no criticism of Greek religion in our extant fragments, but also no compromise of Jewish monotheism. The Gentile messenger refers in authentic terms to 'Titan the Sun' (217), but acknowledges the hand of the 'Most High' on the side of the Hebrews (239), while Raguel is represented sympathetically as a competent interpreter of Moses' dream, declaring it to be a 'good sign from God' (83). The instructions on the Passover clarify the rationale of this most prominent Jewish festival, while omitting details (e.g. the requirement that participants be circumcised) which might alienate

---

[29] On these passages, see Jacobson 1983:73–74, 106–7, 126–27 and Holladay 1989:481–82. For the Egyptian anti-Jewish slanders from the time of Manetho, see above, chapter 2.1.3.

Greeks.[30] Even the references to the 'land' to which the Hebrews travel seem to be apologetically designed. Ezekiel never clarifies the identity of the 'other land' (154) to which the Hebrews depart, and he suggests that they could reach it after a journey of only seven days (167–68). Indeed, it appears that the drama ended not in Judaea but at Elim.[31] The utopian conditions described there, and the portentous appearance of the phoenix, give the play a climactic conclusion without the disgraceful years of wandering in the wilderness or the violent conquest of another land.

The chief symbol of this cultural liaison between Jews and Greeks is Moses, the central figure in the play. From the prologue onwards, he is portrayed in the guise of a tragic hero, a foundling (like Ion) who achieved greatness, even a murderer (like Oedipus) who fled the consequences of his deed but saved his nation.[32] Like other national heroes, he is divinely inspired, confronts opponents on behalf of his people and leads them through adversity by his extraordinary prowess. In the remarkable description of his dream (68–82) he is taken up to a heavenly throne, whose occupant actually vacates it in his favour, enabling him to view the universe and to count the stars. Such a dream vision has precedents in both Greek and biblical literature, but there are aspects which seem to amount to divinization.[33] Raguel's interpretation (83–89) suggests Moses' supreme powers as ruler and seer, motifs which were no doubt more fully developed in the lost sections of the play. In any case, it is in keeping with this heroic representation of Moses that his hesitation to take on his role, and God's resulting anger, are omitted in Ezekiel's version.

[30] I am unpersuaded by Collins' claim that this omission of circumcision indicates that 'Judaism for Ezekiel is not constituted by its distinctive markings' (1986:207–8). In fact circumcision did not distinguish Jews from Egyptians (Herodotus 2.104; Philo, *Spec Leg* 1.2) and Ezekiel may have been loath to draw attention to a rite which associated Jews and Egyptians but appeared absurd to Greeks; see Jacobson 1983:135 and Dalbert 1954:65.

[31] See Jacobson 1983:125–26, 134–35, 152–57.

[32] See Jacobson 1981, highlighting parallels with Sophocles' *Oedipus Coloneus*. Aristotle (*Ars Poetica* 13.5) considered it necessary for the tragic hero to suffer misfortune through some great misdeed.

[33] The passage has attracted considerable attention, with parallels noted in apocalyptic and merkavah literature; see e.g. Meeks 1968, Holladay 1976 and van der Horst 1983. In the dream it appears that God (if it is he – the figure is described as 'a noble man', 70) beckons Moses to his throne and leaves it for him; but the interpretation suggests the acquisition of earthly powers and the ability to interpret past, present and future.

This Hellenized portrait of Moses is an important precursor of Philo's *Life of Moses* (*Mos* 1 and 2) and, in contrast to that of Artapanus, it is drawn without a hint of religious syncretism. In fact, the description of Moses' education neatly sums up Ezekiel's dual commitment to the Jewish people and to Greek culture: from his mother Moses received instruction concerning his 'ancestral lineage and the gifts of God' (35) and in the palace 'a royal upbringing and education' (παιδεύματα, 37). Nothing could more clearly exemplify the stance of a poet 'who was seeking to be at once Greek and Jewish, with one foot in Greek poetry, literature and history and the other in the Jewish tradition' (Jacobson 1983:140). There is no indication that such accommodation involved either religious compromise or a weakening of ethnic loyalties.[34] Ezekiel's was a Judaism fully committed to the Jews' communal text (the Septuagint), their communal story, their national hero and their ancestral customs.[35] His achievement was to present this Jewish heritage within the cultural framework of the classical Greek tradition.

## 6.3 The Letter of Aristeas

The so-called *Letter of Aristeas*[36] is famous for its imaginative account of the translation of the Pentateuch and has often been sifted, with

---

[34] Collins notes Moses' marriage to a non-Jew and Raguel's reference to his son-in-law as a 'stranger' (ξένος, 83), but his conclusion that this 'must be taken to imply a positive attitude towards mixed marriages' is too sweeping (1986:208). To be sure, Ezekiel does not exhibit Demetrius' concern to have Moses marry a descendent of Abraham (*apud* Eusebius, *Praep Evang* 9.29.1), but his strong sense of ethnic identity is clear in the references to race and 'ancestral lineage' noted above.

[35] The absence of the Sinai revelation should not be taken to imply a lack of interest in the law; Philo's *Life of Moses* omits this episode as well. In his instructions concerning the Passover, Moses is shown sufficiently clearly as a law-giver. There are no good grounds for taking the play to present Judaism in the guise of a 'mystery' (*pace* Collins 1986:207–11, following Goodenough). Whatever 'mystical' associations surround Moses' vision, there is no hint that his experience is shared by others, and no clear indication that the phoenix is a symbol of renewal or immortality.

[36] It is, in fact, neither a letter nor by its alleged author, Aristeas. It is a narrative (διήγησις, 1) composed by an unknown Jew, though purportedly written by a Ptolemaic courtier called Aristeas to his brother Philocrates. Since it is tiresome repeatedly to call attention to this well-known fact by referring to 'Pseudo-

meagre results, for clues concerning the origins of the Septuagint.[37] In fact, the story of the translation – its request by the Ptolemaic librarian Demetrius, the appointment of the 72 translators and the welcome afforded to their translation – is only the narrative framework within which the author can assemble a fascinating miscellany of material designed to illustrate the value of the Jewish religion. The librarian's request opens a discussion in the court of Ptolemy II Philadelphus on the relationship of the Ptolemaic dynasty with the Jews, and provides the occasion for a diplomatic mission, equipped with lavish gifts, from the Ptolemaic king to the Jerusalem high-priest Eleazar (9–82). An idealized description of Judaea and of worship in the Jerusalem temple (83–120) is then complemented by a long speech by Eleazar extolling and explaining the Jewish law (130–71). Almost all of the second half of the work is taken up with a stilted account of the king's discussion with the translators, spread over seven banquets, during which all 72 are given the opportunity to answer questions on the topic of good government (187–300).

The whole account is narrated as if from the perspective of a Gentile courtier. In adopting that fictional stance, Aristeas is able to portray Gentile reactions to Jews as if 'from the inside'. We are here given 'access' to the intimate discussions of the court and the private impressions of a courtier as he observes Jewish representatives and Jewish customs. The stance of the narrator, as that of a well-informed and high-level participant in the story, thus lends authority to the massively favourable impression of Jews which the work provides. In no other Jewish document is this fictional perspective so effectively employed; it enables us to see with peculiar clarity how certain Jews wished themselves to be perceived by non-Jews and on what basis they wished their relationships to be conducted.

The Jewish author of *Aristeas* must be taken to be a man of considerable education and high social rank, perhaps even a member of the Ptolemaic court. The literary pretensions of the work, especially the elaborate dedication (1–8), display a well-educated command of Greek. Moreover, the narrative is full of literary *topoi*: detailed descriptions of objects of art (51–82), literary

Aristeas', I have elected to connive in the fiction and use the simple appellation Aristeas. On the text and date of this work see the Appendix on Sources.

[37] For a critical survey see Gooding 1963.

portraits of unfamiliar places (83–120), formal speeches at *symposia*, here on the well-worked theme of 'kingship' (187–300).[38] Such features suggest a rhetorical training of some sophistication, even if their execution here is of no literary merit. What is especially revealing is the explicit valuation of education at key points in the narrative. In the preface, great emphasis is laid on the superior value of culture (παιδεία, 7–8), and the fictional narrator is once directly praised as among that rare breed of 'gentlemen of integrity (καλοὶ καὶ ἀγαθοί) who excel in education (παιδείᾳ διαφέροντες)' (43). Even more striking is the depiction of the Jewish translators as

> men of excellent education (παιδεία) thanks to their distinguished parentage; they had not only mastered Jewish literature but also given considerable attention to the literature of the Greeks... They had a great natural facility for discussions and questions concerning the law and zealously cultivated the quality of the middle way (which is the best) eschewing any crude and uneducated frame of mind (ἀποτεθειμένοι τὸ τραχὺ καὶ βάρβαρον τῆς διανοίας)... (121–22).

In this encomium, which is later echoed by the philosophers in the court (235) and by the king himself (321), we are surely to see the cultural values of the author himself, for whom these translators represent model Jews. This carefully phrased accolade, with its pointed reference to Greek learning, reflects the stance of a Jew who warmly embraces Greek cultural ideals.

A number of details suggest that Aristeas may even have operated within the Ptolemaic court. His description of the behaviour of Philadelphus indicates an accurate knowledge of court procedure and diplomatic protocol, and some aspects of the royal correspondence bear a close relation to official documents preserved on papyrus. His eulogistic portrayal of the Ptolemaic court, and his engagement in the tradition of 'advice to kings on government', may be more than a literary trait: since he is careful to comment on the presence of educated men in the court (124–

---

[38] See the detailed analyses of this passage by Zuntz 1959 and Murray 1967. They illustrate the combination of Jewish and Greek elements and relate this text to the *symposium* debates and treatises περὶ βασιλείας which were common in the Hellenistic period.

25), and on the king's appointment of worthy Jews among them (37), he may himself have fitted into that category. Since we know that Jews rose to prominence in Ptolemaic circles in the second century BCE (see above, chapter 2.2), it is plausible to place Aristeas in such a milieu at such a time.[39]

An obvious symptom of Aristeas' acculturation is his depiction of all the characters in this story – king, courtiers, philosophers, Jewish high-priest and Jewish translators – as inhabitants of the same cultural world, who accord one another the respect of equals. On the basis of their common *paideia*, Jews and Greeks alike prize rational thought above bodily desires (5–8, 130, 140–41, 321), and together extol moderation and self-control (122, 222–23, 237, 256). In their common pursuit of virtue (ἀρετή, 122, 200, 215 etc.), both set a high premium on justice (δικαιοσύνη), which is as great a concern to the Ptolemaic king in his treatment of his subjects (18, 24, 125) as it is to the Jewish high-priest in his explanation of the law (144–49, 168–69). Their shared moral values, with a notable emphasis on clemency and generosity, are underscored throughout the banquet discussions: with monotonous regularity the king applauds the unimpeachable sentiments uttered by his Jewish guests. We witness here the comfortable harmony of fellow 'gentlemen' (καλοὶ καὶ ἀγαθοί), Jews (3, 46, 285) and Greeks (43, 207) alike.

Thus, in Aristeas' world, Jews and Greeks accord one another the greatest respect. The purportedly Gentile narrator records at the outset his admiration for the high-priest, the 'divine law' of the Jews and Jewish piety (3–5). He is lyrical in his wonder at the conduct of worship in the Jerusalem temple, insisting that any observer would be both amazed and transformed by the splendid holiness of the sight (99). He records his acceptance of Eleazar's allegorical explanation of the law (170–71) and his deep admiration for the spontaneous wisdom of the translators, insisting on the accuracy of his account (295–300). And within his narrative all the Greek characters display the same respectful attitude. Demetrius honours the holiness of the Jewish law-book (10, 30–31), philosophers admire the responses of the translators (201, 235, 296), and even Egyptian priests are noted as considering the Jews 'men of God' (140). Most prominently of all, Ptolemy

---

[39] On the date of Aristeas, generally acknowledged on a variety of grounds as during the second century BCE, see the Appendix on Sources.

Philadelphus writes in the friendliest of terms to Eleazar (35–40) and treats his ambassadors with unprecedented courtesy (175). He too shows the highest regard for the law, even bowing seven times at the arrival of the Hebrew manuscripts (177). He sponsors the translation as a lasting favour for all Jews (38) and accompanies this benefit with the release of every enslaved Jew, on incredible financial terms (12–27). Thus here the most brilliant of all the Ptolemaic kings, the patron of the greatest centre of Hellenistic culture, stands in awe of Judaism, whose representatives astound him with their wisdom (200–1, 293–94, 312).

The compliments paid by such Gentiles in their respect of Judaism are fully returned by the Jews. Among the significant virtues of the 72 translators was their disinclination to look down on others with conceit or contempt (122), and such cultured broad-mindedness is the mark of all the Jewish actors in this story. Eleazar writes to the Ptolemaic king in a tone of friendship and love (44), acknowledging the justice in his social legislation (166–67) and even noting his 'piety towards our God' (42, see below). He ensures that sacrifices are offered in the Jerusalem temple for the king and the royal family, accompanied by prayers for God's preservation of his kingdom in peace and glory (45). Similarly, the translators pepper their responses to the king with flattering remarks about his moral excellence (229, 233 etc.) and offer prayers for God's blessing on the royal house (185). Through all this, the Jewish author is doing his utmost to glorify the Ptolemaic regime: he makes notable efforts to exonerate Ptolemy I Soter for his enslavement of the Jews (14, 23) and paints Philadelphus in the most glowing colours as a paragon of virtue (15–16, 26–28 etc.).

The most remarkable feature of this mutual respect between Jews and Greeks is its application to theology. Prominent among the values shared by Jews and non-Jews is 'piety' (εὐσέβεια), which is attributed as frequently to the Ptolemaic court (2, 24, 37, 42, 210 etc.) as it is to Jews (131, 215, 229 etc.). The common ingredient of that piety is the recognition of God as creator (16–17) and as sovereign in his providential care of the world (16–19, 132–33, 201 etc.). Jews and Greeks alike recognize the God who 'blesses the human race, giving them health and food and all other necessities in their season' (190), just as they match each other in noting God's blessing on the Ptolemaic kingdom (15–18, 37, 45). Thus we find here both Jews and non-Jews offering prayer to God, who hears and answers their requests (17–20, 313–16). The latter passage concerns the affliction of Theopompus and Theodectus for their unworthy treatment of the Jewish Scriptures: their awed response typifies Gentile recognition of the divine quality of the Jewish law (cf. 3, 15, 31, 177). Moreover, Philadelphus releases Jews from slavery as a thank-offering to 'the Greatest God' (τῷ μεγίστῳ θεῷ, 19, 37). And in a remarkable statement the courtier Aristeas is made to note that the Jews 'worship the God who is overseer and creator of all, whom all humanity worship, but we, Your Majesty, address differently as Zeus and Dis' (16).[40]

This last passage suggests the recognition, by a non-Jew, that Jews and Greeks worship the same God under the guise of different names. This is the closest the Jewish author comes to implying the complete equivalence of Jewish and non-Jewish religion. Yet – and this 'yet' is crucial for the comprehension of this document – Aristeas is in fact careful to avoid the total identification of his Jewish faith with that of others. The statement just cited is put in the mouth of a Greek, not a Jew. *Greek* recognition that the God whom Jews worship is the one whom Greeks call Zeus may seem logically reversible into *Jewish* recognition that the God whom Gentiles worship (as Zeus) is the same God honoured by Jews. But what is logically consequent may be psychologically intolerable.[41] The strategy of Aristeas, here as elsewhere, is to illustrate Gentile recognition of Jewish religion, but that does not mean that Jews also recognize the validity of Gentile worship. While Gentiles in this story send gifts to the Jerusalem temple, Eleazar does not reciprocate with gifts for an Egyptian temple (here the contrast with Artapanus is illuminating). While Philadelphus' delegates are staggered by the beauty of Jewish worship, Eleazar's delegates are spared the usual ceremonies in the Ptolemaic dining-rooms when 'the sacred heralds, the sacrificing priests and the others whose custom it was to offer prayers' are banished in order to accommodate the sensitivities of the Jews (184). Thus also the reader is tactfully spared any depiction of the practice of non-Jewish cult. The Jewish translators can find some common ground with Philadelphus on the true spiritual essence of worship, 'honouring God ... not with gifts and sacrifices but with the purity of the soul

---

[40] τὸν γὰρ πάντων ἐπόπτην καὶ κτίστην θεὸν οὗτοι σέβονται, ὃν καὶ πάντες, ἡμεῖς δέ, βασιλεῦ, προσονομάζοντες ἑτέρως Ζῆνα καὶ Δία. The translation by Shutt 1985 ad loc. is seriously misleading at this point.

[41] Although, of course, the whole work is written by a Jew, the attribution of this statement to a Greek gives it less significance than if it were from a Jew; note that Eleazar is careful to refer to 'our God' (42).

and of a holy disposition' (234; cf. 170). But it is significant that it is only at this abstract level that they can recognize the validity of the king's religion. If he sends gifts to the Jerusalem temple, they are certainly acceptable, but only on the basis that they are an act of piety to '*our* God' (42)!

This sense of religious incommensurability is evident in Eleazar's long speech on the law, which begins with a haughty dismissal of 'Greek' and 'Egyptian' religion. The Jewish food laws are, he insists, designed to prevent bad associations (130), and the basis for that social distinction is found in the contrast between the Jews' belief that 'God is one' (132), and the fact that 'all other people beside us think that there are many Gods' (134). This blanket indictment of polytheism is then made specific with derogatory comments on the fabrication of statues (people make 'Gods' weaker than themselves), especially since, following the theory of Euhemerus, the 'Gods' so worshipped are only great inventors of the past (whose wisdom is in any case now surpassed!). By thus exploiting euhemerism Aristeas pours scorn on the 'mythmakers' whom Greeks consider the wisest of men (135–37). And having thus dismissed iconic worship and Greek mythology, he can afford merely to sneer at 'the other absurd sorts of people, Egyptians and such like' who offer sacrifice to wild animals and other creatures, dead or alive (138).

The strength of this polemic against 'the rest of humanity' may seem surprising in this generally eirenic document, which is otherwise at pains to portray mutual respect between Jews and Gentiles. One might be inclined to take the derogatory references to 'the others' or 'the majority' (134, 151–52, 222–23) in a reduced sense, to exclude the enlightened Gentiles (Aristeas, Philocrates, the king and his court) who here dialogue with the Jews. There is, perhaps, an element of ambiguity in a key phrase in section 140, where Eleazar notes that Jews are recognized as 'men of God', a title which 'does not apply to the rest, but only to those who worship the true God' (ὃ τοῖς λοιποῖς οὐ πρόσεστιν, εἰ μή τις σέβεται τὸν κατὰ ἀλήθειαν θεόν). This exception clause probably refers only to Jews, but it is just possible to include here such Gentile men of piety whom Eleazar otherwise compliments.[42] If so, it would

---

[42] Thus for instance Boccaccini translates 'which is not ascribed to others, except a few who worship the true God' (1991:177). This reading is partially supported in Meisner's rendition (1977:63: 'Diese (Bezeichnung) steht den übrigen nicht zu, es sei denn, jemand verehrt den wahren Gott'). But Boccaccini seems to

suggest a tolerance of such Gentile worship as Jews considered to be directed towards 'the true God'.

Nonetheless, what is clear throughout this work is that Jewish piety is in key respects superior to any other. In the philosophical discussions at the banquets, Aristeas is careful to have every response by the translators include some reference to God, and he draws special attention to this feature by having first the king, and then the court philosophers, acknowledge the excellence of the Jewish opinions, since 'they take God as the starting point of their answers' (200–1, 235). This supremely theistic philosophy involves acknowledging God's capacity to judge even our secret activities (132, 189), in recognition that he directs, prompts and empowers all human moral activity (195, 255 etc.). God is presented not only as the model for just and generous behaviour (205, 207 etc.) but also, more fundamentally, as the one who creates our moral capabilities, who grants the disposition, as well as the strength, to act justly (193, 197 etc.).[43] In this radically theocentric version of ethics, the Jews are judged to have the edge over all other systems of thought, so that even the philosophers in the most cultured Hellenistic court recognize that they are outclassed (235)!

This sense of superiority, of the Jews' higher spiritual and moral class, is the central motif in Eleazar's speech on the law (130–71). When asked about the distinctive Jewish rules on clean and unclean objects, Eleazar begins by highlighting the twin concerns of 'our lawgiver' for piety and righteousness (εὐσέβεια and δικαιοσύνη, 131). The Jews' superior grasp of monotheism (131–41, see above) thus serves as the foundation for their moral and social distinctiveness which is the theme of the allegorical explanations which follow (142–69). The discrimination in the law between clean and unclean foods has a supremely rational explanation:

> Do not take the discredited [or, outmoded][44] view that Moses created this legislation out of an excessive concern for mice

make Aristeas' exception apply to 'a few' non-Jews more definitely than is warranted by the text.

[43] On Aristeas' 'theology of grace' see Boccaccini 1991:171–74. His essay on Aristeas (1991:161–85) is a rare and skilful attempt to take seriously the theology of this document.

[44] There are good reasons for taking the unusual phrase καταπεπτωκότα λόγον in the sense of 'a viewpoint long refuted'; note the translations by Pelletier (1962, 'l'objection, d'avance écroulée') and Meisner (1977, 'die (längst) zurückgewiesene Auffassung'). Friedländer 1903:95 suggested that Aristeas is

or weasels or such like: all these rules were solemnly arranged for pious investigation and moral correction, for the sake of righteousness (144).

The birds, for instance, which are listed as unclean, are wild and rapacious creatures who lord it over others by brute force; such a bad example is to be shunned and only the tame and gentle birds can be considered clean (145–150). The moral lesson, which the lawgiver indicates symbolically, should be plain to anyone of intelligence (148, cf. 153). Another lesson is to be drawn from the restriction of diet to those animals which 'cleave the hoof'. This 'cleaving' signifies 'distinction' (Aristeas subtly inserts διαστέλλειν ['distinguish'] into his citation of the relevant verse, 150), and this distinction refers in particular to that between Jews and all 'others' (151). The sexual morality of 'the majority of other men' – their promiscuity and homosexual relations – is singled out for notice in this connection (150–52). Thirdly, the reference in the law to animals who 'chew the cud' is taken as a symbol of 'memory', and the Jewish concern with remembering the blessings of God – illustrated by their 'mezzuzoth' and 'phylacteries' – is taken as a sign of their special piety (153–62). Finally, certain unclean animals – mice and weasels – are castigated as peculiarly polluted in their habits, symbolizing, like the carnivorous birds, the corruption and cruelty which are to be avoided (163–69).

This famous passage has been correctly acclaimed as the first extant allegorization of the law; both in its terminology and in its conceptuality it is a significant precursor to the allegorical techniques displayed by Philo and his contemporaries.[45] It indicates Aristeas' concern to make sense of otherwise puzzling injunctions in the law by transposing them into the moral discourse of his environment. In that respect it is a further indication of his acculturation. Yet, the purpose of this exercise is to explain why

---

attempting to refute the suggestion that the Jews did not eat mice and weasels out of respect for them as sacred animals. We know that the weasel was sacred in Egypt (Plutarch, *Isis and Osiris* 380f–381a), and there is evidence that the Jews' abstention from certain meats could be interpreted as a sign of reverence for such animals (Juvenal, *Satire* 6.160).

[45] Note the vocabulary of 'symbol' (σημεῖον, σημείωσις, 150, 161 etc.), and the insistence that the law is neither arbitrary (εἰκῆ) nor myth-laden (μυθωδῶς, 168): rather, it expresses profound and natural reason (λόγος βαθύς, λόγος φυσικός, 143) for those with the intelligence to understand its rationale (148, 153).

Jews are so distinctive in their eating habits, as well as in their moral and religious customs. This fundamental aspect of Jewish distinction is explained in a set of justly famous metaphors when Eleazar declares that

> the wise lawgiver ... hedged us about with impenetrable fences and iron walls (περιέφραξεν ἡμᾶς ἀδιακόποις χάραξι καὶ σιδηροῖς τείχεσιν) to prevent us mixing in any way with people of other nations, being preserved pure in body and soul, separated from false beliefs, honouring the one God who is powerful above the whole creation (139, cf. 142).

This forceful presentation of Jewish separateness comes as something of a shock in the midst of a work which otherwise celebrates the convivial atmosphere enjoyed by Jews and Greeks. Eleazar's speech gives us the clearest possible statement of the function of the food laws in preserving the Jews' distinct identity. Yet a few chapters later his delegates are merrily feasting with Philadelphus and his entourage. What has happened to the impenetrable fences and iron walls? Aristeas is not guilty of complete self-contradiction: when Philadelphus entertains the translators he specifically accommodates *their* dietary requirements, just as he foregoes his normal religious practices before the meal (181–86). That suggests that if Jews and Gentiles are to mix in friendly social intercourse, it has to be *on the Jews' terms*. But one still senses some tension between Eleazar's emphasis on the *distinction* between Jews and 'others' and the *common values* which they share in the rest of the work.

Such a tension is best explained by reference to the analysis of 'Hellenization' offered above (chapter 4; cf. Tcherikover 1958:79–85). Aristeas is a highly acculturated Jew, committed to the values of Greek *paideia*; he cannot accept that Jews are 'barbarian' or in any sense inferior to the cultural standards of his environment. Yet that need not correlate with complete assimilation: despite his high social status, he marks and defends a social boundary over which Jews cannot pass. He is sufficiently aware of sociological realities to know that social intercourse has a profound effect on social identity: 'you see the effect of our modes of life and relationships, how through association with evil persons men become perverted' (130). Though he accommodates his Judaism to many aspects of the Hellenistic tradition, he never abandons the Jewish sense of difference; indeed he uses Hellenistic categories to define the terms of Jewish superiority. By presenting the Jews as purer than others, fenced off from their 'perversions', he defends the preservation of Jewish distinction as a moral and theological necessity.[46]

There has been much dispute on the question of the intended audience for this finely balanced presentation of Judaism. The old consensus held that *The Letter of Aristeas* was an apologetic work, directed to Greeks who were interested in, or alternatively hostile towards, Judaism.[47] However, Tcherikover, in an influential challenge to that consensus, insisted that the work 'was not written with the aim of self-defense or propaganda, and was addressed not to Greek, but to Jewish readers'.[48] In particular, he argued that the positive portrayal of Jew-Greek relationships was intended to encourage hesitant Jews to embrace Greek education and to enter Greek society, while Eleazar's speech also urges educated Alexandrian Jews not to disobey the prescriptions of the law, which are more meaningful than they suspect. Despite some weaknesses, his thesis now constitutes the current consensus.[49]

In fact, it is peculiarly difficult to discern the intention of a pseudonymous document, and it is unnecessary to pose the question as an alternative – either for Jewish or for Gentile readers. There are, in fact, good reasons to hold that Aristeas was hoping to address Gentiles, as well as Jews, presenting Judaism in its most attractive guise for their benefit. It is surely significant that, besides addressing an implied Gentile reader, this document concerns itself repeatedly with Gentile reactions to Jews – by the king, by the court and by Aristeas himself. In particular, Eleazar's speech is directed to Gentile hearers, responding to the queries of 'the majority of men' (128); and the only recorded reaction to his moral explanation of the law is by a Gentile (Aristeas), who admires his

---

[46] It is thus misleading to claim that for Aristeas 'the law ... is one symbolic expression of the truth which can also be approached in other ways' (Collins 1986:181; cf. Hadas 1951:62).

[47] See e.g. Friedländer 1903:84–104; Meecham 1932:109–19; Dalbert 1954:92–102.

[48] Tcherikover 1958:61; this was consonant with his earlier challenge to the whole notion of 'Jewish apologetic literature' (1956).

[49] It is followed in the main by Hadas (1951; he knew the earlier Hebrew version of Tcherikover 1956) and by numerous subsequent scholars, e.g. Bartlett 1985:11–16 and Boccaccini 1991:161–85. However, it seems implausible that Aristeas should adopt a Gentile disguise to address Jews nervous about their relations with Greeks.

'apology' (ἀπολογεῖσθαι, 170).⁵⁰ An 'apologetic' work does not necessarily respond to attacks on Judaism or attempt to win converts. Rather, at a time when Jews were coming into prominence while retaining their distinctive lifestyle, Aristeas creates a narrative to describe the kind of respect Jews could enjoy in élite circles and to explain the reasons for their religious, moral and dietary differences. He seeks understanding and tolerance from interested Gentiles, while portraying (in his own image) the sort of acculturated Jew he thinks his fellow Jews could become.⁵¹

Whatever his intended readership, Aristeas produced a document which demonstrates both the extent of his acculturation and the limits of his assimilation. While supportive of Greek educational ideals, with their moral and philosophical values, Aristeas is unswerving in his loyalty to his fellow Jews, who are bound together by their distinctive 'constitution'.⁵² His pride in the law (i.e. the LXX) is evident throughout, and he has taken care to interpret its more puzzling regulations as both rational and moral. He views Jewish aniconic cult as the supreme statement of monotheism, and considers the theocentric emphasis of Jewish philosophy as qualifying it to outstrip the best that Hellenism could offer. He readily identifies himself with Judaea and its temple, at least as it exists in his imagination.⁵³ For all these reasons he sees no cause to abandon his Jewish identity or to assimilate entirely to

50 Tcherikover 1958:62 asks why Aristeas should choose to explain the particular issues covered in Eleazar's speech, rather than 'circumcision, the Sabbath, the main holidays, and the prohibition of pork'. But since circumcision was practised by some Egyptians, and since the Sabbath seems to have been widely respected in Egypt, there was no need to 'defend' these. The prohibition of pork *is* of course covered in Eleazar's explanation of 'chewing the cud' (Deut 14.8; *Aristeas* 153–62).

51 A subsidiary motive may be suggested by the strong support he gives to the Septuagint translation (especially 301–11), but it is not clear what alternative Aristeas is trying to combat: a Hebrew original? an alternative Greek version produced in Palestine? or a translation made in Leontopolis? The latter is the least likely, *pace* Collins 1986:83–86.

52 He uses the term γένος ('race') once (6), but has Jews refer to each other as fellow 'citizens' (πολῖται, 3, 36, 44, 126). This political metaphor (cf. πεπολιτευμένοι, 31) points to the essence of Jewish unity in a shared mode of life which can cross geographical boundaries. There is no reference to covenant or to salvation-history.

53 The anachronistic and literary tone of his description, and its wild inaccuracies (he thinks the Jordan encircles Judaea and floods annually like the Nile, 116!), make one doubt that Aristeas had ever been to Judaea.

the Greek way of life. He is a fine example of a cultured Greek Jew who thrived in the tensions which Hellenization produced.[54]

## 6.4 Aristobulus

While Artapanus, Ezekiel and Aristeas allow us to measure their socio-cultural stances only through their narratives, the philosophy of Aristobulus gives direct expression to his cultural standpoint.[55] Unfortunately, it is preserved in only five fragments. The first attempts to link the date of the Passover to the position of the sun and moon (*apud* Eusebius, *Hist Eccles* 7.32.16–18). The second and longest (*apud* Eusebius, *Praep Evang* 8.10.1–7) introduces Aristobulus' allegorical method and gives a theological explanation of three Scriptural anthropomorphisms. The third (*Praep Evang* 13.12.1–2) asserts the dependence of famous philosophers on Moses, while the fourth and fifth (*Praep Evang* 13.12.3–8 and 13.12.9–16) are dominated by lengthy citations of poets whose views are deemed to be derived from, and supportive of, Jewish philosophy. Despite their diversity in subject-matter, these passages are bound together by a coherent strategy which combines a bold cultural claim with a creative theological hermeneutic.

The cultural claim, which appears in four of the five fragments, is the assertion that the Jewish 'school of thought' is both prior and superior to any Greek philosophy. Aristobulus refers to the Jewish traditions as 'our philosophical school' (ἡ καθ' ἡμᾶς αἵρεσις, 12.8), which he elsewhere identifies with 'our legislation' (νομοθεσία, 10.8; 12.1 etc.) and which he considers the personal achievement of Moses (10.3; 12.3). It is Aristobulus' boast that Moses' text, the basis of the Jewish way of life, is the well from which the greatest Greek philosophers drew, though they were unable to preserve the purity of the original source. Thus, 'it is

---

[54] I would therefore question Tcherikover's judgment that 'like most of the people who strive to be "citizens of two worlds", Aristeas did not actually belong to either of them' (1958:84). Tcherikover's own stance is evident in his assessment that 'his Judaism is pale and colorless, imbued with foreign influences, and it lacks the inner warmth of a genuine national feeling' (ibid.).

[55] Since Eusebius is less paraphrastic than Clement in citing Aristobulus, his five extracts are generally taken as the most reliable text. For the location of these fragments, and the system of citation here employed, see the Appendix on Sources.

evident that Plato followed the path of our legislation and he clearly spent much energy in investigating its individual aspects' (12.1). Indeed, before Plato and Socrates, Pythagoras 'transferred many of our points into his doctrines and registered them there' (12.1, 4). Even further back, Homer and Hesiod 'borrowed from our books the notion that the seventh day is holy' (12.13), and verses can be cited from Orpheus to indicate also his derivative status (12.4ff.). In general, Aristobulus contends that all people of intelligence admire Moses' wisdom and 'divine spirit', and that it was out of such recognition that 'philosophers and many others, including poets, took from him their significant starting-points'; in fact, it is due to such imitation that they have won their own reputations (10.4)! Thus all the best in the Greek cultural tradition has been plagiarized from Moses. The cultural glory of Greece is only a reflection of the splendid Mosaic original.

We have already found a parallel to this remarkable claim in Artapanus, who depicts Abraham and Joseph as cultural inventors and Moses as the teacher of Orpheus;[56] but nowhere else do we find it mounted in such detail or with such panache. Aristobulus is sufficient of a realist to recognize one aspect of its implausibility: how were Homer and Plato able to gain enlightenment from Moses' Hebrew text? He counters (12.1) with the thesis of an early Greek translation – before the version sponsored by Demetrius of Phalerum, before even 'the Persian conquest' (341 or 525 BCE). The sense of unreality here suggests to modern readers a pseudo-intellectualism, but we should not underestimate the propaganda value of even such preposterous claims in the ancient world.

When subordinating Greek culture to Mosaic authority, Aristobulus is not, of course, rejecting but absorbing its achievements. While the compliment may be weak, he intends to praise Plato for his assiduous attention to Moses, and the examples he proffers suggest his own familiarity with the Greek tradition. Since two of the fragments are addressed to the king, some scholars have suggested that Aristobulus functioned in the Ptolemaic court under the patronage of Philometor. Indeed, a reference to one

---

[56] See above, chapter 6.1. There are similar claims in the writings of Eupolemus (Eusebius, *Praep Evang* 9.26.1) and Pseudo-Eupolemus (*Praep Evang* 9.17), in relation to the invention of writing and astrology. These are all part of a widespread competition among eastern nations to claim the origin of Greek culture; see Walter 1964:45–51.

Aristobulus in 2 Macc 1.10 dubs him 'the teacher of Ptolemy the king'. In fact, the historical value of this notice is questionable and the address to the king may be only literary convention.[57] Even so, his intellectual pretensions and his evident respect for Greek literature suggest a well-educated figure who has the confidence to engage in serious debate with contemporary philosophy.

It is noticeable that twice in these brief extracts Aristobulus offers critical comments on the sources he cites. Noting the common description of wisdom as a 'lantern' in the Peripatetic school, he cannot resist suggesting that 'our ancestor Solomon said in clearer and finer fashion that wisdom existed before heaven and earth' (12.10–11). In a more extensive comment he explains why, in his citation from Aratus' proem, he has altered all references to 'Zeus' to read simply 'God' (ruining the metre as a consequence!). Since, Aratus intended to refer to God, it is better, he claims, to make such reference absolutely clear, lest any wonder whether 'Zeus' is the same as his 'God' (12.7). Yet the alteration is more than just a clarification: it is also a matter of appropriate theological language. Philosophers agree on the necessity of holding 'pure conceptions' of the Deity, but this, Aristobulus asserts, is a point particularly prescribed by Judaism ('our school'), with its characteristic concern for piety (εὐσέβεια, 12.8). The implication is clear enough: to use Greek names for the Deity is to introduce an 'impurity' and 'impiety' from which Jews alone, with their nameless God, are exempt. While Aristobulus is deeply indebted to the Stoic philosophy represented by Aratus, he insists on this textual emendation to signal the superiority of his Jewish tradition.[58]

Besides Aristobulus' claim to cultural priority and superiority, his fragments are characterized by a consistent theological thesis. He is, in fact, the earliest known Jew from the Diaspora to operate self-consciously as a theologian, and is explicitly concerned with proper speech and thought about God (συντηρεῖν τὸν περὶ θεοῦ

---

[57] Bickerman 1988:228. The question of authorship is fully discussed by Walter 1964:35–123. Although he doubts the reliability of the notice in 2 Macc 1.10, he considers it probable that Aristobulus wrote in the reign of Philometor, and possible that he functioned as a scholar in the Museion (39–40). On the date of Aristobulus see further the Appendix on Sources.

[58] The comparison with *Aristeas* 16 is interesting. As we have seen (above, 6.3), Aristeas allows a Gentile to assert the equivalence of God and Zeus. Here, although he is citing a Gentile author, Aristobulus is unwilling to let any 'impure' theological expression stand.

λόγον, 10.12). The theme to which he continually returns is the power and sovereignty of God in the cosmos. If God is 'over all things' (ἐπὶ πάντων) and all nature is subordinate to him (10.10; cf. 10.12; 12.4), he is also operative 'through all things' (διὰ πάντων), which thereby manifest his power and greatness (10.17; 12.7). Divine power (θεία δύναμις) is repeatedly stressed (10.1, 8, 15; 12.4, 7; cf. ἐνέργεια, 10.12) and its field of operation is always natural phenomena (rather than human affairs). Thus the physical structure of the world is a divine 'establishment' (or 'condition', 10.3, 9, 16; 12.3, 4, 9); its order and coherence are directly attributable to God (12.11–12).

So close is the identification of God with nature that Aristobulus can forge remarkably pantheistic statements. Not only is God everywhere (10.15), sustaining all things (12.4, 12), but the very forces of nature can be properly described as 'power from God' (τό παρὰ τοῦ θεοῦ δυναμικόν); fire would not burn if divine power were not added to it (10.15). In accordance with this pantheistic tendency, Aristobulus frequently speaks of God in abstract and impersonal terms: in his discourse, the Deity is depicted as 'divine power' or 'divine stability' more often than as the personal being portrayed in the Jewish scriptures. It is therefore no surprise to find him cite the proem of Aratus' *Phaenomena* with such enthusiasm. While emending the references to 'Zeus', he does not challenge but embrace Aratus' conception of the God *in* nature, who fills all things and sends signals to humanity, his offspring, through changing seasons and weather conditions (12.6). Aratus says in poetry what Aristobulus says in prose, that 'the power of God operates through all things' (12.7). In other words, Aristobulus' theology has been profoundly influenced by Stoic theology and physics.[59]

These two apparently disparate concerns – the originality of Jewish philosophy and the immanence of divine power – combine

---

[59] On the interconnection of physics, theology and logic in Stoicism see Sandbach 1975. The references to the 'sevenfold *logos*' in 12.12, 15 are probably not a token of Stoic psychology (rightly, Walter 1964:68–82), but still display Stoic influence (Hengel 1974:166–67). To be sure, Aristobulus is an eclectic philosopher who draws on Aristotelian, Stoic and Pythagorean motifs. But the extent of Stoic influence on his theology has often been underestimated. If the Orphic poem cited in 12.5 is the text originally quoted by Aristobulus (Walter doubts this), it adds still more examples of pantheism.

to produce Aristobulus' programme of allegorical interpretation.[60] How could Aristobulus reasonably claim that Plato, Pythagoras and Orpheus derived their philosophy from the narratives of the Pentateuch, and how could he discover in these stories his philosophical convictions about God as divine natural power? The opening chapters of Genesis gave some encouragement to Jews seeking to link their tradition to Greek theologies of creation, and Aristobulus makes specific reference to Genesis 1 and 2 (12.3, 9). Yet here he encountered anthropomorphic descriptions of God 'speaking' or 'resting', and such 'mythical' language continues, of course, right through the books of Moses. Aristobulus' cultural claims and his 'physical theology' necessitated a new hermeneutic, the tools for which were made available by Stoic exegesis of Homer.[61] Just as Stoics could claim that Homer's quarrelling and immoral Gods were ciphers for the conflicting forces of nature, so Aristobulus insists that exegesis must retain a 'fitting conception of God' (10.2), recognizing that when Moses appears to speak of human traits in relation to God, he really means 'physical arrangements and the conditions of great things' (10.3).[62] Only an allegorical reading of Moses can enable his readers to perceive the matters of great significance (μεγαλεῖόν τι) about which he spoke (10.5, 9).

Those who lack intelligence appreciate only the literal meaning of Moses' words and thus fail to appreciate such significance (10.5). But in all ages people with capable minds have stood in awe of his wisdom (10.4). When Moses refers to God's hands he has, of course, an elevated meaning (τὸ μεγαλεῖον), 'divine power' (10.7–9). Talk of 'standing' indicates the stability (στάσις) of the cosmos (10.9–

---

[60] Walter has argued (1964:26–31, 44–45; cf. 1980b:263–64) that the motif of Mosaic originality is only prominent because of the particular interests of Clement and Eusebius, whose selections have highlighted a notion which was incidental to Aristobulus' purpose. His thesis is possible but unprovable, since we have only these fragments to go by.

[61] On Stoic exegesis see in general Walter 1964:124–29, and the detailed studies of Whitman 1987:31–47 and Dawson 1992:38–52.

[62] The Greek is hard to translate: φυσικὰς διαθέσεις ἀπαγγέλλει καὶ μεγάλων πραγμάτων κατασκευάς. Given Aristobulus' special focus on the physical nature of divine power, I prefer to give φυσικάς its proper Stoic sense of 'physical/natural'. Similarly in 10.2 and 12.9 I would take the adverb φυσικῶς in the sense 'in physical/natural terms' (with Stein 1929:8) rather than the weaker 'according to its essential meaning' (*pace* Walter 1964:59 n. 3, 130–35). In the light of its usage elsewhere, it makes little sense to translate κατασκευάς in 10.3 as 'preparations' (A. Y. Collins 1985:838).

12).[63] The divine 'descent' at Sinai was only an indication of the ubiquitous divine presence and of the splendour of God's greatness which permeates nature (10.12–17).[64] References to the speech of God signify the creation of things, the establishment of the universe (12.3–4). In each case, by allegorical or other linguistic devices, Aristobulus redefines the meaning of Moses' text to find there the Stoic God who permeates the cosmos, the only God of which one can talk with 'fitting speech' (λόγος καθήκων, 10.1).

It is in accordance with this 'naturalistic' theology that we find Aristobulus justifying two central Jewish institutions – the Passover and the Sabbath – by reference to the physical structures of the world. In the first fragment Aristobulus is reported as linking the date of the Passover to the vernal equinox, when the sun and moon stand opposite each other. Such astrological observations fit Aristobulus' programme perfectly. If the Jewish law describes God in theological terms as the immanent power in the universe, it is entirely fitting that the Jews' most prominent festival should be in tune with the structures of nature. Jewish religious practice thus has an entirely scientific rationale. In the same way the Sabbath is linked with the pervasive principle of nature which Aristobulus calls 'the principle of the number seven' (ὁ ἕβδομος λόγος, 12.12, 15). Of course Gen 2.1–3 already encouraged some speculation on the relationship between the Sabbath and the structure of the world, but here we see Aristobulus claim that not only the Jewish calendar but also the whole cosmos revolves in units of seven (12.13). He proceeds to show how this scientific interpretation of the Sabbath is echoed in Hesiod, Homer and Linus, who borrowed the idea, of course, from the Jewish books (12.13–16).[65]

---

[63] Aristobulus carefully avoids using the verb in relation to God and employs only the noun, whose double sense, 'standing' and 'stability', enables him to shift into description of the condition of the universe.

[64] This difficult passage confounds our expectation of some allegorical explanation of the noun 'descent' (κατάβασις), and provides instead a rationale for the story as a demonstration of pervasive divine power. Aristobulus' treatment suggests that he is not concerned with the consistent application of the 'rules' of allegorical exegesis; his aim is to establish, by whatever means possible, that when Moses talks of God he refers to the energy which rules and empowers the universe.

[65] Some of the verses cited here have been doctored or even invented. It is unclear whether Aristobulus himself is responsible or anonymous Jewish authors who had already collected such 'testimonies' to the truth of Judaism; see below, and the full discussion by Walter 1964:150–71.

The hesitant and inconsistent way in which Aristobulus employs his allegorical method indicates his pioneering role in its application to the Pentateuch. It also suggests that he views it as a means to an end, rather than an end in itself. As an exegete he promises to do the best he can, but if his exegesis proves unpersuasive the blame should be placed not on Moses but on the inadequate interpreter (10.6). That is the classic disclaimer of those who accord ultimate authority to their texts, and Aristobulus' hope is to establish, by whatever means, the supreme value of the Mosaic text. Confident in the brilliance of this 'philosophical' authority, Aristobulus can take pride in his ancestral tradition: together with his 'fellow citizens' (12.1) he highlights the superiority of 'our ancestor Solomon' (12.11).[66] His achievement is not just to 'bring the text up to date' by interpreting it in terms compatible with Hellenistic culture. He also claims that the Hellenistic culture which has moulded his thought is itself dependent on Judaism. He draws out from the text what his Hellenistic education demands must be there, but then asserts that his Hellenistic concepts are themselves derived from Moses' genius. In other words, he claims to own what he has in fact been mastered by.[67]

While engaged in a significant programme of cultural convergence, Aristobulus thus safeguards the uniqueness of his Jewish tradition. His accommodation of that tradition to his intellectual environment by no means undermines its integrity; in fact he employs that accommodation precisely to bolster the claims of Judaism.[68] Such 'aggressive syncretism' (W. L. Knox) was a powerful cultural strategy which enabled Jews to embrace their cultural environment without being overwhelmed by it, gaining from its strengths while adopting a stance of critical superiority. On that basis Alexandrian Jews could play a prominent role in

---

[66] As we have seen, the political metaphor was prominent is Aristeas (above n. 52), and we will find it again in Philo. Aristobulus' references to '*our* law' and '*our* lawgiver' indicate that he views himself as a spokesman for the Jewish people. As Hengel rightly notes (1974:169), there is here 'no weakness which is prepared for assimilation, but a firmly based spiritual and religious self-awareness.'

[67] Cf. Dawson 1992:82. Dawson's analysis of allegory indicates how Aristobulus fits the text to the radically different cultural ideals of his day, and subordinates those new cultural meanings to the authority of his text.

[68] Collins' suggestion that Aristobulus' discussion of the 'sevenfold principle' is intended 'to diminish the markers which would separate Judaism from its Hellenistic environment' (1986:178) appears to misconstrue his strategy.

Ptolemaic Egypt while retaining their ethnic and religious distinctiveness.

Traces of the same strategy can be detected elsewhere among Alexandrian Jews, both in the employment of Greek mouths to speak Jewish truths and in the use of allegory to import Hellenistic meanings into the Bible. Aristobulus' citation of verses ascribed to famous Greek poets appears to reflect an established tradition of collected 'witnesses' to Judaism. Some of these verses appear genuine; others have been suitably emended – changing 'fourth' to 'seventh', for instance, to make Homer speak about the Sabbath! Occasionally verses, and even whole poems, have simply been invented. Thus we find spurious verses attributed to Sophocles, Euripides and Menander, bearing witness to monotheism, divine judgment or Jewish moral principles.[69] In general we know too little to draw conclusions about the creators and collectors of such *gnomologia*, although bold hypotheses have been advanced about Pythagorean Jewish groups fascinated by the number seven, or the 'mystical' tendencies of the authors of an Orphic poem.[70] In broad terms the strategy appears to be like that of Aristobulus: the appropriation of Greek culture in support of specifically Jewish ideas and practices.

The use of allegory to interpret the Scriptures could serve a similar function. Just as Aristeas employed this technique to indicate the moral significance of Jewish food laws, and Aristobulus to prove the sophistication of Moses' theology, so also other Jews used allegory to find all manner of Hellenistic truths embedded in Moses' text. It is clear that between Aristobulus and Philo there lies a long process of development by which the fragmentary and hesitant efforts of the former evolve into the coherent and systematic approach which Philo can take for granted. It takes Aristobulus several laborious sentences to prove that 'the hand of God' is a metaphor for his power, but that is an equivalence which Philo can take as read.[71] As Stein once observed (1929:9), Philo is

---

[69] See the collection and translation of such fragments by Walter 1983 and Attridge 1985, and the discussion of their origins in Schürer 3.656–71.

[70] On the collection of verses relating to the number seven see Walter 1964:150–71. The Orphic poem has survived in several different recensions and unravelling their relationship and sequence is a complex and perhaps impossible task. See the survey of this problem in Schürer 3.661–67 and the conflicting solutions offered by Walter 1964:202–61, Lafargue 1985 and Collins 1986:204–7.

[71] Cf. Walter 1964:58–86, 141–48.

not noted for his laconic style and what he expresses with minimal explanation is clearly for him self-evident. In Philo we find a clear rationale for biblical anthropomorphisms and a regular procedure for dealing with them. We also find the conviction that allegory can be applied to the whole text, not just its difficult passages, and that two layers of meaning – the literal and the allegorical – can co-exist. Etymology is employed to decipher the meaning of biblical characters, and biblical terms and narratives have developed standardized meanings. It appears that little if any of this is the achievement of Philo himself; it is part of a tradition which he can use and supplement. Indeed, he frequently refers to other allegorists and sometimes mentions explanations handed down from of old (e.g. *Spec Leg* 1.8).[72] Unfortunately his references are not specific enough for us to gain a clear profile of the allegorical schools he mentions, or to trace the development of this important tradition.[73] Nevertheless, it is evident that something like Aristobulus' programme continued for up to two centuries after his death. Hellenized Jews in Alexandria used the allegorical method to discover many kinds of truth (theological, ethical, psychological, scientific, even medical) adumbrated in their sacred text. This was not just a defensive move, to make sense of 'outdated' narratives and laws. It was a positive strategy by which they attributed to Jewish 'philosophy' the insights of the Hellenistic civilization they admired.

## 6.5 Philo

### 6.5.1 Philo's Social Context

Philo stood at the peak of the Jewish community in Alexandria and at the climax of a Jewish philosophical tradition which was deeply engaged with Hellenistic culture. His historical treatises, *In Flaccum* and *De Legatione ad Gaium*, provide invaluable information about the Alexandrian crisis of the mid-first century CE (above, chapter 3) and reveal the reactions of a deeply loyal Jew who was shocked to find his community under the gravest threat. The other treatises, numbering more than forty, show us Philo the

---

[72] The best recent survey of this evidence is by Hay 1979–80.
[73] Two famous attempts at reconstruction were offered by Bousset 1915 and Stein 1929.

philosopher, employing philosophy primarily to exegete the Greek text of the Pentateuch, and striving to surpass the long tradition of Alexandrian Jewish theology. Our knowledge of Philo's predecessors is so fragmentary, and the bulk of Philo's surviving work so imposing, that we tend to accord to him an enormous, and perhaps exaggerated, significance. It could be mere accident that only tiny fragments of Aristobulus have survived while many codices of Philo were preserved; and from an historical point of view we would gladly trade several of Philo's more tedious tractates for just one from a previous or contemporary exegete! Yet at least in Philo we have one fully documented example of an upper-class and educated Jew, explaining his tradition and his continuing allegiance to it in carefully framed accommodation with the Hellenistic world.

It should be clear by now that the fullness of our knowledge about Philo cannot be used to construct that myth of lazy scholarship, the 'typical' Diaspora Jew. Philo is not typical of Jews in Alexandria, still less of Egyptian or North African or Mediterranean Jews. Of course, he is not wholly *sui generis*. He draws on a long theological tradition which flourished in the intellectual circles of Alexandrian Judaism, and he frequently mirrors the social attitudes of that élite. To an extent, then, we may take Philo to represent the intellectual and social stance of his own social class. But first he must be considered as an individual, wrestling with the peculiar tensions of his particular calling.

The only datable event in Philo's life is his leadership of the Jewish delegation from Alexandria to Rome in 39–40 CE. Since he describes himself soon after as a grey-haired 'old man' (γέρων, *Legatio* 1), it is reasonable to put his birth date roughly 60 years earlier.[74] Thus Philo's *floruit* coincides with those first few decades of the first century CE when the Jewish community in Alexandria enjoyed its final period of peace and prosperity. And 'prosperity' is a term particularly apposite to Philo's own life. Josephus, in his only reference to Philo, introduces him as 'highly honoured' and the brother of Alexander the Alabarch (*Ant* 18.259). This Alexander we know from elsewhere as a man of fabulous wealth, able to offer a loan of 200,000 drachmas (*Ant* 18.159–60) and to

---

[74] In *Op Mund* 105 a man is judged a γέρων from the age of 57. Of course Philo may not be using the term precisely in *Legatio* 1, whose date of composition is in any case not easily fixed (sometime after 41 CE). We may suggest a birth date around 20 BCE, with a margin of error of at least ten years.

gift massive gold and silver plating for the nine gates of the temple (*Bell* 5.205). His political connections reached as high as the imperial family, since he served as 'overseer' for Claudius' mother, Antonia (*Ant* 19.276–77).[75] Thus Philo belonged to one of the wealthiest families in Alexandria, a Rothschild dynasty whose leadership and sponsorship was no doubt rewarded with the utmost respect. Everything Philo writes, and indeed the leisure he has to write it, reflects that cushion of wealth which protects him from the harsh realities experienced by 'the common herd'. While he struggles to control his appetite at massively indulgent banquets, he finds it hard to appreciate the desperate lot of the beggars he passes every day.[76]

As is typical in the Graeco-Roman world, the privileges of wealth were reflected in the quality of education. Philo talks repeatedly of the training of the gymnasium and of the school education (the 'encyclical training') given to the children of wealthy families.[77] His works demonstrate that he has been well trained in literature, in mathematics, in astronomy, in rhetoric and in music, the subjects which formed the core curriculum of contemporary education. The literature is, of course, the classics of the Greek tradition. Philo shows intimate knowledge of Homer, whom he frequently quotes, and can draw on historians, poets and even Attic law where necessary. But his intelligence took him further. Having mated with the 'slave girl', school education, Philo was intelligent and wealthy enough to devote the rest of his life to a partnership with the 'mistress', philosophy. Thus he acquired that close familiarity with the major philosophical schools which proved so important in his exegesis of Scripture.[78]

There is nothing to indicate that Philo's cultural formation took place in a context other than the schools and sporting institutions shared by other Greek youths of his social class.[79] As we have already

---

[75] On Philo's family see Schwartz 1953 and Morris in Schürer 3.815 n. 14.

[76] On self-control at banquets, see *Leg All* 3.156. He considers 'trivial' the literal sense of the law on the return of the poor man's cloak at night (Exod 22.26–27, discussed in *Somn* 1.92–101).

[77] See e.g. *Spec Leg* 2.230; *Prov* 2.44–46 and *Cong* 74–76; cf. Mendelson 1982. Philo considers it a praiseworthy feature of the translators of the LXX that they had received a 'Greek education', *Mos* 2.32.

[78] The allegory of successive partners, almost a cliché in Homeric interpretation, is the basis of Philo's oft-repeated allegory of Hagar and Sarah (most fully detailed in *Cong*).

[79] So rightly Mendelson 1982:28–33 and Harris 1976:72, 91, against Wolfson 1948:1.78–91.

noted (chapter 3, Excursus), Philo probably enjoyed Alexandrian citizenship and thus passed through the regular training of an ephebe. As an adult he swims in the mainstream of Alexandrian cultural life. He mingles with the crowd at sporting events of all kinds – boxing, wrestling and pancratist contests as well as chariot races – and he frequently uses athletic metaphors for the challenges of life.[80] Similarly, he attends the theatre to watch plays, dances and puppet shows, and knows all about the elaborate private banquets which were the social cement of his class.[81]

But Philo is also intimately acquainted with the life and traditions of the Jewish community in Alexandria. Reared in a Jewish family, he has been 'given the finest training from an early age by divinely gifted men' (*Spec Leg* 1.314).[82] His phenomenal knowledge of Scripture and his familiarity with oral traditions handed on by 'elders of the nation' (*Mos* 1.4) suggest an intensive Jewish education alongside his grounding in Greek culture. He became in time a master of the multiform heritage of Jewish Alexandrian exegesis and surely played his part in the Sabbath expositions of the law, teaching a long-suffering audience the lessons of virtue.[83]

Thus Philo moved easily in a social environment which we perhaps too neatly divide into 'Greek' and 'Jewish' worlds. Although in some respects he feels superior to his non-Jewish friends, the social and intellectual achievements of Alexandria are not alien to him. There is here no hint of a tension between 'Greek' and 'Jewish' values, no fundamental struggle to reconcile the Jew and the Greek within him.

There are, however, indications of another kind of conflict in Philo, pervading his whole life and thought. In a rare autobiographical snippet at the beginning of *Spec Leg* 3, Philo looks back wistfully at a period in his life when he enjoyed uninterrupted philosophical contemplation. At that time, soaring up to the

---

[80] See e.g. *Probus* 26; *Prov* 2.58. Harris rightly considers the detail in Philo's imagery as evidence that Philo 'was a keen and well-informed spectator of the Games at Alexandria, and that he expected his readers to be no less well-informed than himself' (1976:72).

[81] Attendance at the theatre: *Ebr* 177; *Probus* 141. Banquets: *Leg All* 3.143; *Ebr* 217–19 etc.

[82] On training in Jewish customs 'from the cradle' cf. *Spec Leg* 2.88; 4.149–50; *Virt* 141; *Legatio* 115, 210.

[83] See e.g. *Spec Leg* 2.60–64. We will return to Philo's political role in the Jewish community below, 6.5.5.

heights with his soul divinely inspired, he could look down at the maelstrom of ordinary life from which he had gratefully escaped. Now, however, such freedom is his no more:

> As it proved, that deadliest of evils was lying in wait for me, Envy, the enemy of the good; it suddenly set upon me and did not cease violently to drag me down until it had plunged me into a huge ocean of political troubles (αἱ ἐν πολιτείᾳ φροντίδες) in which I am dragged along, unable to get my head above water. (*Spec Leg* 3.3)

In fact, Philo is thankful that there are moments, even now, when he escapes the tyranny of people and affairs and rises up on wings to breathe again the pure air of wisdom; at such moments he occupies himself with the study of Scripture to discover its hidden philosophical sense (*Spec Leg* 3.1–6).

We cannot identify to what specific event(s) Philo here alludes,[84] and this passage is not uninfluenced by rhetorical clichés; yet it reveals clearly enough the forces which pulled Philo in conflicting directions. Philo the philosopher longs for the seclusion of the study, where his mind can range the universe and contemplate eternal truth. He loves solitude and naturally gravitates from the public domain into the recesses of his own home; when visitors plague him even there, he is eager to escape to some familiar but lonely spot in the country.[85] Cities are hateful places, full of vulgar crowds and turmoil, and nothing attracts him more than the lifestyle of the Therapeutae which he so conspicuously idealizes.[86] There may be elements here of a philosopher's pose, a mask of social aloofness donned for professional credibility. A man who so evidently enjoys banquets and sporting contests might have found the Therapeutic lifestyle less congenial than he thought. Yet his testimony is not entirely to be dismissed. If Philo is drawn back into the life of the city, it is less for its social attractions than for the sake of his commitment to the Jewish community. Philo's rootedness in that community provided the counter-balance to his

---

[84] See Goodenough 1926 and 1938:47 n15.

[85] *Abr* 20–25, 85–87; *Vit Cont* 18–21; *Leg All* 2.85 (where, however, he admits that solitude does not always prove fruitful).

[86] *Decal* 2–13; *Vit Cont* 19–20. He advises keeping clear of the masses with their inclination to vice, *Ebr* 26; *Fug* 14; *Mut* 213. Conversely, he knows that 'the common herd' consider his lifestyle both miserable and misanthropic, *Cong* 174.

philosophical detachment, and as tensions mounted in the city his involvement became increasingly political. The catastrophe of the Alexandrian pogrom in 38 CE finally overwhelmed all other concerns and thrust upon him an enormous responsibility as leader of the Jewish delegation to Rome. Philo the recluse became Philo the representative; the philosopher had to breathe the polluted air of politics. However, as I shall argue, it was precisely the pull of such community loyalty which kept Philo from spinning into philosophical abstraction and coupled his universalist vision to the practical and social interests of Alexandrian Jews.

### 6.5.2 Mosaic Philosophy

It is axiomatic for Philo that philosophy is the fount of all good things (*Op Mund* 53), and he is in no doubt where to find its most sublime expression: in the Greek text of Moses. Even in his general philosophical discourses he suggests that his Greek sources have cribbed their best ideas from Moses (*Probus* 57; cf. *Aet* 19; *Mos* 1.1–3). His favourite mode of philosophy is exegesis of 'holy Scripture', and his near complete confinement to the Pentateuch indicates its source of excellence in Moses.[87] If there has ever lived a perfect Sage (Philo knows the Stoic doubts on this matter), it was Moses. Endued with supreme intellectual skills (*Mos* 1.18–29), Moses became the noblest king, the holiest high-priest, the wisest prophet and the finest law-giver of all time (*Mos* 2.1–7). More particularly, in certain key respects he clearly outclassed all other philosophers. Philo is deeply impressed by the biblical accounts of Moses' personal encounter with God on Sinai; where others inferred the existence of God from the design of the universe, Moses uniquely received a vision from the Uncreated Himself and thereby acquired clearer and more perfect knowledge (*Leg All* 3.97–101). There is even a text (Exod 7.1), to which Philo frequently returns, where Moses is described as θεός; even with an attenuated meaning, that unique appellation signals an unparalleled proximity to truth (*Sacr* 8–10; *Somn* 2.189 etc.). Thus, as a philosopher, Philo counts himself 'in the school of Moses' (οἱ κατὰ Μωυσῆν φιλοσοφοῦντες, *Mut* 223).

---

[87]  The end of Deuteronomy is the end of the 'holy Scriptures', *Mos* 2.290. The authority of other biblical texts derives from their authors' 'discipleship' of Moses (e.g. *Plant* 39; *Cong* 177; *Conf* 62); cf. Goodenough 1969:75–77.

In reality, of course, Philo's debt to Plato is just as great, if not greater, than his debt to 'Moses' (modern Pentateuchal criticism would have devastated his religion). Philo's thought is structured by Platonic dualism, in which the visible and sensible world of changing matter is taken to be a copy of an invisible, immaterial universe of 'ideas'. It is axiomatic for him that the conceptual world of eternal truths is the only proper object of study for our equally immaterial souls, which have the misfortune to make our burdensome bodies their temporary home. Philo has studied with particular intensity Plato's cosmogony in the *Timaeus*, but echoes of other dialogues may also be heard on almost every page of his work. The absolute transcendence of God as fashioner of creation, his pure goodness in will and act, the location of truth in invisible realities, the upward soaring of the soul as it sheds the encumbrances of physical existence – such central Platonic themes provide the ground-plan for Philo's philosophy.

To be sure, other philosophical traditions also influenced Philo, whose Platonism reflects the eclectic philosophy of contemporary Alexandria.[88] Pythagorean reflection on the properties of numbers was (almost literally) music to Philo's ears, while his anthropological dualism was strengthened by the Stoic opposition of reason and the passions. Handy items from Peripatetic theology or Stoic ethics are ubiquitous. Occasionally Philo incorporates extraneous or inconsistent material, but he is generally in control of his own theology and critical of ideas he cannot harmonize with Scripture.[89] The statement of his creed in *Op Mund* 170–72 displays his careful choices among current theological options, and includes a characteristic emphasis on providence and a strong affirmation of

---

[88] Philo was 'essentially adapting contemporary Alexandrian Platonism, which was itself heavily influenced by Stoicism and Pythagoreanism, to his own exegetical purposes' (Dillon 1977:182); cf. Chadwick 1970.

[89] Unassimilated material includes the detour into Scepticism in *Ebr* 170–202, but Chadwick is right to insist that 'it is wrong to exaggerate this phenomenon as if Philo were nothing but an uncritical compiler of pre-existing material and his mind a mere junk-shop' (1970:138). Philo is unable to decide whether there is only one 'good', moral virtue (the Stoic position), or whether the welfare of the body and favourable circumstances may also be classed as 'goods' (as Peripatetics held); as Dillon notes (1977:146–49), such inconsistencies are often caused by the text leading Philo now in one direction, now in another. Wolfson's portrayal of Philo as a systematic philosopher (1948) was overblown; see now Nikiprowetsky 1977 and Runia 1986, whose conclusions (pp. 505–519) are especially to be noted.

the unity and transcendence of God. Jewish aniconic monotheism was easily compatible with Plato's Creator God, whose nature could neither be seen nor adequately copied. It was also possible to add theological substance to the Platonic notion of the soul's intuition of the 'forms': according to Philo, it is the grace of God which empowers the soul to rise to the mystic vision of God, a revelation of light granted by the Light itself.[90]

Early Christians were familiar with a Greek saying: 'Either Plato philonizes or Philo platonizes.'[91] It is not hard to decide between these options. Chadwick is right to remark that 'philosophy, especially Platonism, genuinely mattered to him and he could not have expressed his faith adequately without it' (1966:30). But it is also true that without his faith and his sacred text Philo would never have immersed himself so deeply in philosophy. Philo reads Plato not for his own sake but for the reflection of truths he thinks he has learnt from Moses. What *to us* is an imposition of Platonism on a philosophically innocent text, is *to Philo* the exposition of an inner truth concealed by its philosophical author. Moses had in fact left certain clues even on the surface of the text. Are not Genesis 1 and 2 two different creation accounts, and does not the Greek of Gen 1.1–2 describe the first created world as invisible (ἀόρατος)? Does not Gen 2.7 define the constitution of human beings as dust inbreathed with divine spirit? And does not God reveal himself in Exod 3.14 as ὁ ὤν (the Existent One)? Given such hints as these, the exegete was invited to discover the fuller meaning of the whole text, and for that discovery an allegorical method was close to hand.

### 6.5.3 Allegory

On any Greek understanding of philosophy, it is hard to imagine any less philosophical text than the Pentateuch, with its strange and sometimes scurrilous legends, its tedious genealogies and its detailed cultic regulations. Moreover, Philo's Bible was in Greek, a

---

[90]  E.g. *Praem* 40–46. Philo insists (against Stoic moralism) that the attainment of virtue, while rightly striven for, is ultimately a gift from God (e.g. *Leg All* 3.136–37). Goodenough's emphasis on Philo as mystic (1962, 1969) captures an important aspect of Philo's religious experience, although his thesis of a 'mystic gospel' prevalent throughout 'Hellenistic Judaism' is not convincing.

[91]  E.g. Jerome, *De viris illustribus* 11.

clumsy and over literal translation, often obscure in its style as well as its subject matter. It is fortunate that he believes the Greek translation to be inspired and wholly reliable, since he almost certainly had no access to the original himself.[92] Yet oddities in the Greek, easily explained by a Hebraicist, are further puzzles for Philo, requiring rational explanation. He must have spent thousands of hours in intensive study of this Greek text, and he is convinced that not a single word is superfluous (*Leg All* 3.147; *Post* 78 etc.). As we watch him in tractate after tractate spinning intricate intratextual webs, we feel the devotion of a man who has devoted the best years of his life to making sense of this enigmatic text.

The master-key which unlocks the text and releases its philosophical truth is the allegorical method. Philo is confident that 'almost all – or at least most – of the law-book is allegorical' (*Jos* 28). The qualification is interesting: Philo does not have to find an allegorical meaning for everything in the text, although he surely could have done so, if he had judged it necessary. The story of Moses can be told in a eulogistic mode almost entirely free of allegory (*Mos*), and the tractate on Abraham gives considerable space to the literal meaning of the text because Philo considers this suitably encomiastic (*Abr* 217). At the literal historical level Abraham was a supremely wise man, though it is also true that his textual persona is a symbol of the virtue-loving soul (*Abr* 68).

But in general Philo's preference lies with the allegorical. With the élitist prejudices of a professional philosopher he considers the surface meaning of the text (ἡ ... ἐν φανερῷ ἀπόδοσις) to be for the masses (οἱ πολλοί), while he is among the few who look to the hidden meaning to discover truths about the soul, not just the body (*Abr* 147). In part this represents the intellectual pleasure of deciphering a code: the very awkwardness of the text is proof that its 'riddles' conceal some philosophical truth. But in another respect Philo's method is simply the hermeneutical correlate of his Platonic dualism. The literal meaning suits those who remain

---

[92] Some still hold that Philo's knowledge of Hebrew extended beyond 'handbook' knowledge of the Greek meanings of Hebrew names. But *Mos* 2.37–41 strongly suggests that Philo is not himself able to compare the Hebrew with the Greek (note the tell-tale φασι, 'they say', 38); hence the vehemence of his insistence on their exact equivalence. Only sentiment makes him regard Hebrew as his 'ancestral language', *Agr* 95; *Cong* 177 etc.

on the surface of things, who are content with appearances; but allegory is for those who contemplate naked and bodiless truth – those who live for the soul rather than the body (*Abr* 236). In his description of the banquet of the Therapeutae, Philo imagines the President standing to deliver a sermon, much like one of his own allegorical treatises: it proceeds at a leisurely pace, spun out with much repetition for the benefit of the audience who listen with rapt attention (a touch of Philonic optimism!). The content of the sermon is, of course, allegorical exegesis, of which Philo here provides his fullest explanation:

> To these people [and to Philo] the whole law-book is like a living being which has as its body the literal rules and as its soul the invisible sense (νοῦς) which is stored up in its words. In this the rational soul begins to observe the things especially appropriate to itself, seeing in the words as in a mirror the extraordinary beauties of the concepts (νοήματα); it unfolds and unveils the symbols and so brings out naked into the light the inner thoughts for those who are able, with a little reminding, to contemplate the invisible things through the medium of the visible. (*Vit Cont* 78)

Such Platonic epistemology indicates why allegory is the preserve of an intellectual minority: only they have the necessary rational souls capable of discerning the intellectual truths in the text. Only 'the people of vision' (*Plant* 36) can appreciate this sort of exercise; they form a band of 'initiates' inducted into the divine mysteries (*Cher* 48). No doubt the majority found such rarified exercises of little interest or relevance.[93]

For much of the time Philo is content that the common people understand the text at a less exalted level. He recognizes, with only slight condescension, that for some people the consistency of the literal sense is a matter of some importance (*Deus* 133). But there are times when he too is bothered by the plain meaning of the text. On the surface, it is a moral scandal that Noah should pronounce a curse on Canaan in Gen 9.25, when it was not Canaan but his father Ham who had 'looked on his father's nakedness'. Philo supposes that those who examine the details of the text at the literal level will find some explanation for this. He is content

---

[93] There are indications that this majority held Philo and his sort in some contempt: see e.g. *Ebr* 65; *Somn* 1.102; 2.301–2.

to let them go their own way, while he, following correct reason (ὀρθὸς λόγος), will enquire into the inner allegorical meaning (*Sobr* 31–33.). Elsewhere he is simply perplexed by the apparent arbitrariness of the Mosaic law: why are some animals listed as unclean, or why must one set apart for the altar specifically the lobe of the liver, the kidneys and the fat (*Spec Leg* 1.212–14)? It is unthinkable that Moses should write something absurd or irrational and it is only in allegory that Philo can find a reasonable explanation.

Philo is particularly concerned lest the sacred books be taken to be 'mythological'. The term μῦθος (legend, myth, fable) is loaded with fears and prejudices: it is the word he regularly employs to denigrate Greek legends, which he knew very well but considered morally and theologically debased. Philo knew that many stories in the Pentateuch looked remarkably like the fables he censured – God planting a garden, a serpent speaking, angels having intercourse with women, heroes cheating each another, their wives engaging in unseemly quarrels. He consistently gives allegorical explanations of such unworthy features of his sacred text, while typically ignoring the efforts of Greeks to allegorize their own myths and legends.

Of greatest concern, however, is the possibility that the text conveyed an unworthy image of God. LXX Gen 4.16 states that Cain 'went out from the face of the Lord' (a literal rendering of a Hebrew idiom). For Philo any literal understanding of this text would be dangerously irreverent (*Post* 1–7). If God has a face, has he also hands, feet and genital organs? And, once you give God human form, would you blasphemously attribute to him human passions as well? And, in any case, could Cain go away from God, if God fills the universe and there is nothing outside it? Philo concludes that none of this text can have a literal meaning. Elsewhere, literal and allegorical explanations can co-exist as different layers of meaning, suitable for different readers. Here, only those with a firm grasp of truth can make proper sense of the text.[94] At such points Philo is not playing hermeneutical games:

---

[94] *Deus* 60–69 explains such anthropomorphisms on the principle of divine accommodation: like a doctor who lies for the good of his patient, Moses gives a false picture of God's anger for the sake of those who could not understand the truth. Thus Philo holds that the literal sense is useful, but not that it is true; cf. *Somn* 1.228–38.

he is providing an apologetic without which, in his opinion, the text would have to be jettisoned altogether.

Philo's hermeneutic is founded on an absolutist principle: the text is, and must be shown to be, rational and worthy in its every detail. Philo knows critics may pounce on a 'myth' like the tower of Babel and imagines their disgust: 'Can you still be serious when you say that the laws contain the principles of absolute truth? Look, your so-called "holy books" also contain myths, which it is your habit to deride whenever you hear other people recount them!' (*Conf* 2). Moreover, such rational criticisms did not only arise outside the Jewish fold: there are also signs of a theological criticism from *within* the Jewish community. For instance, Philo knows that some people consider aspects of the Scripture dangerously impious (e.g. *Plant* 69–72 on Deut 10.9) – a criticism which could only arise from loyal Jews with an intimate knowledge of the text. We get a glimpse here, and elsewhere, of a Jewish theological critique which attempts to salvage Jewish piety by bracketing or downgrading portions of the text.[95] What is revealing is the strength of Philo's reaction against such sophisticated *Sachkritik*. He brands such people fault-finders whose piety is a pretence: they have wilfully misunderstood the text. Philo has based his life's work on the conviction that *everything* in the sacred text is worthy and profound, and he cannot afford to jeopardize that investment with the least admission of fault (*Det* 13). He will not accept a hermeneutical strategy which discriminates between text and text; it has to be all or nothing. In this sense, while not a literalist, Philo is a textual fundamentalist.

However, it would be misleading to suggest that Philo adopts allegorical techniques only or even primarily for apologetic purposes. While they have apologetic value, they are also simply self-evident to Philo, having long been accepted by intellectual Jews as the highest form of exegesis. The method has become so ingrained that Philo is convinced that he is not creating a meaning for the text, merely discovering its true intent: like an explorer he tracks down an elusive but objectively present sense.[96] And for Philo that sense concerns first and foremost the human condition. While

---

[95] Such internal intellectual criticism of the text may also be evidenced in *Abr* 178–83; *Mig Abr* 44–45; *Leg All* 3.204–6; *Conf* 9–15; and *Somn* 2.98.

[96] On finding the reality (πρᾶγμα) in a text: *Fug* 121; *Conf* 190. On the truth which loves to hide: *Fug* 179 etc.

he knows of some who find scientific knowledge in the text, for Philo there is only one sort of truth worth discovering and that is truth about ourselves. Proper exegesis begins with the assumption that the figures in the text are types of the human condition, body-lovers, perhaps, or wise-thinkers, or, in the case of the patriarchs, the seekers of truth through teaching (Abraham), the naturally self-taught (Isaac) and those who make progress through practice (Jacob).[97] In many cases Philo uses some etymological device to secure this meaning (this is the only time he makes some pretence to know Hebrew). His use of that information is consistently directed towards anthropology and 'the anatomy of the soul' (*Cong* 54).

### 6.5.4 Israel and the Human Race

If the purpose of Philo's allegory is to find philosophical truth in the Pentateuch, its inevitable tendency is to universalize the text. To take Abraham, Isaac and Jacob as individuals only on the page, and in reality as types of soul-condition, is to dehistoricize the patriarchal stories.[98] In Philo's allegories the Bible is read not as a record of history (still less, salvation-history) but as a philosophical analysis of the human condition, a depiction of human types and an instruction in human wellbeing.[99] This move from history to philosophy represents a shift from the particular to the universal; to dehistoricize is to deJudaize. A 'naive' reading of the Exodus would take it as a story of Israel's departure from Egypt and acquisition of a land of her own, but allegorical exegesis dissipates all such particularities. Israel means 'the one who sees God'; the rescue from Egypt is the escape of the soul from the confines of the body; and the land which is entered is the 'territory' of the

---

[97] *Abr* 52 and *passim*; on the figures as τρόποι ψυχῆς, see *Abr* 52, 147 etc. Sandmel 1956:142–43 notes the derivation of these types from Aristotle.

[98] *Abr* 52–55 describes their individuality as merely textual: λόγῳ μὲν ἄνδρες ἔργῳ δὲ ... ἀρεταί. Cf. *Cong* 180; *Quaest Gen* 4.137; *Somn* 1.52. Elsewhere Philo can take Abraham as a real historical figure, and it is crucial that Moses lived in history not just in the text. With figures like Samuel, Philo is not so sure (*Ebr* 144).

[99] Philo protests against taking the story of Terah's migration as a piece of historical information (*Somn* 1.52). And who would be so foolish as to think that Moses is interested in providing genealogies (*Cong* 44)?

virtues.[100] Thus in Philonic allegory there is neither Jew nor Greek. In principle, *anyone* could read the Pentateuch as their 'story', *anyone* could identify with Abraham in his progression from 'encyclical studies' to philosophy, *anyone* could learn to escape the pleasures of the body and cultivate the fruits of the soul.

Or, at least, anyone who counted as a lover of wisdom and a devotee of virtue. Wisdom and virtue had long been recognized as international commodities, but those who claimed to possess them were apt to consider themselves a tiny élite. Although wisdom recognized no racial boundaries, she restricted her favours – by definition – to the educated, to those who distanced themselves from the squalor of the masses. In his most universalistic tract, *Quod Omnis Probus Liber Sit*, Philo can parade an international array of sages – from Persian 'Magi' to Indian gurus, from Heracles to Diogenes the Cynic. The Essenes can take a place in this roll-call of the wise, but they are not introduced specifically as Jews or granted any superior status. Yet, as Philo himself insists, this cosmopolitan list represents a highly selective band: while the world is full of the rich and famous, few can be counted wise, just and virtuous (*Probus* 72). There may be, Philo reckons, a moral minority among Greeks and non-Greeks who practise wisdom; like an ember smouldering in a fireplace, they keep the flame of virtue from total extinction (*Spec Leg* 2.44–48).[101] But when Philo describes the lifestyle necessary for such virtue, we can see why his category is so restricted. Avoiding the hurly-burly of civic life and the gatherings of 'thoughtless people', the wise allow their souls to soar in contemplation of the stars; they ward off bodily desires and unsettling passions, taking pleasure only in moral excellence. Philo may wish that all humanity live like this, but he is describing a lifestyle possible only for philosophers.[102]

Nonetheless, even if the universalism of virtue is in practice somewhat restricted, it is important to observe that Philo's

---

[100] *Somn* 2.255 insists that the promise of land to Abraham in Gen 15.18 does not concern physical territory but 'the better portion of ourselves'; elsewhere (e.g. *Cher* 119ff.) the text is taken to refer to the whole creation. The patriarchs' 'homeland' is heaven, the true home of a wise man's soul, *Agr* 64–65; cf. *Heres* 82.

[101] Cf. *Agr* 103–4; *Ebr* 26; *Mut* 213 The masses, of course, seek nothing more than bodily pleasures, *Agr* 23–25.

[102] Cf. Bassler 1982:105–19. Philo shares the philosopher's assumption that good education is the necessary path to virtue, *Mut* 229.

philosophy always leads *away* from Jewish particularity. Under philosophical influence, the God of the Bible becomes notably abstract, as the Existent One (τὸ ὄν) and the Cause (τὸ αἴτιον), and the greatest emphasis lies on his universal attributes.[103] God is Father of all, Ruler of all and Saviour of all humanity (e.g. *Op Mund* 72, 78, 169). The goodness and generosity of God, which are among Philo's favourite themes, are always universal in scope: God loves to give his gifts to all, including the imperfect (e.g. *Leg All* 1.34). Correspondingly, Philo is concerned about human piety in general, not just Jewish religion: he is exercised by the falsity of showy sacrifices in temples (plural) and by licentious behaviour at religious feasts.[104]

Thus it is immensely important to Philo that his sacred text and its laws are of universal significance. Since the law-book opens with an account of creation, anyone who lives by the law is living according to nature and can count himself a 'citizen of the world' (κοσμοπολίτης, *Op Mund* 3; cf. *Mos* 2.45–52). Thus the biblical commands are the laws of nature – most evidently so with the Sabbath rest (Philo is eloquent about the natural properties of the number 7), but also in relation to other laws and festivals.[105] The fact that people of many races observe Jewish festivals (*Mos* 2.17– 44) is of more than merely apologetic significance: it shows that there is a kindred spirit (οἰκειότης) among humanity, at least among those who value virtue.[106]

The Philo who extols this common 'polity' (πολιτεία) of virtue (*Spec Leg* 2.73) is Philo the philosopher, the Philo who spends hours in solitude on lonely farms outside the city. There he strives to build bridges between his Mosaic text and Hellenistic culture, between the Jewish tradition and the moral values which reason

---

[103] Philo is uneasy with the biblical language which personalizes God as 'your God', *Mut* 27–28.

[104] *Det* 19–21; *Deus* 8–9; *Cher* 91–97. The emphasis here on the purity of the soul, and doubts about the value of a 'building' for God, threaten to undermine all 'outward' forms of religion; cf. *Mos* 2.107–8; *Cher* 98–101; *Sobr* 62–63 etc.

[105] The number 7 constitutes 'the festival not of a single city or country, but of the whole world' (*Op Mund* 89); cf. the whole of *Op Mund* 89–128 and *Decal* 96–105; *Mos* 2.209–11 etc. Natural explanations are offered for circumcision in *Spec Leg* 1.1–11 and the food laws in *Spec Leg* 4.100–25. The festivals are given a dual rationale, one specific to the nation and the other 'universal, in accordance with nature and in harmony with the whole cosmos', *Spec Leg* 2.150; cf. 2.162, 188.

[106] *Mos* 2.17; *Spec Leg* 2.73; 3.155.

had established as the peak of human excellence. The dangers of such a project are clear: synthesizing the Jewish tradition with the common discourse of Hellenism risks suppressing its distinctiveness and subverting its particular social identity. Bridges can carry traffic in two directions, and as many as might be attracted to the Jewish community might leave in order to attain its ideals without its restrictive customs.

In fact, however, Philo's universalism is held in check. Ultimately his allegorical reading of Scripture functions not to submerge Moses' authority in the sea of Hellenism, nor to parallel Moses with Plato as equal sources of truth. Rather the whole gamut of Hellenistic culture is subordinated to Moses, pressed into service to endorse *his* original achievement. In the last resort, as Dawson observes, Philonic allegory 'is an effort to make Greek culture Jewish rather than to dissolve Jewish identity into Greek culture ... Philo's allegorical reading of scripture revises Greek culture by subordinating it to Jewish cultural and religious identity; his interpretation is not a synthesis but a usurpation' (1992:74, 113). The philosophy that finds common ground in human virtue and piety is ultimately employed in the service of one particular community: the philosopher returns to the city and commits himself to his fellow Jews.

It is worth observing the terms of this commitment. Although Philo refers often enough to the Jewish people as a 'nation' (ἔθνος), their ethnicity is defined less in genealogical terms than by reference to their common 'constitution', the holy πολιτεία of Moses.[107] Such an emphasis enables Philo to portray the superiority of Jews in cultural rather than racial terms.[108] Quite simply, the community to which Philo belongs has the best constitution (οἱ ἄριστα πολιτευόμενοι, *Conf* 141).[109] The single most important

---

[107] πάτριος πολιτεία: *Conf* 2 etc; Moses' πολιτεία: *Gig* 59; *Ebr* 109; *Heres* 169; the ἱερὰ πολιτεία: *Mos* 2.211; *Spec Leg* 4.55; *Virt* 87 etc; the πολιτεία of the Jews, *Virt* 108. What unites the nation is a κοινωνία of laws and customs (*Spec Leg* 4.16; cf. 4.159).

[108] It also eases the explanation of proselytism, since the kinship of common values is more significant than the accidents of birth, *Spec Leg* 1.315–317; 2.73; 3.155; *Virt* 147, 206–10. Nevertheless, the Jewish tradition is still 'ancestral', and Jews continue to be blessed by the merits of the fathers, *Spec Leg* 4.180–82; *Praem* 165–67.

[109] On the Mosaic constitution as the ideal constitution of Plato and Aristotle, see Wolfson 1948:2.374–95.

factor here is its unique piety towards God. Philo's summary of this matter is worth noting in detail. The Jewish nation is

> one which makes the greatest profession, to be engaged in the supplication of the One who truly exists, who is the Creator and Father of all. For what disciples of the best philosophy learn from its teaching Jews gain from their laws and customs, that is, knowledge of the highest and most original Cause of all, while they reject the deceit of created Gods. For no created thing is really God; it is only so in men's opinion, since it lacks the most essential quality, eternity. (*Virt* 64–65)

This extraordinary claim encapsulates Philo's pride in Judaism. He considers Jewish theology equal to 'the best philosophy' and is proud to see it embodied in Jewish laws and customs, not just philosophical treatises. Chief among these customs is Jewish aniconic worship: the 'most original Cause of all' is, of course, invisible and it makes excellent sense that there should be somewhere a special place sacred to that One, entirely free of images (*Legatio* 318). Iconic worship, by contrast, can hardly be adequate for the true, invisible God; indeed it can only draw attention away from the Creator to 'the deceit of created Gods'.[110] For all his sense of affinity with Gentile sages and scholars, Philo remains profoundly shocked by the folly of 'idolatry' which he finds prevalent at all levels of Alexandrian society. He can see here only a 'most vital error' which the Jewish nation is privileged to correct: passing over all created objects, they give worship only to the Uncreated and Eternal God (*Spec Leg* 2.164–67). In this sense Jews are the one truly worshipful community in the world; they are the nation with the clearest vision of God, the people thus naturally most God-beloved.[111]

---

[110] In *Decal* 52–80 Philo follows much the same pattern as we will note in *Wisdom of Solomon* 13–15 (below, chapter 7.1), criticizing in turn worship of the cosmos, use of images and Egyptian animal-cults; cf. *Spec Leg* 1.12–31 and numerous other passages. Moses' rule is for those who wish to 'follow genuine philosophy and lay claim to genuine and pure piety (εὐσέβεια)', *Decal* 58. To suppose that physical realities are either eternal or self-powered (αὐτοκρατής) is to commit a most basic philosophical error. See Goodenough 1962:80–85.

[111] *Mos* 2.189; *Plant* 55–60; *Mig Abr* 113–14; *Abr* 98 etc. Since 'Israel' means 'the one who sees God', Philo often refers to the Jewish community as 'the nation which sees' (τὸ ὁρατικὸν ἔθνος).

It is along such lines that Philo understands those scriptural texts which refer to Israel as God's chosen people. Without reference to the notion of covenant, Philo takes the Jewish community to be God's special possession in the world, in the sense that a ruler of a kingdom can own it all, yet have his own particular property.[112] It is important for him, however, to temper this claim by emphasizing Israel's service for all humankind: if Israel is the nation dearest of all to God, she has also received the task of priesthood and prophecy on behalf of all humanity (*Abr* 98). Thus Philo interprets the temple prayers and sacrifices as offered on behalf of all the nations,[113] and holds that 'the Jewish nation is to the whole world what the priest is to the state' (*Spec Leg* 2.163). In other words, Jewish distinction before God is neither arbitrary nor arrogant. Philo professes to be astonished that Jews are accused of 'inhumanity' (ἀπανθρωπία): their universal goodwill is displayed by their supplications for all humanity, and their worship of the truly Existent God is performed not just in their own name, but also in the name of all who evade the service they owe to God (*Spec Leg* 2.167).

The Jews' distinction in piety (εὐσέβεια) is matched by their pre-eminence in virtue (ἀρετή). Given Philo's social context, it is hardly surprising that Egyptians are vilified as irreligious and irrational hedonists.[114] It is more striking that key elements of Hellenistic culture become targets of criticism. Much as he enjoys the games, Philo scorns the exaggerated significance given to athletics: he ridicules their concern with physical prowess and deplores the violence in boxing and pancratist contests (*Agr* 113–19). He charges the theatres with sensuality and the clubs with degeneracy.[115] Sharp contrasts are drawn between the ordered and pious festivals of Jews and the licentious extravagance of Greek festivals.[116] As a foil to the banquet of the Therapeutae, Philo lambasts the morals of Greek dinner-parties, and launches a savage attack on the Symposium of Plato (*Vit Cont* 40–63). In particular, of course, he reacts with horror to its positive image of homosexuality, and on this, and other aspects of sexual morality, he claims for Judaism

---

[112] *Plant* 55–60; cf. *Spec Leg* 4.180–81; *Legatio* 3–4.
[113] *Spec Leg* 1.97, 168–69, 190; *Legatio* 306; cf. *Mos* 1.149.
[114] *Mos* 2.193–96; *Jos* 254; *Flacc* 17, 29 etc. On Philo's identification of himself as 'Greek' rather than 'Egyptian' see Goudriaan 1992:79–86.
[115] Theatres: *Agr* 35; clubs: *Ebr* 20–23; *Flacc* 4, 136.
[116] *Mos* 2.23–24; *Spec Leg* 1.192–93; *Cher* 91–97.

the moral high ground in restraint of pleasure and adherence to the laws of 'nature'.[117] Philo is aware that in these and other matters the peculiarity of Jewish customs brings unpopularity and a reputation for anti-social behaviour (*Virt* 34, 141). Like an orphan among the nations, he writes, the Jewish people have no friends: their exceptional laws demand the highest virtue, an austere standard which is anathema to the pleasure-loving mass of men (*Spec Leg* 4.179–81). The latter, one imagines, would hardly appreciate his slightly priggish tone.

It is a matter of pride for Philo that among the Jews virtue is not the concern only of a few, but is taught to people of every age and class (*Deus* 146–48). In this democratization of virtue the synagogue plays a key role. Here Jews of all types use their leisure to study 'philosophy' and to learn the rules of right conduct; such 'schools of virtue' justify the Sabbath rest and distinguish the Jews as a supremely educated and philosophical nation.[118] By contrast, Greek education is debased by its mythology: impressionable children brought up on immoral tales can hardly be expected to love the truth or follow the path of virtue.[119] Thus any who join the Jewish community as proselytes have a lot of nonsense to unlearn. As 'refugees to piety' they have to abandon their false beliefs and refit their lives in accordance with virtue.[120] Ultimately, then, the Jewish 'polity' is *sans pareil.* One day, Philo hopes, when the fortunes of the Jewish nation are restored, other nations will abandon their customs and adopt the laws of the Jews: 'for when the laws shine brightly with the prosperity of the nation, they will obscure the light of others, as the risen sun obscures the stars' (*Mos* 2.44).[121]

### 6.5.5 Philo and the Jewish Community

Thus, however broad his intellectual horizons, Philo's philosophy is harnessed to the interests of the Jewish nation. His norms and values are the common coinage of Hellenism: an admirable *paideia*, a life of piety and the pursuit of virtue in accordance with nature. But for Philo nowhere are such norms attained or such values

---

[117] Homosexuality as 'unnatural': *Abr* 135–37; *Spec Leg* 3.37–42; *Vit Cont* 59–62. Sexual morality in general: *Jos* 42–45 and *Spec Leg* 3.7–82.

[118] *Decal* 96–101; *Mos* 2.209–16; *Spec Leg* 2.61–63; *Hyp* 7.10–14.

[119] *Post* 165; *Mos* 1.3; *Spec Leg* 1.28–31, 53.

[120] *Spec Leg* 1.51–53, 309; *Virt* 102–4, 175–86, 212–22.

[121] In *Praem* 162–70 the future restoration of the nation is spelled out further in a rare but significant eschatological vision; cf. *Quaest Exod* 2.76.

cherished as among the Jews, where they are to be found embedded in their sacred text and practised in their ancestral customs. Whatever his reclusive tendencies, and however risky his allegorical method, Philo remained a philosopher in and for the Jewish community.

Nowhere is this made clearer than in a famous passage, *Mig Abr* 89–93, where Philo castigates the Jewish allegorists who regard the allegorical sense as the only proper meaning of the law and its literal observance as unnecessary (see above, chapter 5.1). Philo's response is fascinating, not least because he employs arguments which stand in tension with his own philosophical stance and allegorical method. In their concentration on invisible realities, he claims, they have neglected the proper concern with the visible. 'In fact, as if they lived on their own in the desert, or had become disembodied souls, and knew no city or village or home or any company of people at all, they overlook the opinions of the masses (οἱ πολλοί) and search out truth in its naked abstraction' (*Migr Abr* 90). Such people should have been taught by the sacred word to abandon none of the customs fixed by 'divinely empowered men of old'. While the laws have allegorical meanings, their literal observance is not to be abandoned: 'We should think of the literal observance as like the body, and the allegorical meaning as the soul: just as we ought to take care of the body, since it is the home of the soul, so we ought to pay heed to the letter of the law' (*Migr Abr* 93). In this way, he concludes, we will avoid blame and the accusations of the masses.

Hard as it is to credit, this is the same man who elsewhere denigrates the literal meaning of the text and consistently subordinates the visible to the invisible. This is the same Philo who elsewhere wishes *he* could be alone in some lonely spot away from the city, who considers the body an unwelcome tomb of the soul and who urges the importance of living for the soul rather than the body. And this man who here seems so concerned with the opinion of the masses elsewhere cultivates a lofty disdain of his social inferiors and ridicules the worldly man's concern for reputation.[122]

In combating these allegorists, Philo combats a large part of himself and thereby lays bare the tensions inherent in his own life.[123] The tendencies in his own philosophy towards the solitary

---

[122] Note, from this very treatise, *Mig Abr* 9–11, 106–8!
[123] Cf. Sandmel 1956:198 and D. Schwartz 1992:16–18.

search for universal truth are here opposed by the countervailing force of the community and its historical traditions. Philo's anxiety to preserve a good reputation and his profound respect for the customs fixed of old reveal a man whose identity is ultimately defined by the community to which he belongs. The parallels he draws between the bodiless soul and the isolated individual suggest a far-reaching correlation between body and society. Just as he recognizes a necessary role for the body in sustaining the soul, so Philo accepts the social requirements of his Judaism and the dangers inherent in his own allegorical programme. If soul and body live in a necessary symbiosis, so must philosophy and community. If Philo draws back from his ideal of the self-sufficient solitary, it is because all his instincts draw him to a social commitment where his virtues, though vulnerable, are embodied in social reality.[124]

Ironically, it was by committing himself to the instability of community affairs that Philo made his most lasting contribution to the Jewish people. His appointment at the head of the Jewish delegation in 38/39 CE suggests a previous period of experience in political affairs; indeed the rueful reference to submersion in political concerns in *Spec Leg* 3.1–6 indicates not a recent but a long-past alteration in his life-style (Goodenough 1926). It is likely that Philo took a regular place among those 'of special experience' who taught in the synagogue, Sabbath by Sabbath, and it is possible that he also had some judicial functions within the community. Certainly, at an (undatable) moment when there arose a challenge to the observance of the Sabbath, Philo was prominent in the defence. *Somn* 2.123–32 refers to an attempt by a governor of Egypt to pressurize the Jews to perform political services on the Sabbath – for Philo, the thin end of a wedge liable to cause the total dissolution of Jewish life. He personally witnessed the governor's exasperation on this matter (*Somn* 2.124–29), and appears to have undertaken some representative role for the community. This was certainly the case in the crisis of 38 CE. Here we find Philo dealing directly with Flaccus and drawing up a document for Gaius setting out the complaints and claims of the Alexandrian Jews.[125] Thus it

---

[124] Cf. *Ebr* 80–87 and *Fug* 25–38. The social and political constraints on Philo's philosophy are well observed by Goodenough 1938:68–83; Borgen 1965 (and many subsequent essays); and Dawson 1992:106–26.

[125] *Flacc* 97–98, 103; *Legatio* 178–79.

seems to have been natural to appoint him as leader of the five-man delegation sent to argue their case directly with the emperor (*Legatio* 370).

It would be natural to assume that the Alexandrian pogrom and the humiliations endured by the delegation in Rome had a profound effect on Philo. That assumption may indeeed be correct, though our inability to date Philo's treatises confounds attempts to trace developments in his thought.[126] In any case, the man who writes the treatises *In Flaccum* and *De Legatione ad Gaium* has become forever suspicious of the Alexandrian society in which he once moved with such confidence. 'Former friends' have proved to be deadly enemies, 'Alexandrian' has become a term of abuse, and the once frequented theatre is now tainted with the memory of the Jews' appalling sufferings.[127] Such violence has bound Philo's sympathies to all the disparate elements in the Jewish community, and the threat to the temple which emerged while he was in Italy has laid upon him a sense of responsibility for all Jews everywhere.[128] In the historical treatises, the God who watches over human affairs operates his providence specifically for Jews, and those who dare to damage them meet their nemesis in a punishment described in gruesome detail.[129]

Thus the moments when Philo steps forward onto the stage of history display the social and political commitments which were the context for all his work. Much as he might resent such 'political troubles' (*Spec Leg* 3.3), Philo's soul needed a 'body politic' as much as it needed its physical equivalent. In subsequent generations, Philo's allegories ceased to be of interest to Alexandrian Jews who were thrown into cultural and political retreat. They were adopted with enthusiasm only by Christians

---

[126] It is possible that Philo returned to allegorical and general philosophical study after the mission to Rome, though Terian's suggestion (1981:28–34) that most of Philo's work comes from this twilight period is incredible (his dating of *Anim* rests precariously on an uncertain reading of *Anim* 2 and 54).

[127] *Flacc* 62 (former friends); *Legatio* 120, 162–65 (the Alexandrian character); *Flacc* 73–77, 84–85, 95–96 (the events in the theatre).

[128] *Legatio* 184–94, 281–84, 330. Note the references to τὸ Ἰουδαϊκόν (184) and ἡ καθολικωτέρα πολιτεία (194).

[129] God's special providence for Jews: *Flacc* 121, 170, 191; *Legatio* 3, 196, 220, 336–37. Flaccus' fall, exile and death are described with rhetorical glee, occupying nearly one half of *In Flaccum*; and it appears that a similarly vindictive account of the fall of Gaius originally stood at the end of *Legatio*.

who could further deJudaize his universalist interpretation of the Jewish scriptures. But in their original context they expressed the dual commitments of a man whose integration of Judaism into Hellenistic culture was exceptionally profound, but who ultimately turned that synthesis to the advantage and defence of the Jewish community.

# 7

## *Cultural Antagonism*

Our rich supply of literature from the Egyptian Diaspora enables us to place alongside the examples of cultural convergence discussed above a number of documents whose socio-cultural stance is predominantly oppositional and antagonistic. There are elements of cultural antagonism in some of the literature discussed in the preceding chapter: it was partly on that basis that their authors distinguished the Jewish tradition from its cultural environment. But in the literature we will now review antagonism has become the dominant and determinative characteristic. It is worth stressing again that this does not imply a lack of Hellenization in the sense of 'acculturation' (see chapter 4). Some of the authors whose works we will here discuss were clearly familiar with Greek literature and equipped with well-developed rhetorical skills. But our focus here is on their *use* of such acculturation, in particular the posture they adopt in depicting the relationship between Judaism and its social, political and cultural environment. In the four cases we will examine in this chapter, the prevailing ethos can be shown to be antagonistic, with non-Jews presented mainly in the guise of 'enemies', 'aliens' or 'fools'. Although our first case, *The Wisdom of Solomon*, is slightly ambiguous in this regard, in general it can be shown that all the following documents are marked by such an aggressive stance.

## 7.1 The Wisdom of Solomon

*The Wisdom of Solomon* is in many respects an elusive document, hard to categorize and difficult to place in a historical context.[1]

---

[1]   On the date see the Appendix on Sources. For the reasons advanced there, I would favour a date in the period covering the end of the Ptolemaic era and the beginning of the Roman (100 BCE – 30 CE).

Such difficulties are due in part to its variegated contents and styles. Its first section (1.1 – 6.11) begins and ends with a warning to 'rulers' concerning just conduct, but its central focus is on the plight of the righteous. The latter are shown tormented by irreligious opponents but ultimately vindicated in the judgment of God and rewarded with immortality. This theodicy gives way to a rhetorical depiction of Wisdom, the ultimate gift of God (6.12 – 9.18). Adopting the persona of Solomon, the author praises Wisdom's many attributes and offers a humble prayer for God's bestowal of her benefits. In a transitional passage, he gives a list of biblical figures saved by Wisdom, climaxing in the story of the Exodus (10.1–21). The second half of the book (chapters 11–19) gives an extended commentary on incidents in the Exodus, using the pattern of *syncresis* (comparison) to contrast the misfortunes of the Egyptians with the deliverance of God's people. This long section is interrupted near its start by two important digressions, one on the character of God's justice (11.22 – 12.27), the other on the follies of non-Jewish worship (nature worship, idolatry and animal cults, 13.1 – 15.19).[2] In this second half the figure of Wisdom drops from view almost completely and the 'Solomonic' speaker gives way to a confessional 'we'.

Such diversity has led, not surprisingly, to much source-critical speculation and many theories of multiple authorship. The scholarly pendulum has swung to and fro on this issue, but the current consensus, for what it is worth, strongly favours the unity of the work.[3] Despite the uncertainty in this matter, it is safest to analyse the work in its final form, whether its present unity be as originally conceived or as imposed by a compiler or redactor.

---

[2]    The precise division into sections varies to an insignificant degree between different interpreters, chiefly at the transition points (e.g. whether chapter 6, in whole or in part, belongs to the first or second section; whether chapter 10 is the conclusion of the book of Wisdom or the opening of the narrative section). For discussion see Reese 1965, Wright 1967, Winston 1979:9–12 and Kolarcik 1991:1–62. On the diverse literary genres in this work see Reese 1970:90–121.

[3]    Grimm's magnificent commentary (1860) put paid to earlier theories of multiple authorship, but only for a while. The early twentieth century saw a plethora of such theories, but these are now widely considered passé; see e.g. Winston 1979:12–14, Reese 1970:122–45 and Larcher 1983:1.95–119. There have been several suggestions as to the Hebrew (or Aramaic) origin of the early chapters, but none has won substantial support. Georgi, observing both stylistic unity and theological inconsistency, suggests that the work is the product of a school which developed over time (1980:392–94).

My inclusion of this document in the category of 'Cultural Antagonism' may occasion some surprise. It is common to find *Wisdom* cited as an example of the profound Hellenization of Diaspora Jews and their openness to the cultural values of their environment. Its sophisticated vocabulary and its developed rhetorical features are certainly the fruits of a thorough-going Greek education.[4] In his theological concepts, especially in his anthropology and belief in immortality, our author was clearly influenced by Hellenistic philosophy.[5] Moreover, in his encomium of Wisdom, he emphasizes her availability to all: 'she is easily observed by those who love her, and is found by those who seek her' (6.12; cf. 1.1–2; 6.21–23). He also describes her attributes in universal terms. The knowledge she provides encompasses the whole gamut of science (7.17–22); in her range she is limited to no single nation but covers the whole world, and orders all things well (8.1). Thus 'in every generation she enters into holy souls and renders them friends of God and prophets' (7.27), while 'a multitude of wise men is the salvation of the world' (6.24). There is nothing in this 'book of Wisdom' (6.12 – 9.18) which identifies 'Wisdom' with the law or the Jewish people, and even the Jewish identity of the king seems strangely muted, despite the references to people and temple (9.7–8).

Indeed, one of the distinctive features of *Wisdom* is its disinclination to name any of the characters in its story. Even the biblical heroes in 10.1–21 remain anonymous, although identifiable from Scripture, and at no point does the author identify himself, or 'God's children', as Jewish. It is possible to interpret this phenomenon as a deliberate abstention from ethnic labels in the interests of a universal typology of 'the just' and 'the unjust'. Thus Collins suggests that 'the history of Israel provides a paradigmatic example of the experience of righteous individuals or a righteous people but is only an illustration of the workings of the universe … the primary distinction is not between Israel and the gentiles, but between the righteous and the wicked. While Israel is presented as the paradigm of the righteous, it is not necessarily an exclusive

---

[4] See especially Reese 1970:1–31, on the Hellenistic vocabulary and style. The highly-wrought depiction of the Egyptians' fear (17.3–20) is a good example of the author's rhetorical skills and his interest in psychology.

[5] See Reese 1970:32–89 and Larcher 1969:179–327.

paradigm.'[6] Moreover, there is a heavy emphasis in this work on God's *universal* providence and mercy. The repeated stress on God's care for his whole creation (1.13–14; 6.7; 9.1–3 etc.) comes to its climactic expression in the following address to God:

> For you are merciful to all, because you are all-powerful,
> and you overlook the sins of humanity, to lead them to repentance.
> You love everything in existence,
> and you loathe nothing of what you have made...
> You spare everything because they are yours, O Lord, lover of life;
> for your immortal spirit is in all things. (11.23 – 12.1)

Despite such a strong universalist strand, I have been driven to conclude that the predominant theme in *The Wisdom of Solomon* is in fact the social conflict and cultural antagonism between Jews and non-Jews. The extent of the author's linguistic and educational Hellenization is certainly striking, but it is necessary to observe the uses to which that training is put and the interests it is made to serve. As we shall see, the author of *Wisdom* employs his considerable learning not to integrate his Judaism with his environment but to construct all the more sophisticated an attack upon it! While recognizing the universalist tendencies in 'the book of Wisdom', I consider that its present context in this complex (and possibly composite) document drowns its integrative potential in a sea of polemic. It is above all the prominence of 'enemies' and the pervasive emphasis on conflict which incline me to interpret *Wisdom* as an educated and deeply Hellenized exercise in cultural aggression.

1. The opening section of the book (1.1 – 6.11) is flanked by addresses to 'rulers of the earth', but its appeal to adopt the path to wisdom is dominated by warnings of judgment. Although God may be found by those who do not put him to the test (1.2), he also readily convicts the foolish (1.3). Wisdom is a 'kindly spirit' (φιλάνθρωπον πνεῦμα, 1.6) which fills the world, but her chief work here is to observe and convict the blasphemer (1.6–11). Although death is not the design of God, it is the necessary result of ungodliness (1.12–16). Thus kings should be warned that God is

---

[6] Collins 1986:185; cf. Reese 1970:76, 119, 158 on the heroes of biblical history as 'types' of the saved.

watching all they do: his universal providence (προνοεῖ περὶ πάντων, 6.7) means in particular his vindication of the lowly from the injustices of their rulers (6.4–11).

The vindication of the oppressed is, in fact, the central topic of these opening chapters. The author paints a vivid portrait of the ungodly, whose materialistic world-view makes them disregard the possibility of life beyond death, while they viciously abuse, torture and even kill the righteous (2.1–11, 19–20; cf. 5.1). By vivid caricatures of their shallow reasoning and moral indifference, the author depicts a sharply polarized society where 'righteous' and 'ungodly' stand opposed in straightforward antagonism. His chief purpose is to give comfort and encouragement to the oppressed. Immortality is promised as the just reward to those thus persecuted (2.21 – 3.4) and their vindication before God is described at length (3.1–9; 5.15–16). Those who, through lack of children or brevity of life, might seem to have missed the common blessings of life are given particular encouragment (3.13 – 4.15).[7] Conversely, our author predicts the uselessness of the children of the ungodly, and pours venom into his depiction of their end (4.18 – 5.14). The cameo finishes with a frightening vision of God's armed and wrathful assault on his enemies (5.17–23).[8]

There is no explicit identification of the characters in this shocking drama. Like the lament psalms, from which he draws much inspiration, the author is content to depict them in general terms. The oppressed are 'the righteous' (2.10, 12, 16 etc.), 'the holy ones' (4.15; 5.5), 'the elect' (3.9; 4.15) and 'the children of God' (2.13, 18; 5.5). It is only the religious and social context of his audience, and the re-use of such terms in the later description of the Exodus, which will make clear his primary reference to contemporary Jews. Nonetheless, there are already some clues in these opening chapters to the issues on which this conflict arises. When the ungodly complain that the righteous man 'reproaches us for sins against the law (νόμος) and accuses us of sins against our training' (παιδεία, 2.12), it is possible to hear specifically Jewish charges. Moreover, the ungodly find the righteous man's manner

---

[7] The note of compensation here is unmistakable. Those who die young are comforted with the example of Enoch, as one snatched from life to avoid the pollutions of sin (4.7–15); the author omits to mention that Enoch was already 365 years old at the time of his removal (Gen 5.23)!

[8] For a detailed analysis of the flow of thought in these chapters see Kolarcik 1991:63–131.

of life strange (ἀνόμοιος), and object that he considers their ways unclean (ἀκαθαρσία, 2.15–16). Admittedly it is difficult to extract from this welter of polemic any clear profile of the social tensions here dramatized. But in the context of the whole work, and the later identification of the author with 'the people of God', there is good reason to see in these opening chapters a reflection of conflict between Jews and non-Jews.[9]

2. After the 'book of Wisdom' (6.12 – 9.18) and the transitional survey of biblical characters who were saved by Wisdom (10.1–21), the rest of *The Wisdom of Solomon* is devoted to a lengthy meditation on the salvation of God's people in the Exodus (chapters 11–19). Before examining the main contours of this meditation, we can consider first the long excursus on aberrant forms of worship which takes up all of chapters 13–15. Strictly speaking, little of this passage is relevant to its context. The author is contrasting the deliverance of the Jews with the punishment of the Egyptians, and he notes the particularly apposite form of their punishment by means of the very animals they foolishly worshipped as Gods (12.23–27). This reference to the false attribution of divinity acts as the trigger for a wide-ranging attack on all forms of 'false' religion, most of it with no explicit reference to the Egyptians at all. It is as if the author cannot resist the temptation to let loose the most devastating broadside he can direct against non-Jewish religion. In the event he composes one of the most sustained attacks on Gentile religiosity which we have from the pen of a Diaspora Jew.[10]

The excursus is divided into three sections, dealing with three types of error. In the first (13.1–9) the author attacks the folly and ignorance of those whose worship is directed to the physical elements – fire, wind, air, the stars, etc. – rather than to the One who created them. Whatever forms of religion he has in mind here,[11] he considers this a failure of intelligence: 'they lacked the

---

[9] On the possibility that the party of oppressors might also include disaffected Jews, see above, chapter 5.1.

[10] For a detailed analysis of these chapters see Gilbert 1973. The closest parallel is Philo's comment on the first two commandments, *Decal* 52–81; the similar treatment of types of religion in the same order might indicate a common source or tradition.

[11] See Reese 1970:52–62, Gilbert 1973:1–52 and the commentaries of Winston 1979 and Larcher 1983 ad loc. Philo identifies the elements with the Greek pantheon (the air = Hera; the sun = Apollo; the sea = Poseidon etc.), *Decal* 53–55.

ability to know the Existent One from the good things which they saw' (13.1). The Greek argument from analogy (from the beauty and power of the world to the beauty and power of God) is used against all who settle for less than the pure worship of the transcendent God. For a moment he hesitates in his judgment: 'yet little blame is to be attached to such people, for perhaps they go astray while seeking God and desiring to find him' (13.6). But he soon recovers his confidence: 'yet again, not even they can be excused; for if they had the ability to know so much that they could infer the universe, how did they not sooner find the Lord of these things?' (13.8–9).

When he turns to the second category, idolatry (13.10 – 15.17), there is not a moment's hesitation in the powerful flow of rhetoric. 'Miserable, with their hopes set on dead things, are those who call "Gods" the works of human hands' (13.10). The author thinks he knows the origin of such folly – in the sorrow of a grieving parent who makes an image of the child he lost, or the concern of subjects to flatter their monarch by constructing a beautiful statue (14.12–21). Yet this neither excuses the idolatry nor diminishes its damaging effect. The author is confident that the invention of idols is the root of immorality (14.12), a claim which he expands in a list of moral and social corruption, especially in the sphere of sex (14.22–31). The diagnosis is simple enough: 'the worship of unmentionable idols is the beginning, the cause and the end of every evil' (14.27). He thus feels justified in launching a withering attack on all engaged in the manufacture of objects of worship, whether they work in wood (13.11 – 14.7) or clay (15.7–17). In an outburst of invective of which Deutero-Isaiah would have been proud, he lavishes scorn on the fools who imagine that the wood they carve can respond to prayer, or the clay they fashion can save in its lifeless form. The rhetoric depends, of course, on a crude caricature of non-Jewish religion, but the author is confident that 'the impious man and his impiety are equally hateful to God' (14.8–9).

The third section of the excursus (15.18–19), with which the author returns to the flow of his meditation on the Exodus, concerns the Egyptian worship of animals. Where Aristeas' comments had been brief and dismissive (*Letter of Aristeas* 138), *Wisdom* engages in repeated snipes on this topic (11.15–20; 12.23–27; 15.18–19) with the claim that the punishment of the Egyptians by animal plagues was a suitable judgment for their animal cults: it was fitting that God should torture them with their own abominations (12.23)![12] To worship any animal is, he considers, the height of folly (12.24–25), but he judges the Egyptian animal deities particularly lacking in intelligence and beauty: they are in fact the very creatures which the Creator omitted to bless (15.19)!

Inserted into this long and hostile excursus is a paragraph depicting the distinction of the Jews (15.1–6):

> But you, our God, are kind and true,
> longsuffering and governing all things with mercy.
> For even if we sin, we are yours, since we know your power;
> but we will not sin, since we know that we are accounted yours.
> For to know you is the sum of righteousness,
> to recognize your power is the root of immortality.
> For the evil inventions of human art have not deceived us,
> nor the sterile labour of painters ... (15.1–4)

Here the Jews' true knowledge of God is contrasted with the culpable ignorance of the worshippers of nature, while Jewish abstention from representation of God is taken to signal their freedom from idolatrous delusion. With such superior piety, they are marked out as God's own people, entitled to consider God in a special sense as *theirs*.

3. This emphasis on Israel's privileged status, amplified by a catalogue of her enemies' punishments, is the most prominent feature of the depiction of the Exodus in chapters 11–19. While here also the allusive style continues, and there is no explicit reference to 'Jews', the narrative presupposes a detailed knowledge of the biblical account, leaving its implied reader/hearer in no doubt as to the characters involved. Adopting from 10.15 the depiction of Israel as a 'holy people and a blameless race', this narrative is replete with references to 'God's people' (12.19; 16.2, 20; 18.7 etc.) and the 'holy nation' (17.2). With frequent reference to the 'covenants' and 'promises' (12.21; 18.6, 22), Israel's special relationship to God is underlined (cf. 15.1–4). The author also adopts a confessional stance, turning the narrative into direct address to God (from 10.20 onwards) and identifying himself with the story through reference to 'our fathers' (12.6; 18.6 etc.) or

---

[12]  The claim depends on the vagueness of the assertion. There is no evidence that any of the animals mentioned in the Exodus plagues (locusts, frogs, flies, gnats) were reverenced as Gods in Egypt.

simply 'us' (12.22; 15.2 etc.). Adopting the labels employed in the first section of the book, he now makes unambiguously clear whom he has in mind as 'the righteous' (10.20; 11.14; 12.9 etc.), 'the holy ones' (10.17; 18.1, 9 etc.) and 'the children of God' (12.19–21; 16.10, 21 etc.). He fittingly closes the book with a confession of praise:

> For in everything, O Lord, you have exalted your people and given them glory, and you did not neglect to assist them in every time and place. (19.22)

Throughout this section of *Wisdom*, 'God's people' stand in contrast to 'the foolish', 'the ungodly', 'the unrighteous' and 'the wicked'. More particularly, and in structural parallel to the opening chapters, they are opposed by 'enemies' and 'foes' (11.3, 5, 8; 12.20, 22 etc.), now explicitly identified as 'ours' (12.22). The specific charges against them are vague (10.15; 15.14; 17.2; 18.2; 19.13–16), but the structuring of the social world into simple oppositions is unmistakably clear. The author identifies himself and his readers/ hearers with a persecuted people, a nation delivered from implacable enemies by divine power. The conflictual tone of the Exodus stories both matches and shapes his perception of social relations between Jews and Gentiles.[13]

It is generally acknowledged that the narrative units in chapters 11–19 are structured by seven comparisons, in each of which God's punishment of his enemies is paired with some aspect of his deliverance of his people.[14] The author spares no detail in depicting the awesome effects of God's punishments, and frequently refers to the collaboration of nature in this battle against the unrighteous (16.24–25; 19.6 etc.). Not that he does not feel the need to justify God's actions in this story. He insists on several occasions that the punishment of the Egyptians precisely fitted their crimes,[15] even

---

[13] The Exodus stories obviously concerned only the Egyptians, but our author widens his attack to 'the nations' (τὰ ἔθνη) in general (12.12; 14.11; 15.15).

[14] 1. The pollution of the Nile but the provision of water in the desert (11.1–14). 2. Animals bring hunger to Egypt but quails feed Israel (16.1–4). 3. Incurable plagues in Egypt but deliverance from serpents in the desert (16.5–14). 4. Hail and fire on Egypt but manna from heaven for Israel (16.15–29). 5. Terrifying darkness in Egypt but the pillar of fire for God's people (17.1 – 18.4). 6. The plague of death in Egypt but the stemming of the plague in the desert (18.5–25). 7. Death for Egyptians at the Red Sea but deliverance for Jews (19.1–12).

[15] E.g. the impiety of animal worship is punished with animal plagues (11.15–20); the imprisonment of Israel is punished with imprisonment in darkness (18.4); the slaughter of Israel's sons is punished with the death of Egypt's first-born (18.5).

that they were punished by the very instruments of their sin (11.16), and he affirms that God's justice is always proportionate and fair (11.20). These statements open the important digression on the justice of God (11.21 – 12.22) in which the author stresses God's merciful nature, his love for all creation and his provision of time for sinners to repent. He insists that God is righteous and rules justly, and that those on whom his wrath descends are entirely *deserving* of their fate.[16] However, this digression, in which so many 'universalist' statements are to be found, is introduced not to modify God's judgment but precisely to justify its operation.

It thus emerges with unmistakable clarity that God's favour rests preferentially on his people. While he may be described as 'Saviour of all' (16.7), it is his own children whom he saves while punishing their enemies (16.5–14). His nature is all-merciful (11.23), but the ungodly can only experience his 'merciless anger' (19.1). While disciplining his children, he scourges their enemies ten thousand times more (12.20–22). Of course there are good reasons offered for such preferential treatment. The culpable ignorance of nature-worship and the folly of idolatry cannot but invite the wrath of God, while the pure piety of Israel guarantees her status as God's own people (15.1–4). Yet the author displays little openness of spirit towards his religious environment. The anonymity of the characters is not designed to establish a broad typology capable of including the righteous of all nations. It is a stylistic and rhetorical device, in the Alexandrian tradition of literary allusion; the biblically informed audience will know well enough to whom 'God's people' refers.[17]

Since such conflictual and antagonistic passages form the beginning and end of *The Wisdom of Solomon* in its present form, I understand its primary tone as one of cultural antagonism. In this context, the potential of a more integrated cultural vision suggested by 'the book of Wisdom' (6.12 – 9.18) is never fulfilled. Indeed, in their present literary context, the darker notes in that passage concerning the worthlessness of the foolish (7.28; 9.6) take on

---

[16] Note the stress on 'desert' in 1.16; 12.15, 20, 26; 16.1, 9 etc. The digression on God's justice (11.21 – 12.22) is aided by the choice of an extreme example, the purported practice of human sacrifice by the 'accursed' Canaanites (12.3–11).

[17] On Alexandrian allusiveness, see Winston 1979:139–40. For a contrary view, see Ziener 1956:94–97 and Collins 1986:182–87.

fuller and more threatening meaning. It is noticeable that the transitional survey of biblical characters in 10.1–21 depicts the role of Wisdom in *rescuing* the righteous from an evil world. It thus appears that the author's undoubted acculturation – his linguistic, literary and rhetorical training – is enlisted in the service of a vigorous defence of Jewish particularity.[18] In contrast to the generally eirenic stance of *Aristeas* and the universal typologies of Philo's allegories, *The Wisdom of Solomon* fosters a cultural antagonism in which Jews under stress are encouraged to trust that God will vindicate their righteousness and confound their enemies.

The tone of this work fits well its likely dating (on a range of criteria) in the late Ptolemaic or early Roman era (see Appendix). Particularly revealing is the reference in 19.13–16 to Egyptian hostility to strangers (μισοξενία) and her cruel treatment of 'those who had already come to share the same rights' (τοὺς ἤδη τῶν αὐτῶν μετεσχηκότας δικαίων, 19.16). As we have seen, there is evidence for a rise in ethnic tensions towards the end of the Ptolemaic era (chapter 2.2), and the Roman system of taxation heightened conflicts about Jewish political rights (chapter 3.1). The generalized accounts of conflict in this document do not allow us to discern any particular outbreak of violence, but they seem to represent a mood of antagonism, even among Hellenized Jews, which is fully understandable in that historical context. With Scriptural resources from the story of the Exodus, the author holds firmly to 'the light of the law' (18.4) in a world darkened by impiety. He reaffirms his faith in the God who rewards the righteous and vindicates his people through whatever afflictions they endure. His passionate invective against Gentile religion and his strong affirmation of the Jews' identity as the people of God might have played a significant role in enabling the Jewish community to hold steady in such difficult days.[19]

---

[18] If, as many suggest, the depiction of Wisdom in 7.22ff. is dependent on contemporary patterns of Isis-hymnology, our author appropriates this genre while roundly condemning all Isis worship (chapters 13–15). Focke 1913:92–95 underlines the limits of the author's Hellenization.

[19] As Reese notes (1970:146–51), the work makes best sense as directed to educated Jews who were able to identify the biblical allusions in the text. But I doubt that the author intended them 'to incorporate good qualities of pagan culture into their lives' or 'to develop a positive attitude towards their actual situation' (147–48). The aim of encouragement of embattled Jews is better appreciated by Grimm 1860:27–35, Winston 1979:63–64 and Larcher 1983:1.114–19.

## 7.2   3 Maccabees

The lively narrative known (incongruously) as 3 Maccabees is one of the texts most accessible to our form of analysis. Its detailed depiction of relations between Jews and Gentiles, its range of vocabulary in describing both groups and its theological interpretation of their destinies provide a full body of data for the assessment of its social and cultural stance. The story it tells is so evidently fictional as to render it comparatively easy to detect here the fears and aspirations of its Jewish author. Some of the texts we have considered thus far have had to be scrutinized with some subtlety to uncover their social intentions. This one wears its strategy on its sleeve.

Our narrative purports to give an historical account of certain incidents in the life of Ptolemy IV Philopator (220–205 BCE). From the start, however, its rhetorical tone indicates the author's primary interest in drama, pathos and religious propaganda. Victorious at the battle of Raphia, Philopator visits nearby cities and temples to offer sacrifice (1.1–7). The friendly reception of the Jews at Jerusalem is soon turned into crisis as the king persistently demands entry into the Holy of Holies. In a highly-wrought depiction of distress, with brides rushing out of their chambers and mothers abandoning their infants in the streets, the whole of Jerusalem is shown in uproar at the king's profane intent (1.8–29). With the readers brought to this emotional pitch, the narrator records a long prayer by the High Priest Simon, which recalls God's previous acts of redemption and pleads now for rescue from the defilement of arrogant men (2.1–20). In response to such entreaty, God paralyses the king at the moment when he strides towards the sanctuary (2.21–24).

However, such 'just judgment' (2.22) serves only to goad the king into revenge. The Jerusalem crisis is merely the prelude to a plot which threatens all Jews in Egypt, and the narrative now begins its long ascent to a peak of terror. On his return to Egypt the king issues a decree demanding that all Jews offer sacrifice, also branding them with the emblem of Dionysus and reducing them to a condition of slavery. The only alternative is to become initiates in 'the mysteries' with rights as Alexandrian citizens (2.25–30). Since only a few Jews commit such 'apostasy' (2.31–33), the king, furious at his lack of success, orders a round-up of all Egyptian Jews to inflict upon them 'the worst form of death' (3.1). Here the narrator creates an early frisson of horror, but skilfully employs three and a half more chapters revealing its grotesque dimensions. First the popular slanders against the Jews are described (3.2–10), then the king's vicious misrepresentation of events in a letter to his administrators (3.11–30). His harsh tone is matched by the violent and gleeful arrest of the Jews by a hostile population (4.1). With images frighteningly reminiscent of our own century, the author describes the Jews being packed into transport with the utmost cruelty and dispatched to concentration conditions in the Alexandrian hippodrome, there to await an unknown fate (4.1–11). With totalitarian thoroughness, the king orders all Jews to be registered for death, the monstrosity of his aim underscored by the lack of papyrus and pens to fill out the death lists (4.12–21).

It is only now revealed how the Jews' execution is to be conducted: through the intoxication of elephants set to trample them all to death (5.1–2). Once again, however, the narrator uses suspense to great effect. As the elephants are prepared for their task, and the Jews cry out tearfully to God, the king oversleeps and the massacre is postponed (5.1–17). The next day, the elephants are led out in battle array and the crowd gathers expectantly, but the king is struck with amnesia by the all-powerful God and the dénouement is again delayed (5.18–35). Finally, at the climax of this narrative tricolon, the beasts are raised to a frenzy of madness and the king's army advances towards the hippodrome (5.36–47). As the Jews bid one another their tearful farewells, a priest called Eleazar leads the victims in prayer (6.1–15). Like Simon's prayer in Jerusalem (2.1–20), this lengthy petition not only heightens the suspense but clarifies the terms on which God will intervene: he is called to demonstrate his power in defence of his 'elect nation' under threat from the 'impious Gentiles'. Then, just as the elephants enter the hippodrome, 'the most glorious, almighty and true God' sends two angels to terrify the enemies of the Jews; the army is scattered in confusion, trampled to death by their own frenzied beasts, who turn back on those who urge them forward (6.16–20).

After such a miraculous rescue, it only remains to rectify the wrongs suffered by the Jews. Shifting the blame onto his advisers, the king orders the Jews' release, makes all necessary provision for a feast at the site of their intended execution, and writes another letter which mirrors and cancels his first (6.21 – 7.9). For the Jews, after joyfully disposing of three hundred apostates, all is feasting and celebration as they return to their homes, treated with new respect even by their enemies (7.10–22). The theme of the narrative is appropriately summarized in the closing ascription of praise: 'Blessed be the deliverer of Israel for ever and ever! Amen' (7.23).

It should be evident even from this synopsis – as it certainly is to any reader of the text – that this narrative is chiefly shaped by theology and rhetorical invention. To be sure, it is possible at various points to detect the impress of historical events. The description of the battle of Raphia in chapter 1 resembles that of Polybius in certain details, and we know from papyri of a Dositheos, son of Drimylus in the king's employ (1.3; *CPJ* 127; see above, chapter 5.1). There is also some evidence that Philopator was a devotee of Dionysus, and issued decrees to regulate and promote his cult.[20] The story of the elephants has a well-known parallel in Josephus, *C Ap* 2.51–55, where the Jews of Alexandria are condemned to be trampled by drunken elephants – a plan which backfired with the king himself subject to a 'terrible apparition'. Josephus, however, places this story in the reign of Ptolemy Physcon (Euergetes II), where, as we have seen, its historical origins more likely belong (above, chapter 2.2.1). Both Josephus (*C Ap* 2.55) and 3 Maccabees (6.38–40) connect the event to a Jewish festival, and it is easy to conceive how similar but not identical legends could be passed down in the Jewish community and how the author of 3 Maccabees could imaginatively connect them with stories he had heard about Philopator.[21]

Another topic in which 3 Maccabees might be founded on history is with regard to a 'census' or 'poll tax' (λαογραφία, 2.28). Tcherikover argued (1961b) that the author's connection of this 'census' with the choice offered to Jews between 'slavery' and 'citizenship' reflects the introduction in 24/23 BCE of the new Roman system of taxation; under this regime new fiscal distinctions caused most Jews to feel demoted in status and induced a minority to struggle to have their citizen rights confirmed (see above, chapter 3.1). The author of 3 Maccabees considers any Jews pursuing the latter option to be 'apostates', a view which we may consider somewhat partial (cf. chapter 3, Excursus and chapter 4.1).

In fact the references in 3 Maccabees to this 'census' are extraordinarily garbled. In 2.28–30 religious and political factors

---

[20] See above, p. 32. On these and other historical echoes in 3 Maccabees see Hadas 1953:16–21, Tcherikover 1961b, and Paul 1986:312–19.

[21] Josephus' account shows that he also knew of more than one version: the king's concubine is called Ithaca in some accounts and Irene in others (*C Ap* 2.55).

are mingled with such imprecision that the author appears to imagine the Dionysiac emblem as a brand signalling royal enslavement, and the offer of Alexandrian citizenship as open to Jews of all social classes.[22] Moreover, the 'registration' referred to here is soon superseded by a (curiously unnecessary) registration for execution (4.14), while 7.22 indicates yet a third type of register for the confiscation of property! One has the impression of an author stitching together legends of varied origin, creating a patchwork of events which make no historical sense in this strange amalgam.[23] The outlines and patterns of this narrative are chiefly the products of his imagination. The world which he portrays, of vulnerable Jews and implacable enemies, thus expresses his own perception of the position of Jews in an 'alien' environment.

The atmosphere which pervades this narrative is full of threat and hostility. The initial friendliness between Philopator and the Jerusalem elders (1.8) is only a foil to its subsequent rupture as the 'impious', 'brash' and 'lawless' man prepares to assault the sanctity of the temple. Simon's prayer compares the king's desire to the arrogance of the giants, the insolence of Sodom and the pride of Pharaoh (2.1–8). Together, narrative characterization and petitionary phraseology make of Philopator an ogre, who can then be suitably scourged for his monstrous pride and impudence (2.21). It is necessary for the narrative, of course, that he does not subsequently repent (2.24): instead, in a motif which will recur throughout, he breathes dire threats against the Jews. His decree against the Jews is his first act of revenge, and even the offer of citizen rights is only, the narrator insists, an attempt to cover his hostile purpose (2.30). With an explosion of anger, the 'impious man' extends his hostility to Jews in the country as well (3.1), such anger (cf. 4.13; 5.1, 30) as invites comparison with the savagery of

---

[22]　The interpretative problems of 2.28–33 are immense. All Jews have to sacrifice (to whom?) or are barred from their 'temples' (2.28; could ἱερά mean synagogues?), yet they are also brought (regardless?) εἰς λαογραφίαν καὶ οἰκετικὴν διάθεσιν (these two items somehow regarded as equivalent). How could the Jews bribe their way out of 'registration' and why does the author describe that course of action as 'fearless' (2.32)? To add to the problems, 2.31 requires textual emendation to make any sense at all!

[23]　I am largely persuaded in this matter by Tcherikover 1961b, though even more sceptical than he about the possibility of finding history in 2.28–33. Kasher's attempt (1985:211–32) to treat 3 Maccabees as an historically coherent account of conditions in the third century BCE is wholly implausible. See further Anderson 1985a:510–12.

Phalaris, the ultimate tyrant (5.20, 42; cf. 3.8; 6.24; 7.5). The more the Jews suffer, the more the king is pleased (3.11; cf. 4.16; 5.16–17, 36). His letter (3.12–29) not only distorts the 'true' account of the events in Jerusalem, but vilifies the Jews as 'accursed' and 'impious', enjoining sadistic measures for their dispatch to Alexandria.

This lurid depiction of Philopator is worthy of comparison with the greatest caricatures of Second Temple literature – the Maccabean Antiochus, Esther's Haman, and Philo's Flaccus or Gaius. Like them all, Philopator is engaged in a hopeless contest with God. Foolhardy in his ignorance of God's power (3.11), the king's misguided idolatry leads him into blasphemy of the 'God Most Great' (4.16). The reader sees with pleasure his impotence before God, who tricks him first with sleep, then with amnesia (5.1–35), before finally shaking him with terror (6.20). Yet the king is not alone in his hostile intentions against the Jews. In his court, his friends and associates share his corrupt lifestyle and his hatred of the Jews (2.25–26; 5.3, 21–22). In the country, slanders are spread by enemies of the Jews (3.2), and the king's first letter is welcomed with public feasts, the open expression of long-held hatred (4.1). The army (5.5; 6.19), the Alexandrian crowd (5.24) and the registrars (6.34) join the catalogue of hostile parties, to which the Jewish apostates too are added as 'enemies of the nation' (2.33). Thus even when the king's wrath is finally turned to pity (6.22), and his earlier orders countermanded, the hostility of others remains. The registrars groan with shame (6.34) and the enemies of the Jews now treat them with respect (7.21), but enemies they remain. The narrative ends with an enforced truce, not a genuine harmony of races.

The one exception to this portrait of social antagonism is a reference to Alexandrian 'Greeks' (οἱ κατὰ τὴν πόλιν Ἕλληνες) who are grieved at the treatment of the Jews and, as friends, neighbours and business associates, offer to give what help they can (3.8–10). The inclusion of this reference is intriguing: such 'Greeks' in fact take no further part in the narrative, and their insignificance is already suggested by notice of their powerlessness under a tyrannical regime (3.8). It is possible that this cameo reflects some historical reality, but its primary function is rhetorical. Like Philo and Josephus, though with less sophistication, the narrator seeks to ally the Jews with 'Greeks' and so to represent hostile parties as something else (Philo and Josephus would specify

'Egyptian').[24] In fact, of course, the king, the court and the higher echelons of the army and administration were all, in the Ptolemaic period, exclusively 'Greek', but it suits the author's purpose to reserve the term 'Greek' for a friendly class of people. He is conscious of accusations that Jews are 'barbarian enemies' of the state (3.24) and wants to ally them as far as possible with the cultured and right-minded people called 'Greeks'.

The reference to the 'Greeks' is thus primarily a rhetorical ploy, and one which the author cannot weave convincingly into the pattern of the plot. The primary social division depicted in the narrative is straightforwardly between Jews and 'Gentiles' (τὰ ἔθνη in the sense of 'the other nations'/'non-Jews'). When the king's orders are received, there are public feasts for 'the Gentiles' (τοῖς ἔθνεσιν) whose joy reveals their long-standing hatred of Jews (4.1). When the Jews are bound in the hippodrome, they pray for God to reveal his might to the 'proud Gentiles' who consider them defenceless (5.6, 13). This motif is central to Eleazar's prayer, where God is urged to manifest himself to 'those of the nation of Israel' who are maltreated by 'detestable and lawless Gentiles' (ὑπὸ ἐβδελυγμένων ἀνόμων ἐθνῶν, 6.9; cf. 6.13, 15; 7.4). In such phrases it becomes clear that the author's world is structured by the binary contrast of 'Jews' and 'Gentiles', whose relationship is chiefly defined by hostility.[25]

The framework within which our author places such relationships is that of competing ethnic groups. The Jews are a 'nation' (ἔθνος, 1.11; 2.27, 33), with fellow Jews defined as 'fellow nationals' (ὁμοεθνεῖς, 4.12; 7.14) and non-Jews as 'those of another nation' (ἀλλοεθνεῖς, 4.6). Jews may also be defined as a 'race' (γένος, 1.3; 3.2 ,6; 6.4, 9, 13; 7.10; φῦλον, 4.14; 5.5), with a similar distinction between those of the same racial origin (ὁμόφυλοι, 3.21) and those of another (ἀλλόφυλοι, 3.6). [26] Correspondingly, the work is full of references to 'ancestral' figures and traditions (1.23; 2.12; 6.32; 7.16), with the Jews described as 'the seed of Abraham' (6.3) and

---

[24] Cf. Philo, *Flacc* 29; *Legatio* 166–70; Josephus, *C Ap* 2.68–70. See Collins 1986:107–8.

[25] I would thus dissent from Collins' assertion that 'the author perceives no intrinsic enmity between the Jews and the gentiles as such' and that 'the crisis is ascribed to the mad insolence of an individual ruler and can be resolved when he passes away or comes to his senses' (1986:108–9).

[26] The political terminology (πολῖται, 1.22; πολιτευόμενοι, 3.4) proves in context to be a subset of this ethnic conceptuality, not a rival to it.

'the children of Jacob' (6.3, 13). The author uses the two pivotal prayers to rehearse Israel's place in salvation-history and to identify the Jews as God's 'holy people Israel' (2.6), and 'the people of your sanctified inheritance' (6.3). Indeed, it is clear throughout the narrative that God exercises particular care for the Jews, not just because they are oppressed, but because they are his special people. He is *their* God and the God of their fathers (5.13; 6.11, 29; 7.16), and his saving power (6.29, 32; 7.16, 23) is shown in operation only in their favour. His 'providence' and 'aid' are continually at their service (4.21; 5.30, 35), for they are loved by God (2.10; 6.11). The whole narrative is designed to indicate in spectacular fashion how 'the heavenly God shields the Jews, as a father his children, in continual alliance with them' (7.6; cf. 6.15). Although he uses no precise terminology, the author's indebtedness to traditional concepts of covenant and election is crystal clear.

An important feature of Jewish identity projected by this product of Egyptian Judaism is the sense of solidarity with Jews in Judaea. The opening crisis in Jerusalem does not simply provide the pretext for the king's decrees in Egypt, but displays the wider loyalties of the Egyptian Jews. The king recognizes them to be 'fellow nationals' with the Jews of Judaea (3.21), and threatens to cap the destruction of Egyptian Jewry with an expedition to Judaea to flatten the Jerusalem temple (5.43). The similarities between the prayers of the Jerusalem priest Simon and the Egyptian priest Eleazar also indicate the theological unity of the two communities. To our Egyptian author, Jerusalem is 'the holy city', chosen and sanctified by the God who created all the earth (2.9, 16; 6.5).

Such geographical loyalties, and the pervasive sense of alienation, explain the expressions of misplacement with which 3 Maccabees characterizes the residence of Jews in Egypt. Eleazar talks of God's sanctified people perishing unjustly, 'a stranger in a strange land' (ἐν ξένῃ γῇ ξένον, 6.3), indeed 'in the land of their enemies' (ἐν τῇ γῇ τῶν ἐχθρῶν, 6.15; cf. Lev 26.44). And this perspective is mirrored by the narrator when he twice recounts that festivals were established in Egypt 'for the period of their sojourn' (ἐπὶ πᾶσαν τὴν παροικίαν αὐτῶν, 6.36; cf.7.19).[27] It is

---

[27] Hadas' translations 'for all their community' (6.36) and 'for the duration of their community' (7.19) are rare slips; contrast his recognition in the introduction (1953:25) that the term *paroikia* means 'a sojourning in a foreign land'. The sense of 'foreignness' here is rightly recognized by Grimm 1853a and Anderson 1985a *ad loc.*; cf. Tcherikover 1961b:25.

not clear when or how the author envisaged the return of Egyptian
Jews to their real homeland (cf. Deut 30.1–5); but it is evident that
Egypt is for him a foreign residence and not a home.

The depiction of such hostility between Jews and Gentiles, and
of the Jews' eventual redemption, graphically portrays the fears
and aspirations of this Egyptian Jew. He senses with fear the ease
with which anti-Jewish slanders can be spread (2.26–27) and in a
particularly revealing passage allows us to see just where such
slander could inflict most damage:

> The Jews continued to preserve their goodwill toward the
> kings and their unswerving loyalty. But since they worshipped
> God and were governed by his law, they kept themselves apart
> in matters of food, for which reason they appeared hostile
> [or, odious] to some. By their fine behaviour in righteousness
> they ordered their social life and established a good
> reputation among all. But although the fine behaviour of
> the nation was commonly talked about, those of other races
> took no account of it. They talked instead about the
> differences in worship and food, claiming that such people
> were not bound in loyalty (ὁμοσπόνδους) to the king or his
> army, but were ill-disposed and bitterly opposed to his affairs.
> (3.3–7)

The social significance of food regulations is as evident here as in
*The Letter of Aristeas.* The author perceives the observance of Jewish
food laws as a major impediment to social integration (cf. 2.31)
and later criticizes 'apostates' for transgression in this matter 'for
the sake of the stomach' (7.11). The close link in this passage
between religion and food is also revealing, given the common
practice of religious rites at the meal table: the term ὁμοσπόνδους
(3.7) perhaps echoes the use of libations (σπονδαί) at meals as
well as in oaths of loyalty, and it indicates how the Jews' principled
abstention from eating with non-Jews could be readily interpreted
as hostile or politically subversive. With remarkable candour, the
author recognizes the Jews' inability to quash this suspicion despite
their generally upright behaviour.

The political effects of the Jews' social distinction are also
emphasized here, and this is a subject on which our author shows
particular sensitivity. Not only is he careful to claim unimpeachable
loyalty to the Ptolemaic house, but he places in the mouth of the
king no less than four times a recognition of the Jews' loyal service
to the throne (3.21; 5.31; 6.25–26; 7.7). The author is conscious of

charges that the Jews were not just ill-disposed towards others (cf. 3.25; 7.4) but also politically dangerous, actual, or at least potential traitors to the Ptolemaic state (3.24; 4.10; 6.12; 7.3, 5). That is an accusation which he knows could greatly threaten their security.

Indeed it is the general sense of vulnerability which is the most striking characteristic of this text. 3 Maccabees conjures up nightmarish visions in which Jews are persistently slandered, in which registrars draw up Jewish death lists, and Gentiles greet Jewish misfortunes with glee. Although this nightmare is probably influenced by the parallel stories in Daniel, Esther and the Maccabean literature, the fact that our author can imagine this scenario taking place in Egypt indicates his sense of insecurity in that environment. He is not confident that all Jews would hold firm under such pressure, and he knows that 'apostates' could greatly debilitate the community (hence his glee at their execution, 7.10–16). Were it not that his sensational style was a common feature of popular historiography, one might be tempted to regard him as paranoid.

But what of his social and cultural aspirations? He cannot imagine that Alexandrian citizenship, or honour in the court of the king, could be acquired except at the expense of fidelity to Judaism (1.3; 2.30–31).[28] His expectations of social integration seem limited, and he is content to hope that Gentiles will respect Jews for their moral lifestyle, tolerate their differences in religion and food and recognize their loyalty to the state. From the king in particular he can hope for support for the Jewish festivals (6.30–40) and public acknowledgement of their political loyalty, even some recognition of the Jews' God as the powerful God of heaven and history (6.28; 7.2, 6, 9). But the chief impact of that recognition is not some moral or religious transformation, but merely greater caution in dealing with the Jews in future! Ultimately his confidence is not in the inherent justice of the state, nor in the military resources of the Jews (who remain passive throughout), but in the superior power of God over all the forces of evil. The theology of

[28]　While it may be overstated to claim that the author's view is 'in direct opposition to that of the official representatives of the Alexandrian community' (Tcherikover 1961b:23), it clearly stands in opposition to those who did hold Alexandrian citizenship while remaining loyal Jews (*pace* Collins 1986:110); see above chapter 3, Excursus. Kasher's claim that 'III Maccabees contains no echo of any controversy among the Jews for or against Alexandrian citizenship' (1985:226) is extraordinary.

3 Maccabees is remarkably focused on the theme of divine power: the God of the Jews is 'king' (βασιλεύς, 3x), 'lord' (δεσπότης or cognate verb, 5x), 'all-powerful' (παντοκράτωρ or equivalents, 6x) and 'most great' (μέγιστος, 6x). The heart of the narrative is the conflict between the puny authority of the Ptolemaic king and the overwhelming power of the Creator God. In his last recorded words the king acknowledges that 'if we devise any evil against them [the Jews], or harm them in any way, we shall have as our adversary no human being but the Most High God, the Lord of all power, who will take comprehensive and inescapable revenge on all our actions' (7.9). If our author's motto is 'In God we trust' it is also, as for the Scots, 'Nemo me impune lacessit'![29]

Given the many points of comparison between 3 Maccabees and *The Letter of Aristeas*, it is instructive to note the wholly contrasting ethos of the two texts.[30] Both have as their central figure a Ptolemaic king, both tell of his relations with the Jerusalem temple and with Jews in Egypt, both feature high priests and both touch on the topic of Jewish food laws. Yet the contrasts could hardly be greater. Aristeas tells of a positive collocation of events in which a Ptolemy arranges that Jews be released from slavery, the court sponsors the translation of the Jewish law and the king holds friendly banquets with the translators. 3 Maccabees tells of near sacrilege in Jerusalem, wide-scale persecution and an attempted holocaust. But the authors' different subject matter reflects deeper divergences in their perception of relations between Jews and non-Jews. As we have seen (chapter 6.3), Aristeas' narrative constructs a world in which Jews and Gentiles in the Ptolemaic court hold each other in the highest respect, and in their common concern for education (παιδεία) share values of piety, justice and moderation. For the author of 3 Maccabees, on the other hand, the desire to associate with the king is tantamount to apostasy (2.31–33)! He shows no interest in Hellenistic philosophy or ethics and considers the Jews' righteous lifestyle to be largely ignored by the hostile non-Jewish world (3.3–7). While he wishes to claim some support from 'Greeks', he mostly expects a deep-rooted hostility from all Gentiles.[31] Aristeas, by contrast, considers cordial relations to be

---

[29] In Scots paraphrase, 'Wha dare meddle wi' me?'

[30] The comparison has been pursued by e.g. Tracey 1928, Hadas 1949 and, most effectively, Tcherikover 1961b.

[31] As Tcherikover observes, 'The hatred of the gentiles towards the Jews serves as the main framework for the whole story in III Macc.', 1961b:24.

the norm: his only reference to Gentile hostility (22–25) is the exception to the rule by which he otherwise displays Gentile admiration of Jews, even recognition of their philosophical pre-eminence. While both documents refer to the social barrier created by the Jewish food laws, *The Letter of Aristeas* provides a lengthy explanation in the terms of Hellenistic culture and portrays Jews feasting in the court, at least on Jewish terms. 3 Maccabees simply highlights the issue as a question of fidelity to the law, and shows no attempt to meet Gentile sensibilities half way.[32] Again while Aristeas combines a rejection of Gentile polytheism with respect for Gentile piety, the author of 3 Maccabees displays an undifferentiated scorn for the 'abominations' worshipped in Gentile temples (2.18) and castigates Gentiles for their worship of 'follies' (6.11). In general, while Aristeas identifies points of contact with the Hellenistic culture he admires, the author of 3 Maccabees portrays a Jewish community ill at ease in its social and cultural environment.[33]

It is possible that such contrasting views could be held within the Alexandrian Jewish community at the same time. In fact, there is some evidence to place 3 Maccabees after *The Letter of Aristeas*, possibly, as Tcherikover argued, at the beginning of the Roman era (see Appendix). In this historical context, the author's sense of vulnerability was not unjustified. As we have seen (chapter 2.2), in the final century of the Ptolemaic era the Jews were increasingly exposed politically, and some events made them appear as politically disloyal as they are charged with being in this text. The Roman era, with its new system of taxation, undoubtedly caused anxiety to Jews whose social and political rights were not secure, and it coincided with an increase in anti-Jewish sentiment, not least in Alexandria (chapter 3.1). 3 Maccabees is clearly related to an annual Jewish festival in which deliverance from a terrible fate at the feet of elephants was celebrated with days of feasting (6.38–40; 7.17–20). As the Jewish community reflected on such a miraculous deliverance, 3 Maccabees served both to underline their social vulnerability and to inspire confidence that God would remain their protector (7.9). Like the festival-orientated narratives

---

[32] In the final scenes the king does donate some provisions to the Jews (6.30, 40) and holds banquets himself (6.33), but the two parties never feast together!

[33] Paul 1986:311–33 draws a similar conclusion in comparing the two texts; he observes that in 3 Maccabees 'loin d'y avoir synthèse il y a affrontement' (332).

of Esther and 2 Maccabees, whose introduction into Egypt in the first century BCE may have influenced our author, 3 Maccabees builds around the celebration of such festivals strong walls of social and cultural defensiveness.

The parallels between the narrative of 3 Maccabees and the Alexandrian crisis of 38–41 CE have led some scholars to suggest that the text originates in those events and mounts a veiled attack on the emperor Gaius under the guise of Ptolemy Philopator.[34] In fact, however, the text's association with Jewish festivals indicates that it belongs to a much older tradition, and, for all the similarities with Philo's accounts of the Alexandrian pogrom, there are too many discrepancies to take the text as a coded history of recent events.[35] Rather, the parallels between 3 Maccabees and the traumatic events of 38–41 CE indicate how nearly our author's nightmare became a reality. In those fateful years, Flaccus and the Alexandrian civic leaders were able to exploit precisely that vulnerability felt by the author of 3 Maccabees, and Gaius was to bring to a new peak the long-felt fear of the desecration of the temple. History came uncannily close to confirming fiction. The difference was that Gaius' plan was not foiled by a heaven-sent paralysis, but by his own lack of conviction, or the skill of his Syrian legate, or the assassin's dagger (or a combination of all three). More significantly, there was no divine intervention to save the Alexandrian Jews from the pogrom of 38 CE; our author's confidence that God would save his people proved to be ill-founded. It is no surprise that, when opportunity arose in 41 CE, some members of the Jewish community took it upon themselves to pursue the 'comprehensive and inescapable revenge' (7.9) which God had so far failed to exact. Unfortunately, such hostilities fed a cycle of violence which climaxed in the uprising of 116–117 CE. In those years, as we have seen (chapter 3.3), our author's worst fears for the Jewish community in Egypt were tragically and finally fulfilled.

---

[34] So most recently Collins 1986:104–11 following the theses of Ewald and Willrich 1904; Grimm also espoused this view (1853a:217–19), but with some hesitancy.

[35] Despite the similarities between the image of Philopator and Philo's portraits of Flaccus and Gaius, our author makes no use of the topic of self-deification which would have fitted the events of 38–41 CE exactly. Also the destruction of Alexandrian synagogues and the insertion of imperial images find no echoes in 3 Maccabees.

## 7.3 Joseph and Aseneth

The book of Genesis records that when Pharaoh elevated Joseph to high office in Egypt 'he gave him as his wife Aseneth, the daughter of Petephres, the priest of Heliopolis' (LXX Gen 41.45; MT: 'Asenath, daughter of Potiphar, priest of On'). Such a marriage, with its disregard of patriarchal warnings and Mosaic rules against exogamy, inevitably attracted comment and anxious explanation.[36] For a certain Egyptian Jew (of indeterminable date between 100 BCE and 100 CE) that text was an invitation for an imaginative literary exercise in which themes from Greek romance were combined with a detailed portrayal of Aseneth's conversion. The stilted product of this fusion, now known as *Joseph and Aseneth*, was to enjoy remarkable success, circulating eventually in many different recensions.[37] Its significance for us is in demonstrating the use of a Hellenistic form to launch a stinging attack on Hellenistic religion.

The narrative opens with clichés of the romance genre. Aseneth, raised in a wealthy family, is a virgin of spectacular beauty, energetically wooed by all the most eligible men in the world (chapter 1). She lives in opulent conditions (her rooms and property are described with the detail characteristic of this genre),[38] but one thing blocks the path of love. In Greek novels such obstacles are the very stuff of the genre, though of many different kinds, physical and social. In this case, the heroine shows worrying tendencies towards sexual asceticism and despises the man (Joseph)

---

[36] See Aptowitzer 1924 noting, alongside our document, haggadic tales that Aseneth was the daughter of Dinah.

[37] As a result, it has proved peculiarly difficult to reach agreement on the original form of the text. Different editions use varying texts and different systems of reference. I here follow Burchard's analysis of the textual history, his reconstruction of the text and his reference system (1965, 1979, 1985). On the date of the work see Appendix on Sources. Its popularity among Christians has raised the question of Christian interpolations in the work, as posed for instance by Holtz 1967–68. Although Burchard has given cogent reasons for confidence that the work is still authentically Jewish (1965:99–107), Holtz's arguments have yet to receive the detailed consideration they deserve. Burchard's longer text (1979) invites more suspicion than the shorter version favoured by Philonenko 1968. See the survey of this problem by Chesnutt 1995:36–41, 65–71.

[38] Such detail is not a strong argument for female authorship (*pace* Kraemer 1992:110–12), though that cannot, of course, be ruled out.

whom her father wants her to marry (chapters 2–4). Bowled over, however, by her first sight of Joseph, she then finds herself rejected as an alien and idolatrous woman (chapters 5–8). The typical anguish of the heroine (when smitten by love, disappointed by misfortune or foiled by her own mistakes) finds its counterpart here in a week of bitter remorse, in which Aseneth repudiates her former religion and begs for mercy from the God of the Hebrews (chapters 9–13). Receiving tokens of acceptance from the hands of a heavenly man (chapters 14–17), she can fittingly welcome Joseph on his return and receive his recognition as a convert. The two are, of course, happily married with all due ceremony (chapters 18–21). After this climax it is a little surprising to find several more chapters loosely attached at the end (chapters 22–29). However, they continue in the novelistic vein and feature the envy of rival suitors (here Pharaoh's son), the trials endured by the lovers (a plot hatched with the support of four of Joseph's brothers) and their miraculous escape from danger (the attackers' swords disintegrate in answer to Aseneth's prayer!). Here, as in the earlier chapters, there are many parallels with the extant Greek and Roman romances.[39]

Yet even the most sympathetic reader of *Joseph and Aseneth* would have to acknowledge some aesthetic disappointment in comparing this story with the tales to be found in the romances. This is not only because of the stilted prose or the somewhat prudish depiction of the heroes, who are allowed no more than kisses and the occasional hug (19.10 – 20.1). The real cause of the failure of the narrative as romance is that it has been overwhelmed by the theme, and the elongated depiction, of Aseneth's conversion. Having fallen in love with Joseph at first sight, Aseneth is brought into his presence, only to be repulsed by Joseph's hands and by this hefty theological statement:

> It is not fitting for a man who worships God (ἀνὴρ θεοσεβής), who blesses with his mouth the living God, who eats blessed bread of life and drinks blessed drink of immortality and is anointed with blessed ointment of imperishability to kiss an alien woman (γυναῖκα ἀλλοτρίαν) who blesses with her mouth dead and dumb idols, who eats from their table bread of strangulation and drinks from their libations drink of

---

[39] For a valuable synopsis of the parallels see Burchard 1970:66–81 and West 1974.

entrapment and is anointed with ointment of destruction. (8.5)

This formidable sentence (the Greek is as cumbersome as this translation!) sets the agenda for the following ten chapters – the heart of the work. When Joseph prays for her conversion (8.10–11) we are already pointed to the resolution of the drama, and we are told immediately both that Aseneth repents and that Joseph will return to see her in a week (9.1–5). In a story now devoid of suspense, the author presents at length the rituals and prayers of Aseneth's repentance (chapters 10–13) followed by the arrival of the commander of God's army, who hails Aseneth as the 'City of Refuge' for all future converts and feeds her from a magical honeycomb (chapters 14–17). Throughout these chapters it is Aseneth's relationship with God rather than her relationship with Joseph which is the focus of attention, and even the eventual wedding celebrations are capped by a psalm (in the text reconstructed by Burchard), in which Aseneth remembers her former sins and celebrates her new life (21.10–21).

Religion also plays an important role in Greek and Roman romances. In such narratives sacrifices and prayers are as frequent as in everyday life, and heroes and heroines recognize the assistance of particular deities in their eventual success.[40] Nowhere is the religious theme more deeply interwoven into the text than in Apuleius' *Metamorphoses*, where Lucius' eventual salvation by the intervention of Isis, and the matching myth of Cupid and Psyche, give a deeply religious interpretation to the story.[41] Although, even here, religion is by no means as prominent as in *Joseph and Aseneth*, commentators have often pointed out parallels between Lucius' Isis-initiation and Aseneth's conversion. Like Aseneth, Lucius offers a prayer of appeal, which is answered by a heavenly apparition and issues in the revelation of mysteries. Like Aseneth, he is 'reborn' in both a physical and spiritual transformation which brings the assurance of divine protection for the future. The merciful God(dess) pities and redeems the suffering supplicant.

---

[40] Note, for instance, the prayer of thanks to Aphrodite at the conclusion to Chariton's *Chaereas and Callirhoe*.

[41] See the fine analysis in Walsh 1970, whose balanced assessment refutes Merkelbach's attempt to find religious myth or ritual behind numerous details in the narrative.

Yet precisely this comparison reveals how distinctive is the world-view of *Joseph and Aseneth*. Although Apuleius' priest points out the 'moral' of Lucius' wayward lifestyle, with its excessive *libido* and dangerous *curiositas* (*Met* 11.15), there is nothing faintly comparable to the grovelling humiliation of Aseneth's repentance and her total repudiation of her past. Although *Metamorphoses* Book 11 is one of the few places where one might legitimately speak of 'conversion' in relation to Graeco-Roman religion,[42] even here there is nothing like the sense of complete reversal depicted in *Joseph and Aseneth*. What is more, the 'piety' which is the eventual salvation of Lucius is precisely that which Aseneth repudiates! Isis, to whom Apuleius shows genuine religious devotion, is to our Jewish author among the 'dead and dumb Gods of the Egyptians' which are the obstacle to Aseneth's salvation. And whereas Isis, the 'Queen of Heaven', represents and encompasses all the Gods and Goddesses, and tolerates quite cheerfully Lucius' initiation into further cults (*Met* 11.2, 5, 27–29), Aseneth encounters the 'God of Heaven' as a 'jealous God' who 'hates all those who worship idols' (11.7–8). Thus not only is *Joseph and Aseneth* a novel with a peculiarly strong religious interest; it also seems designed to counter whatever religiosity is to be found in its 'pagan' counterparts. This is not just a novel which employs Jewish subject-matter and adapts a Greek form for Jewish readers.[43] It so reshapes the genre as to issue in propaganda fiercely antagonistic to all non-Jewish religion.

The aggressive stance of the narrator is already clear in the description of Aseneth's living quarters in chapter 2. A prominent feature of her tower residence is the presence of 'Gods of the Egyptians fixed to the walls, countless Gods of gold and silver; and Aseneth used to worship them all and feared them and offered sacrifices to them' (2.3). The disdain of polytheism (countless

[42] See the famous study by Nock 1933 who regards Apuleius' religion (second century CE) as a new phenomenon created by the rival power of Christianity.
[43] Apart from the pervasive influence of the LXX, the narrative so often takes for granted the readers'/hearers' knowledge of the biblical story that it is hard to see how it could communicate to other than a biblically literate audience. In contrast to the informative introductions of Greek novels, *Joseph and Aseneth* begins 'It happened in the first year of the seven years of plenty' (1.1), as if one was simply expected to know what those 'seven years' refer to and who is the Joseph who supervises Egypt at that time; cf. other examples at 23.14 and 24.1–5 and Delling 1984:3–4. Contrast the careful introduction of character and context in Ezekiel's *Exagoge*.

Gods, all worshipped) and of iconic worship (the Gods themselves are the images, *fixed* to the walls) is patent, and Aseneth seems to be deliberately portrayed in near-priestly guise as wholly immersed in their worship. Later, when she dresses to meet her parents, her very clothing is emblazoned with idolatry, with the names of the Gods engraved on her jewelry and 'the faces of the idols carved on them' (3.6). Aseneth is as tainted as she can be, and so, by extension, are the Egyptians, whose Gods these are (their namelessness enabling the charge to be as general as possible). When Joseph arrives for a meal at Pentephres' house, he is given a table for himself alone, 'because he did not eat with Egyptians, since this was an abomination (βδέλυγμα) to him' (7.1). Here our author subtly inverts an embarrassing text in Genesis, according to which the Egyptians would not eat with the Hebrews since to do so was an abomination to *them* (Gen 43.32)!

The unacceptability of Aseneth's condition is heightened by the arrangement of the plot. At first the obstacle to the marriage between Joseph and Aseneth is presented as Aseneth's refusal to countenance such a man ('a shepherd's son from the land of Canaan', 4.10). However, even when she falls in love, the problem is not resolved because it now emerges that Joseph refuses to countenance such a woman. This sudden reversal throws all the emphasis on the religious incompatibility of the two central characters. When Aseneth is encouraged by her father to kiss Joseph as her 'brother', he physically repels her and excoriates her 'defiled mouth' in the terms we have already cited. In this connection the author makes interesting play with the notion of what is 'alien' (ἀλλότριος). When Joseph arrives at the house, the gates are locked to keep 'aliens' out (5.6), but the absence of Aseneth from the party leaves her status unclear. Seeing her watch him from her window, Joseph demands her removal ('Let her leave this house', 7.2), wearied by the unwelcome attentions of Egyptian women and mindful of his father's instruction to be wary of every 'alien woman' (γυνὴ ἀλλοτρία), whom to marry would be ruin and destruction (7.5). Pentephres, however, manages to persuade Joseph that Aseneth is not an 'alien woman' in the sense that she is his daughter and a virgin who hates all men and therefore constitutes no threat. As an equally ascetic man, he can surely be a 'brother' to such a girl. However, this fiction of moral kinship is soon exploded: as soon as Aseneth approaches to kiss Joseph, as 'sister' to 'brother', he rejects her with horror as a 'alien woman' who blesses dead and dumb idols (8.5). 'The man who worships

God will kiss only his mother and his natural sister and the sister of his clan (φυλή) and family (συγγένεια) and the wife who shares his bed, who bless with their mouths the living God' (8.6). This makes unmistakably clear the religious parameters of primary social relations. The only legitimate forms of kinship are with those who, through birth or marriage, share the religious orientation of the Jew. All others, whatever their moral virtue or physical attractiveness, remain irreducibly 'alien'.

It is thus necessary that, in the period of repentance which follows, Aseneth wholly repudiates her former religion, both physically and verbally. Stripping off her idol-imprinted clothing she flings it out of the window, and immediately pulverizes her numberless Gods of gold and silver, dispensing of them too through the window, for the beggars to gather the dust (10.12). Even her royal food, tainted with idolatry, must go the same way, fit only for 'alien' dogs (10.13). After seven days of mourning, with the scattering of ashes and a shower of tears to turn them into mud, she is finally brave enough to address the living God, though anxious lest he refuse to accept prayer from such a defiled mouth (11.7–11). Now she adopts Joseph's evaluation of her former religion as the worship of 'dead and dumb idols' (11.8; 12.5), pleading for mercy, forgiveness and protection from 'the wild old lion, the father of the Gods of the Egyptians' (12.9). Her conversion constitutes, in the terms of Joseph's prayer, a transition from darkness to light, from error to truth and from death to life (8.9). In fact, the death/life imagery is prevalent throughout the narrative: as she turns from 'dead Gods' to 'the living God', so life is created out of her spiritual deadness (8.5, 9; 12.1–2; 15.4–5; 16.8, 14; 20.7; 27.10). Thus, at the last, she may kiss Joseph (his kisses impart life, wisdom and truth, 19.11) and may welcome him to a meal in her house: now when the doors are shut to keep out 'aliens', she is inside ready to meet him (19.1–5).

It is at first sight curious that this narrative, with its wholly negative portrayal of Aseneth's pre-conversion life, should include a more positive portrayal of other Egyptian characters. Thus Pentephres, despite recognition of his office as a (non-Jewish) priest, is introduced as a man of wisdom and gentleness (1.3). He is keen for his daughter to marry Joseph, whom he recognizes as 'the Powerful Man of God' (3.4; 4.7) on whom 'the spirit of God' and 'the grace of the Lord' rest (4.7). His respect for Joseph is accompanied by respect for 'the God of Joseph' (3.3) and, on seeing his transformed daughter dressed as a bride, he (and his family) 'gave glory to God who gives life to the dead' (20.7; cf. Paul in Rom 4.17–20). In similar terms Pharaoh, who had appointed Joseph to his office (4.7), arranges the marriage of Joseph and Aseneth and even pronounces a blessing on them in the name of 'the Lord God, the Most High' (21.2–7). For the subsequent wedding banquet he invites 'all the leaders of Egypt and all the kings of the nations' (21.8) to a feast in which nothing is heard of separate tables or abominable company. At the very end of the story, Joseph, who had previously been hailed as the saviour of Egypt (4.7), is recorded as inheriting the throne, at least for a 48-year regency (29.9).

Although this depiction of friendly relations seems somewhat out of step with the antagonistic spirit in the account of Aseneth's conversion, it is not, I think, a serious discrepancy. Pentephres and Pharaoh are peripheral to the story (indeed, Pentephres and his family are 'off-stage' from 10.1 till 20.6), and their friendliness towards Joseph is to a large extent necessary for the narrative to work at all.[44] Without Pentephres' insistence, Joseph and Aseneth would never have met, and the clash of religious cultures could never have been played out. Pharaoh's arrangement of the marriage is a detail required by the biblical text from which this whole story developed (Gen 41.45). It is crucial to the dynamic of the story that Pentephres and Pharaoh recognize Joseph's God, but also that he never recognizes theirs; and though described as priest, Pentephres, unlike his daughter, never performs a religious act. In other words, the giving of honour is almost entirely one-sided – from non-Jews to Jews and not vice versa.[45] There is nothing here like the mutual respect which we saw to be characteristic of

---

[44]  Similarly, in the final chapters most of the characters follow stereotyped roles necessary for an exciting narrative. I am unconvinced by the attempt of Sänger 1985 and Collins 1986:89–91 to read the details of these adventures (a friendly ruler [Pharaoh], hostility in high places [Pharaoh's son], Jewish military power [the armed prowess of Levi and Simeon]) as 'evidently paradigmatic of Jewish-Gentile relations in the Egyptian Diaspora' (Collins 1986:90). While the general shape of legends can reveal social and cultural conditions, I doubt that the details of characterization can be pressed in this way.

[45]  A Jewish author, of course, likes to imagine that people of importance recognize the validity, and even the superiority, of the Jewish religion. Philonenko 1968:56–57 and Sänger 1985:97–98 take Pentephres and Pharaoh as representatives of 'God-fearers'; but if they fit into this broad category, they rank only with those whose connections with Judaism are minimal (Cohen 1987a; 1989).

*The Letter of Aristeas*. And if the wedding is celebrated with common feasting, the missing reference to separation at table is a function of narrative necessity rather than religious laxity: while the earlier disjunction of Joseph at the meal table (7.1) was an important symbol of social alienation, it will not do to insert a jarring note of disharmony into an otherwise happy ending.

Thus the strong sense of alienation between Jews and non-Jews which governs the relations of Joseph with the unconverted Aseneth is not an exception to a rule of generally harmonious relationships. Rather, the encounter of Joseph and Aseneth, and the issue of the kiss, bring to the surface the sense of cultural antagonism which is the predominant tone of this document. When one considers the numerous frictionless ways in which this marriage could have been portrayed, the humiliating experience which Aseneth is made to undergo indicates just how strongly the author wishes to communicate this message.

Aseneth's acceptance before God is indicated by the appearance of a heavenly figure, who allows her to partake of a miraculous honeycomb (chapters 14–17). Although this last event occupies a comparatively small proportion of the narrative (15.13 – 17.3), it has fascinated scholars and spawned a plethora of speculations.[46] The link between the honeycomb and the formulaic statements about 'eating bread of life, drinking a cup of immortality and being anointed with ointment of imperishability' (16.16; cf. 8.5, 9; 15.5; 19.5) has led to suggestions that this text reflects the practice of a Jewish mystery cult, associated by some with the Therapeutae or Essenes, by others with groups not otherwise attested.[47] In certain respects the text does invite comparison with mystery-initiations: besides the reference to 'the ineffable mysteries of God' (16.14), the theme of rebirth and the accompanying visions, reclothing, sacred meals, and miraculous symbols all have parallels in Lucius'

---

[46] The mysterious bees in 16.17–23 seem to invite some allegorical explanation, but no interpretation has gained a consensus.

[47] For a critical survey see Burchard 1965:121–26 and Sänger 1980; the latter concludes that the text portrays not the rites of a mystery initiation, but certain standard procedures in the admission of proselytes. This position has now been supported by the full-length investigation of Chesnutt 1995. The similarity of these phrases to New Testament statements on the Lord's Supper has been a further reason for the interest in such passages; see Burchard's judicious assessment (1987). The question of Christian interpolation must also be raised here (see above, n. 37).

initiation in *Metamorphoses* 11. Yet these probably represent not a reflection of specific cultic activities but a literary effort to portray Judaism as a 'mystery religion' with its secrets, sacred meals and promise of eternal life. Philo uses similar 'mystery' language (*Leg All* 3.27, 71, 219; *Virt* 178 and *passim*) though he does not utilize it, as here, in a narrative form. If our author adopts symbols and formulae current in his religious environment (as he arguably employs the image of the Sun God, Helios, in describing Joseph, 5.4–7; 6.2), he does so to appropriate them for a new Jewish use – an appropriation which simultaneously cancels their value in cults of the 'dead and dumb Gods' fostered by non-Jews.[48]

In some respects this individualistic idiom of 'mystery-initiation' appears to overshadow the social and communal aspects of Judaism. In the terms of the narrative, Aseneth's conversion is followed by her 'mystical experience' and her marriage to Joseph, not by her incorporation into a Jewish community. Nonetheless, there are good reasons to believe that this narrative arises from a context in which Judaism represents not just the individual's safe passage to eternity but also her/his incorporation into a communal tradition. As Burchard has argued, the formula about blessed bread, wine and oil is best taken to refer to the staples of Jewish life, its food, drink and (multi-purpose) oil, concerning all of which many Jews were careful to avoid defilement from non-Jewish religion.[49] Thus the antithesis in 8.5 between 'pagan' food, drink and oil as tokens of death, and their Jewish equivalents as tokens of life, does not refer to rival cultic rituals, but to two spheres or patterns of life. The contrast is no doubt rhetorically overdrawn (not least in representing *all* Gentile food as tainted by sacrifice to 'idols'), but the very exaggeration represents a concern to preserve the Jewish way of life uncontaminated by exposure to 'idolatry'. And when we begin to ask how Jews were to gain access to this 'blessed bread

---

[48] Thus even if Philonenko 1968 is right to detect parallels in our document with Egyptian depictions of the Goddesses Neith and Isis, this hardly amounts to 'an open attitude conceptually toward certain aspects of pagan religion and culture' (Kee 1976:188). The question is not what our author has borrowed, but for what purposes and within what framework of thought.

[49] Burchard 1965:121–33, now slightly modified in 1987:109–117. He concludes that 'the passages mentioning blessed bread, cup and ointment ... refer ... to the special Jewish way of using the three chief elements of human subsistence, namely, food, drink and ointment. The special Jewish way is to pronounce benedictions over them before use' (1987:117). On Jewish concern for purity of food, drink and oil, see below chapter 14.3.2.

of life', and in what contexts the requisite 'blessings' to the living God were to be made, we are brought back to the social life of Jewish communities cemented by their common dietary concerns and their prayers before and after meals.

Another indication of the social ramifications of Aseneth's conversion is her own expression of the social dislocation entailed. A remarkable feature of her lament in chapters 11–13 is her assertion that

> everyone has come to hate me, and with them even my mother and father, because I have come to abominate their Gods and have destroyed them ... And therefore my mother and father said 'Aseneth is not our daughter' and my whole family and all people hate me because I have destroyed their Gods. (11.4–5; cf. 12.10–15)

Since there is in fact no reference in the narrative to the hostility of Aseneth's parents (in fact the opposite, 20.7), this complaint must represent a stereotypical depiction of the social consequences of becoming a proselyte.[50] But if converts experience such dislocation of their former social ties, where do they now belong? In the terms of this narrative, Aseneth belongs to Joseph her husband, but also therefore to his family (note her acclaim of Jacob as her father, 22.7–9) and beyond that to the 'Hebrews', to whose God she appeals (11.10).

Indeed, it is striking how frequently in this narrative 'God' is used in genitival clauses: if there are Gods of the Egyptians ('their Gods' – see citation above), there is also the God of Joseph, otherwise known as the God of Jacob/Israel, the God of the Hebrews. And this suggests that Aseneth's marriage to Joseph is a symbol (or means) of her incorporation into the Jewish people, just as earlier her disdain was coloured by prejudice against his family and his roots (4.9–10). The terms in which Joseph prays for her are thus entirely fitting:

> Lord, bless this virgin,
> And renew her by your spirit,
> And form her anew by your hidden hand,
> And revive her by your life,
> And let her eat the bread of your life

---

[50]  Cf. Philo, *Spec Leg* 1.52; 4.178; *Virt* 102–4.

And drink the cup of your blessing,
And *number her among your people,*
   Which you have chosen before all things came into being,
And let her enter your rest,
Which you have prepared for your chosen ones. (8.9)

His prayer is answered when Aseneth is hailed as 'The City of Refuge', in which 'many peoples trusting in the Lord God will be sheltered' (15.7) and 'the sons of the living God will dwell' (19.8; cf. 17.6). By such references the narrative points beyond this particular hero and heroine to the social world of the community they represent.[51]

The admission of Aseneth as a paradigmatic convert indicates that this community is not, in the author's view, confined within ethnic boundaries. However, we should not conclude that his conception of Judaism was 'nonethnic' in every sense.[52] When Aseneth converts, her lament suggests that she is fully uprooted from her Egyptian environment, as indeed the epithet 'Egyptian' is a term of abuse throughout. In 1.5 it is claimed that she 'was nothing like the daughters of the Egyptians'; her religious practices were her only tie to Egyptian culture and that was severed at her conversion.[53] The same passage compares her beauty not, as in Greek novels, with famous Greek women or Goddesses, but with the Hebrew matriarchs: 'she was in every respect similar to the daughters of the Hebrews, as tall as Sarah, as handsome as Rebecca and as beautiful as Rachel' (1.5). Such statements surely suggest the ethnic pride of an author who can think of no higher standard of beauty than that of his ancestresses.[54]

---

[51] Note also the writing of Aseneth's name in 'the book of the living in heaven', 15.4. Douglas 1988:36–38 rightly interprets the visit of the heavenly man as a symbol of 'aggregation' into a new community.

[52] *Pace* Collins 1986:214–18 who considers that Judaism is here 'a universal religion freed from the restrictions of race' (215) and a 'nonethnic religion of monotheism' (217).

[53] Thus I cannot accept Collins' claim that 'Aseneth has at once both a Jewish and an Egyptian profile. She does not lose her Egyptian identity when she converts' (1986:217).

[54] Both Collins 1986:214 and Kee 1983:410 suggest that the scurrilous behaviour of Joseph's brothers in chapters 22–29 indicates that Jewish birth is no guarantee of moral righteousness. But it is doubtful if the author wished to emphasize this point (the brothers largely follow the biblical roles), and 8.6 makes clear the foundational significance of the family and clan.

By the same token, we may speak of an 'open attitude toward Gentiles'[55] only if we recall that they cannot receive an intimate welcome unless they have been changed by conversion. Joseph's physical repulsion of Aseneth hardly conveys an image of 'openness'! God is the God of pity and compassion, but he hates all those who persist in 'idol-worship' (11.7–10). The demand for conversion is a peculiarly aggressive form of welcome, an 'openness' only to the extent of allowing contact to enable a 'catch' (note the fishing metaphor in 21.21). Aseneth's painful process of repentance shows how costly such a 'welcome' is felt to be by 'aliens' undergoing such a fundamental resocialization. To be sure, this is a more 'open' attitude than if no proselyte were to be admitted at all (as at Qumran, 4QFlor 1.4; but cf. CD 14.4). But the author's care in describing the depth of Aseneth's conversion indicates that he could accept no casual or compromised commitment from those wishing to be numbered among God's people.

Since it is difficult to establish the date of this document (see Appendix), its *Sitz im Leben* can be fixed only in the most general terms. So much biblical knowledge is presupposed that it is unlikely to have been designed as a missionary tract, but it may reflect discussion in the Jewish community on the legitimacy of, and conditions for, proselytism.[56] There is an evident concern to discourage exogamy (both male and female options are mentioned, 8.6–7), at least without the thoroughgoing conversion of the non-Jewish spouse; we have already noted the social and religious threat which intermarriage posed (above, chapter 5.1). As we have seen, the use of 'mystery' language suggests an understanding of Judaism as a path to personal transformation, but this is more likely to be an interpretation of the Jewish way of life as a whole than an esoteric doctrine of a mystical group.[57] The

---

[55] Kee 1976:186; cf. West 1974:77–78 who considers the writer's attitude to the non-Jewish world 'tolerant and unimpassioned ... Aseneth's confession is long, but the only specific offences mentioned are idol-worship and malicious talk about Joseph.' But, given the significance of religion in Graeco-Roman life, our text's denigration of 'idol-worshippers' is extremely far-reaching.

[56] So Chesnutt 1988 and 1995.

[57] Kee finds links with 'merkavah mysticism' and posits 'an esoteric group of upper-middle class Jews and converts' (1983:410); cf. Philonenko 1968. But the assumption that a particular religiosity is the product of a distinct religious group is unwarranted. Apuleius' mystical and Platonizing religiosity did not distance him from traditional religious practices. As Walsh comments on Apuleius: 'The picture emerges of the Neoplatonist vividly conscious of the

author believed that Judaism made possible personal contact with the Divine and rebirth to eternal life; but he did so in support of the Jewish community as a whole and in competition with other and attractive forms of religiosity. He is determined to retain the religious exclusivity expressed in his dismissal of 'dead Gods', whatever that may cost both converts and Jews.[58] He is confident that God will protect true worshippers and that the pattern of repentant conversion here described will be followed by other Gentiles (15.7; 19.5). It was precisely the religious confidence necessary to sustain a community whose minority religious status created many pressures and temptations.

## 7.4 The Egyptian Sibylline Oracles

One of the most remarkable products of Egyptian Judaism is a collection of oracular pronouncements in the style of epic verse, attributed to a Sibyl. These date from the mid-second century BCE onwards,[59] and constitute a literary tradition which became popular in certain Jewish centres. It was also later utilized and supplemented by Christians, who in subsequent centuries continued to imitate the Sibylline style in predicting doom for the world and glory for God's people.

According to Plutarch, Heraclitus once asserted that 'Sibylla, with raving mouth, uttering gloomy words, rough and unadorned, yet reaches a thousand years by her voice on account of God'.[60] The citation illustrates many typical features of Sibylline prophecy in the ancient world. The Sibyl (the term was sometimes a personal name, sometimes a class of prophetess) was considered a woman

---

existence of the other world, and worshipping the truest reality under the conventional Roman labels for divinity' (1970:185). Philo is a good example of a similar phenomenon in Judaism, and there is no reason to treat the author of *Joseph and Aseneth* otherwise.

[58] The cost to converts is clear in chapters 11–13, which are full of references to abandonment, ostracism and persecution. It is possible that the emphasis on not returning evil for evil in the later chapters (23.9; 28.5, 14; 29.3) reflects a social context where Jews are under pressure and tempted to take retaliatory measures.

[59] For the complex questions of date see further below and the Appendix on Sources.

[60] Plutarch, *Moralia* 397A. For what follows see the comprehensive discussion of Sibylline prophecy in Parke 1988.

of immense longevity whose age accorded her great authority, while her ancient origins gave to her 'prophecies' of historical events the impression of accurate prediction. Her predominant mood was despair, and she larded her doleful predictions of natural and political disaster with contemptuous comments on the follies of humanity.[61] One did not consult the Sibyl for entertainment. From her 'raving mouth' issued a medley of allusive prophecies, their very incoherence a token of her inspiration. Her oracles were taken seriously by all social classes, and could be politically influential at moments of social or military crisis. But their natural milieu is not the refined circle of scholars or courtiers, but the popular ambience of oracle-mongers and diviners.[62] While typically circulating in written form, it was easy to adapt and augment the tradition in accordance with new conditions. Herodotus (7.6) tells of an interpolator caught supplementing the oracles of Musaeus, but there were many whose concoction of Sibylline oracles passed unseen into the collection of her pronouncements.

It is ironic that the Jewish and Christian imitations of the Sibyl are the only extended Sibylline oracles to survive. While the Greek oracles have come down to us only in isolated fragments, the songs of the Jewish/Christian Sybil fill several books, compiled and edited in the sixth century CE. These texts are, however, exceptionally difficult to interpret. In the first place, our manuscripts are frequently incomplete or corrupt, forcing editors to resort to conjectural emendations of varying worth.[63] Even with a secure text, however, it is peculiarly difficult to disentangle this medley of

---

[61] Her pronouncement at the pyre of Croesus was typical: 'Miserable men, why do you pursue what is impious?' (cited by Parke 1988:60). To explain the popularity of her 'grim forecasts', Parke suggests that 'when a disaster happened, it was a comfort to feel that this was not simply some arbitrary catastrophe. It had been foreseen and foretold' (1988:18).

[62] This is certainly suggested by their crude poetry and their importance at times of popular disturbance; see e.g. Parke's discussion of the influence of Sibylline oracles in the Peloponnesian War and in moments of crisis in Rome (1988:102–6, 136–143). Parke suggests that 'the sombre utterances of the Sibyl emerged as popular literature at times of disaster. This fact ... showed that they satisfied a popular need and implies that they were themselves a form of folk-literature ... we must imagine the Sibyl's utterances as distributed not so much in literary circles as in the lower strata of society' (1988:17).

[63] The standard text is that of Geffcken 1902a, whose *apparatus* indicates the many complexities. Sometimes the uncertainty of the text greatly impedes our ability to grasp its meaning.

material. Since oracles were constructed by imitation and readily updated, it is a delicate business to decide which oracles are of Jewish and which of later Christian origin, also where 'pagan' originals have been incorporated, and in which cases older oracles have been supplemented in view of subsequent history. Add to this their typical opacity and their use of teasing metaphor, and it is easy to appreciate how rarely these Sibylline oracles can be located in specific historical contexts. Although certain conclusions have become established in scholarship, on many issues there is little agreement, and alternative viewpoints are easily propounded with little chance of proof or refutation.[64] Here, however, we may follow the consensus which assigns books 3 and 5 to an Egyptian provenance; the other books whose dates and origins are much less easily discerned will have to be omitted from our discussion.

The *Third Sibylline Book* is generally agreed to contain the oldest Jewish material. In its present form it is a patchwork of oracles, some directed against cities and nations, others reviewing world history, others again praising the Jews and predicting future crises and redemptions in their history. The whole work is attributed to a Sibyl who identifies herself as the daughter-in-law of Noah (3.809–29). To what extent this compilation is unified and to what extent it has been cobbled together from disparate sources is a moot point.[65] It is safest to steer a middle course and to recognize, with manuscript evidence, the secondary nature of 3.1–96 (which includes specific attacks on Rome), while accepting the bulk of the rest of the book as originating in the second century BCE, with some additions and modifications in the following century. If the references to the seventh king of Egypt (3.192–93, 318, 608–9) can be dated to the reign of Ptolemy Philometor (180–145 BCE), that would give us a total temporal span from the 170s to the end of the first century BCE.[66] The ease with which such oracles could be

---

[64] For classic treatments see Geffcken 1902b and Rzach 1923; on the differing interpretations of Book 3 see below.

[65] For contrasting views see e.g. Geffcken 1902b:1–17 and Nikiprowetzky 1970, the latter arguing for a wholly unified document. See the survey of opinions in Schürer 3.632–38.

[66] Note the careful argumentation of Collins 1974, summarized in 1983. Nikiprowetzky's dating to 42 BCE (1970) is a tour de force which depends on taking the 'seventh king' as an allusion to Cleopatra VII. Nonetheless, his book exposes many weaknesses in the arguments employed by others. For a survey of suggested datable allusions see Fraser 1972:1.708–13 with notes.

adapted makes it impossible, in my opinion, to reach greater precision in dating any single passage within this historical period.[67]

Nonetheless, the oracles in Book 3 provide important evidence of the social and political attitudes of certain Egyptian Jews during this period. We may take as examples three of the central oracles which offer a coherent perspective on the place of the Jews in world history.

1. Our first passage, **3.162–294**, opens with a typically Sibylline overview of world kingdoms, here beginning with the rule of the 'house of Solomon' (167) and running through the unjust regimes of Greece, Macedonia and Rome till the point when, at the seventh reign of a king of Egypt, 'the nation of the Great God will again be strong, and will be guides in life for all mortals' (192–95). The special status of the Jews is then underscored by an announcement of woes on various peoples, which concludes with the prediction that evil will fall also on 'the pious people who live around the great temple of Solomon, the offspring of righteous men' (213–15). However, before describing this fate (the exile), the Sibyl digresses to eulogize the Jewish nation, highlighting their religious good sense (they do not succumb to sorcery or astrology, 220–33) and their moral virtue (their concern for justice and the welfare of the poor, 234–47). Paraphrasing biblical texts, the Sibyl refers directly to the Exodus, to the leadership of that 'great man', Moses, and to the gift of the law at Sinai (248–58). Indeed, with almost deuteronomistic zeal, she highlights the rewards of obedience to the law and predicts the exile as Israel's punishment for her idolatrous sins (259–281). However, the prophecy finishes on an optimistic note, promising to those who 'trust in the holy laws of the Great God' (284) the restoration of the temple and, in general,

---

[67] 3.171–95 is a good example of the difficulties here. Its 'preview' of history runs through the era of Greeks and Macedonians and includes a lengthy critique of the Romans before apparently climaxing in the 'seventh reign' of an Egyptian king. Although Roman power was becoming visible already after the battle of Pydna (168 BCE), the critique of Roman homosexual practices looks odd at so early a date. While Collins places the oracle in the second century BCE, and Nikiprowetzky, with equal confidence, in the first (Geffcken had suggested excising the reference to the seventh king), it is possible that this oracle began in the reign of Ptolemy Philometor but 'grew' over subsequent decades. See the discussion of this passage in Collins 1974:31–32 and 1986:64–65, Nikiprowetzky 1970:199–201, 210–12 and Momigliano 1975a:1081–82.

'a good end and very great glory, as the immortal God has decreed for you' (282–83).

While this last passage (282–94) clearly has in mind the post-exilic restoration, it is the sort of prophetic oracle which takes on fuller meaning in its eschatological context.[68] The future glory of Israel is assured: her moral and religious superiority distinguish her as the one nation exempt from the disastrous fate awaiting the other kingdoms of the world.

2. A similar pattern of thought governs a later oracular sequence, **3.489–600**. A lengthy prediction of woes on other nations concludes with cosmic disasters destroying two-thirds of humanity (489–544) and issues in a call for repentance directed to Greece (545–72; cf. 624–31). Here, as elsewhere in the Sibyllines, the chief criticism of other nations concerns their 'idolatry' – that great 'error' by which they offer sacrifice to 'dead Gods' and thereby fail to 'honour the name of the Begetter of All' (550). The call to repentance sets before the Greeks the threat of encounter with the full force of God's wrath, but also, through that experience, the possibility of acknowledging his power and offering sacrifice in his temple (556–72). In contrast to the sinful Greeks, the Sibyl again praises 'a race of pious men who attend to the will and intention of the Most High and fully honour the temple of the Great God' (573–75). Besides their proper worship (shunning the 'empty deceits' of idolatry), the Jews are noted for 'sharing the righteousness of the law of the Most High' (580). Special attention is given to sexual morality where the Jews' abstention from pederasty distinguishes them from the nations of transgressors – Phoenicians, Egyptians, Romans, Greeks, Persians, Galatians, all Asia and 'many nations of others' (596–600)! In such a bleak moral environment, the Jews, of course, 'far exceed all others' (μέγα δ' ἔξοχα πάντων / ἀνθρώπων, 594–95).

3. Our final passage from Book 3 is the climactic scenario with which it concludes, **3.657–808**. Here the Sibyl predicts a gathering of kings with hostile intent against 'the temple of the Great God' and the 'excellent men' who inhabit the land (657–68). However, God's judgment, accompanied by massive convulsions of nature,

---

[68] See, in general, Nolland 1979a, though his suggested correspondences with contemporary Judaean history are probably over-specific.

will defend his temple and his 'sons', scattering those who, in ignorance of his laws, attacked the sanctuary (669–709). Such a cosmic display of wrath will lead some to offer worship in the temple and to 'ponder the law of the Most High God' (718–19) and thus usher in a golden age when God 'will raise up a kingdom for all ages among men' (767–68). In the idyllic conditions of this new world (the description draws heavily on Isaiah 11), there will be universal peace between men and among all creatures. As a chastened humanity observes God's 'common law' (758), God's temple will be the sole locus of worship:

> From every land they will bring frankincense and gifts to the house of the Great God. There will be no other house to be recognized among men, even for future generations, save that which God gave to faithful men to honour. (3.772–75)

Our summary of these three pivotal passages in Book 3 reveals the chief concerns of the Jews among whom such oracles circulated. These Egyptian Jews clearly retained an affiliation with the land of Judaea ('the holy land of the Great One', 734–35), and in particular with the Jerusalem temple. The unique sanctity of this temple is repeatedly emphasized, and its central place in the final sequence indicates a theological commitment to Jerusalem greater than any we have so far encountered in Jewish literature from Egypt. Also remarkable is the repeated reference to 'the holy law', whose observance is the central feature of Israel's special identity.[69] As 'the people of God' (725) and 'sacred race' (573), the Jews have a special destiny in world history. 'To them alone did the Great God give wise counsel and faith and good reason in their breasts' (584–85), and their pure piety and special knowledge of the law (580, 768–69) bear witness to this privilege. In the eschatological crisis in Jerusalem, all nations will recognize 'how much the Immortal One loves those men, for everything fights on their side and aids them' (711–12). Taken together, such oracles express as clearly as one could expect in this genre the traditional notion of Israel's election.

Adopting the scornful Sibylline mask allows these Jewish oracle-mongers to launch a vigorous attack on other nations. Their sins

---

[69] The temple is prominent in 3.214, 265–94, 302, 556–79, 665, 703, 718, 772–75. The law features in 3.234–64, 275–76, 284, 580, 600, 686–87, 719, 768–69. These references show how frequently the two themes go in tandem.

and follies are amply recounted, most often, as we have seen, in the categories of 'idolatry' and moral licence.[70] Only occasionally are charges laid for specific offences against the Jewish nation (301–2, 313–14). In general the Jews' moral and social differences are so pronounced that 'everyone will be offended at your customs' (272). Such social alienation is writ large across every page of these doom-laden oracles. To be sure, the final oracle includes a vision of world-wide repentance and the worship of all nations at the temple of God. But that can only come about when they abandon idolatry and recognize the unique sanctity of the Jerusalem temple. Such hopes of radical conversion are the correlate of a cultural antagonism which recognizes no value in the religious practice of non-Jews. If this is propaganda, it represents a proselytization by fear.[71]

Given this predominant mood of cultural and social alienation I find unconvincing Collins' suggestion that the repeated references to the 'seventh king' of Egypt (3.192–93, 318, 608–9), and the isolated notice of 'a king from the sun' (652–56), mark a positive appreciation of the Ptolemaic dynasty and 'a distinctly favourable attitude towards Egypt'.[72] Collins suggests that a Jew living in the hospitable conditions of the reign of Philometor (180–145 BCE) expected that the king, or his successor, would usher in a messianic age. There is of course a precedent in Deutero-Isaiah for the identification of a Gentile king as a messianic figure, and there may even be an allusion to Cyrus in this role in 3.286. However, in the case of the Sibylline Oracles the evidence is far from convincing. The three references to the 'seventh king' or 'seventh reign' signal only the time in which *other events* occur: there is little if any suggestion that the king himself is an agent of transformation.[73] The only reference to royal agency in the

---

[70] Idolatry is condemned in 3.545–55, 586–90, 604–6, 720–23, and other forms of religion in 3.221–33. (The attack on idolatry in 3.8–45 may be from a separate and later collection.) The sexual immorality of other nations features prominently in 3.185–86, 594–600, 764–66.

[71] See Simon 1983.

[72] The thesis is first advanced in Collins 1974:38–44 and repeated in 1983:354–59 and 1986:64–72 (with some modifications). The citation is from 1974:76. Collins' view is partially foreshadowed by Fraser 1972:1.708–16, though the latter draws a distinction between the favourable view of Philometor and the critical stance towards Egyptians.

[73] *Pace* Collins 1974:42–43. 3.191–5 indicates the coming greatness of God's people when a seventh king of Egypt will rule, but not that he will enable or support such an event. 3.314–19 describes a period of affliction in Egypt 'in

establishment of the new age is the brief oracle about 'the king from the sun' (3.652–56). It is by no means clear that this figure is the same as the 'seventh king', and, though the title may be of Egyptian origin, it is not necessary to take it as referring to a Ptolemaic king.[74] When we find throughout this book of oracles recurrent criticism of the Greeks and Macedonians (3.171–74, 381–83, 545–49), when we find Egypt and Alexandria threatened with destruction (348–49, 611–15) and the whole religious structure of Ptolemaic Egypt scorned as vain idolatry, it is hard to see how these Sibylline authors could be considered supporters of the Ptolemaic ideology.[75]

Much more plausible is Momigliano's thesis that Book 3 of the Sibylline Oracles reflects a revival of Jewish nationalistic sentiment in the wake of the Maccabean revolt.[76] While the oracles make no reference to the Maccabees or to their revolt (beyond a possible echo in 194–95),[77] the dating to the reign of the seventh Egyptian king (Philometor, 180–145 BCE) would fit this context admirably; moreover, the echoes of the book of Daniel confirm this general ambience.[78] Whatever their views on the Maccabean family, these Sibylline oracles emphasize the Jews' national greatness, centred on temple and law, in parallel to Maccabean ideology. At a time of

the seventh generation of kings', to be followed by rest. 3.601–18 depicts God's judgment 'whenever the young seventh king of Egypt rules his own land'; the land will be ravaged by a great king from Asia before men convert to the worship of the true God.

74  Collins 1974:41 cites parallels in Isa 41.2, 25 and the use of the identical phrase in *The Oracle of the Potter* (cf. Collins 1994). This potent title was certainly adopted by the Ptolemies, but also by the author of *The Oracle of the Potter* with reference to a native (non-Ptolemaic) king. There is no strong reason to suggest that the Jewish Sibyl followed Ptolemaic propaganda in this regard.

75  Contrast the real spirit of friendship towards the Ptolemies in *The Letter of Aristeas*. One of the awkward features of Collins' thesis is that he is required to hold that these expectations of a seventh Ptolemaic king were preserved despite their manifest failure to materialize. He also has to posit a sea-change in the attitude of the Sibyllines during or after Cleopatra's reign (1974:66–71), despite the continuity of theme and style in the oracles in this tradition.

76  Momigliano 1975a; cf. Collins' response in 1986:64–72. It is not necessary to follow Momigliano's general thesis (that this book constitutes a response to a request for support from Palestine) to see the force of his association between these oracles and the aspirations raised by events in Judaea.

77  Momigliano 1975a:1081; cf. Nolland 1979a.

78  3.396–97 obviously echoes Daniel 7; it is notable that Collins brackets out these verses as 'a Jewish addition to this oracle' (1983:371 note u2) without specifying their date or context.

turmoil in Judaea and uncertainty in Egypt (which suffered two invasions by Antiochus Epiphanes in the 160s BCE), we can imagine Jewish observers in Egypt adopting the Sibylline genre to express their expectation that God would intervene to punish evil-doers and vindicate his people.

Of course, the adoption of the Sibylline genre form indicates some degree of acculturation. The use of epic hexameters suggests some knowledge of Greek literature and the Jewish Sibyl is not averse to using Homeric epithets in describing God. Moreover, in their imitation of the Erythaean Sibyl (3.813–18), these oracles are willing to paraphrase passages current in Gentile circles.[79] Yet this Hellenization in theme and form should not be confused with the careful accommodation achieved by such figures as Aristobulus and Aristeas. Because the Third Sibylline Book has its origins in the same era as these Jewish luminaries, and in a period of Jewish prominence in Egyptian affairs, it is often suggested that it, too, represents an attempt to develop common ground with contemporary Graeco-Egyptian culture.[80] Yet both in level and tone it is far removed from the court-culture of those documents. The natural milieu of Sibylline oracles is the street, not the academy, and the semi-scholarly facade of these unliterary verses masks 'a popular literature circulating among the lower reading public' (Parke 1988:167). Moreover, the choice of the Sibylline genre enables the Jewish author(s) to adopt that contemptuous tone towards humanity which is the hallmark of the Sibyl. Like the biblical oracles against the nations, these oracles skilfully wrap their nationalist message in the garb of an international oracle. Using the ancient authority of the Sibyl, their Jewish authors developed a powerful medium through which to launch a religious and social critique of their contemporaries and to express their own expectations of national revival. It was with such scorn of non-Jews and such national aspirations that lower-class Alexandrian Jews sustained their conflict with Alexandrians in the late Ptolemaic and

---

[79] This is most evident in 3.110–55 (Cronos and the Titans) and 401–88 (the Trojan War and Homer). Scholars continue to debate whether such passages have been lifted wholesale from earlier sources. On such thematic and literary 'syncretism' see Nikiprowetzky 1970:112–94.

[80] E.g. Collins 1974:53–55; 1987:438: 'the positive and optimistic relations between Jews and gentiles which originally prompted the use of the Sibylline form as a common medium'; 1986:63, 'attempting to bridge two cultures'.

early Roman eras (see above chapters 2.2 and 3.1). It is here, perhaps uniquely, that we can glimpse the sort of inspiration which led the ordinary population of Egyptian Jews to resist the cultural pressures of their society and to develop the resilience which sustained them through the early Roman period.[81]

The continuing vitality of this Sibylline tradition is indicated by the injection of new oracles reflecting conditions in the first century BCE. As Roman power became more prominent in the Eastern Mediterranean, so the hostility of the Sibyl was directed against this new example of impious brutality. It is generally recognized that the prediction of Asian triumph over Rome in 3.350–80 originated in the first century BCE, and the introduction to Book 3 (lines 1–96) is full of premonitions of the destruction of Roman power. The Sibyllist awaits the time when 'a holy prince will come to wield his sceptre over the whole world for all ages, as time hurries on. And then implacable wrath will fall on Latin men' (3.49–51).[82] If such anti-Roman sentiments circulated among the Jewish population in Alexandria, one can understand the strength of their physical resistance in the upheavals of 41 and 66 CE (see above, chapter 3).

Since the Jerusalem temple played a central role in the eschatological drama of the early Jewish Sibyllines, its destruction in 70 CE was bound to ignite an explosion of fury. We can observe the effect of this disaster in the *Fifth Sibylline Book*. This tapestry of oracles, dating from 80–130 CE,[83] is woven with unusual consistency around this central motif: 'I saw the second Temple thrown headlong, soaked in fire by an impious hand, the ever-flourishing guardian Temple of God, made by holy people' (5.398–401). Nowhere do we see more clearly the shock waves of this catastrophe rippling out into the Diaspora than in these emotional oracles.

---

[81] I am unpersuaded by Collins' attempt to link *Sib Or* 3 with the Oniads and the community at Leontopolis, 1974:44–53. The suggestion that Alexandrian Judaism was uniformly 'academic' and typically 'spiritualizing' (1974:53; 1983:355–56) is unwarranted, and it would be surprising to find future hopes so resolutely focused in the Jerusalem temple in a community which worshipped at Leontopolis. Of course Alexandria was not the only centre of Jewish population in Egypt, but as the largest it remains the most likely provenance.

[82] For the probable dating of this and other passages in 3.1–96 at the turn of the Ptolemaic-Roman era in Egypt see Collins 1974:64–70.

[83] See Appendix on Sources and the analysis of the material by Geffcken 1902b:22–31, Rzach 1923:2134–40, and Collins 1974:73–95.

The blame is liberally applied: on Nero (5.150–54), on Titus (5.408–13), on the Gauls (5.200–5), on the Romans in general (5.159–61) and on all humanity. 'For murder and terrors are in store for all men because of the great city and a righteous people, which is preserved through everything, which Providence has exalted' (5.225–27). It is, of course, precisely the failure of 'Providence' which underlies the hurt and confusion expressed in such oracles.

Even more clearly than in Book 3, the Sibyl in Book 5 portrays her social maladjustment to Egyptian life by predicting the destruction of her environment: when the Nile rises to smother the land (5.52–74), the great Egyptian cities will be demolished (5.179–99). After decades of political conflict in Egypt (especially Alexandria), there are now special grievances concerning the maltreatment of Jews (5.68–70). Besides the now familiar insults against iconic or zoomorphic religion (5.75–85, 276–80, 351–60, 403–5), the Sibyl directs specific barbs at the famous cult of Isis ('thrice-wretched Goddess') and Serapis (5.484–91). In fact she imagines a mass conversion to 'the true God' (5.492–503), with priests urging the population to 'change the terrible customs we have learnt from our ancestors' (5.494). Details of the future are not entirely clear. In some oracles there appears to be a promise of a new temple in the 'holy land' (5.418–33), and Judaea is repeatedly hailed as the land of God's special grace (5.247–85, 328–32). Elsewhere, there is the prospect of a 'great holy temple in Egypt', though this too will be subject to destruction (5.492–511). Perhaps the sack of once 'inviolable' Zion has made future prospects harder to predict. But, in any case, the removal of the 'unclean foot of Greeks' (5.264) and the silencing of Egyptian Gods (5.484–91) indicate the triumph of the 'divine and heavenly race of the blessed Jews' (5.249).

A special feature of the Fifth Sibylline Book is its use of current speculation on the return of Nero.[84] In four separate oracles (5.93–110, 137–54, 214–27, 361–85) his dramatic return from the East is predicted, with a full measure of vengeance on all in his path. His threatening potential has been magnified by his role in the Jewish War and by his rumoured ambitions on Judaea (5.104–10, 150–54; cf. Suetonius, *Nero* 40.2). He is also used here both as the

---

[84] On the origins and influence of this speculation see MacMullen 1966:143–45 and Collins 1974:80–87.

instrument of judgment on Rome and as the symbol of all her wickedness. Romans are warned of judgment for their sexual perversions, and the destruction of the Temple of Vesta is gleefully acclaimed (5.386–96). In one of the most politically subversive statements in antiquity, the Sibyl announces the annihilation of the imperial city:

> Alas, city of the Latin land, unclean in all things ...
> You have a bloodthirsty heart and an impious mind.
> Did you not know what God can do, what are his designs?
> But you said, 'I am unique and no-one can wipe me out'.
> But now the eternal God will destroy you and all your people,
> And there will no longer be any sign of you in that land ...
> Remain unique, you lawless one. Mingled with the flames of fire
> Inhabit the lawless nether regions of Hades. (5.168–78)[85]

It is strange to think that at precisely this time Josephus was enjoying the patronage of the imperial court in Rome and explaining the heaven-sent success of this 'doomed' city (see below, chapter 12.2.1)!

Such are the dimensions of the 'Antichrist' figure in these oracles that the Sibyl imagines a forthcoming war of devastating proportions. At two points she portrays a coming messianic figure, 'a certain king sent from God to destroy all great kings and all the finest men' (5.108–9), 'a blessed man from heaven' who will redistribute wealth and build a massive tower in the city of God (5.414–33). Such messianic eschatology matches the historical events in Egypt we have outlined above (chapter 3.3). For it is surely in this Fifth Sibylline Book that we come closest to the ideology which inspired the Diaspora Revolt of 116–117 CE.[86] The Jewish destruction of Egyptian temples fits these pronouncements against Isis and Serapis, and the Sibyl's predictions of a cataclysmic world war (5.362, 462) are mirrored in the zeal with which Jews demolished the property of 'unclean Greeks', and in the spread of the revolt through Cyrene, Egypt and Cyprus. Loukuas' royal

---

[85] The echoes of the attack on Babylon in Isa 47 (cf. Rev 18) are noted by Fuchs 1964:67–68.
[86] See especially Hengel 1983. The destructive war, the messianic expectations, the hatred of Rome and of Egyptian religion, and the military significance of the East (Trajan was engaged in a difficult Parthian campaign in 115 CE) are all themes in this document which link it to the Diaspora Revolt.

title suggests that many considered him to be precisely that 'king sent from God' which the Sibyl announced. In the event no Egyptian priests preached repentance to the population of Egypt and no great Jewish temple replaced the damaged shrines of Serapis. Instead the Roman troops and Egyptian peasants all but wiped out the 'impious' Jews of Egypt. It is somehow fitting that the violent propaganda of this Sibylline Book concludes with the bleak prospect of a starless sky (5.531).

# PART TWO

# THE DIASPORA IN OTHER MEDITERRANEAN SITES

# 8

## *Cyrenaica and Syria*

No region of the Mediterranean Diaspora can compete with Egypt in its wealth of evidence pertaining to Jews. The combination of epigraphic, papyrological and literary sources which enables us to paint so detailed a picture of the Egyptian Diaspora has no parallel elsewhere. While the number of Jewish inscriptions discovered in other regions continues to mount year by year, and synagogue buildings are occasionally unearthed, they rarely compensate for the near total lack of papyri from outwith Egypt. What is more, the varied portfolio of Jewish literature which we know to emanate from the Egyptian Diaspora has no counterpart in other regions. What other documents we know (or suspect) to come from outwith Egypt are either uncharacteristic of Jews in their particular locations (Josephus; Paul) or are of indefinable origin (Pseudo-Phocylides; 4 Maccabees).

In our present state of knowledge there are only four other locations in the Mediterranean Diaspora where we may offer a moderately full account of Jewish life: Cyrenaica, Syria, the province of Asia and the city of Rome. We know from isolated inscriptions or passing literary references that Jews lived in very many other parts of the Mediterranean world. Cyprus, Cilicia, Pontus, the Bosphorus, Macedonia, Greece, Illyricum and Italy (beyond Rome) all have some attestation in our sources; but in all such cases the evidence is too fragmentary to enable us to construct a coherent account of Jewish life there (see above, chapter 1, p. 10–11). Even in the four locations we will now study (chapters 8–10), there are massive gaps in our knowledge and huge periods of silence which will severely restrict our efforts. But in these cases there is just enough material to justify an investigation of Jewish history and the relations of Diaspora Jews with their social and political environments.

## 8.1 Cyrenaica

The region of Cyrenaica (part of modern-day Libya) constituted an island of Hellenism whose origins lay in an early period of Greek colonization. In our period its five main cities – Cyrene, Apollonia, Ptolemais, Teucheira and Berenice – were of independent character, sometimes referred to collectively as the Pentapolis, sometimes simply as Cyrene. (It is thus often unclear whether a reference to 'Cyrene' refers only to that city or to the region as a whole.) Turning from Egypt to Cyrenaica for information about Jews, we are immediately struck by the paucity of information left to us by history. Josephus is either ignorant of, or uninterested in, the fortunes of Jews in Cyrenaica until an incident in 73 CE in which he was personally implicated; thus he provides only snippets of information and, on the incident in question, two highly partisan (and not wholly consistent) accounts (see below). Fortunately, archaeology in this region has proved to be of particular value to the historian. The appearance of Jewish names on epitaphs and on lists of ephebes in several sites gives us a starting point for analysis, and three lengthy inscriptions from Berenice enable us to draw some conclusions concerning the Jews' social location in that city. Moreover, the violent uprising of Jews in Cyrenaica which started the Diaspora Revolt (116–117 CE) has left so many traces in the archaeological record as to enable us to piece together aspects of that event which proved so disastrous to the cities and to the local Jewish communities.[1]

The migration of Jews to Cyrenaica appears to have come about in consequence of their sizeable presence in Egypt. Since Cyrenaica was ruled by the Ptolemaic dynasty until 96 BCE, it is reasonable to assume, as Strabo suggests, that Jewish settlement in the towns of the Pentapolis took place from (or at least through) Egypt (*apud* Josephus, *Ant* 14.118). Whether this took place with the active encouragement of Ptolemy I (323–282 BCE), as Josephus claims (*C Ap* 2.44), is uncertain, given Josephus' general tendency to claim royal support for Jews from the earliest possible date. But since we

---

[1] Applebaum 1979 gives the fullest analysis of the evidence, with a particularly valuable description of the Diaspora Revolt. His tendency to extract more from the Jewish inscriptions than is reasonable is corrected in the more sober and up-to-date collection of the evidence by Lüderitz (with Reynolds) 1983. Lüderitz has announced a forthcoming comprehensive treatment of Jewish history in Cyrenaica.

know that Jews were employed in the Ptolemaic army and at various levels of administration in Egypt (see chapter 2.1), it is not unreasonable to suggest that their presence in Cyrenaica was of similar value to the dynasty.[2]

Sadly, our sources leave us almost entirely ignorant of the social, political and intellectual development of Jews in Cyrenaica during the Ptolemaic period, which was so significant for Egyptian Jews. The only individual known to us is Jason of Cyrene, whose five volumes of history on the Maccabean revolt were summarized in the volume we know as 2 Maccabees (see 2.19–32). Unfortunately, the author of 2 Maccabees has introduced many of his own characteristics into his epitome of Jason, such that it is hard to assess Jason's own aims and perspectives.[3] At most we can assert that Jason's work indicates advanced educational skills among some Jews in Cyrene and an acute interest in the Maccabean struggle. We have no way of telling whether this 'nationalist' sentiment was typical of Cyrenaean Jews; it is not even certain whether Jason wrote in Cyrene or simply came from there but lived and worked in Judaea. But his work could be taken as evidence for contact between Cyrenaica and Judaea in the second century BCE, a contact which we know continued in subsequent centuries and which proved to be of decisive significance on later occasions.[4]

Our knowledge of Jews in Cyrenaica only begins to acquire depth in the Roman era. When Ptolemy Apion bequeathed the region to Rome at his death in 96 BCE, the cities were allowed their freedom and the region was left comparatively unsupervised until its reorganization as a province in 74 BCE. This period of freedom proved far from peaceful, as rivalries within and between the cities caused civic unrest: on his arrival in Cyrene in 87/86 BCE, Sulla's

---

[2]  Applebaum speculates on their status as cleruchs on royal land, but admits the absence of reliable evidence for the Ptolemaic period (1979:130–38).

[3]  The epitomator claims in 2.23–31 merely to have shortened Jason's narrative, but the character of his work, with its long florid episodes, suggests otherwise. He describes himself as a painter (2.29) who aims to gratify (2.25) and provide enjoyment for the reader (16.39). The work may have undergone further editorial revision when the two Jerusalem letters were added as a preface (1.1 – 2.18). Doran 1981:77–84 probably underestimates the alterations introduced by the summarizer. In reality, 'we do not know how much is due to the reviser and how much to the original author' (Schürer 3.532); cf. Tcherikover 1961a:381–90; Hengel 1974:95–99.

[4]  Excavation has unearthed one Jewish coin from the Maccabean era in Ptolemais (see Kraeling 1962:268). Applebaum's argument for a second wave of Jewish immigration in the Maccabean era is tenuous, 1979:138–44.

lieutenant Lucullus found its citizens 'harassed by successive tyrannies and wars' (Plutarch, *Lucullus* 2.3). A reference in Josephus may indicate (the text is uncertain) that the Jewish community played a significant role in this unrest, even that they were the main culprits as far as Lucullus was concerned (*Ant* 14.114).[5] In this connection Josephus cites Strabo to indicate that in Cyrene (the city or the whole region?) 'there were four [classes?], the citizens, the peasants, the metics and, fourth, the Jews' (*Ant* 14.115). It is hard to know what to make of this crude social categorization, but it might suggest that the Jewish community in Cyrene was a large and independent body, distinct from the citizens, but distinct also from other groups of settlers (metics). We cannot tell precisely what legal status it had, nor how it was organized, although evidence from Berenice suggests the existence of a *politeuma*-organization (Lüderitz 1994:210–21). Strabo suggests that Cyrenaica had particularly fostered the Jews as organized groups (συντάγματα) who followed their ancestral laws (*apud* Josephus, *Ant* 14.116). Such a significant group could well have exercised some influence in the troubled decades after Apion's death and, by taking sides, won enemies as well as friends.[6] But our evidence allows us to draw no firm conclusions beyond the existence of well-established and prominent Jewish communities in the early Roman period. It is no surprise to find such communities playing a significant role in the later history of Cyrenaica.

It is in the early imperial era that our inscriptional evidence begins to shed light on the Jews' location in Cyrenaean society. From the city of Cyrene we have two lists of ephebes (one from the late first century BCE, the other from 3/4 CE) which include Jewish names, Jesus son of Antiphilos, for instance, and Eleazar son of Eleazar (Lüderitz 6–7). This proves the entry of Jews into the citizen body of Cyrene, though it is impossible to say what attitude they took to the religious aspects of their training (each

---

[5]  Most texts read: ἐπὶ τὴν ἐν Κυρήνῃ στάσιν τοῦ ἔθνους ἡμῶν ὧν ἡ οἰκουμένη πεπλήρωτο. But codex P omits ὧν and on that basis Niese (1887–1895) ad loc. posits a lacuna after στάσιν; that would make unclear what involvement, if any, Jews had in the civic unrest. Plutarch makes no reference to Jews in this connection.

[6]  Compare Jewish involvement in Egyptian politics discussed in chapter 2.2. On the nature of the troubles in Cyrenaica, which are largely obscure, see Romanelli 1971:39–51, Applebaum 1979:63–66, 201–4 and Braund 1985. Cf. the inscription honouring Apollodorus for his benevolent role in a period of 'anarchy' in Berenice, Reynolds no. 3 in Lloyd 1981.

list of names is dedicated to the Gods of the gymnasium, Hermes and Heracles). A similar phenomenon is probably discernible in Teucheira, where among the names scratched on the walls of the gymnasium are some which are almost certainly Jewish (Lüderitz 41).[7] Moreover, the rise of individual Jews into positions of civic responsibility is demonstrated by two inscriptions. In one (Lüderitz 36) Simon son of Simon (probably a Jew) is part of a two-man delegation from the city of Ptolemais to a Roman business-man, A. Terentius, in Lanuvium; in the other we find in the list of Cyrene's 'guardians of the law' (νομοφύλακες) El(e)azar son of Jason (Lüderitz 8; the date is 60/61 CE). It appears that Eleazar's position entailed considerable responsibility, requiring education, experience and the confidence of the civic leaders.[8] To find a Jew in this position attests the integration of wealthier Jewish families into the civic life of Cyrene.[9]

Inscriptions concerning individual Jews and their acquisition of citizen status demonstrate that the Jewish communities and the citizen bodies were not mutually exclusive entities; but otherwise they give us little indication of the relationship of Jews in general to their social environment. The discovery of large numbers of Jewish tombs in Teucheira might have shed some light on this matter, but the inscriptions consist merely of names, and nomenclature is not a sufficient indication of ethnic identity. Thus it is unclear whether we have unearthed a wholly Jewish cemetery (with Jews bearing a mixture of Jewish and Greek names), or whether the Jewish tombs are mixed in with others, and some individual Jews (e.g. as slaves) buried with Gentile families.[10] The

---

7   Lüderitz modifies some of Applebaum's claims but argues that Theodotus and Dositheos are almost certainly Jewish names in this context (1983:64–66). The names in pairs, including one Dositheos, may indicate homosexual relationships.

8   See Applebaum 1979:186–90.

9   The inscription opens with a list of civic priests and was almost certainly dedicated to Apollo Nomios, Aphrodite and Homonoia. Thus the question of Eleazar's religious practice is raised (though hardly answered). Schürer 3.131 reminds us that we cannot be sure that Eleazar and his like have maintained their Jewish practices. Applebaum writes that 'it may be supposed that he had not renounced his faith, since he did not follow a common fashion of changing his name to a Greek one, as did many Cyrenean Jews' (1979:186). We know indeed of many Cyrenaean Jews with Greek names, but did Jews ever *change* their names to indicate their alienation from the Jewish community?

10  See the cautious discussion by Lüderitz 1983:69–145 (inscriptions 43–69) which now takes precedence over Applebaum 1979:144–60. The tombs are mostly

Jewish families in the Teucheira cemetery show frighteningly high rates of child mortality, but probably no higher than the average.[11] An inscription from Cyrene concerning one 'Sarra proselyte' (Lüderitz 12) indicates that Jewish communities could grow by conversion as well as by reproduction.

Most revealing are three major inscriptions from Berenice which record the formal business of the Jewish community there. The first (*SEG* 16.931 = Lüderitz 70) records the thanks of the Jewish *politeuma* to one Decimus Valerius Dionysius who, as his contribution to the *politeuma*, has paid for the stucco flooring (?) and the plastering and painting of the walls of the 'amphitheatre'. He is henceforth to be freed from his 'liturgy' obligations and to be crowned at every meeting (σύνοδος) and new moon, and the inscription is to be placed by the rulers of the community at a prominent place in the amphitheatre. The second (*IGRR* 1.1024 = Lüderitz 71) lists nine rulers (*archontes*) of the community, and records thanks to Marcus Tittius, son of Sextus, who had been present in the province on public affairs and had shown exemplary consideration for all, responding to the appeals of citizens and also showing valuable patronage to the Jews' *politeuma*, both to the group and to individuals; again he is to be honoured at each meeting and the inscription to be placed at a prominent location in the amphitheatre. The third (*SEG* 17.823 = Lüderitz 72) records a list of donors to a fund for the restoration of the Jewish synagogue in Berenice, the list beginning with ten *archontes* and a priest.[12]

The third inscription displays merely the internal affairs of the community, though the list of names shows that many of its leaders bore Gentile theophoric names and others had names which were common in their Cyrenaean environment.[13] For our interpretation

---

arranged in burial courts, and the relations between those buried together in these conditions are not known. Only a fraction can be identified as 'certainly Jewish'; but if these make up a considerable proportion of a certain burial court, are the rest to be taken as Jewish as well? Lüderitz concludes that at least four of the courts here are Jewish.

[11] See van der Horst 1991:73–84.

[12] In this inscription, the term συναγωγή is used to refer both to the meeting of the Jews and to the building in which they met – the earliest known inscription to employ this usage (55 CE). The precise dating of the other two inscriptions is problematic, since it is uncertain which era their numbering relates to; but they are probably from the first century BCE or early first century CE.

[13] Among Gentile theophoric names are Serapion, Ammonos and Isidora; as Reynolds comments (in Lloyd 1981:244), 'the impression is of a group which sought a degree of integration with its Greek neighbours.'

of the first two inscriptions much hinges on the identification of the 'amphitheatre' mentioned in both texts: is this the civic amphitheatre of Berenice, or is it a Jewish building given this name because of its shape? Many have found difficulty with the notion that the Jews of Berenice mounted dedicatory inscriptions in the civic amphitheatre and paid for its upkeep. One need not hold that the Jews held their own meetings in such a setting, or that they paid for the gladiatorial contests which took place there.[14] It could simply be that they were expected to help pay for the upkeep of the amphitheatre, so that the Jew Decimus Valerius Dionysius could make his contribution to the Jewish *politeuma* by paying for the building works here listed. It is certainly possible to imagine that the Jewish community in Berenice was sufficiently prominent and integrated into civic life to share in the use of major civic amenities; a century later there is evidence that Jews in Miletus (Asia) had their own block of theatre seats (*CIJ* 748).

However, it is marginally more likely that the 'amphitheatre' was a specifically Jewish building. It is doubtful whether there was a permanent civic amphitheatre in Berenice at this time, and one would not expect an amphitheatre to have a stucco floor; one may also question whether Jews could mount their own dedicatory inscriptions there.[15] Thus, despite the lack of parallel for such a name, it is probable that the 'amphitheatre' here is a Jewish building, perhaps a meeting place for members of the *politeuma*, who appear to have been a select 'council' of community representatives.[16] Nonetheless it is significant that they honoured here not only their own member (Decimus Valerius Dionysius) but also a visiting Roman official (Marcus Tittius), whom they praised for bringing some benefit both to the city as a whole and to the Jewish *politeuma*. Jews and Romans are here honoured in identical formulae, which also match the standard phraseology of contemporary Greek inscriptions.

---

[14] The first alternative was raised as an objection by Applebaum 1979:165, the second by Robert 1940:34 n. 1.

[15] See Lüderitz 1994:213–14. The question of the flooring is discussed by Reynolds in Lloyd 1981:247 and Tracey in Horsley 1987:208–9 (the latter suggesting a floor not in the amphitheatre itself but in an adjoining room).

[16] Lüderitz 1994:210–21. The structure of this building might thus have been similar to the synagogue (?) building in Gamla (see Sanders 1992:200).

Thus, even if the 'amphitheatre' is their own, it seems that the leaders of the Jewish community in Berenice were willing to identify themselves in large measure with the interests of the whole civic community. Some, like Decimus Valerius Dionysius, were Roman citizens, others (as we have seen) were citizens of their particular cities. It thus appears that some Jews in Cyrenaica had been successful in their assimilation into Greek political life. The fact that the Jewish community as a whole honoured such Jews indicates that their measure of assimilation was not considered illegitimate in the only court that mattered.

In or soon after the period of these inscriptions from Berenice Josephus records a dispute in Cyrenaica concerning the Jews' temple tax (*Ant* 16.160–61, 169–70). As so often, Josephus' vague terminology gives us little aid in interpretation. He refers to the Jews' former 'equality of rights' (ἰσονομία) and Augustus' grant of 'equality of taxation' (ἰσοτέλεια), but does not indicate whether these are identical or what either really meant. It is also unclear how much his generalized remarks in *Ant* 16.160 relate to Cyrenaica (which he brackets here with Asia) and to how much of that province they apply; the only relevant document here cited is a letter from Agrippa to the city of Cyrene (*Ant* 16.169–70, c. 14 BCE). The document suggests that, at least in that city, the Jews had been accused of non-payment of taxes and had contested their liability to pay. An earlier ruling from Augustus had been ignored by the city, or interpreted in a way unfavourable to the Jews, and the Jewish community had been brought to court on the matter, had lost their case and had had some of their 'sacred money' (destined for the Jerusalem temple) confiscated as a result.

We cannot tell whether this issue affected other cities or even what exactly was a stake in Cyrene. But if we may take our bearings from parallel cases in Asia (on which see below, chapter 9), it appears that the Jewish community, because of its wealth and prominence, was considered liable to financial contributions, from which it claimed exemption. In fact about this time the Cyrenaean cities appealed to Augustus also against Roman citizens who claimed exemption from taxation and 'liturgy' duties.[17] The cities

---

[17]  *SEG* 9.8, section III; in this case their appeal was successful. Were some wealthy Jews who had liturgy obligations in the Jewish community (as Decimus clearly had in Berenice) declining to perform liturgies for the citizen body as well? Baldwin Bowsky 1987 links the Berenice inscription honouring Marcus Tittius (Lüdertiz 71) with the Jews' successful appeal against the cities, but her case depends on a doubtful chain of argumentation concerning the date of the inscriptions.

were engaged in a war between 20 and 2 BCE against native tribesmen; that must have put them under severe economic pressure which no doubt exacerbated these financial disputes.[18] We do not how the Jews' dispute was resolved, nor what were its repercussions; but it serves to indicate that, despite the generally harmonious relationships between Jews and Gentiles, the Jews' separate communal organization and their financial identification with Jerusalem could become causes of disharmony in Jew-Gentile relations.

There is evidence, both in the New Testament and in inscriptions, for continuing contact between Cyrenaean Jews and Judaea in the first century CE.[19] Unfortunately such contact was to have fatal effects in the aftermath of the Jewish War. We do not know whether Cyraenean Jews fought in Judaea during the War, but a half-shekel coin from the second year of the war, with the inscription 'The freedom of Zion', has been found in Cyrene.[20] The presence of nationalist fervour in the province is indeed a necessary presupposition of the story to be found in Josephus (*Bell* 7.437–53; *Vita* 424) that a weaver called Jonathan, a refugee from Judaea, stirred up a considerable uprising in Cyrenaica in the aftermath of the War (probably 73 CE). Josephus' account is not entirely satisfactory (in one version the rebels are unarmed, in another they have weapons), but it appears that Jonathan was a charismatic figure who was able to raise the expectations of a large number of local Jews, and led them into the desert with promises of 'signs' (*Bell* 7.438). Josephus' account has obvious class biases, but he is probably correct to claim that Jonathan's supporters were mostly the poorer members of the community, and Applebaum has argued that their discontent had substantial economic causes besides their national and religious fanaticism.[21]

---

[18] On conditions in the province in this period see Romanelli 1971:69–91; Kraeling 1962:11–15.

[19] From the New Testament, note Simon of Cyrene in the gospels (Mark 15.21 and parallels) and Jews from Cyrene who had settled in Jerusalem and established their own synagogues there (Acts 2.10; 6.9; cf. 11.20 and 13.1). Lüderitz 35 is a Jerusalem inscription concerning Sara daughter of Simon who hailed from Ptolemais; cf. Applebaum 1979:126.

[20] Healy 1957 and Lüderitz 27.

[21] Applebaum 1979:201–41 argues that many Jews were former tenants on royal land, whose ownership had proved a matter of dispute during the first century CE. He postulates that it was the landless Jewish 'proletariat' who were the most susceptible to Jonathan's propaganda.

The wealthier Jews, some of whom were, as we have seen, more socially integrated, had more to lose from civil commotion; they distanced themselves from the movement and collaborated with the authorities in its suppression. We find the same class divisions here as we have noted in Alexandria in this period (see above, chapter 3.2), but in this case the Jewish upper classes were unable to dispel the suspicion that they were responsible for the trouble. Although the Roman governor, Catullus, was able to quell the Jewish insurgency (causing, according to Josephus, 2000 Jewish casualties), his retaliatory measures extended to propertied Jews as well. Josephus, who has to assert his own innocence in this affair, claims that Catullus was motivated by personal pique against certain individuals and by a desire for glory in conducting his own 'Jewish War'. But it is significant that his drastic measures against the upper-class Jews in Cyrenaica – according to Josephus he had 3000 killed and their property confiscated – were never legally challenged. Vespasian investigated Jonathan's claims of an international Jewish plot (which had implicated Josephus) and dismissed them (*Bell* 7.447–50); but he took no action against Catullus. Catullus, therefore, may have had some grounds for his measures, or at least the support of local interest groups who perhaps used the Jews' communal solidarity and their identification with Judaea to discredit them all.[22]

Whether Catullus' punitive measures were justified or not, they constituted a devastating blow to the Jewish communities in Cyrenaica. The families ruined by his executions and confiscations were presumably those which had provided leadership to the synagogues. They were also those whose status had inclined them to the sort of social and cultural integration which we have witnessed in the inscriptions. Without such leadership, and with grievances harboured by Jews of all classes in the aftermath of the Jonathan affair, we must presume that the Jews of Cyrenaica became socially and politically disaffected. We have no direct knowledge of them during the following generation, but some such social alienation must be presupposed to explain the extraordinary explosion of violence which broke out in 115/116 CE and sparked off the 'Diaspora Revolt'. Our literary sources for this catastrophic

---

[22] It was perhaps in this period that the Jewish high priest, Ishmael ben Phabi, was executed in Cyrene (*Bell* 6.114); his family were fully involved in the Judaean War, and a rabbinic source (b Pesahim 57a) records his reputation for 'zeal'.

event emphasize the savagery of the Jewish uprising,[23] and its devastating effects are well evidenced by archaeology, which indicates wholescale destruction of many public buildings in Cyrene, not least the temples.[24] The damage to the infrastructure of the province (many roads had to be rebuilt after this 'tumultus Iudaicus') might suggest that the Jews involved meant to make the province their home no longer. Some indeed migrated into Egypt, and there are good grounds for supposing that their ultimate intention was to press on to Judaea.[25] At their head was a leader called Loukuas,[26] whose designation as 'king' surely indicates some messianic claim. It appears that the biblical prophecies of a coming king and a return from the Diaspora had captivated Cyrenaean Jews, who were perhaps stirred by the eschatological expectations of a final war which we have witnessed in the *Sibylline Oracles* (see above, chapter 7.4).[27] The fury with which they conducted their campaign indicates their mood of utter conviction, even desperation.

This highly organized uprising was a tragic finale to the story of Jewish life in Cyrenaica. Despite inflicting heavy losses on the Roman troops they encountered, their incursion into Egypt was to end in defeat at the hands of Marcius Turbo, who had been hastily dispatched from Parthia by Trajan. To repair the devastated province of Cyrenaica was to absorb considerable time and expense (we have several inscriptions marking Hadrian's assistance in the process), and the extent of the casualties in Cyrenaica may be indicated by the need to introduce new settlers and to found a

---

[23]  Dio Cassius 68.32 talks of the Jews forcing their opponents to fight wild beasts, and even of their cannibalism and the skinning of enemy corpses! He records 220,000 casualties in Cyrene. Of course, his account is probably rhetorically overblown.

[24]  See the survey by Applebaum 1979:272–94 and Smallwood 1981:397–99. Even the *nomophylakeion* in which Eleazar had worked seems to have been destroyed by fire in the revolt! Archaeologists have not been able to excavate the public buildings in cities other than Cyrene, but we may guess that a similar trail of destruction would be found there.

[25]  So Fuks 1961:103–4; Applebaum 1979:335–37; Hengel 1983:660–61.

[26]  Eusebius, *Hist Eccles* 4.2; Dio Cassius refers to Andreas (68.32), perhaps another leader who stayed in Cyrene; see above, chapter 3 n. 67.

[27]  *Sib Or* 5.195–99 refers to the destruction of cities in Cyrenaica; see Hengel 1983:665–79. As Applebaum concludes, 'the spirit of the movement was messianic, its aim the liquidation of the Roman régime and the setting up of a new Jewish commonwealth, whose task was to inaugurate the messianic era' (1979:260).

new city, Hadrianopolis, on the coastal plain. We may judge that few Jews survived to witness this reconstruction, and any that did must have lived in disgrace. As far as we know, Cyrenaica had never experienced such devastation before and cannot have quickly forgiven the Jews who had caused it. Thus ended several hundred years of Jewish prosperity in Cyrenaica, centuries in which occasional disharmony between Jews and Greeks had never seriously impeded Jewish social integration. Through nationalist fervour in the aftermath of the Jewish War, and as a result of Catullus' excessive revenge in 73 CE, an alienated Jewish community finally rose in anger, sweeping the province into chaos and taking with it to destruction thousands of Greek and Roman lives.

## 8.2 Syria

Josephus asserts that 'the Jewish race, while dispersed in considerable numbers among native populations throughout the world, is especially numerous in Syria, because of its proximity' (*Bell* 7.43). There is no reason to question this generalization, except to note that to describe Syria as 'proximate to' the Jews' homeland is a little misleading. For most of the period we are studying, the Jews' home territory was generally considered *part of* Syria, rather than an adjacent, independent country. Jews from Judaea who settled, for whatever social, economic, or political reasons, in Damascus, Ascalon, Tyre or Antioch were not considered by most of their contemporaries to have 'entered' Syria, simply to have moved from one part of it to another.

In truth, the term 'Syria' was somewhat vague, not least because of the historical vicissitudes of the region. In the wars following the dismemberment of Alexander's kingdom, the coastal district which forms the eastern edge of the Mediterranean was the subject of continual disputes between the Ptolemaic and Seleucid dynasties. The division of the region after 302 BCE left Palestine and Phoenicia (sometimes called 'Coele-Syria') in the hands of the Ptolemies and northern Syria under the Seleucids, but after the battle of Panium (200 BCE) the region was reunited under Seleucid rule. It was only when the Seleucid dynasty began to disintegrate that the Hasmoneans could establish something approximating an autonomous Jewish kingdom, extending far beyond the original 'temple-state' of Judaea. But their territory was considerably reduced and brought firmly under Roman control by Pompey

(63 BCE). After this point only the kingdoms of Herod (37–4 BCE) and (in smaller scope) Archelaus (4 BCE – 6 CE) and Agrippa (41–44 CE) established periods of semi-independent Jewish rule. For the remainder of the Roman period, the district was simply one part of the province of Syria.

The chequered history of the region and the continual expansion and contraction of what could be considered 'Jewish' territory make it peculiarly difficult here to distinguish between 'homeland' and 'Diaspora'. When large numbers of Jews settled in the Greek coastal cities, could they consider these as properly 'Jewish', even 'holy land', or were they, in such a Hellenized environment, in the 'Diaspora'? At different points in time, one might have given different answers to this question, depending on whether the city in question was under Greek/Roman control, or in the power of Alexander Jannaeus or Herod the Great. But even under Jewish rulers, the Greek history, constitution and ambience of such cities made the question difficult to answer, and, as we shall see, such ambiguities could become the cause of strife between Jews and non-Jews. For our purposes, it seems best to include in our study not only those Jews who lived in Syrian cities which were always outside Jewish control (e.g. Antioch, Damascus, Tyre, Sidon, Ptolemais) but also those who resided in the Hellenistic cities of the coastal plain, the Decapolis and Peraea, where the majority of the population was Gentile and the cultural environment was predominantly Syro-Hellenistic.[28]

For our period of interest our sources of information about Jews in the Syrian Diaspora are surprisingly limited. The Jewish population in Antioch in this period was especially large (Josephus, *Bell* 7.43), and there has been extensive excavation of the site; but we have no identifiably Jewish remains from the city. Thus our knowledge of the fortunes of Jews in Antioch is limited to incidental remarks by Josephus, together with brief references in the work of

---

[28] Eleazar's speech at Masada places Jews in Caesarea, Scythopolis and Damascus alongside those in Egypt as residents in an 'alien land' (ἐπ' ἀλλοτρίας γῆς, Josephus, *Bell* 7.361–69). The influence of Hellenism in Judaea itself is not, of course, to be underestimated; but the difference in the Hellenistic cities was more than a matter of degree, since there it involved also the ethos and the self-understanding of the civic community. Although Galilee had a sizeable non-Jewish population, the preponderance of Jewish villages and the influence of Jews even in its cities (Sepphoris and Tiberias) make it inappropriate to consider this region in the category of 'Diaspora'.

the sixth century CE chronicler, Malalas, whose reliability is often in doubt. As we shall see, there are moments when Josephus and Malalas describe the Jews' history in Antioch from opposed but equally partisan viewpoints. We have much fuller evidence from Christian and Greek sources in a later period (the fourth century CE), which is of no use to our enquiry. Outside Antioch, a number of inscriptions record Jewish presence in Syrian towns, although again most are outside our chronological limits. Rabbinic references to Jewish presence in Antioch and other cities doubtless contain some historical reminiscences, but the majority relate to the very different conditions after the Bar Kochba revolt (132–135 CE). Thus, we are mostly dependent on the detailed but tendentious witness of 1 and 2 Maccabees for the Hasmonean period, and the histories of Josephus, who was naturally partisan but at least contemporary to some of the events he records. Early Christian writings add very little to the picture: their absorption in the progress of the tiny Christian movement restricts their ability to reveal much of the larger picture of Jews' relations with the Graeco-Roman world.

## 8.2.1 The Hellenistic Era

As we have just noted, for the duration of the third century BCE Syria was divided between Seleucid and Ptolemaic empires. In the Ptolemaic portion of the region, the papyri (e.g. the Zeno papyri) indicate conditions not unlike those we have seen in Egypt (chapter 2.1). The acquisition of Jews, among other Syrians, as slaves, and the use of Jews in military units probably led to a sizeable dispersion of Jewish personnel into the Phoenician and Greek cities on the coastal plain which bore allegiance to Egypt. As in Egypt, Jews were also to be found at various levels of administration; the most famous example is the Tobiad family in the Transjordanian region, whose legends are recorded by Josephus (*Ant* 12.160ff.). The Hellenization of the whole region, and especially its upper classes, has been documented in full by Hengel (1974).

As for the Seleucid portion of Syria, our evidence is limited to Antioch. Here, as in relation to Alexandria, Josephus makes multiple and not entirely consistent claims concerning the settlement and rights of Antiochene Jews. It is possible that, as Josephus claims, (Babylonian?) Jews fought in Seleucid armies and some of these may have been settled on favourable terms in the city of Antioch (*Ant* 12.119). If so, we cannot tell what these terms were or whether they amounted to citizenship (Josephus' claims are suspect and inconsistent).[29] Whatever citizen rights individual Jewish families may have acquired, these did not belong to the Jewish community as such, which may however have received certain 'rights' (*Bell* 7.110: to follow 'ancestral customs'?) though we cannot tell at what date.[30] That the Jewish community became numerically and socially significant at an early date may be indicated by the decision of the high-priest Onias to take refuge in Daphne (a suburb of Antioch) in 170 BCE, and by the Jews' effective complaint at his assassination (2 Macc 4.32–38). But we are unable to go beyond this meagre observation.[31]

The reunification of the region of Syria under Seleucid rule at the very beginning of the second century BCE must have facilitated movement between Antioch and Palestine, but it probably made little difference to the processes of cultural interaction between Jews and non-Jews in the Syrian cities. However, one event above all was to transform Jew-Gentile relations not only in Judaea but

[29] Both *Ant* 12.119 and *C Ap* 2.38–39 refer to the Jews' rights of *politeia* in Antioch since Seleucus I; but we have noted the suspect nature of such claims in relation to Alexandria (chapter 2.1.3 n28), and the appeal to the fact that Jewish residents in Antioch are called 'Antiochenes' (*C Ap* 2.39) looks like an attempt to blur legal distinctions. *Ant* 12.119–24 refers to the rights of Jews in the first century CE to receive money from the gymnasiarch in lieu of Gentile oil, which they considered polluted. This may refer to Jews training in the gymnasium, preparing to be citizens in Antioch (see further below, n. 63). But that indicates nothing about the status of the Antiochene Jewish community as a whole, and certainly nothing relevant to the third or second century BCE.

[30] *Bell* 7.43–44 suggests some recognition of the Jewish community by 'the successsors of King Antiochus', but it is unclear which 'Antiochus' is meant! The reference here to sharing of rights in the city (7.44) is both more modest and more plausible than the blanket references to citizenship (*politeia*) in *Ant* 12.119–20 and *C Ap* 2.38–39. See the discussion by Marcus in Appendix C to Josephus Loeb volume VII; Tcherikover 1961a:328–29; and Kraeling 1932:137–39. Kasher 1985:297–309 defends Josephus, claiming that by *politeia* he meant no more than the right of the Jewish *politeuma* to exist alongside the Greek citizen body. But if Josephus meant this, his language is, at the very least, disingenuous; and there is, in any case, no evidence that the Jews in Antioch were constituted as a *politeuma*.

[31] The story may be evidence for Jewish settlement in Daphne; so Downey 1961:109–10. Rabbinic efforts to associate Antioch with places and events in biblical history are naive, but may signal the early importance of Antioch in Jewish history; see Krauss 1902:29–33. Kraeling 1932 assembles all the evidence for Jewish residence in Antioch and provides still the best summary of Jewish history in the city, though it has been supplemented by Meeks & Wilken 1978.

also in all the contiguous territories. From c. 175 BCE there began the well-known attempt to Hellenize the religion and culture of the Jewish people, led by certain factions in the Jerusalem priesthood and supported by Antiochus Epiphanes. When this process led to the suppression of traditional Jewish practices (167–163 BCE), Mattathias and his sons instigated a popular revolt which was to have enormous consequences. As Hellenizing priests transformed the temple cult in contradiction of Jewish norms, and as Syrian troops enforced the suppression of Jewish laws (in particular, diet and circumcision customs), the Maccabean backlash created a cultural polarization in which 'Judaism' and 'Hellenism' were portrayed by both sides as mutually exclusive. The complex currents of Jewish opinion, and the alliances of political interest groups, are now barely detectable through the filter of the Maccabean literature. But what proved to be of lasting significance was the military success of the Maccabean cause and the upsurge of Jewish ethnic pride, in which was fostered a sense of contrariety to Greeks and to their 'alien' cultural practices.[32]

Soon after the start of the revolt, some of the Greek cities found themselves at odds with the Maccabean soldiers. Since the cities helped supply the troops ordered to suppress the insurgency, and since they apparently put pressure on their Jewish residents to renounce the Maccabean cause, the Maccabean commanders began to be engaged in fighting well beyond the boundaries of Judaea.[33] Violence is reported in Joppa, in Jamnia, in the region of Tyre and Sidon, in Galilee, in the Transjordan and in Idumaea, with the Maccabean brothers fighting on all sides to rescue their fellow Jews (1 Macc 5.1–68; 2 Macc 12.2–31). Doubtless territorial disputes, economic grievances and the settling of personal scores were just as important as ethnic/religious factors, but every new skirmish and every reported atrocity built up stores of animosity which were not easily dispersed. Moreover, once the Hasmoneans' power was consolidated in Judaea, they were drawn into the Seleucid wars of succession and thus found themselves entrusted

---

[32] See the survey and assessment of scholarly opinion on the Maccabean revolt and its causes in Grabbe 1992:246–93.

[33] See e.g. 1 Macc 5; 2 Macc 10.15–23; 12.2–31. The tendency in this literature always to portray Gentiles as initiating spiteful attacks on Jews (cf. 1 Macc 12.53) means its witness should be treated with great caution. To what extent 2 Macc 6.8–9 reflects a general assault on Jewish residents in the coastal cities is disputed; see e.g. Bickerman 1979:79 and Kasher 1990:56–57.

with new territory (1 Macc 10.74–89; 11.54–62; 12.33–34). After Simon's capture of Joppa there arose a conscious strategy of territorial expansion, in which cities were systematically Judaized and Gentile populations forcibly removed (1 Macc 13.11, 43–48; 14.5–7, 34–36). Eventually, exploiting the political power vacuum in the region, Alexander Jannaeus (103–76 BCE) established himself the master of nearly all the cities on the coastal plain up to Mount Carmel, together with the whole region of Idumaea, and, in the north and east, Samaria, Galilee and several towns across the Jordan (Josephus, *Ant* 13.395–97). Any cities which resisted the imposition of Jewish customs were treated harshly.[34]

It was in this extended period of military and cultural warfare that there arose that implacable hatred between Jews and 'Syrians' which was to fester through subsequent generations. For the inhabitants of the Greek cities surrounding Judaea, the expansion of Jewish power constituted not only a military but also a cultural threat. To the city élite who were long accustomed to Greek education and the refinements of Hellenistic entertainment, the encroachment of Jews from the hills of Judaea was politically threatening and culturally abhorrent.[35] When Jewish soldiers destroyed the city's temples (as in Azotus, 1 Macc 5.68; 10.82–85; Gazara, 1 Macc 13.47–48; and later Gaza, Josephus, *Ant* 13.356–64), or when Gentile populations were deported wholesale (as in Joppa, 1 Macc 13.11), fear and hatred of the Jews became endemic. If, as Kasher maintains, these Hasmonean campaigns were motivated by the genocidal commands in the Jewish Scriptures, we may explain the fury with which the Jews attacked their 'Canaanite' and 'Philistine' foes, and the shock with which the Hellenized cities experienced these 'barbaric' assaults.[36] To be sure,

---

[34] E.g. Pella (Josephus, *Ant* 13.397) and Gaza (*Ant* 13.356–64). Josephus (or his sources) probably exaggerated the extent of Hasmonean destructiveness; for Pella, contrast *Ant* 13.397 with *Bell* 1.156. The archaeological record, where it exists, does not suggest mass destruction. Perhaps only civic institutions and buildings were destroyed, with Greek citizens disenfranchised but not deported *en masse*.

[35] On the cultural achievements of the cities in question see Schürer 2.29–52, 85–183. Bickerman notes that 'twenty centuries ago the highland Jews of Palestine were rough peasants and shepherds who had grown up in an inhospitable country; they were known for their boldness and ruthlessness in war, and like the Arabs they terrified neighbouring agricultural countries by their inroads' (1962:137).

[36] Kasher's apologetic for this attempt to 'purify the land of Gentile abominations' (1990:313) is spectacularly lacking in sensitivity to the Gentile point of view.

such religious motivations were bound up with many more mundane economic and political disputes;[37] yet what distinguished Jews most clearly from other tribes in the region (Arabs, Ituraeans, Idumaeans etc.) was their religious intolerance and their apparent hostility to all things 'Greek'. That this impression took root even while the Hasmonean kings became Hellenized is one of the many ironies in the history of the Hasmonean state.

Josephus refers on numerous occasions to the Syrians' ingrained hatred of the Jews (e.g. *Bell* 1.88; 2.461, 478, 502; 5.550–51, 556; 7.367), and he clearly includes in the category 'Syrian' not only the native Semite population but also the Greeks and their descendants in the cities.[38] It is in this context of Hasmonean expansion that we find Greek complaints about the Jews' 'banditry' and 'seizure of others' property' (Strabo, *Geographica* 16.2.37) and vigorous attacks on their separateness and 'xenophobia'. According to both Josephus (*Ant* 13.245) and Diodorus (epitome of book 34, 1.1–5), Antiochus Sidetes VII was once urged, when besieging Jerusalem (134 BCE), to destroy the Jews on the grounds of their 'hatred of humanity'. Moreover, the Greek presentation of Antiochus Epiphanes as a champion of civilization, who attempted to eradicate the misanthropic customs of the Jews, is clearly part of the same anti-Jewish propaganda.[39] It was probably in the Syrian cities that there arose the malicious tale that Antiochus discovered in the temple a Greek who was being fattened for an annual ritual, in which the Jews would feast on the flesh of a foreigner and swear an oath of hostility to Greeks (Josephus, *C Ap* 2.89–96). The creation and circulation of such a myth is comprehensible in the context of an ideological warfare between Jews and Greeks, spawned by the success of the Maccabean uprising.[40]

---

The Maccabean literature is full of anachronistic references to 'Philistines' (e.g. 1 Macc 3.24; 5.66), which may spring from the biblical 'zeal' of the movement.

[37] For a fine example of what can be reconstructed in some specific cases, see Theissen 1992:61–80 on relations between Jews and Greeks in the region of Tyre.

[38] Cities with particular records of hostility include Ascalon (Josephus, *Bell* 3.10; Philo, *Legatio* 205), Tyre (Josephus, *C Ap* 1.70) and Strato's Tower/Caesarea (Josephus, *Bell* 7.361–63).

[39] See Bickerman 1979:12–14 and Gabba 1989:643–46. It is likely that the common source for Josephus and Diodorus was Posidonius, a native of Apamea in Syria; see Stern 1.184.

[40] The extent to which this ideological warfare reflected social reality is difficult to determine. The Hasmonean kings moved comfortably in the circles of

The expansion of Jewish power must have been resented chiefly in the cities immediately affected. To what extent it altered the relationships of Jews and Greeks in more distant Syrian towns is difficult to assess. It appears that Jewish prisoners were brought to Antioch,[41] but there is no evidence of any 'persecution' of Jews in Antioch in the time of Antiochus Epiphanes corresponding to that in Judaea. In fact in subsequent years the bronze utensils which Antiochus Epiphanes had appropriated from Jerusalem were given to the Antiochene Jews (Josephus, *Bell* 7.44). We know of only one incident in Antioch in this period which affected the Jews. At some point in the late 140s BCE, Demetrius II appealed for help to his ally Jonathan after a rebellion of his own troops. According to our sources (1 Macc 11.41–51; Josephus, *Ant* 13.135–42), Jonathan's detachment of 3000 soldiers played a decisive role in suppressing the uprising in the city and ended up burning much of Antioch. When the Jewish soldiers returned to Jerusalem with their spoils it is hard to believe that they were as popular in Antioch as 1 Maccabees claims (11.51). The story is reminiscent of the fateful role which Onias' soldiers played in Egyptian political affairs at precisely this time (see above chapter 2.2.1), but we do not know what effect this incident had on Antiochene Jews.

## 8.2.2 The Roman Era[42]

When Pompey settled the affairs of Syria in 63 BCE, he judged the Hasmonean state to have benefited too much from the chronic instability of the region. Although he allowed Hyrcanus' rule to continue, he greatly reduced his territory, freeing nearly all the coastal cities together with the most important cities to the north and east of Judaea.[43] This appears to have been a popular act, not least because Gabinius subsequently supported the rebuilding of many cities which had suffered damage in the Hasmonean

Hellenistic potentates (Bickerman 1962:153 refers to 'Maccabean Hellenism') and Alexander Jannaeus at least employed Gentile troops (Josephus, *Bell* 1.93).

[41] The city became associated with the 'third captivity' in rabbinic tradition, j Sanhedrin 10.6.

[42] See now the comprehensive survey of the region by Millar 1993.

[43] Josephus, *Bell* 1.156–57 names Hippos, Scythopolis, Pella, Samaria, Jamnia, Marisa, Azotus, Arethusa, Gaza, Joppa, Dora, and Strato's Tower. He goes so far as to say that Pompey restored these cities to their 'legitimate inhabitants'; cf. *Ant* 14.75–76 and Jones 1971:256–59.

conquests (Josephus, *Bell* 1.165–66). The sense of relief at liberation from Jewish rule is marked by the adoption of new dating eras in many of these cities.[44] It is likely that the non-Jewish population was significantly increased in the wake of this civic reconstitution.

However, with the establishment of Herod as the client king of Judaea (37–4 BCE) a new and more ambiguous relationship developed.[45] Augustus granted Herod possession of a number of important cities and created for him a kingdom almost as large as that of Alexander Jannaeus (*Bell* 1.396). But Herod's concern to foster an image of munificence led him to promote, rather than to suppress, the aspirations of his Gentile subjects. The list of Herod's donations to Syrian cities is extensive (*Bell* 1.422–25) and the line of the central street in Antioch which he paved is still clearly discernible.[46] One should imagine, as Kraeling suggests, that in Antioch and other locations favoured by Herod 'the prestige and self-importance of the local Jewry will have risen to a point scarcely reached before or after this time' (1932:147). Yet we know that Herod was distrusted by many of his Jewish subjects and to watch this Idumaean 'Jew' reconstitute Strato's Tower as Caesarea, a Greek city complete with amphitheatre, gymnasia, statues and temples, must have aroused anger among those who considered this territory part of the 'holy land'.[47] The ambiguities of Herod's legacy, with its simultaneous Jewish and Hellenistic glory, was to create tensions which remained unresolved until the bloodbath of 66–70 CE.[48]

The establishment of direct Roman rule in Judaea after the deposition of Archelaus (6 CE) served to enforce peace in the region, but not harmony. The insensitivities of Roman procurators of Judaea and the use of Syrian soldiers in the Roman auxiliary units who garrisoned the territory only inflamed Jew-Gentile

---

[44] Schürer 2.91: 'the Roman invasion meant deliverance from a hated domination.'

[45] In the meantime there is some evidence for the appropriation of Jewish territory by Tyre and Sidon during the confused days of the Roman civil wars; see Josephus, *Ant* 14.306–23, especially 314.

[46] Josephus claims that Herod both paved this street and adorned it with *stoai* for its entire length (*Bell* 1.425; *Ant* 16.148); cf. Downey 1961:173–76.

[47] Cf. Josephus, *Ant* 15.267–91; *Bell* 2.85. See Levine 1975:11–18 on the Herodian refoundation of Caesarea, highlighting Josephus' ambiguity on the status of the city.

[48] There were some complaints against Herod even from the side of the Greeks, e.g. the charges of 'tyranny' laid against him by the city of Gadara, Josephus, *Ant* 15.351–58. Herod's army was of mixed ethnic origin, *Ant* 14.394.

relations in the region.[49] We have record of a number of incidents which broke out in Syrian cities in the years 39–44 CE, some perhaps 'copy-cat' riots in the wake of the Alexandrian pogrom of 38 CE (see chapter 3.1), others possibly reflecting resentment at the installation of a Jewish king (Agrippa I). At Jamnia, Gentile residents built an altar (probably to the emperor) which so provoked the majority Jewish population as to rouse them to destroy it (Philo, *Legatio* 200–5). According to Philo, the incident raised the issue of the sanctity of the city as part of the 'holy land' (*Legatio* 202) and thus brought to the surface deep tensions concerning the identity of such cities.[50] When news arrived of Gaius' decision to erect an image in the temple of Jerusalem, the atmosphere in the province inevitably soured, and only the skilful procrastination of the governor Petronius prevented the outbreak of a revolt yet more violent than the Maccabean uprising. We have distant echoes of civil disorder in Antioch at this time, recorded in fantastic terms by Malalas, but probably containing an element of truth in referring to violent attacks on the Jewish community.[51] Whatever may have been the differences of opinion among Jews under Antiochus Epiphanes, none could have welcomed Gaius' self-deification and its manifestation in this vindictive plan against the Jews; but the prospect may have encouraged those Gentiles who already had grievances against the Jews. As Petronius' troops gathered in Antioch to carry out the project, Jewish protests may well have attracted resentment of their 'subversive' refusal to honour the emperor in his chosen form.[52] The whole incident clearly shook

---

[49] For the history of Judaea in the period see e.g. Smallwood 1981:144–80, 256–92. On the Syrian soldiers, Josephus, *Bell* 2.186, 268, 502; *Ant* 19.364–66 and Schürer 1.362–67. The insults of the soldiers in *Bell* 2.223–31 illustrate the ethnic tensions which affected relations between Jews and 'Roman' troops.

[50] Philo's characterization of the non-Jews in Jamnia as 'intruders' and 'settlers' (μέτοικοι, *Legatio* 200) manifestly distorts the character of the place as an old Greek city, now in the possession of the imperial family; see Schürer 2.110 n. 129.

[51] Malalas 244,18 – 245, 21. The incident is discussed and some residue of truth distilled by von Stauffenberg 1931:189–92; Kraeling 1932:148–50; and Downey 1961:192–95. The notice of an expedition by Phineas from Jerusalem is fanciful, but that Jews were killed and some synagogues burned is not implausible. It is possible that the violence erupted around images of the emperor as in Alexandria, Jamnia (?) and Dora (see below).

[52] This aspect of Malalas' story receives possible confirmation in the fact that Claudius' decree in 41 CE urging tolerance of the Jews was expressly addressed to Syria as well as to Alexandria (Josephus, *Ant* 19.279); that suggests there was significant pressure on Syrian Jews at this time.

the Jewish population throughout the province of Syria (Josephus, *Ant* 18.261–309; *Bell* 2.184–203) and underlined the insecurity of their national traditions under Roman rule.

Although Gaius' plan eventually came to nothing, it left a deep impression on Gentiles in the province, as well as Jews. Early in the reign of Claudius, the Gentile population of Dora erected an image of the emperor in the Jews' synagogue (Josephus, *Ant* 19.300–11). Although Agrippa was able to elicit a swift rebuke from Petronius, the incident illustrates the widespread hostility towards Jews, and the tendency to copy others' methods in causing them embarrassment. Petronius' reaction indicates Roman fears lest the Jews, 'under the pretext of self-defence', cause insurrection in the province (*Ant* 19.309). When, in this same period, territorial disputes broke out between Jews and Gentiles near the city of Philadelphia (*Ant* 20.1–5), we can appreciate how economic, political and cultural competition could all contribute to the instability of the province.

The short reign of Agrippa I (41–44 CE) in some respects exacerbated the tensions in the region. Although, like Herod, Agrippa acted as a benefactor to many cities (*Ant* 19.328–30), he made no attempt to hide his Jewish loyalties. The same king whose ostentatious display in Alexandria had ignited sufficient fury to spark off the pogrom of 38 CE (see chapter 3.1.1) made such enemies among his soldiers in Caesarea as to cause them to indulge in outrageous celebration at his death (*Ant* 19.356–58). Presumably they danced for the same reasons as the Jewish population mourned (19.349): this Jewish king was set to favour the interests of his Jewish subjects.[53] The Jews' disappointment at his death was compounded by the reversion of their territory to direct Roman control. Mounting Judaean nationalism and the callous insensitivity of Roman governors combined to create a dangerously explosive atmosphere.

One location where we can chart such a rise in tension is Caesarea, the city where Agrippa died. As the procurator's base and the chief barracks for his soldiers, Caesarea was bound to be the most important interface for Jew-Gentile relations in the region; and since the city was established on Hellenistic lines, yet had a majority Jewish population, it provided a litmus test for intercommunal relations. At some point in the 50s CE, the long-

[53] Levine 1975:28–29.

running disputes in the city were crystallized in the legal question whether Jews or 'Greeks' should control the city's affairs (Josephus, *Bell* 2.266–70; *Ant* 20.173–78).[54] The strength of feeling on both sides ensured that this political issue was first fought out on the streets, where the Jews' numbers and resources proved superior. However, the local Greek/Syrian population had the support of the soldiers stationed in the city, many of whom were themselves residents of Caesarea. Both sides appealed to the role of Herod in the refounding of the city: the Jews claimed him as a Jew (it was a valuable argument in retrospect), while non-Jews pointed to the manifestly Greek character of the city he had built (*Bell* 2.266; but cf. *Ant* 20.173). Having struggled in vain to control the intercommunal violence, the procurator Felix referred the matter to Rome. When Nero's decision went against the Jews (*Bell* 2.284; *Ant* 20.182–84, probably 61–62 CE) the scene was set for an explosion of violence; the imperial verdict seemed to demonstrate to Jews throughout the province that all they could rely upon now was their own ability to fight.

Before describing the explosion in 66 CE, we should note that it would be over-simplified to depict relations between Jews and Gentiles in the Syrian cities as wholly antagonistic. In the very period when these tensions were mounting, we have evidence to suggest that there were also friendly relations which drew Gentiles towards the Jewish community. Josephus claims that at the outbreak of the war each Syrian city had its 'Judaizers', an 'equivocal' (ἀμφίβολον) and 'mixed' (μεμιγμένον) element, who were neither clearly Jewish nor anti-Jewish (*Bell* 2.463). This generalization receives some confirmation from two specific examples: in Damascus, he claims, all but a few of the wives of the Damascenes had 'submitted to the Jewish religion' (*Bell* 2.559–61), and in Antioch the Jews were constantly attracting to their religious practices 'a considerable body of Greeks, whom they had in some measure made a part of themselves' (*Bell* 7.45). While such claims are probably exaggerated, it does not seem possible to dismiss them outright: we have independent evidence suggesting, for instance, the existence of proselytes in Antioch (Nicolas, Acts 6.5) and Gentile sympathizers in Caesarea, even among the military

---

[54] Josephus' two accounts are not entirely compatible and remain vague on detail; it is not at all clear, for instance, what the issue of *isopoliteia* (*Ant* 20.183) entailed. For a full discussion of the affair see Levine 1974.

(Cornelius, Acts 10.1–2)![55] No doubt relations between Jews and Gentiles differed according to local histories and conditions. Yet even in the locations where our sources indicate some positive relations (Damascus, Caesarea and Antioch) we will find that the Jews became the targets of assault in 66–67 CE.

The best explanation for the varying qualities of relation between Jews and Gentiles is to posit distinctions between social levels. Josephus indicates that the upper-class Jews in Caesarea were eager to maintain peace and anxious to restrain the rasher elements in their community (*Bell* 2.267, 287; *Ant* 20.178); and although this is a regular feature in his depiction of affairs, it probably corresponds to the truth. It is in such circles that there were likely to develop closer relations to Gentiles. John the tax-collector in Caesarea (*Bell* 2.287) would necessarily make business and other social contacts across the ethnic divide far more readily than fellow-Jews of humbler means. The ease with which Agrippa I moved in both Gentile and Jewish worlds was only an extreme example of the social integration desired by many Jews of high social status.[56] We may therefore suggest that Josephus' general comments on 'Judaizing' applied especially to Gentiles who moved in these higher social echelons and had significant relationships with Jews of their own class.[57] Thus the eruption of violence in 66 CE represented primarily the antagonisms of the lower social classes (both Jews and Gentiles), whose vehemence outweighed the more friendly relations established by some of their social superiors.

[55] Gentile association with Christian Jews in Antioch (Acts 10.19–26; Gal 2.11–14) may reflect a general pattern of interaction, although the Christian movement seems to have specially fostered such contact. From an earlier period (second to first century BCE) note Meleager's complaint that his (probably Gentile) lover has been charmed by a Jew (Stern 43; the location is either Gadara or Tyre).

[56] Saul, the spokesman of the Jews in Scythopolis who fought alongside Greeks, is noted by Josephus as a man of social importance (*Bell* 2.469). The community at Antioch seems to have included wealthy families (*Bell* 7.45) and may have covered the same social range as we find there at a later time (Meeks & Wilken 1978:10–13). Among the Jewish Christians in Antioch, Manaen and Barnabas (Acts 13.1; cf. Acts 4.36–37) were apparently men of means.

[57] In Josephus' story (*Bell* 2.559–61), the Damascene wives attracted to Judaism were surely from a high social level: only so would they have enjoyed the freedom to explore different religious traditions and only so could they have caused such concern to the city authorities. Cornelius (Acts 10.1–2) was a centurion (with considerable financial means), not a soldier from the ranks.

If Josephus is to be believed, it was a fresh outburst of violence in Caesarea which sparked a succession of massacres in the cities surrounding Judaea; and these marked the start of the Jewish War.[58] Having gained victory in the case before Nero, Gentile harassment of Jews in Caesarea reached such a pitch as to provoke a full-scale uprising of the Jewish community. The immediate issue was access to a synagogue in the city, and the ultimate provocation a sacrifice on its steps erected on a makeshift altar (*Bell* 2.284–92). In the violence which erupted the Roman troops were unable (or unwilling) to protect the Jewish community (whose bribery of the procurator proved ineffective). Not long after, the Caesarean mob were able to exploit such vulnerability. When news came that Jews had slaughtered Roman troops in Jerusalem, the city rose in fury on its Jewish inhabitants, the families and comrades of the dead no doubt eager to exact revenge. According to Josephus as many as 20,000 Jews were killed and the rest rounded up in captivity (*Bell* 2.457). Philo does not claim such casualties even in the Alexandrian pogrom.

It was now evident that the Jews who were resident in the Syrian cities were fatally exposed and could expect no mercy either from fellow citizens or from Roman troops. Thus a wave of Jewish reprisals now rippled around the country. Josephus gives a list of locations affected, remarkable in its extent though not exhaustive: Philadelphia, Heshbon, Gerasa, Pella, Scythopolis, Gadara, Hippos, Gaulanitis, Kedasa (a Tyrian village), Ptolemais, Gaba, Caesarea, Sebaste, Ascalon, Anthedon and Gaza (*Bell* 2.458–60).[59] It is not clear what precisely were the aims of these Jewish attacks, but we must imagine here the unleashing of anger after decades of grievance. In some places the Jewish assault was sufficient to gain control of the city; in others, it merely invited a yet more terrible revenge. Although Josephus' accounts of these events are unreliable, the fact of full-scale intercommunal war can hardly be doubted.[60]

---

[58] Rappaport 1981 suggests that this Jew-Gentile conflict was indeed the chief cause of the war.

[59] Josephus, *Vita* 66–67, 410 adds Tiberias and villages in the Decapolis. See Kasher 1990:268–87.

[60] *Bell* 2.461–80, 559–61; 7.361–68; *Vita* 24–27. Josephus is inconsistent on the number of casualties (e.g. in Damascus, *Bell* 2.561; 7.368) and has contrary explanations for the decision of the Jewish inhabitants of Scythopolis to fight with, rather than against, the Greek citizens (*Bell* 2.466–76; *Vita* 26).

It was naturally the cities closest to the ferment in Judaea which were most caught up in the fray; Sidon, Apamea and Antioch were initially free of violence (*Bell* 2.479). In Antioch, however, feeling was bound to run high since the city served as the provincial capital and the mustering point for the legions detailed to put down the Jewish revolt. It was when Vespasian arrived to command the army's assault on Judaea (67 CE) that trouble broke out in Antioch (*Bell* 7.46–53). Certain Jews were accused by Antiochus, the son of the chief Jewish magistrate, of plotting to burn the city. Josephus' story makes best sense if this Antiochus was a military officer (he was entrusted with soldiers by the governor) and thus caught up in the anti-Jewish sentiment of the army.[61] At first Antiochus merely denounced certain Jews (including his father!) of revolutionary intentions – an action not unlike the concern of high-ranking Jews in Alexandria and Cyrenaica to distance themselves from zealot agitators (chapter 3.2; 8.1). But the anti-Jewish feeling in the capital was bound to give this accusation greater momentum. Before long Antiochus was advocating that leading Jews be forced to prove their loyalty by sacrificing 'in the manner of the Greeks' (*Bell* 7.50),[62] and he attempted to suppress Sabbath observance (*Bell* 7.52–53). It was probably in this context that efforts were made to abolish the privilege of Jews in the gymnasia to buy their own (non-Gentile) oil (Josephus, *Ant* 12.120).[63] It was a particularly galling symbol of the 'separateness' of the Jews – so vividly manifested at that moment in the Revolt – that Jewish citizens should disdain as 'impure' the oil distributed by the gymnasiarchs.

[61] See further below, chapter 11.1. Smallwood 1981:361–62 argues that Antiochus must have been a citizen and even a magistrate (though she does not consider a military post); her suggestion that Antiochus' victims were mostly converts to Christianity is unsupported.

[62] Josephus does not make clear to whom this test was applied, but it probably only affected the most prominent Jews, perhaps only citizens. Josephus says that only a few Jews were prepared to sacrifice and the rest were killed (*Bell* 7.51), yet the Jewish population was still thriving in subsequent years. The sacrifice was perhaps a test of loyalty, when leading Jews were under suspicion of giving support to the Jewish insurgents in Judaea.

[63] The Mucianus mentioned in this passage was governor of Syria in 67–69 CE. Josephus records that Jews who were unwilling to use 'foreign' oil were permitted to 'receive a fixed sum of money from the gymnasiarchs amounting to the cost of the oil' (*Ant* 12.120). It is possible that this refers to the general oil supply of the city (so Tcherikover 1961a:329, 516 n91; Kasher 1985:303–4), but I judge it more likely to concern Jews training in the gymnasium, for two reasons: i) It is unlikely that the gymnasiarchs would have a monopoly over

That the Jewish community in Antioch survived this ordeal – and even retained for its Antiochene citizens the privilege concerning oil – is striking testimony to the control exercised by the Roman governor, Mucianus. Antiochus was clearly in a position to inflict great damage on his community, and the city was ready to believe the worst of the Jews. Indeed (in what appears to be a separate incident) when a fire actually destroyed some parts of the city, Antiochus attached blame to the Jews and a massacre of terrible proportions would have ensued but for the swift intervention of the Roman authorities (Josephus, *Bell* 7.54–62).[64]

At the conclusion of the Jewish War, the Jews in Antioch, like Jews in other Syrian cities, can hardly have avoided the sense of disgrace which attached to their nation. As was natural for a victor in a hard-fought war, Titus displayed his Jewish captives in many Syrian cities (Josephus mentions Caesarea and Berytus, *Bell* 7.20, 36–40, 96), using his spoils to decorate the cities and employing his captives to provide entertainment through their deaths. Our sources present his behaviour in Antioch from two quite different perspectives. Malalas (260,21 – 261,14) records the erection of the Cherubim on a city gate and the construction of a theatre with the inscription 'From the spoils of Judaea'. Josephus, on the other hand, recounts only Titus' refusal to disadvantage the Antiochene Jews, despite appeals by the city to have them expelled, or at least their rights abolished (*Bell* 7.100–11). Malalas' witness, though hostile to the Jews, is believable, considering Titus' use of spoils from the war elsewhere. Josephus' one-sidedness is suspect – it was of strategic importance to display Titus as favourable to all but militant Jews – but his story is also probably true in essence. It was

the complete oil supply of so large and complex a city as Antioch, even if the gymnasia were important consumers of the product. ii) The only context in which oil was freely supplied to consumers (and thus money had to be granted for alternative supplies) was the gymnasium institution. (Alternatively, we would have to suppose that the Jews were granted a refund of some 'oil-tax' payable by the general populace, Kraeling 1932:139.) Thus it is likely that this concession applied to those Jews who were training in the gymnasia (on the way to Antiochene citizenship) and who caused offence by this demand for special treatment. Josephus' obscures the issue by generalizing it, and implausibly dates the origin of the privilege to the time of Seleucus I. On the reasons for the impurity of Gentile oil see Goodman 1990b.

[64] Kraeling 1932:150–52 suggests that the two stories of threatened and then actual fire in the city are variants of one and the same incident; but cf. Downey 1961:586–87.

not in the Romans' interest to deport Jews from Diaspora cities, nor to encourage insurrection through appearing to humiliate them. Although Titus and the Antiochenes (and Josephus) recognized that the Jews resident in Antioch had their 'home-country' (πατρίς) in Judaea (*Bell* 7.109), to return them to its damaged conditions would only have incited further trouble. The Roman policy of *parcere subiectis* was here as elsewhere crucial to the establishment of a lasting peace.

Since the suppression of the revolt involved the destruction of the temple, Jewish resentment in the province of Syria was bound to run deep. It was, perhaps, the presence of Roman soldiers rather than the acquiescence of the Jews which prevented further outbreaks of violence. The refoundation of Joppa (as Flavia Joppa) and the promotion of Caesarea to the status of Roman colony indicate the determination of Rome to keep the cities under their control. At the time of the Diaspora Revolt (116–117 CE) there is some evidence for trouble in Judaea, but the vague and fragmentary nature of our evidence suggests that it was nipped in the bud.[65] There is nothing to indicate that Antioch or any other Syrian town was caught up in the same mad fury as engulfed Egypt, Cyrenaica and Cyprus. Subsequently, in the Bar Kochba uprising (132–35 CE), it was only in Jerusalem and in the hills and caves of Judaea that the insurgents could gain control.[66] However, we must presume that throughout this period Jews in the province were regarded with some suspicion. It was impossible for Jews in the Syrian Diaspora to avoid the effects of the national struggle in Judaea, which influenced the history of their relations with Gentiles from the time of the Maccabees right through to the revolt of Bar Kochba. It was to take many generations before their revolutionary reputation could be shed. In later centuries, however, they emerge in, for instance, Caesarea and Antioch, as strong and confident communities, with the past history of intercommunal violence now only a distant memory.[67]

---

[65] See Smallwood 1981:421–27.

[66] There is evidence for fighting in Galilee and Scythopolis and possible indications of Jewish sabotage in Caesarea, but it is clear that the heart of the revolt was the hill-country of Judaea; see Smallwood 1981:441–49.

[67] On Caesarea in the third to fourth centuries CE see Levine 1975; and on Antioch in the same period, Kraeling 1932:152–60 and Meeks & Wilken 1978.

# 9

## The Province of Asia

What do we know about Jews in Asia in our period of interest (323 BCE – 117 CE) and how reliable are the sources we possess? To pose such questions is immediately to reveal the paucity and fragility of our evidence. The past century has seen remarkable progress in the archaeology of Asia Minor, some of its finds proving to be of great significance for the understanding of the Diaspora: the excavation of the Sardis synagogue and the discovery of a list of contributors to a Jewish institution in Aphrodisias are two of the most spectacular examples from recent years.[1] Unfortunately, however, nearly all such discoveries relate to a period some time after that covered in this book, dating in most cases from the third century CE or later. A few inscriptions shed light on conditions in the first century CE and will be utilized here; but isolated inscriptions are usually of limited value.

In common with most other locations outside Egypt, there are no papyri from Asia with which to construct a profile of the social and economic conditions of Jews. There is only one piece of Jewish literature in our period, *Sibylline Oracles* 1–2, which could be linked to Asia Minor, though its provenance is not certain and, of course, no single piece of literature can be taken as 'typical' of Asian Jews.[2]

---

[1]  For the Sardis synagogue, discovered in 1962, see Seager and Kraabel 1983; for the Aphrodisias *stele*, Reynolds and Tannenbaum 1987. Both finds have been extensively discussed in recent literature. Schürer 3.17–36 gives a survey of all the information relating to Jews in Asia Minor, but we are fortunate now to possess a fine analysis of the Diaspora in this region by Trebilco 1991. Cf. also the forthcoming contribution by Levinskaya 1996.

[2]  The Jewish substratum of *Sib Or* 1–2 (from around the turn of the era; it has a later Christian overlay) has often been associated with Phrygia, because of the claim that Phrygia was the first land to emerge from the flood (1.196–98, 261–67); see Geffcken 1902a:50; Collins 1983:330–34; Trebilco 1991:95–99. I do not consider this a particularly strong basis for attributing the work to Phrygian Jews.

We have to accept that our knowledge of what Jews in Asia actually thought is extremely limited.

Most of our historical information has to be derived from literary sources which, though not written by Asian Jews, tell us something about their social and religious conditions. Covering our period of interest we have fragments of information in one of Cicero's speeches (*Pro Flacco* 66–69) and some observations on Jews by the Asian rhetorician, Apollonius Molon.[3] Incidental comments in early Christian writings (Acts; Revelation; Ignatius) give rudimentary but partisan information relevant to the last century of our period. Otherwise, we are entirely dependent upon the material supplied by Josephus. Since almost all our evidence concerns towns which lay (at some point in their history) in the Roman *province of Asia*, I will narrow our focus in what follows to this one area. Other regions of 'Asia Minor' more broadly defined (i.e. the Anatolian peninsula, or, roughly, modern Turkey) give us little more than isolated epigraphs: thus, Bithynia, Pontus, Galatia, Cappadocia, Cilicia and Pamphylia will not figure in what follows although we know that they too had a Jewish presence.[4]

An investigation of Josephus' notes on the early history of the Jews in Asia confronts us immediately with his deficiences as a historical source: his evidence is anecdotal and partial (in both senses of the word), and he depends on documents whose authenticity is a matter of controversy. His earliest reference to Jews in Asia is an anecdote from Clearchus of Soli concerning a meeting between Aristotle and a Hellenized Jew in the region of Mysia (*C Ap* 1.177–82). It is unlikely that this story is of historical value in relation to the fourth century BCE, and, even if it is, the Jew concerned appears to be a traveller from 'Coele-Syria': his presence is no indication of settled Jewish communities in Asia.[5] More significant might be Josephus' claims that Jews were settled in cities of Asia by Seleucus I (or Antiochus II, or, more vaguely,

---

[3] The relevant passages are to be found in Stern 68 and 46–50 respectively.

[4] So Philo, *Legatio* 281 and Acts 2.9–10. For the meagre inscriptional evidence see Schürer 3.32–36. Of course, the boundaries of each of these provinces varied over time, according to political conditions. For the purposes of this discussion, I am including the district of Phrygia within the province of Asia, as at various times it was administratively incorporated. For a comprehensive history of Asia see Magie 1950.

[5] Tcherikover 1961a:287; cf. Hengel 1974:59, 257–58; Stern 15. Reference in Obadiah 20 to the exiles of Jerusalem in 'Sepharad' has sometimes been connected to Sardis, but not reliably so; see Schürer 3.20.

the 'Diadochi') and given equal rights with Macedonians and Greeks (*Ant* 12.119, 125–26; 16.160; *C Ap* 2.39). In fact, however, these broad claims are as suspect as those he presents for the status of Jews at the founding of Alexandria (see above, chapter 2.1.3 n. 28); his inconsistencies and unreliable 'proofs' are a sure sign of his dubious credibility at this point.[6]

Thus the earliest piece of evidence which can make a serious claim to reliability is a letter cited in *Ant* 12.147–53. This contains instructions from Antiochus III (223–187 BCE) to his governor, Zeuxis, concerning the transportation of 2000 Jewish families from Mesopotamia and Babylonia to fortresses and other strategic places in Phrygia and Lydia: they are each to be given plots of land and permitted to 'use their own laws' unmolested. Precisely here, however, we encounter the question, heavily debated, of the authenticity of the documents cited in Josephus' *Antiquities*.[7] In this particular case, there are grounds for suspicion in some formal details of the letter and in its emphasis on the Jews' 'piety towards God' and fidelity to the king; it is likely that the document has been edited or possibly even concocted by Jews with an apologetic interest.[8] However, it is entirely possible that Jews served in Seleucid armies (as they certainly fought for the Ptolemies), and later evidence indicates that Jewish communities in Asia had already grown to a considerable size by the first century BCE. Some perhaps could trace their origins to the military garrisons of the late third century BCE indicated by this letter. The permission here granted

---

[6]  Careful analysis of *Ant* 12.125–26 indicates that it was probably only Greeks who claimed citizenship from the time of Seleucus II, though Josephus' ambiguous phraseology is designed to suggest that Jews did too; the passage could indicate, however, that some Jews were citizens in Ionian cities in the late first century BCE (see below). For a critical discussion of Josephus' vague and exaggerated claims see Marcus, Appendix C in Josephus Loeb volume VII; Tcherikover 1961a:328–30; Trebilco 1991:167–69.

[7]  Already in 1914 Juster noted that the literature on this issue was 'fort abondante', 1914:1.132 n. 4. There is a useful survey of representative opinions on the Antiochus III texts in Appendix D of Josephus Loeb volume VII, and a select bibliography on the Roman decrees in Appendix J. For widely differing conclusions, and divergent interpretations of scholarly biases, see Bickerman 1980:24–43 and Moehring 1975.

[8]  Despite the defence of the document by Schalit 1959–60 and Bickerman 1980:24–43 (an essay written in 1955), Gauger 1977:1–151 has mounted such detailed objections to its authenticity that his case will require an equally thorough refutation; see the brief response by Momigliano 1982:258–59 and the hasty dismissal of Gauger's work in Schürer 3.17 n. 33.

to 'use their own laws' unmolested was, however, to prove a matter of controversy in their subsequent relations with Asian cities.

Since the bulk of our evidence about Asian Jews is to be found in documents of the Roman era assembled in Books 14 and 16 of Josephus' *Antiquities*, it is important to establish at the outset what evidential value they possess. In a broadside against scholarly gullibility ('pseudohistory'), Moehring (1975) has challenged the apologetic interests of scholars who make use of these sources, highlighting the uncertainties surrounding Josephus' acquisition of such documents and the textual corruptions in their present state. To be sure, there are many features of these documents which incline one to caution. Although they are arranged in roughly chronological order, Josephus (or his source) has an insecure grasp of the history of the period; for instance, confusing Hyrcanus I with Hyrcanus II, he has included a Pergamene decree of the late second century BCE (*Ant* 14.247–55) in the midst of material from the middle of the following century. It was no help to him (nor us) that the documents were mostly undated and several only fragmentary. In some cases dates can be inferred from the persons named in the decrees, but sometimes these bear no relation to, or even contradict, the historical facts; and it is a moot point whether these should be corrected to make them fit with history (presuming textual corruption of originally authentic material) or whether the impossible names and titles are themselves signs of inauthenticity.[9]

Josephus' lack of control over his material is evident in certain cases (e.g. the repetition of identical decrees in *Ant* 14.228–40), and these give the impression of an assembled portfolio of all material deemed in the least relevant.[10] For it is obvious that such letters, decrees and *senatus consulta* are cited only for their contribution to Josephus' apologetic cause. In Book 14 Josephus is concerned to display evidence of the alliances between the Jewish nation and the Romans (*Ant* 14.185–89) and to demonstrate the Romans' benefactions to the Jews (*Ant* 14.265–67, 323). Thus he

---

[9]  Many suggested 'corrections' are to be found in Juster 1914:1.132–52 and in the notes to the Loeb edition; but note Moehring's objections to this procedure, 1975:134–40.

[10]  Where did Josephus acquire this material? Niese's suggestion (1876) that he drew on the portfolio put together by Nicolas of Damascus for his speech before Agrippa (*Ant* 16.31–57; cf. 12.125–27) remains attractive, although it is insufficient to cover all Josephus' records. Presumably the Jewish communities themselves treasured the verdicts which went in their favour. See the discussion in Moehring 1975:147–54, Smallwood 1981:558–60 and Rajak 1984:110–11.

cites only those decrees and resolutions which mention the Romans;[11] obviously, he would take care to omit reference to those occasions (e.g. the decision of Flaccus which we know from Cicero) on which Roman rule was less accommodating to Jewish sensibilities. In Book 16 he uses his material from the imperial era to highlight the Romans' tolerance of Jewish customs and to suggest the possibility of mutual toleration between Jews and Greeks throughout the Empire (*Ant* 16.174–78); it would clearly have been impolitic to cite, here or elsewhere, Claudius' rebuke of the Alexandrian Jews which we know from his papyrus letter (*CPJ* 153)! Thus at the very least Josephus gives a highly partisan selection of material. He (or his sources) may also have emended the material he cites, for instance by the omission of inconvenient sections, the addition of flattering clauses or the generalizing of originally limited statements.[12]

Although each document needs to be separately assessed, there is sufficient material here of probable authenticity to give us solid ground on which to build.[13] Moreover, even those documents which fall under suspicion are useful in indicating the kind of points at which Asian Jews felt vulnerable and, like Nicolas' speech to Agrippa (*Ant* 16.31–57), they give us a reasonable impression of the issues which caused difficulty between the Jewish communities

[11] It is rarely noted that this emphasis on Rome is the decisive factor in the selection of material in *Ant* 14.185–267: all the material is either by Roman magistrates or makes explicit reference to the Romans. Thus all the decrees of the cities cited here (Delos, Laodicea, Pergamum, Halicarnassus, Sardis and Ephesus) refer to Romans and their concern for the Jews; it is possible that some of these references have been added by Josephus or his source.

[12] Watching Josephus' use of *The Letter of Aristeas* (in *Ant* 12) gives us some indication of his willingness to alter his sources, and comparing Philo's cited documents (*Legatio* 311–15) with those in Josephus (e.g. *Ant* 16.171) indicates the sort of emendations which such sources could undergo. Thus even Bickerman acknowledges the likelihood of Josephus' adaptation of his sources, 1980:34–35. In the one place where we can compare one of Josephus' decrees with a genuine text (*Ant* 19.280–85 with *CPJ* 153) it is likely that Josephus' version has been partly falsified.

[13] Rajak 1985:19–20 is incorrect to suggest that Moehring considers all Josephus' documents to be forgeries: he merely urges that 'the question of their authenticity has to be decided in every single instance' (1975:156). But she is right to claim that the analysis of their formal features gives some grounds for confidence, although this applies chiefly to the *senatus consulta*. For recent attempts to date and order these documents see Smallwood 1981:127–43 and Saulnier 1981.

and their host cities. Indeed, it is ironic that the very material which Josephus cites to establish the favourable position of Jews in Asia enables us to perceive how controversial were their claims and practices at this time: his citations of solutions indicate how widespread and continuous were the problems! When we have examined the evidence he provides, in the context of what we know of contemporary conditions in Asia, we will have to consider whether it is representative of the social situation of Asian Jews in the first century BCE.

Our first indication of the influence of Jewish communities in Asia comes in a decree of the city of Pergamum (*Ant* 14.247–55) which probably dates from the end of the second century BCE.[14] Here we find envoys from Judaea making the most of the alliance between Hyrcanus I and the Roman Senate in drawing support from Asian cities. Although no direct reference is made to a Jewish community in Pergamum, a sudden reference to one Theodorus who impressed on the council the merits of Hyrcanus (14.252–54) probably signifies a local community of Jews prominent enough to have their representative invited to address the council.[15] If so, we catch a glimpse here of a social dynamic in which Roman favour for the current regime in Judaea could bring important benefits for Jewish communities in areas under Roman rule – a dynamic which would encourage such Diaspora communities to affirm their identification with their Judaean 'homeland'. In this case, Pergamum appears to have been willing to honour and support such networks of allegiance. In subsequent decades, economic, social and political factors conspired to render such relationships much more problematic.

The Romans created the province of Asia out of the vast kingdom of Pergamum, which they inherited on the death of Attalus III in 133 BCE. After limited initial warfare, the region enjoyed peace, although the new conditions were not necessarily to its advantage. Rapidly discovering the economic potential of the new province, Roman speculators came into Asia in their thousands. Following

---

[14] Juster 1914:1.134–35. All scholars accept that the Hyrcanus here is Hyrcanus I; the only question is which Antiochus is involved. The letter cited in 1 Macc 15.15–24 has also been taken to indicate Jewish residence in Asia (e.g. Tcherikover 1961a:288; Schürer 3.4); but the address to the cities and regions there listed concerns conditions in Judaea and is no indication of local Jewish residence.

[15] Trebilco 1991:7–8.

the laws of Gaius Gracchus (123 BCE), the Senate allowed consortia of business-men to bid for the rights of tax-farming in Asia, and thus arose the notorious *publicani* whose unscrupulous methods of extortion caused deep resentment throughout Asia. On the whole, Roman governors were powerless to check the excesses of these *publicani* and in any case typically used their year of office for their own enrichment, so that the economic condition of the Asian cities began to look precarious.[16] One single event, however, was to devastate the province for decades to come. In 88 BCE Mithridates VI invaded Asia from Pontus, posing as a liberator from Roman rule, and he won sufficient support to induce many cities to comply with his order to massacre all resident Romans, men, women and children, on a single day. Our sources suggest that as many as 80,000 died in this holocaust, which the Romans did not allow their subjects to forget for generations to come.[17]

In the terrible years of this first Mithridatic War, and in the settlement subsequently imposed by Sulla, the cities of Asia were financially ruined. Those cities which supported Mithridates were required to provide men and supplies for his army; most of those which resisted were sacked by his superior army. After Mithridates' withdrawal, Roman troops plundered the province as captured territory. Sulla saw no reason to impose other than the harshest terms on the treacherous cities, allowing very few to remain 'free', and imposing fines and hefty taxes which were the subject of complaint for decades. 'Never, since the days of the Persians, had Asia Minor been treated so harshly' (Magie 1950:238).[18] As tax-farmers swarmed in 'like harpies which snatched at the people's food' (Plutarch, *Lucullus* 7.6), the Asian cities were driven into debt

---

[16] On the *publicani* see Magie 1950:164–66; on the governors' predatory habits and their fear of impeachment in Roman courts see Magie 1950:159–60, 172–75, 246–49, 251–53, 378–81, 488–89.

[17] Appian, *Mithridatic Wars* 12.21–23; thirty years later Cicero casts up the incident as a slur on the fidelity of the Asian Greeks (*Pro Flacco* 59–61), and it doubtless remained etched on Roman memories long after that.

[18] Magie details the 20,000 talent fine extracted from Asia and Sulla's personal booty of 1,500 pounds of gold and 115,000 pounds of silver, as well as the tax regime which Lucullus became famous for trying to ameliorate (1950:237–40). The *publicani* now enjoyed increased scope for their operations, while pirates raided the islands and coastal cities. Magie's analysis of the Asian economy in the 60s and 50s BCE concludes that 'in spite of instances of prosperity in many places, the exploitation of Asia by the Roman Republic wrought great harm to the inhabitants of the country' (1950:258).

at such high rates of interest that they were forced to sell works of art, to mortgage public buildings and to suspend normal civic activities. Seventy years later there were buildings still lying in disrepair (Josephus, *Ant* 16.18).

It is in this context of economic stringency, which lasted, with only limited periods of relief, throughout the rest of the first century BCE, that we must place the persistent financial disputes in which the Asian Jewish communities were involved. Josephus cites a passage from Strabo indicating that, when he captured Cos, Mithridates appropriated the money he found there, including '800 talents of the Jews' (*Ant* 14.110–13). It is possible that, although Josephus claims otherwise, this was money deposited by Egyptian rather than Asian Jews; but if Josephus is right about its origin, and if the figure is even remotely correct, it indicates that the Jewish communities in Asia had together accumulated huge financial resources.[19] How they recovered from this loss we do not know, but it is an indication of their continuing prosperity that in 62 BCE the governor Flaccus confiscated well over 100 pounds of gold which the communities had collected in four centres to send to Jerusalem.[20] Even if we allow for several years' arrears in this temple contribution (given the unsettled state of Judaea), this figure represents several large communities: 100 pounds of gold is worth over 100,000 drachmae, and annual contributions of 2 drachmae per head were made only by males aged between 20 and 50 (though some perhaps made larger donations). More to the point, the fact that the Jewish communities could amass such sums of money must have caused some envy among non-Jews. That they transported this money to a foreign country and thereby drained such cash away from impoverished local communities must also have been a matter of local concern. How much one could do with 100 pounds of gold for the benefit of the cities in which the Jews enjoyed

[19] Strabo did not indicate the source of the Jews' money and Josephus' interpretation was challenged by Willrich 1904. If we accept Josephus' claim concerning its Asian origin, we cannot accept his assertion that it was all composed of contributions for the Jerusalem temple; the figure is far too large. Following Reinach 1888 one must see here more general funds deposited by Asian Jewish communities; cf. Marshall 1975:147–48..

[20] Cicero, *Pro Flacco* 28.68: at Apamea a little less than 100 pounds of gold; at Laodicea a little more than 20 pounds; at Adramyttium and at Pergamum a small amount (see Mitchell 1993:2.33 n186). These four cites were *conventus* centres and perhaps collected from several local communities. But Jews in other locations (e.g. Ephesus) apparently escaped the governor's attention.

residence! On this occasion the governor Flaccus confiscated the money on the grounds that the Jews were breaking an edict forbidding the export of gold from the province.[21] But we may guess that Flaccus had the support of the relevant city authorities for the discovery of the Jews' illegal activity and for the enforcement of his edict.[22] For cities struggling to meet their tax obligations and unable to repair their own temples, it must have been galling to discover that such sums were regularly donated to a foreign temple.

As the Asian economy reeled under multiple blows, we find the Jews continuing to encounter difficulty with regard to their temple contributions and other financial affairs. As well as the regular predations by governors, Asia suffered a series of impositions in the middle decades of the first century BCE which further depleted her resources. At the start of the Roman civil war (49 BCE), Pompey's associates raised troops and gathered cash in Asia: by imposing poll-taxes and taxes on doors and porticoes, and by requisitioning supplies, they doubled debt in Asia over two years.[23] Although Julius Caesar dealt leniently with the province and reduced the power of the *publicani*, his successors once again milked Asia ruthlessly, with first Cassius and then Anthony demanding from the cities their next 10 years' taxes in advance! The Parthian invasion in 40 BCE only added to the misery of the province. With the continuous demand for money, ships and men, and with the burden of billeting Roman troops, most cities were thrown into the hands of money-lenders whose rates were never lower than 12% and sometimes as high as 48% compound interest![24] It was well into the Augustan period before such crippling burdens of debt could be removed.[25]

---

[21] See the full explanation by Marshall 1975 which indicates that the Jews could claim no exemption from the senatorial decisions (*pace* Smallwood 1981:126–27), if they were interpreted by the governor to require control of the economy of the provinces. He shows that the Jews 'were caught red-handed in their attempt to defy Roman law' (143); cf. Trebilco 1991:14–15.

[22] Cf. Marshall 1975:148–49, who notes also the cities' resentment of the special levy (for ships) imposed on them by Flaccus in 62 BCE.

[23] Magie 1950:402–4.

[24] Magie 1950:250–53, 385–95 (a notorious case at Salamis), 418–31.

[25] See Magie 1950:441–42, 469–74 on the slow but steady recovery under Augustus; there were major earthquakes in the region in 28 BCE, 12 BCE and 17 CE.

It is precisely in this period of acute economic hardship in Asia that we find the Jewish communities continually challenged on their acquisition and use of funds. In (probably) 46 BCE the proconsul has to instruct the city of Miletus not to interfere with the way the local Jews manage their funds (καρποί, *Ant* 14.244–46).[26] In the same period, the people of Parium (or Paros) are instructed to permit the Jews to live in accordance with their customs, which are specified to include the right to collect money and to hold communal meals (*Ant* 14.213–16). Again, after Caesar's assassination, Dolabella tells Ephesus to allow the Jews to make their 'offerings for sacrifice' (*Ant* 14.223–27). A further flurry of cases are known to us from nearer the end of the century in which Ephesus (*Ant* 16.167–68), Sardis and Ephesus (*Ant* 16.171; Philo, *Legatio* 315) and Ephesus again (*Ant* 16.172–73) are instructed to allow the Jews to keep and guard their 'sacred money', and to transport it to Jerusalem; any who steal or otherwise appropriate it are to be accounted guilty of temple robbery. According to *Ant* 16.162–65 (cf. Philo, *Legatio* 311–13), Augustus had to issue a general decree relevant to the whole of Asia announcing the inviolability of the Jews' sacred money and the seriousness of theft from their synagogues.

The social and economic realities underlying this recurrent point of dispute are, I think, revealed in the speech of Nicolas of Damascus before Agrippa in Ionia in 14 BCE (*Ant* 16.31–57). Among the Jews' grievances concerning Gentile high-handedness is the complaint that the Jews have been deprived of their money collected as offerings for Jerusalem and have been forced to contribute to military expenses and public duties ('liturgies'), and to spend their sacred money on such things (16.28). Nicolas insists that Jewish prosperity should not arouse envy (16.41); he also indicates that the Jews' sacred money has been taken from them by the imposition of taxes (16.45). Here an important aspect of the controversy emerges. The Jewish community clearly had a reputation for prosperity. It contained extremely wealthy individuals, who would normally be held liable to contribute to 'liturgies', and it made sizeable collections of money for its annual tribute to Jerusalem. At a time of financial stringency, with the cities

---

[26]　See Juster 1914:1.147 and Saulnier 1981:172 on the difficulty in dating this document. καρποί could refer to temple dues, funds in general or food supply (Sanders 1990a:296–97); if the first, we can imagine that the Jews' failure to win their appeal against Flaccus had set a precedent difficult to overturn.

only beginning to recover from decades of debt, it seems to have been extremely irksome to Greeks to witness this large and apparently wealthy community fail to pull its weight for the benefit of the city. The Jews made no contributions for the dilapidated temples in their own cities: they sent their money to a temple elsewhere. Indeed it appears that they refused in general to undertake certain 'liturgy' obligations, which were normally required of wealthy citizens as their contribution to the welfare and honour of the city.[27] In some cities the authorities took steps to rectify this 'injustice' – with what legal proceedings we cannot now tell – and seized the temple collections in lieu of money they reckoned owing to them. The Jews bitterly resented such confiscations, as they had resented those by Flaccus. Sometimes they won support from the imperial authorities to have the practice stopped, though the repetition of the same order to the same cities indicates that the city magistrates sometimes chose to ignore or circumvent Roman rulings. It appears that, so long as the financial crisis lasted, the Jews' large collections were too tempting a cherry to resist, and their apparent failure to assist in the economic restoration of their host cities continued to be a cause of resentment.

This economic bone of contention was, in fact, only part of a more general challenge to the rights of the Jewish communities within the cities. A number of Josephus' decrees concern the rights of Jews in the cities to meet, to own 'sacred' property and to enjoy some measure of self-government. In Sardis (where our evidence on this issue is most full) there was some dispute about the Jews' entitlement to hold an 'association' (σύνοδος) and to own a 'place' (τόπος) of their own where they could settle their affairs and adjudicate their own legal disputes (*Ant* 14.235, probably 49 BCE). On some (undated) occasion, the city agreed to allow them this measure of self-government, together with the right of assembly on stated days and permission to build communal buildings; it also undertook to provide suitable food in the markets (*Ant* 14.259–61). Rights of assembly were also a matter of dispute in some other cases: at Parium (or Paros), where the rights of Jews to share common meals (and organize associated finances) is affirmed by

---

[27] On 'liturgy' obligations in Asia see Magie 1950:167–68, 582–91, 651–54. On later imperial measures to restrict exemptions from such duties, see Millar 1983.

reference to Caesar's permission in Rome for Jewish *collegia* (θίασοι, *Ant* 14.213–16),[28] and in Halicarnassus, where Jewish festivals, feasts and gatherings (σύνοδοι) are permitted to take place (*Ant* 14.256–58). In fact, as regards Asia as a whole, Augustus was called upon to justify the Jews' permission to meet in associations (Philo, *Legatio* 311–12), and he insisted that their money and their sacred books were 'holy' property which it would be sacrilegious to steal (*Ant* 16.162–65). It appears from these cases that in many parts of Asia the legal status of the Jewish communities became a matter of intense controversy, with some factions in the cities contesting their social and religious rights.

Bound up with many of these cases is also the specific issue of the Jews' observance of the Sabbath (and other feasts). The Sabbath is one of the main grounds on which Jewish Roman citizens in Asia managed to claim exemption from enrolment in the legions which were recruited for the Roman civil wars – an exemption which the relevant authorities seem to have been willing to grant (*Ant* 14.238–40, 223–27, with reference to the Sabbath and Jewish diet). Even in the routine life of the cities, however, the Jews' peculiar calendar and, in particular, their refusal to take part in public events on the Sabbath were sufficiently irksome to cause numerous legal disputes, requiring repeated intervention by Roman authorities. Thus in the 40s BCE Miletus has to be reminded of an earlier ruling to allow the Jews to observe the Sabbath (*Ant* 14.244–46); Laodicea is pressured into granting permission, while recording the strong resistance of the city of Tralles (*Ant* 14.241–43); and Jews in Ephesus have to petition the governor to prevent being fined for their observance of the Sabbath (*Ant* 14.262–64). In addition, Halicarnassus offers to fine anyone preventing the Jews from observing the Sabbath (*Ant* 14.256–58) and in the Augustan era Nicolas of Damascus makes a detailed complaint to Agrippa that Jews in Ionia are being forced to appear in court and conduct other business affairs on their 'holy days' (*Ant* 16.27, 45).[29]

---

[28] Some aspects of this ruling are suspect, not least the claim that the Jews *alone* were granted exemption from Julius Caesar's ban on *collegia*; contrast Suetonius, *Iulius* 42.3: 'cuncta collegia praeter antiquitus constituta distraxit.'

[29] Cf. Augustus' ruling that no-one require Jews to give bond (ἐγγύας ὁμολογεῖν) on the Sabbath or even on 'the day of preparation' after the ninth hour (*Ant* 16.163; cf.16.168). ἐγγύας ὁμολογεῖν is a technical expression for giving security or a guarantee. This could relate to many kinds of commercial deals, and is not necessarily a bond to appear in court (as in the Loeb translation).

How can we explain these long-running disputes and the recurrent opposition which Jews encountered regarding such basic rights as synagogue assembly, self-adjudication and Sabbath observance? Such issues could only arise if the Jewish communities were a significant presence in the cities concerned and if at least some of their members were of social and economic importance. A small and insignificant community can be ignored by the city magistrates, even if its lifestyle is peculiar; or, if not ignored, it can be coerced into submission. Here, one senses the presence of Jews sufficiently prominent in city life for it to be exceptionally awkward when they refuse to attend court or do business on the Sabbath; and these are Jews sufficiently articulate and well-connected (and with sufficient funds) to be able to take their protests to the highest authorities, with at least occasional success. Such impressions are supported by our scanty information on the social status of the Asian Jews. As well as the indicators of wealth already noted in connection with the Jerusalem collections, we can note that some Jews in Ephesus and other Asian cities possessed Roman citizenship – sufficiently many to make it worthwhile to issue special directives about them (*Ant* 14.228–40).[30] There are also clues which indicate that certain individuals possessed citizenship in particular cities: in Sardis, for instance, two of Josephus' documents probably refer to Jewish citizens, and at Iasus there was at least one and probably several other Jewish ephebes.[31] Although Josephus' description of the issue is confusing, the Ionians' complaint that if the Jews wished to be their 'fellows' (συγγενεῖς) they should worship the same Gods (*Ant* 12.125–26) makes best sense as a protest against Jewish citizens who demanded exemption from civic religious practices.[32] The

---

[30] On this episode see Schürer 3.120, with discussion of Jews holding Roman citizenship, 132–35. It is not clear why Smallwood holds that 'the number of Jews involved must have been infinitesimally small' (1981:127–28). Two inscriptions indicate Jews in Asia possessing Roman citizenship in our period: *MAMA* 6, 264 concerns one P. Tyrronius Cladus (80s or 90s CE) and *CIJ* 770 a Jew from a later period, T. Flavius Alexander, whose name indicates that a forebear acquired citizenship in the Flavian era; cf. Trebilco 1991:172–73.

[31] Sardis: Josephus, *Ant* 14.235, where the text is uncertain but makes better sense as 'citizens of yours'; 14.259, where Tarn suggested omitting πολῖται but without sufficient cause. The Iasus inscription mentioning one Ioudas (early imperial period) was published by Robert 1937:85–86. See the discussion, with slightly different conclusions, in Trebilco 1991:167–73.

[32] Since the issue of citizenship is dropped in the account of Agrippa's decision (12.126) and does not occur at all in the fuller account in 16.27–65, it is possible that Josephus has introduced it gratuitously. But it is just as likely that he

same issue perhaps lies behind the refusal of Jews to provide 'liturgies', although wealthy and prominent enough to do so (*Ant* 16.28).

Whatever the precise legal status of individual Jews, what mattered to the cities was that these capable and influential communities were less than fully supportive of the city where they resided. We have two sources which may give some insight into the sort of objections which were made against Jews in Asia at this period. First, the remarks of Apollonius Molon, who was born in Caria and taught rhetoric at Rhodes in the first part of the first century BCE, might be taken to represent ideas circulating in the élite circles of Asian city life. He was, it appears, quite well informed about the Jews and their biblical history (Eusebius, *Praep Evang* 9.19.1–3) but in his various references to Jews (to which Josephus responds in *C Ap* Book 2) he clearly denigrated them. Apollonius objected above all to the Jews' exclusivity – their refusal to worship the Gods whom others worshipped, to accept those who had different ideas about God or to socialize with those whose customs were different (Josephus, *C Ap* 2.79, 258). Thus he levelled against Jews the twin charge of 'atheism' and 'misanthropy' (*C Ap* 2.148), to which he apparently joined particularly venomous invective against the Jewish religion: he appears to have circulated the legend about the annual sacrifice of a Greek in the Jerusalem temple, he denigrated Moses as a 'charlatan', he vilified the Jewish nation as especially stupid and culturally bankrupt, and he castigated Jewish laws as lessons in evil (*C Ap* 2.89–96, 145, 148).[33] We seem to hear in such charges not only the typical Greek disdain of 'barbarians' but also the wounded pride of a Greek cultural tradition shocked

refrained from further comment because the decision did not prove as favourable for the Jews as he would have liked (Smallwood 1981:141)! The Ionian complaint is sufficiently close to that of Apion in Josephus *C Ap* 2.65 to suggest a similar issue in both cases: individual Jews gained citizenship but caused offence by abstaining from participation in civic religion. Citizenship could be granted by cities on the basis of benefactions or merit, or, in some cases, it could be bought; once gained it would be inherited by successors. Paul may have been a citizen of Tarsus in Cilicia (Acts 21.39), but it is not clear in what sense Luke uses the term πολίτης; see Tajra 1989:78–80 and Hengel 1991:4–6.

[33] It is a little unclear in *C Ap* 2.79–96 who precisely is reponsible for which blasphemies about the Jerusalem temple; but the plural *isti* in 2.90 suggests Apollonius, as well as Apion, are to blame for the myth of the cannibalistic feast in Jerusalem. If this story circulated in Asia, it could only have inflamed the opposition of the Greek cities to the Jews' dispatch of funds to Jerusalem.

by the dogged refusal of Jews to co-operate in its religion or to integrate fully in the social affairs of its civic life.

Our second source of information on the hostility of non-Jews is gained by a careful reading of Nicolas' defence of the Jews, delivered, according to Josephus, in Ionia in 14 BCE (*Ant* 16.31–57). Nicolas refers to others' envy of the Jews' financial success and of the privileges they enjoy in preserving their ancestral customs (16.41). He insists that the Jews' customs are not anti-social (ἀπάνθρωπον οὐδέν ἐστιν, 42) and that there is nothing secretive about their rules (43). He defends the observance of the Sabbath as necessary for the proper study of the laws which guide their righteous behaviour, and he claims that such customs are both good and ancient, 'even though some may not believe this' (43–44). At the end of the speech, the Greeks, according to Josephus, could mount no proper reply but merely asserted that the Jews 'by spreading all over the country were ruining everything' (πάντα νῦν ἀδικοῖεν, 59). This hardly does justice to the seriousness of the complaints which underlie Nicolas' speech. In particular, it appears that exception was taken to the special privileges claimed by the Jews. Why should they alone be allowed exemption from the duties and services which were incumbent on all good residents in these cities? Why did they alone celebrate a different calendar, whose seven-day cycle interrupted their civic and business responsibilities? Why did they need the whole day off and what right of antiquity could they claim for it anyway? It appears that it was precisely because the Jews were becoming more numerous and prominent ('spreading all over the country') that their distinct behaviour was regarded as a sign of their hostility to the customs which were treasured by these Greek cities.

Such hostility as we find in Apollonius Molon and as the foil to Nicolas' speech is particularly understandable in the social and political circumstances of the first century BCE. During this turbulent century the Greek cities found themselves overrun by successive armies, exploited by tax-farmers and money-lenders and humiliated by debt. At various points in the course of the century many cities lost their right to claim 'freedom and autonomy', which they were desperate to regain, not simply for its tax advantages but for the pride of observing their own 'ancestral laws'. These were cities boastful of their histories, tracing their origins back to mythical heroes, and fiercely competitive with their neighbours.[34]

---

[34] See Mitchell 1993:1.206–11.

We should not overlook the centrality of religion in the maintenance of such civic patriotism. In many cases a local cult with a world-famous temple was central to the city's identity and crucial to its economy. In Ephesus a city mob could respond with fervour to the cry 'Great is Artemis of the Ephesians', reacting violently to a threat to the city's honour and its massive religious revenues (Acts 19.23–41). Much the same could have occurred in any Asian city. The most obvious means for Roman rulers or wealthy citizens to gratify the cities was to enhance their religious glory, through some festival or contest, some temple erected or restored, or some priesthood endowed.[35]

At a time when civic pride was wounded by political circumstances, the Jews' abstention from such 'idolatry', and their limited participation in the main currents of civic life, were their fundamental crimes in the eyes of the Greeks.[36] For civic communities struggling to revive their political fortunes, the presence of burgeoning sub-communities less than fully committed to the social and cultural life of the city was an irritant. Like larger-scale nationalism, civic pride can respond violently to the influence of 'aliens', when society itself suffers deprivation or decline. In the case of the Asian cities, the Jews, scattered as they were in different locations, in which different issues arose at various times, were spared any major or concerted onslaught.[37] But they had to contend with repeated violations of their 'rights', as time and again their communal institutions were challenged and their religious customs ignored. To this extent they were victims of the social, economic and political pressures bearing upon the Greek cities in these decades.[38]

---

[35] See, in general, Lane Fox 1986:64–82, and for the significance of the temples in Asian cities, Magie 1950:417, 432–33, 441–42, 582–91. On Ephesus and its affirmation of identity through the cult of Artemis, see Rogers 1991; cf. the essays on cults in Asia in *ANRW* II.18.3.

[36] It is difficult to tell to what extent the Jews also lived separately. The Sardis decree might indicate a Jewish area of residence (*Ant* 14.261, οἴκησις); and it is possible that the Jews in Halicarnassus clustered around their synagogues by the sea (*Ant* 14.258). There is evidence for communal eating (*Ant* 14.213–16; 16.164, reading ἀνδρῶνος) but we do not know with what regularity or social significance. The celebration of Jewish festivals (*Ant* 14.216) was obviously noticed as a distinctive public practice.

[37] Was violence ever used against the Jews? There are possible hints of such in *Ant* 14.245; 16.60, 160–61, but none are unambiguous.

[38] Rajak 1984:122–23 is right to insist that the Jews' difficulties are insufficiently explained by appeal to their 'intractable exclusiveness', but her suggestion

It is important to note that the evidence we have been considering thus far concerns only the first century BCE: our reports of Jewish difficulties come precisely in those decades when the province of Asia was at its nadir. In subsequent centuries, when socio-economic conditions were vastly improved, the Jewish communities seem to have prospered, gaining both tolerance and respect in the Asian cities (see below). Is it possible, however, that our perceptions are distorted by the nature of the evidence available to us? As we have noted already, Josephus' decrees in *Ant* 14 and 16 were designed to show the favour in which Jews were held by the relevant authorities, yet ironically reveal a series of disputes in which Jewish rights were questioned or ignored. How representative is this evidence? Does it give too one-sided a picture of Jewish social discomfort?

We must acknowledge, of course, that when Jews and Gentiles lived harmoniously there was no need for intervention from civic or Roman authorities and therefore no record of council decrees or imperial legislation which Josephus might cite. Moreover, some centres of Jewish residence (e.g. Pergamum, Apamaea, Adramyttium) do not feature in Josephus' record and could be held to be trouble-free. However, here, as elsewhere, 'silence is a deceptive witness',[39] and we must search for corroborating evidence either way, if such can be found. In fact, I think there is plenty to suggest that the image of intercommunal conflict which we gain from Josephus' documents is an accurate reflection of reality in the first century BCE. In the first place, of course, Josephus cites only such decisions which went in the Jews' favour.[40] We know from Cicero (not, of course, Josephus!) that Roman governors were sometimes unsympathetic to the Jews' claims. We hear of the Flaccus case only because legal proceedings were initiated primarily by non-Jews and on issues unconnected with the Jews; we cannnot tell in how many other cases Jews were unable to appeal against proconsular decisions.[41] Moreover, Josephus' own evidence indicates that

that in many cases Roman protection was necessary 'only because of deliberately engineered attacks on Jewish practices' is to give too simple an account of events (albeit one which Nicolas of Damascus proffered, *Ant* 16.45).

[39] Smallwood 1981:143, though she appears to use it rather freely at an earlier point in her argument (127).

[40] Elsewhere, Josephus notes Nero's decision against the Jews of Caesarea (*Bell* 2.284), but tactfully omits its wording!

[41] *Ant* 16.27 suggests that it was only because of the presence of Agrippa and Herod that Asian Jews felt free to air their grievances in 14 BCE.

individual cities sometimes passed decrees against the Jews' interests (*Ant* 14.213, 245) and that they objected to Roman rulings on the matter (*Ant* 14.242, 245). The mere fact that certain topics recur so frequently in these decrees is also, of course, eloquent witness to their limited force. If cities threaten to fine their citizens for disturbing Jewish practices, or a governor removes the right of asylum for synagogue-thieves, we must surely imagine that the Jews have suffered repeated abuse (*Ant* 14.258; 16.168).[42] If we may believe him, Josephus could have cited many more decrees on such matters (*Ant* 14.265–66), as indeed his own documents make reference to others not here collected (e.g. *Ant* 14.230, 260); they would no doubt have broadened our perceptions of the Jews' difficulties, but could hardly have lessened our impression of their seriousness. When we add the evidence for anti-Jewish sentiment which we find in Apollonius Molon and in the speech of Nicolas, our deductions from Josephus' documents receive strong confirmation. That we can make sense of such conflicts in the social and economic conditions of the first century BCE makes the case for strained relations between Jews and Gentiles in certain Asian cities as secure as it can be.

This is not to say that the Jews were a powerless minority, easily trampled upon by their opponents. In fact all the evidence we have viewed inclines us to regard their communities as significant entities, represented by influential individuals able to fight for redress. In some cases they had powerful patrons in the cities – Marcus Alexander in Halicarnassus (*Ant* 14.256), for instance, or Prytanis in Miletus (*Ant* 14.245) – who could move motions in their favour in the city councils or report their injustices to the Roman governor.[43] It is no insignificant community which can ensure that the market-officials (ἀγορανόμοι) in Sardis supply the right foods for their use (*Ant* 14.261)! As we have seen, there is evidence for Jews both as Roman citizens and as citizens of their own cities, and in general one can only explain Gentile hostility on the grounds that the Jewish community was of influence and importance – perhaps growing importance – within the life of the city.[44] The

---

[42]　See Rajak 1984:118–20.

[43]　Cf. John the tax-collector in Caesarea (*Bell* 2.287–88), in his case resorting to bribery!

[44]　Some rulings appear to reflect the growth of the Jewish community and corresponding *new* requirements (e.g. *Ant* 14.261); cf. the friction in Caesarea when the Jewish community attempted to buy new property (albeit adjoining the synagogue), Josephus, *Bell* 2.285–86.

controversies which arose in these Asian cities reflect the significant integration of such Jews into civic life: it is as business-partners, litigants, market-users, even potential 'liturgists' that the Jews are noticed and their peculiarities resented.

To gain redress, the Jews repeatedly appealed to Roman authorities, who alone could overrule the decisions of Greek city councils in Asia. In the case of Flaccus and his confiscation of Jewish gold, we can see how powerless the Jewish communities were if the Asian governor was able to interpret his anti-Jewish activity as in the interests of the Roman state. But on many occasions the Jews in Asia were able to benefit from current Roman favour towards Judaea and the pacts of friendship between Roman and Judaean rulers. Thus the Pergamum decree (*Ant* 14.247–55) shows the value of the alliance between the Senate and Judaea revived by Hyrcanus I. Despite Jewish armed resistance to Pompey, Judaea was cultivated by Rome as a valuable client. Julius Caesar in particular gained important support from Hyrcanus II and Antipater, which he rewarded in a number of decrees benefiting not only Hyrcanus and Judaea (*Ant* 14.190–212) but also Jews in Rome (see chapter 10.1) and in Asia (*Ant* 14.213–16). Hyrcanus was able to intercede with Dolabella for the benefit of Asian Jews (*Ant* 14.223–27), and, at a later period, the friendship between Herod and Agrippa was obviously significant for the Ionian Jews in winning their case in 14 BCE (*Ant* 16.27–65).[45] Each example of friendship towards the Jews could be used as a precedent on future occasions. We find Augustus referring back to Caesar's decisions (*Ant* 16.162) and Nicolas of Damascus making skilful use of this device in his speech to Agrippa (*Ant* 16.48–54).

Nicolas' speech is the best example of the sort of tactic used by Jews in requesting Roman support. By means of the appeal to precedent, the Greek cities could be presented as flouting the authority of their Roman masters and, since all were dependent on Roman 'privileges', the cities could be warned lest they endanger their own rights (*Ant* 16.31–40). Highlighting the significance for all races of their ancestral customs, Nicolas presents Roman rule as the guarantor of the religious rights of all, the underwriter of religious tolerance (*Ant* 16.35–38). In this case he can also make much of Agrippa's successful visit to Judaea and the

---

[45] For a justly cautious view of Josephus' idyllic presentation of the relationship between Herod and Agrippa see Roddaz 1984:450–63.

splendid hospitality of Herod (*Ant* 16.50–56). In conclusion he insists that what the Jews require is only the defence of the honour of Rome, which is a consistent benefactor of the Jews (*Ant* 16.57).

There is no hint here, or elsewhere, of a 'Charter' of Jewish rights established by Caesar or any other Roman ruler.[46] Rather, the generalities of Roman support for the Jews' 'ancestral customs' had to be brought to bear each time on individual cases. Senatorial decisions, imperial edicts and personal friendships all had to be confirmed and their relevance to the immediate circumstances proved. For such a procedure it was advantageous for the Jews to assert their ethnic bonds: it mattered to the Jews in Asia what Agrippa did for the Jews in Judaea (οἱ ἐκεῖ Ἰουδαῖοι, *Ant* 16.55), and in these circumstances at least they were pleased to acclaim Herod as '*our* king' (*Ant* 16.50). When relations between Rome and Judaea were sweet, the solidarity of the Jewish 'nation' (ἔθνος) was to the advantage of Diaspora Jews: it was as *an ethnic and ancestral tradition* that they sought to defend their way of life.

It is possible that such tactics, while sometimes successful, could exacerbate the difficulties in the Jews' relationships with local city councils. As the 'autonomy' of the 'free' Greek cities became increasingly nominal during the course of the first century BCE, there may have been some resentment at Roman interference in their internal affairs; such, at least, may be guessed from the cities' unwillingness to comply with the Roman rulings on the Jews' behalf. However, after the anti-Roman uprising during the first Mithridatic War, there is no evidence of serious opposition to Roman power. If the Jews were caught in an awkward triangle of relationships, it was not as serious here as for their compatriots in Egypt, whose fatal entanglement in Alexandrian hatred towards Rome we have already studied (chapter 3.1).[47] Whether the Jews' emphasis on their ethnic unity with Jews in Judaea and Rome antagonized Greeks we can only guess; but it cannot have helped them shake off their reputation for separateness, as we find it expressed by Apollonius Molon and his like.

---

[46] So, rightly, Rajak 1984 against, e.g., Juster 1914:1.216–17, 233–35 and Smallwood 1981:128–38.

[47] Cicero claims that Asian Greeks hate Roman power (*Pro Flacco* 8.19), but his remarks seem to be confined to the economic sphere and are in any case moulded by his rhetorical purposes. *Sib Or* 3.350–80 and 4.145–51 reflect an expectation of Asian revenge on Rome, but such passages are difficult to place or date.

The *Pax Romana* created by Augustus was of enormous benefit, socially and economically, to the province of Asia. From his principate onwards Roman rule appears to have enabled Asia to prosper, in marked contrast to its depressed condition in the last decades of the Republic.[48] It is consistent with the analysis offered above that the slow recovery of the province should coincide with a relaxation of pressure on the Asian Jewish communities. For it is noteworthy that Josephus' supply of decrees detailing Roman intervention on behalf of the Jews dries up at the very beginning of the first century CE. Of course, such an argument from silence can bear little weight, and it is frustrating that our evidence for Asian Jews in the first century CE is so paltry. Notices concerning Asian Jews in the earliest Christian literature do not tell us about much more than their presence and their rejection of the Christian mutation of their tradition.[49] The polemical tenor of these sources inclines us to read them with some caution, but Luke may be right to indicate that Jews were sufficiently respected in Anatolian cities to be able to influence the local Gentile population (Acts 13.50; 14.2). Moreover, his repeated references to Gentile 'God-fearers' in the synagogues, including some of significant social standing, might suggest that Jews were a respectable segment of the population (Acts 13.16, 48–50; 14.1; cf. 16.14; 17.4, 12).[50] At about this time (the middle of the first century CE) an inscription from

---

[48] See Magie 1950:469–74 (Augustus), 541–46 (Claudius), 566–72 (Vespasian), 576–82 (Domitian), 631–39 (Antoninus); the peace since Actium 'had introduced an era of prosperity such as the country had never known even under its native kings' (582).

[49] Acts 6.9–11; 19.8–10, 33–34; 21.17–36; Rev 2.9; 3.9. For a thorough trawl of such evidence see Trebilco 1991:20–27.

[50] Despite the theological biases in Luke's work, he intends to paint a picture plausible to his first century readers. *Pace* Kraabel 1981, 'God-fearers' in Asia (under varying titles) are not a Lukan invention, as the Aphrodisias inscription has shown (see Reynolds and Tannenbaum 1987:48–66; Schürer 3.150–76; Mitchell 1993:2.8–9, 31–32). It is possible to interpret the action of Alexander in Acts 19.33–34 (Ephesus), and the opposition of the synagogues to the churches in Rev 2.9 (Smyrna) and 3.9 (Philadelphia), as attempts to dissociate the Jews from the more socially subversive Christians. Some have also found in the crowd's reaction to Alexander (Acts 19.34) evidence of continuing Gentile hostility to Jews. But the historical value of this Lukan scene is questionable (see Haenchen 1971:570–79). A connection between the texts in Revelation and Domitian's clamp-down on 'Judaizing' non-payers of the tax (J. T. Sanders 1993:166–80; see below, chapter 10.4) is unlikely; we have no evidence for *delatores* or trials on this matter outside Rome.

Acmonia indicates that an extremely prominent Gentile, Julia Severa, donated a synagogue building to the Jewish community.[51] This is scanty evidence from which to generalize, but it might indicate a more friendly pattern of relationships between Jews and Gentiles in the Asian cities.

Certainly, from the second century onwards (and thus into the period beyond the purview of this book), there is mounting evidence that Jews gained prestige in Asian society. That Ignatius' Asian Christians are tempted towards the synagogue may have religious as much as social causes,[52] but it may be significant to find in Miletus that Jews (and, or possibly as, 'the God-worshippers') have prominent seats in the theatre which they obviously frequent.[53] The third and fourth centuries supply an ever increasing range of inscriptions indicating that the Jews received financial and political support from important Gentiles,[54] but also that they themselves played a prominent part in the life of the cities they inhabited. Naturally, conditions varied between different cities, but the size and prominence of the Sardis synagogue is proof enough of the social integration and civic prestige of the Jewish community in at least that location.[55]

---

[51] *MAMA* 6,264 (a better reading than *CIJ* 766); see Trebilco 1991:58–60 and Mitchell 1993:2.8. Julia Severa was almost certainly a Gentile (she and her husband were chief priests in the imperial cult three times during Nero's reign), though I consider it just possible that she was a Jew (married to a Gentile), whose exogamy and involvement in 'idolatry' were condoned by the Jewish community because of the value of her patronage.

[52] Ignatius, *Philad* 6.1; 6.2; *Magn* 8.1; 9.1–2; 10.3. The power of the synagogues to attract Christians is further attested in the writing of Melito of Sardis, the composition of treatises against the Jews by Apollinaris of Hierapolis and Miltiades (all second century CE) and by the canons of the Council of Laodicea (fourth century); see the discussion by Trebilco 1991:27–32, 53–54, 101–3 and Simon 1986:306–38.

[53] *CIJ* 748, an inscription much discussed since its discovery; see Deissmann 1927:451–52; Schürer 3.167–68; Trebilco 1991:159–62. Cf. the late second-century inscription from Hypaepa marking 'the Jewish *neoteroi*' (*CIJ* 755), which suggests an association of Jewish young men who had completed ephebe training.

[54] The Aphrodisias inscription is the most striking example (nine city councillors are listed among the Gentile 'God-worshippers' who support this Jewish cause), but it is by no means the only one: cf. the patronage of Capitolina for the Jews in Tralles (*CIG* 2924; discussed by Trebilco 1991:157–58).

[55] However, it seems that the Jews did not acquire this synagogue before the 270s CE, and perhaps in the aftermath of an economic crisis in the province; see Bonz 1990 who questions Kraabel's thesis of a steady increase in Jewish wealth and influence from Hellenistic times.

If we may put such fragmentary evidence together, we may suggest that the easing of social and economic tensions in the province of Asia did much to release the pressure on the Jewish communities. With the cities' pride restored, it was easier to allow pluralist conditions in which the Jewish communities could practise their own customs unhindered. At the same time, such reduction in hostility enabled the Jews' greater integration and acculturation in the cities they inhabited. Like the Jews in early Ptolemaic Egypt they probably explored means by which to remain both Hellenized and faithfully Jewish, and they lived in communities unafraid to express their identity in social and cultural harmony with their environment. The fact that, as far as we know, the Asian Jews gave no support either to the Jewish revolts in Palestine or to the 'Diaspora Revolt' of 116–117 CE may be an indication that their mood was far removed from the antagonistic spirit which came to dominate in Judaea, Egypt and Cyrene. With multiple indications in these later centuries of the Jews' sense of belonging in their Asian environment, we can picture strong and respected communities who made significant social contributions without compromising their Jewish identity.[56]

---

[56] See, in general, the mass of evidence for this later period assembled in Trebilco 1991, who contrasts later Jewish prestige with the troubles of the first century BCE (183–84, 188).

# 10

## *Rome*

Our final observation point on the Mediterranean Diaspora is at the heart of the Roman empire, the city of Rome. Although archaeology has uncovered scattered evidence for the presence of Jews in other parts of Italy (Noy 1993), it is only in Rome itself that we can build a moderately full profile of the Jewish communities, stretching over an extended period of time. Even here our information, literary and non-literary, has many limitations, but it ranks second only to Egypt in its depth and breadth.

The literary evidence derives from both Jews and non-Jews. On the Jewish side, Philo and Josephus each contribute some information on the history of the Jews in Rome. Philo visited Rome as the leader of the Jewish delegation from Alexandria in the reign of Gaius (see above, chapter 3.1.2), and Josephus lived in Rome under Flavian patronage after the Jewish War. Thus they both speak with some first-hand knowledge of Roman conditions, although their experiences also colour the facts they present.[1] From non-Jews we have a far richer supply of comment on Jewish life in Rome than we have for any other Diaspora location; and whereas elsewhere we have only isolated snippets of opinion, in Rome the corpus of Latin literature is sufficient to contextualize remarks about Jews to a far greater degree. Of course, that literature is chiefly representative of the élite, whose often hostile perceptions of Jews give us all too partial an angle of observation. It is, in fact, a good deal harder to discern the opinions of ordinary members of the Roman *plebs* concerning Jews in the city than it is to see the reactions of city mobs in Alexandria or Caesarea. Nonetheless,

---

[1] Thus Philo, in his *Legatio*, emphasizes Jewish privileges in Rome for apologetic reasons. Josephus, despite his lengthy residence in Rome, says surprisingly little about the Jewish community there; on his special circumstances and socio-cultural stance see chapter 12.2.

Roman authors provide a precious resource for any reconstruction of the realities of Jewish life in Rome.

The early Christian literature is less informative for our purposes than we might have hoped. While the book of Acts contributes one item of information (Acts 18.2) to our scanty knowledge of the Claudian era, its portrayal of Paul's meeting with the Jewish community in Rome (Acts 28.17–28) is suspiciously stylized. We possess, of course, Paul's letter to the churches in Rome, dating from the mid-50s CE. In it he appears reasonably cognizant of the affairs of the churches and shows some appreciation of the sensitivities of their Jewish members (e.g. Romans 9.1–5; 14.1–15.13; 16.3–16). His attempt to counteract the tendency of Gentile Christians to despise Jewish traditions (Romans 11.17–24; 14.1–2) might be a pointer to the tide of opinion in the capital, but in general the wider background of Jewish life in Rome remains, as it were, off screen. The same can be said for *1 Clement* (written from Rome in the 90s CE). Although Jews (and the Jewish tradition) played a significant role in the earliest stages of the Christian movement in Rome, Nero's targeting of Christians after the fire of Rome in 64 CE (Tacitus, *Annals* 15.44) suggests a differentiation from the synagogues within a comparatively short time.[2] Thus the story of the Christian house-churches cannot be subsumed under the category of Jewish history in Rome.

The non-literary evidence for Jewish life in Rome is, in numerical terms, particularly impressive. Besides some coins of relevance to Jewish concerns, we are fortunate to possess over 500 Jewish inscriptions which, together with some accompanying art-work, derive from the six Jewish catacombs which have been discovered to date in Rome. The character and location of such Jewish cemeteries, and analysis of their design and furnishings (though all had been looted), have been of some value in assessing the nature of Roman Jewish life; and analysis of the epitaphs themselves (their language and design) and the nomenclature of the deceased and their families has yielded valuable cultural and demographic information.[3] The references to synagogues and to a number of

---

[2]  See especially Lampe 1987:4–9, 53–63. In the Roman churches at least Andronicus, Iunia, Herodian, Aquila and Priscilla were Jews (Romans 16.3, 7, 11), and Rom 14.5–6 might suggest continued synagogue attendance; see Barclay 1996.

[3]  The inscriptions were edited by Frey in *CIJ* 1, with an introduction on the Roman Jewish community. Leon 1960 offered a more cautious assessment of

different synagogue offices have also given us a rare chance to perceive the institutional framework of Jewish life.[4] Of course, by their nature, epitaphs give us only limited information; we have, by comparison, no dedicatory or honorific inscriptions from Rome such as have been found in Asia, Egypt and Cyrene. It is also difficult to judge how representative were the Jews interred in these tombs. Yet as a body of evidence recording the names and deaths of a mass of Jewish individuals, such material is a valuable supplement to the generalizing comments of our literary sources.

The chronological boundaries of this book make our use of this catacomb evidence problematic. Analysis of lettering and brick-stamps suggests that the catacombs were in use primarily in the third and fourth centuries CE, with only some interments taking place before our limit of 117 CE.[5] Yet the precise dating of individual inscriptions is usually impossible. If it would be churlish to reject all the catacomb evidence because of this uncertainty, it would also be unwise to use this material over-confidently as a basis for the reconstruction of conditions in, for instance, the first century CE.[6] Whether the linguistic profile and the institutional structures of the Jewish communities in Rome remained constant over the two or three centuries represented by these epitaphs, we simply cannot tell.

the evidence and a more thorough analysis. Some further inscriptions have been discovered since Leon wrote; see Fasola 1976 and Horsley 1981:114–19. David Noy is due to publish a new edition of the Roman inscriptions and there is now a full analysis of Jews in third and fourth century CE Rome in Rutgers 1995. For the methodological problems in assessing the catacomb inscriptions see Rutgers 1992 and Rajak 1994.

4   We have as yet no material remains of a syngagogue building in Rome, although one has been excavated at its port, Ostia (see Kraabel 1979:497–500). On the institutional structures suggested by the catacomb inscriptions see Williams 1994a and 1994b.

5   On the problem of dating see Frey in *CIJ* 1.liv–lvi, 212–17; Rutgers 1990; Williams 1994a:176 n74; Solin 1983:694–95. The evidence from brick-stamps is not conclusive: old bricks can be reused many years after their manufacture. Yet some of the unmarked tombs may be earlier than those dated, on palaeographic grounds, to the third century CE.

6   The point is not often recognized by those eager to use such material to shed light on circumstances in Rome contemporary with the earliest stage of Christianity: see e.g. Wiefel 1991. Penna 1982 gives an excellent summary of the sources on Roman Judaism; he is cautious in using the catacomb evidence to illuminate conditions in the first century CE.

## 10.1 Republican Rome

The origins and early history of the Jewish community in Rome are almost entirely obscure. As Rome began to gain international importance in the second century BCE, it inevitably drew visitors and settlers from all over the Mediterranean world. Formal contacts and friendship treaties between the Maccabean leaders and the Roman Senate from 161 BCE necessitated embassies (e.g. that recorded in 142 BCE, 1 Macc 14.24; 15.15–24), and may have encouraged Jewish settlement in the expanding city. Unfortunately, the first record of Jews in Rome is of very uncertain value. Valerius Maximus (who wrote in the early first century CE) appears to refer to an expulsion of Jews in 139 BCE by the praetor Cornelius Hispalus (1.3.3). But this account is textually uncertain and has survived only in two epitomes, which differ in their description of the event. According to one (by Nepotianus, fourth – fifth century CE), the praetor ejected Jews (together with Chaldeans) since 'they tried to transmit their sacred rites to the Romans', and he threw down their 'private altars from public places'. According to the other (by Paris, fourth century CE), 'he compelled the Jews, who were trying to infect Roman customs with the cult of Jupiter Sabazius, to return to their homes'. On the basis of the latter statement scholars have erected elaborate theories of a Jewish Sabazios syncretism (of Asian origin), but it is far more likely that the confusion between the Jewish cult and the cult of Jupiter Sabazios arose in the sources used by Valerius Maximus.[7] It is also possible that the link has been created by a copyist's error, since some manuscripts omit all reference to the Jews in this context and the epitomator may have wrongly combined the various textual traditions he had available.[8] Given this uncertainty and the conflicting depictions of the event in the two cryptic epitomes, it would be exceptionally hazardous to draw conclusions about the nature of Roman Judaism from this evidence.[9]

---

[7]  For the syncretism theory, developed by F. Cumont, see Hengel 1974:263 and Simon 1976:52–56; a Gentile confusion of the divine title 'Sabaoth' with Sabazius has been frequently mooted as an alternative explanation (e.g. Schürer 3.74). For a Roman perception of Jews as worshipping Jupiter, see on Varro below, p. 286.

[8]  So Lane 1979, followed by Trebilco 1991:140–41.

[9]  Speculations on the meaning of 'private altars' (synagogues? altars erected by non-Jews under Jewish influence?) and on the possible connection with the

There is room for doubt that an expulsion of Jews took place at all,[10] but if it did, it is impossible now to assess its scale or its rationale.[11] One may refer in general to the nervousness in the Roman republic concerning cults and customs which bypassed the normal channels of power in the state,[12] but it is unclear to what extent at this early stage Judaism could be considered such a threat. It is striking that Varro (116–27 BCE), the champion of ancient Roman *mores*, appears to have honoured Judaism as an enlightened cult which preserved old-fashioned aniconic worship, and he understood the Jews to worship Jupiter, only under another name.[13] There is no hint here, in the figure most sensitive to the danger of religious novelties, that Jews or Judaism could be considered a threat to the Roman way of life. That impression is not evidenced before the first century CE.

Our earliest secure information on the Jews' presence in Rome is to be found in Cicero's speech in defence of Flaccus (59 BCE). We have already noted the information in this passage (*Pro Flacco* 28.66–69) which relates to the Jews in Asia (see above, chapter 9, pp. 266–67), since one aspect of this lawsuit concerned Flaccus' confiscation of the temple-dues of various Jewish communities in the province of Asia. Indulging his penchant for theatricality, Cicero lowers his voice at this point in his speech, claiming that the attendant crowd will be packed with Jews who have come to support the interests of their compatriots in Asia (*Pro Flacco* 28.66). What realities lie beneath this rhetoric it is hard to tell, but the jury must have been able to sense some truth in Cicero's claim that the Jews generally stick together and wield influence in informal political meetings (*scis quanta sit manus, quanta concordia, quantum valeat in*

recent Jewish embassy to Rome (in 142 BCE) are of little value; see the discussion of the evidence in Vogelstein 1940:10–14; Leon 1960:2–4; Stern at 147; Smallwood 1981:128–30; and Goodman 1994:82–83.

[10] Alessandri 1968 considers the story highly dubious and suspects a retrojection of events from Tiberius' reign; her scepticism is shared by Marshall 1975:140–41.

[11] Both the epitomes of Valerius Maximus suggest that the cause was Jewish proselytizing activity; but this may be influenced by events in 19 CE contemporary to Valerius Maximus (see below, 10.3).

[12] For an analysis of the social and political factors in the suppression of the Bacchic cult groups in 186 BCE see North 1979.

[13] Unfortunately we know his opinions on this matter only through the filter of others' (chiefly Augustine's) reports; see Stern 72–75.

*contionibus, Pro Flacco* 28.66).[14] Pandering to the snobbery of the jury, Cicero represents the Jews as a turbulent influence in Rome, liable to oppose any 'decent-minded' public figure (*in optimum quemque, Pro Flacco* 28.66). But since he nowhere refers to Jews in his voluminous correspondence (or takes cognizance of their views in his works on theology), one suspects that their influence is here greatly exaggerated.[15] However, such references indicate at least that the Jews were by now well established in Rome, sufficiently organized to send money each year to Jerusalem (*Pro Flacco* 28.67), and gaining a reputation for their social cohesion – a feature which later and more malevolent observers would interpret as clannishness or misanthropy.

The other notable feature of Cicero's depiction of the Jews is his haughty dismissal of their religion as a 'foreign superstition' (*barbara superstitio, Pro Flacco* 28.67) and his depiction of the Jewish cult as alien to the Romans and their power. Each state, Cicero remarks, has its own religious scruples, 'and we have ours' (*sua cuique civitati religio ... est, nostra nobis*). The Jews' sacred rites were simply 'incompatible with the glory of the Roman empire, the dignity of the Roman name and the ancestral institutions' (*Pro Flacco* 28.69). The recent war in Judaea, when Pompey had had to battle against the forces of Aristobulus fortified in the temple (63 BCE), gives Cicero reason to underline this incompatibility; it shows, he says, what they think of our empire. And with a final sarcastic jab he notes that the Jews' defeat, enslavement and submission to Roman taxation indicates how much the Gods care for them: *quam cara dis immortalibus esset docuit, quod est victa, quod elocata, quod serva facta* (*Pro Flacco* 28.69).[16]

To depict Cicero as a hardened anti-Semite on the basis of this passage would be to misunderstand its character. As a rhetorician of consummate skill, Cicero indulged in ethnic *vituperatio* whenever

---

[14] Cf. *Pro Flacco* 28.67: *multitudinem Iudaeorum flagrantem non numquam in contionibus*. On the *contiones* in Roman politics see Stambaugh 1988:104.

[15] The *optimum quemque* may indicate Cicero's perception that Jews sided more with the *populares* than with the *optimates*, but this is no more than one would expect of a group of foreign origin in Rome at this time. The *populares* were of course no more 'democratic' than their opponents (*pace* Leon 1960:8), but the Jews' later allegiance to Julius Caesar makes sense on these terms.

[16] Cf. his remark on Jews and Syrians as 'nations born to slavery', *De Provinciis Consularibus* 5.10 – the only other reference to Jews in Cicero's enormous corpus.

it served his argumentative purposes, frequently, as here, in discrediting witnesses for the case he opposed. This same speech pours scorn on the character of the Greeks, whom elsewhere he lauds (when it suits his case against Verres), and whose culture he admired. He himself warns us not to take his court-room remarks as expressive of his own personal opinions.[17] It is also important to note that although Cicero depicts the Jews' religion as inferior to the Romans', and although he can cite their resistance to Pompey as proof of their religious incompatibility, there is no suggestion here, as we will meet it later, that the Jewish way of life could *undermine* Roman customs. Cicero's remarks encourage the jurors to display an amused disdain of foreign customs, but hardly to fear Judaism as a hostile or corrupting influence. His tone is scornful but not venomous.[18]

Cicero's explicit identification of Roman religion with Roman power constitutes an important presupposition of the religious beliefs of most Romans. In an age when the validity of religion was proved by its success, the Romans could only conclude from their repeated military victories that their religion and piety were superior to all others. If the Jewish nation fought (in the cause of their temple) and lost, that just shows how much the Gods care for them! If the Romans won, the same statement could be made of them, without irony. Since tending 'the peace of the Gods' was a constant concern of the state, any diminution of the pious scrupulosity of the citizen body, especially among the prominent Roman families, was bound to elicit concern. The flexibility of polytheism encouraged the constant aggregation of new cults as the boundaries of the empire expanded; newly conquered peoples had their own deities which their traders or captives brought to Rome, and scrupulous Romans were concerned to take these too

---

[17] *Pro Cluentio* 139, cited by Wardy in the course of a useful discussion of Cicero's statements on the Jews, 1979:596–613.

[18] If its attribution is reliable, we may also note here Cicero's joke about Caecilius, recorded in Plutarch, *Cicero* 7.6. Plutarch reports that Quintus Caecilius Niger, who was quaestor during Verres' government of Sicily (73–71 BCE), was open to the charge of 'Judaizing', and that Cicero in the trial of Verres joked: *quid Judaeo cum verre* (*verres* meaning 'pig'). This would indicate that the Jews were already known in Rome for their abstention from pork and that some individual Romans showed a degree of interest in Jewish customs (to what extent in this case we cannot tell: Cicero's joke does not depend on Caecilius being a proselyte). Cicero reckons this will cause amusement. (On the possible confusion in our sources between this and a later Caecilius, see Schürer 3.703.)

under the Roman wing. Although antiquarians might bewail the gradual obsolescence of old rites, such new cults of themselves never constituted a threat to the religious 'health' of the city.[19] It was only a cult which rejected Roman religion *tout court* and scorned the worship even of the mighty Jupiter Capitolinus which could be properly perceived as a threat to the Roman way of life (and thus to her military, political and economic security). In Cicero's day, Judaism was no more than a *barbara superstitio* practised by a foreign group in Rome. It was only when its presence began to be felt among citizens – and especially among citizens of influence – that it was to experience a backlash such as we will find in the first century CE.

Cicero's reference to the Jewish nation as 'enslaved' reflects the arrival of numerous Jewish slaves in Rome as war-captives. Pompey's captives included Aristobulus and his children, but also many of humbler status (Josephus, *Ant* 14.70–71, 79). Indeed, Jews must have featured prominently in the Roman slave-markets not only in the immediate aftermath of Pompey's victory, but also as a consequence of continuing fighting in Judaea during which both Gabinius and Cassius took large numbers of prisoners (Josephus, *Ant* 14.85, 119–20).[20] This significant influx of Jewish slaves helps explain Philo's observation that the majority of Roman Jews were former war-captives who had, by his time, attained manumission and Roman citizenship (*Legatio* 155). Philo is writing in the principate of Claudius, referring to the situation when he visited Rome a few years earlier in Gaius' reign (37–41 CE). His reference to the Jews as 'freedmen' probably includes those who were descendants of freedmen, and it indicates that within the four generations from Pompey to Gaius large numbers of Jews had arrived in Rome as slaves and subsequently attained their freedom, perhaps even outnumbering those Jews whose residence in Rome was older. Thus the Jewish community in Rome gained enormously from the Roman victories in Judaea and from the liberal offer of

---

[19] See especially Wardman 1982:22–62.
[20] The figures (e.g. 30,000 in *Ant* 14.120) may be exaggerated, as Smallwood notes, 1970:235–36; she also refers to the capture of Jerusalem by Sosius in 37 BCE and the numismatic evidence for further captives at that time.

manumission which was typical of Roman slavery. There is no reason to believe that Jewish slaves were freed particularly quickly,[21] but they would benefit, as would slaves of any national origin, from the grant of Roman citizenship to any slave formally manumitted.[22] When Philo refers to such Jews as Roman citizens (*Legatio* 155, 157) he may be generalizing somewhat, but his reference to the collection of the dole (*ibid.* 158) confirms that at least some Jews acquired citizenship.

Thus the Jews in Rome became securely established as part of its increasingly cosmopolitan *plebs*. Philo indicates that by Augustus' time they were settled predominantly on the right bank of the Tiber, in an area of generally poor residences across the river from the civic heart of Rome (the area now known as Trastevere).[23] This suggests, as we would expect, a generally humble mode of life, though it does not rule out individual attainment of higher status. It was important for the new Jewish immigrants to find an established community already present in Rome, whose 'prayer-houses' (*proseuchae*) they could join and supplement. The fact that this national group gathered in its own places of prayer every seven days, organized collections for the temple in Jerusalem and arranged its own places of burial suggests an impressive degree of communal cohesion. Recent slave immigrants from Judaea might seek to retain their links with their homeland, and some, it appears, returned there on their manumission.[24] In any case, the temple dues and their transportation to Jerusalem (Cicero, *Pro Flacco* 28.67; Philo, *Legatio* 156) maintained the sense of indebtedness to the geographical centre of their traditions. Whatever the tendencies of individuals towards assimilation, the Jewish community

---

[21] Despite frequent but baseless assertions that their dietary and Sabbath practices must have made them awkward as slaves: thus, La Piana 1927:345; Leon 1960:4; Smallwood 1981:131. Vogelstein 1940:16 thought that 'some may have quickly won the favor of their masters by their deft service'. See the proper corrective to such opinions by Fuks 1985:29–30.

[22] Only formal manumission delivered citizenship, while an informal grant of liberty gave only *peregrinus* status, though after the *Lex Junia* (17 BCE or 19 CE?) Latin or Junian status; see Smallwood 1981:131–32.

[23] Note the study of this crowded lower-class district by MacMullen 1993.

[24] Such is suggested by the reference to a synagogue of *Libertini* in Jerusalem (Acts 6.9), although it is possible that some of its founders had been in slavery to Romans in eastern locations.

successfully established structures for the maintenance of its social distinction.

A crucial factor in the development of the Jewish communities in Rome was the patronage they gained from Julius Caesar. What benefit Caesar derived from the support of the Roman Jews we cannot tell, but his policy in the East was dependent to an important degree on the co-operation of the Judaean rulers, and it appears that the Roman Jews were able to benefit from this alliance on the basis of their common nationality. At the outbreak of the civil war (49 BCE) Caesar attempted to trade on the Hasmonean hatred of Pompey by releasing Aristobulus to fight against the Pompeian forces (Josephus, *Ant* 14.123–25). His protégé was shortly poisoned by Pompey's agents, but soon Pompey himself was dead, and his appointees in Judaea, Hyrcanus II and Antipater, were quick to switch their allegiance to Caesar. Their support proved to be crucial for Caesar's campaigns in the East, especially in the Alexandrine War where they provided troops and eased Caesar's passage through the Jewish military settlements on the Egyptian border (Josephus, *Ant* 14.127–39). This display of friendship elicited such gratitude from Caesar as to be mentioned in later decrees, confirming Hyrcanus as high-priest and ethnarch and bestowing significant tax advantages on the Judaean state (Josephus, *Ant* 14.190–212).

Such recognition of the Jews as 'friends and allies' could work to the advantage of Jewish communities outside Judaea. As we have seen (chapter 9), Josephus records a number of decrees from the period during or shortly after Caesar's reign, indicating the success of the Jewish communities in Asia in affirming their rights to meet, to enjoy the Sabbath unmolested and to send funds to Jerusalem. In one of these (addressed to Parium or Paros, *Ant* 14.213–16), reference is made to the permission granted to Jews in Rome to meet, to hold common meals and to collect contributions of money. The names and titles in this decree are garbled, and the suggestion that the Jews, alone of all societies (θίασοι), had been granted such permission is suspiciously parochial. Yet it is possible to link this passage with Suetonius' notice that Caesar banned all the *collegia* except those of ancient foundation (*cuncta collegia praeter antiquitus constituta distraxit, Iulius* 42.3), and some such exemption extended to the Jews helps to explain their special grief at Caesar's death (*Iulius*, 84.5). Thus it appears that, in his clamp-down on the *collegia* (whose political activities had contributed greatly to the disintegration of the Republic), Caesar had judged the Jews' gatherings as sufficiently ancient or a-political (or supportive of his regime) to permit their continuation; he thus safeguarded what was, as we have seen, the mainstay of Jewish communal identity in Rome.[25] Given his brief period of power in Rome, such action might have been of limited value; but the victory of his adopted son, Octavian, in the subsequent wars ensured that Caesar's favour to the Jews set a precedent likely to be heeded in the early years of the principate.

## 10.2 The Augustan Era

The Augustan era was characterized by a calculated effort to revive traditional Roman religion and by a certain suspicion of foreign cults.[26] The fictitious speech of Maecenas to Augustus found in Dio Cassius Book 52 warns against permitting novelties in religion, since those who despise the Gods will not honour anything else, and their meetings will spawn conspiracies (52.36.1–4). Nonetheless, there is nothing to suggest that Augustus took any measures to restrict Jewish activities in Rome; in fact what evidence we have suggests his favourable stance towards them. Although Philo is an interested party, concerned to portray the imperial tradition as uniformly favourable to Jews (until the aberration that was Gaius), we have no reason to doubt his word that Augustus preserved the rights of association which the Jews had enjoyed hitherto (*Legatio* 155–57).[27]

In fact, in one particular Augustus extended their rights still further, by allowing those Jews who were Roman citizens and

---

[25] On the *collegia* and Caesar's actions in their regard see Yavetz 1983:85–96; he recognizes the dubious features in Josephus' text (at *Ant* 14.213–16) but notes its compatibility with our other knowledge of Caesar's activities (1983:95). Juster argued that the Jewish communities were too distinctive to be considered *collegia* at all (1914:1.413–24), but it seems the term was flexible enough to cover such institutions as the synagogue community; see Guterman 1951:130–56 and Smallwood 1981:133–35.

[26] For an analysis of 'Augustanism' in politics and religion see Wardman 1982:63–79.

[27] Thus we must take it that when Augustus banned all but the 'ancient and legitimate *collegia*' (Suetonius, *Augustus* 32.1) the Jews again enjoyed exemption. Augustus' decree on the rights of the Jews in Asia (Josephus, *Ant* 16.162–65) grants the entitlement to observe their 'ancestral customs' (with special reference to Sabbaths and Jerusalem collections); that may mirror the permission granted to Jews in Rome.

entitled to the monthly dole to collect their corn-handout on the following day when the distribution happened to fall on a Sabbath (*Legatio* 158). This is in many respects a striking concession. Apparently a significant number of Jews were entitled to such corn-handouts, but were also scrupulous enough in their observance of the Sabbath not even to collect their dole on that day. It would be hard to find clearer testimony to the significance of the Sabbath and its faithful observance in Rome. At the same time, Augustus obviously decided that this Jewish law was not incompatible with the rights of Roman citizenship enjoyed by such Jews: as Philo points out (with a view to the different story in Alexandria), he did not take away their Roman citizenship because they cared about their Jewish one (*Legatio* 157). The holding over of the dole until the following day probably necessitated an official list of citizen Jews, documenting their double identity as Jews and Romans. The fact that such Roman Jews (or should we say, Jewish Romans?) paid no respect to the Roman Gods, but sent money to a temple far from Rome, and even, perhaps, enjoyed immunity from service in the Roman army,[28] does not seem to have prejudiced Augustus against them, although it may have irritated others, whom Philo admits were not always well disposed towards the Jews (*Legatio* 159). Augustus' personal goodwill to Jews is further suggested by the special donations which he and his wife made to the Jerusalem temple, and by the fact that a synagogue in Rome was named 'the Augustesioi' in his honour.[29]

Just as Caesar's benevolence to the Jews was linked to his political alliance with Hyrcanus II, so Augustus' policy in such matters was probably influenced by his close relations with Herod. Augustus

---

[28] Such may perhaps be inferred from the exemption granted to Jewish Roman citizens in Delos and in various cities in Asia in 49 BCE (Josephus, *Ant* 14.223–34), and from the objections raised by Jews to their conscription under Tiberius (Josephus, *Ant* 18.84).

[29] Philo (*Legatio* 157, 317) claims that the emperor personally funded daily sacrifices in Jerusalem which had been maintained ever since; Josephus mentions a twice-daily sacrifice for Caesar and the Roman people (*Bell* 2.197), although he says it was at the expense of the whole Jewish people (*C Ap* 2.77). On the contributions of Julia Augusta see Philo, *Legatio* 319 and Josephus, *Bell* 5.562–63; she also had a Jewish slave girl, Acme (*Ant* 17.138–41). The synagogue of 'the Augustesioi' is attested in *CIJ* 284 and five other inscriptions. Whether the synagogue of 'the Agrippesioi' (*CIJ* 365, 425, 503) was named in honour of Marcus Agrippa or of one of the Jewish kings named Agrippa it is impossible to say; see the discussion of these two synagogues in Leon 1960:140–42.

(as Octavian) had been influential, together with Anthony, in ensuring Herod's recognition as king (Josephus, *Ant* 14.381–89), and we have already had occasion to note Herod's reciprocating pro-Roman stance and his special friendship with Marcus Agrippa (chapter 9, p. 277). It was fitting, therefore, that several of Herod's children were brought up in Rome. Alexander and Aristobulus, sons of the Hasmonean Mariamme, were raised in the house of (C. Asinius?) Pollio and were well-known to Augustus (*Ant* 15.342–43); Antipater was entrusted to Agrippa to take to Rome and to become a friend of Augustus (*Ant* 16.86–87; 17.52–53), while Antipas, Archelaus and Philip were also brought up in Rome (*Ant* 17.20–21). One might imagine that an upbringing in such circumstances would destroy all vestiges of Jewish identity. Yet it appears that Asinius Pollio was a supporter of the Jewish nation and that even the Herodian family was known for its refusal to eat pork.[30] Jewish differences appear to have been tolerated even at this social level.

The circle of friends, associates and clients gained by these royal offspring must have been considerable and of lasting value to the Herodian house.[31] What relations these Herodians had with the rest of the Jewish population in Rome is difficult to assess, but their presence in the city maintained interest in Judaean affairs among Roman Jews. When, at Herod's death (4 BCE), Archelaus came to Rome to have his succession confirmed, there were, according to Josephus, as many as 8000 Jews in Rome who staged protests against him, perhaps scandalized by recent news from Jerusalem (*Ant* 17.300–3). By contrast, when, at some point in the following decade, an imposter claimed to be Herod's son, Alexander (executed in 7 BCE), crowds of Roman Jews thronged to greet him and to accompany him through their narrow streets (*Bell* 2.101–10; *Ant* 17.324–38). No doubt wealthier Jews in Rome (as in Crete

---

[30] On Asinius Pollio see Feldman 1953 and Horbury 1991:139–41 (detailing the debate on the identity of this Pollio). Macrobius, *Saturnalia* 2.4.11 records Augustus' joke that he would rather be Herod's pig than Herod's son! Cf. Juvenal, *Sat* 6.153–60. However, the offspring of Alexander appear to have abandoned Judaism (Josephus, *Ant* 18.139–42).

[31] On the Herodian friends in Rome (and the possibility of a Jewish festival in Rome celebrating a Herodian accession day, Persius, *Satire* 5.179–84), see Horbury 1991:123–46. Aristobulus' wife, Berenice, was to rank high among the friends of Antonia (wife of Drusus the elder) – a friendship which later proved extremely valuable for her son, Agrippa (*Ant* 18.143–44, 164–65); see further below, p. 302.

and Melos) hoped to gain by their support of this potential king, and others perhaps hailed him as a revival of the Hasmonean line. In any case, their enthusiasm suggests a high level of concern for the fate of their home-country and a continuing sense of identification with the interests of (fellow) Judaeans. To what extent this rebounded against the Roman Jews when Alexander was unmasked as a pretender we can only guess. But conditions in Augustan Rome were sufficiently favourable to ensure that they did not receive the public abuse which was experienced by the Alexandrian Jews when they paraded another king, Agrippa I, in 38 CE.

All such evidence suggests that the Jewish community in Rome flourished during the Augustan era, maintaining its distinct Jewish identity while gaining in numerical and social significance. Estimates of numbers are notoriously hazardous. Josephus' 8000 protesting against Archelaus (*Ant* 17.300) can be no more than a guess, but we may treat with some seriousness his figure of 4000 men of military age conscripted by Tiberius to fight in Sardinia (*Ant* 18.84), since it is (independently?) attested by Tacitus (*Ann* 2.85.4, though his figure may include Egyptians; see below). If there were 4000 men of citizen or Junian status aged between 18 and 45 we must take the total Jewish population as at least 30,000.[32] In a total civic population of roughly 1 million,[33] that remains only a small percentage, but still a sufficient number to make its presence felt. If such a foreign group could, through the Herodian family or other social contacts, acquire significant patrons, its influence could stretch much further than its numerical mass.[34]

In fact we have striking testimony to the influence of Jews in Augustan Rome in the comments of two Augustan poets, Horace and Ovid. In a famous sentence Horace finishes one satire (*Sermones* 1.4:140–43) by playfully threatening his critic with a crowd of poets

---

[32] Estimates of the numbers of Roman Jews vary from 20,000 (Penna 1982:328; Vogelstein 1940:17) to 40,000 – 50,000 (Leon 1960:135) or even 60,000 (Juster 1914:1.209). See the full and suitably cautious discussion by Solin 1983:698–701.

[33] Stambaugh 1988:89–91.

[34] As we shall see, the evidence from the beginning of Tiberius' reign suggests that the Jews had acquired notable supporters over a period of time. It is intriguing to find that one of the most famous orators and literary critics of the Augustan age, Caecilius of Calacte, was a Jewish freedman (see Schürer 3.701–4); he is recorded in the Suda as 'Jewish in his religion', but his relationship to the Jewish community in Rome is impossible to determine.

who will 'compel' him into line, like the Jews (*ac veluti te / Iudaei cogemus in hanc concedere turbam*, 142–43). This has usually been taken to be an allusion to Jewish proselytizing, but the reference to compulsion suggests a broader application: the Jews are noticed as a social body able to pressurize others, with perhaps religious, but also social (and political?) consequences.[35] What sort of social pressure the Jews might exercise is nicely illustrated by another passage (*Sermones* 1.9:60–78), where Horace's friend, Fuscus, refuses to rescue him from a bore, claiming his inability to converse because 'today is the 30th Sabbath; do you want me to insult the circumcised Jews?'. When Horace replies that he has no such scruples, Fuscus teases by responding that he, however, has, since he is 'somewhat weaker, one of the many' (*sum paulo infirmior, unus / multorum*, 71–72). Fuscus is being mischievous, of course, but the joke would fail if there were not some general perception that the Sabbath was a superstition observed by many ordinary Romans.[36]

That this was indeed the case is confirmed by several references to the Sabbath by Ovid. His remarks about the 'seventh day rites of the Syrian Jew' (*Ars Amatoria* 1.75–76) presuppose a general familiarity with the Sabbath (cf. *Remedia Amoris* 219–20),[37] and it is striking that in this latter passage the Sabbath is considered a day on which non-Jews might be reluctant to travel. Even more fascinating is the assumption underlying *Ars Amatoria* 1.413–16. Here Ovid is discussing good days on which to court a girl, and recommends particularly the Allia (a mournful commemoration of a Roman defeat at the hands of the Gauls) and the Sabbath. The reason for highlighting such days is that shops will be shut, and one will not therefore be impoverished by the girl's demands for presents! Ovid considers the Sabbath to have such general effect as to cause a significant closure of shops and businesses on that day (*quaque die redeunt rebus minus apta gerendis*, 415), presumably

---

[35] See Nolland 1979b, who, however, makes too sharp a distinction between religion and politics.

[36] The reference to the thirtieth Sabbath remains obscure; does it represent some confusion between the celebration of the new moon and the observance of the Sabbath? See Stern 1.326.

[37] The concession to Jews over the distribution of the corn-dole must have brought their Sabbath observance further into public view. It may also help to account for the fact the Jews were considered by many to fast on the Sabbath (see Suetonius, *Augustus* 76.2 and Pompeius Trogus, epitome 36.2.14, among others).

Gentile as well as Jewish.[38] It is probable that the observance of such Sabbath prohibitions was more common among the lower social ranks, as Fuscus' *infirmior* and *unus multorum* suggest. The phenomenon may be linked to the unofficial observance of the seven-day planetary week, which was coming into vogue at just this time; for the Jewish Sabbath coincided with Saturn's day, known to be specially inauspicious. The two systems of counting, the planetary week and the Sabbath week, thus reinforced each other and it is likely that, as Colson comments,

> the existence of the planetary week and the fact that the day on which the Jew abstained from work coincided with the day of the planet most adverse to enterprise promoted Sabbatarianism, and served to confirm many outsiders in the belief that it and Judaism in general deserved their respect and imitation.[39]

Although Horace can ridicule Jewish credulity (*Sermones* 1.5.100–1), the tone in which both he and Ovid discuss the Sabbath is one of amusement rather than hostility. Of course, this reflects their own genres and characters (Ovid is hardly a spokesman for Augustan ideology!), but it may also indicate a general perception that the Jewish way of life, though prominent and gaining influence in the lower orders of the Roman population, was not (yet) a serious threat to the Roman way of life. In literary circles widely varying perceptions of the Jews were coming to Rome from the East. Alexander Polyhistor (mid–first century BCE) had collected information about the Jews in apparent sympathy with their literature and religion, while the writings of Pompeius Trogus (around the turn of the era) show how the anti-Jewish sentiments which we have found in Egyptian, Syrian and Asian sources were

---

[38] The implication is noted by Hollis 1977:108, who remarks on the impact of Judaism on the social and economic life of Rome.

[39] Colson 1926:41; cf. Balsdon 1969:59–65. See especially Dio Cassius 37.16–19 where the Jewish Sabbath is taken to be the day of Saturn (or Kronos), whose observance in a seven-day cycle had become traditional among Romans by Dio's day (second to third century CE). Stern 1.319 considers Tibullus' allusion to an 'accursed day' (1.3.15–18) to refer directly to the Sabbath, but it is as likely that Saturn is the predominant influence here. Cf. Tacitus, *Histories* 5.4.4 where the Sabbath is connected with Saturn, the most powerful of the seven stars which rule the human race.

percolating into the Roman consciousness.[40] When Agrippa warned that he would grant the Jews their privileges provided they did not harm Roman rule (Josephus, *Ant* 16.60), we sense the Jews' political vulnerability: if Roman governors or emperors chose to interpret Jewish activities as detrimental to the interests of the state, they would have no compunction about applying all necessary force against them.

## 10.3 From Tiberius to Claudius

After the peaceful conditions of the Augustan era, the Jews in Rome did indeed experience something of a backlash in the reigns of Tiberius (14–37 CE), Gaius (37–41 CE) and Claudius (41–54 CE). According to sources of varying origin, whose story is mostly consistent, a major disruption of Jewish life in Rome occurred in 19 CE when Tiberius (or, more exactly, the Senate) conscripted 4000 Jews into the army to serve in Sardinia, and banished many others from Rome.[41] The reasons for this sudden assault on Roman Jewry can be deduced with a fair degree of certainty.[42] Josephus records the event as the result of a scandal in which a Roman noblewoman, Fulvia, the wife of a prominent senator, adopted Jewish practices

---

[40] On Alexander Polyhistor, see Freudenthal 1875 and Stern 51–53; on Pompeius Trogus, who repeats, alongside biblical traditions, the Egyptian libel of leprosy and the Greek charge of misanthropy, see Stern 136–39.

[41] The principal sources are: Josephus, *Ant* 18.65–84; Tacitus, *Ann* 2.85.4; Suetonius, *Tiberius* 36; Dio Cassius 57.18.5a. For a thorough analysis of their characteristics see Williams 1989. Although Josephus' dating is vague and could be taken to mean c. 30 CE, the dating in Tacitus is secure. Tacitus and Josephus agree on the figure of 4000, and the military duty in Sardinia, on which Suetonius is (typically) more vague. In his survey of imperial relations with the Jews, Philo omits to mention this incident, choosing to refer only to later anti-Jewish measures allegedly planned by Sejanus, which Tiberius overturned (*Legatio* 159–61). His dishonesty here is a warning not to place too high an estimate on the historical value of his writings.

[42] I am unpersuaded by Williams' attempt (1989) to discount the proselytizing motif as an invention of the sources and to suggest that Jews were simply more troublesome than most in this year of food shortages (cf. Newbold 1974). Although they differ in detail, all of our sources indicate that proselytes (Josephus), 'those who converted to Jewish ways' (Dio), those 'infected with this superstition' (Tacitus) or those who 'followed similar practices' (Suetonius) were involved in this incident. Williams' thesis depends on the Jews being perceived as particularly turbulent and does not explain why none of our Roman authors mention rioting in connection with the Jews.

under the influence of four Jews in Rome, who then stole the money and purple cloth which they induced her to donate to the Jerusalem temple (*Ant* 18.81–84). That so great a reaction should follow from this single incident is unlikely (and Josephus' story is written in novelistic vein); Dio may be closer to the mark when he asserts that the expulsion took place because the Jews were converting *many* Romans to their customs (57.18.5a). Josephus, Tacitus and Suetonius all connect this action against the Jews with simultaneous measures against the cult of Isis (or Egyptians in general), and from a passing reference in Seneca we gain the impression that the early years of Tiberius' reign saw a strong reaction against 'foreign cults' (*alienigena sacra, Letter* 108,22).[43] The story about Fulvia probably represents heightened concern at this time that the foreign element in Rome was becoming all too influential and its practices spreading into the ranks of equestrians and senators. The whole incident thus expresses Roman fear of cultural invasion, the insecurity felt by the guardians of the Roman tradition who had acted often in the past against the Isis cult, but here for the first time took measures to curb the influence of Jews as well.[44]

The Isis cult was fairly easily repressed by demolishing her sanctuaries, destroying her images and punishing her priests. But Jewish customs were not so easily subdued. Even if one razed the Roman synagogues and expelled their officials, that would still leave a large Jewish population whose ethnic identity was strong and who would continue to observe their 'foreign' customs even without their synagogues and officials. Thus the Senate elected to remove from Rome as many Jews as they could expel without complicated legal procedures. Citizens or those with Junian rights could not simply be expelled without due legal process, but they could be conscripted into the army and dispatched to a foreign region: thus 4000 men of military age were sent to Sardinia to counter bandits on the island. Foreigners without civic rights (*peregrini*) could simply be expelled, and it appears that many Jews in this category, and

---

[43] Seneca recalls here the Pythagoreanism of his youth, and the insistence of his father that he abandon his vegetarian practices lest they be mistaken for the observance of a foreign cult (perhaps abstinence from pork, as adherence to Judaism). The incident shows how Gentiles could be taken to be 'Judaizing' when they in fact intended no such thing!

[44] On previous action against the Isis cult see Moehring 1959, who also gives a valuable analysis of Josephus' narrative of the relevant scandals.

others suspected of Jewish tendencies, were summarily removed from the city.[45] Thus the Senate attempted to check the burgeoning Jewish influence in the city by removing as many as possible of the adherents of the Jewish cult.[46] Although military service and expulsion orders could never be made permanent, the Senate apparently hoped to debilitate the Jewish community, numerically and psychologically, such that it would never again threaten to 'corrupt' the Roman way of life.

Whatever the short-term effect on Roman Jewish communities, subsequent evidence indicates the failure of the Senate's policy. Forty years later Seneca was to complain about the spread of Jewish customs, in terms of the familiar Roman complaint that the vanquished had given their laws to the victors (*victi victoribus leges dederunt*).[47] The resilience of Judaism in Rome is only partially explained by the fact that, despite the expulsions, considerable numbers of Jews must have remained in the city, and no doubt many deportees subsequently returned.[48] The reconstitution of Jewish life in Rome after this serious assault on its existence can only be explained by the peculiar tenacity of Roman Jews. The fact that, according to Josephus, many of those enlisted for military service refused to serve on religious grounds is confirmation of their faithfulness to their tradition, even in the face of severe punishment (*Ant* 18.84). While upper-class Jews like Josephus might dismiss the event as an unfortunate aberration, or like Philo prefer to forget it altogether, we may guess that many whose lives were

[45]　Although Tacitus says 'from Italy', we should probably follow the agreement of our other sources that the expulsion was only from the city of Rome. On the legal questions of expulsion see Merrlll 1919, followed and supplemented by Smallwood 1956a and 1981:201–10.

[46]　It seems that the measure was directed more against Jewish customs than against Jews *per se*. According to Tacitus, any who renounced their practice of the Jewish rites within ten days were allowed to remain in Rome; conversely, Suetonius suggests that non-Jews were involved in the expulsion if they were known to practise Judaism: he refers to Jews and *similia sectantes*. Abel's argument (1968b) that *only* proselytes were expelled might seem justified by Tacitus' account (cf. Radin 1915:307–8), but is historically implausible (Williams 1989:769–72).

[47]　From his *De Superstitione, apud* Augustine, *De Civitate Dei* 6.11 (Stern 186).

[48]　Those remaining in Rome despite the Senate's action would include the families of the army conscripts, citizen males above and below military age, and Jewish slaves, together with any Jews who simply could not be traced. It is not clear whether Tacitus' notice that the 4000 conscripts were *libertini* is to be taken literally or as a Tacitean slur on the origins of all Roman Jews; cf. Solin 1983:686–88.

seriously disrupted by this affair would become still more tenacious in their commitment to Judaism, only now more wary of the Roman authorities.

The events of 19 CE represent the first public recognition that Judaism constituted a threat to the Roman way of life. Over the next 100 years we will meet several representatives of the conservative upper-classes who will echo this perception in their outright hostility towards Jews. It appears that after the Augustan era it became fashionable in certain literary and aristocratic circles to insult Jews openly; but at the same time (and as one reason for the hostility of their detractors), Jews found friends at all levels of Roman society, even in the imperial court. Thus the period from 20 to 120 CE will provide us with a bewildering range of evidence in which the individual inclinations of Roman emperors or senators brought sometimes favourable, and at other times highly damaging, results for the Jewish community in Rome. As if in illustration of the new unpredictability of Roman attitudes, we find, just ten years after the expulsion order of 19 CE, evidence for a new crisis in Rome which was averted at the last minute. According to Philo (*Legatio* 159–61), Tiberius' chief minister Sejanus had launched serious accusations against the Jews in Rome and was planning measures 'to wipe out the whole nation'; fortunately these were rescinded just in time at his fall in 31 CE. Philo's vague and sensationalized description of the affair leaves its nature wholly uncertain.[49] But the incident does show that the Jews could no longer be confident about the emperor's attitude to their concerns, and that the influence of particular individuals in the imperial court could largely determine their fortunes.

Tiberius' successor, Gaius, raised Jewish fears to their peak. In his short reign (37–41 CE), characterized by his megalomaniac obsessions, Gaius made it clear that he had little sympathy with Jewish scruples concerning iconic worship, especially if they threatened to detract from worship of his own divinity. The Alexandrian delegations which came to Rome in this period surely

[49] *Flacc* 1 suggests he wrote a whole treatise on the subject, which is now lost. Although some have considered the Sejanus affair to be the same as that in 19 CE, the dating is incompatible (Sejanus did not have sufficient power that early) and the incidents appear entirely separate; see Smallwood 1981:208–9. Hennig 1975:160–79 rightly questions the reliability of Philo's tendentious account, but it is likely that Philo is exaggerating rather than inventing facts; cf. Solin 1983:688 n. 218b.

caused concern among Roman Jews, not least because the anti-Jewish poison injected into the imperial court by Apion (the leader of the Greek delegation) and Helicon (an imperial slave) were bound to prejudice the emperor against Jews. An even greater threat was caused by the announcement that the emperor intended to erect his statue in the temple in Jerusalem. Philo's depiction of the Jews' shock at the news of this decision (*Legatio* 184ff.) restricts our view to his delegation and the Jewish prince Agrippa; but if Jews of this degree of assimilation were devastated by the news, we may guess that the mass of Roman Jews were enormously troubled. That the danger was, in the event, averted, removed the possibility of large-scale civic unrest in Rome (as elsewhere in the empire), but the incident certainly shook the Jews' confidence in the imperial house; as Tacitus comments, there remained the fear lest another emperor repeat the order (*Ann* 12.54).

Among the factors which staved off Gaius' project for the Jerusalem temple was the personal intervention of Agrippa I. This Jewish prince, a grandson of Herod and son of Aristobulus, had been brought up in Rome in Augustus' reign, where he had been a special companion of Drusus and in favour with the powerful Antonia. After Drusus' death (23 CE) he left Rome, owing a huge sum of money (Josephus, *Ant* 18.143–60). On his return, and with a loan from Antonia to pay off his debts, he became a particularly close friend of Gaius, an association widely known but eventually resented by Tiberius, who even put Agrippa in prison (*Ant* 18.161–223; Dio 59.24.1). His friendship with Gaius, however, paid off when the latter gained power and immediately crowned the prisoner king (*Ant* 18.224–39). We have already noted the influence of such events on the riot in Alexandria in 38 CE (chapter 3.1.1), but we may recognize in this context Agrippa's far more positive influence on Jewish affairs during the temple crisis. Although their accounts differ, both Josephus (*Ant* 18.289–309) and Philo (*Legatio* 261–338) indicate that Agrippa played an important role in persuading Gaius to reconsider his decision. The creation of links between the Herodian family and the imperial court was never of greater significance for Jews in Judaea, Rome and elsewhere than in these crucial conversations between Gaius and Agrippa.

In fact this well-connected Jewish king was even to have an influence on the imperial succession, after the assassination of Gaius in January 41 CE. Agrippa appears to have played a role in the delicate negotiations between Claudius and the Senate (Josephus, *Ant* 19.236–47; *Bell* 2.206–10), and was rewarded with a kingdom even larger than Herod's, together with consular insignia (*Bell* 2.214–16; Dio 60.8.2–3). In fact, his friendship with the emperor may have influenced Claudius' decisions concerning the Jews in Alexandria and his promulgation of a decree to ensure the safety of Jews in the Diaspora (Josephus, *Ant* 19.279–85 and 19.286–91).[50] Since Claudius intended from the start to repudiate Gaius' policies and to reinstate the ideals of Augustus, their association perhaps only confirmed Claudius' own inclinations. In any case, Agrippa's influence over the emperor was not to last much longer; his death in 44 CE deprived the Jews of their most important ever advocate in the imperial court.

The decade of the 40s saw further difficulties for the Jews in Rome, though their precise nature and date are a matter of some controversy given the sparse and inconsistent evidence provided by our sources. Our direct evidence consists of only four items:

(1) Acts 18.2 records the arrival of Aquila and Priscilla in Corinth from Italy, 'because Claudius had ordered all the Jews to leave Rome'. Luke's account suggests that they were Christian believers before they arrived in Corinth. He records their arrival as nearly simultaneous with that of Paul, whose 18–month stay ended with a hearing before Gallio (to be dated 50–51 CE). If we can trust this narrative, we would be inclined to place their expulsion from Rome at the end of the 40s. But it is just possible that they spent time in Italy between expulsion from Rome and arrival in Corinth, and doubts have also been raised about the reliability of the chronology in Acts 18.[51] Thus this piece of evidence, though our earliest, is not unproblematic.

(2) Suetonius (*Claudius* 25.4) mentions in a famous sentence that the Jews were expelled from Rome since 'they were constantly rioting at the instigation of Chrestus' (*Iudaeos impulsore Chresto*

---

[50] In the introduction to the first and the text of the second Agrippa is specifically named (together with Herod of Chalcis). For the suspicion that surrounds these decrees and comparison with the papyrus Letter of Claudius, see above chapter 3.1.2. One should note also the important friendship between Claudius and Alexander the Alabarch who looked after the estate of Antonia, Claudius' mother (Josephus, *Ant* 19.276).

[51] On the peripatetic possibilities for Aquila and Priscilla see e.g. Leon 1960:25. The chronology of Acts 18 has been challenged in a full discussion of the evidence by Lüdemann 1984:164–71. For alternative views see Jewett 1979:36–38 and Lampe 1987:4–8.

*assidue tumultuantis Roma expulit*). Unfortunately, he gives no date for this event. The majority of scholars take the *impulsore Chresto* as a garbled echo of disputes in the Roman synagogues concerning Christ, but it is possible that this discovery of a Christian dimension is a mirage.[52] Suetonius leaves unclear whether all Jews were expelled, or only those involved in the 'tumults'.

(3) Dio Cassius (60.6.6) records that Claudius did not expel the Jews, since they were too numerous, and an expulsion would have caused disorder; instead he ordered them not to hold meetings. This notice is given in connection with, though not explicitly dated to, the first year of Claudius' reign (41 CE).

(4) Orosius (*Adversus Paganos* 7.6.15–16) asserts that Josephus records Claudius' expulsion of Jews in the 9th year (i.e. 49 CE). There is in fact no such report in Josephus, and it is not clear whence Orosius derived his date. His reliability is obviously suspect.

Since these four statements are the only direct references to some Claudian action against Roman Jews, we cannot be sure about what, if anything, happened or when. As indirect (and therefore even less certain) evidence, we may note that:

(5) Dio mentions no action against the Jews in 49 CE, though this portion of his work is only partially extant.

(6) Tacitus' account of affairs in 41 CE is missing. We have his record of the year 49 CE, but this makes no mention of an expulsion or any other order against the Jews.

(7) Claudius' Letter to Alexandria (*CPJ* 153), dating to 41 CE, warns the Jews in Alexandria against fomenting 'a common plague for the whole world' (lines 99–100). This could be taken to echo Claudius' anger with the Jewish community in Rome at this time, but need not be interpreted in that way.

(8) In his *Legatio*, written in the early years of Claudius' reign and

---

[52] The majority can claim the considerable weight of Momigliano's opinion in their favour, 1961:32–33. But Benko 1969 has shown that the case is not closed; Suetonius knew something about the Christians and could call them by their proper name (*Nero* 16.2); cf. Radin 1915:313–15 and Solin 1983:659, 690.

possibly intended specially for Claudius, Philo makes much of the fact that Augustus did not expel the Jews from Rome or prevent them from meeting in their synagogues (157). He also omits to mention Tiberius' expulsion of the Jews in 19 CE. These diplomatic touches could reflect Philo's awareness of threats against the Jews in Rome at the time of writing.

How are we to put this flimsy and contradictory set of evidence together? We have a large array of options advocated by various scholars, which we may reduce to two types of solution. One is to give credence to all of our four direct sources and to posit two different events in Claudius' reign. Thus Momigliano, Bruce, Smallwood and many others conclude that Claudius acted to repress but not expel Jews in 41 CE (with Dio), but later, after the provocation created by Christian preaching, expelled Jews from the city in 49 CE (combining Suetonius, Acts and Orosius). The silence on this expulsion in 49 CE in Dio and Tacitus (and Josephus) could indicate that only a few Jews were expelled (despite Acts' 'all'), perhaps only or especially Christian Jews.[53] The other type of solution is to take all our sources as referring confusingly and contradictorily to the same event. Advocates of this solution give varying weight to Dio and Suetonius. Some accept Dio's account that no expulsions took place but only some restrictions on Jewish gatherings. Others conclude that, despite Dio, some expulsions, perhaps partial or temporary in nature, were carried out.[54] Forced to opt for one or other date, some accept Dio's account of events but Orosius' date (49 CE), others follow Suetonius' account but accept Dio's date (41 CE).[55]

It is not easy to find any firm ground amidst this welter of hypotheses. I would hesitantly add my support to the first solution, proposing seperable events, a ban on meetings in 41 CE and a (limited) expulsion in 49 CE. It is difficult to know whence Acts and Suetonius derived (independently?) their story of an expulsion, if none took place, and equally awkward to override

---

[53] Momigliano 1961:31–38; Bruce 1961–62:309–26; Smallwood 1981:210–16. See also Slingerland 1989, though he discounts the Christian dimension to these events.

[54] See the discussion of these options by Leon 1960:24–27; Stern 1974:180–83; Lüdemann 1984:165–66.

[55] For these two options see e.g. Schürer 3.77 and Janne 1934.

Dio's conviction that no expulsion took place in 41 CE.[56] Perhaps Claudius acted against a restive Jewish population in Rome in 41 CE, imposing a ban on synagogue gatherings in order to diffuse tensions arising from Gaius' threat to the temple.[57] As the decade progressed and the Jewish communities became embroiled in controversy over the new Christian message, he decided on firmer but selective measures in 49 CE, perhaps disbanding certain synagogues or expelling known 'trouble-makers'. Luke's assertion that *all* the Jews were expelled (Acts 18.2) is clearly exaggerated: not even in 19 CE were all Jews expelled, and Claudius lacked the political will to uproot tens of thousands of Roman inhabitants, citizens and non-citizens alike.[58] It is probable, therefore, that the measures of the 40s – the temporary ban on meetings and the selective expulsion of trouble-makers – were a much less serious blow to the Jewish community in Rome than Tiberius' actions in 19 CE. All our evidence suggests the continuing influence of the Jewish communities in Rome and even some of those expelled seem to have returned after a few years (Aquila and Priscilla, Romans 16.3).[59] Yet Claudius' actions underlined the insecurity of the political status of Jews in Rome and rendered them susceptible to suspicion or scorn.

## 10.4 From Nero to Trajan

In the following decades up to the reign of Domitian (i.e. from 49 to 81 CE) there is no record of official action against the Roman Jewish community, but plenty of evidence to confirm our

---

[56] I have deliberately set out the evidence in full and described the alternative options, in order to give readers the basis on which to make their own decisions on this most difficult case.

[57] Dio mentions only the increase in the Jewish population as the cause of Claudius' clamp-down, but he places it in the context of Claudius' suppression of clubs and his closure of taverns. Slingerland 1989:306–16 gives strong support to Dio's dating (41 CE). On Claudius' religious policy see Scramuzza 1940:145–56 and Momigliano 1961:20–38.

[58] See especially Smallwood 1981:215–16.

[59] The synagogue of the 'Augustesioi', probably founded in the Augustan era, is still found functioning in the inscriptions of the third century CE, despite the disruptions in the Julio-Claudian era. It is likely that the synagogues of the 'Hebrews' and of the 'Vernaculae' were also early foundations, whose continuance is also well evidenced; see Leon 1960:147–49, 154–57. Dio correctly notes the resilience of the Roman Jews despite occasional repression (37.17.1).

impression of the Jews' ambiguous position in Roman society. They emerge as a thriving community winning admirers and imitators among ordinary citizens and even, in certain cases, in the higher echelons of society, but also subject to hostile comment in conservative literary circles. Both aspects of their experience can be seen in the comments of the philosopher Seneca (d. 65 CE). Seneca resented the popularity of Jewish customs in Rome, singling out for adverse comment especially the observance of the Sabbath and the custom of lighting Sabbath lamps, a visible and apparently attractive feature of Jewish observance in Rome.[60] Seneca's hostility to Jews is evident in his reference to their 'utterly heinous nation' (*sceleratissima gens*), but he also rues the fact that the Jews knew the rationale for their customs.[61] Thus, although he and later authors could misrepresent Jewish customs as laziness (on the Sabbath), worship of the pig (because of their abstention from pork) and honour of the sky (for the nameless, heavenly Deity),[62] it is evident that others, of varying social classes, found Jewish customs reasonable and admirable.

In fact it is during these decades that we hear of some notable figures whose support for Jews became public knowledge. Tacitus refers to an accusation of *superstitio externa* in 57 CE against a high-class woman, Pomponia Graecina (*Ann* 13.32), though whether this refers to Jewish practices is not certain. Better documented is the case of Poppaea Sabina, the mistress (and later wife) of the emperor Nero. According to Josephus, she exerted her patronage on behalf of Judaean priests who had been sent to Rome on trial,

---

[60] Seneca, *De Superstitione, apud* Augustine, *De Civitate Dei* 6.11. The lighting of lamps is also remarked upon, in a hostile tone, by Persius, *Satire* 5.180–84, who suggests that non-Jews were apt to mark the Sabbath (or a festival in honour of a Herodian king?) in this way; this provides some support for Josephus' claim concerning the same custom in *C Ap* 2.282.

[61] *De Superstitione, apud* Augustine, *De Civitate Dei* 6.11. The passage ends with the statement: *illi tamen causas ritus sui noverunt; maior pars populi facit, quod cur faciat ignorat.* Even if the second half of this sentence refers to the imitation of Jews by an ignorant populace (*maior pars populi!*; see Stern 1.432) we know that Jews had developed explanations for their customs, perhaps in the context of their synagogue instruction (Philo, *Legatio* 156–57). We have already noted early Alexandrian examples in Aristeas and Aristobulus; Josephus indicates that he was preparing four volumes on 'Customs and their Reasons' (*Ant* 20.268).

[62] For such misrepresentations see e.g. Petronius (fragment 37 = Stern 195); Plutarch, *Quaestiones Conviviales* 4.5; Juvenal, *Sat* 14.96–106; Tacitus, *Hist* 5.4. On Juvenal and Tacitus, see further below.

and extended her benefaction to him as their advocate (*Vita* 16). Elsewhere, he records her support for Jerusalem priests on another occasion, and refers to her as 'God-worshipping' (θεοσεβής, *Ant* 20.195). The meaning of this accolade is disputable, and it is possible to dismiss Poppaea's interests as merely superstitious.[63] But her intervention on both occasions in support of Jewish priests indicates that she had at least some cause to favour the Jewish community; whether her interests were more political than religious it is impossible to tell.[64] In fact, here, as in the case of other prominent supporters and 'sympathizers', it is impossible to distinguish 'political' from 'religious' motivations (Cohen 1989). Support for the Jews as an ethnic community involved support for their distinctive customs, but not necessarily personal practice or belief.

As the case of Poppaea illustrates, the influence of the Jews reached even the imperial court. There is no record of Nero's discrimination against Jews in any respect, and in the great fire of Rome (64 CE) it was the adherents of the new Christian 'superstition', not the Jews, who were made the scapegoats (Tacitus, *Ann* 15.44; contrast the fire in Antioch a few years later, Josephus, *Bell* 7.41–62). A Jewish actor, Alityros, was a special favourite of the *princeps* (Josephus, *Vita* 16). The Herodian family was also known and honoured in the court even after the death of Agrippa I (44 CE). Agrippa II, his son, had been brought up with Claudius and, although too young to be granted his father's kingdom, he was important enough to intercede with the emperor on behalf of the Jews on several occasions (Josephus, *Ant* 19.360–62; 20.10–12, 134–36). One (hostile) perception of their friendship is provided by the fragments of an Alexandrian 'thriller', in which Isodorus and Lampon, on trial before Claudius, bemoan the influence of Agrippa ('this cheap-jack Jew') in the court (*CPJ* 156b).[65] After the

---

[63] See Smallwood 1959, highlighting Poppaea's notorious immorality and her involvement in Roman religion.

[64] Williams 1988 refutes most of Smallwood's arguments, but admits that Poppaea's attachment to the Jewish religion 'was very unspecific indeed' (109). The element of political patronage is in any case clear: note the reference to εὐεργεσία in *Vita* 16.

[65] They also accuse the emperor of being the cast-off son of Salome (Herod's sister, *CPJ* 156d)! There has been much discussion over the dramatic date of this largely fictitious narrative, which could belong to 41 or to 53 CE; see Tcherikover in *CPJ* 2.67–70 and above, chapter 3 n. 51.

Jewish War (in which he had sided with the Romans, not the revolutionary Jews), Agrippa was prominent in Rome and accorded the rank of praetor (Dio 66.15.3–4).

Two of Agrippa's sisters were also to become well-known in Rome. Drusilla was married to Felix (the procurator of Judaea, *Ant* 20.141–44), while Berenice almost effected a more spectacular match. After three previous marriages, Berenice became a famous unattached princess, whose closeness to Agrippa caused rumours of incest but whose charms made her a new 'Cleopatra' in the East. In particular, her affair with Titus caused considerable comment. After their first encounter in 68 CE, Titus became infatuated and brought her to Rome after the Jewish War, where she was established as his mistress (Tacitus, *Hist* 2.2.1; Dio 66.15.3–4). It appeared at this point that a marriage was imminent (some said Titus had promised it), but a significant body of opinion in Rome disapproved of the relationship, partly out of political envy but partly, it seems, because of opposition to the notion that a Jewish princess should attain such influence in the court.[66] Thus Titus had to send her away from Rome in 75 CE, and probably again in 79 CE when he became emperor (Dio 66.18.1). Having come within an ace of this ultimate prize, the Herodian family was never again to exert much influence in the Roman court.

The fact that Titus could dally with a Jewish princess even after the Jewish War may seem surprising. Although Rome had been somewhat distracted by its own civil wars at the end of the Jewish War, Vespasian's successful bid for power naturally focused attention on his exploits, and those of his son, in Judaea. We know that histories of the War circulated in Rome with understandable flattery of the Romans and denigration of the Jews (Josephus, *Bell* 1.2). The massive triumph celebrated in Rome (*Bell* 7.123–62), displaying Jewish nobles and temple furniture, and the proclamation of the submission of Judaea on coins and in sculpture (Titus' arch) must have discredited the Jews in the eyes of the Roman population, much as Cicero years earlier had joked about

---

[66] On the political factors involved see Crook 1951. Opposition to such significant Jewish influence is suggested by Smallwood 1981:385–88, noting the popular concern voiced even in the theatres. Despite her dubious sexual morality, Berenice had been a staunch defender of the sanctity of the temple (Josephus, *Bell* 2.310–14, 402–5). Since her previous Gentile husband had been required to get circumcised (*Ant* 20.145–46), there may have been some alarm in Rome lest Titus too submit to the Jewish rite!

the Gods' care of the Jews when they fought against Pompey and lost. The influx of prisoners must have been large (*Bell* 7.118), though no doubt Rome disposed of many of the 97,000 (*Bell* 6.420) in the East. To what extent the Jewish population in Rome suffered from ill-feeling we cannot tell. Since there had not developed in Rome anything like the animosity towards Jews that we have noted in Antioch and Alexandria, we hear of no requests for reprisals such as were addressed to Titus in those eastern cities. There is also no evidence of agitation sparked by refugees, such as we have seen in Alexandria and Cyrene. Upper-class Jews in Rome perhaps shrugged off the revolt as a terrible mistake perpetrated by irresponsible hot-heads, and when they were joined by the historian Josephus (who was given high-class lodging in Rome, together with citizenship and a pension), they gained a spokesman for their conciliatory point of view (Josephus, *Vita* 422–29; see further below, chapter 12.2).

Thus, despite the disaster in Judaea, Roman Jews seem to have been allowed to carry on their lives without change, or at least with only one. That single change was the transformation of the annual contribution to the temple into the Jewish tax, payable into the *fiscus Iudaicus*, initially for the rebuilding of the temple of Jupiter Capitolinus. We have already noted the effect of this tax as a public humiliation, and increased financial burden, on Jews throughout the empire (see above, chapter 3.2), but we can imagine the particular gall for Roman Jews in watching the reconstruction of the temple of the God (Jupiter) who had been victorious over their own, at their own expense![67] In the long term, the destruction of the Jerusalem temple and the cessation of contributions and pilgrimages to the 'holy city' may have weakened the geographic loyalties of the Roman Jews to a 'foreign' country. At least it was more possible now for outsiders to understand the Jewish way of life in religious and cultural rather than mainly national terms. Thus, paradoxically, the destruction of the temple may have helped to maintain, rather than diminish, the attractiveness of Jewish customs to non-Jews.

The imposition of the tax and the continuing attraction of Judaism contributed to a new crisis for Roman Jews in the reign of Domitian (81–96 CE). According to Suetonius, Domitian, eager to

---

[67]  Martial, *Epigrams* 7.55.7–8 enjoys the humiliation of 'burnt Solyma, lately condemned to pay tribute'.

raise new funds, exacted the Jewish tax with 'special severity' (*Iudaicus fiscus acerbissime actus est*) and closed off possible loopholes by which he thought some had evaded its payment (*Domitian* 12.2).[68] Suetonius mentions two categories of 'tax-dodgers': (a) those who were considered to live 'the Jewish life' without admitting themselves to be Jews (*qui ... inprofessi Iudaicam viverent vitam*); and (b) those who hid their origins in order to avoid paying the tax imposed on their race (*dissimulata origine imposita genti tributa non pependissent*). Although the precise reference of these two categories has caused some dispute, it seems reasonably clear that the first (a) refers to non-Jews whose 'Judaizing' lifestyle (perhaps even in trivial particulars) could be used in evidence against them, while the second (b) was intended to catch all Jews by birth, whether or not they practised Judaism.[69] In the atmosphere of terror encouraged by Domitian and in this heyday of informers, it appears that investigations were conducted with considerable brutality and false charges laid on such a scale as to cause widespread concern: such at least is suggested by the fact that Nerva saw fit at his accession to power (96 CE) to mint coins proclaiming the end of all such witch-hunts, with the legend *FISCI IUDAICI CALUMNIA SUBLATA* ('The Cessation of Malicious Accusations relating to the Jewish Tax').[70]

Although the connection is somewhat obscure, this rigorous extraction of the Jewish tax was apparently combined with a general move against prominent Roman citizens who adopted (or could

---

[68] See especially Smallwood 1956b and 1981:371–85, and Williams 1990; whether one describes Domitian's action as an *extension* of the tax-base (Smallwood) or merely a clamp-down on tax evasion (Williams) may be a matter of perspective. It is difficult to know whom Vespasian had thought liable to the tax, given that Josephus' note on this is vague (*Bell* 7.218) and Dio's account (66.7.2) was written long after the event, reflecting conditions in his own day.

[69] Besides Smallwood and Williams (see previous note), see also Bruce 1964 and Thompson 1982, whose alternative solutions are, however, much less convincing. Thompson takes both clauses to refer to 'apostates' and non-Jewish *peregrini*, with the second referring specifically to those who were circumcised. But it is difficult to imagine that apostates would let themselves be caught under the first heading, although, in relation to the second, he may be right that anyone found circumcised, whatever the cause of the operation, was taken to be a Jew (and therefore liable to the tax).

[70] See Mattingly 1936, nos. 15, 17, 19. As an example of brutality, note Suetonius' story of the stripping of a 90-year old at a tribunal, to see if he was circumcised (and thus taxable), *Domitian* 12.2.

be charged with adopting) Jewish customs.[71] Dio notes that Nerva abolished all proscriptions on the charge of 'impiety' or 'Jewish lifestyle' ('Ιουδαικὸς βίος, 68.1.2). He had earlier recorded the trials of Flavius Clemens and Flavia Domitilla (cousins of the emperor and the parents of his heirs) on a charge of 'atheism' (ἀθεότης), on which also many others had been charged who had drifted into Jewish customs (67.14.1–2). This purge of the imperial family was probably motivated primarily by political rather than religious considerations, but it appears that Domitian was able to seize on any Jewish 'leanings' as a sign of disloyalty to the (Roman) Gods and insult to his own divine status (*maiestas*).[72] The trials seem to have been directed at 'Judaizing' non-Jews rather than Jews themselves, but nonetheless the propaganda depicting Judaism as 'atheism' and the bad feeling surrounding the Jewish tax seems to have fostered a general spirit of anti-Judaism in the capital.[73] Quintilian and Martial, whose works reflect the atmosphere in Domitian's Rome, are noted for their snide remarks about Jews, and the repeated emphasis in Martial on circumcision may echo Roman amusement surrounding the 'unmasking' of 'tax-dodgers' among Jewish males.[74] It is not necessary to posit here some plot

---

[71] How Judaizing Roman citizens could be charged both with tax-evasion (suggesting the legality of their behaviour provided they paid the tax) and also with 'atheism' (illegal, whether or not they paid the tax) is a question which Smallwood's analysis of the facts left unclear (see 1956b:1–6); note the criticism of her position by Rajak 1979:192, Thompson 1982:335–37 and Williams 1990:206–7. Williams suggests that tax-cases were lodged against lesser people and 'atheism' charges against the politically important, and that in any case logic played little part in the extraordinary treason trials of Clemens and Domitilla (208–9). This may be correct, though Nerva's coins suggest that the tax-cases were of major significance; we simply lack sufficient information to comprehend the basis or the nature of the charges in the trials of Clemens and others of his ilk.

[72] Despite Christian tradition, there is no good reason to regard Flavius Clemens and (this) Domitilla as Christians rather than simple (or at least alleged) 'Judaizers'; on this matter see Smallwood 1956b, Keresztes 1973 and Lampe 1987:166–72.

[73] There is no evidence that the issue of tax-evasion or 'atheism' was pursued outside Rome (see Williams 1990:201 n29); J. T. Sanders' use of such evidence to speculate about conditions in Asia at this time is, as far as I can see, unjustified (1993:166–204).

[74] Quintilian, *Institutio Oratoria* 3.7.21 refers to Jews as 'a race which is a curse to others' (*perniciosa ceteris gens*). Martial excoriates the stench of 'Sabbath-fasting women' (*Epigrams* 4.4) and repeatedly ridicules the circumcised (e.g. 7.30.5; 7.35.3–4; 7.82.5–6; 11.94). He laughs at the unsuccessful attempts of an actor,

against all Jews in the capital, but the evidence we have surveyed does suggest an atmosphere in which Judaism was presented as un-Roman and even anti-Roman.[75]

The death of Domitian (96 CE), and the strong reaction against his policies which ensued, must have relieved the situation of the Jews considerably. As we have seen, Nerva even advertised the end of the trials relating to the Jewish tax, though this was not, of course, the end of the tax itself, which continued in place until the fourth century CE. But the anti-Jewish poison which had accumulated during the 1st century in certain circles, and which was augmented both by the Jewish War and by the reign of Domitian, was not so quickly drawn. We meet it most dramatically in two writers who flourished at the end of the first century CE and the beginning of the second: Juvenal (c. 60–130 CE) and Tacitus (c. 56–120 CE).

Juvenal's *Satires* contain several famous passages about the Jews of Rome, expressed in that caustic tone which is his hallmark. *Satire* 3 is a complaint about the insufferable conditions of the city, in which Juvenal flaunts all his xenophobic prejudices. Jews are included among the Greeks, Syrians and other 'effluent' which has flowed into the Tiber from the East. At the Porta Capena, where Juvenal meets his departing friend, the sacred grove which was once the scene of a native Roman myth has been hired out to Jewish beggars, whose basket and hay signal their alien Sabbath customs (3.10–18).[76] This combination of cultural and class snobbery is

---

Menophilus, to hide his circumcision by means of a pin (*fibula*), 7.82. Although representative of upper-class disdain of Jews, Martial's obscenities are also driven by a particular set of sexual fears and distastes. See Sullivan 1991:185–210, who also points out that circumcision was performed for other than Jewish reasons (189); cf. Cohen 1993b:41–43.

[75] References in rabbinic literature to a visit to Rome by four important rabbis from Palestine are too vague and too insecure historically to suggest a sudden crisis in Rome, as reconstructed by Vogelstein 1940:68–74 and Smallwood 1956b:8–11. Although Josephus claims that he received support from Domitian and Domitia (*Vita* 429), it is notable that his sponsor for the *Antiquitates* (published 93–94 CE) is not imperial (as was the *War*), but one Epaphroditus. The apologetic tone in this work (which was poorly received in Rome, *C Ap* 1.2–3) and in its sequel, *Contra Apionem*, indicates a strong tide of opinion in Rome running against the Jews.

[76] As the scholion on the parallel passage (6.542) indicates, the hay and basket are probably intended to keep food warm on a day when it is forbidden to light fires; see Courtney 1980:158. As Highet notes, in this brief passage Juvenal manages to combine invective against foreigners, greed, extravagence and the destruction of Roman traditions (1954:69).

repeated elsewhere, with insinuations that the synagogue is a haunt of beggars (3.296), and a caricature of a Jewish fortune-teller, offering the benefits of her high-sounding lore at a knock-down price (6.542–47).[77] But it is the sense that Jews are weakening Roman traditions which is most powerful in the opening to *Satire* 3 and which becomes particularly prominent in *Satire* 14.96–106. Here, in a context where he bemoans the evil influence of fathers on their sons, Juvenal depicts the vices of the 'Judaizing' father, notably his laziness on the Sabbath, his absurd abhorrence of pork and his nebulous worship of the heavens: all these encourage the son to go still further. The 'further' depicted here is circumcision (i.e. proselytism), which Juvenal describes as if it constituted a major threat to the Roman way of life. Such converts are taught to 'despise Roman laws' (*Romanas autem soliti contemnere leges*), since they now revere Jewish commands, handed down in Moses' esoteric book (14.100–2). Such, indeed, is their social alienation that they refuse to perform the common decencies of life, except for members of their circumcised sect (14.103–4).[78] In this vivid and well-informed vignette, Juvenal has neatly summarized the social, cultural and religious factors which made Judaism, in his view, both despicable and dangerous.[79]

A remarkably similar tone is struck in the famous description of Jews, Judaism and Judaea at the opening of Tacitus' *Histories* Book 5 (1–13). In this ethnographic digression, a prominent place is given to the description of Jewish customs, in which Tacitus mixes by now common explanations of Jewish practice with his own cynical imputation of their motives. In explaining Jewish origins Tacitus highlights the Egyptian fable of the expulsion of lepers, but adds that Moses attempted to secure their allegiance by giving them novel rites contrary to the rest of humankind (*Hist* 5.4.1). This is amplified by a striking sentence which indicates Tacitus' particular Roman sensitivities: 'Among the Jews everything that

---

[77] Cf. Martial's depiction of a Jewish beggar, *Epigrams* 12.57.13. Juvenal knows about high-class Jews too, and mocks the customs of the Herodian family, 6.153–60.

[78] Here 'showing the way' and 'directing to the fountain' are clichés indicating basic civilized behaviour (see Courtney 1980:572); Josephus refutes precisely this charge in *C Ap* 2.211.

[79] Sherwin-White (1967:97–99) rightly insists that Jews (unlike some other foreign groups in Rome) were not an economic or political threat to upper-class Romans like Juvenal; but he underestimates the cultural threat reflected in the passages we have considered.

we hold sacred is considered profane, and everything permitted to them is abhorrent to us.'[80] The personal pronouns (*nos, nobis*) are revealing: Tacitus assumes among his readers a common Roman identity, which is scandalized by the incompatibility and sheer contrariety of the Jews' religion. The same note is struck elsewhere,[81] and driven home most forcibly with reference to the conversion of Romans to the Jewish rites. After outlining Moses' original rules which, though odd, were at least ancient (*Hist* 5.5.1), Tacitus proceeds to list some 'depraved customs' of more recent origin, the first of which is the practice of the proselyte:

> For all the worst kind of people, abandoning their ancestral religion, contribute dues and donations; for this reason Jewish wealth has increased, as also because of their stubborn loyalty, their readiness to show pity (to each other), and their hatred and enmity towards all others (*Hist* 5.5.1).

After further reference to the Jews' distinctive customs (separate eating, no mixed marriage, and circumcision 'to mark their difference'), Tacitus returns to the converts, who learn to 'despise the Gods, shed their patriotic loyalties and treat their parents, children and siblings as of no account' (*contemnere deos, exuere patriam, parentes liberos fratres vilia habere, Hist* 5.5.2). Nothing could indicate more clearly the basis for Tacitus' vilification of all things Jewish: while the Jewish revolt could be disposed of simply enough, her religion threatened to spread like a cancer in the body politic, destroying the very organs – religion, nation and family – by which Rome had been made great. Such invective testifies to the insecurity which had plagued Roman culture ever since Rome began to gain dominance over the Mediterranean world. Speaking at the very height of the empire, Tacitus writes with the disdain of one who had seen Roman power conquer every opponent, but knew that a contrary cultural tradition was living and growing in the capital.[82]

---

[80] *Profana illic omnia quae apud nos sacra, rursum concessa apud illos quae nobis incesta, Hist* 5.4.1.

[81] Note for instance the interpretation of the Jews' sacrifice of rams as a mark of their contempt for Ammon (*Hist* 5.4.2), and the suggestion that Jerusalem was well defended because its founders foresaw frequent wars arising from their difference in customs (*Hist* 5.12.2)!

[82] The impression of *growth* is felt both in financial (*Hist* 5.5.1) and in numerical terms (*Hist* 5.5.3). Besides the accession of converts, Tacitus can ascribe the numerical increase only to the Jews' lust, and their reluctance to expose

Our impressions from both Juvenal and Tacitus are of a Jewish community successfully maintaining its social identity in faithfulness to its ancestral traditions and gaining admirers, imitators and even converts from among non-Jews. And such impressions are fully supported by the inscriptional evidence, though most is of a later date. Here we find synagogue communities with a host of functioning and honorific officers, their service to the community proudly listed in their epitaphs.[83] At least eleven synagogues are attested in the inscriptions (only some of which can be securely dated before the second century CE), and geographical indicators in their names, in the location of the catacombs and in literary references indicate a spread over several parts of the city.[84] It is unclear whether there was any central body to hold these communities together,[85] yet some links clearly existed between Jews of different synagogue communities and we have no evidence of Jewish disunity.[86] One may imagine that their chequered fortunes in the first century CE encouraged Jews to identify with one another in their common fate.

Juvenal's complaint about Jewish devotion to their law and to their own people is neatly mirrored in a verse epitaph celebrating the virtues of one Regina (*CIJ* 476; end of second century CE), notably her 'love for her people' (*amor generis*) and her 'observance of the law' (*observantia legis*). Elsewhere individuals are commemorated as 'lovers of the people' (φιλόλαος, *CIJ* 203, 509) and 'lovers

---

unwanted children. It is instructive to compare Tacitus' opinion of the Jews with his more favourable impression of the Germans (see Sherwin-White 1967); the Jews appear more dangerous as 'the enemy within'. Tacitus can find nothing admirable in their cult (*mos absurdus sordidusque, Hist* 5.5.5); see Wardy 1979:629–31.

[83] On the offices listed and their meaning see Frey in *CIJ* 1.lxxxii – ci; Leon 1960:167–94; Schürer 3.92–107; Williams 1994b.

[84] Leon 1960 rightly dismissed many fanciful interpretations and insecure readings of the synagogue names. On the geographical spread of the synagogues, covering at least the Trastevere district, the Campus Martius, the Subura, the Porta Capena and the Porta Collina see Leon 1960:136–38 and Lampe 1987:26–28.

[85] No conclusive proof of a central communal organization has been discovered; even the recent discovery of an inscription honouring an ἀρχιγερουσιάρχης does not overturn this, see Solin 1983:696–97. Yet one can scarcely be confident either way on the basis of this lack of evidence; see Applebaum 1974:498–501.

[86] Beturia was honoured as the 'mother' of two different synagogues (*CIJ* 523), and we find several communities sharing the same catacomb; see Williams 1994a.

of the law' (φιλέντολος etc., *CIJ* 132, 509; cf. 72, 111, 113); one woman 'lived well in Judaism' (*CIJ* 537).[87] Although some Jews appear to have suppressed their Jewish identity in evading payment of the tax, the story we have traced shows the general tenacity of Jews in keeping to the 'arcane volume of Moses' (Juvenal).[88] As Philo suggests (*Legatio* 156), the Sabbath expositions of the law laid the foundation of Jewish identity in Rome; only the temporary ban by Claudius caused any disruption to this socio-religious tradition, which could easily survive the destruction of the temple in Jerusalem.

There is also plenty of evidence to confirm the attractiveness of Jewish customs in Rome at the end of our period, of which Juvenal and Tacitus complained. We have already noted the 'atheism' trials from Domitian's era, in which 'drifting into Jewish customs' had become a political crime. The new regime announced by Nerva's coins appears to have dissipated the controversy. Josephus' *Contra Apionem* (late 90s CE) is not only sponsored by an interested Gentile in Rome, Epaphroditus (*C Ap* 1.1), but also makes a powerful case for the respectability of the Jewish tradition in its Roman environment. Josephus may exaggerate when he speaks of widespread Judaizing (*C Ap* 2.282, cf. 2.210, 261), but not much later Epictetus speaks of Gentiles who adopt some Jewish habits, and others who become Jews through baptism (*sic*, Arrian, *Diss* 2.9.19–20). It is not necessary to posit a full-scale or self-conscious Jewish mission to imagine how Romans continued to imitate Jewish customs and, in some cases, underwent a major change of identity in becoming proselytes.[89]

---

[87] Note also the evidence for schools of learning in *CIJ* 201, 333 and 508; many inscriptions portray scrolls of the law.

[88] Even in the Roman churches, where they congregated with Gentiles, Jewish believers were clearly adamant in their observance of Jewish food laws and Sabbath customs (Romans 14.1–15.13). On the controversy surrounding circumcision in these congregations see Marcus 1989.

[89] There are seven cases of proselytes in the Roman inscriptions: *CIJ* 21, 68, 202, 222, 256, 462 and 523. This may seem very few (out of over 500 inscriptions) but there are plausible reasons for under-reportage (e.g. the unwillingness of the deceased's families to bury them among Jews). We simply do not know the statistical significance of proselytes in Rome. Goodman 1994 has argued that, before 100 CE at least, there was no concerted Jewish mission to the Gentile world; this may be true (on his definition of 'mission'), but it does not gainsay the fact that Gentiles were attracted to Judaism to varying degrees throughout our period and probably aided by Jews in the process. I am unpersuaded that

The winning of converts and the attraction of sympathizers indicates that Jews were not as 'ghettoized' as might be supposed from their maintenance of separate cemeteries.[90] Information on the social and economic location of Roman Jews is, in fact, particularly sparse. In the catacombs the scratching of names and the crude spelling of epitaphs might indicate a generally humble status, but some sarcophagi and family burial chambers are of fine decoration.[91] Juvenal may comment scornfully on the Jewish beggars and pedlars of cheap prophecies, but an encounter with Josephus would have reminded him that some Jews in the city were people of considerable means. One cannot explain the attraction towards Judaism of the likes of Fulvia or Clemens and Domitilla unless they had met Jews of similar social standing. Jewish scholars (Caecilius of Calacte), actors (Alityrus) and poets (Martial, *Epigr* 11.94) indicate some penetration into the mainstream of Roman society, and it would be gratuitous to assume that here, uniquely, such integration was necessarily bought at the cost of fidelity to Judaism. Fragmentary as it is, such evidence as we possess indicates that the Jewish community in Rome ranged across the social strata, from Greek-speaking illiterates to Romanized court favourites. Whatever their social locations, Jews seem to have been able to attract the attention of their social peers, either for good or ill.

Our survey of the history of Jews in Rome has been conducted largely on the basis of 'snapshots' derived from particular events and individual literary perceptions. Yet these have provided for the most part a remarkably coherent picture. As one among many immigrant minorities in Rome, Jews were subject to the cultural and social snobbery of the Roman élite, even though exceptional Jewish individuals were known in the imperial court. However, the durability of the Jews' ancestral customs, and their particular attractiveness to Romans of many social classes, were special features of the Jewish profile in Rome, sufficiently important to

there was a significant change in this regard around the end of the first century CE (Goodman 1994:42–48, 120–28, an argument depending almost entirely on inference). See above pp. 298–99 on the attractiveness of Jewish customs as the cause of Tiberius' expulsion in 19 CE.

90  *Pace* Frey in *CIJ* 1.lxii – lxiv, and Solin 1983:684–85, 716–20. Cf. now Rutgers 1995 who presents multiple evidence for the interaction of Jews with their cultural environment in late antique Rome.

91  See the summary by Leon 1960:75–92 and 233–38.

attract hostile attention from Tiberius, Claudius and Domitian. Before the crisis of 19 CE, however, and even as a rule thereafter, Roman Jews were allowed to retain their own customs in the vast multicultural mixing-bowl of the Roman population. At no point were the Roman Jews so numerous or so threatening to the Roman *plebs* or the governing classes as to occasion the sort of violence we have witnessed in Syrian, Egyptian and Cyrenaean cities. With their hands clean of the wars in Judaea and the Diaspora Revolt of 116–117 CE, the Jewish community in Rome could sustain an unbroken history, which has lasted to the present day.

# 11

## *Levels of Assimilation among Diaspora Jews Outside Egypt*

In chapter 5 we drew together evidence which indicated different levels of assimilation among Egyptian Jews, plotting the range of positions on a spectrum of high, medium and low assimilation; we also saw the difficulty in some cases of assigning any category at all. Within Egypt there were varying social environments in which such assimilation took place (there were differences, for instance, between the *chora* and Alexandria), and in each environment variations in social level. With the limited information at our disposal, some rough categorizations had to suffice: the precise location of individual examples was less important than the demonstration of variation among Egyptian Jews.

It would be nice to be able to provide such an analysis of assimilation in each of the other Diaspora locations, where the experiences and social circumstances of the Jewish communities were, as we have seen, extremely diverse. Unfortunately we lack the breadth of evidence to provide an analysis of this sort for any single Diaspora location outside Egypt during our period. Our evidence from the individual sites we have surveyed is simply too scanty, too piecemeal or too obscure to fill even our rough categories with meaningful examples. I have therefore decided, in accord with the shape of this book, to gather together material from all the non-Egyptian Mediterranean locations. The breadth in the field of vision will inevitably result in less precision of focus than was possible in relation to Egypt, and the scanty and haphazard nature of our sources should discourage still further any pretence to provide a rounded picture of social realities. Yet perhaps a rough and hesitant sketch is better than an empty canvas. As in chapter 5, we will arrange our evidence in the general categories of 'high', 'medium' and 'low' assimilation, with the same definitions as there employed. Once again there will be some material which is suggestive but too obscure to place anywhere except under the heading 'unknown'.

## 11.1 High Assimilation

As noted in relation to Egypt (p. 104), many cases of high assimilation among Jews may be lost to our sight, simply because such individuals successfully merged with the non-Jewish population and became unrecognizable as Jews. Nonetheless, there are some examples which do come to our attention and which we may group into a number of forms.

1. *Participation in non-Jewish cult.* In a number of cases we may suspect Jews of participation in Graeco-Roman religion, merely from the public roles they played. Thus Eleazar the νομοφύλαξ of Cyrene in the mid-first century CE (see above p. 235) held a public post which typically required some religious participation; certainly, the inscription which names him begins with a list of civic priests (Lüderitz 8). Similarly, it is difficult to imagine how Alityrus gained popularity in Nero's court as an actor (μιμολόγος, Josephus, *Vita* 16) without also taking part in the religious rituals of that environment. Yet in these and other cases we have only our suspicions to go on, and it is just possible that special arrangements and exceptions were made to accommodate the scruples of such Jews. Thus they cannot be placed with certainty in this category. Nor may they be dubbed self-evidently 'apostates' without evidence of how they were regarded by contemporary Jews.[1]

In at least three cases, however, we have some direct evidence of Jewish integration in non-Jewish cult. In Oropus (Greece) an inscription was erected in the third century BCE recording that Moschos, son of Moschion, who identified himself as a Jew ('Ιουδαῖος), received instructions in a dream from the Gods Amphiaraos and Hygieia (*CIJ* 1.82); since the inscription was erected in the temple of Amphiaraos we may presume that Moschos honoured and worshipped these Gods even while he proclaimed

---

[1]  On Eleazar see Schürer 3.131. Smallwood considers that Alityrus was 'without doubt an apostate, even if he retained enough national consciousness to befriend Josephus', 1981:281 n. 84. On the difficulties in applying the label 'apostate' see above, chapter 4.2.

his identity as a Judaean/Jew.[2] A second example comes from Iasus in Asia: there in the second century BCE a man named Nicetas, son of Jason, from Jerusalem (thus probably a Jew), is to be found among other metics contributing to a Dionysiac festival (though only 100 drachmae, *CIJ* 749).[3] One may infer that after paying his contribution he enjoyed the feast which he helped finance.

The third and most striking example of participation in Gentile cult is Antiochus in Antioch in the late first century CE. As we noted in recounting the history of Jews in Syria (pp. 256–57), the outbreak of the Jewish revolt in 66 CE caused immense difficulty for Jews in Antioch, which was the mustering point for the Roman army (Josephus, *Bell* 7.46–53). Josephus suggests that a particular cause of trouble for the Antiochan Jews was when Antiochus, the son of a magistrate (ἄρχων) in the Jewish community, accused his father and other Jews of plotting against the city. Josephus' story makes best sense if we suppose that Antiochus was an officer in the Roman army: only on this supposition can we explain the governor's willingness to entrust soldiers to his control (*Bell* 7.52). Whether he had already drifted away from the Jewish community we cannot tell (Josephus claims that he was highly respected among Jews for the sake of his father, *Bell* 7.47), but we can appreciate the acuteness of his dilemma as a Jew of high social rank in a military establishment which was currently being mobilized to fight his fellow countrymen. When charges against suspected 'revolutionary' Jews gathered momentum, Antiochus is recounted as renouncing his ethnic traditions. He proved his 'conversion' (μεταβολή) and his 'hatred' of Jewish customs by offering sacrifice 'after the manner of the Greeks' (τὸ ἐπιθύειν ὥσπερ νόμος ἐστὶ τοῖς ῞Ελλησιν, *Bell* 7.50). Moreover, he then attempted to force other Jews to do likewise, and banned the Jewish observance of the Sabbath (*Bell* 7.51–53).[4] This calculated renunciation of Judaism is the most extreme case of assimilation known to us (though it may be parallel to the 'Jewish critics and opponents of Judaism' in Egypt noted

---

[2]  The inscription and dream related to the manumission of a slave; see Schürer 3.65.

[3]  See discussion in Tcherikover 1961a:352 and Schürer 3.25, where however some doubt is raised about Nicetas' ethnicity.

[4]  It seems likely that only the leading Antiochene Jews were involved in the sacrifice 'test' (see above p. 256 n. 62); those who did succumb to this pressure may also be counted in this category of high assimilation.

above, chapter 5.1). Its violent character reflects the particular pressures at the time of the outbreak of the revolt.[5]

2. *Social Climbers.* Our sources describe a number of cases of Jews who abandoned the Jewish life-style, or at least crucial aspects of it, in order to ease some social dilemma or gain promotion in society. Among the Herodian offspring who were brought up in Rome, Josephus indicates that some 'right from their birth abandoned the native customs of the Jews and transferred to those of the Greeks' (*Ant* 18.141). Their subsequent careers in the imperial administration, or as client kings in eastern nations, were no doubt aided by their (or their parents') decision to discard Jewish ways.[6] We cannot tell whether Berenice, the Jewish princess who became the mistress of Titus (see above, p. 309), also abandoned Judaism entirely, but her intimacy with the future emperor suggests at least a high degree of assimilation to Roman customs.

At two points in the history of Roman Jews we hear of those who were willing to abandon Jewish customs in order to avoid shame or disaster. At the time of the expulsion of Jews by Tiberius (19 CE), we hear from Tacitus that any who were willing to renounce the 'profane rites' of Judaism were spared (*Ann* 2.85.4; see chapter 10.3). The phraseology suggests that some did take this option. Later, after the imposition of the tax for the *fiscus Iudaicus*, Domitian attempted to catch those who had so far evaded payment. Among those mentioned in this connection by Suetonius were those who avoided payment by hiding their racial origins (*dissimulata origine*, *Domitian* 12.2; see above p. 311). Suetonius provided an example of a 90-year-old man who was stripped in court to prove he was circumcised. If this individual was a Jew (it is possible he was circumcised for other reasons), he appears to have been among a number of Jews in Rome who endeavoured to hide their Jewish origins in order to avoid the new burden of tax imposed after the Jewish War.

But it did not require such special social pressures to induce Jews to assimilate to a high degree. The comic actor, Menophilus,

---

[5]   At the same point in time Josephus refers to the ἀπόστασις of Jews in Scythopolis, who opted to fight with the local Greeks against an advancing party of Jews (*Bell* 2.466–76; *Vita* 26); but their decision seems to have been primarily political, rather than a renunciation of their Jewish heritage.

[6]   *Ant* 18.139–40; on their careers see Smallwood 1981:391 n. 8.

whom Martial taunts for trying (unsuccessfully) to hide the fact
that he was circumcised (*Epigrams* 7.82; Stern 243) was probably a
Jew attempting to conceal his Jewish origins; presumably he also
avoided any public behaviour which would have identified him as
of Jewish origin.[7] Similarly, the circumcised poet born in Jerusalem
whom Martial lambasts in another poem (*Epigrams* 11.94; Stern
245) may be regarded as highly assimilated: if we may trust Martial's
invective, he swore by Jupiter and practised homosexual relations.
Such cases indicate the pressures to conform faced by socially
successful Jews. In the decrees which Josephus cites concerning
the military conscription of Jews in Asia, there are references to
Jewish Roman citizens 'who practise Jewish rites' (*Ant* 14.234, 239),
with the implication that there were others who had ceased to do
so.[8] Further, we may be sure that the assimilatory tendencies against
which 4 Maccabees is directed (see below, chapter 12.3) were not
a figment of the author's imagination. Perhaps we may also include
in this category those proselytes whom Josephus indicates as failing
to sustain the Jewish lifestyle (*C Ap* 2.123); his reference to their
lack of 'endurance' (καρτερία) perhaps indicates the social
pressures which they faced following their change of commitment.[9]

3. *Exogamy*. In discussing cases of high assimilation in Egypt, we
noted the particular threat to Jewish loyalty posed by intermarriage
with non-Jews (pp. 107–8). We know of some cases outwith Egypt
where such intermarriage took place to the detriment of Jewish
observance. Acts 16.1–3 recounts the case of Timothy, a native of
Derbe or Lystra (Lycaonia), whose Jewish mother had married a
Greek. Timothy had not been circumcised as a boy and we may
well wonder whether in other respects also the customs of the family
departed from Judaism.[10] In another case of intermarriage
Josephus recounts that Drusilla, sister of Berenice and Agrippa II,

---

[7]   However, note the questions on the interpretation of this passage raised by
      Cohen 1993b:42–43.
[8]   Cf. also a decree from Halicarnassus which allows 'those Jewish men and women
      *who so wish* (βουλομένους)' to keep the Sabbath and observe other Jewish laws
      (*Ant* 14.258). Does this suggest that there were known cases of Jews who did
      not so wish?
[9]   One example of a lapsed proselyte is Polemo the king of Cilicia, who was
      circumcised in order to marry Berenice, but when deserted by her 'was released
      from his adherence to Jewish customs' (Josephus, *Ant* 20.145–46).
[10]  On this case and the question of matrilineal descent in first century Judaism
      see Cohen 1986.

left her husband to marry Felix, the Roman procurator of Judaea, apparently without requiring that he become circumcised; later the family lived in Italy (*Ant* 20.141–44). Josephus records this marriage as a transgression of the ancestral laws (*Ant* 20.143) and we may guess that the household of Drusilla and Felix was not entirely governed by Jewish customs.[11]

4. *Isolated Jews.* Just as we noted some categories of isolated Jews in Egypt, so there were also Jews elsewhere in the Mediterranean Diaspora whose isolated social circumstances necessitated a high level of assimilation. This would probably apply to any Jews in the Roman army, though it may have been uncommon for Jews to enlist: as we have seen, Roman soldiers in Asia were able to claim exemption from conscription at least during the civil wars (Josephus, *Ant* 14.234–40). The Roman Jews sent to Sardinia in 19 CE clearly served in the army, though perhaps in large Jewish units, not in isolated conditions. It is possible that the Rufinus whose military record was found in the Via Appia Pignatelli catacomb (*CIJ* 79) was a Jew; but there is room for doubt whether this catacomb (or this grave) was Jewish.[12]

We may be more certain about the isolation typical of Jewish slaves in a Gentile household. We know that considerable numbers of Jewish captives were scattered around the Mediterranean after the numerous wars in Judaea – Pompey's capture of Jerusalem, the subsequent wars of Gabinius and Cassius, and the Jewish Revolt. The vast majority of these must have ended up as slaves in non-Jewish households. Of course, it was not impossible for these slaves to retain their Jewish identity. We do not know whether slave-owners forced their slaves to participate in household cults, and Philo claims that a large proportion of the Jewish community in Rome was made up of freedmen who 'were not forced to alter their native customs' (*Legatio* 155). We have one inscription (from Aquileia, Italy) of a freedman who proclaims himself a 'Iudaeus' (*CIJ* 643 = Noy 7), though we cannot tell what that appellation meant in

---

[11] For further possible examples of intermarriage, see Kraemer 1989:48 n. 37; several of these cases involve women named Sabbatis or the like, on which see below, 11.4. Note also the depiction of the sin of Israelites with Moabite women in Josephus, *Ant* 4.131–51, which, as van Unnik 1974 has shown, probably reflects the situation of those who in Josephus' day broke away from Judaism through intermarriage.

[12] See Leon 1960:234.

practice. But it cannot have been easy to continue practising Jewish customs in such circumstances. We can only speculate how it worked out for such as Claudia Aster, a captive from Jerusalem, commemorated in an epitaph from Naples (*CIJ* 556 = Noy 26), or for Acme, the Jewish slave of Julia (Livia), the wife of Augustus (Josephus, *Ant* 17.134–41).

5. *Christian Jews.* While it is dangerous to generalize about the behaviour of Jews who joined the Christian movement, there are several indications that it was not uncommon for such Jews to associate with Gentile believers on terms which indicate quite a high level of assimilation. The issue of commensality was central to many disputes within the early Christian movement (Acts 10–11, 15; Galatians 2.11–14; Romans 14–15) and here at least some Christian Jews associated with Gentiles in ways that concerned or even scandalized other Jews. Paul's particularly assimilationist stance on this issue stands out most clearly, and will be considered more fully below (chapter 13). In Romans 14.1–15.6 we find him defending the right of Christian Jews in Rome to observe Sabbath and food regulations, but the passage reflects the pressures on Jewish believers to abandon aspects of their ancestral customs which impeded fellowship with their 'brothers and sisters in Christ'. If such Jews formed their primary relationships more among Gentile fellow Christians than among the Jews of their synagogues, they were bound to appear (from a Jewish perspective) highly assimilated.

## 11.2 Medium Assimilation

As in relation to the Egyptian material (chapter 5.2), this rather broad category is designed to include Jews with significant social ties to the non-Jewish world who nonetheless preserved their Jewish identity. As we have seen, many Jews in Cyrenaica and Asia (and some Syrian cities) were well integrated into civic life in various capacities; yet the Jewish communities in these locations did not dwindle or disappear. As Trebilco notes in relation to Asia Minor: 'A degree of integration did not mean the abandonment of an active attention to Jewish tradition or of Jewish distinctiveness. It was as *Jews* that they were involved in, and a part of, the life of the cities in which they lived' (1991:187). The material from Asia Minor which Trebilco analysed is mostly from a period beyond our time-span, but we have some evidence which points to the same conclusion from our period. Again we may distinguish a number of different types, though many Jews may have fallen into more than one sub-category.

1. *Jewish Ephebes and Citizens.* In discussing the evidence from Cyrenaica and Asia, we have already noted the probable presence of Jews among ephebes in Cyrene and Teucheira (above pp. 234–35) and in Iasus (Asia; p. 271 and n. 31). It is possible that some of these had begun to renounce their Jewish customs, but it does not seem necessary to assume so. Certainly at a date just beyond our limits an inscription from Hypaepa (Asia) indicates the existence of an association of Jewish youths (*CIJ* 755), apparently ephebes who have graduated from the gymnasium but retained their Jewish identity.[13] Correspondingly, we have noted some evidence for Jews as citizens of various Mediterranean cities. Paul of Tarsus may be a case in point (depending on how we interpret Acts 21.39), and there is other suggestive evidence from Asia.[14] Regarding Antioch, we have seen reason to reject Josephus' claim of Jewish citizenship for the whole Jewish community (above pp. 244–45), but the dispute about oil probably points to individual Jewish citizens (pp. 256–57 n. 63). If any of these cases concern citizens, they also indicate that citizenship did not necessarily entail loss of Jewish distinctiveness. Whether Jews in this position were willing to make some cultic compromises cannot be ascertained, and perhaps individuals followed their own paths through the complexities of daily life.[15] Some, however, seem to have caused offence precisely because they combined citizen rights with Jewish particularities (Josephus, *Ant* 12.125–26).

Jews are also to be found as Roman citizens, both in Rome itself and in other cities in the empire. Josephus was one but certainly not the only Jew granted Roman citizenship in Rome (*Vita* 423). Many of the Jews who were entitled to the corn-dole in Rome (Philo, *Legatio* 158) probably gained their citizenship on manumission. Most of these must have been rather less assimilated than Josephus, who had access to exalted political circles, but they

---

[13] See Trebilco 1991:176–77.
[14] See above pp. 271–72, with reference to Josephus, *Ant* 12.125–26; 14.235, 259; 16.28; cf. Trebilco 1991:172.
[15] For an assessment of the options facing Jewish citizens and civic officials see the fine discussion by Trebilco 1991:173–85.

nonetheless took their place in Roman political life, while maintaining the Sabbath and no doubt other Jewish customs. Elsewhere in the Roman empire the legal right of Roman citizenship may not have entailed significant social assimilation, but we may note in this connection such examples as Paul (if we may believe Acts on this matter, Acts 16.37) and those Jews noted in the decrees recorded by Josephus, *Ant* 14.228–40.

2. *Jews prominent in civic life.* In a category overlapping with that just discussed, we may note here the evidence for Jewish participation, and even prominence, in civic life, especially in Cyrenaica and Asia. In the former we have noted individuals like Simon (probably a Jew) who represented Ptolemais on a Roman delegation (Lüderitz 36) and Eleazar from Cyrene (Lüderitz 8; see pp. 235 and 321 above on Eleazar). In Asia the decrees cited by Josephus indicate that Jews were regularly liable to attend court and conduct business deals, but were scrupulous enough to refuse to do so on the Sabbath (*Ant* 14.262–64; 16.27, 45).[16] Josephus also indicates that certain wealthy Jews were considered liable to perform 'liturgy' duties (*Ant* 16.28), a role which suggests a high degree of civic responsibility. These were clearly the sort of figures who, like John the tax-collector in Caesarea (Josephus, *Bell* 2.287), could represent their fellow Jews in important political matters. They seem to have been loyal enough to their Jewish traditions to cause frustration to some non-Jews of their social class.

Only in a very few cases can we put names to this class of assimilated Jew, whose presence and significance we sense in most Diaspora locations. In Roman political circles we may note, besides Josephus, Caecilius of Calacte, who is recorded as being 'Jewish in his religion' while also a notable orator (see Schürer 3.701–4). We have also recorded the significance of members of the Herodian family resident in Rome, some of whom seem to have been influential in court circles while also faithful in their observance of Jewish customs (see above, pp. 293–94). The two Agrippas stand as the prime examples of this *modus vivendi*, which apparently gained the respect both of Roman emperors and of (most) observant Jews.

---

[16] Note also the Jewish theatre-goers from Miletus, evidenced from *CIJ* 748, on whom see Schürer 3.167–68 and Trebilco 1991:159–62.

*3. Jews who gained patrons, supporters or converts among non-Jews.*
Further evidence for the kind of assimilation we are here discussing
is the fact that Jews throughout the Mediterranean Diaspora won
interest, sympathy and support among Gentiles. That can be
explained only if there was considerable social interaction between
Jews and non-Jews, a meeting of interests, occupations and social
networks in which Jews nonetheless retained their social and
religious identity as Jews. The many facets of Gentile sympathy or
support for Jews are too complex to be discussed in detail here; it
is impossible, and probably unhelpful, to distinguish between the
social, political and religious aspects of such a phenomenon.[17]
Although some forms of 'imitation' of Judaism by Gentiles may
have taken place with minimal social interaction (e.g. the
observance of the Sabbath/Saturn's Day in Rome, above p. 297),
other examples of Gentile support for Jewish customs or
communities presuppose extensive social intercourse. The Jews in
Acmonia (Asia) who won the patronage of Julia Severa in funding
the construction of their synagogue (first century CE) must have
had extensive dealings with her at a social level. Similarly, Jewish
communities in Damascus and Antioch which had gathered a
penumbra of Gentile sympathizers (Josephus, *Bell* 2.463, 559–61)
could hardly have done so if they were wholly ghettoized. To cite
another individual case, the Jewish teacher of the law in Rome who
won the interest and eventually the conversion of Fulvia (*Ant* 18.81–
84) must have been closely associated with her over a period of
time to achieve this result. On the whole, the patterns of life we
have observed in the Mediterranean Diaspora suggest that Jews
were neither socially and culturally isolated nor simply blended
into some social amalgam. While their boundaries may have been
defined variously in differing circumstances, it was precisely the
ability to maintain these boundaries while continuing everyday
social contacts with non-Jews which was the peculiar achievement
of the successful Diaspora communities.

*4. Artistic Assimilation among Roman Jews.* Finally we may mention
one very particular form of assimilation which was brought to light
in the Roman catacombs (though most and perhaps all of the
examples are from beyond our chronological limits). Although

---

[17] See Cohen 1989 and the evidence for 'sympathizers' amassed by Feldman
1993:288–341.

most of the tombs in the catacombs were undecorated, or decorated with purely Jewish symbols, some tombs were adorned with forms of art common among non-Jews. In the Via Appia catacomb, for instance, there are painted chambers whose plaster walls and ceiling are decorated with human and animal figures with no specifically Jewish associations (as far as we can tell). The most striking case portrays Victory garlanding a young man, together with the figure of Fortuna holding a cornucopia and (apparently) a libation disk.[18] Since these paintings are located in a Jewish catacomb, we may conclude that those who commissioned them were Jewish, and perhaps also the artists (cf. *CIJ* 109 for a Jewish painter). They clearly found it possible to combine their Jewish commitments with such mythological art.[19]

In a similar fashion, some sarcophagi used by Jews bore elaborate carvings with common Gentile motifs; the most intriguing example appears to depict Dionysus, with the typical accoutrements of his cult.[20] We cannot tell whether such a sarcophagus was specifically commissioned by a Jew or simply used without reflection on its artistic design. Thus it would be dangerous to draw far-reaching conclusions from the use of these works of art, but it is important that some Jews found such artistic assimilation unobjectionable. As Rutgers comments, 'one cannot simply suppose that the non-Jewish elements in Jewish art from Rome by themselves show that Roman Jews were receptive to Roman society and its values. Yet, the fact remains that it must have been perfectly normal for a Jew to walk into a non-Jewish workshop to order a sarcophagus' (1992:108). There is also evidence to suppose that some Jews allowed epitaphs to be inscribed with 'D M' (=Dis Manibus, 'To the Divine Shades') without scruples about such a funerary cliché.[21]

---

[18]  Descriptions and illustrations in Goodenough 2.17–20 and 3.737–56; Leon 1960:204–5 and figures 13–16.

[19]  See, however, Rutgers 1995:44, 54–55, indicating that these chambers may not have been Jewish in origin, though they were in reuse.

[20]  Goodenough 2.43 and 3.833–34; Leon 1960:215 and figure 45. Since the original provenance of this sarcophagus is not certain, it may not have been used by a Jew. Another sarcophagus, with a menorah in the central medallion, but with otherwise typical 'pagan' designs, is certainly Jewish: see Goodenough 2.26–27 and 3.789; Rutgers 1995:77–81.

[21]  Frey omitted many possible cases from *CIJ*, considering them non-Jewish on this ground alone; see Goodenough's objections, 2.137–40. Even Frey, however, included some arguably Jewish cases (*CIJ* 287, 464?, 524 [a 'metuens'], 531?, 678). Note the discussion of this matter in Kraemer 1991:155–58 and Rutgers 1995:269–72.

Unfortunately we cannot trace what, if anything, this might represent in relation to other social facets of their lives.

## 11.3 Low Assimilation

We know of no segregated Jewish communities outwith Egypt comparable to the community of the Therapeutae. However, we may point to two social phenomena like those noted in chapter 5.3, which tended to restrict Jewish assimilation in other Diaspora locations.

1. *Jewish Residential Districts.* As in Egypt, there is evidence in some locations for a Jewish preference to live together. The Jews in Sardis, for instance, seem to have won the right to establish a close communal life, with defined religious and legal rights focused around a τόπος (Josephus, *Ant* 14.259–61). It is not clear whether this refers to a (synagogue) building alone, or also a segment of the city. The fact that the same decree orders the market-officials of the city (ἀγορανόμοι) to ensure the supply of suitable food for Jews indicates that Jews in Sardis used the same ἀγορά as everyone else, but would frequent only certain shops within it. These are clearly not ghetto conditions, but still the care with which Jewish communal facilities are protected indicates the desire of the community to maintain close social bonds. Strabo attests that Jews in Cyrene were not only a distinct legal entity (alongside peasants, metics and citizens) but were also encouraged to form organized groups (συντάγματα) following their own national laws (*apud* Josephus, *Ant* 14.115–16). Unfortunately we cannot tell what this meant in practice and to what degree such social arrangements restricted assimilation. In Rome, there is reason to believe that the Jewish communities were concentrated in certain districts of the city (above p. 316 n. 84). If Cicero's *quanta concordia* (*Pro Flacco* 28.66) bears any relation to social reality, we can imagine quite tight-knit communities whose social networks ensured concerted action on matters of common concern.

Residency in a Jewish district of a town did not mean, of course, that all such Jews had minimal links with non-Jews. Such were the crowded conditions in an immigrant quarter like Trastevere in Rome that Jews could not help encountering people of other nationalities at every turn.[22] But common residency did make it

---

[22] See Rutgers 1992:116–17.

possible for those who so wished to minimize social contacts with 'outsiders'. The Jewish catacombs in Rome indicate that even in death it was possible to remain largely within the boundaries of a Jewish community.

2. *The Effects of Social Conflict.* Here the same social dynamic applies as was suggested in relation to Egypt (chapter 5.3): conflict both expresses and breeds social alienation. The ethnic hatred which built up in Syria in and after the Maccabean wars led to levels of hostility in some cities which seem to have affected all but the upper echelons of society. The Jewish youths engaged in street battles with 'Greeks' in Caesarea in the years before the Jewish Revolt were clearly estranged from non-Jewish society. Similarly, the ethnic violence which broke out in other Syrian cities in 66 CE suggests that Jewish and Greek communities had pulled apart socially over a period of time; certainly, the effects of the conflicts must have ruined community relations for years thereafter. That process of social alienation is evident in Cyrenaica, where the Jewish revolt led by Jonathan in 73 CE, and its merciless suppression, seem to have created an atmosphere of such bitterness as to fuel the hugely destructive uprising of 116–117 CE. The Jewish insurgents led by Andreas who in the years of the Revolt destroyed temples, roads and civic buildings in Cyrenaica must be counted at the extreme end of our spectrum of assimilation, along with their imitators in Egypt and Cyprus.

## 11.4 Unknown Assimilation

As in Egypt, there are some cases where it is not certain whether our evidence concerns Jews at all or, if it does, what precisely it signifies about their assimilation. We will not discuss further here Jewish use of magic, which is certainly attested outside Egypt, but on which sufficient has been said in chapter 5.4.[23] Rather we will note three categories which have been taken in the past as examples

---

[23] For examples of Jewish magic throughout the Diaspora see the survey by Alexander in Schürer 3.342–79; examples of amulets are given in *CIJ* 743 and Noy 159 (probably later than our period). On Jewish exorcists in Ephesus (Acts 19.11–17) see Trebilco 1991:24, 214 n. 32; cf. the Cypriot Jews associated with magic in Acts 13.6–12 and Josephus, *Ant* 20.142.

of extreme Jewish assimilation, but which turn out to be far from clear in their significance.

1. *'Former Jews or Judaeans'*? In an inscription from Smyrna (Asia), to be dated probably just after our period, a list of citizens who donated money to the city includes a category of people recorded as οἱ ποτὲ ᾿Ιουδαῖοι (*CIJ* 742). Frey regarded this as clear evidence of Jews who had renounced their Jewish traditions.[24] Recently, however, several scholars have questioned this interpretation; they consider the inscription to mean nothing more than 'former inhabitants of Judaea' (i.e. immigrants to Smyrna from Judaea).[25] While this alternative interpretation is not unattractive, it cannot be said to be securely established, at least without parallels to the phenomenon of referring to immigrants as 'formerly' some other nationality. Millions of Jews had settled outside their homeland in the Diaspora but they were generally referred to simply as ᾿Ιουδαῖοι; I am not aware of any others being described, either by themselves or by others, as '*former* Judaeans'. Thus the interpretation of this cryptic phrase must remain an open question.[26]

2. *Syncretistic Worshippers of God 'Hypsistos'*? A number of inscriptions from Asia Minor record dedications 'to the Most High God', some in clearly Jewish contexts referring to the Jewish God but others in contexts which indicate that other Gods are being worshipped. It was once common to regard such inscriptions as evidence that Jews in Asia were involved in a thoroughgoing syncretism, especially associated with the cult of the God Sabazios. However, it has now been shown with some certainty that this hypothesis (originally propounded by Cumont) is unfounded.[27] Although both Jewish and non-Jewish cults can use the epithet ὕψιστος ('Most High') of the supreme object of worship, that is no proof that Jews, in so doing, were merging their cultic practice with that of non-Jews. And the evidence that Jews worshipped the God Sabazios rests on little more than the garbled text of Valerius Maximus concerning Jews in Rome, which we have already shown to be historically

---

[24]   *CIJ* ad loc.:'Il y eut donc à Smyrne des Juifs qui renoncèrent à professer le judaïsme et acquirent le droit de cité.' Cf. Smallwood 1981:507.

[25]   So e.g. Kraabel 1982:455; Solin 1983:647–49; Trebilco 1991:175.

[26]   See also the doubts of Cohen 1990:221–22 n. 5.

[27]   See most fully Trebilco 1991:127–44; cf. J. T. Sanders 1993:191–96.

dubious (above, p. 285). Thus it may be that the inscriptions bear no evidence for Jewish religious assimilation at all. On the other hand, it would be a mistake to rule out *a priori* the possibility that Jews were involved in such non-Jewish cult. It is no more impossible that Jews should set up dedications in a non-Jewish context to the 'Most High God' than that they should record their thanks to 'God' in a temple of Pan (above, pp. 99–100). Thus again we are forced to profess our ignorance of the social realities which such inscriptions represent.

3. *Syncretistic Jews called Sabbatis, Sabbata, etc.?* In chapter 5.4 we noted the interpretative problem posed by persons in Egypt called 'Sambathion' (or the like) who appeared in otherwise wholly Egyptianized contexts. Parallel phenomena occur outside Egypt where individuals whose names appear to derive from the Jewish institution of the Sabbath are to be found in inscriptions of otherwise purely non-Jewish character.[28] As in Egypt, this may be accounted for by the general popularity of the Jewish Sabbath (especially in Rome), so that such names could easily be used by non-Jews (e.g. for children born on that day). But again it would be a mistake to rule out *a priori* the possibility that figures with this name in 'compromised' associations might be Jews.

Indeed, if we have learned anything from the range in the spectrum of assimilation both in Egypt (chapter 5) and elsewhere (this chapter), it is that we cannot rule in advance what was or was not possible for Jews in their assimilation. While global theories of 'Sabazios-syncretism' have proved unfounded, we can establish no limits for the possible assimilation of particular Jews in individual circumstances. The evidence collected here for 'high assimilation' has to be taken just as seriously as all the evidence for the careful preservation of Jewish distinction. In the past, interpretation of ambiguous evidence, especially inscriptions, has been governed by (often unspoken) assumptions about what was possible or impossible for Jews. Yet, as Rajak has noted, 'to determine in advance what is Jewish and what is not (or even "probably" not) is to operate with a preconception of Jewish identity, when our task is, precisely, to seek to define that identity. The relative infrequency of such material, as against material which can readily be taken as Jewish, does not mean that the marginal material is unimportant' (1994:240). As a result, it is often impossible to determine the

---

[28] See e.g. *CIJ* 63\*, 68\*, 69\*, 71\*, 73\*.

significance of fragmentary information.[29] Our surveys of the range of assimilation among Diaspora Jews should help to keep options open where they are sometimes prematurely closed.

---

[29] See also Kraemer 1991 on the problems in identifying inscriptions as Jewish, 'pagan' or Christian.

# 12

## *Cultural Convergence and Cultural Antagonism Outside Egypt*

In the last chapter we considered a selection of material relating to the assimilation of Jews from Mediterranean locations outside Egypt. Here we may gather together literature from the same geographical net whose socio-cultural stance we wish to examine. As indicated in chapter 1.3, we will include here any literature which cannot be assigned to Egypt with certainty – both literature which is definitely from elsewhere (the works of Josephus, from Rome) and that whose provenance is uncertain, but not definitely Egyptian (Pseudo-Phocylides, 4 Maccabees). Since we will examine here only these three authors, it is possible to include them within a single chapter, encompassing both cultural convergence and cultural antagonism (in Egypt we could devote a chapter to each, chapters 6 and 7). Of our present trio, Pseudo-Phocylides (12.1) is most evidently in the category of cultural convergence and 4 Maccabees (12.3) in that of cultural antagonism (on the definition of these categories, see chapter 4.5). Josephus (12.2) is appropriately placed between the two, since, as we shall see, his work contains elements of both, in almost equal measure. Paul of Tarsus is so anomalous as to require a chapter of his own (chapter 13).

### 12.1 Pseudo-Phocylides

The didactic poem written in the name of Phocylides is an intriguing example of Jewish acculturation, though one whose precise socio-cultural stance is difficult to assess. To begin with, it is not easy to establish the correct text of the work, which has undergone many corruptions and alterations over time. There is even some doubt surrounding the opening couplet, which identifies the poem as the work of Phocylides (without which it would be anonymous). But these lines are probably original to the poem and the ascription certainly fits its style as a more or less loosely arranged collection of moral instructions, in the diction and metre of antique Greek didactic poetry.[1]

While the work is generally in character with the authentic sentences of Phocylides, the sixth century BCE Milesian, there is no doubt that the ascription is fictional and that the poem comes from a Jewish source.[2] The authorship may be single or multiple, but in any case it reflects the perspective of a Hellenized Judaism, proud of its Scriptures and traditional moral values but unafraid to find common cause with aspects of the Hellenistic moral tradition, or to attribute its inspiration to a famous dispenser of wisdom from Greek antiquity. While its provenance is often taken to be Alexandrian, this assumption depends on an uncertain inference from a single verse. V.102 ('it is not good to dissolve the human frame') is usually understood to refer to dismemberment or dissection of a corpse, and because Alexandria is the only site in antiquity where dissection is known to have been practised, most scholars have taken this sentence as a criticism of local practices by an Alexandrian Jew. But that is a slender argumentative thread. The crucial verse may be better taken, in context, to refer to secondary burial, and even if dissection is here in view, one did not have to live in Alexandria to abhor it.[3] Since Jews outside Alexandria could acquire the sort of acculturation necessary to construct a poem of this character, I have opted to follow caution and to treat this work separately from the literature of definite Egyptian provenance.

The contents of Pseudo-Phocylides are diverse, as is typical in such gnomological literature. The poem touches on a range of topics affecting social relations (e.g. envy, modesty, consideration

---

[1] On the status of vv. 1–2 see van der Horst 1978:107–10 and Derron 1986:xlv–xlvii.

[2] The fiction was first exposed by Scaliger in the early 17th century and the poem received its first significant exposition as the product of a Hellenized Jew by Bernays (1885, first published in 1856). I have found his seminal work still worthy of detailed consideration 140 years after its initial publication. See the survey of the history of interpretation by van der Horst 1978:3–54, updated in 1988. On the date of Pseudo-Phocylides see the Appendix on Sources.

[3] On v. 102 see van der Horst 1978:183–84 and Wilson 1994:109 n. 122. On the question of provenance see also Schürer 3.690 and Derron 1986:lxiii–lxv; the later notes the possibility of a Syrian origin for the work.

of the poor) and personal values (e.g. attitudes to money, misfortune and death), usually in pithy snippets of advice rather than extended disquisitions. Only at the end of the poem are the sentences held together around general themes – the necessity of hard work (vv. 153–74), sexual ethics (vv. 175–206), and relations in the household (vv. 207–227). But even here the genre encourages bare moral instruction with minimal philosophical or theological explication. Because of such conventions, and in light of the generality of much of the ethical content, the social and cultural commitments of the author are not easy to ascertain.[4]

Yet careful study reveals that Pseudo-Phocylides owes an enormous debt to the Jewish tradition, for amidst all the general material of common currency in the ancient world there are certain features of the work which bear an ummistakably Jewish stamp. Some verses in the poem are derived directly from the LXX, either in concept or in vocabulary. Thus, for instance, Septuagintal language is evident in v. 10 (μὴ κρῖνε πρόσωπον, lit. 'do not judge the face', i.e. partially) and in v. 53 ('do not pride yourself on wisdom, strength or riches'; cf. LXX Jer 9.22 and I Regn 2.10). Elsewhere, teaching contained in the poem is paralleled uniquely in the Jewish Scriptures: the instruction not to take both chicks and mother from a bird's nest (vv. 84–85) can only be drawn from Deut 22.6–7; the advice to help raise an enemy's fallen beast (v. 140) has a specificity explicable only from Exod 23.5; and the warning against eating meat torn by wild beasts (vv. 147–48) is clearly dependent on LXX Exod 22.30, while expressed in epic Greek vocabulary.[5]

Other passages show the influence of the Jewish tradition in a less specific but equally significant way. Thus, for instance, the collection of verses inculcating care for the poor (vv. 9–41) takes its inspiration from the many Scriptural commands on this subject.

[4]   On the gnomological tradition and its international character, see Derron 1986:vii–xxxi. Wilson 1994:15–41, 178–99 takes the genre to be that of a gnomological poem which also serves as an epitome of ethical instruction. He also argues that the poem is much more tightly structured than has been previously appreciated (e.g. vv. 9–131 are arranged under the headings of the four cardinal virtues), but I do not find his case wholly persuasive.

[5]   See van der Horst (1978) ad loc. in each case: vv. 84–85 are 'thoroughly Jewish', as was recognized by Porphyry in a comment on this custom; v. 140 has 'no Greek or Roman parallels'; vv. 147–48 are 'typically Jewish' even while 'it is clear that Ps-Phoc. does his utmost to write archaic language.' Van der Horst's broad collection of parallels (now supplemented in 1988) has been tabulated by Derron 1986:35–54.

When the poem urges its readers to 'give to the poor man at once, and do not tell him to return tomorrow; fill your hand, give alms to the needy' (vv. 22–23), we are hearing the distinctive social conscience of the Jewish Scriptures.[6] Similarly, the sexual morality taught in the poem is typically, even if not uniquely, Jewish. The ban on homosexual relations (v. 3, 190–92) and bestiality (v. 188), the outline of forbidden degrees of marriage (vv. 179–83), and the strong condemnation of abortion and the exposure of unwanted children (vv. 184–85) are all typical of the Jewish tradition, distinguished, either by emphasis or by simple contrast, from the normal standards of Graeco-Roman morality.[7] The presence of these Jewish characteristics in the poem makes it likely that its opening (vv. 3–8) is modelled on the Decalogue and that some influence from the LXX is present even in those passages which could be drawn equally from Jewish or from non-Jewish moral traditions (e.g. commands to honour the elderly and bury the dead).[8] In any case, one does not have to exaggerate Jewish parallels to conclude that the poet has learned to draw his moral boundaries according to the traditions and example of the Jewish community.

In this connection it is worth noting the marked parallels between the instructions in Pseudo-Phocylides and the distillations of Jewish morality which we find in two Jewish apologetic works: Josephus, *C Ap* 2.190–219 and Philo, *Hypothetica* (in Eusebius, *Praep Evang* 8.7.1–9). All three texts emphasize sexual morality (Josephus like Pseudo-Phocylides rules against homosexual acts, abortion and sex during pregnancy), all three stress duties to the elderly and the poor, and – most strikingly – all three include the minor rule against taking the parent bird with its young from the nest (Pseudo-Phocylides vv. 84–85; Josephus, *C Ap* 2.213; Philo, *Hyp* 7.9). Such similarities, amidst some differences of content and emphasis, can

---

[6] See van der Horst 1978:128–30, drawing attention to the parallel in Prov 3.27–28 and the Septuagintal use of ἔλεος to mean 'alms'. He rightly comments that 'the notion of special duties towards the poor is under-developed in Greek ethics' (126).

[7] See again van der Horst (1978) ad loc., noting the dependence in several cases on Lev 18 and 20, whose rules are expanded to take in new realities in the Hellenistic world (e.g. concubines, v. 181, and lesbian sex, v. 192). Although several passages in these verses on sexual and family matters (vv. 175–227) have parallels in Greek and Roman ethics, the severity in condemnation of some sexual practices appears to be uniquely Jewish and the ban on infanticide was noticed by Tacitus, *Hist* 5.5.3 as typically Jewish.

[8] On the use of the LXX here, and the special concentration on Exod 20–23 and Lev 18–20 see Niebuhr 1987:5–31.

best be explained if all three authors were drawing on a common Jewish source.[9] Thus the evidence indicates that Pseudo-Phocylides is dependent on Jewish tradition not only for individual *sententiae* but also for the inspiration to construct a moral compendium. But here, unlike in Josephus and Philo, the compendium is never identified as Jewish nor presented as proof of the excellence of the Jewish law; rather, it is generously attributed to a *Greek* poet!

Indeed, a study of the contents of Pseudo-Phocylides indicates that alongside its typically (or even uniquely) Jewish ingredients, and besides those maxims whose character is equally Jewish and Greek, there are some verses whose style and content are unambiguously Greek in origin, and a few that appear distinctly strange in a Jewish work. The whole poem is shaped by the conventions of metre and vocabulary of ancient didactic poetry, and some verses are drawn more or less straight from the poetry of Homer or Theognis; thus even in the midst of the Jewish-tinctured sexual precepts there is an echo of a famous Homeric comment on the splendour of a harmonious marriage (vv. 195–97; cf. Homer, *Odyssey* 6.182–85).[10] The poem inculcates moral virtues such as moderation (σωφροσύνη, v. 76) and equality (ἰσότης, v. 137) which are central to the Greek moral tradition, while also suggesting goals (e.g. the control of passions, vv. 59–60) and moral distinctions (e.g. between types of anger or zeal, vv. 63–67) which derive from the Stoic tradition. Thus, in terms of content, Pseudo-Phocylides represents a confluence of Jewish and Hellenistic traditions effected by an author (or circle) just as much at home in Greek epic/didactic poetry as in the Septuagint. Although the combination of these traditions occasionally introduces some conceptual confusions (e.g. on life beyond death, vv. 103–115),[11] the cultural synthesis effected by our author is generally neither unnatural nor strained.

It is in the theology of the poem – although theological statements are rare – that the Judaism of our author has been regarded as most compromised. In general, God is referred to in the singular (e.g. vv. 8, 29, 106; cf. v. 54); indeed, there is even an

---

[9] The parallels between these three texts were first noted by Wendland and have often been discussed since: see e.g. Crouch 1972:84–101; Küchler 1979:207–35; and Niebuhr 1987:5–72.

[10] See van der Horst 1978:241–42, and for other literary echoes see e.g. v. 48 with Homer, *Iliad* 9.312–13 and vv. 199–204 with Theognis vv. 183–90.

[11] See van der Horst 1978 ad loc. and Fischer 1978:125–43.

attempt at demythologization in the statement that 'Eros' is not a God (οὐ γὰρ ἔρως θεός ἐστι, v. 194). Yet the poem also mentions 'Gods' (θεοί, vv. 104; cf.v. 98?), as well as 'the heavenly ones' (Οὐρανίδαι, v. 71) and 'the blessed' (μάκαρες, vv. 75, 163) which would normally be taken in Greek literature to refer to the Gods. The presence of such statements has led some to doubt that the poem could be Jewish at all, while others have used textual emendation to remove the offending remarks.[12] In fact, the problems are not particularly acute. The suggestion that after death men become 'gods' (θεοί, v. 104) is striking, but not wholly impossible in Jewish circles where the dead could be considered angels, and angels could be styled 'sons of God'.[13] And although among Greeks 'the heavenly ones' and 'the blessed' would usually be taken to refer to the Olympian Gods, it appears that our poem means nothing more here than the heavenly bodies (vv. 71–75), which were typically regarded as animate.[14] Thus Pseudo-Phocylides does not encourage polytheism, and the whole poem could be read without embarrassment within the framework of Jewish monotheism. Yet it makes no attempt to *exclude* a polytheistic interpretation and it shows an interesting laxity in theological terminology.[15] What is more, there is no hint of a polemic against idolatry or polytheistic cult.

The fact that this poem, while covering so many aspects of life, fails to repudiate 'idolatry' has been much discussed since Bernays first raised the issue (1885). Bernays noted the inclusion of all the

---

[12] Kroll 1941:508: 'Undenkbar im Munde eines Juden ist auch die Auffassung der Gestirne als Götter' (vv. 71, 75). Bernays 1885:199–205 emended θεοῖσι (v. 98) to γόοισι and θεοί (v. 104) to νέοι. See the full discussion in van der Horst 1978:180, 186–88; he follows Bernays at v. 98 but not at v. 104.

[13] See Hengel 1972:297 with parallels from Qumran, taking the phrase as 'eine freie Redeweise'; cf. van der Horst 1978:186–88 and Fischer 1978:129–43. V.98 μέτρα δὲ τεῦχε θεοῖσι is almost certainly textually corrupt. See the emendations (and reconfigurations) discussed by van der Horst 1978:180 and Wilson 1994:105 n. 102.

[14] Vv. 71–75 clearly refer to sun, moon and earth which are not unnaturally referred to as 'heavenly ones'; compare Philo's reference to them as 'manifest and visible θεοί' (*Op Mund* 27)! The denotation of the μάκαρες in v. 163 is not so clear-cut; see van der Horst 1978:221.

[15] Note also the impersonal reference to God as 'Justice' (Δίκη, v. 77; cf. Philo, *Flacc* 104) and the reference to divine wrath as δαιμόνιος χόλος, v. 101. Collins 1986:146 notes that 'no warning is given to the non-Jewish reader that vv. 98, 104, or 163 should not be read in a polytheistic sense' (v. 98 should be omitted from this list), and concludes 'evidently, Pseudo-Phocylides was more concerned with the ethics one practiced than with the gods one worshipped.'

elements of the Decalogue in vv. 3–8 except the rejection of images and the Sabbath command, and showed how, although much of vv. 9–41 is based on Lev 19, again our author omits texts which attack other cults, as well as references to the Sabbath and dietary laws (1885:226–34). He considered this an attempt to suppress anything specially connected to Jewish nationality (1885:227), and explained the poem as an attempt to propagandize among Gentiles without causing offence or giving the work an obtrusively Jewish identity (1885:248–54). Estimates of the purpose of this poem have in fact varied widely since Bernays' day, some considering it a tract aimed to instruct Gentiles in a moral life, others as intended for a Jewish audience (see further below). It is possible to explain the omission of reference to 'idolatry' on either thesis – either, as Bernays suggested, as a tactful approach to non-Jews, or as unnecessary in an environment where the repudiation of 'idols' was taken for granted. Yet, however much can be attributed to rhetorical strategy, the omission, alongside the laxity in theological vocabulary, also indicates something of the socio-cultural stance adopted by our author.

Comparison of Pseudo-Phocylides with parallel material helps to indicate the range of possibilities open to someone writing in this genre. We have noted the similarities between this poem and apologetic passages in Josephus and Philo which suggest a common source for all three. It is interesting that neither Josephus nor Philo engage *in this context* in any explicit polemic against 'idolatry'. Yet Josephus, at least, is careful to highlight the imageless nature of Jewish worship and the 'impiety' of attempts to conjecture God's likeness (*C Ap* 2.190–91), while Pseudo-Phocylides makes no gestures in this direction. Perhaps in a work ascribed to a Greek (Phocylides) it would have been felt inappropriate to include remarks prejudicial to Greek religious practice: as we have seen, Aristeas can incorporate rejection of iconic cult only by citing a speech from a Jewish representative (*Letter of Aristeas*, 128–38; see above, chapter 6.3). Yet it was possible for Jews to insert polemic against 'idolatry' even into supposedly Greek works. Part of our poem is, in fact, found embedded in *The Sibylline Oracles* (2.56–148) and there some verses have been added (2.59, 96) which attack the worship of 'idols'.[16] Perhaps our author was just too

---

[16] Cf. the verses attributed to Sophocles in Pseudo-Hecataeus, which have the Greek tragedian inveigh against 'statues of Gods made of stone, bronze, gold or ivory' (*apud* Clement, *Stromata* 5.14.113,2; translation in *OTP* 2.825).

sophisticated to destroy his pseudonymity with such obviously implausible sentiments, but it was surely possible to make some positive reference to the oneness of God and the value of imageless worship if so desired.

In fact, as Bernays noted, Pseudo-Phocylides also omits reference to some other characteristics of Jewish communities, notably the observance of the Sabbath and the food laws.[17] It is not quite accurate to say that the poem omits everything that is uniquely Jewish, since many of its moral emphases, and some of its particular instructions, are uniquely or distinctively Jewish in origin. Yet it contains nothing that would link it unambiguously with *the Jewish community*.[18] While charity to the poor and the refusal to practise abortion may have been distinctively Jewish traits, an individual's lifestyle along such lines would not have identified her so clearly as a member of the Jewish community as, for instance, refusal to eat pork or to work on the Sabbath. Why is this latter, characteristically Jewish, behaviour unmentioned in this poem? Perhaps it would have been difficult to make a positive case for Sabbath rest while praising the value of labour (vv. 153–74).[19] Yet the reference to abstinence from meat torn by wild beasts (vv. 147–48) could surely have been expanded to include other kinds of food which Jews considered impure; and the moral interpretation of such food laws current since the days of Aristeas could have been employed effectively in this genre.

It appears that the poem represents a Jewish ethos, broadened to embrace elements of the Greek moral tradition and universalized to pass over anything which might tie it to the specific environment of the Jewish community. Both Josephus and Pseudo-Phocylides discuss the raising of children, but while Josephus highlights the

---

[17] Circumcision is also omitted, but this is less surprising: it is hard to see how it could have been included in this treatise on the moral foundations of the good life.

[18] The distinction here is between the *Jewish origin* of much of the material and its *social implications*, the latter linking the practitioner unambiguously with *the Jewish community*. There are specific practices of Jewish origin mentioned in this poem, but some were too rarely or too privately performed to define the practitioner's social identity, while others were sometimes performed also by non-Jews.

[19] Philo adds to his summary of Jewish morality a long section on the Sabbath day and Sabbath year (*Hyp* 7.10–20), but his disquisition requires detailed justification of the practice which might have been difficult to express in the form of didactic poetry. Yet, as we have seen in relation to Aristobulus (chapter 6.4), epic verses could be cited or invented on the value of the seventh day.

need to teach children 'the laws and deeds of their fathers' (*C Ap* 2.204), our poem omits any such particularity (vv. 206–217). Its universalizing tendency is also evident in cases where it makes general application of Scriptures originally specific to Jewish concerns. Thus, for instance, Pentateuchal laws about the treatment of 'idolaters' are broadened into a general warning against association with 'evildoers' (vv. 132–34; cf. Deut 13.6–11).[20] Similarly, the Jewish experience of the Exodus, which functions so often in the Torah to motivate care of strangers (e.g. Lev 19.33–34; Exod 23.9), is here placed on a universal plane:

> Strangers should be regarded with equal honour as citizens. For we all experience the poverty which comes from much wandering, and nowhere is there a secure place on earth for humanity. (vv. 39–41)

Here the Jewish Exodus is taken to typify the experience of all humanity, and the Jewish Scriptures are read not as a handbook of moral instruction for the Jewish community but as the epitome of a moral code applicable to all. If the poem's instructions contain the 'mysteries of righteousness' (v. 229), these are never identified with the Jewish law, although so many of them are actually drawn from it. Our Jewish author is content to give Phocylides ('the wisest of men') the credit for expressing these 'decisions of God' (vv. 1–2). He wears the Gentile mask not as a camouflage to smuggle Judaism into Greek culture, but because he believes the moral tradition of Judaism is sufficiently universalizable to be plausibly credited to a famous ancient Greek.[21]

Where, then, would the author of this poem belong in our spectrum of Jewish responses to Graeco-Roman society and culture? Although some have considered him an 'apostate' Jew,[22] there is no good reason to believe that he has repudiated his Jewish identity. He is committed to the Jewish social ethic concerning the poor (although himself of high social status, vv. 95–96), and he retains some of the socially awkward features of the Jewish sexual ethic. These are aspects of Judaism which an upwardly-mobile Jew,

---

[20] Bernays 1885:237 noted that the author 'hat es [the law] von dem jüdisch religiösen Boden hinweg in das Gebiet der allgemeinen Criminaljustiz gezogen.' Cf. van der Horst 1978:203–4 with further parallels.

[21] Cf. Wilson 1994:151–53, 196–97.

[22] E.g. Sebestyén (see van der Horst 1978:17–18).

becoming assimilated into Gentile society, might be expected to abandon. In truth, it is peculiarly hard to gauge from a poem of this character the social commitments of its author, but there is nothing here to indicate that he has abandoned the Jewish community. When the poem concludes that purity concerns the soul, and not the body (v. 228), this could be read as a repudiation of Jewish purity practices, with retention only of their spiritual value (cf. the pure allegorists criticized by Philo, *Mig Abr* 89–93). But without knowledge of the author's actual behaviour in relation to the temple, ritual washing and 'impure' foods, we are not able to assess the practical impact of such a sentiment.[23]

It is best to conclude that our author was a highly acculturated Jew, educated in the Greek literary and moral tradition and willing to explore the common ground between his Jewish heritage and his Hellenistic education. He does not use his Greek learning explicitly to bolster or to defend his Judaism, but neither has he lost his respect for his Jewish sources. In line with the Jewish wisdom tradition, he explores a way of distilling the moral values of Judaism in a universalistic form, neither asserting the superiority of the Jewish tradition (through eulogy of the law or polemic against 'idolatry') nor undermining its cultural integrity. His moral commitments, which were shaped by the Jewish Scriptures, are expressed in the form of the Greek gnomological tradition, in a cultural convergence which affirms the value of both. Most recent scholars have taken the poem to be designed for the Jewish community; and if this is correct, such a universalized inter-pretation of the Jewish tradition would not in the least undermine Jewish integrity.[24] Nonetheless, what he provides for his fellow Jews

[23] In fact, the text here is not certain and its meaning as it stands unclear. See van der Horst 1978:258–60 and 1988:27–29; cf. Walter 1983:216 and Wilson 1994:147 n. 1, 173–74. *The Letter of Aristeas* 234 looks equally radical in its spiritualization of the notion of purity, but earlier passages in the work indicate that the author still valued the Jerusalem temple and observed the food laws. In the context of these *gnomai* in Pseudo-Phocylides, it is impossible to discern the social correlates of such a sentiment as v. 228; see also Räisänen 1983:36–38.

[24] Older theories of propaganda to Gentiles (e.g. Seeberg, Wendland – see van der Horst 1978:3–54) failed to take account of the author's decision to write under Phocylides' name and to hide his Jewish identity. It is now common to take the work as directed to the Jewish community, for instance to encourage Hellenized Jews that their tradition was already supported by the famous poet of the sixth century BCE: so e.g. Walter 1983:176–80, 191–93 and Niebuhr 1987:66–72. Van der Horst 1978:70–76 declined to choose between the various

is not circumscribed by the special characteristics of the Jewish community. He encourages them to be proud of behaving in accordance with the 'mysteries of righteousness' (v. 229) *because Phocylides taught them*, quite beside the fact that they are mostly drawn from the Jewish law. In this sense our author understands his Jewish moral heritage to be an integral component of his Hellenism.

## 12.2 Josephus

### 12.2.1 Josephus' Social Context

Josephus counts as a Diaspora Jew by adoption, not birth, making his home in the Diaspora for the second but most productive half of his life. Although he was raised and educated among the aristocracy of Judaea, the debacle of the Jewish War, and his own inglorious role within it, required him to live abroad, for a short time accompanying Vespasian to Alexandria, for a longer period as an imperial protégé in Rome. It was in Rome that he wrote all his surviving works, and even if he rarely mentions his Diaspora environment it influences his literary output in many ways. His (lost) Aramaic account of the War was written for (among others) Jews in the Eastern Diaspora (*Bell* 1.3–6). Its Greek form, the *Bellum Iudaicum*, had a broad reading public in view – Greek speakers throughout the Roman empire, *Bell* 1.3 – and is influenced both by the special relationship Josephus had formed with his Roman benefactors, Vespasian and Titus, and by the opprobrium which Judaean Jews had brought upon their compatriots throughout the world. His *magnum opus*, the *Antiquitates Iudaicae*, was written for Greeks (*Ant* 1.5, 9; 16.174) and displays the sensitivities of a Diaspora Jew who was concerned to defend the reputation and rights of Jews living among Gentiles. Its appendix, the *Vita*, indicates Josephus' own insecurities, as rival accounts of the War threatened to undermine his position in Rome more than twenty years after the event.[25] His last work, the *Contra Apionem*, is an effective

---

options, but in 1988:15–16 followed the suggestion of Derron (1986:xlvii–li) that the author is providing a 'pagan' text suitable for use in Jewish schools, the pseudonym being required by the genre of the material.

[25] I take the *Vita* to date from the mid 90s CE, appearing with or soon after the publication of the *Antiquitates* (93 CE). For the dating of Josephus' works, see the Appendix on Sources.

response to the ethnic and cultural slurs which were endured by Jews throughout the Diaspora, not least in Rome. Thus, while remaining self-consciously a Judaean priest, and although he refers to Judaea, even after decades of absence, as 'the land which we inhabit',[26] the Josephus we encounter in his works is a man who has had to take his Diaspora location seriously as a social and political fact. We are fortunate to be able to watch his complex response to this fact in his voluminous literary output.

Josephus' account of his upbringing suggests that his intelligence was initially channelled more towards his national Jewish traditions than to the cultural resources of Hellenism.[27] His education gave him expertise in the Jewish legal tradition (*Vita* 7–9) and, while one may smile at his claims to the status of child prodigy, there is little reason to doubt that his aristocratic priestly family encouraged this promising youth to gain the skills which counted for most among Jerusalem priests. Years later, on completion of his *Antiquitates*, Josephus boasted of his expertise in native Jewish learning (ἡ ἐπιχώριος καὶ παρ' ἡμῖν παιδεία, *Ant* 20.263) and insisted, revealingly, that although he has laboured to acquire some literary skills in Greek, the Jewish people do not specially admire the acquisition of others' languages but 'give credit for wisdom only to those who have an accurate knowledge of the law and are able to interpret the meaning of the Holy Scriptures' (*Ant* 20.264). This is, of course, a highly partisan definition of 'wisdom', and we have encountered other Diaspora Jews, such as Aristeas and Philo, whose broader conception of *paideia* would have made them reject this contrast between Jewish and Greek learning. The fact that Josephus thinks that only two or three Jews have ever mastered the Greek literary tradition (*Ant* 20.265) testifies to his lack of awareness (or appreciation) of the thorough acculturation which we have found elsewhere in the Diaspora.[28]

---

[26] E.g. *C Ap* 1.1, 315; in the same work he refers to Judaea as 'our land' (1.132), as every Jew's 'homeland' (πατρίς, 2.277), and even as 'this land' (1.103), as if he were actually there.

[27] Cf. the careful analysis of Josephus' family, education and cultural formation by Rajak 1983:11–45, who concludes that 'the Graeco-Roman features seem to be outweighed by those of markedly Jewish character' (45).

[28] He clearly knew the letter of Aristeas, which he paraphrases in *Ant* 12; but his literary improvements in 'Atticizing' its style perhaps indicate that its Greek seemed to him unimpressive. While he knew of Philo as a prominent Alexandrian Jew who was 'not unacquainted with philosophy' (*Ant* 18.259),

Josephus' Scriptural education, his study of the main Jewish sects and his three-year discipleship to an ascetic named Bannus (*Vita* 10–12) did not provide much grounding in Graeco-Roman literature, rhetoric or philosophy. It is not accidental that his first account of the War was written in Aramaic, and that the effort of transposing this into a work of Greek historiography required the aid of literary assistants (*C Ap* 1.50).[29] This does not mean that he could not speak Greek fluently as a young man – indeed he must have been able to do so to be sent to Rome (aged 27) to plead on behalf of some fellow priests (*Vita* 13–16; 64 CE). There he was able to make contacts within the imperial household, gaining the patronage of Nero's mistress, Poppaea, through the actor Alityrus. But the incident is symptomatic of the social and cultural commitments which formed Josephus' character. He went to Rome not to gain education or political experience but to aid fellow Judaean priests, and in admiration for their rigorous commitment to the Jewish law (when offered Gentile fare, they ate only figs and nuts, *Vita* 14). Thus his upper-class social skills were put to the service of his national religious tradition.[30] Poppaea's new Judaean client spoke Greek with a Hebraic accent, which he retained to the end of his life (*Ant* 20.263). His commitment to the Jewish people and their interests was equally enduring, we shall argue, despite the traumas he was to undergo.

Chief among those traumas was the outbreak of the War in 66 CE, Josephus' brief, controversial and disastrous period of command in Galilee, his captivity, and his subsequent role in advising Titus

there is no unambiguous evidence that Josephus had read any of his works, and his lack of interest in allegory suggests that he would hardly have appreciated them if he had. It is intriguing to find that Josephus refers to some Hellenized Jewish authors as Greeks rather than Jews (*C Ap* 1.215–18), though whether he does this from ignorance or for rhetorical convenience it is hard to say.

[29] Thackeray's conviction that he had discovered the hand of two assistants in different sections of the *Antiquitates* (1929:100–124) now commands very little assent; see e.g. Rajak 1983:233–36. In fact, Josephus only admits to receiving assistance for the *Bellum*, and he may have acquired sufficient literary expertise over two decades in Rome to write the *Antiquitates* unaided. Yet he still records being daunted at the thought of writing in Greek, a 'foreign and strange tongue' (*Ant* 1.7); that is an expression one cannot imagine on the lips of Alexandrian Jews like Ezekiel or Philo.

[30] It is usually maintained, on the basis of *Vita* 12, that Josephus was also committed to Pharisaic practices and theology. However, Mason 1989 has shown that the passage means only that in his political activity Josephus deferred to the Pharisaic school.

at the siege of Jerusalem. Josephus describes these events fully in the *Bellum* and returns to some aspects of the story in his *Vita*, but the discrepancies between the two accounts and their clearly apologetic purposes have led to widespread cynicism concerning the reliability of either.[31] In truth, it appears that from the start of the revolt Josephus was torn by conflicting loyalties, not (it should be noted) between the interests of Jews and non-Jews, but between his general loyalty to all his compatriots and his particular loyalty to the Jewish aristocracy, who had the most to lose from the outbreak of hostilities. He appears to have shared Agrippa II's pessimism concerning the chances of defeating the Roman army.[32] Yet he did not, like Agrippa, desert the Jewish revolutionaries, but was appointed (as he claimed), or thrust himself forward (as his detractors charged), to defend the region of Galilee. In the chaotic conditions of the year 66–67 CE, his concern for the return of property pillaged from wealthy members of his class laid him open to the charge of treachery against the Jewish cause.[33] But he did commit himself and his troops to the defence of Jotapata which at least delayed the Roman advance.

His surrender to the Romans in the cave at Jotapata, despite entering a suicide pact with his fellow soldiers, has often and perhaps rightly been criticized as a wholly unscrupulous act.[34] It is easy to see why those who felt they were fighting for the Jewish nation and the integrity of the Jewish law considered Josephus' decision the act of a coward and renegade.[35] The venom with which

[31] See e.g. Cohen 1979, in line with the classic suspicions of Josephus' veracity. Rajak 1983 attempts to redress the balance, sometimes over-apologetically. See the survey of scholarship on this and other matters in Bilde 1988.

[32] Classically expressed in the long speech placed in Agrippa's mouth in *Bell* 2.345–401. Whether Josephus realized that the revolt was doomed from its very inception it is impossible now to tell, but as his efforts to organize the defence of Galilee faltered, it did not require all that special insight to see which way the war would end (*Bell* 3.136, 351).

[33] See e.g. *Bell* 2.595–613 where his intention to return the money stolen from Agrippa's steward made many suspect him of treason; cf. *Vita* 63–69 on the goods looted from Herod Antipas' palace in Tiberias.

[34] It sits uncomfortably beside Josephus' own assertion that by Jewish law a general should die rather than surrender (*Bell* 3.400), and that he would rather have died a thousand deaths than betray his country and surrender his command for the sake of a better lot among his enemies (*Bell* 3.137). He later admires the sentiment of the high-priest Jesus that he would rather die nobly than live as a captive (*Bell* 4.250).

[35] See *Bell* 2.393 for the motivation of the revolt. *Vita* 140 indicates that Josephus was considered a traitor to the nation and to the ancestral laws even before

the defenders of Jerusalem rejected his appeals to surrender indicates clearly enough how they viewed his comfortable position in the Roman camp.[36] Yet Josephus insists that his motives were pure. His excuse for his survival – that he had to act as God's messenger to announce to Vespasian his future elevation to imperial power (*Bell* 3.399–408)[37] – seems embarrassingly poor, yet Josephus was to convince himself that he could continue to serve as God's agent even in the Roman camp (*Bell* 3.354). He perhaps hoped that he could help save Jerusalem and its sanctuary by persuading its defenders to lay down their arms. The fact that he was regarded with some suspicion in the Roman camp during the siege of Jerusalem (*Vita* 416) suggests that he gave evidence of his pro-Jewish sympathies.

Unfortunately, events were to shatter Josephus' hopes and destroy his credibility among fellow Jews. With the collapse of the revolt, the burning of the temple and the devastation of Jerusalem, Josephus' aid to the Roman cause appeared all too successful, and when he himself was ensconced in Rome with an imperial pension there was every reason to believe that he was being rewarded for his treachery. That perception motivated numerous Jewish efforts to discredit Josephus, as first Jonathan in Cyrene and later many others attempted to 'expose' Josephus as a double agent (*Bell* 7.447–50; *Vita* 424–25, 428–29). It is striking that Josephus makes no reference to the Jewish community in Rome, and his silence may betray his failure to gain its confidence even through 30 years' residence in the city. It would have been easy enough for Josephus to assimilate fully into élite Greek-speaking circles in Rome as had some of the Herodian offspring, who abandoned 'the native Jewish ways to go over to the customs of the Greeks' (*Ant* 18.141). Yet the evidence suggests that he did no such thing. When he requested permission from Titus to retrieve from Jerusalem some 'sacred books' (*Vita* 418), he was not in search of souvenirs but was gathering resources for a continuing commitment to his ancestral traditions. Once, before the walls of Jerusalem, he claimed that he would never be so degraded a captive as to abjure his race or to

Jotapata. On the reception of the news of his surrender see *Bell* 3.438–42 and Rajak 1983:171–72.

[36] See e.g. *Bell* 5.375, 541–47.

[37] There is, understandably, much debate in Josephan scholarship regarding the meaning and timing of such a prediction; for two recent, though contrasting, discussions, see Rajak 1983:185–91 and Mason 1992:45–49.

forget his ancestral customs (*Bell* 6.107). The claim was greeted with derision at the time, but, unless we charge him with utter hypocrisy, his literary productions in Rome suggest that he amply fulfilled that promise.[38]

### 12.2.2 Bellum Iudaicum (*The Jewish War*)

Josephus' first productions, his Aramaic and Greek accounts of the War, have often been regarded with the greatest suspicion as works of imperial propaganda. Comfortably settled in Vespasian's former house, gifted with Roman citizenship and a pension, Josephus, it may seem, was practically commissioned to compose a flattering account of the War, with the added aim of warning off potential revolutionaries in the East (*Bell* 1.3–6, with 3.108). His submission of his work to Vespasian and Titus (*C Ap* 1.50–52), and Titus' signature and request for publication (*Vita* 361–63), look as close to an imperial *imprimatur* as one can imagine.[39]

Nonetheless, whatever was the case with the lost Aramaic work, our Greek *Bellum* is actually a more complex work than these aspects of its production would lead us to expect. To be sure, there are sycophantic descriptions of the bravery and clemency of the emperors (especially Titus), and a somewhat desperate concern to exonerate them from responsibility for the destruction of the temple (see below). But Josephus intends more here than mere flattery. As the preface indicates, he is disturbed by accounts of the War which, in flattering the Roman victors, have denigrated the Jews (*Bell* 1.2, 7–8) and he is responding to an atmosphere in Rome which, in the aftermath of the triumph (71 CE), is full of anti-Jewish slanders. We may recall Cicero's sarcasm concerning the Jewish race following Pompey's capture of Jerusalem (63 BCE): *quam cara dis immortalibus esset docuit, quod est victa, quod elocata, quod serva facta est* (*Pro Flacco* 28.69; see above, chapter 10.1). In the present case the Romans had not simply captured and inspected the temple, they had completely destroyed it, and as a priest whose symbolic world had hitherto centred on the glory of the temple,

---

[38] Laqueur's cynical reading of Josephus' motivation (1970:245–78), as an imperial stooge who then turned patriot for financial reasons, has rightly now fallen out of favour. It is impossible here to summarize the content of Josephus' works; a valuable summary can be found in Attridge 1984.

[39] For an eloquent presentation of this case see Thackeray 1929:23–50; it has been challenged by Rajak 1983:174–222.

Josephus deeply mourns its loss. He is unable (or unwilling) to hide his emotion on this subject (e.g. *Bell* 1.9–12; 6.111); it raised the most fundamental questions about God's providence and his promised commitment to his people and the holy city.

Thus Josephus' composition of the *Bellum* rested on a complex web of commitments: to the emperors who had treated him so favourably, to the Jewish nation whose reputation he wished to salvage and to the God whose purposes he struggled to comprehend. His chief strategy in reconciling his social commitments was to place the blame for the suffering of Jerusalem squarely on the shoulders of the 'bandits' and 'tyrants' who seized control of the revolt, and to represent the Romans as *unwilling* agents in the destruction of the city. This thesis is stated unambiguously in the preface (*Bell* 1.9–12) and is repeated in later editorial comments which maintain that it was the revolution (στάσις) which captured the city and the Romans who captured the revolution: 'the tragedy of the affair may be fairly assigned to her own people, the justice to the Romans' (*Bell* 5.257; cf. 5.442–45). In heaping blame on the revolutionaries, whose reign of terror spawned horrific acts of cruelty, Josephus is not just retaliating against his political foes, who had opposed his leadership in Galilee, murdered his friends and abused him from the walls of Jerusalem. He is also exonerating 'right-thinking' leaders like himself and the mass of ordinary Jewish citizens whom he here represents as forced into the revolt by a power-crazed clique of murderers. Although the whole Jewish people had suffered, they were not all equally to blame. Josephus here attempts to deflect the blanket condemnation of Jews then current in Rome onto an (unrepresentative) cadre of fools.

Corresponding to this concentration of blame, Josephus emphasizes the reluctance and innocence of the Romans, a claim so remarkable that Josephus is compelled to repeat it with nauseous regularity. It was the Jewish 'tyrants', Josephus insists, who drew upon the holy temple the unwilling hands (χεῖρας ἀκούσας) of the Romans (*Bell* 1.10); and while the 'tyrants' were brutal towards their fellow-countrymen, the Romans showed exemplary clemency to the Jews, though they were of a different race (*Bell* 1.27). Although he records the insensitivity of some of the later procurators of Judaea, Josephus insists that the Romans as a whole respected the temple and were concerned to preserve the laws and piety of the Jews; they proved in fact more pious that the self-styled defenders of the temple (*Bell* 4.180–84; 5.363; 6.101–2). This exoneration of the Romans reaches its high point in the whitewashing of Titus, whom Josephus portrays as desperate to preserve the city, eager to come to terms or to fight elsewhere out of respect for the sanctuary (*Bell* 1.10, 27–28; 6.124–28 etc.). This 'naturally humane' man (6.324) is represented as the recipient of 'melancholy' instructions to besiege Jerusalem from his 'reluctant' father (*Bell* 6.344, ἄκων again).

Particularly sensitive is the question of responsibility for the burning of the temple. Here Josephus goes out of his way to distance Titus from this drastic act, depicting him in the council as arguing against the destruction of the sanctuary and then dismayed when torches were irresponsibly applied (*Bell* 6.236–70). This notorious feature of Josephus' account is certainly 'economical with the truth' and possibly a complete fabrication.[40] It clearly suited Titus' purposes to celebrate his victory over the Jews and to parade items from their temple in his triumphal procession and then be cleared by Josephus of the charge of impiety, which might attach to his destruction of a venerable temple. At this point, one can only suspect that Josephus is acting as an imperial toady.

Whatever the human cause of the destruction of the temple, Josephus still has to grapple with the theological question of God's withdrawal of his promised protection. Here he can draw on biblical resources in reflection on the destruction of the first temple, and can sharpen his critique of the 'tyrants' by accusing them of so defiling its precincts that it simply had to be destroyed. Early in the narrative he introduces the notion of the pollution of the city which invites divine wrath (*Bell* 2.455), and he alludes mysteriously to an 'ancient saying' that civil strife defiling the temple would seal its doom (*Bell* 4.381–88; 6.109–10). Thus the destruction of the sanctuary by fire can be represented as its necessary *purgation*, for which purpose God abandons his sanctuary and gives aid to its assailants. These themes come to their fullest expression in the speeches Josephus attributes to himself before the walls of Jerusalem (*Bell* 5.363–419) and in front of the temple (*Bell* 6.96–110). In the former, harping on the pollutions of the temple,

---

[40] The alternative account of Sulpicius Severus, like those of the rabbis, presents Titus as the chief instigator of the destruction; whether this is more reliable historically continues to be a matter of dispute (see e.g. Feldman 1984a:850–51 and Rajak 1983:206–11). But the destruction of the temple in Leontopolis (*Bell* 7.420–21) indicates that the Romans had few scruples about the elimination of religious centres which had been or could become foci of disaffection.

Josephus concludes that 'the Deity has fled from the holy places and has taken his stand with those against whom you fight' (*Bell* 5.412); in the latter, after a bitter reproach of the defenders for their impiety, he issues his final words before the destruction of the temple: 'It is God, then, God himself, who is bringing with the Romans a fire to purify the temple and who is ravaging a city full of so many pollutions' (*Bell* 6.110).

It is here, in his political and theological affiliation with the Romans, that Josephus accommodated himself most fully with his social and political environment. There are also, to be sure, some literary aspects of the *Bellum* which indicate a measure of cultural accommodation to the requirements of Graeco-Roman historiography. The use of speeches, the drawing out of the emotive and grotesque features of the story, and the inclusion of numerous literary conceits drawn from the Thucydidean tradition, all indicate a concern (no doubt aided by the assistants) to present a narrative which is recognizably consonant with the best in the Greek tradition (cf. *Bell* 1.13–16). In the same vein, Josephus endeavours to present the Jewish parties as philosophical 'schools', with differing views on fate and freewill (*Bell* 2.119–66), and he repeatedly refers to the influence of fortune (τύχη) and fate (εἱρμαρμένη) on the events he records.[41] But these are minor phenomena, with minimal impact on Josephus' theology, compared to the massive political and theological adjustment which led him to place himself and his God on the side of those who had just destroyed his city and its temple.

Josephus' viewpoint here is no doubt influenced by the sheer invincibility of the Roman empire, its supremacy having been proved once more by the crushing of the Jewish revolt. It is not accidental that Agrippa's speech surveys the provinces and nations subdued by the Romans (*Bell* 2.358–87) or that Josephus includes a long excursus on the organization of the Roman army (*Bell* 3.70–109). Experience, not least his own in Galilee, had proved that Roman power was, quite simply, irresistible (*Bell* 5.364–66). But it is the theological judgment which accompanies this assessment which is remarkable in its boldness: 'Fortune has passed over from all sides to them, and God, who brings round sovereignty to nations in turn, now stands over Italy' (*Bell* 5.367).[42] The conviction that

---

[41] On the role of 'fate' in relation to God see Lindner 1972:42–49, 89–94.

[42] It is possible to read the 'now' here as suggesting that Josephus still entertained hopes for the future glory of the Jewish nation, in succession to that of the Romans. But this is uncertain; on Josephus' future hopes see de Jonge 1974.

God is on the side of the Romans, and was with them in their victory in Judaea, is expressed by Agrippa (*Bell* 2.390) and Titus (*Bell* 3.484; 6.38–39), as well as by Josephus himself (most fully in *Bell* 5.363–419). Most dramatically, at his surrender at Jotapata, he records his 'silent prayer' in these terms:

> Since you who created the Jewish race have decided to bring it to its knees,[43] and fortune has passed completely to the Romans, and since you have chosen my spirit to declare the future, I surrender myself to the Romans willingly and choose life, but I call you to witness that I go not as a traitor but as your servant. (*Bell* 3.354)

In his choice of surrender (rather than death) Josephus was widely considered more a traitor than a servant of God. It is easy to see how his theological endorsement of the power which had crushed his nation could be taken to negate his purported loyalty to the Jewish people. The 'future' he here feels committed to declare concerns not the future restoration of the Jewish nation but the elevation of her enemy, Vespasian, to the imperial throne. Later he interprets an oracle which other Jews took to refer to a Messiah as indicating instead the sovereignty of Vespasian (*Bell* 6.312–15). When Josephus coolly records Titus' triumph in Rome, with its display of sacred objects from the Jerusalem temple (*Bell* 7.123–57), one is entitled to ask what has become of his commitment to his nation (*Bell* 1.9–12). Has his tactful endorsement of the Roman victory obliterated his Jewish patriotism?

The correct answer would be, I believe, in the negative, but only because Josephus' aspirations for his people are no longer for their political freedom but merely for their social toleration. While the final scenes of *Bellum* Book 7 record the heroism of the Zealot defenders of Masada, Josephus knew that the future of Judaism did not lie in such suicidal nationalism. By recording Titus' visit to Antioch and his refusal to allow there any reduction in Jewish privileges (*Bell* 7.100–11), Josephus indicates how he sees the future of his people. While the nation has been 'brought to its knees', it has not been destroyed, and Josephus is hopeful that Roman power

---

[43] Thackeray, the editor of the Loeb text, follows one MS in reading 'to break' (κλάσαι); some other MSS read 'to punish' (κολάσαι) but the rest (supported by Niese and Naber) read ὀκλάσαι. This last reading, which I follow, appears to mean 'to make someone crouch or squat'; hence the translation above.

will preserve, not threaten, its distinct identity.[44] In this regard Josephus' *Bellum* integrates his Jewish with his Roman social commitments. Given the circumstances of its composition, it is not surprising that it remains the most forthright expression of Jewish-Roman political accommodation known to us.

### 12.2.3 *Antiquitates Iudaicae (Jewish Antiquities)*

In his preface to the *Bellum*, Josephus had elevated the recording of contemporary events (like the *Bellum*) above the works of historians who simply retold ancient history, reworking schemes adopted from others (*Bell* 1.13–15). Nonetheless, when he published his *Antiquitates* (93/94 CE), he presented to the Greek-reading world an account of Jewish history which, for fully half its length, reworked the biblical account (Books 1–10), and for subsequent periods often followed already existent national records (*The Letter of Aristeas*, 1 Maccabees, the Herodian history of Nicolas of Damascus etc.).

This shift in genre seems to signal more than merely a change of subject matter. To devote this much effort to the retelling of one's national story suggests a desire to promote its reputation and to enhance (or defend) its pride, in an age when 'national histories' were an important form of political and cultural propaganda. As has often been noted, Josephus' *Antiquitates Iudaicae* is in some respects comparable to the *Antiquitates Romanae* of the Augustan historian Dionysius of Halicarnassus, both in scope and in literary characteristics.[45] But there are also important parallels between Josephus' *magnum opus* and the historiographical products of Hellenized orientals, like the Babylonian Berossus and the Egyptian Manetho, who reworked their national records in order to promote their cultural and ethnic claims.[46] Josephus' uncritical dependence on his main source, the Jewish Scriptures, shows that his method bore little resemblance to the critical sifting of sources typically practised by Greek and Roman historians, and in this and other respects his *Antiquitates* might well be dubbed 'apologetic historiography' (Sterling).

---

[44] The theme of Roman concern for the sanctity of the temple and, more generally, the laws and customs of the Jews, recurs regularly: see e.g. *Bell* 4.180–84; 5.363, 402–6; 6.101, 123, 333–34.

[45] See Shutt 1961:92–101 and Attridge 1976:51–56.

[46] These similarities have been emphasized by Rajak 1982 and Sterling 1992:226–310.

However, Josephus' preface to the *Antiquitates* indicates that his task is not simply to portray the merits of his forefathers; he also has a lesson to preach. In *Ant* 1.14 he spells out what he conceives to be the moral of the story he will tell: that

> those who follow the will of God and who are not so rash as to break the laws which have been excellently established prosper in everything beyond belief, and as their prize receive from God good fortune (εὐδαιμονία); but, insofar as they rebel against the careful observance of these laws, possibilities become impossible and whatever imagined good they strive to achieve turns into utter disaster.

This moral perception of history, as a process of divine reward and punishment, has its roots in both Jewish and Greek traditions. To some degree it echoes the Deuteronomistic conception of Jewish history, and the emphasis here on *laws* betrays a characteristically Jewish understanding of virtue. At the same time, Greek tradition also found history a field of moral instruction and delighted in stories of the crushing of arrogant impiety. Both traditions could employ in this connection the theme of providence (πρόνοια), a motif which Josephus uses extensively in this work.[47] Thus Josephus' preface appears to signal his concern to present Jewish history in terms which will receive widespread acceptance and which suggest that the Jewish story is paradigmatic of the ways of God with all humanity.

In recounting the biblical story Josephus consistently dresses his narrative in Hellenistic garb. Biblical figures are given characterization through speeches and analyses of their inner motivation, and a premium is placed on emotion, pathos and suspense. Erotic and other novelistic features creep into the story at several points (e.g. Joseph and Potiphar's wife), and biblical material is rearranged to enhance its narrative power. In certain stylistic traits Josephus appears to pander to the tastes of a sophisticated readership. Thus, in relation to the supernatural, he takes an apparently non-commital stance ('on these matters everyone can form his own opinion', *Ant* 1.108; 2.348 etc.), although he usually indicates that he himself is convinced of the veracity of the biblical history. It is another question, however, how far such narrative

---

[47] The term appears as many as 120 times in *Ant*, 57 of which refer to divine providence. Although it does not wholly replace expressions about 'fate', it outweighs them in significance; see especially Attridge 1976:154–65.

techniques reflect an inner re-conceptualization of the Jewish story. While adopting Hellenistic vocabulary in ethics and philosophy (ἀρετή, εὐδαιμονία, πρόνοια, etc.), there is little to indicate any significant philosophical engagement on Josephus' part. He considers that some enigmatic parts of Moses' legislation may have an allegorical meaning (*Ant* 1.24–25), but he makes minimal use of this form of explanation.[48] While he has clearly worked hard since his arrival in Rome to acquaint himself with the Hellenistic literary tradition, Josephus cannot be said to have acquired the degree of acculturation we have found in Alexandrian authors like Ezekiel or Aristobulus.[49]

In fact, many of the alterations Josephus makes to the biblical story have an apologetic motivation. This is most obvious in his omission of embarrassing events in Jewish history – the Golden Calf, for instance – but it operates also in much subtle redrafting of the narrative. Since he was the object of persistent slanders in the Graeco-Roman world, Moses is an especially important figure in Josephus' narrative. He is praised in the most fulsome terms at the start of the story (*Ant* 1.18–26) and accorded a fine eulogy at his death (*Ant* 4.327–31), while in between his virtues as general, legislator and leader of the people are repeatedly emphasized. Stains on Moses' character (e.g. his murder of the Egyptian, Exod 2.11–14) are carefully removed, and details which might give support to his detractors (e.g. the incident of the leprous hand, Exod 4.6–7) are edited out. In general, Josephus displays a gallery of heroes (Abraham, Joseph, Moses, Samson, Solomon, even Saul), whose qualities are recognizable as much by Greeks as by Jews; together they create a composite model of the ideal Jew, dispelling the negative images which Josephus and his contemporaries were continually forced to combat.[50]

---

[48] The only extended passage of allegorization is in explanation of the high-priest's robes (*Ant* 3.179–87), a passage which appears to reflect an older Jewish tradition (cf. the similar explanation in Philo, *Mos* 2.117–30). It is possible that the promised work on 'Customs and their Reasons' (see *Ant* 1.25; 20.268) would have included philosophical and allegorical explanations, but these play a minimal role even in the *Contra Apionem*.

[49] On the familiarity with literature indicated by *Ant* see Schwartz 1990:45–57.

[50] Feldman has conducted many individual studies of the Hellenizations in Josephus' portrayal of biblical figures and gives an overview in 1984a:794–804. On the figure of Joseph see especially Niehoff 1992:84–110. It is notable that Solomon's prayer is modified to make explicit the openness of the temple to non-Jews, thus rebutting the notion that the Jews were anti-social (*Ant* 8.116–17).

The moral thesis outlined at the start of the work (*Ant* 1.14, see above) requires Josephus to highlight wickedness or virtue wherever they reap their just reward, and this affects the way he handles the biblical notion of covenant. In fact the term 'covenant' is entirely omitted by Josephus, and biblical passages where it constitutes a prominent feature of the narrative are completely rewritten (e.g. Gen 15 in *Ant* 1.183–85; Gen 17 in *Ant* 1.191–93). While Josephus often portrays God as the providential 'helper' and 'ally' of the people of Israel, it appears that the *unconditionality* inherent in the concept of a covenant bond was felt to be too much at odds with the notion that God rewards the virtuous on the basis of their virtue alone. The ambiguities in Josephus' treatment of this matter can be seen most clearly in his version of Moses' farewell speech (*Ant* 4.176–95, a paraphrase of the book of Deuteronomy). Here Moses points to the single source of blessing *for all humanity*, the gracious God who rewards the worthy and punishes those who sin (*Ant* 4.180). Israel's duty is to remain faithful to her laws, and not to be enticed by any other. But if she keeps on this path of virtue, she will be invincible among the nations, with a fame which outstrips all 'foreigners' (*Ant* 4.181–83). The Jews' glorious destiny is not unconditionally assured, yet they will enjoy a special role in history if they properly fulfil their task. Moses here warns that disobedience will lead to expulsion from the land and a scattering throughout the world as slaves (*Ant* 4.190–91). Yet if they are ruthless in rejecting the attractions of other cultures, and if they preserve the Mosaic laws (νόμοι) and constitution (πολιτεία), they will be accounted the most fortunate of all nations (*Ant* 4.191–93).[51]

This reference to expulsion from the land echoes a Deuteronomic curse (Deut 28.63–68), but also reflects Josephus' ambiguous attitude to the biblical promises concerning the land. Although he preserves some of the patriarchal promises in this connection, Josephus omits reference to the scope of the land and takes care to delete notions of its covenanted status.[52] This probably reflects political realism: in the aftermath of the War, it was impossible to represent the land as inviolable, and though he still owned property in Judaea (*Vita* 429), Josephus' Jewish identity now had to be

---

[51] For other references to the special status of the Jewish race, cf. *Ant* 3.313; 4.114, 126–28. Note the discussion by Attridge 1976:71–107.

[52] See Amaru 1980–81.

defined in a Diaspora context. Thus, in paraphrasing Balaam's predictions, Josephus highlights the positive aspects of the Diaspora (as a 'permanent home', *Ant* 4.115–16), while repressing the Messianic expectations which could be derived from Num 24.17. Elsewhere, too, Josephus is carefully restrained on the theme of Israel's national expectations (e.g. *Ant* 10.210 on a Danielic prophecy). It was crucial to represent Jewish tradition as a matter of 'law' and 'constitution' which could and should be maintained wherever Jews made their home.

In fact, Josephus is moderately confident that Jewish life in the Diaspora can be sustained in an atmosphere of toleration. He hopes that the *Antiquitates* will be favourably received by Greeks (*Ant* 1.5; 16.174), and takes encouragement from the warm reception given to the translation of the Scriptures in the court of Ptolemy Philadelphus (*Ant* 1.10–12). In fact Josephus is pleased to record many moments in Jewish history when the temple and the nation had been honoured by Gentile kings.[53] Although he rarely responds with appreciation of the Greek cultural tradition,[54] it is of the utmost importance for him to show that Judaism has long been recognized and protected by the rulers of other nations.

In this connection Josephus has collected numerous letters and decrees in favour of the Jews, the majority grouped into two collections in *Ant* 14.185–267 and 16.160–78 (see above, chapter 9). The first of these is a miscellany of Roman rulings in favour of the Jews, intended to refute those who scorned their significance or questioned their rights (14.185–89); Josephus here proves to his own satisfaction the Jews' long-standing friendship with the Romans (14.265–67). The second is concluded with a fascinating statement of principle, which perhaps reveals most fully Josephus' goals in the composition of the *Antiquitates*:

> I frequently make reference to these decrees in order to reconcile the nations (ἐπιδιαλλάττων τὰ γένη), and to remove those causes of hatred which are ingrained in unreasonable people among both us and them. ... It is most advantageous for all men, Greeks and non-Greeks alike, to

---

[53] See the survey by Moehring 1984 and Cohen 1987.
[54] Small gestures in this direction are to be found generally when he is following sources; e.g. *Ant* 1.240–42 (citing Cleodemus on the relations between Abraham's offspring and Heracles) and *Ant* 12.21–22 (a paraphrase of *The Letter of Aristeas* 16). The universalistic reference to the kinship of all humanity in *Ant* 2.94 is a rarity.

practise justice; our laws are specially concerned with this matter and they make us (if we keep to them sincerely) kind and friendly to all. Thus we properly expect the same attitude from them, for foreignness (τὸ ἀλλότριον) should not be defined by difference in customs but in relation to one's proper attitude to civilized behaviour (καλοκαγαθία); for this is common to all and it alone enables society to survive. (*Ant* 16.175–78)

It is intriguing to find here Josephus' recognition that the problems in community relations have come from both sides ('unreasonable people among both us and them'); he knows that Jews have not always kept to the standard of 'justice' and 'civilized behaviour' which the law requires. He here cites Roman decrees, which he hopes will encourage some 'reconciliation', but he also reaches out for a common standard of morality (καλοκαγαθία) which can be honoured by Jews and non-Jews alike. It is here that Josephus comes closest to the notion of a shared moral discourse between Jews and Gentiles which we found in *The Letter of Aristeas* (a document he clearly knows well, *Ant* 12.11–118). Unlike Aristeas, Josephus writes in the awareness that this ideal has often been shattered in intercommunal violence, both in Judaea and in the Greek cities of the Mediterranean, but he is confident that it can still be realized under Roman rule. Both in the decrees (e.g. *Ant* 14.247, 257) and in Nicolas' speech before Marcus Agrippa (*Ant* 16.31–57) Josephus represents the Romans as benefactors of the whole world, and emphasizes their role in upholding the rights of individual nations to preserve their own traditions. Universal Roman power has made possible a tolerant pluralism: 'your single rule over all makes good-will effective and ill-will ineffective' (16.46). In his presentation of the Jewish Scriptures and of Jewish history in the *Antiquitates* he has done his best to increase the chances of the good-will which he craves.[55]

### 12.2.4 *Contra Apionem* (*Against Apion*)

Josephus' last extant work, the *Contra Apionem*, functions as the sequel to the *Antiquitates* and indicates in fact its failure as a piece

---

[55] It is possible that the death of Titus and the hostile atmosphere in the reign of Domitian made it uncertain how much good-will Jews would receive (see above, chapter 10.4). Although he claims to have received personal support from Domitian and Domitilla (*Vita* 429), Josephus' patron now is Epaphroditus.

of apologetic. In his preface to the new work, Josephus tells how he has been stung by criticism of his efforts in the *Antiquitates* (just as he is still smarting from criticism of his *Bellum, C Ap* 1.47–56): his assertions about the antiquity of the Jewish race have been met with incredulity from scholars who have pointed to the silence concerning Jews in Greek history (*C Ap* 1.1–2). Josephus, it seems, has paid dearly for his decision to present the early history of the Jewish people in the *Antiquitates* on the basis only of Jewish records (the Scriptures), a procedure required in part by the dearth of non-Jewish confirmatory evidence but also by his own attempt to present the story of the Jewish people on their own terms and from within their own traditions.[56] As an apologetic strategy, it was unrealistic to expect non-Jews to give much credence to the Jewish (biblical) story, at least without some critical assessment of its veracity by comparison with other histories. The many alternative accounts of the Exodus, for instance, were simply too well known and too well received among Greeks and Romans to be outweighed by Josephus' revamped version of the biblical account. Moreover, in association with these alternative accounts, the degree of prejudice against Jews in literary circles required a far more explicit and concerted response. The apologetic aspects of the *Antiquitates* had been too disjointed and too indirect to make a serious impact on Josephus' intended audience.

Thus the *Contra Apionem* combines a double defence, first proving the antiquity of the Jews (1.1–218), then responding to four of their Egyptian detractors (Manetho, Chaeremon, Lysimachus and Apion, 1.219 – 2.144), reserving for one final case (Apollonius Molon) an *apologia* in the form of a positive portrayal of the Jewish 'constitution' (2.145–286). That Josephus should feel it necessary in Rome to respond to the anti-Jewish slanders of these non-Roman *literati* from generations, even centuries, before his time is an ironic tribute to their enduring influence. It may also indicate that, as we have suggested above (chapter 10.4), the climate of opinion among upper-class Romans at this time (the end of the first century CE) was markedly anti-Jewish. It is striking to set alongside each other Josephus' defence of Jews in the *Contra Apionem* and the collection of anti-Jewish prejudices presented by Tacitus a few years later in his *Histories* 5.1–13. The comparison indicates that almost every item of criticism voiced by Tacitus is

[56] On this aspect of *Antiquitates* see Rajak 1982.

known to Josephus. The 'Egyptian' slanders to which Josephus responds clearly influenced Tacitus and his contemporaries, and some aspects of Tacitus' critique which reflect the biases of upper-class Romans are also matched in Josephus' response.[57] In other words, the evidence from Tacitus suggests that Josephus' apology here is more than a rhetorical show: it engages precisely with the contemporary Roman disparagement of Jews.

Josephus' account of the early history of the Jews had been disbelieved largely on the grounds that it was uncorroborated by the best-known Greek historians (*C Ap* 1.2), and this manifestation of Greek cultural snobbery spurs Josephus into an attack on 'Greeks' more wide-ranging than anything found in his earlier works. His counter-attack is on three fronts. In the first instance, he attacks Greek historiography (*C Ap* 1.7–46) on the grounds that, compared to those of oriental nations, Greek records are of recent manufacture and preserved in unsatisfactory conditions. What is more, their historians are content to make conjectures about the past, with more attention to style than accuracy. Jews, by contrast, have unanimous records which have been carefully preserved. In point of fact, Greek culture is largely derivative from the East. So much, then, for 'the best known Greek historians'!

A second front emerges later in the work, in Josephus' criticism of Greek religious practice and belief. In explaining the Jews' refusal to erect statues (even of the emperors), Josephus comments with amusement on the willingness of Greeks ('and others') to make statues of just about anyone, and then refers to the Mosaic veto on the construction of images 'out of contempt for a practice which profits neither God nor men' (*C Ap* 2.73–75). Later, a critique of painters and sculptors forms part of a hefty broadside against Greek religion (*C Ap* 2.236–54). Here Josephus ridicules the fables of the Gods in Greek mythology, and blames the Greek legislators for giving these poets licence to teach the masses such erroneous theology. He finishes this section with an ironic comment on the passing fashions in Greek religion: 'Gods who

---

[57] Among the Egyptian aspects, Tacitus employs Egyptian accounts of the Exodus (*Histories* 5.3), criticism of Jewish sacrifices (5.4.2) and negative comparisons with Egyptian religion (5.5.3–4). Tacitus' critique of Jewish 'laziness' (5.4.3), fanaticism (5.5.3) and general 'contrariness' (5.5) springs from his particular Roman sensitivities and is reflected in every case in Josephus' apologetic response.

formerly reached a peak of respect have now grown old' (*C Ap* 2.253).

The third aspect of Josephus' critique of the Greeks concerns their lack of commitment to their laws. This is the theme which dominates both the beginning (*C Ap* 2.220–35) and the end (*C Ap* 2.271–78) of the lengthy passage where Josephus compares Jewish and Greek constitutions (*C Ap* 2.220–86). Here the unshakeable Jewish commitment to the law is contrasted with the Greek failure to take seriously the (easier) requirements of Plato's legislation, and with the fact that even the vaunted Spartan constitution was abandoned in adverse political circumstances. The famed toughness of the Spartans is still inferior to the endurance of Jews, and the generally lax Greek attitude to inherited laws is roundly condemned: 'With most people, breaking the laws has become a fine art! Not so with us' (*C Ap* 2.276–77).

Such criticism of 'Greeks' gives the *Contra Apionem* a more aggressive stance than other Josephan works, but even here such cultural antagonism is not as serious as it seems. Many of the points outlined above were stock criticisms of Greeks, often repeated, in fact, by Greeks themselves. Thus, as Josephus recognizes (*C Ap* 1.8), the Greeks acknowledged the greater antiquity of eastern nations (Egyptians, Chaldaeans, Phoenicians – Josephus would like to add 'the Jews'), and it was standard procedure for any self-respecting Greek historian to criticize other Greek historians for their uncritical use of sources. Likewise, in his attack on Greek mythology, Josephus knows that he is following in the steps of Greek intellectuals (especially Plato, *C Ap* 2.238–39, 242, 256–57), and when one compares what other Jews had said about idolatry (e.g. *Wisdom of Solomon*) Josephus' comments on images appear relatively mild. It is also noticeable that the examples Josephus chooses are generally from the old 'classical' Greece rather than from contemporary life. While Josephus thus undercuts the exaggerated cultural claims of his Hellenized contemporaries, he leaves undefined the targets of his attack in the present day.

In any case, it is clear that, in the final analysis, Josephus needs the support of (the best in) the Greek tradition and it is not in his interests to create an absolute contrast between Jews and Greeks. Against the charge that the best Greek historians did not mention Jews, it will not do simply to dismiss their evidence as inaccurate, for an important section must be devoted to the discussion of Greeks who *did* in fact mention Jews (*C Ap* 1.161–218). It is no matter that some of the references to Jews which are here brought forward are of minimal value or somewhat forced: it is still of importance to have 'the most trustworthy' Greeks on the right side (*C Ap* 1.4). Similarly, the comparison with Greek religion and law depends on an assumption of *shared* values concerning piety and law-observance. It must be conceded by all that 'the proof of virtue is obedience to the laws' (*C Ap* 2.226), for only on that basis can it be shown that Jews attain the goals which Greeks also aim for, but fail to reach. In the same vein, it is of great significance to Josephus that the Jews' rejection of contrary beliefs and customs is no different from that practised by the best of the Greeks: Plato's censorship of Homer and the poets, the Spartans' wariness of foreigners and the Athenians' rejection of Socrates are all, for Josephus, worthy parallels to Jewish attitudes in this matter (*C Ap* 2.255–70).[58]

In fact Josephus' comments on Greeks are continually restrained by his concern not to allow Judaism to appear antagonistic or 'anti-social'. His sensitivity concerning the Jewish reputation on this score is evident in his repeated response to the charge of 'misanthropy' (e.g. *C Ap* 2.209–13, 148, 261, 291), and he devotes some time to refuting the myth of the ritual murder of a Greek in the Jerusalem temple (*C Ap* 2.89–111). At the beginning and end of his comparison of Jewish and Greek constitutions he offers an apology for his critical tone (*C Ap* 2.150, 287) and insists that Jews are required to refrain from abuse of other people's customs (*C Ap* 2.144) and from blasphemy against their Gods (*C Ap* 2.237; cf. *Ant* 4.207). In refuting the notion of a Jewish oath of hostility to Greeks, Josephus goes so far as to say that 'we are separated from the Greeks more by our location than by our customs [!], so we neither hate nor envy them' (*C Ap* 2.123). In this connection Josephus highlights (and perhaps exaggerates) the phenomenon of Greeks adopting Jewish customs (*C Ap* 2.123–24; cf. 1.166; 2.209–10, 257–61, 280–86). For this proves not only the superiority of the Jewish constitution but also the openness to outsiders which Jews are criticized for failing to display.

The character of Josephus' attack on 'Greeks' in his *Contra Apionem* can best be appreciated by contrast with, on the one hand,

---

[58] See Schäublin 1982, who highlights the aspects of Athenian and Spartan propaganda which Josephus employs, even if this sometimes involves him in self-contradiction. It is odd, for instance, to hail the Athenians for rejecting Socrates (*C Ap* 2.263–64) and for their supreme piety (2.130), and then to blame them for admitting new foreign Gods (2.251)!

his abusive remarks about Egyptians, and, on the other, his consistent praise of Romans. His venom against Egyptians is based on the long history of mutual hatred (*C Ap* 1.223–26) which lay at the root of the contrary legends concerning the Exodus and which had contributed to the hostilities in Alexandria. Since one of Josephus' chosen opponents is the Alexandrian rhetorician Apion, he can display his considerable skills in *vituperatio* in personal abuse of this 'impudent dog' (*C Ap* 2.3–7, 28–32, 41–42, 80–82, 85 etc.). His favourite tactic is to ridicule the Egyptian animal cults as divisive, demeaning and senseless (*C Ap* 1.224–25; 2.65–67, 81–86), with the implication that the Egyptians are as irrational and sub-human as the animals they worship (*C Ap* 1.225; 2.66). By contrast, the Romans are spared even the moderate criticism levelled at the Greeks. Wherever they are mentioned, Romans are praised as the undisputed masters of the world (*C Ap* 2.41, 125–26) whose magnanimity and moderation allow subject races to preserve their own customs (*C Ap* 2.73–78, in relation to the emperor cult). Josephus is pleased to be able to link the Romans with the Jews as races whose origins were unknown to the Greeks (*C Ap* 1.60–68), a tactic which suggests his awareness that Roman resentment of Greek cultural hegemony was in some respects parallel to the feeling of the Jews. Most revealing is the fact that the critique of 'Greek' religion and mythology is not widened (as it could have been) to include the Romans: to say that 'the Greeks and some others think it good to make statues' (*C Ap* 2.74) looks like a studied attempt to *avoid* including the Romans in his critique of religious images.

Thus Josephus' comments on non-Jews in the *Contra Apionem* are carefully tailored to fit the historical context in which he wrote and the rhetorical exigences of his work. His strategy is to present Judaism as a superior form of civilization, and for this purpose he here defines it as a 'constitution' (πολιτεία).[59] By portraying the Jewish tradition within this framework, Josephus can present the specific commands of the law (summarized in *C Ap* 2.190–219) as

---

[59] The term πολιτεία was used to introduce the summary of the Mosaic laws in *Ant* 4.196–98. But it is only in the *Contra Apionem* that we find extended reflection on the virtues of the Jewish way of life *qua* 'constitution'. Josephus has found a partial model in Plato's *Laws*, which he cites in this context; see Schäublin 1982:335–41.

the expression of a distinctive political philosophy which has, in his view, the following three advantages (*C Ap* 2.145–286).[60]

In the first place, the Mosaic constitution is superior in its unique blend of written laws and everyday customs (*C Ap* 2.168–89). Whereas Spartans and Cretans emphasized the practice of customs, and Athenians and other Greeks concentrated on the framing of laws, Moses combined both in a way which overcame the Greek antithesis of 'word' (λόγος) and deed (ἔργον). Josephus places particular emphasis on the way this enables the principles of right belief to be embodied in the daily life of ordinary Jews, and he notes how the regular rituals of domestic life were designed to create commitment to the law even from infancy (2.168–74). Thus he can boast that Jews are far more knowledgeable about their constitution than other nations, and are trained to take it much more seriously than the comparatively slap-dash Greeks.

Thus, the second special virtue of the Jewish constitution is the degree of faithful commitment which it has received. Perhaps the most insistent theme running through this entire work is the Jews' constancy in observance of their laws (*C Ap* 1.42–43, 60–61; 2.82, 149–50 etc.). That means both a refusal to allow changes to an already perfect constitution (*C Ap* 2.182–89) and a willingness to defend the laws even to the point of death (*C Ap* 2.218–19, 232–35 etc.). Against charges of cowardice or fanaticism (*C Ap* 2.148), Josephus insists that there is no nation more courageous in defending its customs and nothing more admirable than a self-sacrificing commitment to the established laws. Siding here with the Spartan tradition (*C Ap* 2.225–31), Josephus claims that Jews even outshine Spartans in this regard.

Thirdly, Josephus portrays the Jewish constitution as uniquely shaped by piety (εὐσέβεια), in holding that the whole of life is governed by the will of God (*C Ap* 2.160). In this connection he famously coins the term 'theocracy' (θεοκρατία, *C Ap* 2.165), by which he means not the rule of the priests but the sense of God's immediate rule, such that 'no action and no secret thought can escape his knowledge' (*C Ap* 2.166). While Josephus' vocabulary here is shaped by Hellenistic theology, this sense of the all-

---

[60] The laws selected in *C Ap* 2.190–219 may be drawn from a traditional summary, since they have many points in common with Pseudo-Phocylides and Philo's *Hypothetica* (see above pp. 339–40); but Josephus' emphases reflect his apologetic concerns (see Kamlah 1974).

pervasiveness of religion was indeed a special feature of the Jewish way of life, based on a strong sense that Jewish customs were directly ordained by God (*C Ap* 1.42). Josephus' skill lies in making a virtue of this 'religiosity' as the sign of a supremely noble constitution, and to suggest (not unlike Aristeas and Philo) that Jews outclass all others in their reverence for God. It is this theme which opens and closes the final encomium of the Jewish constitution:

> I would therefore be bold to say that we have introduced to the rest of the world very many of the finest things. For what is finer than inviolable piety? What is more just than obedience to the laws? What is more beneficial than to be in harmony with one another and neither to split apart under difficulties nor to become arrogant and factious in prosperity? In war we despise death and in peace we devote ourselves to crafts and agriculture, and we are convinced that God is everywhere, watching and directing all things. (*C Ap* 2.293–94)

Thus the final word we hear from Josephus is bursting with Jewish pride, using the literary and cultural resources of the Greek tradition to outbid the Greek claim to cultural superiority. Josephus has fulfilled his promise not to abjure his people or forget his ancestral customs (*Bell* 6.107). There were easier ways he could have passed his time in Rome than in the labour of writing the *Antiquitates* and in the controversies courted by the *Contra Apionem*. These works show us a Diaspora Jew making a supreme – and in fact the last extant – effort to interpret Judaism for non-Jews in the Graeco-Roman world. Although not as acculturated as some of his predecessors, Josephus attempted to use what Hellenistic forms and concepts he knew to make his Judaism both intelligible and attractive to his contemporaries. In his political alignment with his Roman patrons he came close to subverting the national cause he had once supported, but he discovered in Rome new ways to express his Jewish commitments. It is hard to say whether his work is characterized more by cultural convergence than by cultural antagonism – even in the *Contra Apionem*, as we have seen, the antagonism is carefully channelled or restrained. But it is quite clear that Josephus would never have allowed his Jewish heritage to be melted into some general cultural amalgam. Even in the *Bellum* Josephus never abandoned his loyalty to the Jewish people, and at the last he fought as effectively as any other Diaspora Jew for the honour of the Jewish 'constitution'.

## 12.3   4 Maccabees

4 Maccabees is an anonymous work (for centuries wrongly ascribed to Josephus) which inculcates faithfulness to the law by retelling the story of Eleazar, the seven brothers and their mother, whose martyr deaths had been portrayed in 2 Maccabees 6–7. The distinctive feature of the work is the attempt to place these martyrdoms within the framework of the thesis that 'religious reason is master over the passions' (αὐτοδέσποτός ἐστιν τῶν παθῶν ὁ εὐσεβὴς λογισμός). This thesis, stated in the very first verse of the work, is the leitmotiv which runs through the entire piece, helping to bind together the philosophical discussion in the opening section (1.1–3.18) and the narrative of the martyrs' deaths which occupies the bulk of the remainder (3.19–17.6).[61] This combination of philosophical theory and Jewish history bears some similarities to the achievements of Aristeas and Philo; but, as we shall see, the level of acculturation here is distinctly inferior and certain features of the work define its mood more as defiance and defensiveness than as cultural convergence.

Already in the *exordium* (1.1–12) the author announces that he is to illustrate his thesis by reference to Jewish martyrdom (1.8–9). Thus the rest of the philosophical introduction, which defines his terms and illustrates the defeat of passions through scriptural examples, can function only as a 'trailer' to the 'main feature' to come. In fact the rhetorical techniques of the piece have much in common with the dramatic conventions of the screen. After giving a panoramic view of the context of the drama (3.19–4.26), the camera zooms in on the individuals concerned, Antiochus the 'tyrant' on one side, the nine Jewish martyrs on the other, with close-up studies of their motivation as they engage in ferocious dialogue. The viewers' emotions are skilfully engaged as the horror of each victim's torture is portrayed and the camera lingers long to extract the full pathos in each case – the indignity in the suffering of an aged priest, the tragedy of young men going to their deaths, the bitter sorrow of a mother witnessing the death of her sons.

---

[61]   17.7–18.24 may be taken as the *peroratio* and *recapitulatio*; see the full structural analysis by Klauck 1989:648–53. The material in chapter 18 has often been assessed as misplaced or as a glossator's addition: see e.g. Grimm 1853b:368–70; Freudenthal 1869:155–59; Dupont-Sommer 1939:152–53. But significant voices in recent years have rehabilitated this chapter as a loose collection of summarizing material; see Breitenstein 1978:154–57 and Klauck 1989:657–58.

Like a 'voice over', the author provides commentary and reflection (6.31–7.23; 13.1–14.10; 16.1–17.6) which point the moral of the story (6.31; 7.16; 13.1; 16.1).

It is not easy to deduce whether this highly rhetorical piece was designed initially for a 'live audience', or whether it was always a literary product. Certain features, like the references to 'this occasion' (1.10; 3.19) and the direct address to 'you children of Israel' (18.1), have led some scholars to conclude that we have here the transcript of an actual speech, perhaps connected to an annual celebration of the Maccabean martyrs.[62] Given the prevalence of 'literary speeches' in the Greek and Roman traditions, one may remain uncertain of such a conclusion, and in general the *Sitz im Leben* of this piece is difficult to define. It could be placed almost anywhere in the Diaspora, although its linguistic 'Asianisms' might suggest a location in the north-east of the Mediterranean, and the later evidence for a tomb of Maccabean martyrs in Antioch has inclined many scholars to suggest that its origins lie in that city.[63] It may be dated to the end of the first or early in the second century CE, thus allowing us to relate it tentatively to the story of the Jewish Antiochene community which we have touched on above (chapter 8.2).[64]

Since the very first word of the piece proclaims its subject as 'thoroughly philosophical' (φιλοσοφώτατον, 1.1), we are entitled to ask to what extent 4 Maccabees is engaged in the philosophical issues of its cultural milieu and what degree of acculturation it attests. The topic it thematizes, the relation between reason and the passions, is indeed a central issue in contemporary (particularly Stoic) philosophy, and the care which the author takes in the opening chapters to define wisdom (1.16), to list the passions (1.20–28), to enumerate the cardinal virtues (1.18 etc.) and to raise objections to the thesis (2.24–3.5) gives the impression of an author familiar with fundamental aspects of the Hellenistic philosophical

---

[62] E.g. Freudenthal 1869:4–36; Dupont-Sommer 1939:67–75; Hadas 1953:103–9; but the thesis has been attacked by Breitenstein 1978, Anderson 1985b:534–37 and Klauck 1989:663–64.

[63] Grimm's assumption of an Alexandrian origin 1853b:293 was rightly questioned by Freudenthal 1869:111–13. See the discussion in Dupont-Sommer 1939:67–75; Hadas 1953:109–13; and Klauck 1989:666–67, who all incline to an Antiochene origin. Anderson 1985b:534–37 prefers to leave the matter open; van Henten 1986 suggests a Cilician provenance.

[64] For the evidence and arguments on the dating see the Appendix on Sources.

tradition. It is important to this author that Judaism is a 'philosophy' (5.22, 35; 7.7, 9, 21). His inventive vocabulary and his developed rhetorical skills confirm the picture of a Jew with an advanced Greek education who has gained a thorough training in rhetoric and a familiarity with the core disciplines of a Hellenistic schooling.[65]

On closer inspection, however, the philosophical claims of the work appear somewhat pretentious and its achievements limited in scope. None of the objections raised to the thesis are in fact properly answered, and the efforts towards terminological definition are weakened by the fact that the key word πάθος is required to carry several meanings (e.g. 'passion', 'emotion', 'experience') to hold the thesis together. The Stoic ethos of the piece is modified and mixed in various respects, and the author's eclectic approach appears to be evidence not of his command of the different schools of thought but of his dependence on current popularizations of philosophy.[66] It is likely that the many inconsistencies and repetitions are the result not of interpolation or textual corruption (as has often been thought), but of the author's inability to sustain a controlled and organized treatise.[67]

More particularly, it is clear that the 'philosophy' of the treatise is present only to serve the interests of the author's Jewish commitments. The general philosophical tone of the opening chapters is barely sustained throughout the piece, where even the philosophical interludes between the martyr-narratives only partially reflect the terms of the initial discussion.[68] As the work

---

[65] Van Henten 1986:146 comments: 'Der stark rhetorische Charakter von 4 Makk setzt voraus, dass der Autor ziemlich gebildet war und zumindest die übliche Ausbildung als Ephebe genossen hat.' Yet he disapproved of the erection of a gymnasium in Jerusalem (4 Macc 4.20).

[66] It is generally acknowledged that Stoicism forms the chief philosophical framework of the document, and even the apparent departures from Stoic 'orthodoxy' (e.g. the view that the passions are to be countered not extirpated, 3.5) can be paralleled within the diverse Stoic tradition; see especially Renehan 1972, who also suggests dependence on Posidonius. Hadas' emphasis on Platonic features 1953:115–18 was excessive, and the author's eclecticism is rightly noted by Breitenstein 1978:131–43, 158–67 and Klauck 1989:665–66.

[67] See e.g., in contrast to Dupont-Sommer 1939, Breitenstein's analysis of the author's intellectual weaknesses and his untidy use of *variatio* 1978:134–43, 152–57.

[68] So Breitenstein 1978:148–57 and Lebram 1974, who argues that the genre is not that of philosophical diatribe but of graveside encomium (*Epitaphios Logos*). Klauck 1989:649–50 lists the points of continuity between 1.1–3.18 and the

progresses, the emphasis lies increasingly on faithfulness to the law as an end in itself,[69] and by the final appeal to the 'offspring of Abraham' to 'obey this law and live godly lives in every respect' (18.1) the repetition of the philosophical thesis (18.2) has become stilted and of marginal significance.

Even in the opening chapters it is clear that the author views the philosophical virtues as not simply illustrated in the law but dependent for their realization on its practice. Thus, having issued a classic definition of wisdom as 'knowledge of divine and human affairs and their causes' (1.16), our author adds immediately 'and this wisdom, to be sure, is education in the law (αὕτη δὴ τοίνυν ἐστὶν ἡ τοῦ νόμου παιδεία), through which we learn divine affairs reverently and human affairs as is good for us' (1.17). The identification of 'wisdom' (σοφία), 'education' (παιδεία) and (Jewish) law (νόμος) is revealing, and the first person plural ('we learn') indicates the author's commitment to, and confidence in, the Jewish community. Such a statement suggests that the only form of 'wisdom' or 'philosophy' in which our author is interested is that known and practised by Jews. Despite his claim to be able to draw proofs from 'many diverse sources' (1.7), all the *exempla* in chapters 1–3 are biblical, with many serving not just to illustrate but also to prove the point at issue. If Jews ('we') resist the allures of forbidden food, does that not prove that reason rules over desires (1.32–35)? If the law tells us not to covet, then reason really must be able to control covetous (and other) desires (2.4–6). Indeed, the commands in the law indicate not just *one* mode of rational behaviour but the *essential* route to virtue. God enthroned the intellect (νοῦς) as the necessary control over passions and inclinations, but it is vital to add that 'he gave to it the law, so that someone who is governed by it can reign over a realm of moderation, righteousness, goodness and courage' (2.22–23). There is no indication that such virtue could be achieved in any other way.

In this connection it is significant that the author repeatedly defines the 'reason' he lauds as '*godly* reason' (ὁ εὐσεβὴς λογισμός,

---

subsequent chapters, but the discontinuities in vocabulary and theme are really more striking.

[69] The prologue talks of dying for 'virtue' (ἀρετή, 1.8) and 'nobility' (καλοκαγαθία, 1.10), but later the definitions of the purpose of the martyrdoms focus more on the law (13.9), 'godliness' (9.7) and God (16.19).

1.1; 5.38; 7.16 etc.).[70] The adjective 'godly' occurs so frequently in this treatise, together with the noun 'godliness' (εὐσέβεια) and the verb 'to honour God' (εὐσεβεῖν), that they may be taken to represent the central motif of the whole piece.[71] When reason is applauded, its efficacy is dependent on its 'godliness', and in the crucial debate between Antiochus and Eleazar (see below), Eleazar's reason is superior to that of Antiochus precisely because it rests on an unwavering commitment to God (5.14–38). And this indeed makes clear – what is implicit throughout – that the 'godliness' in question is more precisely *Jewish* godliness. While sharing the Stoic belief that religion is an ingredient of reason, 4 Maccabees defines that religiosity in the specific terms of the Jewish religion, as practised in exemplary fashion by Jewish heroes of the past.[72] In his final comment on the martyrdom of Eleazar (7.16–23) our author argues that 'those who take care for godliness with their whole heart, they alone can control the passions of the flesh, believing that to God they do not die, as did neither our patriarchs, Abraham, Isaac and Jacob, but they live to God' (7.18–19). There can be no failure among those who 'live in a philosophical way in accordance with the full rule of philosophy and trust in God' for they conquer the passions 'on account of godliness' (διὰ τὴν θεοσέβειαν, 7.21–22). In other words, philosophy reaches its potential when expressed in 'godliness', the sort of godliness displayed by the Jewish patriarchs (and by Eleazar). Supreme philosophical achievement and unswerving belief in God are distinctively Jewish phenomena.

In fact it is striking how frequently reference is made in 4 Maccabees to the Jewish nation. The 'fathers' of the nation are repeatedly recalled, not just for their moral example, but as the guardians of Israel's integrity who will welcome and praise the martyrs after death (5.37; 13.17; 18.23). Jews refuse to violate their ancestors' oaths to keep the law (5.29) and cannot bear to bring

---

[70] The adjective is peculiarly difficult to translate and is variously rendered as 'pious', 'devout', 'religious' and 'reverent'. I have chosen 'godly' since it brings out most clearly the relationship to God which is central to the author's use of the term and its associated noun and verb.

[71] Dupont-Sommer's word index lists 11 examples of the adjective, 4 of the verb and 46 of the noun. The phrase ὁ εὐσεβὴς λογισμός occurs in Greek literature only in this document; Lauer 1955 suggests that it means 'reasoning which follows the rules of piety' or 'reasoning for the sake of piety'.

[72] See Breitenstein 1978:168–71. He comments: 'Ueber dem griechischen ἀρετή-Begriff steht somit alles überragend die (jüdische) Frömmigkeit' (170).

shame upon them (9.2). As a spur to courage they bid one another 'remember whence you came' (13.12) and address each other as 'Abrahamic offspring' (6.17, 22; 9.21; 18.1 etc.). The sense of belonging to a nation (ἔθνος) is accordingly strong (the term occurs 17 times) and the martyrs are called to bear witness on its behalf (16.16). Such blood bonds are dramatized most clearly in the loyalties of the family, and here the author emphasizes the brothers' filial responsibility to encourage each other to martyrdom despite their natural inclination to save each other (9.23; 10.2–3; 12.16–17; 13.19–27). Their common training in the law (13.22–24) is emphasized again in the final chapter, where their father's instruction is described (18.10–19).

Thus the law is here extolled not simply as the path to virtue but as the 'ancestral law' (πάτριος νόμος) which binds the Jewish people to their past and, in the present, to one another (4.23; 5.33; cf. 8.7; 9.1; 16.16). Even God is here described as 'the ancestral God' (ὁ πατρῷος θεός, 12.17), who acts in accordance with 'our just and ancestral providence which has cared for the nation' (9.24). As the servant of God (12.11), Israel may expect divine providence to be her salvation (17.22). There is no indication that Gentiles may lay claim to any such status or entertain any such hopes.

Thus the 'philosophy' which 4 Maccabees teaches is designed purely to bolster the claims of the Jewish people and to confirm their commitment to the Jewish way of life. What the author has gained from his Hellenistic training he has put to the exclusive service of his own ethnic and religious tradition. The conventional terms with which he describes this tradition suggest that his engagement with Hellenism has touched only the surface of his faith; it has not brought about any fundamental reconceptualization of Judaism. Whereas Aristeas can depict Jews and Gentiles as sharing a common culture of education, philosophy and honourable conduct, 4 Maccabees displays no admirable Gentiles and makes little effort to re-interpret the Jewish tradition in line with Hellenistic concepts.[73] Aristeas shows Jews surpassing Gentile philosophers but in a context of shared values and goals; 4

---

[73] It is noticeable that no attempt is made to show the value of the law by allegorical exegesis. In 1.30–35 the signficance of the food-laws lies in their literal observance alone, not in their 'deeper' meaning; it is possible that 5.26 hints at allegorical interpretation (so Klauck 1989:713) but this is by no means explicit. Fischer 1978:85–105 considers the eschatology and anthropology of the work only superficially Hellenized.

Maccabees asserts that 'only the children of the Hebrews are invincible in the cause of virtue' (9.18). Whereas Aristeas and Philo develop a Jewish accommodation which employs Hellenistic concepts to redescribe the value of Judaism, the author of 4 Maccabees has absorbed his education only insofar as it will support the literal meaning of his Scriptures and the traditional concepts of his Jewish heritage. His acculturation does not lead to significant cultural convergence.[74]

However, would it be correct to describe the dominant stance of 4 Maccabees as 'cultural antagonism'? Inasmuch as the work depicts and reflects upon struggle, it is clearly characterized by an ethos of opposition. Utilizing the Stoic motif of the struggle of the sage, the author depicts the Jewish martyrs as called into a contest for the sake of the nation and the law (16.16) – a 'divine contest' (ἀγὼν θεῖος, 17.11–16) in which Eleazar first entered the lists, followed by the rest, and all nine faced 'the tyrant' as their opponent (ὁ τύραννος ἀντηγωνίζετο, 17.14).[75] Antiochus is consistently referred to simply as 'the tyrant', and although he is not made the sole cause of the persecutions (3.21–4.1; 4.19–21), he is repeatedly portrayed as a cruel and proud man (10.17; 11.4; 18.20 etc.), notwithstanding his occasional bursts of pity (5.6–15; 8.4–11; 12.2–5). Thus the martyrs' deaths are interpreted as the necessary response to the power of evil, a response of unyielding faithfulness which succeeds in defeating the tyrant and his tyranny (1.11; 8.2 etc.).[76] The judgment of Antiochus, though not immediate, was bound to come in full and fitting measure (9.9, 24, a warning repeated by each of the seven brothers!).

Yet the contest is depicted here largely as *single combat* between each martyr and the king. Some general references are made to the king's courtiers (5.1–2) and to a wider audience (15.20; 17.14), yet the camera scarcely strays from the two figures on stage at each moment. The soldiers are necessary adjuncts to apply the torture

---

[74] Hadas talks of 'the exploitation of novel methods for the traditional tasks of exhortation and admonition ... the [philosophical] framework is essentially mere scaffolding for a spiritual message' (1953:123); cf. Anderson 1985b:537–38 and Schürer 3.589–90. Heinemann 1928:803–5 concludes: 'So stolz der Verfasser offenbar auf seine griechische Bildung ist, so ist er doch weit weniger stark als andere philosophierende Juden von ihr berührt' (805).

[75] See Pfitzner 1967:57–65; earlier the author had described the struggle against the passions in similar terms (3.5).

[76] On Antiochus as 'tyrant' and the use in this document of standard features of this theme from the Greek tradition, see Heininger 1989.

(6.1, 8; 9.11, 28 'like savage leopards'), although they also admire and pity the victims and offer to help them out of their plight (6.11–15; 9.16 etc.). Otherwise the wider social context of these events, the Gentile society which surrounds and threatens the Jewish heroes, is noticeable by its absence. The martyrs are pitted against 'the tyrant' (and his human tools) but not against Gentiles or the Gentile world, and nothing is said to disparage non-Jews as such on moral or religious grounds. There are two general references to 'the enemies of our nation' (17.20; 18.4), but these are rooted in past conditions, recalling Maccabean history, and they are not taken up in rhetorical appeals to resist such 'enemies' in the present.

Thus, despite the general atmosphere of struggle and the gruesome detail with which the victims' deaths are portrayed, 4 Maccabees does not employ its theme to portray as broad or as fundamental a social antagonism between Jews and Gentiles as one might have expected. It is interesting to compare its ethos in this regard with that of 2 Maccabees, from which it derived its narrative. In the depiction of the martyrdoms themselves, 2 Maccabees does not look beyond the immediate confrontation between Antiochus and his victims, but the surrounding material is full of references indicating general hostility between Jews and Gentiles. In 2 Maccabees Gentiles defile the temple (2 Macc 6.4) and neighbouring Gentile cities attempt to wipe out their Jewish populations (2 Macc 6.8–9; 12.2–9). The Maccabean fighters are ranged against 'impious', 'barbarous' and 'blasphemous' Gentiles (2 Macc 8.1–7, 16–17; 10.2–5; 13.9–12 etc.) and the author compares God's favourable chastisement of Jews with his ruthless treatment of other nations (2 Macc 6.12–16). It is striking that this general perspective is *not* represented in 4 Maccabees, for even if Antiochus is described as 'the tyrant of the Greeks' (18.20), 'Greeks' or 'Gentiles' are not themselves described in derogatory terms. The atmosphere here may also be contrasted with that of 3 Maccabees, which, as we have seen (chapter 7.2), is full of hostile crowds and 'lawless Gentiles'.

Thus the story of persecution on which 4 Maccabees reflects is not used, as it might easily have been, to encourage Jewish readers to view their social world as implacably hostile. Yet the work does reflect a Judaism which is wary of social pressures and the author is obviously concerned lest Jewish faithfulness be compromised. Particularly revealing here are the speeches which form the prelude to the martyrs' deaths. In his source, 2 Maccabees 6–7, our author had found a brief speech of Eleazar on being urged to make pretence of eating forbidden food (2 Macc 6.24–28); and that he was happy to utilize and expand (4 Macc 6.16–23). But he has created *de novo* an earlier dialogue between Antiochus and Eleazar which reveals with special clarity the issues at stake in this test of Eleazar's faithfulness (5.6–38).

First, in 5.6–13, Antiochus is given a speech which raises significant questions about the validity of the Jewish way of life. Eleazar's refusal to eat pork is here considered irrational, since no-one could criticize this harmless pleasure, and morally wrong, since it means rejecting one of nature's good gifts (5.8–9). The first charge is used to undercut Eleazar's claim to be a 'philosopher': in the king's eyes his is a senseless and stupid philosophy (5.7, 11) which amounts to no more than 'empty opinions concerning the truth' (κενοδοξῶν περὶ τὸ ἀληθές, 5.10; cf. 8.5; 10.13). The second goes to the heart of the matter by challenging the rationale for the Jews' dietary laws: if to eat such food is 'natural', on what grounds could they possibly refuse it? In the further suggestion that God would forgive a minor lapse committed under pressure (5.13, repeated in 8.14, 22, 25) we sense the temptations experienced by the author's Jewish contemporaries, and the unique reference in this context to 'the Jews' (5.7, elsewhere 4 Maccabees uses the archaic term, 'the Hebrews') confirms that he has here his contemporary context in mind.

We may presume, therefore, that Eleazar's reply to this challenge (5.16–38) will reveal our author's most important convictions on the rationale for Judaism. His opening riposte is the most crucial:

> We, Antiochus, have been convinced that our lives must be governed by the divine law and thus we regard no compulsion stronger than the requirement that we obey the law; so in no way can we justify transgression. Even if our law, as you suppose, were not truly divine, but we merely considered it to be divine, even so it would not be right for us to destroy our reputation for godliness. (5.16–18)

It is the Jews' belief that their law is divine which rules out any possibility of compromise, however small it might seem (5.19–21). As it is divine, the law simply overpowers any alternative authority and nullifies considerations of expediency. It is interesting to find this bold claim so clearly stated (cf. 5.25), even in the awareness that it is disputed by others. Indeed it is striking that our author, while allowing the hypothetical denial of Jewish belief on this matter ('even if our law, as you suppose, were not truly divine'), underlines the importance for the Jewish community of the *claim* that the law is divine, since, he asserts, Jews must at all costs maintain their religious reputation. In his view, without this claim to be faithful to the divine will the Jews would lose their right to respect in the Graeco-Roman world, which is founded on their 'godliness' (εὐσέβεια). Elsewhere he repeats this concern for the Jews' reputation (δόξα, 6.18; 7.9) even though he knows it lays them open to the charge of 'vanity' (κενοδοξία, 8.19, 24; cf. 5.10). Without this conviction that its way of life was ruled by divine law, the Jewish community would lose, in our author's view, its *raison d'être*.

Eleazar's supplementary arguments meet Antiochus' objections head on. Is the Jews' philosophy 'irrational'? No, since their way of life inculcates moderation, courage, righteousness and godliness, four of the standard philosophical virtues (5.22–24). Are their practices contrary to nature? No, since the law-giver is the creator of the world who regulates the law in accordance with nature (κατὰ φύσιν): 'whatever is suited to our souls he has allowed us to eat, and whatever is contrary he has forbidden' (5.25–26).[77] And if Antiochus thinks he can simply force obedience by the weight of his authority, he must think again: Eleazar looks for moral direction not to the king but to the Jewish community, whose forefathers swore to keep the law and will welcome him, unsullied, after death (5.29, 37). His sense of obligation to the 'ancestral law' (πάτριος νόμος, 5.33) and to the youth in the Jewish community (6.19) easily outweighs the pressures of Gentile society.

In this crucial exchange between Antiochus and Eleazar we gain our clearest impression of the social context of 4 Maccabees and the cultural stance of its author. Although the work concerns an extreme case of persecution, there is little to indicate that either the author or his community are threatened to quite this degree: they look back on these events with a shudder (14.9) from the relative security of a later time. Yet the story is told with the awareness that it is not easy to maintain one's faithfulness to the Jewish tradition, and the author seems conscious of the need to bolster Jewish commitment among those of his own social class. Thus, as Klauck has noted, the work is designed to counter the

---

[77] The Greek is a little difficult in 5.25, though the general point is clear enough; on the translation see Klauck 1989:712 (in contrast to Hadas and Anderson) and Redditt 1983:256–57.

temptations to assimilation among acculturated Jews.[78] Wrapping its message in attractive philosophical garb, it parades the example of faithful Jews who resisted the offer of compromised social advancement (2.15; 8.7; 12.5), who stayed faithful to the Jewish food laws (the greatest impediment to social integration) and who could counter the reasoned objections of Gentiles with effective apologetics. He assures them that their principled stance is not irrational but highly philosophical, and even suggests that it will be admired by non-Jews (17.23–24).

Thus even if this work is not characterized by the degree of hostility which we have found in some other examples of 'cultural antagonism', its dominant mood is that of wariness, the expectation of danger for Jews living in a Graeco-Roman environment. Although well versed in the linguistic and rhetorical conventions of the Greek tradition, our author is concerned lest Jews be tempted to 'renounce the ancestral rule of your constitution, sharing in the Greek way of life and changing your patterns of behaviour' (8.7–8; cf. 4.19–20; 18.5). He is determined that he and his fellow Jews resist such pressure to 'disown Judaism' (4.26). If they resist, they will display the power of 'godly reason' over the 'passions' and prove the philosophical excellence of the Jewish tradition. But such resistance is also, and perhaps more fundamentally, simply what is required of those who belong to the Jewish community and share in its heritage.

If we may place our author in Antioch at the end of the first century CE, we may observe that he had good reason to adopt this defensive stance. As we have seen (chapter 8.2.2), the Jewish community in Antioch came under extreme pressure during the Judaean War (66–70 CE), and the treachery of one of its prominent members, Antiochus, led to formidable pressure on leading Jews to renounce their Judaism. According to Josephus, Antiochus 'sacrificed in the manner of the Greeks' and tried to force other Jews to do likewise, while also attempting to ban the observance of the Sabbath (*Bell* 7.50–53); some Jews resisted to the point of death. While the Jewish community survived this ordeal and managed to regain its rights, the experience cannot have been swiftly forgotten, and in the aftermath of the Judaean War Jews of social rank must

---

[78] Klauck 1989:664–65; cf. Redditt 1983:264–70 and already Grimm 1853b:290–91. Note how 13.22 assumes the acquisition of both Greek παιδεία and Jewish training in the law.

have faced considerable pressure to disown their heritage. Perhaps the events in Antioch revived the memory of the Maccabean martyrs (there was a similar test of 'idolatry' and even another Antiochus!). In any case, our author appears to have suspected that educated Jews would find their Jewish loyalties difficult to maintain. With considerable rhetorical skill he retells an old tale in such a way as to establish their cultural claim to 'philosophy' while cementing their commitments to the Jewish nation.

# 13

## *Paul: An Anomalous Diaspora Jew*

There is nothing strange about including Paul in our gallery of Diaspora Jews. While he played a decisive role in shaping the new Christian movement, he was also, of course, a Jew. Moreover, for the period of his life of which we are best informed, he was a Diaspora Jew, in the sense that his residence and life-commitments were in the Diaspora. According to Acts, Paul was born in the city of Tarsus (in Cilicia, Acts 21.39; 22.3) and thus even in terms of origins he may be counted among Diaspora Jews. However, we do not know how long he lived in Tarsus before moving to Jerusalem (Acts 22.3), and if the rest of his life had been spent in the Jewish homeland he could hardly have merited inclusion in this book. In fact, however, after his call experience Paul spent very little time in Jerusalem or Judaea but travelled to the north and west around the Mediterranean basin, usually staying in cities where there were communities of Jews. During these thirty years (about half of his life) Paul can properly be regarded as a Diaspora Jew and compared with other Jews living in this social environment.[1] Whether his initial formation took place in Tarsus or in Jerusalem, the Paul who preaches, disputes with Jews and Gentiles and writes to members of his churches is a Jew at work in the Diaspora. By observing him in this, his primary social context, we can plot his social and cultural location amongst other Diaspora Jews. As we shall see, his position there is distinctly anomalous.[2]

---

[1] Paul's call/conversion is usually dated in the years 33–35 CE and his death in the mid 60s. Since he was probably in the age range 25–35 at his call (Hengel 1991:67), that leaves half of his life lived mostly in the Diaspora. For the chronology of his life see Jewett 1979.

[2] Recent interpretation of Paul has been strangely reluctant to explore this sort of comparison. Davies 1948 and Sanders 1977 restrict their attention to rabbinic and Palestinian comparisons (as also, in the main, does Segal 1990), while conversely Collins 1986 omits Paul from his survey of Jews in the Diaspora. Comparisons between Paul and Philo have been pursued by Goodenough 1968

Our knowledge of Paul is based on two kinds of source – his own letters and the portrait of his life and message in the book of Acts. The portrait of Paul in Acts contains exaggerations and apologetic traits which leave the 'Lukan Paul' open to question on a number of scores, though not wholly worthless historically.[3] Of the letters attributed to Paul, not all can be claimed as authentic; we will follow the usual critical judgments on this matter, which leave us with a textual base of seven (see the Appendix on Sources). Even these are not unproblematic in their evidential value. They tell us what Paul said to his own converts but not, except by implication, how he spoke to non-Christian Jews or Gentiles. Moreover, each represents (though to varying degrees) situational rhetoric, where consistency or 'balance' were less important than the management of an immediate problem. In his judgments on the Jews and his Jewish heritage we find Paul writing now in anger (Phil 3.2–11; Gal 4.21 – 5.12), now in anguish (Rom 9.1–5), and we would like to know which is the 'real' Paul. Are we to posit a process of development (maturation?), or was the 'real' Paul precisely this vacillating?

Despite such difficulties, our sources shed enough light on Paul's life and thought to enable us to assess his social and cultural posture. Paul tells us that he was brought up in a Jewish family ('circumcised on the eighth day, of the people of Israel', Phil 3.5), indeed one where Hebrew/Aramaic was apparently as well known as Greek: such seems to be suggested by his claim to be a 'Hebrew born of Hebrews' (Phil 3.5; 2 Cor 11.22; cf. Acts 22.2). In Acts (but only Acts) he is introduced as a πολίτης of Tarsus (Acts 21.39), but it is unclear what meaning is to be attached to Luke's term, which could mean 'citizen' or merely 'resident'.[4] There is a good case to be made that Paul had Roman citizenship (as Acts repeatedly claims), which was probably inherited from a father or grandfather given formal manumission; it is possible that one of Paul's ancestors had been taken captive in the upheavals following Pompey's arrival in Syria (see above, chapter 8.2.2) and taken to

---

and Sandmel 1979b, but the parallels adduced are frequently strained.

[3] See the famous essays on this topic by Vielhauer 1966 and Bornkamm 1966; a recent addition is Lentz 1993. Note the careful weighing of the issue by Barrett 1994:3–8, 161–66.

[4] See Tajra 1989:78–80 and Hengel 1991:4–6. Paul's apparent ignorance of the classics of Greek literature, which were central to a citizen's education, makes it doubtful that he was a citizen in the technical sense.

Tarsus in slavery.[5] Thus Paul's family may have been resident in Tarsus for only two or three generations, and it is no surprise to find him, like some other Diaspora Jews, returning to Jerusalem to undergo education there (Acts 22.3).[6]

Paul's education may only be guessed at from the cultural level of his letters and from his autobiographical statements, but the two match each other reasonably well. His letters are written in good, but not polished, Greek prose, argumentatively effective but not stylistically grand. He does not give the impression of one who has undergone the literary and rhetorical training which was characteristic of the gymnasium. It seems he had no more than a rudimentary knowledge of Greek literature (contrast Ezekiel and Aristobulus, not to mention Philo): the occasional literary tag (Menander in 1 Cor 15.33) reflects only popular parlance.[7] While his letters sometimes display popular styles of debate (e.g. diatribe in Romans, and ironic comparison in 2 Cor 10–13), they rarely if ever employ the stylized techniques of a trained orator.[8] Paul admits to being an 'inexpert speaker' (2 Cor 11.6) and it is clear that Apollos and other Jews known to the Corinthian church were more impressive than he in this respect (Acts 18.24; 1 Cor 1–2; 2 Cor 10–13).

At no point does Paul prize the Greek *paideia* which was valued so highly by Jews like Aristeas and Philo. Instead he refers with some pride to his 'progress in Judaism beyond many of my own age among my people, being exceptionally zealous for the traditions of my fathers' (Gal 1.14); he also lists among his credentials 'as to the law, a Pharisee' (Phil 3.5). As Hengel has argued, his Pharisaic education must have taken place in Jerusalem, in a school of Torah-interpretation, probably in Paul's case in the

---

5    Hengel 1991:6–15.
6    Since the descendants of freedmen could experience widely varying fortunes, Paul's ancestry gives us few clues to his economic status. It appears that his financial condition varied greatly during his eventful life (Phil 4.11–12), although his favoured occupation as a leather-worker (Acts 18.3) placed him in the general stratum of mobile artisans, who were somewhat despised by the leisured classes (1 Cor 4.12); see Hock 1980 and Hengel 1991:15–17.
7    Malherbe 1983:41–45; Hengel 1991:34–37.
8    The parallels with rhetorical handbooks, which are nowadays frequently adduced, may only signify that their authors noted the characteristics of effective speech, which Paul knew from experience; see Litfin 1994:255–57, Classen 1991:26–31 and the authoritative judgment of Norden 1909:2.492–502.

Greek language.[9] Here Paul acquired his extraordinarily intimate knowledge of the Scriptures, and learned the range of exegetical methods which he was later to display in his letters. Thus the evidence points to a Greek-medium Jewish education, in which the broad spectrum of Hellenism entered Paul's mind only through the filter of his conservative Pharisaic environment.

Paul's early commitment to the integrity of the Jewish nation and its 'ancestral traditions' is evident from the 'zeal' with which he harassed the early Christian communities (Gal 1.13; Phil 3.6). However, the direction of his life was fundamentally altered by his 'call' experience in or near Damascus (Gal 1.15–17; Acts 9.1–22; 22.3–21; 26.2–23).[10] His call was to be an apostle to the Gentiles (Gal 1.16; Rom 1.15; 11.13), and in fulfilment of his new mission Paul developed a life-style and a theology which questioned the authority of the 'ancestral customs' which he had once vigorously defended. In his most revealing comment on his mission strategy (1 Cor 9.19–23), Paul claims that he adapted his behaviour to his audience: among Jews he became a Jew, in order to gain them, but among Gentiles ('those without the law') he became 'as one without the law, though not lawless before God, but acting "lawfully" to Christ' (τοῖς ἀνόμοις ὡς ἄνομος, μὴ ὢν ἄνομος θεοῦ ἀλλ' ἔννομος Χριστοῦ, 1 Cor 9.21).

Such tactical adaptability (or 'inconsistency', cf. Gal 1.10) enabled Paul to justify a degree of assimilation which brought him into continuous controversy with fellow Jews. At Antioch he advocated eating with Gentiles on terms which came under strong attack from Jews (Christian and non-Christian alike) and were eventually repudiated even by his long-time associate Barnabas (Gal 2.11–14). Although the precise contours of that dispute are now obscure,[11] Paul's behaviour in Antioch was probably consistent with his statement elsewhere (concerning food) that 'I know and am persuaded in the Lord Jesus that nothing is unclean of itself' (Rom 14.14). This radical principle contrasts sharply with the commitment to the Jewish dietary laws which we have found both in defensive Diaspora documents like 3 and 4 Maccabees and in

---

[9]    Hengel 1991:18–62. The reference to Paul's training 'at the feet of Gamaliel' (Acts 22.3) is not implausible, but it leaves unclear at what age Paul moved to Jerusalem for his education; see the investigation by van Unnik 1962.

[10]    For the analysis of this 'call' as also a conversion experience see Segal 1990.

[11]    See the discussion by Dunn 1990:129–82 and Sanders 1990b.

the sophisticated treatises of Aristeas and Philo. Unlike the latter, Paul develops no allegorical explanation of the law, on which basis he might have claimed to 'fulfil' the law in its moral sense: he simply asserts his freedom from this central Jewish tradition. To be sure, in Rom 14 he indicates his willingness to renounce such freedom for the sake of law-observant believers, just as in 1 Cor 8–10 he would give up eating meat offered to 'idols' if it impeded faith. But such tactical concessions could not mask a fundamental freedom (ἐξουσία, 1 Cor 8.9), which Josephus would have dubbed a 'self-determination' (αὐτεξουσία) deeply corrosive to the Jewish way of life (*Ant* 4.145–49).

Paul's assimilation took place in private rather than in public affairs: he was probably not an ephebe or citizen in a Greek city nor did he ever hold a civic post. Although he did not care to enquire about the 'idolatrous' origins of the food he ate in others' homes (1 Cor 10.23–33), his invectives against 'idolatry' (1 Cor 10.14–22; Rom 1.18–32) indicate that he could never have participated directly in Gentile cult. Neither did he marry a Gentile. Nonetheless, he did form primary relationships with Gentile believers (like Titus and Onesimus, Gal 2.1–3; Phlm 10–12) who became his 'brothers in Christ' with bonds of affinity equal to those he formed with Jewish believers. In the intimate atmosphere of his house-churches Paul and his (mostly Gentile) converts shared common meals, joined in prayer and worship, exchanged spiritual gifts and greeted each other with the 'holy kiss' (1 Cor 16.20; Rom 16.16 etc.). To associate with Gentiles in such intimacy without requiring that they come under the authority of the Jewish law was to stretch Jewish openness to 'strangers' far beyond its usual limits (cf. Josephus, *C Ap* 2.209–10).

In fact, Paul explicitly describes his aim as the creation of communities in which 'there is neither Jew nor Greek' (Gal 3.28). In the context of their new community, the ethnic identity of Paul's converts was simply irrelevant: they were to choose their mates, for instance, 'in the Lord' (1 Cor 7.39) regardless of their ethnic origin. This does not mean that Jewish Christians were pressured to abandon law-observance or prized away from their synagogues: in Rom 14.1 – 15.6 Paul goes to some lengths to defend the right of law-observant Christians to attend synagogues on the Sabbath and to keep Jewish dietary laws.[12] Yet the significance of such

---

[12] See Barclay 1996.

obedience to the law is now hugely reduced: theirs is simply one way of 'honouring the Lord' (Rom 14.5–6) and, in Paul's view, a symptom of 'weak' faith (Rom 14.1–2). In undercutting the ideological basis of their faithfulness to the law, Paul also induces his Jewish converts to transfer the core of their allegiance to the church community which now sets the parameters of legitimate behaviour (Rom 14.17; cf. Gal 2.14).[13]

In social reality Paul's churches were distinct from the synagogues, and their predominantly Gentile members unattached to the Jewish community.[14] If Paul forbade his Gentile converts to get circumcised (1 Cor 7.18; Gal 5.2–12) he also gave them no encouragement to attend synagogues or to contribute to their financial needs. Paul's congregations had an alternative cult ('the true worship', Phil 3.3) in which the reading of Scripture was not obscured by the veil of misunderstanding which he thought hampered the teaching of the synagogues (2 Cor 3.15). It was to 'the household of faith' that believers bore their primary responsibilities (Gal 6.10). Although Paul gathered a collection for 'the saints' in Jerusalem (Gal 2.10; 2 Cor 8–9; Rom 15.25–33), his Gentile converts knew no obligations to the temple in either tax or pilgrimage; they were encouraged, rather, to think of themselves as 'the temple of God' (1 Cor 3.16–17; 6.19–20; 2 Cor 6.16). Paul is even so bold as to redefine the term Ἰουδαῖος such that it applies not to the physically circumcised but to the 'hidden' reality of a circumcision of the heart, in the Spirit (Rom 2.25–29). Such a one-sided emphasis on the 'symbolic' meaning of Jewish practices was, of course, precisely what Philo criticized in those we have called 'pure allegorists' (*Mig Abr* 89–93; see above chapter 5.1). Where Philo insists that a good Jew should preserve his/her reputation in the eyes of the Jewish community ('the masses'), Paul boldly asserts that what counts is praise from God, not men (Rom 2.29).

Such a radical stance on law-observance obviously derives from Paul's mission and his formation of multi-ethnic Christian

---

[13] It is striking that, although Paul's churches contain some Jews (including himself), he often *distinguishes* them from 'the Jews' (1 Cor 10.32), otherwise known as 'the sons of Israel' (2 Cor 3.13–16) or 'Israel according to the flesh' (1 Cor 10.18). It is only in Romans 9–11 that he struggles to describe how the church and Israel could again be coterminous.

[14] This is properly recognized by Meeks 1985 and given pointed, though sometimes over-schematized, expression by Watson 1986.

communities. But that is not to say that it is merely a question of pragmatism. Paul's theology of the law, though sometimes baffling in its expression, is clearly an attempt to clarify the rationale for his revolutionary praxis.[15] In Galatians, his most heated letter on the subject, Paul drives a wedge as far as he dare between the Jewish law and faith in Christ, confining the former to the period between Moses and Jesus, and according it a merely temporary, indeed 'enslaving' role. His tone is more measured in Romans, which affirms the sanctity of the law (Rom 7.12, 14), yet even here Christians are in important senses released from its authority (Rom 7.1–6; 14.1ff.). If Christ is the 'fulfilment' of the law (Rom 10.4), that τέλος ('end'/'goal') includes important elements of 'finality'. Even in this most positive letter Paul's tone is radically different from that total commitment to the law which we have found in writers as diverse as Aristeas, Josephus, Philo and the author of 4 Maccabees. Unlike these other Diaspora Jews, Paul cannot acclaim the law as the highest path to virtue or the supreme instruction in piety. He is too impressed by its weakness and its vulnerability to the power of sin (Rom 7.7 – 8.4). He even criticizes those who boast in the law as the best expression of the will of God (Rom 2.17–24). The adulation accorded to Moses by Artapanus, Ezekiel, Philo and Josephus is impossible for Paul, for whom the law-giver has been eclipsed by Christ. In Paul's theology the pattern of the Scriptures has been reconfigured to make Abraham rather than Moses its seminal figure (Gal 3; Rom 4).

Thus in terms of his social behaviour and his relationships with Gentiles, Paul is a highly assimilated Diaspora Jew, and his letters make clear that this was no accidental or merely pragmatic state of affairs: he had developed a new reading of the Scriptures which justified precisely his norm-breaking assimilation. Yet Paul makes little attempt to express his new commitments in the terms or categories of Hellenistic culture. Despite years of association with Gentiles, Paul's letters show little acculturation in the core of his theology, and he rarely attempts to effect any cultural synthesis with the Graeco-Roman world he sought to evangelize. One might expect a Jew who thought deeply about his formation of multiethnic communities to draw on the heritage of Hellenism, through

---

[15] The literature on 'Paul and the law' has vastly increased since Sanders 1977; see the survey in Westerholm 1988. Influential variant positions can be found in Sanders 1983, Räisänen 1983 and Dunn 1990.

which, as other Diaspora Jews had found, a universalized form of Judaism could come to expression. One might also expect some blurring of the traditional categories by which Jews had demarcated themselves from the rest of humanity. Instead, we find in Paul a strongly antagonistic cultural stance, combined with a radical redefinition of traditional Jewish categories. It is this anomaly we must now explore further.

Paul most commonly categorizes humanity in terms of the simple biblical division between 'Jews' and 'Gentiles/the nations' (τὰ ἔθνη, Gal 2.8–9; 1 Cor 1.23; 2 Cor 11.26; Rom 3.29; 9.24, etc.), with the latter often referred to simply as 'the foreskin' (ἀκροβυστία, Gal 2.7–9; 1 Cor 7.18–19; Rom 2.25–29 etc.). The biblical disdain for 'uncircumcised Gentiles' is evident in the associations Paul builds around these terms. He contrasts Jews with 'Gentile sinners' (ἐξ ἐθνῶν ἁμαρτωλοί, Gal 2.15), and assumes that the latter have minimal moral standards (a certain sexual sin is found 'not even among the Gentiles', 1 Cor 5.1); indeed, he summarily dismisses them as 'Gentiles who do not know God' (1 Thess 4.5). Although he understands himself to be 'an apostle to the Gentiles', he considers his converts as somehow lifted out of this negative category: the Corinthian Christians were, he says, '*formerly* Gentiles' (ὅτε ἔθνη ἦτε, 1 Cor 12.2).[16] Although his life's work consists of establishing communities made up of Jewish and non-Jewish believers, each of equal dignity, Paul retains the assumption that the non-Jewish world is a cess-pit of godlessness and vice (Rom 1.18–32; Phil 2.15).

Thus Paul's success in winning Gentile converts does not cause him to redraw his conceptual map of the world, simply to move the chosen few among the Gentiles into the territory traditionally ascribed to Jews. The Corinthian Christians are addressed as 'the church of God in Corinth' (1 Cor 1.2, the term ἐκκλησία being drawn from the LXX); they are the 'saints' who are 'called' and who 'call on the name of the Lord' (1.2, cf. Joel 3.5 LXX). They are the people who 'love God' (1 Cor 2.9), God's building, even

---

[16] One may compare past European missions to evangelize 'the heathen'. Paul does of course talk about the salvation of the ἔθνη (and of God as the God of the ἔθνη, Rom 3.29), but in terms that make clear that the only good members of these 'nations' are those who are saved. Once saved, Paul typically addresses them in the Scriptural language applicable to Jews (see below), except when he needs to distinguish Gentile from Jewish converts (Gal 2.12, 14; Rom 11.13; 15.27; 16.4).

his temple (1 Cor 3.9–17; 6.19). Similarly, the Philippians are taught to consider themselves God's children (2.15), and are assured that they constitute the true circumcision, the community that worships God in spirit (3.3). In the letter to the Galatians, whose argument turns on the question of his converts' identity, Paul's argument is thick with Scriptural proof that all believers are 'children of Abraham' (3.6–29), sons of God and heirs of the promises (4.1–8), the proper line of descent from Abraham and Isaac (4.21–31); they are even addressed as the 'Israel of God' (6.16).[17] The same themes are found, in yet richer and fuller exposition, in the letter to the Romans, where, in chapters 4 and 9–11, Paul clarifies how Gentiles can be considered among the descendants of Abraham and how they may be grafted into the 'olive tree' of God's historic people (Rom 11.17–24). As Hays has shown (1989), Paul continually weaves into his language biblical citations and allusions in order to clothe his Gentile churches in scriptural garb; even Gentile converts are encouraged to think of the patriarchs as 'our fathers' (1 Cor 10.1; Rom 4.1).

Thus Paul adopts precisely that traditional biblical language which we have found in documents like 3 and 4 Maccabees. He makes little if any attempt to place his definitions of the people of God within the framework of Hellenistic culture. As we have seen, Josephus could locate Judaism within its wider cultural environment by using categories such as *politeia* ('constitution') with which to describe the Jewish way of life. Aristeas and Philo could present Jews as exemplary advocates of morality and philosophy, and Ezekiel could suggest a comparison between the Exodus and a defining moment in Greek history. Even 4 Maccabees could attempt to place Jewish faithfulness to the law within the framework of Stoic ethics. All these varied cultural syntheses were employed to define and support the Jewish community. Paul radically expands – indeed threatens – the boundaries of that community, yet is far less open to any such cultural engagement. Although he creates and addresses communities which cross ethnic and cultural boundaries, Paul's theology employs traditional Jewish categories. His heritage shapes his perceptions of the world, even while its categories are violently redefined by the social effects of his mission.

---

[17] Commentators continue to baulk at this remarkable transference of terminology; compare Barclay 1988:98 and Dunn 1993:344–46.

To turn to Paul after reading most other Diaspora literature is to be struck by his minimal use of Hellenistic theology, anthropology or ethics. To be sure, one may point to elements of Paul's pastoral advice which have similarities to themes discussed by popular philosophers. But the letter in which such parallels have been most diligently sought (1 Thessalonians) has as its theological core (1 Thess 4.13 – 5.10) a depiction of salvation whose apocalyptic concepts are far removed from the main currents of Graeco-Roman thought.[18] In fact, the prominence of apocalyptic in this passage is no isolated phenomenon. It dominates also the main theological passages in 1 Corinthians, where Paul pits the message of the cross against all forms of human wisdom (1 Cor 1–4), portrays Christ's cosmic warfare with the 'powers' (1 Cor 15.20–28) and insists on the notion of a bodily resurrection with almost no concession to Hellenistic anthropology (1 Cor 15.35–58). Philo would have found all such language thoroughly distasteful.

In attempting to explain the 'Hellenization' of early Christianity, a number of scholars have argued that Paul's theology shows Hellenizing traits, especially in his anthropology and sacramentalism.[19] In fact, careful analysis of the texts rarely points in this direction,[20] and comparison of Paul with other Diaspora authors only shows how little his theology is influenced by Hellenism. The anthropology of *The Wisdom of Solomon* and Philo is far more Hellenized than Paul's, and both Philo and *Joseph and Aseneth* use 'mystery' concepts much more readily than he. Certainly Paul can speak of self-sufficiency (Phil 4.10–19) and detachment (1 Cor 7.25–31) in Stoic-sounding phrases, and he discusses obligation and service (1 Cor 9) in ways which parallel Stoic ideology. But it is clear in each case that his ethical foundations are quite different from those of the Stoics: he has neither aimed at nor achieved anything like that cultural

---

[18]  See Malherbe 1989, with the concession on the content of 1 Thess 4.13–5.10 at p.64.

[19]  At least since Lüdemann 1872, Paul's anthropology has been scrutinized in this way; see the survey of research in Barclay 1988:178–215. Earlier attempts to identify the influence of the 'mystery religions' have been revived by Maccoby 1991.

[20]  For a recent appraisal of the 'mystery religions' hypothesis see Wedderburn 1987. Boyarin's emphasis on Pauline dualism and allegory, as symptoms of a quest for Greek universals comparable to Philo (1994), is wide of the mark. Paul does not spiritualize Israel's heritage but transfer it from one community to another.

convergence we have found in Aristobulus and Philo.[21] It is revealing how little Paul uses allegory in his interpretation of Scripture, and what he finds when he does so (1 Cor 9.9–11; Gal 4.21–31) bears little relation to the theological or ethical mainstream of Hellenistic thought. Paul's ethics are not significantly shaped by the cardinal Greek virtues (the term ἀρετή appears only in Phil 4.8). He makes no attempt to relate his moral values to that common ethic to which Aristeas, Pseudo-Phocylides and others made appeal.

In fact, one might say that the main thrust of Pauline theology was inherently antipathetic to any such attempt to find common cause with Hellenistic culture. Far from Aristeas' appreciation of *paideia*, Paul derides the 'wisdom' of the Greeks (1 Cor 1.18–25) which he considers to have been overturned by the cross of Christ. With extraordinary boldness, he divides humanity into 'those perishing' and 'those being saved' on the sole ground of their response to his message (1 Cor 1.18). If believers gain access to a wisdom, this is an esoteric possession of those graced by the Spirit (οἱ πνευματικοί), unavailable to 'ordinary people' (οἱ ψυχικοί, 1 Cor 2.6–16). The world outside the church is the domain of Satan (1 Cor 5.5; 2 Cor 4.4), in which one is hardly to find either moral or theological illumination.

Paul's comparative lack of openness to Hellenistic culture can be seen through a comparison of Romans 1–2 with the Lukan speech attributed to him in Acts 17. In the Lukan portrait Paul is a preacher taken seriously by Epicurean and Stoic philosophers in Athens. He obliges his audience with a Stoicizing portrait of human religiosity, which he represents as a common quest for the unknown God. He even cites Aratus with approval (as had Aristobulus), affirming the common identity of humankind as the offspring of God (Acts 17.28). By contrast the real Paul, although he utilizes the Stoic notion of creation as design, lambasts all humanity as disobedient to the truth (Rom 1.18–22), and reacts to Graeco-Roman religion not with the indulgence of the Areopagus-speaker but with Jewish abhorrence (Rom 1.23; cf. Gal 4.8–10; 1 Cor 12.2 etc.).[22] In Romans 2.12–16 Paul is at his most Stoic in suggesting

---

[21] The essays by Malherbe and Engberg-Pedersen in Engberg-Pedersen 1994 show some similarities between Paul's patterns of thought and those of Stoicism, but these rarely touch the fundamentals of Paul's thought. Cf. Sevenster 1961 and Pohlenz 1949.

[22] For the contrast between Acts 17 and Romans 1 see especially Dibelius 1956:57–64.

that Gentiles have access to a 'natural law', equivalent to that known by the Jews. But this notion is raised only in order to enhance the indictment of Jews (2.27), and the fact that this passage stands like an erratic block on the landscape of Romans indicates how little Paul wished to pursue such concepts.[23] Indeed the thrust of Romans 1–3 is not to identify common categories in which Judaism could be viewed alongside other cultural traditions, but precisely to demolish the religious and cultural claims of both Jews and Gentiles. Thus Paul operates a sort of negative universalism: his aim is not to subsume Judaism (or his Christian mutation of it) within Hellenistic moral or theological categories; rather, he assaults all contemporary cultures – Jewish or Gentile – with an antagonism scarcely less ferocious than that we have found in the Sibylline Oracles.

Thus, in the spectrum of voices we have heard from the Diaspora, it is those we have placed in the category of 'Cultural Antagonism' which most approximate to the character of Paul's theology. At certain points (notably Romans 1–2) Paul's writings are so close in expression to *The Wisdom of Solomon* (e.g. chapters 13–15) that his dependence on this document has often been suggested. Like *Wisdom*, Paul connects idolatry and immorality (Rom 1.18–32) and interprets humanity as divided between 'the sons of God' and the rest. But Paul is considerably less acculturated than the author(s) of *Wisdom*, whose stylistic sophistication and dualistic anthropology bear much closer comparison with Philo. Although the polemic against idolatry in *Wisdom* is more extended than any in Paul, it is also more subtle in noting different forms of non-Jewish cult; and although *Wisdom* knows of the devil (2.24) it lacks Paul's developed demonology. The most striking aspect of their difference is that Paul lacks any parallel to the divine 'Wisdom' which can be found by all who seek her (*Wisdom* 6–10). For Paul, Adam was not saved by Wisdom (*Wisdom* 10.1–2) but subjugated to the reign of death, from which only Christ can bring deliverance (Rom 5.12–21). Even if there are faint outlines of a universal salvation in Paul's thought (Rom 5.18; 11.32; 1 Cor 15.20–22), they are predicated on the notion that God's grace will reach a wholly powerless and disobedient humanity.

---

[23] Sanders' suggestion that Paul includes in Romans 2 'homiletic material from Diaspora Judaism' (1983:123–35) is unproven. But the awkwardness of this chapter in its context indicates how crude most of the rest of Paul's theology may have appeared by comparison to such culturally sensitive reflections.

There are many similarities between the conceptuality employed by Paul and that familiar to the author of 3 Maccabees: for both, 'Gentiles' are by definition 'lawless' and immoral. Like the author of that Maccabean novel, Paul understands the 'elect' to be threatened by a hostile world, for it is clear that he regards suffering and persecution as the norm (which he is surprised to find unrealized in Corinth).[24] Not unlike 3 Maccabees, he can interpret his converts' suffering as a sign of their salvation, and equally proof of the 'destruction' of their opponents (Phil 1.28). But Paul places such experiences into an apocalyptic framework in which the hostilities are given a theological rationale and viewed from a cosmic perspective. Apocalyptic turns his gaze continually to the future and it no longer matters to Paul if his churches are vindicated in the historical and political realm (as it mattered for the author of 3 Maccabees and his Jewish community in Egypt). Paul's *politeuma* is not in Alexandria (or any other city) but in heaven (Phil 3.20). What is more, its members are both Jews and Gentiles, whose common identity is defined not by the law but by their shared allegiance to Christ.

Here, then, we encounter the truly anomalous character of Paul. In his conceptuality Paul is most at home among the particularistic and least accommodated segments of the Diaspora; yet in his utilization of these concepts, and in his social practice, he shatters the ethnic mould in which that ideology was formed. He shows little inclination to forge any form of synthesis with his cultural environment, yet he employs the language of a culturally antagonistic Judaism to establish a new social entity which transgresses the boundaries of the Diaspora synagogues. By an extraordinary transference of ideology, Paul deracinates the most culturally conservative forms of Judaism in the Diaspora and uses them in the service of his largely Gentile communities.

It is hardly surprising that this anomalous Jew should meet both puzzled and hostile reactions in Diaspora synagogues. However scriptural he claimed his theology to be, and however much it was couched in traditional Jewish terminology, Paul's assimilating practices and his lax (or at least inconsistent) observance of the law earned him suspicion, opposition and even punishment in the synagogue. If Philo attacks those who abandon Jewish customs, and

---

[24] On the contrast between Corinth and Thessalonica in this regard see Barclay 1992b.

bears witness that the 'pure allegorists' were liable to criticism from 'the masses', it is understandable that Paul was frequently, as he put it, 'endangered' by Jews (2 Cor 11.26). He considered himself 'persecuted' because of his stance on circumcision (Gal 5.11; cf. 4.29; 6.12), and in one (disputed) passage he mentions being 'banished' by Jews and 'prevented from speaking to Gentiles' (1 Thess 2.15–16). We might be inclined to dismiss these comments as the product of paranoia were it not for the precise information in 2 Cor 11.24 that he had received on five occasions the synagogue discipline of the 39 lashes. That indicates that at least five times Paul was on trial in a synagogue, denounced as a sinner (LXX ἀσεβής) in the terms of the Deuteronomic warrant for this punishment (Deut 25.1–3).[25] Five times he was judged guilty, despite no doubt offering a robust defence. Such punishment represents the response of a synagogue to an erring member, not quite the expulsion and ostracism of one judged wholly apostate.[26] But if Paul continued in the practice which earned him this punishment, the synagogue authorities must eventually have decided to ostracize him (cf. 3 Maccabees 2.33 and 3.23). As a comparative newcomer to the synagogues he visited, and without a power-base in the Diaspora communities, Paul was in too weak a position to resist such repudiation.

The tensions created by this experience and by the anomaly of his own stance are reflected in Paul's varying descriptions of his identity. On occasions he proudly asserts his Jewishness, proclaiming himself a Hebrew, an Israelite and of the seed of Abraham (2 Cor 11.22). It is essential to his argument in Romans 11 that he is an Israelite, of the seed of Abraham and the tribe of Benjamin, and therefore part of that 'remnant' which ensures the continuity of God's dealings with his people (11.1). Yet elsewhere he talks of his *former* (not his present) life in Judaism (Gal 1.13–14), and in Phil 3.2–11 he lists his Jewish credentials only to declare them all 'loss', indeed 'dung', for the sake of knowing Christ. Obviously rhetorical factors influence such variant self-descriptions,[27] but they also reflect the turmoil into which he was thrown by his mission and its rejection in the synagogues.

---

[25] See Harvey 1985 and Gallas 1990.
[26] Sanders 1983:192; on expulsion, see Horbury 1985.
[27] See the full analysis by Niebuhr 1992.

It would have been natural for one so repudiated to cut all ties with the Jewish community. In fact, however, Paul kept returning to Diaspora synagogues, as is evidenced both by his *repeated* repudiation there and by the fact that, in his most extended reflection on the topic (Romans 9–11), he resolutely identifies himself with the Jewish people.[28] The anguish Paul expresses over the unbelief of fellow Jews is inexplicable unless it represents his dual sense of loyalty, both to the Jewish communities and to the churches of believers. Paul never lost his sense of belonging to, and even representing, the Jewish people and it was presumably this sense of loyalty which drew him back again and again to the synagogue. Unfortunately, his efforts to preserve his association there only strengthened the reaction against him. The more he identified with the synagogue and the more he defended there what he understood to be a new development of the Jewish tradition, the more dangerous he appeared. He was, in their eyes, not just an 'apostate' but one who led others astray, who 'taught apostasy from Moses' to the Jews who live among the Gentiles (Acts 21.21). The very fact that Paul could speak so persuasively in the traditional Jewish idiom, made him all the more insidious a foe to those who judged his teaching subversive.[29] The majority of Paul's Jewish contemporaries (both Christian and non-Christian) found his mutation of the Jewish tradition incomprehensible or unattractive.[30] The majority of his Gentile converts, and most subsequent readers of his letters, could only see their distance from, not their common destiny with, Jews. Thus, mostly unwittingly, Paul fostered the fateful division between Christianity and Judaism.

---

[28] It is sometimes argued (e.g. Sanders 1983:179–90) that Paul rarely attended synagogues, and that Acts invents such visits for its own theological purposes. While granting that Acts may exaggerate and over-schematize the facts, it is hard to understand how Paul could have run into trouble among Diaspora Jews so often unless he was known and treated as a synagogue member. Paul counts time in Sabbaths (1 Cor 16.2) and in relation to Jewish festivals (1 Cor 16.8), both of which suggest continuing association with the Jewish community.

[29] Cf. Segal 1990:125–26: 'Paul's peculiar combination of departure from Pharisaic Judaism and strenuous and public reliance on rabbinic method to demonstrate Christianity was a dangerous path to choose. It was bound to cause trouble in the Jewish community. It became even more dangerous because Paul insisted that he remained a Jew.'

[30] The opposition of Christian Jews is evident throughout Paul's letters, as well as (slightly muted) in Acts; see Lüdemann 1983.

# PART THREE

# JEWISH IDENTITY IN THE MEDITERRANEAN DIASPORA

# 14

## *Jewish Identity in the Diaspora: A Sketch*

Our studies of the Mediterranean Diaspora have illustrated the diverse conditions in which Diaspora Jews lived and the variety of ways in which they responded to those conditions. We have observed the distinct histories of Jewish communities in our five different locations (Egypt, Cyrenaica, Syria, Asia and Rome) and, in each location, the changes in circumstance over time. Political, social, economic and cultural factors have all been seen to influence the fortunes of Diaspora Jews. In political matters we have noted the varying relations of Jews with the Ptolemaic dynasty in Egypt, the effect of the Roman annexation of that land and the political tensions which destroyed the relative prosperity of Jews in Alexandria. We have also noted the variable relationships between Jews and Roman officials, who in some cases favoured their cause (e.g. Julius Caesar, most Roman governors in Asia and Antioch) and in some cases did not (e.g. Flaccus in Alexandria, Catullus in Cyrenaica). In social and economic affairs, we have noted the successful integration of Jews into Alexandrian society in the Hellenistic era but their alienation and marginalization at the end of our period in both Egypt and Cyrenaica. We have also traced the economic roots of the difficulties experienced by Jews in first century BCE Asia, but noted their success elsewhere and in other periods in gaining patronage and respect. Culturally, we have observed the varied influence on Jewish fortunes of Hellenistic pluralism, Egyptian hostility and the cultural conservatism of the Roman élite. Thus, there were no 'typical' Diaspora conditions. Understanding the social milieu of Diaspora Jews requires attention to each individual site and period as well as the peculiar circumstances of Jewish individuals and communities in each environment.

It is equally impossible to generalize about Jews' reactions to their Diaspora environments. As we have seen, the spectrum of social responses spreads all the way from total assimilation to near total isolation: at one end, a Tiberius Julius Alexander wholly integrated into the social life of the Roman world, at the other, one of the 'Therapeutae' meditating on the law in the monastic conditions described by Philo. In the literature which we have studied we have also found a rich diversity in the socio-cultural stances adopted by Diaspora Jews, some developing elements of convergence with their non-Jewish cultural milieu, others adopting a largely antagonistic stance. As circumstances differed, so did the reactions of the local Jews, but even in the same location and circumstance we have found Jews of different social levels and differing individual preferences giving widely divergent reactions. It is clear that in such matters no single Diaspora Jew could ever be taken as typical of all the rest.

Such an accent on diversity is consonant with dominant trends in the current study of Judaism, which properly reacts against the generalizations spawned by previous generations of scholars. The greater the precision in attention to detail, the more generalizations will appear impossible: if you look at a wood closely enough, you will find that every tree – indeed every leaf – is different. Yet it is possible to become mesmerized by such concentration on detail and so fail to see the landscape of the Diaspora in broader perspective. In particular, we have yet to explain what held Jews in the Diaspora together and what linked them to other Jews elsewhere and across time. Diversity is not the only characteristic of the Diaspora, and some explanation is required for the way that Jewish communities survived *as coherent and enduring entities*. What bound Jews together and prevented the disintegration of their communities? And what were the boundaries which made clear to themselves and to others the difference between a Jew and a non-Jew?

In this concluding chapter I wish to consider the elements which constituted Jewish identity in the Diaspora, risking for once combining evidence from varied times and places (though not totally ignoring local diversity). 'Jewish identity' is, of course, a multi-faceted phenomenon. Jews had (and have) a triple identity: how they viewed themselves, how they were viewed by other Jews and how they were viewed by outsiders.[1] Moreover, Jewish identity

---

[1]    Each of these, of course, includes many complexities. For instance, Herman 1977:30 (following D. Miller) notes the difference between objective public identity (how a person appears to others) and subjective public identity (how a person perceives his/her appearance to others).

could be presented differently according to context: conversation with fellow Jews is a different discourse from conversation with Gentiles, whose anticipated response might affect the presentation considerably. Such varying Jewish profiles do not necessarily represent different 'Judaisms': one and the same socio-religious phenomenon can wear many masks.[2] In his allegorical exegesis Philo can present Judaism in a mystic and philosophical guise quite different from that adopted in his political and apologetic presentation of Judaism; but Philo the politician recognized Philo the philosopher as authentically Jewish. He also recognized the literalist Jewish populace in Alexandria as fellow Jews even if he disdained them for their intellectual limitations. For all the diversity which we have noted in the Jewish Alexandrian literature, we have found no evidence of a splintering of the community along ideological lines, except perhaps in the double delegation to Claudius (chapter 3.1.2).[3] If Judaism is defined – as it should be – as a *social* and not just an *intellectual* phenomenon, it is hard to see how the plural 'Judaisms' could apply to the Diaspora.

In identifying the bonds which held Diaspora Jews together, we will find ourselves most confident at those points where the perceptions of 'outsiders' match those of 'insiders'. If non-Jews repeatedly commented on Jewish characteristics which were also held by Jews to be essential to their way of life, we can be sure that such items were indeed integral to the identity of Diaspora Jews. If it can be shown that the features we identify also functioned *in social reality* to clarify Jewish distinction, we can be further assured that we have located the critical phenomena.

[2] Thus, like Sanders 1990a:255–56 and Bauckham 1993, I find it neither necessary nor helpful to refer to 'Judaisms' (plural) in this period, at least in the Diaspora. Collins 1986 may mislead if his fine book gives the impression that 'national and political' Judaism was necessarily different *in social reality* from the Judaism defined as 'ethics', 'philosophy' or 'the mysteries of God'. Models drawn implicitly from Christian denominations or from contemporary varieties in Judaism may lead the historian astray at this point.

[3] Even the Leontopolis community does not seem to have functioned in opposition to, or disjunction from, other Jews; as we have seen (above pp. 37–38, 40 n. 64), Leontopolis Jews identified themselves readily with Jews in Alexandria and with the high-priest as the leader of Palestinian Jews. The tensions among Alexandrian Jews in 66 CE, and among Cyrenaean Jews in 70 CE, perhaps reflect differing social levels and expectations, comparable to the division in 41 CE which led to the double delegation to Claudius. Yet these are not clear evidence of substantially different 'Judaisms'.

This chapter is labelled a 'sketch' in two senses. In the first place, I can draw here only the outlines of a huge and complex reality which requires much further analysis and the inclusion of a wider range of evidence. But it is a 'sketch' also in the sense that, like every artist's impression, it is inevitably drawn from an individual perspective. Despite advances in historical knowledge of post-biblical Judaism, scholarship has yet to grapple fully with the problems inherent in describing its subject matter, which has been placed in many different frameworks, all potentially distorting. Whatever theological or anthropological categories we use – defining Judaism as 'covenantal nomism' (Sanders 1977), or by reference to its 'pillars' (Dunn 1991), or in terms of its 'stories, symbols and praxis' (Wright 1992) – the framework is likely to prove inadequate and open to challenge.

In every sketch certain lines define the shape of the picture. Here I wish to investigate first what I consider the core of Jewish identity in the Diaspora, the ethnic bond which held Diaspora Judaism together (14.1). I will then identify some social and symbolic 'resources' on which Diaspora Jews consistently drew (14.2), before concluding with investigation of the 'practical distinctions' which defined their social identity (14.3). Of course, as an interdependent social system, Diaspora Judaism defies all such categorizations. It was a complex tapestry, and while examining each thread separately we must take care not to obscure the interweaving of its multiple strands, which gave it its rich texture and composite strength.

## 14.1 The Ethnic Bond

The terms 'race' and 'ethnicity' have become problematic in the modern world, and their usage varies somewhat among contemporary social scientists (see Rex 1986). 'Race' normally draws attention to biological and genetic characteristics whose physical manifestations are often immutable. 'Ethnicity', where it is distinguished from 'race', typically takes into consideration the broader cultural features displayed by a kinship group, whose practice is a matter of choice not birth. In line with this usage, I here take 'ethnicity' to refer to a combination of kinship and custom, reflecting both shared genealogy and common behaviour. Thus, in asserting the significance of the 'ethnic bond', I am claiming that Jewish identity in the Diaspora was not merely a matter of ancestry nor simply a question of cultural practice but was based on a combination of these two interlocking factors.

It has been rightly observed that the Jewish tradition underwent an important development in the Hellenistic era, in which it became possible to define Judaism not simply as an ancestral trait but also as a 'mode of life' which could be voluntarily adopted or abandoned.[4] This change came about partly under the influence of Hellenism. If, within Hellenism, a 'Greek' could be defined more by language, education and life-style than by birth, it was possible for Hellenized Jews to portray Judaism also as a pattern of life, a *politeia*, rather than simply a trait determined by genealogy.[5] It was also in the Hellenistic era that there emerged two phenomena of some social significance. First, some Jews by birth assimilated to the non-Jewish world to the extent of abandoning Jewish customs. Dositheos, son of Drimylos, for instance, is recorded as being a 'Jew by birth' (τὸ γένος 'Ιουδαῖος) who 'changed his customs and abandoned his ancestral opinions' (μεταβαλὼν τὰ νόμιμα καὶ τῶν πατρίων δογμάτων ἀπηλλοτριωμένος, 3 Macc 1.3; see above, chapter 5.1). Secondly, besides the special case of the Idumaeans and Ituraeans, some individuals without Jewish ancestry joined themselves to the Jewish community to such a degree that it became possible to talk of such 'becoming Jews'. For instance, Josephus refers to Izates, king of Adiabene, deciding to get circumcised in order to be 'assuredly a Jew' (εἶναι βεβαίως 'Ιουδαῖος, *Ant* 20.38).[6]

---

4  See the suggestive comments by Schwartz 1992:5–15 and the careful analysis by Cohen 1990.

5  As Cohen 1990:218 demonstrates, in Jewish literature *politeia* can have a meaning much wider than 'constitution', embracing the social and political aspects of a 'way of life' or 'culture'.

6  At what point such adherents could be described as 'becoming Jews' seems to have varied in different cases and according to different perspectives. See the discussion of degrees of adherence to Judaism and the differences in depiction of such phenomena in Cohen 1989. Ethnicity can be (variously) ascribed as well as inherited. Kraemer 1989 has suggested that some inscriptions referring to 'Jews' could apply to merely 'Judaizing' Gentiles. There was, of course, a penumbra of Gentile 'sympathizers' who gave varying support to the Jewish community in social, political and religious matters (Siegert 1973; Cohen 1989). The existence of this phenomenon is clear enough in the sources, even if the precise terminology often associated with it (e.g. 'God-fearers') was not standardized until after our period (and perhaps not even then; see Reynolds & Tannenbaum 1987:48–66 on the θεοσεβεῖς in Aphrodisias, third century CE). At what point this interest and support could be considered significant enough to consititute entry into the Jewish community may not have been universally agreed, but Josephus indicates that some boundaries were drawn

If it was possible to be a Jew yet abandon one's heritage, or to be a non-Jew and yet somehow become one, the old one-to-one correspondence between the nation and the Jewish way of life could no longer hold.

Both Josephus and Philo were aware of this complexity. Josephus refers to the welcome which should be accorded to 'those who desire to live under the same laws as ourselves' since 'belonging together' (οἰκειότης) is 'not a matter of birth alone but also of choice of lifestyle' (*C Ap* 2.210). Similarly Philo, in discussing 'nobility' (εὐγένεια) in *Virt* 187–227, emphasizes the limited significance of ethnic descent: true nobility is a matter of the soul, not of inheritance (cf. *Praem* 152). There are hints that Roman authorities too were aware that Jewish descent did not necessarily correspond to observance of Jewish laws: references in some decrees to 'Jews who have and do Jewish customs' (e.g. *Ant* 14.234) seem to imply the existence of Jews who do *not* keep such customs (see above, chapter 11.1). Also, as Goodman has argued (1989; 1990a), the imposition of the *fiscus Iudaicus* in 70 CE and the disputes about its applicability in and after the reign of Domitian (see above, chapter 10.4) clarified the distinction between Jewish descent and Jewish practice: some Jews manifestly no longer practised Judaism and some non-Jews did. Subsequently, he suggests, Judaism was treated (at least by tax-collectors) as a religion and not simply as a matter of ancestry.[7] Perhaps other factors, like disputes over the identity of Jewish Christians, also clarified the distinction between ancestry and custom.

Nonetheless, although such a distinction could now be made, the evidence indicates that it was ethnicity – precisely the *combination* of ancestry and custom – which was the core of Jewish identity in the Diaspora. This can be shown by at least five strands of evidence: the 'ethnic' terminology typically employed by Diaspora Jews in describing themselves; Gentile perceptions of Jews

---

at this point (*C Ap* 2.209–10), and the Aphrodisias *stele* places proselytes, but not Gentile θεοσεβεῖς, among the Jews. As the Izates case indicates, circumcision was often considered the key entry requirement for men (see further below, 14.3.3).

[7]   Cf. Goodman 1994:120–28. His interesting suggestion is slightly marred by exaggerating this moment (the end of the first century CE) as the first point at which it became important for Jews to know who was really a fellow Jew. As we shall see (and as Goodman partially acknowledges, 1990a:194), well before this point Jews needed to know who was a Jew, at least for the purposes of marriage.

as an ethnic group; the thorough resocialization of proselytes who joined the Jewish community; the recognition of the importance of endogamy (marriage within the ethnic group); and the training of children in the Jewish way of life. We will briefly examine each of these in turn.

1. Almost all the literature from the Diaspora indicates the significance of the 'nation' as the bearer of the Jewish tradition. In 3 Maccabees, for instance, the prayers are full of references to the Jewish 'nation' (ἔθνος; φῦλον), 'race' (γένος) or 'people' (λαός), and throughout the narrative the distinction between Jews as 'fellow nationals' (ὁμοεθνεῖς and ὁμόφυλοι) and non-Jews as 'foreigners' (ἀλλοεθνεῖς and ἀλλόφυλοι) is spelled out in unambiguously ethnic terms. The same applies to *Joseph and Aseneth, The Wisdom of Solomon* (at least in its later chapters), *The Sibylline Oracles* and 4 Maccabees (see above, chapters 7.1, 7.3, 7.4, 12.3).

It may be no surprise that these documents, which we have found to be among the least accommodated of our Diaspora literature, should focus so explicitly on the ethnic characteristics of Judaism; such, after all, reflects the traditional ideology of the biblical text. What is more significant is that even comparatively acculturated and accommodated authors show that ethnicity is the core of their Jewish identity. Josephus, for instance, although he portrays Judaism as the supremely good *politeia* (*CAp* 2, *passim*), is consistent in his depiction of the Jews as members of a nation, who recognize fellow Jews as 'people of the same race' (ὁμόφυλοι) and non-Jews as 'people of other races' (ἀλλόφυλοι, ἀλλοεθνεῖς or ἀλλογενεῖς). To be sure, there may be some apologetic factors in this presentation of social reality: Josephus knew that Jewish practices were tolerated by the Romans only on the basis that they were 'ancestral customs' (τὰ πάτρια ἔθη), so it suited his purposes to present Judaism in largely ethnic terms. Yet few readers of Josephus' prologues will doubt that he speaks quite naturally of 'our ancestors' (*Ant* 1.9; cf. *Bell* 1.17) as a proud member of the Jewish people whose national history it is his business to record. Similarly, Ezekiel (the Tragedian), for all his Hellenistic sophistication, refers repeatedly to the Jews as a 'race' (γένος, lines 12, 35, 43 etc.) or 'people' (λαός, 107, 112 etc.) and to God as the God of their ancestors (104–8, 213 etc.). Even Aristobulus, while using (and perhaps preferring) the political metaphor of 'citizenship' (πολῖται, 12.1), proudly introduces Solomon as 'one of our ancestors' (12.11).

Philo's representation of Judaism is, as we have seen, double-sided (chapter 6.5). On the one hand, his allegorization of the text can de-Judaize its referents to the extent that the only γένος in view is the γένος of the whole human race; as a philosopher, he hints at a common standard of virtue which Jews and Gentiles together recognize and strive towards. Yet in his more literal renderings of the text, and in his apologetic and historical works, he is as resolute a defender of the Jewish nation (ἔθνος) as any other Diaspora Jew. He looks forward to the time when the fortunes of his nation will be restored, when other people will abandon their ancestral customs to adopt those of the Jews (*Mos* 2.43–44). Also, and significantly, while castigating those who have rejected the benefits of their Jewish birth, he hopes for their repentance and restoration: and the ground of his hope is not just the mercy of God but also the intercessory prayers of 'the founders of the nation' (ἀρχηγέται τοῦ ἔθνους, *Praem* 166).[8]

Of the works we have surveyed, the only ones where the ethnic dimension of Jewish identity largely disappears from sight are *The Letter of Aristeas* and Pseudo-Phocylides. It may be no accident that both of these are presented as the products of Gentile authors. As a collection of ethical maxims, Pseudo-Phocylides is naturally reticent about particular ethnic affiliations: it is a genre in which national identity is inevitably suppressed. In the case of *The Letter of Aristeas*, though the Jews are introduced as a γένος (6), the narrator, the high-priest and the king all refer to Eleazar's fellow-Jews as 'citizens' (πολῖται, 3, 36, 44, 126), and the metaphor may be carefully chosen to throw emphasis on the political and cultural, rather than the genealogical, aspects of Judaism. This is consistent with the fact that Aristeas proved to be one of the most accommodated of the Diaspora authors we surveyed.

Thus, with only occasional exceptions, all the Diaspora literature here analysed portrays Jews (past and present) as bound together by a common ethnicity. It is no accident that the leader of the Alexandrian community should be known as an ἐθνάρχης (Josephus, *Ant* 14.117) or that a Jewish inscription at Leontopolis should record an individual's leadership of the whole *ethnos* (ἀρχῇ

---

8   Similarly, the fact that Paul, despite his radical questioning of Jewish ethnic privileges, wrestles over the fate of his fellow Jews and retains the notion that God's elect people are beloved by God for the sake of the patriarchs (Rom 9.1–5; 11.1, 28) indicates how deeply ingrained is his sense of identification with his 'kin'.

πανδήμῳ ἐθνικῇ, Horbury & Noy 39);[9] similarly, in Rome, epitaphs praise the deceased for their love of 'the people' (*amor generis, CIJ* 146; φιλόλαος, *CIJ* 203). The description of Jewish loyalty in such ethnic terms seems to have come readily to mind.

2. Equally significant is the consistency with which non-Jewish authors and authorities refer to Judaism as an ethnic entity. A few examples may suffice to illustrate the point. Among Greek writers, Strabo refers to the spread of the Jewish 'tribe' (φῦλον) throughout the world (*apud* Josephus, *Ant* 14.115); among Romans, Cicero speaks of them as a *natio* (*De Provinciis Consularibus* 5.10) and Seneca (*apud* Augustine, *De Civitate Dei* 6.11) and Tacitus (*Hist* 5.4.1) as a *gens*. In imposing the tax payable to the *fiscus Iudaicus* after 70 CE, the Romans identified all Jews throughout the empire with the Judaeans they had just defeated: it was, as Suetonius remarks, a tax on the whole *gens* (*Domitian* 12.2). As we have noted, Domitian's rigorous extraction of the tax brought to light the fact that some Jews by descent were no longer practising Judaism, while some non-Jews were. But it seems that these 'anomalies' never undermined the fundamental assumption that Judaism was at core an ethnic tradition. In the third century CE Dio Cassius noted that 'people of other races' (ἀλλοεθνεῖς) could be called 'Jews' through imitating Jewish customs; yet he still refers to the Jewish people as a γένος and implies that their customs are to be understood as an ethnic, and not merely a religious, peculiarity (37.17.1–2).

This last point was, indeed, a crucial aspect of the Jews' relationship to Roman (and Greek) political authorities. Whenever the rights of Jews to assemble, to celebrate the Sabbath or to send money to Jerusalem were challenged, the basis of their appeal, and the grounds on which it was granted, was the right to practise their 'ancestral customs' (τὰ πάτρια ἔθη) or to live in accordance with their 'ancestral laws' (οἱ πάτριοι νόμοι). For instance, a survey of the decrees relating to Asia (see above, chapter 9) would indicate that, apart from some references to Jewish 'superstition' (*Ant* 14.232), the majority of judgments refer to 'ancestral' laws or customs (e.g. *Ant* 14.235, 258, 260, 263). We should note the force of the epithet πάτριος in such cases: it indicates what is hereditary, what is passed down from one's ancestors, what is embedded in

---

[9] For an alternative, though less plausible, interpretation see Lüderitz 1994:208–10.

one's familial and ethnic tradition. Indeed the notion of 'ancestral customs' precisely encapsulates that combination of kinship and custom which we have taken to define ethnicity. It was on this basis that the Romans respected Jewish peculiarities and privileges, on the principle that time-honoured ethnic practices should never be disturbed.[10]

3. Thus internal and external sources agree in depicting Judaism as primarily an ethnic tradition. A further indication of the significance of 'ethnicity' is that when non-Jews adopted Judaism as proselytes they underwent such a thorough resocialization as to acquire in effect a new 'ethnicity' in kinship and custom. If Diaspora Judaism had attracted large numbers of proselytes who had retained their previous ethnic identities, its own ethnicity would have been diluted and perhaps destroyed. The number of proselytes is in fact notoriously difficult to assess, and many different estimates have been offered.[11] But whatever the statistical facts, what is significant is that, on conversion, the identity of proselytes was so thoroughly redefined as to transfer them, practically speaking, into the Jewish nation. When Philo describes the process of conversion, he indicates that 'incomers' (προσήλυτοι, or, more often, ἐπήλυται) come over to a new and better *politeia* (*Spec Leg* 1.51; *Virt* 108, 175) by virtue of the fact that they renounce their previous customs, with all their 'mythical' and 'idolatrous' associations (*Spec Leg* 1.309; 4.178; *Virt* 102, 211–22; cf. *Mos* 2.44). It is particularly noticeable in this regard that he emphasizes the social dislocation which such a 'conversion' entails. Converts abandon their families and friends and all the social ties which had encouraged their former 'error' (*Spec Leg* 1.52; *Virt* 178) by a transference of loyalties which is bound to make their families hostile (*Spec Leg* 4.178). For this reason Philo notes the special care which Moses commands to be accorded to such people, who are not only to be taught better customs and rules for their moral

---

[10] Cf. the terms of Claudius' statements in the Alexandrian decree, *CPJ* 153, lines 85–86; *Ant* 19.283–4, 290. See further Rajak 1984 and 1985.

[11] Feldman 1993:288–341 presents the maximal case, which is of varied strength (arguments from numerical increase in the Jewish population being particularly precarious). On proselytes in Rome, and the difficulty in assessing their numbers, see above chapter 10.3 and p. 317 n. 89. An emerging new consensus questions whether Judaism is rightly to be considered a 'missionary' religion (e.g. McKnight 1991 and Goodman 1994), though here the definition of 'missionary' partly determines the conclusions drawn.

transformation (*Quaest Exod* 2.2; *Virt* 180–86), but are also to be welcomed as members of the Jewish community with equal rights (*Spec Leg* 1.51–53), as sharers in its joys and griefs (*Virt* 103). When Philo urges that incomers be accorded alternative citizenship, family and friendship (μὴ ἀμοιρείτωσαν ἑτέρων πόλεων καὶ οἰκείων καὶ φίλων, *Spec Leg* 1.52; cf. *Virt* 103) he interprets the biblical legislation to imply the provision of a new kinship as well as a new culture.

The same is implied in other Diaspora literature.[12] As we saw in our analysis of *Joseph and Aseneth*, Aseneth's conversion is presented as a thoroughgoing deracination, an abandonment of her Egyptian identity and a social realignment so complete as to lose (in theory) her ties with family and friends (see above, chapter 7.3). It is possible, of course, that this picture is rhetorically overdrawn (and the narrative indicates continuing support from her family), but, at least for this author, conversion entails a radical change from her previous status as an 'alien' (ἀλλοτρία). Much the same emerges from Josephus' only extended description of proselytism, his account of the conversion of the royal house of Adiabene (*Ant* 20.17–96). Here he depicts Izates contemplating circumcision, knowing that his subjects would take it ill if their ruler practised 'strange and foreign customs'; circumcision would render him 'assuredly a Jew' (βεβαίως Ἰουδαῖος) and thus a foreigner to his compatriots (*Ant* 20.38–39). It is clear that 'becoming a Jew' means far more than adopting certain religious customs: it entails a complete realignment of social commitments, which in this case at least had significant political implications. Josephus records the political and economic aid given by Izates and Helena to the people of Judaea (e.g. *Ant* 20.49–53); some members of the royal family even fought with Judaeans in the Jewish War (*Bell* 2.520; 6.356). His references to such converts as 'kinsmen' (ὁμόφυλοι, *Bell* 2.388) indicate how fully he considers them to have been integrated into the Jewish nation.

The social and cultural redefinition of a proselyte's identity is mirrored in the hostile comments of Juvenal and Tacitus. Juvenal complains that circumcised converts become accustomed to 'despise Roman laws' in their transition to the Jewish law (*Romanas*

---

[12] Inscriptions relating to proselytes indicate that some went so far as to change their names on conversion: see e.g. Sara a proselyte in Cyrene (Lüderitz 12) and Veturia Paulla, renamed Sara in Rome (*CIJ* 523).

*autem soliti contemnere leges / Iudaicum ediscunt et servant ac metuunt ius*, 14.100–101); the transition here from 'Roman' to 'Jewish' signals his perception of a cultural change so great as to alter the convert's ethnic loyalties. The same is evident in Tacitus' particularly venomous comments on the 'scoundrels' who 'abandon their ancestral religious customs' (*spretis religionibus patriis*) and learn at once to 'despise the Gods, shed their patriotic loyalties and treat their parents, children and siblings as of no account' (*contemnere deos, exuere patriam, parentes liberos fratres vilia habere, Hist* 5.5.1–2). The association of religion, family and patriotism indicates Tacitus' perception of their radical shift in kinship and cultural affiliation.

Thus, although Gentiles could adopt Jewish practices to varying degrees, some with little practical difference to their ethnic identity, it is clear that 'to Judaize' (ἰουδαΐζειν) could entail, at its greatest level of commitment, much more significant change than its nearest equivalent, 'to Greekize' (*Graecari*).[13] Similarly, 'Judaism' ('Ιουδαϊσμός) is much closer to an ethnic descriptor than its supposed equivalent 'Hellenism' (Ἑλληνισμός). Where we find the term 'Judaism' in our sources (2 Macc 2.21; 8.1; 14.38; 4 Macc 4.26; Gal 1.13–14; *CIJ* 537, 694), the context makes clear that the term denotes no mere cultural life-pattern cut loose from kinship associations; it represents, as Paul says, commitment to *ancestral traditions* (Gal 1.14) whose principal carrier is the Jewish nation.[14]

4. In this connection we should note the concern among Diaspora Jews to keep marriage bonds within the nation, or at least to accept only Gentiles committed to join it. The ban on exogamy was founded on several passages in the Pentateuch (Gen 34; Exod 34.15–16; Num 25; Deut 7.1–4) which were interpreted in a broad sense to refer to all Gentiles.[15] Of course there were cases when Jews did marry Gentile spouses (see the examples collected above, chapter 5.1 and 11.1). But the sensitivity of Diaspora Jews on this matter is evident not only in *Joseph and Aseneth* (which could be

---

[13] See Yavetz 1993:17.

[14] See Amir 1984, who considers that for a Jew in the Hellenistic world 'his Judaism united him with the other members of his ethnic group within invisible boundaries which divided an inner region of the world from an external one' (40).

[15] Cf. Ezra 9–10 and Tobit 4.12–13. On the processes of interpretation here see Cohen 1983.

dismissed as extreme) but also in the careful depiction of Moses' marriage by Demetrius (fragment 3, Eusebius, *Praep Evang* 9.29.1), and in Philo's comments on the corrupting influence of exogamy (*Spec Leg* 3.29). There are also several statements on this matter by Josephus, who highlights Solomon's transgression of Moses' law which 'prohibited marriage with those of other races' (*Ant* 8.191) and elsewhere notes that the law forbids Jews to have intercourse with 'foreign women' (*Ant* 12.187). Josephus also gives a lengthy description of the disaster brought about by the Midianite women (Num 25; *Ant* 4.131–55) and comments negatively both on Anilaeus' marriage to a Gentile (*Ant* 18.340–52) and on Drusilla's marriage to Felix (*Ant* 20.141–43).

In this matter, as in others, some Diaspora Jews were more assimilated than others, but it seems that mixed marriage was generally discouraged. Tacitus supports this conclusion with his (hostile) observation that Jews 'sleep apart' and 'refrain from intercourse with foreign women' (*discreti cubilibus ... alienarum concubitu abstinent, Hist* 5.5.2). It is obvious that the preservation of the Jewish tradition owed much to this effort to keep the nation 'pure' (*nostrum genus permansit purum*, Josephus, *C Ap* 2.69). Sociological studies of the effects of exogamy in contemporary Jewish communities have shown time and again its debilitating effect on Jewish affiliation in the immediate or the following generation,[16] and Philo and Josephus understood this well enough.

We should note in this context the importance of circumcision, though its connection to this topic is rarely noticed. One of the most important functions of circumcision was in identifying with whom a Jewess may have sexual intercourse. A foundational text here was the story of Dinah and the Shechemites (Gen 34): that makes clear that Dinah could not be married to a man with a foreskin (Gen 34.14), while if the Shechemites were to institute circumcision they could freely intermarry, and could count as members of the same race (34.15–16).[17] In line with this tradition, Josephus records examples of Gentile men who were required to get circumcised and adopt Jewish ways before marrying members of the Herodian family (*Ant* 20.139, 145–46). The social function of circumcision is made explicit in Josephus' remark that it was instituted to prevent Abraham's offspring from mixing with others

---

[16] See e.g. Ellman 1987, among many others.

[17] This story and the significance of circumcision is commented on extensively in the fragments of Theodotus (*apud* Eusebius, *Praep Evang* 9.22.1–11).

(*Ant* 1.192). It fulfilled this function by making it taboo for Jewish women to receive from an uncircumcised man what Philo calls 'alien seed' (*Quaest Gen* 3.61). As Esther (in the Greek version) suggests, Jewish girls were taught to shudder at the thought of a sexual encounter with an uncircumcised man (Add Esther 4.17u).

Such a taboo would obviously most affect Jewish women, though there may also have been some sense that the daughters of Gentile men were tainted by their fathers' uncircumcision and thus 'out of bounds' for Jewish youths (see e.g. Gen 34.16 and Judg 14.3).[18] In any case, the issue of exogamy was more critical in the case of Jewish girls since in pre-Mishnaic Judaism (as Cohen 1986 has argued) the offspring followed the ethnic status of the father rather than the mother. Thus the greatest responsibility for the ethnic continuity of Judaism lay with Jewish girls (or rather, their fathers, who preserved their virginity and arranged their marriages). Since circumcision was, in most contexts, a uniquely Jewish practice (see below, 14.3.3), the insistence on circumcised partners played a crucial role in keeping the nation 'pure'.[19]

5. Finally, we may note the importance of the socializing of children within the Jewish tradition, a task which ensured that Judaism would be continued as an ethnic phenomenon. The education of children was already emphasized in the Pentateuch (e.g. Deut 6.6–7, 20–25; 11.19; 31.10–13) and it features prominently among the concerns of later rabbinic Judaism.[20] In the Diaspora literature, family solidarity is an important feature of 4 Maccabees, undergirded by the father's teaching of his sons (4 Macc 18.10–19: instruction in law and prophets, singing of psalms and reciting of proverbs).[21] Philo indicates that synagogue instruction in the law (on which see below, 14.2.3) was passed on by Jewish men to their wives, children and slaves (*Hyp* 7.14) and he also mentions, as a matter taken for granted, that Jews have been trained 'from a

---

[18] See also Philo, *Legatio* 72 on the importance of marriage ties in binding families together socially.

[19] We do not need to imagine premarital inspection of prospective bridegrooms(!): in most contexts it could be taken for granted that men were uncircumcised unless they had immediate Jewish ancestry.

[20] See e.g. Safrai 1976 and Yarbrough 1993:41–49, the latter with a large range of evidence.

[21] Cf. Susannah 3: her parents had taught her 'in accordance with the laws of Moses.'

very early age' to honour the One God and to observe the laws (e.g. *Legatio* 115, 195, 210; *Praem* 162; *Spec Leg* 1.314; 2.88; 4.149–50; cf. *Mos* 1.31–33). Indeed he speaks of the laws and the 'ancestral customs' as 'engraved' on the soul of every young Jew (*Legatio* 210; *Spec Leg* 4.149; cf. 2.228).

Children's education is a matter of pride also to Josephus. He lists among Jewish boasts their 'training of children' (παιδοτροφία, *C Ap* 1.60; cf. Paul in Rom 2.20) and indicates how in the customs of the home, from infancy upwards, children learn to obey the law in all its practical details (*C Ap* 2.173–74). Like Philo, he claims that the result is the 'engraving' of the law on Jewish souls (*C Ap* 2.178). He also describes more formal education in which Jewish children learn to read and are instructed in 'the laws and the deeds of their forefathers' (*C Ap* 2.204). The celebration of festivals in the homes of Diaspora Jews must also have provided opportunities for the induction of the next generation into the lore of the nation.

Such investment of effort in the home indicates the assumption that those of Jewish ancestry will be the principal bearers of their customs and culture for the future, even if they are augmented by 'incomers' to some degree. As Goodenough commented, Jews in the Diaspora were less concerned with theological orthodoxy than with the social requirement that members of the community be 'propagating Jews' (Goodenough 2.290), raising the next generation as practising Jews who in turn would do the same for their offspring. The success of Jewish families in this regard ensured that ethnic bonds constituted the core of Jewish identity through all the centuries we have surveyed.

## 14.2 Social and Symbolic Resources

We have considered thus far the central thread of Jewish identity in the Diaspora. However, its strength lay in the fact that it was closely interwoven with other supporting strands. These we must now explore as we examine the chief social and symbolic resources on which Diaspora Jews drew in affirming their identity. Among the social resources we must consider first the local community of Jews, then, at a wider level, the networks which joined Jews in diverse communities together. A special category here is the association of the Diaspora with the temple and the 'homeland', whose significance requires careful assessment. Besides such social resources, certain symbolic resources deserve attention, notably the Law (or Scriptures) and the figure of Moses.

## 14.2.1 The Local Community[22]

It is impossible to generalize about the shape and size of local communities of Diaspora Jews, which differed from place to place and changed over time. Some gathered enough resources to build their own προσεύχαι ('prayer houses'), others appear to have met more informally in the open air or in private houses. Some were formally consitituted with ἄρχοντες, πρεσβύτεροι, ἀρχισυνάγωγοι and a range of other officials (Schürer 3.92–102), others may have developed nothing like this degree of institutionalization (our literary and epigraphic evidence only records the most organized communities). As we have seen (above, pp. 25–27), some appear to represent local concentrations of Jews in streets and sections of towns, while others may have drawn together Jews whose living conditions were more isolated. At its lowest level 'community' meant merely the informal recognition by Jews that it was helpful to associate with one another in social, economic and political affairs; at its highest it entailed legally constituted entities which we find operating their own courts, keeping their own archives, managing their own catacombs, maintaining their own buildings, electing their own officials, voting their own decrees, and negotiating with civic authorities over their communal rights (see above, chapters 2–3, 8–10).

How individual Jews related to other Jews in their locality cannot now be traced in full, and must have varied according to local conditions and individual inclinations. However, we may suggest that in general the greater the range and permanence of local expressions of community, the stronger was the support available for such Jews who wished to maintain their Jewish identity. Thus, for instance, the physical and financial commitments involved in constructing a *proseuche* must in themselves have strengthened the ties of association for local Jews. Similarly, the availability of official

---

[22] For the significance of the family, the most basic unit of social support for Diaspora Jews, see above pp. 410–13 and, in general, Cohen 1993a. The legal and constitutional aspects of Diaspora communities are discussed in Juster 1914:1.409–85, Applebaum 1974 and Schürer 3.107–25. Lüderitz 1994 has questioned the common assumption that the term πολίτευμα was typically used for Jewish communities, which probably went under different names in different locations and historical periods.

(often honorific) positions within the community served to crystallize the commitments of wealthier Jewish families, whose patronage surely established social and economic networks among local Jews. The organization of community gatherings for meals, festivals and fasts, and the establishment of decision-making bodies which regulated community affairs, also served to reinforce, on a regular basis, the sense of Jewish belonging. In particular, we may trace the significance of three aspects of Jewish communal life which bound local Jews together in religious, social and financial affairs:[23]

1) *Festivals and Fasts.* We hear of special local festivals celebrated by the Jewish community in Alexandria, both in commemoration of the translation of the law (Philo, *Mos* 2.41–43) and in celebration of deliverance from persecution (3 Macc 6.30–36; Josephus, *C Ap* 2.55). However, such Alexandrian (and no doubt other local) specialities only supplemented the main festivals of the Jewish calendar, which seem to have been observed throughout the Diaspora. Besides general references to feasts (Josephus, *Ant* 14.257–58; 16.27, 45; cf. Gal 4.10; Col 2.16), our sources indicate the particular significance of Passover, Tabernacles and the Day of Atonement.[24]

The *Passover* (with its peculiarly Jewish name, τὸ πάσχα) is attested in a wide range of sources in our period (and before it, at Elephantine, *CAP* 21). It is central to the religion of Aristobulus (fragment 1), and through its association with the Exodus it features prominently in Ezekiel's play as 'the beginning of months and seasons' (192; cf. *Wisdom of Solomon* 18.9). In line with the terms of its institution, it may have been a purely domestic celebration (outwith Jerusalem), its 'hymns and prayers' (Philo, *Spec Leg* 2.145–49) a family event.[25] Even so, fixing its date and the preparations for such a celebration were shared experiences in the community

---

[23] For common meals (associated with Sabbaths or festivals?) see Josephus, *Ant* 14.214–15; 16.164 (reading ἀνδρῶνος); *CPJ* 139.

[24] Note also the evidence for celebrations of the new moon: Philo, *Spec Leg* 2.140–44; Lüderitz 70 and 71; Col 2.16; Epistle to Diognetus 4.1, 5; see Thornton 1989.

[25] Our sources might indicate that, despite Deut 16.1–8, Jews in the Diaspora actually sacrificed animals in their homes at Passover (Philo, *Spec Leg* 2.145; *Mos* 2.232; Josephus, *Ant* 14.260); see Sanders 1992:133–34. On the celebration of Passover and Pentecost at a later date in Hierapolis (Asia) see *CIJ* 777. For Passover as a time of pilgrimage, see below, 14.2.2.

as a whole, binding its constituent families together. It was certainly well enough known in Rome for Tacitus to comment on it (*Hist* 5.4.3). The feast of *Tabernacles* (known to Plutarch, *Quaest Conviv* 4.6.2) was even more clearly a public and community event, well attested in Egypt (*CPJ* 452a; Philo, *Flacc* 116–18) and the occasion of a meeting of the *politeuma* in Cyrene (Lüderitz 71). Finally, the *Day of Atonement* appears to have been taken very seriously in the Diaspora communities: it is attested in Delos (*CIJ* 725) and treated with awe by Josephus (*Ant* 3.240–43) and Philo (*Spec Leg* 2.193–203).[26] Josephus suggests that it was well enough known to be imitated by non-Jews (*C Ap* 2.282), and Philo indicates that, like today, Jews who were otherwise non-observant held this day in particular regard (*Spec Leg* 1.186).

These annual Jewish observances enabled Diaspora Jews to express their solidarity with one another on occasions of celebration or religious awe which answered to deep human needs. Their attractiveness to non-Jews (attested by Philo, Josephus, Paul and in later evidence of Gentile Christian 'Judaizing') indicates how prominent such events could be.[27] As a counterpart to the calendar of Gentile religion, Jewish festivals and fasts afforded Diaspora Jews an alternative identity, which was reinforced with sufficient frequency to secure its endurance through all kinds of circumstance (Philo, *Flacc* 116–18).

2) *Sabbath Gatherings.* We shall have more to say about the Sabbath as a 'Jewish distinctive' below (14.3.4), but here we may note the importance of the weekly gatherings in the life of the local community. Philo suggests that in Alexandria such meetings were attended more by men than by women or children (*Hyp* 7.14), but women were clearly present (and honoured with official positions) elsewhere.[28] Such regular association was of immense social significance. Despite some claims to the contrary, it is likely that the Sabbath 'prayer-house' meetings included elements of prayer and worship,[29] but this was combined with an activity given

---

[26] Other fasts could be called as occasion demanded: see e.g. Josephus, *Vita* 290–95 for a special fast day in Tiberias.

[27] E.g. Philo, *Mos* 2.41–43; Josephus, *C Ap* 2.282; Paul in Gal 4.10; Col 2.16. For later Judaizing by Gentile Christians see Wilson 1992.

[28] See Brooten 1982 and Kraemer 1992:106–7.

[29] McKay 1994 questions the existence of Sabbath *worship*, and rightly notes the limited evidence on this topic. However, some elements of Sabbath worship are suggested by: i) the association between Sabbaths and 'religious rites' and

greater emphasis by Philo and Josephus: communal instruction in the law. It was for Philo a proud boast (and one of the chief purposes of the Sabbath) that every seven days Jews gathered in their 'prayer-houses' to hear the law expounded. By such instruction in their 'ancestral philosophy', he insists, Jews were equipped for life-long and steadfast observance of their customs (*Legatio* 156–57 [Rome], 312–13 [Asia]; *Somn* 2.127; *Hyp* 7.11–12 [Egypt]; *Mos* 2.216; *Spec Leg* 2.62–63 ['in every city']; *Probus* 81–82 [Essenes]; *Vit Cont* 30–33 [Therapeutae]). Such passages suggest that this regular instruction played a crucial role in legitimizing the Jewish way of life and socializing its adherents. Josephus strengthens that impression by referring to such Sabbath instruction as the opportunity for Jews to 'gain thorough and accurate knowledge' of their legislation (*C Ap* 2.175), enabling them to avoid transgression (*Ant* 16.43). The number of occasions on which Sabbath instruction features in the New Testament (e.g. Mark 1.21–22; Luke 4.16ff.; Acts 13.42; 15.21; 17.2; 18.4) reinforces our sense of the ubiquity of this custom and its importance in Jewish social life. Such regular gatherings bound the community together in common loyalty to their distinctive way of life.

3) *Collections of Temple Dues.* The financial organization of local Jewish communities no doubt varied according to their size (and degree of investment in buildings) and may have concerned mainly a few wealthy families. In one matter, however, all communities were engaged in financial arrangements which involved every adult male: the annual collection for the Jerusalem temple. The liability of each Jewish male to pay the 'half-shekel' tax was established on the basis of Exod 30.11–16, and there is good evidence that the collection of this money, supplemented by extra donations from the wealthy, was scrupulously undertaken by Diaspora communities. As we have seen (chapter 8.1 and 9), the collection and dispatch of this money caused political difficulties for the communities in Cyrenaica (Josephus, *Ant* 16.169–70) and Asia (Cicero, *Pro Flacco* 28.66–69; Josephus, *Ant* 16.162–68, 171–73 etc.), and their struggle

---

'prayers' in Josephus, *Ant* 14.245, 258; ii) Ovid's references to *culta septima*, *Ars Amatoria* 1.76, 416; iii) the special Sabbath worship evidenced at Qumran (4Q504; see McKay 1994:51–56); iv) the multiple evidence that prayer took place in synagogues on many occasions (e.g. Matt 6.5; Josephus, *Vita* 290–95; Philo, *Flacc* 121–24); and v) the general likelihood that the most important weekly gatherings in a 'prayer-house' would include prayers.

to win their 'rights' in this regard indicates how important this tradition had become. Elsewhere, the collection of dues was less problematic and faithfully fulfilled: Philo attests to its significance in Egypt (*Spec Leg* 1.76–78) and Rome (*Legatio* 157, 291, 312–13) and notes the convoys which brought the collected revenues from the Eastern Diaspora (*Legatio* 216; cf. Josephus, *Ant* 18.312–13). In fact, the general observance of this 'ancestral custom' in the Diaspora is attested by the Roman assumption that all Jews were liable to contribute – hence their diversion of the temple tax into the *fiscus Iudaicus* after the destruction of the Jerusalem temple.

As Philo attests, the collection of this money had, for the individuals concerned, a vital religious meaning: the money constituted for each man a 'ransom for his soul' (λύτρα τῆς ψυχῆς αὐτοῦ, Exod 30.12) and was contributed in the belief that it would bring physical or social 'salvation' (*Spec Leg* 1.77–78). But as the same passage makes clear, it also helped bind each individual contributor to the local community. The money was apparently given at various times during the year and deposited in a communal bank, from which the annual total was drawn and transported to Jerusalem. In this way the local community acted as the broker of Jewish commitment to the temple (on which see below, 14.2.2), with every financial contribution serving to reinforce the individual's sense of belonging to a local social unit. The fact that this tax involved not only rich benefactors but every adult male ensured that this financial bond tied all the families of the community together. When, after 71 CE, the tax was transmuted into contributions for the *fiscus Iudaicus*, it became necessary for every individual, man, woman and child, to be publicly identified as a 'Jew'. The stigma was unwelcome, but it served to make Jews ever conscious of their social and political distinction in the Roman empire.[30]

## 14.2.2 Links with Jerusalem, the 'Homeland' and other Diaspora Communities

Discussion of the temple tax has highlighted an important aspect of Diaspora identity: the link with Jerusalem. The practical and symbolic value of this link must now be assessed, as the most important factor connecting Diaspora Jews with their 'homeland'. But we may also note other types of contact with Jews elsewhere in the Diaspora, which helped to reinforce Diaspora Jewish identity.

---

[30] See further Goodman 1989 on the social effects of the *fiscus Iudaicus*.

1) *The Diaspora and the Temple.* We have just noted the importance of the annual collection of dues for the temple, for which the Jewish communities were well known (Tacitus, *Hist* 5.5.1). As well as the 'half-shekel' tax (interpreted in Egypt as equivalent to 8 drachmae), we know of other gifts, both great and small, which Diaspora Jews contributed to the temple. Among the large-scale offerings we hear of donations from the Adiabene royal family (Josephus, *Ant* 20.49–50; *Bell* 4.567; 5.55 etc.), from a certain Nicanor from Egypt (b Yoma 38a) and from Alexander the Alabarch (Josephus, *Bell* 5.201–5). We hear by chance that Fulvia, a wealthy proselyte in Rome, was induced to donate expensive materials to the temple (Josephus, *Ant* 18.82), and that case may indicate that wealthy Jews in the Diaspora, unable to display their benefactions in local temples, commonly sent prestigious gifts to Jerusalem. Smaller gifts may be indicated by obscure references to 'first-fruits', which may sometimes refer to extra Diaspora donations (Philo, *Mos* 1.254; *Spec Leg* 1.153–54; in Egypt the Romans extracted a 1-drachma supplement of 'first-fruits' for the *fiscus Iudaicus*).[31]

Closely associated with such gifts were the pilgrimages for the major festivals (Passover, Pentecost and Tabernacles), when the safe passage of the money was ensured by large convoys travelling from all parts of the Diaspora. The fact that, each year, tens of thousands of Diaspora Jews flocked to Jerusalem on such festival occasions indicates the strength of the magnetic field established by the temple: Jews (both male and female) were drawn there from all points of the compass,[32] and even those who were unable to travel (for reasons of expense, age or infirmity) can scarcely have been unaffected by the departure of those who conveyed their money to its sacred destination. We cannot tell what percentage of Diaspora Jews ever visited Jerusalem, or how frequently (Philo only lets out in passing that he has been there, *Prov* 2.64), but the uniqueness for Jews of the Jerusalem temple ('one temple for the one God', Philo, *Spec Leg* 1.67; Josephus, *C Ap* 2.193) suggests that its symbolic value was powerful even when its impact on daily life was weak.[33]

---

[31] Cf. Josephus, *Ant* 18.313 and see on this topic Sanders 1990a:295–99.

[32] Cf. Acts 2.5–11; 6.9 and the collection of evidence in Jeremias 1969:62–71, relating to both pilgrimage and long-term residence in Jerusalem by Diaspora Jews. On women pilgrims see *Bell* 5.199.

[33] Attachment to the Jerusalem temple was one of the key factors distinguishing 'Jews' from 'Samaritans'. The significance of this distinction in Alexandria is hinted at in Josephus, *Ant* 13.74–79; we can only speculate on its practical effect on relations between Jews and Samaritans who lived in close proximity elsewhere (e.g. in Delos and Thessalonica).

Diaspora literature of varying hues shows a deep respect for the sanctity of the temple. Aristeas (83–120) depicts the beauties of Jerusalem and the perfections of the temple in lyric prose, with much embellishment of reality. For him, as for Josephus and Philo, it mattered greatly that important monarchs had graced the temple with their benefactions and thereby honoured the whole Jewish people (cf. Josephus, *Ant* 13.242; Philo, *Legatio* 157). Both 3 Maccabees and the Sibylline Oracles affirm God's special protection of his chosen city, and the Oracles look forward to a new and glorified temple as the climax of history (see above, chapter 7.4). Although Philo can provide allegorical interpretations of the temple and its sacrifices, and is anxious to dispel the impression that good sacrifice makes up for a bad soul (e.g. *Mos* 2.107–8), he defends the special holiness of the temple in its literal sense against pure allegorists (*Migr Abr* 92). Indeed his commitment to it, and its symbolic value to the whole Diaspora, is evident in the horror with which he greeted the news that Gaius intended to 'defile' it with his statue (*Legatio* 184ff.). Philo considers the possible fate of the temple much more important than the grievances of Alexandrian Jews (*Legatio* 193–94): he cannot imagine any greater disaster for Jews throughout the world than that the temple should be thus defiled (*Legatio* 198).

It is legitimate to enquire how deep and how universal was this 'zeal for the temple' (*Legatio* 212) in the light of the existence of an alternative temple in Leontopolis and the fact that few Diaspora Jews hurried to defend Jerusalem in 70 CE. Moreover, Diaspora Judaism by no means collapsed when the temple was destroyed. In fact, the Leontopolis edifice, if it served as an alternative, had a limited sphere of influence even in Egypt (it appears to go unmentioned in Egyptian Jewish literature). As for the defence of Jerusalem, its fate was perhaps sealed too quickly by a siege which allowed none to enter from outside, though there clearly was a possibility of military support from the Eastern Diaspora (Josephus, *Bell* 1.5). That Diaspora Judaism survived the destruction of the temple indicates the strength of its other resources; and that it continued in most respects unchanged suggests that the temple had always been of greater symbolic than practical significance. Few if any aspects of Diaspora Jewish life had been governed by Jerusalem priests,[34] and the symbolic functions of the temple could

---

[34] See Sanders 1990a:255–57, against a common older view, as represented by Safrai 1974 (using later rabbinic sources quite uncritically) and Hegermann

be continued in nostalgia (Josephus, *C Ap* 2.102–9, 193–98), in hopes for its restoration (possibly a motivating factor in the Diaspora Revolt), or, diffused, in a residual orientation to 'the homeland'. This latter demands separate treatment.

2) *The Diaspora and 'the homeland'*. Social and political links between the Diaspora and Palestine can be documented easily enough, though it is harder to assess what place Palestine held in the affections of Diaspora Jews. Our survey of the history of Egyptian Jews (chapters 2 and 3) noted the refugees, traders and slaves who travelled between Egypt and Palestine, besides the influence of the Maccabean events on Egyptian Jews, and the involvement of Palestinian Jews in the political disturbances of 41 and 70 CE. We may also note here Palestinian literature introduced into Egypt (e.g. the translation of Sirach and the Greek version of Esther) and letters requesting observance of Palestinian festivals (2 Macc 1.1–9; the colophon of Greek Esther). Syrian Jews also retained close connections with Palestine, the geographical proximity ensuring a continual passage of personnel. Jews in more remote Diaspora locations had less opportunity for contact with Palestinian affairs, though the regular pilgrimages (noted above) and the special religious and educational activities in Jerusalem preserved social contact for as long as the temple stood. In Rome special factors prevailed: the presence of members of the Herodian family and the influx of large numbers of Palestinian slaves ensured that the Roman Jewish population was never out of touch with Palestinian affairs. The interest of Roman Jews in the succession to Herod and the pretender Alexander shows the strength of these connections (Josephus, *Ant* 17.300, 324–31). In general, since Rome was the legal and political centre of the empire, it was easier for Roman Jews to remain in touch with Palestine than for Jews in many other parts of the Diaspora, such as Asia, Cyrene or Greece.

How important, however, was Palestine as the 'holy land' or 'homeland' for Diaspora Jews? The centrality of the land and the hope of return from 'Diaspora' are clearly enough expressed in the Scriptures which were read and studied in Diaspora synagogues

---

1989:155: 'Jews in the Diaspora continued to take their bearings from the religious authorities in Jerusalem.' Priests in the Diaspora, whose marriages were recorded in Jerusalem (Josephus, *C Ap* 1.32–33), were perhaps an exception in this regard.

everywhere. The annual celebration of Passover and the regular pilgrimages would also reinforce the special value of the promised land. Indeed, the Jews' very name ('Ιουδαῖοι) linked them to the land ('Ιουδαία) from which they could be thought to derive.[35] It is therefore no surprise to find Diaspora literature expressing a strong emotional attachment to the land. Even such an Egyptianized author as Artapanus refers to Palestine as the Jews' 'ancient homeland' (27.21), while Ezekiel recounts the Exodus as the return of the Jews to 'their own land' (167). For the Jewish Sibyl, Judaea is a glorious and 'holy' land (e.g. 5.281, 328–32), while in *The Wisdom of Solomon* it is sacred territory, the most precious of all to God (12.3, 7). For Philo also, Palestine is 'holy' (e.g. *Heres* 293; *Legatio* 202, 205, 330) and Jerusalem the 'mothercity' (μητρόπολις) from which the whole Diaspora traces its origin (*Flacc* 45–46; cf. Josephus, *Ant* 3.245; *Bell* 7.375).

But precisely these passages indicate that an emotional attachment to 'the motherland' did not preclude for Diaspora Jews a strong sense of rootedness in their present environment, and even a pride that Jews had proved so numerous and successful as to spread throughout the world. In *Flacc* 45–46 (cf. *Legatio* 281–83; *Mos* 2.232) Philo represents the Diaspora as the dispatch of colonies from an overcrowded homeland, and defends the rights of Jews to consider their new locations their 'fatherland' (πατρίς; cf. *CPJ* 151). Apologetic considerations no doubt played some part in this representation of affairs, but it would be a mistake to conclude that Philo here masks his real feelings. To be sure, he hopes for an eventual return to the homeland, in accordance with the scriptural promise (*Praem* 162–72), but he is realistic enough to treat such notions as a distant hope (cf. *Mos* 2.43; *Quaest Exod* 2.76). In the meantime he belongs to 'our Alexandria' (*Legatio* 150) as much as to Jerusalem, and he defends the notion of Jewish 'double citizenship' (*Legatio* 157).

Van Unnik (1993) was correct to insist that the term 'Diaspora' generally retained a negative valence from its Scriptural association with judgment and its connotation of divine 'scattering'. But not all Diaspora Jews employed this term to characterize their present condition. Those with shallow roots in their present environment eagerly awaited the promised return to the 'holy land' (e.g. *Sib Or*

---

[35] Later synagogues were physically orientated towards Jerusalem and their prayers expressive of its special place in Jewish piety; to what degree this was true in our time-period we cannot tell.

5.260–85) and understood their present condition as 'sojourning' in an 'alien' land (e.g. 3 Macc 6.3, 10, 15, 36; 7.19).[36] Those who were more deeply embedded celebrated their 'colonizing' as a political achievement and considered the whole world as their *eternal* home (Josephus, *Ant* 4.115–16)! Thus, while for most Diaspora Jews 'the holy land' retained some religious significance, the strength of their attachment to Palestine as 'home' probably varied in accordance with their social and political conditions.

3) *Contacts around the Diaspora.* When the Jerusalem temple drew Jewish pilgrims from all over the Diaspora, it also introduced them to each other as fellow members of an international *ethnos*. Both Philo (*Spec Leg* 1.69–70) and Josephus (*Ant* 4.203–4) comment on the friendships forged in the convivial atmosphere of Jerusalem festivals, and such international assemblies must have made as large an impact on participant Jews as modern gatherings of Muslims in Mecca. Even the collection of temple revenues in provincial centres, and the passage of pilgrims on their way to Jerusalem, must have done much to connect Diaspora Jews with one another across national boundaries.

The international contacts of Diaspora Jews were, indeed, an important resource on several counts. On a personal level, the ability to find lodging and trading-partners for travelling Jews fostered an important sense of mutual dependence (e.g. Paul and two Jewish leather-workers in Corinth, Acts 18.2–3). In a Mediterranean world full of dealers, merchants, delegates and myriad other travellers, the ability of Jews to recognize one another as 'fellow nationals' helped connect communities in widely separated locations. In the political sphere such links could count for much: according to Cicero (*Pro Flacco* 28.66), Jews in Rome were prepared to agitate on behalf of Asian Jews, who later probably aided one another in their appeals to Roman governors. Agrippa I (Philo, *Legatio* 261ff.) and Josephus dedicated time and skills on behalf of fellow Jews throughout the Diaspora. For such diplomacy, aristocratic families with their international contacts proved immensely important: Philo's family, the Herodian royals and the Adiabene dynasties are obvious cases in point. Such social networks, though merely hinted at by our sources, operated the levers of power in the Roman world.

---

[36] For the significance of the hope for return from the Diaspora as the 'imaginative preparation' for the Diaspora Revolt see Horbury forthcoming.

At a broader level, the willingness of Jews to band together militarily is impressive evidence of their social cohesion. When Claudius complains that Egyptian Jews from the *chora* are interfering in Alexandrian affairs (*CPJ* 153), we sense the crossing by Jews of that otherwise stubborn social barrier between city- and country-dwellers. The co-operation among Jews in the Syrian cities affected by the crisis of 66 CE is also notable. Most dramatic, however, is the unity of purpose in the Diaspora Revolt, which appears to have joined Jews in Cyrenaica, Egypt and Cyprus in a common cause. Here, as in other respects, the unity of Diaspora Jews was a function not of sameness but of interdependence. For all their diversity, Diaspora Jews recognized one another as working for a common purpose, whether that entailed struggling for their civic rights, or, more fundamentally, fighting for their lives.

## 14.2.3 The Law/Jewish Scriptures

Every year the people of Alexandria witnessed a celebration unique among the multifarious festivals of the Graeco-Roman world. On a certain day a large Jewish crowd (with non-Jewish onlookers) crossed to the island of Pharos, site of the famous lighthouse, for a mass picnic on the beach. The rationale for this event was what constituted its peculiarity: it was to celebrate the rendering into Greek of the Jewish Scriptures. According to legend, Pharos was the place where the translation had been made, a location whose symbolism was easily exploited: here Jews honoured 'that place in which the light of that translation first shone out, thanking God for his gift, old yet ever new' (Philo, *Mos* 2.41). Never before in the history of religion had a *translation* been the focus of such religious celebration. It was only among Jews that written documents were accorded such direct revelatory significance, and only among Diaspora Jews, unable to read their original script, that their Greek version could be the object of such respect.[37]

A community celebrates what it honours, and honours what it needs. The annual pilgrimage to Pharos is but one example of the dependence of Diaspora Jews on their key religious resource, their written 'constitution'. A visitor to the synagogue in Ostia (first

---

[37] The variant legends about the production of this translation attest to its living significance among Diaspora Jews: Aristeas' version is largely repeated by Josephus (*Ant* 12.11ff.), while another is recorded by Philo (*Mos* 2.25ff.).

century CE) would draw the same conclusion from the prominence accorded to 'the ark of the holy law' (Noy 22–24). Roman writers knew about Moses' 'arcane book' (Juvenal, *Sat* 14.101–2) and those who planned Titus' triumphal procession were correct in placing as the final and climactic 'spoil' a copy of the Jewish Scriptures (Josephus, *Bell* 7.150). Throughout the Diaspora, from Alexandria to Ostia, and from the synagogue in Caesarea (Josephus, *Bell* 2.291) to the 'amphitheatre' in Berenice (Lüderitz 70–71), the Jewish communities looked to their 'holy books' for instruction in their distinctive way of life.

Both Josephus (*Ant* 3.223) and Philo (*Legatio* 210) record the widespread Jewish conviction that their laws were given by God, and Philo even suggests that the LXX was written under divine dictation (*Mos* 2.37). For Aristobulus, the descent of God at Sinai to give the law was a moment of the greatest theological significance (fragment 2). As we have seen (chapter 6.4; 6.5.3), the long allegorical tradition which we can trace from Aristobulus to Philo is predicated on the supreme authority, accuracy and profundity of the Scriptures, most especially the five books of Moses. In the other authors we have examined we have often had cause to mention their dependence on the Septuagint (Ezekiel, *Wisdom of Solomon*, Pseudo-Phocylides, even Artapanus); it constitutes the basis for much of their own narrative or instruction. Philo's 'oracles of God' are as unquestionable as the Sibyl's 'holy laws', despite the social and cultural gulf which separates the two authors. From this common scriptural quarry many different edifices could be built, representing divergent interests in history, law or philosophy. The range of interpretative constructions surveyed in our studies of Diaspora authors indicates the extraordinary adaptability of this biblical material. Whether as legislation, mystery, constitution, philosophy, founding legend or moral guide, the Jewish Scriptures were integral to all the social and intellectual achievements of Diaspora Judaism.

We have already had occasion to note the seriousness with which Diaspora communities treated instruction in the law, both in the home and in the weekly Sabbath gatherings. It was Josephus' special boast that, by contrast to other nations, the Jews were uniquely well versed in their 'ancestral constitution', which was engraved on their hearts by both practice and precept (*CAp* 2.171–78). In its regulation of home life and in its status as focus of discourse at the Sabbath assemblies, the law was indeed imprinted deep onto the lives and minds of Diaspora Jews, and it is not surprising to find Seneca complain that, by contrast to the ignorance of the Roman populace, Jews seem to be well informed about the rationale for their pattern of life (*apud* Augustine, *De Civitate Dei* 6.11). Such familiarity goes a long way to explain the peculiar tenacity with which Jews preserved their way of life through the centuries, in varied social and geographical contexts. As Philo commented, 'everyone guards their own customs, but this is especially true of the Jewish nation' (*Legatio* 210). Of course, both he and Josephus minimize, for rhetorical reasons, the degree of transgression by individuals (*Legatio* 211; Josephus, *C Ap* 2.82, 149, 176–78), but it would be hard to deny that, *in general* and *as communities,* Jews in the Mediterranean Diaspora successfully preserved the distinctive customs which were enshrined in their law. The public unrest in Egypt at the undermining of the Sabbath (Philo, *Somn* 2.123ff.), the spirited defence of Jewish customs against obstructive civic authorities in Cyrenaica and Asia, the refusal to collect the corn dole on the Sabbath in Rome – above all, the consistency with which Jews throughout the Diaspora were recognized (and abused) for their distinctive traits – these all indicate that Josephus' claim of unflinching loyalty to the law was not an empty boast (*C Ap* 2.271–78).

## 14.2.4 The Figure of Moses

If the law was the focal point of Diaspora Judaism, it was natural that Jews should find their identity defined by Moses, the man believed to be its human author and the figure most prominent in its narratives. In Moses Diaspora Jews discerned the skills of a lawgiver (comparable to Solon, Lycurgus or Minos of Crete), the profundity of a philosopher (like Pythagoras or Plato) and the nobility of a king (combining multiple Hellenistic ideals). As Philo's *Vita Mosis* displays, his character could in fact be made to shine with all the glory of an idealized Jewish Hellenism. Correspondingly, non-Jews would identify Moses as the figure most responsible for the Judaism they observed, admiring or vilifying him according to their response to that Judaism (Gager 1972). Thus for both Jews and Gentiles, much was at stake in the characterization of this representative figure.

Jews and non-Jews identified Moses as the author of the law (Pentateuch), and hence the 'legislator' of the Jewish nation.[38] The

---

[38] For Moses as author of the law in Philo, see Amir 1983:77–106. The identification of text and author is strong enough to make Moses the author even of the account of his death (Philo, *Mos* 2.290–91; cf. Josephus, *Ant* 4.326).

law is simply 'the law of Moses' and it is 'Moses' who is read each
Sabbath in the synagogues (Acts 15.21). For Juvenal, what proselytes
learn is 'Moses' arcane book' (*Sat* 14.101–2) and he can be
popularly portrayed, bearded, with a book in his hands (Diodorus
34.1.3). As author, Moses is preeminently the law-giver and, as far
as Josephus is concerned, the finest law-giver in the history of
humanity: not only did he create the best 'constitution' (πολιτεία)
ever devised, he also designed the most effective method of
instruction for the whole nation (*C Ap* 2.151ff.). Josephus knew
that among non-Jews Moses' laws had a mixed reputation: some
accorded him recognition as a 'wise' lawgiver, others traced what
they despised in Judaism to Moses' 'malicious' influence (Gager
1972:25–112). It was therefore necessary to take every opportunity
to praise him in praising 'his' Judaism.

For those of an intellectual bent, Moses' books were more than
simply a legislative code. It was important to Philo (*Mos* 2.51–52;
*Op Mund* 1–3) and to Josephus (*Ant* 1.18–26) that Moses began
with a depiction of creation: that indicated the cosmic scope of
his subject and the harmony between nature and the law. This
suggested that his contribution was as much philosophical as legal,
and by the application of allegorical techniques Moses could indeed
be given a truly philosophical voice. We have traced above, in
commenting on Aristobulus and Philo, the significance of 'Mosaic
philosophy' for such Hellenized intellectuals, for whom Moses'
historical antiquity even suggested that he was the font of all that
was true in the Greek philosophical tradition. Philo's works indicate
the depth of engagement which Moses' philosophy could attract
and the height of admiration in which he was held. As we have
seen, Philo is unendingly amazed at the profundity which his own
ingenious mind 'discovers' in Moses.

But the Mosaic books are not only *by* Moses: they are also largely
*about* him, since he features in them as national hero to a far greater
degree than any other individual. The biblical stories, embellished
by a rich tradition of legend (Philo, *Mos* 1.4), portrayed so many
facets of Moses' virtues, that almost every ideal could be illustrated
by some aspect of his life. The laconic account of his youth lent
itself to imaginative reconstructions of his charmed life in the
Egyptian palace. His confrontation with Pharaoh and the Egyptian
'magicians' suggested a miracle-worker capable of changing the
course of nature. His military role at the Red Sea and in the battles
in the desert prompted admiration of a supreme military
commander. His ascent of Sinai to receive the law invited his

portrayal as a mystic and mystagogue with unusually direct access to God. His establishment of Israel's cult secured his reputation as the supreme priest. These and many other flattering labels (inventor, judge, king and seer) cluster around Moses in the multiple Diaspora portraits of his life, sometimes mixed as in Artapanus' racy narrative, sometimes neatly packaged as in Philo's four-part presentation of his hero.[39] Indeed, in Philo (*Mos* 1.27; *Sacr* 9–10 etc.), and in Ezekiel's vision of Moses' enthronement (68–89) Moses comes as close to 'divinity' as it is possible to imagine in Jewish authors committed to maintain the clear distinction between humanity and God.

Once again, the background to such eulogies of Moses is the denigration of his reputation among some non-Jews. The Egyptian counter-myths of the Exodus presented Moses as leper and blasphemer, and Moses' miracles were vulnerable to representation as magical deceit. The tradition of anti-Mosaic slanders stretches from Manetho to Tacitus, through such masters of defamation as Lysimachus and Apion (Gager 1972:113–33). Moses' reputation thus became a rhetorical battle-ground on which opposing sides fought over the character of the Jewish nation and the quality of the Jewish laws. For better or worse, Jews were followers of Moses: in the competitive environment of Graeco-Roman religion his positive presentation could significantly enhance their social and cultural pride.

## 14.3 Practical Distinctions

Thus far we have assessed the significance of the ethnic bond as the core of Diaspora Judaism, and highlighted certain social resources and religious symbols which, woven around that core, gave it strength and stability. In this final part of my sketch, I wish to highlight four features of the Jewish pattern of life which, by their regular practice, marked off Diaspora Jews from their neighbours and thus gave definition to Jewish identity. Not *every* Jewish distinctive was of sufficient public importance to make a noticeable social impact. We know that Jews (uniquely) disapproved

---

[39] As king, law-giver, priest and prophet, *Mos* books 1 and 2. Surveys of Philo's and Josephus' presentation of Moses may be found in e.g. Meeks 1967:100–46 and Feldman 1993:243–85.

of abortion (Josephus, *C Ap* 2.202), but such a stance was unlikely to affect relations with non-Jews to a significant degree. What we need to isolate here are those practices in which Jewish difference was visible, habitual and of social importance, and I shall argue that that was supremely true of Jewish cultic abstention, separatism at meals, male circumcision and Sabbath observance. Even if Jews were not, as a rule, *immediately* recognizable in public, social acquaintance would soon reveal their identity on these four counts (three for women) – provided, of course, they were faithful to the Jewish tradition.[40] Here again, the congruence of 'insider' and 'outsider' perspectives demonstrates the importance of each of these Jewish characteristics.

## 14.3.1 Rejection of Alien, Pluralist and Iconic Cult

To define Jewish religious distinction simply as adherence to 'monotheism' seems inadequate on a number of grounds. The term 'monotheism' places the emphasis on a concept – the belief that there is one, and only one, being rightly called 'God' – and obscures the significance of *cultic practice* in defining acceptable or unacceptable religion. While Philo could go to some lengths to define Jewish monotheism conceptually (*Op Mund* 170–72), even he was occasionally loose in his use of the term θεός (e.g. in reference to the sky and stars, *Aet* 10, 20, 46–47). What concerned him (and *a fortiori* less intellectual Jews) was not nomenclature so much as the *worship* of beings other than the one, invisible Deity (e.g. *Decal* 52–65). Moreover, Jews were not alone in asserting the governance of the universe by One God, yet in practice few Jews would join in Gentile cult addressed to the One God, nor would they contemplate worshipping the One God with the aid of images. Jewish distinction thus has to be defined more precisely, and in

---

[40] Cohen 1993b has questioned the possibility of recognizing Jews in public, but most of his points concern *immediate* recognition, and he underplays the role of social networks in revealing an individual's habitual patterns of behaviour. Also, while none of the following four features were decisive identifiers on their own (Cohen notes that not every circumcised man was a Jew), cumulatively they marked the boundaries between Jews and non-Jews clearly enough. We need not discuss again those Jews who abandoned some or all of these distinctive markers (see above, on 'High Assimilation', chapters 5.1 and 11.1); what follows is what was true in general of the majority of Diaspora Jews. Delling 1987:9–18 surveys these issues and notes the corresponding charges of Jewish ἀμιξία.

negative terms, as the rejection of alien, pluralist and iconic cult. We shall examine each of these facets in turn.

1) *Rejection of Alien Cult.* The *Letter of Aristeas* adopts, as we have seen (chapter 6.3), an eirenic attitude towards non-Jews, whom it represents as honouring the God whose providence brings benefits to all humanity. Yet Jewish distinction is make unmistakably clear in a trenchant passage which contrasts Jews with 'the rest of humankind', who believe there are many Gods, make images of wood or stone, create absurd mythologies or (in Egyptian fashion) worship animals (*Letter of Aristeas* 134–38). What does this 'grapeshot' denunciation of non-Jewish religion signify? That Moses 'hedged us about with impenetrable fences and iron walls, to prevent us mixing in any way with people of other nations, being preserved pure in body and soul, separated from false beliefs, honouring the one God who is powerful above the whole creation' (139; see the discussion above, pp. 145–48). What is striking here is the parallel between 'people of other nations' and 'false beliefs'. It is simply assumed that the religion of 'others' is wrong, both in theology and cult, and that Jewish integrity demands at this point clear lines of demarcation. Only Jews can be trusted to worship the One God correctly.

Here Aristeas is in tune with the biblical tradition in which Jews are warned away from 'other nations' and 'their Gods' (e.g. Deut 6.14; 12.30–31; 29.17, 25). The biblical demand for 'monolatry' (worship of Israel's God alone), while it could be explained in philosophical terms, remained powerful in the simplicity of its criterion: Jews may worship God only according to Jewish tradition.[41] In some Diaspora literature, God is identified specifically as 'the God of Israel' or 'the ancestral God' (e.g. 3 Macc 5.13; 7.16; 4 Macc 12.17; Ezekiel 213; *Joseph and Aseneth* 7.5; 11.10). Correspondingly, Josephus characterizes the rejection of Judaism by Jews as 'sacrifice *in Greek fashion*' (*Bell* 7.50) or as revering *others'* Gods (*Ant* 4.137–38). It would not matter how sophisticatedly monotheistic was the conception of the God thus worshipped: what mattered was that it was an *alien* cult.

Philo occasionally acknowledges that others have a correct conception of God (*Virt* 65; *Spec Leg* 2.165), yet he refuses to accept

---

[41] On this biblical tradition, and its developments in other definitions of idolatry, see Halbertal & Margalit 1992.

the validity of their cult. In the latter passage he credits to all, Greek and barbarian, recognition of the supreme, invisible 'father of Gods and men', yet he immediately convicts all non-Jews of honouring 'created Gods' (*Spec Leg* 2.165–66). If only Jews can correct this error, only the Jewish temple can be regarded as sacred to the One God. Both Philo (*Spec Leg* 1.67) and Josephus (*C Ap* 2.193) affirm that there is only 'one temple for the One God'; were that defiled, Philo argues, there would be left no trace of the reverence paid to the one true God (*Legatio* 347). For all his capacity for abstraction, Philo cannot regard what goes on elsewhere as proper worship.

Such rejection of 'alien cult' did not have to be voiced in aggressive terms to be perceived by non-Jews as intolerance. Egyptian resentment of the fact that Jews disdained their cult is reflected in legends of Moses' iconoclasm (e.g. Lysimachus *apud* Josephus, *C Ap* 1.309), and it is clear that the LXX translation of Exod 22.27 ('you shall not disdain [others'] Gods') was framed to minimize conflict on this score.[42] Josephus admits that Jews have a reputation for 'slighting the Divinity which others claim to honour' (*Ant* 3.179), and that may be confirmed by the critical comments of Claudius (*Ant* 19.290) and Pliny (13.46, *contumelia numinum insignis*). Charges of religious exclusivity thus arise quite naturally: Josephus imagines the complaints of the Midianites, and reports those of Apion and the Ionians, that the Jews refuse to worship the same Gods as the rest of humanity (*Ant* 4.137–38; 12.126; *C Ap* 2.65–67; cf. 2.79, 117). It was a charge that Jews could not deny and struggled to empty of its 'anti-social' implications.

2) *Rejection of Pluralist Cult.* The rejection of alien cult was not, of course, without its rationale. Most prominent in this regard was the Jewish critique of the worship of many, or 'created', Gods. Gentile polytheism was not simply an intellectual error (the false belief that there was more than one God); it was also an insult to the true God that worship should be offered to what were, at most, his agents and subordinates (Philo, *Conf* 168–73). In this regard, Jews could adopt a stance of philosophical purism (cf. Josephus' *purissima pietas*, *C Ap* 2.82), insisting on the unity, singleness and uniqueness of the Divine. Such could be expressed with varying

---

[42] Philo cites this verse (*Quaest Exod* 2.5) to counter accusations that the Law breaks down the customs of others; cf. *Mos* 2.205; *Spec Leg* 1.53. Josephus employs it for a similarly apologetic purpose, *C Ap* 2.237; cf. *Ant* 4.207.

degrees of sophistication, ranging from the simple slogan of the *Shema'* to Philo's philosophical expositions of the Monad. Although Jews stood here on common ground with most philosophers, it was of immense importance that this stance enabled them to reject both Graeco-Roman mythology and the practice of Graeco-Roman cult, both of which were irreducibly polytheistic.

In criticizing the immoral and cantankerous divinities of myth (e.g. Josephus, *C Ap* 2.239–54), Jews could also castigate Gentiles for worshipping created things, for it was evident to Philo (and affirmed by at least some Greeks) that the Gods depicted in the myths and worshipped in popular cult represented the elements of the universe (*Decal* 52–65; *Spec Leg* 1.12–20). The rebuke of such 'nature worship' articulated by Philo and by *The Wisdom of Solomon* (13.1–9) could highlight the incongruity of worshipping the creation rather than the creator. But its real target was the worship of Apollo, Poseidon, Hera, Demeter and the like, whose very plurality (corresponding to the many natural elements) constituted, in Jewish eyes, a confusion of the truth.

It is significant that in his list of 'nature' deities (*Decal* 52–57) Philo does not include the name of Zeus. Zeus constituted, in a sense, an embarrassment and a temptation for Jews, for in the worship of this supreme God it was possible to find a Gentile parallel to Jewish monotheism. As we have seen, Aristeas has a Gentile reckon that what the Jews worship as God is what Greeks call Zeus (16), while Aristobulus, more cautiously, deletes the name of Zeus from his citation of Aratus, preferring to substitute 'God' (fragment 4). Other Gods, of course, could also be deemed 'solo' and 'supreme', and it was not always easy for Jews to retain a linguistic and conceptual distinction in their monotheism. Once again, what mattered was cultic practice, and since it was rare for non-Jews to restrict their worship to one cult, all could be castigated as 'polytheists' whatever they understood their worship to mean. The counter charges of 'atheism' and 'impiety' are only what should be expected from Gentiles who found their multiform religiosity categorically rejected.[43]

---

[43]  For charges of 'atheism' see e.g. Apollonius Molon *apud* Josephus, *C Ap* 2.148 and the survey by Fascher 1963. References to 'impious Jews' during the Diaspora revolt (e.g. *CPJ* 438) no doubt referred to their iconoclastic activities, but may be rooted in broader perceptions. See further Bickerman 1988:243–56.

3) *Rejection of Iconic Cult.* This third strand of religious distinction is closely interwoven with the others, insofar as alien polytheistic cult was typically adorned with visual representations of the Divine. The ban on images in the second commandment (Exod 20.4–6; Deut 5.8–10) could be variously interpreted by Jews: as a global ban on images for any purpose, or as relating only to the use of images *in worship,* as applying only to sculpture and statue or as covering also painting and other figurative art.[44] In general it appears that the greatest sensitivity was aroused by the proximity of images to worship, with the temple and the 'holy city' of Jerusalem arousing deepest anxiety.[45] In the Diaspora we hear no complaints about images on coins, but the introduction of the emperor's statue into Alexandrian synagogues is considered the grossest defilement (chapter 3.1.1).

What mattered for Jewish self-definition was the ubiquity of statues and figurines in non-Jewish cult, and criticism of such images is a regular theme in Diaspora literature. The most extended polemic is found in *Wisdom of Solomon* 13.10–15.17, whose link between 'idolatry' and 'immorality' is reproduced also by Paul (Romans 1.18–32). Similar, though less extended, scorn is expressed in *The Letter of Aristeas* 135 and by Josephus (*C Ap* 2.73–78, 190–92). We have already noted the visceral disgust with 'Egyptian idols' in *Joseph and Aseneth* (chapter 7.3), which is matched by verbal assaults on all Gentile 'idolatry' in the Egyptian Sibylline Oracles (3.8–45, 545–600 etc.; 5.75–85, 351–60 etc.). Philo has the fullest philosophical critique of visible representations of God, which obscure, he insists, the character of God as incorporeal, invisible and uncreated (*Leg All* 3.36; *Post* 165–69; *Decal* 66–76 etc.).

In the polemic against representation of God in human (or animal) form, Diaspora Jews could confidently assert their moral and intellectual superiority over 'cruder' forms of religion. In return, their imageless cult was interpreted by non-Jews as worship

---

[44] There are well-known disparities between the rabbinic ban on images and the frequent use of paint and mosaic images in later synagogues (especially in Galilee and Dura Europos); these may in fact represent variant interpretations of this command (cf. Tatum 1986). Philo takes the ban to cover painting (*Ebr* 108–1C: *Heres* 168–70; *Spec Leg* 1.28–31 etc.), whereas Josephus seems concerned only with the plastic arts.

[45] The controversy surrounding Herod's eagle on the temple gate (*Ant* 17.149–63) indicates that there was no unanimity even among Jerusalemites over the implications of the commandment; Agrippa's statues in his Tiberias palace (*Vita* 65) may have been of concern to very few.

of the sky or clouds (Hecataeus *apud* Diodorus 40.3.4; Juvenal, *Sat* 14.97; Strabo 16.35; Petronius frag. 37 etc.). More seriously, the refusal to include cultic images was potentially of the greatest political embarrassment in relation to the imperial cult. Gaius' reign (37–41 CE) first raised this problem to crisis level, both in Alexandria (when imperial statues were maliciously placed in synagogues) and in Syria/Palestine, where the Jamnia incident and the threat of the statue in the temple gave this issue the widest possible publicity (see chapter 3.1 and 8.2.2 respectively). Jewish resistance to Gaius revealed the world-wide solidarity of the Jewish nation, and made a sufficient impression on Claudius to win imperial permission for their peculiarity on this score (Josephus, *Ant* 19.284–85). Nonetheless, Jews remained vulnerable to suspicion as politically disloyal (Josephus, *C Ap* 2.73). Even those, like Tacitus, who admired the purity of an imageless cult, could still exploit this point (*non Caesaribus honor, Hist* 5.5.4).

## 14.3.2 Separatism at Meals

In the Graeco-Roman world many ethnic groups retained customs banning foods of one kind of another, typically certain meats.[46] However, the intellectual atmosphere of the Hellenistic age made it increasingly necessary to justify such taboos (lest they appear merely superstitious), and the cosmopolitan ethos of the cities (at least among the élite) made it difficult to preserve separatist customs. It was precisely here that an important Jewish distinctive made itself felt.

The Jewish 'constitution', read and expounded each week in the synagogues, contained explicit prohibitions of certain foodstuffs. The lists of forbidden foods (Lev 11 and Deut 14, modernized in the LXX version), are explained by Aristeas (142–71) and Philo (*Spec Leg* 4.95–131), while pork, their most awkward item, became the subject of frequent comment by Gentiles. The biblical ban on the eating of blood (trapped in strangulated carcasses, e.g. Deut 12.16, 23–24) is less easily traced in our literature, though it makes an appearance in Acts 15.20, 29 and *Joseph and Aseneth* 8.5 (cf. Philo, *Spec Leg* 4.122–23).[47] More generally,

---

[46] This is one of the main topics in Plutarch's *Quaestiones Conviviales*, in which Jewish dietary laws are discussed alongside those of other nations; the Egyptians were notorious for their fussiness on this score. Cf. also *The Letter of Aristeas* 128; Philo, *Legatio* 361–62; Erotianus fragment (= Stern 196).

[47] On this topic see especially Sanders 1990a:278–79.

the biblical narratives (e.g. Exod 32; Num 25) reflect uneasiness about the association between food and 'idolatry', and, given the frequency of meals in temples and the common association between food and sacrifice (even in private homes), it was natural that the Jewish stance against 'alien cult' (see above) should spill over into rejection of 'tarnished' foodstuffs.[48] Our evidence indicates that this wariness could include Gentile wine (commonly offered in libations) and even, at least in Syria, Gentile oil.[49]

Such restrictive customs were not observed by all Diaspora Jews. It was not always possible to obtain foodstuffs entirely free of suspicion, if, for instance, the civic authorities were uncooperative (Josephus, *Ant* 14.245(?), 261) or if Jews had to live off army rations (*Ant* 14.226). More generally, in the pressure towards assimilation, the dietary taboos must have been among the first to be discarded, in whole or in part. It was possible for Jews to eat with Gentiles without transgressing their laws if, for instance, Jews were the hosts, or brought their own food to Gentile homes, or ate only certain foods from the fare provided by Gentiles, or if the normal libations were dispensed with.[50] But given the requirement of *reciprocity* in giving and receiving hospitality, it was hardly possible to cement friendships without accepting Gentile invitations, and choosing separate or select food did not accord with common notions of sociability. Thus the pressure on socially ambitious Jews must have been great, and our Diaspora literature indicates, openly or by implication, that not all Jews were faithful to their tradition on this score.[51]

---

[48] On the common cultic associations of meals, both in temple dining rooms and in private houses, see Gooch 1993.

[49] Wine is rejected in Dan 1 and Add Esth 4.17x (specifically for its association with libations); cf. Josephus, *Ant* 4.137. The issue of 'impure' Gentile oil is reflected in Josephus, *Vita* 74; *Bell* 2.591; *Ant* 12.120, all concerning Jews in Syria. The reasons for this taboo are not entirely clear, but probably concern association with 'idolatry'; see Goodman 1990b and Sanders 1992:520 n12.

[50] Bringing one's own food and wine: Judith 12.1–4, 19. Eating only certain foods (e.g. vegetables and fruits): Josephus, *Vita* 14; Rom 14.1–2. Dispensing with prayers and libations: *The Letter of Aristeas* 184–85. Cf. also sitting at separate tables: *Joseph and Aseneth* 7.1 (presumably with distinct food). It was possible also for Gentile hosts to provide only such food as was acceptable to Jews: such seems to be imagined in the banquet in *The Letter of Aristeas* (181) and required by Paul in Rom 14.1 – 15.6. But it is doubtful if this was practical except on special occasions or for special causes. See the discussion of such matters in Sanders 1990b.

[51] See the discussion by Sanders 1990a:272–83, who rightly points out that 4 Maccabees is an hortatory document designed to counteract assimilationist

Nonetheless, there is reason to believe that, in general, Jewish dietary laws were kept in the Diaspora (at least in key respects) and that such customs did create an habitual distinction between Jews and non-Jews. It is significant that many well-known Jews, although assimilated to a considerable degree, upheld the chief Jewish food laws. Philo and Aristeas provided an allegorical explanation for the list of unclean foods, but neither individual discarded its literal observance: on the contrary, they found in allegory good cause to maintain the traditional customs. Whatever embarrassment he received from Gaius, Philo was not tempted to abandon the Jewish taboo on pork (*Legatio* 361–62), which was also upheld by the Herodian family (Macrobius, *Saturnalia* 2.4.11; Juvenal, *Sat* 6.157–60). Similarly Josephus, though he moved in elevated circles in Rome, makes Jewish discipline in diet a matter of pride (*C Ap* 2.173–74, 234, 282). Thus, even if 4 Maccabees and *Joseph and Aseneth* seem somewhat extremist in their presentation of the issue, there is no reason to believe that their insistence on Jewish meal-separatism represents a minority viewpoint. In fact, it seems that in general the Jewish populace was more conservative on such matters than the educated élite (Philo, *Migr Abr* 89–93).[52]

The reality of Jewish distinction in this matter is further confirmed by the regular comments of non-Jews. If Jewish women in Alexandria were tested (or tortured) by being made to eat pork (Philo, *Flacc* 96), they were obviously known to be scrupulous in abstaining from such meat. In Rome such Jewish abstention was notorious and gave rise to speculation that Jews had special reverence for the pig.[53] In fact, Jews were considered unsociable, even misanthropic, for the social distinctions created by their dietary laws. They sit, Tacitus complains, 'at separate tables' (*separati epulis*, *Hist* 5.5.2), and for Diodorus nothing better illustrates the Jews' general 'hatred of humanity' than their refusal to share in meals with other nations (34.1.2). Josephus imagines the Midianite girls complaining about the Jews' alien mode of life, where their

tendencies in this matter (see above, chapter 12.3). Note also the examples of assimilation in 3 Macc 7.10–11 and among Christian Jews in Antioch (Gal 2.11–14).

[52] Only on the assumption of general Jewish observance of these laws is it possible to explain the fact that early Christianity engendered such controversy on this matter; see e.g. Acts 10–11, 15; Gal 2.11–21; Rom 14–15; cf. Esler 1987:71–109.

[53] See Petronius fragment 37; Juvenal, *Sat* 6.160; 14.98–99; Plutarch, *Quaest Conviv* 4.5 and, in general, the texts collected in Whittaker 1984:73–80.

peculiarities of food are matched by their refusal to worship others' Gods (*Ant* 4.137–38).[54] Philostratus (*Vita Apollonii* 33) similarly objects that Jews live an unsociable life, 'sharing no common table-fellowship with others, nor libations, prayers or sacrifices'.[55] It is impossible to understand how such complaints could be raised in different locations and across the centuries (from the first century BCE to the late second century CE) unless Jewish separatism at meals was commonly practised.

In fact, Jews themselves knew very well that their food regulations served to distinguish them from non-Jews. Even in the biblical text it is clear that the food laws are intended to 'sanctify' the Jewish nation (Lev 11.44–45): by making a distinction between the clean and the unclean animal, Jews also distinguished themselves from other nations, being made 'holy to the Lord' (Lev 20.24–26). Aristeas was fully in tune with this Levitical viewpoint when he understood the Jewish dietary rules to establish 'impenetrable fences and iron walls' between Jews and Gentiles (139–42). Even the biblical rule about what 'parts the hoof' is taken by Aristeas, allegorically, to signify the importance of Jewish 'parting' from other people (150–52). In the same vein, 3 Maccabees comments candidly on the 'separation' (χωρισμός) created by Jewish food regulations, even acknowledging that this makes Jews 'hateful' in the eyes of some (3.4). Josephus, proud that the law covers every department of life, links the distinction between acceptable and unacceptable food with the distinction between acceptable and unacceptable company (*C Ap* 2.173–74; cf. *Ant* 4.137–39).

Such separation from Gentiles could be explained by many means: Gentiles may be shunned, for instance, as unclean, uncircumcised, idolatrous or immoral. But what mattered socially was the simple function of the food laws in separating Jews from non-Jews in such a regular and important matter as the taking of food. Even if not every Jew maintained this demarcation, it typically served to bind the Jewish community together in distinction from others and thus to solidify Jewish ethnic identity on a daily basis.

[54] For analysis of this passage as encapsulating the pressures on Jews to assimilate, and the complaints against them if they did not, see van Unnik 1974.

[55] General remarks on Jewish unsociability, which may also reflect the food issue are to be found in e.g. Hecataeus *apud* Diodorus 40.3.4 and Apollonius Molon *apud* Josephus, *C Ap* 2.148, 258.

### 14.3.3 Male Circumcision

Circumcision was often, though not always and everywhere, a distinctively Jewish practice. Roman authors give the impression that circumcision was known in Rome as a uniquely Jewish characteristic, such that a man's circumcision could alone prove his Jewish origin. Only on this basis is it possible to explain how, in a Roman court, a man could be examined physically for his liability to the *fiscus Iudaicus* (Suetonius, *Domitian* 12.2) or how Petronius can represent men who want to disguise themselves suggesting they be circumcised 'to look like Jews' (*ut Iudaei videamur, Satyricon* 102.14). Thus, also writing in Rome, Tacitus suggests that Jews have adopted circumcision 'that they be recognized by this difference' (*ut diversitate noscantur, Hist* 5.5.2). In the Roman environment, then, circumcision constituted, for males, a practically unambiguous token of Jewish identity.

In the eastern Mediterranean, however, circumcision had once been common among many ethnic groups and appears to have continued in use in certain native traditions. In the fifth century BCE Herodotus had claimed (2.104) that circumcision was common among Ethiopians, Egyptians, Colchians and Syrians. In the Hellenistic era the practice was maintained chiefly in unHellenized sections of the population or in strongly 'nativistic' circles, for instance among Egyptian priests (Josephus, *C Ap* 2.141).[56] Where the population became Hellenized, they apparently adopted the Greek dislike of physical 'mutilation', bowing to a cultural pressure that was successfully resisted in the Maccabean revolt. In these circumstances, Jewish circumcision was not wholly unique but, in Hellenized circles, unusual. Even in the East, then, Jewish men who moved in Hellenized society were physically 'marked' as different from their social and intellectual peers.[57]

Whenever it is commented on by non-Jews, circumcision is derided, either as a peculiar 'mutilation' (on a par with castration,

---

[56] Philo's claim that circumcision is 'zealously observed' by many nations, especially the Egyptians (*Spec Leg* 1.2; or Egyptians, Arabs and Ethiopians, *Quaest Gen* 3.48) is either an exaggeration or refers to those of the native population who had not come under significant Hellenistic influence. Certainly the Hellenized Egyptian, Apion, was not circumcised (until near his death for medical reasons), Josephus, *C Ap* 2.142–44; cf. the evidence on eastern circumcision gathered in Stern 1.3–4.

[57] Cohen 1993b:12–22 rightly insists that Jews in the East were not *wholly* distinctive in this matter, but he appears to overlook the social and cultural dimensions of the practice.

according to Hadrian's later rescript) or, perhaps, as a 'barbarian' rite properly abandoned by 'civilized' men.[58] For Philo's Hellenized peers, such as Apion, the Jewish practice was laughable (Philo, *Spec Leg* 1.2; Josephus, *C Ap* 2.137). For Jews to maintain this 'ancestral custom' under such circumstances was therefore in itself a strong affirmation of their distinct ethnic tradition. The fact that the custom is not mentioned by all our Diaspora authors does not indicate its insignificance (*pace* Collins 1985b): it was not a topic that naturally arose in the genre in which many of them wrote. Josephus makes no mention of the rite in his presentation of Judaism in *C Ap* 2.145ff., but that is not because he considers it dispensable. In fact, he considers it of maximum importance for the maintenance of the ethnic identity of Jews (*Ant* 1.192), and promises a fuller explanation in a treatise on 'Customs and their Reasons' which he seems never to have written. Philo does provide some rationale for circumcision, and in typical fashion adds to traditional medical explanations some moral and allegorical reasons for the practice (*Spec Leg* 1.1–11). But he, too, is aware of its social significance, and in his criticism of pure allegorists (*Migr Abr* 89–93) he sides with the conservative majority of Jews in insisting that this Jewish trait be preserved.

I have already indicated (pp. 411–12) what I consider to be one of the most important social functions of circumcision: by marking Jewish males, it limited the sexual relations and marriage-options of Jewish girls and thus discouraged exogamy. It was important that this sign of Jewish identity was sometimes visible (in the baths and athletics, for instance, or for slaves whose naked condition was known to their owners), but nakedness was not often on public display. In general, its notoriety as a permanent sign of Jewish identity made circumcision an important token of commitment for men who contemplated becoming proselytes. Despite some ambiguous evidence, it is tolerably clear that male proselytes were required to get circumcised (to be 'assuredly Jewish', Josephus, *Ant* 20.38) and that circumcision stood as the mark of commitment to the whole Jewish way of life (Josephus, *Ant* 13.257–58; Gal 5.3).[59] Thus, like the other distinctives we are considering, circumcision was not an isolated cultural trait but was closely integrated with other strands of Jewish identity, including the fundamental ethnic bond.

[58] See the collection of sources in Whittaker 1984:80–85.
[59] For fuller discussion see Barclay 1988:45–60.

## 14.3.4 Sabbath Observance

Of all the festivals celebrated by Diaspora Jews, the Sabbath was, in social terms, by far the most important, since its observance was so regular, so noticeable and so socially problematic, affecting, as we shall see, not only personal but also financial, legal and political relationships. The special Jewish name for the seventh-day festival (a rare transliteration of Hebrew among Greek-speaking Jews, Josephus, *Ant* 1.33) was in sufficiently regular usage to be known by non-Jews like Ovid (*Remedia Amoris* 220) and Pompeius Trogus (36.2.14). But it was not just the peculiar name of the Sabbath that impressed non-Jews: it struck them as extraordinary that Jews should cease to work one day in seven, a regularity which to hostile minds suggested stupidity or laziness, or both (Whittaker 1984:63–73). As we have seen (above, chapter 10.2), there is evidence that in Rome the gradual introduction of the astrological week, and the conviction that Saturn's day was unlucky, coincided with Jewish practice, such that the Sabbath could be thought to be observed by more than just Jews. Nonetheless, even in Rome, and certainly elsewhere, Jewish Sabbath observance was well-known, and frequently resented, as an ethnic peculiarity which marked off Jewish communal life from that of all other peoples.

The observance of the Sabbath is, of course, demanded by the Jewish Scriptures, in both law (e.g. Exod 20.8–11) and narrative (e.g. Exod 16.22–30; Num 15.32–36), and the representation of God himself observing Sabbath rest (Gen 2.1–3) gave the practice the highest possible sanction. In fact, the Genesis text not only identifies the seventh day as 'sacred' (Gen 2.3); it also suggests that the seven-day cycle is built into the structure of the universe, thus encouraging philosophers like Aristobulus (fragment 5) and Philo (*Op Mund* 90–127; *Decal* 102–5 etc.) to extol its 'natural' value and to explore, under Pythagorean influence, the significance of the number 7. While we need not imagine that every Diaspora Jew was scrupulous in observance of the Sabbath, we should not forget the social pressure which a community can exercise on an individual in this matter. That is already exemplified in the biblical narrative (Num 15.32–36, a passage of which Philo takes special note in *Spec Leg* 2.249–51 and *Mos* 2.209–20), where the application of the death penalty on a transgressor further underlines the seriousness of the custom. When Philo notes the conservative opinions of the majority of Alexandrian Jews (*Migr Abr* 89–93) and records the Jewish outcry when a governor of Egypt tried to prevent its observance (*Somn* 2.123–24), we are given the strong impression that the Sabbath was generally observed. The popularity of Jewish names derived from the term is also striking. It appears that Jews in general took seriously the fact that the Sabbath was a sign of their unique identity and unique relationship to God (Exod 31.12–17).

Among the social functions of the Sabbath, we have already observed the significance of the weekly Sabbath gathering and instruction in the law (above, 14.2.1). Here we may focus on the simple but fundamental fact of abstention from work. It is clear that 'work' could be differently defined by different authorities (there are notable variations among our Palestinian sources), but in the Diaspora the impact of this prohibition is evidenced especially in military service and in financial and legal affairs.

As regards military duty, Jews had a reputation for unwillingness to bear arms or to march on the Sabbath (*Ant* 14.226; cf. Agatharcides *apud* Josephus, *C Ap* 1.209; Plutarch, *De Superstitione* 8). From Josephus' comments it appears that, during the Maccabean wars and at least on some occasions since, Jews felt justified in taking *defensive* military action on the Sabbath (*Ant* 12.274–77; 14.63–64), but even this degree of latitude must have been too restrictive for Gentile commanders. Presumably Jews in the Ptolemaic army were unable to insist on Sabbath observance (except perhaps in Jewish units, like that based at Leontopolis), and in the Judaean War Jewish scruples seem to have been sacrificed to military expediency (Josephus, *Bell* 2.456, 517). But in Asia at least, in the first century BCE, it was possible for Jews to claim exemption from service in Roman armies on the basis of their Sabbath scruples (*Ant* 14.226, 228, 232, 234 etc.), and Roman concessions here (at a time when citizens were being frantically conscripted) indicate that this 'conscientious objection' could be sympathetically heard.

A form of abstention of much broader impact was the Jewish reluctance to engage in financial or legal affairs on the Sabbath. One form of work clearly prohibited in the Scriptures is the lighting of fires (Exod 35.3), and Philo interprets this to include, by implication, all forms of work, craft or business which involved money or earning one's livelihood (*Mos* 2.211, 219). This particular exegesis may not have been universally accepted, but we have strong and widespread evidence that Diaspora Jews did typically abstain from their normal employment and from other financial affairs on the Sabbath. From Egypt we have the striking testimony of *CPJ*

10 that even a Jew employed in the building trade was scrupulous in observing a Sabbath rest. Higher up the social scale, Jewish officials in the bureaucracy of the Roman governor were loath to give up their Sabbaths even under considerable pressure (Philo, *Somn* 2.123ff.). From Asia we have evidence, which we have discussed above (pp. 270–71), indicating that Jews typically refused to undertake legal or financial commitments on the Sabbath, even when that damaged their business affairs (and possibly made them forfeit legal suits, Josephus, *Ant* 14.262–64; 16.27, 163, 167–68). The vigour with which Asian Jews defended their Sabbath customs indicates the depth of their commitment, as is also vividly displayed by Roman Jews in their refusal to collect the dole on the Sabbath (Philo, *Legatio* 158). So also in Antioch, when Antiochus tried to harm his fellow Jews during the Judaean War, his attempt to make them work on the Sabbath 'exactly as on other days' (Josephus, *Bell* 7.52) demonstrates their normal practice of declining to do just that. It may be doubted whether Jews typically went about on the Sabbath with their hands tucked under their cloaks (as the governor of Egypt charged, Philo, *Somn* 2.126; cf. *Vit Cont* 30). Yet there is no reason to doubt that abstention from work on the Sabbath was a typical and highly visible feature of Jewish distinction in the Diaspora.

The fact that Jews had to fight for their right to observe the Sabbath in Asia and Antioch indicates their vulnerability in relation to a custom which could clearly cause social and cultural offence. Yet what is fought for is also most highly treasured, and becomes more treasured precisely in the fight. In such circumstances the Sabbath became for Jews a token of their entitlement to observe their πάτρια ἔθη, the customs which they had inherited and intended to maintain unchanged. Philo considered the abolition of the Sabbath the breach which could destroy the whole Jewish tradition (*Somn* 2.123). By contrast, with every concession won, the Sabbath became more firmly fixed as an anchor-point for Diaspora Jewish identity, and in its practice each family was bound yet more tightly into the distinctive ethos of the community.

## 14.4 Conclusion

It should by now be clear that each of the strands of Jewish identity which we have examined in this chapter was interwoven with others to form a web of social and religious commitments. The fact that we have frequently needed to refer across from one section to another is an indication of the interdependence of these Jewish characteristics. The fundamental bond of ethnicity was reinforced each time Jewish distinctions were maintained as τὰ πάτρια, as customs passed down from previous generations and requiring faithful transfer to the generations to come. In the education of children and the regulation of family life, the law functioned to bind Jews to one another as an ἔθνος, while circumcision served to keep marriage partnerships within the community. Whenever Diaspora Jews encountered fellow Jews as pilgrims, and every time they abstained from alien cult or the table-fellowship of non-Jews, their distinctive ethnic identity was further confirmed. Thus the ethnic bond, the central thread of Jewish identity, was protected and preserved in the daily habits of Diaspora Jews. Similarly, the Scriptures, the precious legacy of Moses, pervaded every aspect of Jewish life – as the topic of communal Sabbath instruction, and as the 'constitutional' basis for all the Jewish distinctives. Each Sabbath bound Jews by association with one another, and dissociated them from others; their peculiar marking of time and their use of this day for synagogue teaching revived each week their sense of ethnic difference. Indeed each custom we have observed was linked with others to support the social fabric of Diaspora Judaism, and it is surely the combined strength of this fabric which explains the survival of Diaspora communities in the diverse conditions which we have surveyed.

Supported by this strong web of practice and community, Diaspora Jews could intepret their traditions in many different ways. It was not necessary, for instance, to interpret the ethnic bond only in terms of 'election' and 'covenant'. Other metaphors, derived from historical (Ezekiel) or political (Aristeas) spheres, could serve equally well so long as they fulfilled the requisite social functions.[60] In our discussion of Diaspora literature we have noted much diversity in Diaspora interpretations of Judaism, and it appears that hermeneutical unanimity was unnecessary so long as the web of custom was preserved intact. Only where important strands of this fabric began to unravel was there danger for Judaism (e.g. in Artapanus), and only in Paul's unpicking of key supporting threads

[60]  Thus Collins 1986:13–15, 244–46 is right to object to Sanders' prioritizing of 'covenantal nomism' as *the* basic metaphor for Jewish existence (Sanders 1976; 1977).

did we find the fabric beginning to tear. Such internal coherence made Judaism a remarkably durable tradition, not by total isolation from its surrounding milieu but by clarity of differentiation at socially decisive points.

Unfortunately, it was this very strength which rendered Diaspora Jews liable to the resentment of other ethnic groups and the hostility of Greek cities, for whom the presence of the Jewish community as an unassimilable entity was a social and political offence. Thus if Diaspora Judaism was vulnerable, its greatest danger lay not in internal collapse or incoherence but in exposure to hostility from its environment. The cycle of violence into which Egyptian Jews were drawn, and through which they were mostly destroyed, demonstrates this single facet of vulnerability in extreme political conditions. Nonetheless, the resilience of Jewish tradition has enabled its Diaspora survival through a further two millennia, despite intolerance, discrimination and violence even more extreme than that experienced in Roman Egypt. Today that tradition continues, threatened by disunity and greater uncertainty, perhaps, than ever before, but still weaving new social, religious and intellectual patterns from its strong and multiplex thread.[61]

---

[61] On the peculiar challenges facing modern Judaism, arising from assimilation and secularization, from controversies over Jewish identity and disputes over the establishment of the state of Israel, see e.g. Sacks 1993.

# Appendix on Sources

## Aristeas

1. *Text.* The standard critical edition, with section numbers, was prepared by Wendland in 1900 and was utilized by Thackeray in Swete 1914, whose text I have here employed. English translations are available in Hadas 1951 and Shutt 1985, but the latter is unreliable.

2. *Date.* This has been the subject of considerable debate and remains disputed, although the parameters are now recognized to be either end of the second century BCE. Criteria for fixing its date more precisely within that period include:

a) its linguistic traits, including the style of salutation and closing formulae in the official letters;

b) its relation to Aristobulus (both erroneously associate the LXX translation with Demetrius of Phalerum). However, their relative priority, or independent use of common tradition, is variously assessed;

c) its depiction of the relationship between Jews and the Ptolemaic dynasty (but opinions differ as to whether Aristeas' portrayal reflects contemporary reality or his hopes for the future);

d) its silence concerning the Maccabean crisis and the Leontopolis temple (though some detect veiled allusions);

e) its depiction of conditions in Judaea and Jerusalem in 83–120 (though most consider this passage too idealized to be validly sifted for historical references).

For a full discussion of these factors see Bickerman 1930, Meecham 1932:94–109, Hadas 1951:9–54, Murray 1967, Fraser 1972:2.970–72, Collins 1986:81–86 and Schürer 3.679–84. With the latter it is wisest to conclude that 'the author can ... therefore only be dated with certainty to some time in the second century B.C.' (684).

3. *Bibliography.* Schürer 3.685–87.

## Aristobulus

1. *Text.* 5 fragments, found in Eusebius, *Hist Eccles* 7.32.16–18; *Praep Evang* 8.10.1–17; 13.12.1–2; 13.12.3–8; 13.12.9–16. For the numbering of

the fragments and for the parallels in Clement see Walter 1964:7–9. For the sake of convenience, and because there is no danger of confusion, I cite references only by chapter and section in Eusebius; thus 10.5 = *Praep Evang* 8.10.5 and 12.6 = *Praep Evang* 13.12.6. An English translation may be found in A.Y. Collins 1985.

2. *Date.* Walter 1964 dispelled earlier doubts concerning the authenticity and pre-Philonic dating of these fragments. Aristobulus refers to the king whom he addresses as a descendant of Ptolemy Philadelphus (12.2). Clement and Eusebius claim that he dedicated the work to Ptolemy Philometor (180–145 BCE) and 2 Macc 1.10 implies that he served in Philometor's court. Although Walter questions the historical value of these external witnesses, he accepts the probability that Philometor is the king addressed. A more precise dating has been attempted, a) by noting the dedication to the king alone (i.e. in the period of his sole reign, 176–170 BCE), and b) by arguments concerning the relative priority of Aristeas and Aristobulus. In neither case can precision be attained and we can go no further than a probable association with Philometor. For discussion see Walter 1964; Fraser 1972:1.694 and 2.963–65; Hengel 1974:2.106–7 n. 378; Schürer 3.579–80.

3. *Bibliography.* Schürer 3.586–87.

## Artapanus

1. *Text.* 3 fragments, found in Eusebius, *Praep Evang* 9.18.1; 23.1–4; 27.1–37. I cite references only by chapter and section in Eusebius. The text has been edited, with commentary, by Holladay 1983. Besides his translation, see also Collins 1985a.

2. *Date.* Artapanus must be placed after the LXX translation and before Alexander Polyhistor, i.e. between 250 and 100 BCE. Attempts to define the date more precisely are reviewed by Collins 1985a:890–91, who tentatively suggests the end of the third century BCE; but cf. Schürer 3.523–24 and the survey of alternatives by Sterling 1992:168–69.

3. *Bibliography.* Collins 1985a:896 and Schürer 3.524–25.

## Ezekiel

1. *Text.* 17 fragments, excerpted by Alexander Polyhistor and found in Eusebius, *Praep Evang* 9.28 and 29. I cite using the line reference which has become standard. The text may also be found in Jacobson 1983 and Holladay 1989, in both cases with English translation and commentary. A verse translation is given by Robertson 1985.

2. *Date.* Ezekiel is to be dated after the LXX (on which it draws) and before Alexander Polyhistor, i.e. between 250 and 100 BCE. Some have

argued for a third-century date on the basis of the reference to the phoenix (lines 254ff.), which reputedly appeared in Egypt in the reign of Ptolemy Euergetes I (246–222 BCE), but that can hardly fix its date securely. See the full discussion in Jacobson 1983:5–13, who argues for a second century BCE date, in view of the relationships with Greeks and Egyptians assumed in the work and the lack of reference to Judaea (which was under Seleucid rule from 198 BCE).

3. *Bibliography.* See Jacobson 1983 and Holladay 1989.

## Joseph and Aseneth

1. *Text.* The differences between the longer text printed by Battifol 1889–90 and the shorter by Philonenko 1968 are considerable. Burchard has made considerable progress in unravelling the textual problems (1965; summarized in 1985:178–81), making use of the early Syriac and Armenian versions. He has published a preliminary text (1979) which is the basis of his German (1983) and English (1985) translations. It is not clear whether the differences between the longer and shorter versions of the text are to be explained in terms of accretions in the longer or omissions from the shorter. Given the complexities of this matter, I have opted to follow Burchard's text.

2. *Date.* The use of LXX Zechariah puts a probable upper limit around 100 BCE and the confident depiction of conversion might suggest a date before the Diaspora Revolt (116 CE) and Hadrian's ban on proselytism (135 CE; see Burchard 1965:143–51). Within that period all attempts at a more exact dating lack conviction. Linguistic considerations, the absence of reference to baptism and comparison with Greek novels require cross-reference to factors which are themselves difficult to date. The attempts by Sänger 1985 and Collins 1986:89–91 to find contemporary political conditions mirrored in the narrative of chapters 22–29 are methodologically suspect and, in any case, inexact (they reach different conclusions!). Other suggestions are to be found in West 1974:79–81 and Aptowitzer 1924:305. See the full discussion of the matter in Chesnutt 1995:80–85. It is hard to remain other than agnostic within the parameters of 100 BCE and 100 CE.

3. *Bibliography.* See Burchard 1983:619–28 and Chesnutt 1995.

## Josephus

1. *Text.* The Loeb text (Greek and English, 10 vols. edited by H. St.J. Thackeray et al.) is largely, though not entirely, based on the edition of the Greek text by Niese 1887–95.

2. *Date.* Josephus was born in 37/38 CE; his date of death is unknown. The *Bellum* has usually been regarded as composed between 75 and 79 CE, but it is not clear from *Vita* 361 whether Josephus had completed the whole work by the time of Vespasian's death (79 CE). Thus Cohen has argued (1979:84–90) that Books 1–6 date from Titus' reign (79–81 CE) with Book 7 even later, in the reign of Domitian (81–96 CE). The *Antiquitates* are easily dated from *Ant* 20.267 to 93/94 CE. The *Vita* is linked to the *Antiquitates* as an appendix (*Ant* 20.266; *Vita* 430). It must be dated after the death of Agrippa II (*Vita* 359), and since a ninth-century source (Photius) dates that event to 100 CE it has been suggested (notably by Laqueur) that it was added as part of a second edition of the *Antiquitates*. However, all other evidence seems to point to 92/93 CE as the date of Agrippa's death (see Schürer 1.481–83) so there is no reason to adopt such a complex theory. See the discussion in Cohen 1979:170–80 and Rajak 1983:237–38. The *Contra Apionem* is clearly a sequel to the *Antiquitates* but after what interval we cannot tell. Given Josephus' age, a date at the end of the 90s CE seems most plausible. See further Schwartz 1990:13–22.

3. *Bibliography.* This is provided on a massive scale by Schreckenberg (1968/ 1979) and Feldman (1984b, arranged in subject categories and annotated).

# 3 Maccabees

1. *Text.* Greek text in the Septuagint, e.g. A. Rahlfs (ed.), *Septuaginta* (Stuttgart: Deutsche Bibelgesellschaft, 1982). There are modern English translations in Hadas 1953 (with facing Greek text) and Anderson 1985a.

2. *Date.* Bickerman 1928 argued from the formulae in the letters contained in 3 Macc that its *terminus post quem* must be 100 BCE; but estimates after that date still vary. Literary relationships between 3 Macc and the Greek text of Esther have been variously assessed and cannot determine the matter. Tcherikover's argument (1961b) that the term λαογραφία (3 Macc 2.28) indicates a date after the introduction of the Roman poll-tax (24/23 BCE) has been accepted by most, but not all. The claims of Ewald, Willrich, Grimm and Collins that the text arose in a period of intense social conflict and reflects specifically the crises of 38–41 CE have been considered but rejected in the text above (p. 203). It is probably best to follow Tcherikover 1961b in suggesting a date at the end of the first century BCE. For further discussion of this issue see Willrich 1904; Cohen 1941; Hadas 1953:18–21; Anderson 1985a:510–12; and Schürer 3.539–40.

3. *Bibliography.* Schürer 3.541–42.

# 4 Maccabees

1. *Text.* Greek text in the Septuagint (see above, under 3 Maccabees).

Modern English translations in Hadas 1953 (with facing Greek text) and Anderson 1985b.

2. *Date*. Dependence on 2 Maccabees and vocabulary usage suggest a date no earlier than the first century CE. Scholarship has been divided between those who propose an early date (before 50 CE) and those favouring one rather later (90s–130s CE). The former consider the text to presuppose the temple to be still functioning, and have followed Bickerman's argument (1976:275–81) that the reference to the governor of Syria, Phoenicia *and* Cilicia (4 Macc 4.2) must reflect circumstances when the provinces were administratively united, i.e. between 20 and 54 CE. The latter take the temple to be past, find similarities in vocabulary with literature at the end of the first century CE and consider Bickerman's argument insecure. Appeals by either side to political conditions (e.g. the temple incident under Gaius, the Diaspora Revolt or the Bar Kochba Revolt) are of little weight. Advocates of the early date include, besides Bickerman, Hadas 1953:95–99, Collins 1986:187 and Schürer 3.591. The later date was proposed by Dupont-Sommer 1939:75–85, 139–43 and has gained powerful support from Breitenstein 1978:171–85 and van Henten 1986. The latter's refutation of Bickerman is impressive and tips the balance in favour of a date around the end of the first century CE; see the summary of the debate by Klauck 1989:668–69 (suggesting 90–100 CE).

3. *Bibliography*. Schürer 3.592–93; Klauck 1989:680–85.

## Paul

1. *Text*. The Greek text used is Nestle-Aland 26th edition, Stuttgart: Deutsche Bibelstiftung, 1981. English translations abound.

2. *Date*. All the letters date from the late 40s to the early 60s CE, though the precise date of some, and thus their sequence, remains a matter of controversy (Jewett 1979; Lüdemann 1984). See the full discussion of each letter in Kümmel 1966, who also gives the grounds on which scholars consider some pseudonymous. I here follow the current consensus which accepts as authentic Romans, 1 and 2 Corinthians, Galatians, Philippians, 1 Thessalonians and Philemon.

3. *Bibliography*. Simply enormous!

## Philo

1. *Text*. The Greek text of Cohn and Wendland (1896–1914) has been followed almost entirely by the Loeb translators (10 volumes), whose text is followed here. The supplementary Loeb volumes (*Quaest Gen* and *Quaest Exod*) are translated from the Armenian version (the only surviving witness

to those treatises). Terian 1981 has edited the *De Animalibus* and Hadas-Lebel 1973 the *De Providentia*.

2. *Date.* Philo's birthdate is c. 20 BCE, give or take 10 years (see above p. 159 n. 74); his date of death is unknown. Although his historical works (*In Flaccum* and *De Legatione ad Gaium*) obviously date after the events of 38 and 41 CE, they cannot be precisely dated nor indeed can any of the philosophical or exegetical treatises.

3. *Bibliography.* Collected and annotated by Radice and Runia 1988 and regularly updated in editions of *Studia Philonica*.

## Pseudo-Phocylides

1. *Text.* The text established by Young is printed in van der Horst 1978 (without textual apparatus) accompanied by an English translation on facing pages. The most recent critical text is given by Derron 1986 (with apparatus). Wilson 1994 provides another English translation.

2. *Date.* Dependence on LXX Proverbs and Jeremiah and the presence of late Hellenistic vocabulary suggest a date after 100 BCE, and parallels with contemporary philosophers might put the upper limit around 100 CE. See the discussion by van der Horst 1978:81–83 (updated in 1988:15) and Derron 1986:lxi–lxvi.

3. *Bibliography.* A survey of the history of interpretation is to be found in van der Horst 1978:3–58 (updated in 1988); besides the bibliography in that volume see Walter 1983:193–96 and Wilson 1994.

## Sibylline Oracles

1. *Text.* I have used the critical edition by Geffcken 1902b. There is an English translation by Collins 1983.

2. *Date.* Because of the complex history of this compilation of oracles, each Book must be separately assessed for its date and provenance, and within each Book passages of varying dates are to found. The Books of concern to us may be dated as follows:

*Book 3*: The references to the seventh king (3.192–93, 318, 608–9) suggest an original core of oracles in the reign of Philometor (180–145 BCE) or Euergetes II (145–116 BCE). Numerous additions have been made, updating the oracles in the first century BCE, but the final edition of the book appears to have been made before the turn of the era. See discussion above pp. 218–19 and in Nikiprowetzky 1970; Collins 1974 and 1983; and Schürer 3.632–38.

*Book 5*: The references to the destruction of the temple date this book after 70 CE, and most scholars take the generous comment about Hadrian

(5.48) to indicate a date before 132 CE (the Bar Kochba Revolt). However, 5.1–51 may be an addition to an earlier collection of oracles. See Collins 1974 and 1983; and Schürer 3.652–54.

3. *Bibliography.* Collins 1987:456–59 and Schürer 3.652–54.

## Wisdom of Solomon

1. *Text.* Greek text in editions of the Septuagint (see above, under 3 Maccabees) and in J. Ziegler, *Sapientia Salomonis*, Septuaginta XII 1 (Göttingen: Vandenhoeck & Ruprecht, 1962). English translations are available in any Bible which includes the Apocrypha.

2. *Date.* It is universally accepted that the text is to be placed in the period between 150 BCE and 50 CE, but within that 200–year span opinions diverge. Some of the factors appealed to in this connection are:

a) Its relationship to other literature: e.g. apocalyptic texts, wisdom literature (e.g. ben Sirach), the New Testament (especially Paul) and Philo. Such comparative dating is, however, an uncertain business. Compared to Philo, the work is philosophically unsophisticated, but does it then represent a more primitive stage in Alexandrian Judaism, or is it simply the product of a less exalted literary circle? It is uncertain whether Paul used *Wisdom* or simply drew on traditions also utilized by its author.

b) Its allusions to contemporary political circumstances: the reference to 'kings' (6.1 etc.) need not imply a Hellenistic dating, but some have taken the lack of any clear reference to Roman power as an indication of a Ptolemaic date. Conversely, others have interpreted 6.3 and 14.17–20 as a veiled allusion to Roman rule and emperor worship (or even the image of Gaius proposed for the temple). The only feature which can be reasonably associated with political conditions is the acute sense of opposition (chapters 1–5, 10–19) and oppression (19.13–16). Claims to see here reflections of the crisis in 38–41 CE (Winston 1979) are not convincing; the rise in tension through the last decades of Ptolemaic rule and the first decades of the Roman era is a more likely *Sitz im Leben.*

c) Its vocabulary: many items are otherwise attested only in the Roman era (Winston 1979:22–23). But the lack of comparative material from the first century BCE makes this an insubstantial argument.

d) The probable use of LXX Proverbs and Trito-Isaiah: that suggests a *terminus post quem* of c. 100 BCE.

I doubt that it is possible to fix the date more precisely than c. 100 BCE – c. 30 CE. For a discussion of the issue see Winston 1979:20–25 and Larcher 1983:1.141–61, who specifies a date at the beginning of the Roman era in Egypt (30–10 BCE). For an alternative viewpoint see Georgi 1980:394–97 who suggests a date at the end of the second century BCE and also questions the assumption of an Egyptian provenance (suggesting Syria as an alternative). But the Egyptian motifs are too prominent (in the Exodus paraphrase and in repeated attacks on animal cults) to raise serious doubts on that matter.

3. *Bibliography.* There are formidable lists in Winston 1979:70–96; Larcher 1983:1.11–48; and Schürer 3.576–79.

# Bibliography

Abel, E. L.
  1968a    'The myth of Jewish slavery in Ptolemaic Egypt', *REJ* 127, 253–58
  1968b    'Were the Jews banished from Rome in 19 A.D.?', *REJ* 127, 383–86

Albright, W. F.
  1937    'A Biblical fragment from the Maccabaean Age: The Nash Papyrus', *JBL* 56, 143–76

Alessandri, S.
  1968    'La presunta cacciata dei Giudei da Roma nel 139 a. Cr.', *Studi Classici e Orientali* 17, 187–98

Alexander, P. S.
  1986    'Incantations and Books of Magic', in Schürer 3.342–79

Amaru, B. H.
  1980–81    'Land Theology in Josephus' *Jewish Antiquities*', *JQR* 71, 201–29

Amir, Y.
  1983    *Die hellenistische Gestalt des Judentums bei Philon von Alexandrien*, Neukirchen-Vluyn: Neukirchener Verlag
  1984    'The Term Ἰουδαϊσμός (IOUDAISMOS): A Study in Jewish-Hellenistic Self-Definition', *Immanuel* 14, 34–41

Anderson, H.
  1985a    '3 Maccabees', in *OTP* 2, 509–29
  1985b    '4 Maccabees', in *OTP* 2, 531–64

Applebaum, S.
  1974    'The Organization of the Jewish Communities in the Diaspora', in S. Safrai and M. Stern (eds.), *The Jewish People in the First Century*, Compendia Rerum Iudaicarum ad Novum Testamentum I.1, Assen: Van Gorcum; Philadelphia: Fortress Press, 464–503
  1979    *Jews and Greeks in Ancient Cyrene*, Leiden: Brill

Aptowitzer, V.
  1924    'Asenath, the Wife of Joseph – A Haggadic, Literary-Historical Study', *HUCA* 1, 239–306

Attridge, H.
  1976    *The Interpretation of Biblical History in the Antiquitates Judaicae of Flavius Josephus*, Missoula: Scholars Press

| 1984 | 'Josephus and his Works', in M. E. Stone (ed.), *Jewish Writings of the Second Temple Period*, Compendia Rerum Iudaicarum ad Novum Testamentum II.2, Assen: Van Gorcum; Philadelphia: Fortress Press, 185–232 |
| 1985 | 'Fragments of Pseudo-Greek Poets', in *OTP* 2, 821–30 |

Aune, D. E.
| 1976 | 'Orthodoxy in First Century Judaism? A Response to N. J. McEleney', *JSJ* 7, 1–10 |
| 1980 | 'Magic in Early Christianity', in *ANRW* II.23.2, 1507–57 |

Aziza, C.
| 1987 | 'L'utilisation polémique du récit de l'Exode chez les écrivains alexandrins (IVème siècle av. J.-C. – Ier siècle ap. J.-C.)', *ANRW* II.20.1, 41–65 |

Baldwin Bowsky, M. W.
| 1987 | 'M. Tittius Sex. F. Aem. and the Jews of Berenice (Cyrenaica)', *AJPh* 108, 495–510 |

Balsdon, J. P. V. D.
| 1934 | *The Emperor Gaius*, Oxford: Oxford University Press |
| 1969 | *Life and Leisure in Ancient Rome*, London: The Bodley Head |

Barclay. J. M. G.
| 1988 | *Obeying the Truth: A Study of Paul's Ethics in Galatians*, Edinburgh: T & T Clark |
| 1992a | 'Manipulating Moses: Exodus 2.10–15 in Egyptian Judaism and the New Testament', in R. P. Carroll (ed.), *Text as Pretext: Essays in Honour of Robert Davidson*, Sheffield: JSOT Press, 28–46 |
| 1992b | 'Thessalonica and Corinth: Social Contrasts in Pauline Christianity', *JSNT* 47, 49–72 |
| 1995 | 'Deviance and Apostasy: Some Applications of Deviance Theory to First Century Judaism and Christianity', in P. F. Esler (ed.), *Modelling Early Christianity*, London: Routledge, 114–27 |
| 1996 | '"Do we undermine the Law?" A Study of Romans 14.1–15.6', in J. D. G. Dunn (ed.), *Paul and the Mosaic Law*, Tübingen: J. C. B. Mohr (Paul Siebeck) |
| forthcoming | 'Who was Considered an Apostate in the Jewish Diaspora?', in G. N. Stanton and G. Stroumsa (eds.), *Tolerance and Its Limits In Early Judaism and Early Christianity*, Cambridge: Cambridge University Press |

Barnes, T. D.
| 1989 | 'Trajan and the Jews', *JJS* 40, 145–62 |

Barraclough, R.
1984 'Philo's Politics. Roman Rule and Hellenistic Judaism', in *ANRW* II.21.1, 417–533

Barrett, C. K.
1994 *Paul. An Introduction to his Thought*, London: G. Chapman

Barth, F. (ed.)
1969 *Ethnic Groups and Boundaries: The Social Organization of Cultural Difference*, London: Allen & Unwin

Bartlett, J. R.
1985 *Jews in the Hellenistic World: Josephus, Aristeas, The Sibylline Oracles, Eupolemus*, Cambridge: Cambridge University Press

Bassler, J.
1982 *Divine Impartiality. Paul and a Theological Axiom*, Chico: Scholars Press

Battifol, P.
1889–90 'Le Livre de la Prière d'Asenath', in *Studia Patristica* 1.1–87; Paris: Le Roux

Bauckham, R.
1993 'The Parting of the Ways: What Happened and Why?', *Studia Theologica* 47, 135–51

Becker, H. S.
1963 *Outsiders. Studies in the Sociology of Deviance*, New York: Free Press

Bell, H. I.
1924 *Jews and Christians in Egypt: The Jewish Troubles in Alexandria and the Athanasian Controversy. Illustrated by Texts from Greek Papyri*, Oxford: British Museum

Benko, S.
1969 'The Edict of Claudius of A.D. 49 and the Instigator Chrestus', *Theologische Zeitschrift* 25, 406–18

Bernays, J.
1885 'Über das phokylideische Gedicht', in *Gesammelte Abhandlungen* (ed. H. Usener) vol. I, Berlin: Wilhelm Hertz, 192–261 (originally published in 1856)

Betz, H. D.
1986 *The Greek Magical Papyri in Translation*, Chicago: University of Chicago Press

Bevan, E.
1927      *A History of Egypt under the Ptolemaic Dynasty*, London: Methuen

Bickerman, E.
1928      'Makkabäerbücher (III)', in *PW* 14.1, 797–800
1930      'Zur Datierung des Pseudo-Aristeas', *ZNW* 29, 280–98
1962      *From Ezra to the Last of the Maccabees*, New York: Schocken
1975      'The Jewish Historian Demetrios', in J. Neusner (ed.), *Christianity, Judaism and Other Greco-Roman Cults*, Leiden: Brill, vol. 3, 72–84
1976      *Studies in Jewish and Christian History*, Part One, Leiden: Brill
1979      *The God of the Maccabees*, Leiden: Brill
1980      'Une question d'authenticité: Les privilèges juifs', in *Studies in Jewish and Christian History*, Part Two, Leiden: Brill, 24–43
1988      *The Jews in the Greek Age*, Cambridge, Mass.: Harvard University Press

Bilde, P.
1988      *Flavius Josephus between Jerusalem and Rome*, Sheffield: JSOT Press

Blau, L.
1914      *Das altjüdische Zauberwesen*, 2nd edition, Berlin: Louis Lamm

Boccaccini, G.
1991      *Middle Judaism: Jewish Thought 300 B.C.E. to 200 C.E.*, Minneapolis: Fortress Press

Bohak, G.
1995      '*CPJ* III, 520: The Egyptian Reaction to Onias' Temple', *JSJ* 26, 32–41

Bonner, C.
1950      *Studies in Magical Amulets*, Ann Arbor: University of Michigan Press

Bonz, M. P.
1990      'The Jewish Community of Ancient Sardis: A Reassessment of Its Rise to Prominence', *Harvard Studies in Classical Philology* 93, 343–59

Borgen, P.
1965      *Bread from Heaven. An Exegetical Study of the Concept of Manna in the Gospel of John and the Writings of Philo*, Leiden: Brill

1994 ' "Yes," "No," "How Far?": The Participation of Jews and Christians in Pagan Cults', in T. Engberg-Pedersen (ed.), *Paul in His Hellenistic Context*, Edinburgh: T & T Clark, 30–59

Bornkamm, G.
1966 'The Missionary Stance of Paul in 1 Corinthians 9 and in Acts', in L. E. Keck and J. L. Martyn (eds.), *Studies in Luke-Acts*, Nashville: Abingdon Press, 194–207

Bousset, W.
1915 *Jüdisch-christlicher Schulbetrieb in Alexandria und Rom*, Göttingen: Vandenhoeck & Ruprecht

Bowman, A. K.
1990 *Egypt after the Pharaohs*, Oxford: Oxford University Press

Box, H.
1939 *Philonis Alexandrini, In Flaccum*, Oxford: Oxford University Press

Boyarin, D.
1994 *A Radical Jew: Paul and the Politics of Identity*, Berkeley: University of California Press

Braun, M.
1938 *History and Romance in Graeco-Oriental Literature*, Oxford: Blackwell

Braund, D.
1985 'The Social and Economic Context of the Roman Annexation of Cyrenaica', in G. Barker, J. Lloyd and J. Reynolds (eds.), *Cyrenaica in Antiquity*, Oxford: B. A. R., 319–25

Breitenstein, U.
1978 *Beobachtungen zu Sprache, Stil und Gedankengut des Vierten Makkabäerbuches*, 2nd edition, Basel: Schwabe & Co. Verlag

Brooten, B. J.
1982 *Women Leaders in the Ancient Synagogues: Inscriptional Evidence and Background Issues*, Chico: Scholars Press

Brown, P.
1972 *Religion and Society in the Age of Saint Augustine*, London: Faber & Faber

Bruce, F. F.
1961–62 'Christianity Under Claudius', *BJRL* 44, 309–26

Bruce, I. A. F.
1964 'Nerva and the *Fiscus Iudaicus*', *PEQ* 96, 34–45

Burchard C.
1965 *Untersuchungen zu Joseph und Aseneth*, Tübingen: J. C. B. Mohr (Paul Siebeck)
1970 *Der dreizehnte Zeuge*, Göttingen: Vandenhoeck & Ruprecht
1979 'Ein vorläufiger griechischer Text von Joseph und Aseneth', *Dielheimer Blätter zum Alten Testament* 14, 2–53
1983 'Joseph und Aseneth', in *JSHRZ* II.4, Gütersloh: Gerd Mohn
1985 'Joseph and Aseneth', in *OTP* 2, 177–247
1987 'The Importance of Joseph and Aseneth for the Study of the New Testament: A General Survey and a Fresh Look at the Lord's Supper', *NTS* 33, 102–34

Burr, V.
1955 *Tiberius Iulius Alexander*, Bonn: Rudolf Habelt

Casey, M.
1991 *From Jewish Prophet to Gentile God. The Origins and Development of New Testament Christology*, Cambridge: James Clarke and Co.

Chadwick, H.
1966 'St. Paul and Philo of Alexandria', *BJRL* 48, 286–307
1970 'Philo', in A. H. Armstrong (ed.), *The Cambridge History of Later Greek and Early Medieval Philosophy*, Cambridge: Cambridge University Press, 137–157

Charlesworth, J. H. (ed.)
1983, 1985 *The Old Testament Pseudepigrapha*, 2 vols., London: Darton, Longman & Todd

Chesnutt, R. D.
1988 'The Social Setting and Purpose of Joseph and Aseneth', *JSP* 2, 21–48
1995 *From Death to Life. Conversion in Joseph and Aseneth*, Sheffield: Sheffield Academic Press

Classen, C. J.
1991 'Paulus und die antike Rhetorik,' *ZNW* 82, 1–33

Cohen, J.
1941 *Judaica et Aegyptiaca: De Maccabaeorum Libro III Quaestiones Historicae*, Groningen: de Waal

Cohen, S. J. D.

1979       *Josephus in Galilee and Rome. His Vita and Development as a Historian*, Leiden: Brill

1982       Review of A. Kasher, *The Jews in Hellenistic and Roman Egypt* (original Hebrew edition), *JQR* 72, 330–31

1983       'From the Bible to the Talmud: the Prohibition of Intermarriage', *Hebrew Annual Review* 7, 23–39

1986       'Was Timothy Jewish (Acts 16.3)? Patristic Exegesis, Rabbinic Law, and Matrilineal Descent', *JBL* 105, 251–68

1987a      'Respect for Judaism by Gentiles according to Josephus', *HTR* 80, 409–30

1987b      *From the Maccabees to the Mishnah*, Philadelphia: Westminster Press

1989       'Crossing the Boundary and Becoming a Jew', *HTR* 92, 13–33

1990       'Religion, Ethnicity and "Hellenism" in the Emergence of Jewish Identity in Maccabean Palestine', in P. Bilde, T. Engberg-Pedersen et al. (ed.), *Religion and Religious Practice in the Seleucid Kingdom*, Aarhus: Aarhus University Press, 204–23

1993a      (ed.), *The Jewish Family in Antiquity*, Atlanta: Scholars Press

1993b      '"Those Who Say They are Jews and Are Not": How Do You Know a Jew in Antiquity When You See One?', in S. J. D. Cohen and E. S. Frerichs (eds.), *Diasporas in Antiquity*, Atlanta: Scholars Press, 1–45

Cohen, S. J. D. and Frerichs, E. S. (eds.)

1993       *Diasporas in Antiquity*, Atlanta: Scholars Press

Cohen, S. M.

1983       *American Modernity and Jewish Identity*, New York: Tavistock Publications

Collins, A. Y.

1985       'Aristobulus', in *OTP* 2, 831–42

Collins, J. J.

1974       *The Sibylline Oracles of Egyptian Judaism*, Missoula: Society of Biblical Literature

1983       'Sibylline Oracles', in *OTP* 1, 317–472

1985a      'Artapanus', in *OTP* 2, 889–903

1985b      'A Symbol of Otherness: Circumcision and Salvation in the First Century', in J. Neusner and E. S. Frerichs (eds.), *"To See Ourselves as Others See Us". Christians, Jews, "Others" in Late Antiquity*, Chico: Scholars Press, 163–86

1986          *Between Athens and Jerusalem: Jewish Identity in the Hellenistic Diaspora*, New York: Crossroad
1987          'The Development of the Sibylline Tradition', in *ANRW* II.20.1, 421–59
1994          'The Sibyl and the Potter: Political Propaganda in Ptolemaic Egypt', in L. Bormann, K. del Tredici and A. Standhartinger (eds.), *Religious Propaganda and Missionary Competition in the New Testament World. Essays Honouring Dieter Georgi*, Leiden: Brill, 57–69

Colson, F. H.
1926          *The Week*, Cambridge: Cambridge University Press

Courtney, E.
1980          *A Commentary on the Satires of Juvenal*, London: Athlone Press

Cowley, A. E.
1923          *Aramaic Papyri of the Fifth Century B.C.*, Oxford: Clarendon Press

Crook, J.
1951          'Titus and Berenice', *AJPh* 72, 162–75

Crouch, J. E.
1972          *The Origin and Intention of the Colossian Haustafel*, Göttingen: Vandenhoeck & Ruprecht

Dalbert, P.
1954          *Die Theologie der hellenistisch-jüdischen Missionsliteratur unter Ausschluss von Philo und Josephus*, Hamburg: H. Reich

Daniélou, J.
1958          *Philon d'Alexandrie*, Paris: Librairie Arthème Fayard

Davies, W. D.
1948          *Paul and Rabbinic Judaism*, London: SPCK

Davis, S.
1951          *Race-Relations in Ancient Egypt: Greek, Egyptian, Hebrew, Roman*, London: Methuen

Dawson, D.
1992          *Allegorical Readers and Cultural Revision in Ancient Alexandria*, Berkeley: University of California Press

de Jonge, M.
1974          'Josephus und die Zukunftserwartungen seines Volkes', in O. Betz et al. (eds.), *Josephus-Studien*, Göttingen: Vandenhoeck & Ruprecht, 205–19

Deissmann, A.
1927      *Light from the Ancient East*, revised edition, London: Hodder & Stoughton

Delia, D.
1991      *Alexandrian Citizenship during the Roman Principate*, Atlanta: Scholars Press

Delling, G.
1984      'Die Kunst des Gestaltens in "Joseph und Aseneth"', *NovT* 26, 1–42
1987      *Die Bewältigung der Diasporasituation durch das hellenistische Judentum*, Göttingen: Vandenhoeck & Ruprecht

Derron, P.
1986      *Pseudo-Phocylide, Sentences*, Budé edition, Paris: Société d'édition 'Les Belles Lettres'

Dibelius, M.
1956      *Studies in the Acts of the Apostles*, London: SCM Press

Dillon, J.
1977      *The Middle Platonists. A Study of Platonism 80 B.C. to A.D. 220*, London: Duckworth

Doran, R.
1981      *Temple Propaganda: The Purpose and Character of 2 Maccabees*, Washington, DC: Catholic Biblical Association of America

Douglas, R. C.
1988      'Liminality and Conversion in Joseph and Aseneth', *JSP* 3, 31–42

Downey, G.
1961      *A History of Antioch in Syria*, Princeton: Princeton University Press

Droge, A. J.
1989      *Homer or Moses? Early Christian Interpretation of the History of Culture*, Tübingen: J. C. B. Mohr (Paul Siebeck)

Dunn, J. D. G.
1990      *Jesus, Paul and the Law*, London: SPCK
1991      *The Partings of the Ways between Christianity and Judaism and their Significance for the Character of Christianity*, London: SCM Press
1993      *The Epistle to the Galatians*, London: A & C Black

Dupont-Sommer, A.
1939                 *Le Quatrième Livre des Machabées. Introduction,*
                     *Traduction et Notes,* Paris: Librairie Ancienne Honoré
                     Champion

Ellman, Y.
1987                 'Intermarriage in the United States', *JSS* 49, 1–26

Engberg-Pedersen,
T. (ed.)
1994                 *Paul in his Hellenistic Context,* Edinburgh: T & T Clark

Esler, P. F.
1987                 *Community and Gospel in Luke-Acts,* Cambridge:
                     Cambridge University Press

Fascher, E.
1963                 'Der Vorwurf der Gottlosigkeit in der Auseinandersetzung
                     bei Juden, Griechen und Christen', in O. Betz, M. Hengel
                     and P. Schmidt (eds.), *Abraham unser Vater. Festschrift für*
                     *Otto Michel,* Leiden: Brill, 78–105

Fasola, U. M.
1976                 'Le due catacombe ebraiche di Villa Torlonia', *Rivista*
                     *di Archaeologia Cristina* 52, 7–62

Feldman, L. H.
1953                 'Asinius Pollio and his Jewish Interests', *TAPA* 84, 73–80
1960                 'The Orthodoxy of the Jews in Hellenistic Egypt', *JSS*
                     22, 215–37
1984a                'Flavius Josephus Revisited: the Man, His Writings,
                     and His Significance', in *ANRW* II.21.2, 763–862
1984b                *Josephus and Modern Scholarship 1937–1980,* Berlin: de
                     Gruyter
1993                 *Jew and Gentile in the Ancient World,* Princeton:
                     Princeton University Press

Fischer, U.
1978                 *Eschatologie und Jenseitserwartung im hellenistischen*
                     *Diasporajudentum,* Berlin: de Gruyter

Focke, F.
1913                 *Die Entstehung der Weisheit Salomos,* Göttingen:
                     Vandenhoeck & Ruprecht

Frankfurter, D.
1992                 'Lest Egypt's City be Deserted: Religion and Ideology
                     in the Egyptian Response to the Jewish Revolt (116–
                     117 C.E.)', *JJS* 43, 203–20

Fraser, P. M.
1972                 *Ptolemaic Alexandria*, 3 vols., Oxford: Clarendon Press

Freudenthal, J.
1869                 *Die Flavius Josephus beigelegte Schrift über die Herrschaft
                     der Vernunft (IV Makkabäerbuch)*, Breslau: Schletter'sche
                     Buchhandlung (H. Skutsch)
1875                 *Alexander Polyhistor und die von ihm erhaltenen Reste
                     judäischer und samaritanischer Geschichtswerke*,
                     Hellenistische Studien 1–2, Breslau: H. Skutsch
1890                 'Are there traces of Greek Philosophy in the
                     Septuagint?', *JQR* 2, 205–22

Frey, J.-B.,
1936, 1952          *Corpus Inscriptionum Iudaicarum*, Rome: Pontifical
                     Institute of Biblical Archaeology; vol. 1 revised with
                     prologue by B. Lifshitz, New York: Ktav, 1975

Friedländer, M.
1903                 *Geschichte der jüdischen Apologetik als Vorgeschichte des
                     Christentums*, Zürich: Schmidt
1905                 *Die religiösen Bewegungen innerhalb des Judentums im
                     Zeitalter Jesu*, Berlin: Georg Reimer

Fuchs, H.
1964                 *Der geistige Widerstand gegen Rom*, 2nd edition, Berlin:
                     de Gruyter

Fuks, A.
1961                 'Aspects of the Jewish Revolt in A.D. 115–117', *JRS*
                     51, 98–104

Fuks, G.
1985                 'Where have all the Freedmen Gone? On an Anomaly in
                     the Jewish Grave-Inscriptions from Rome', *JJS* 36, 25–32

Gabba, E.
1989                 'The growth of anti-Judaism or the Greek attitude
                     towards Jews', in W. D. Davies and L. Finkelstein
                     (eds.), *The Cambridge History of Judaism. Volume Two:
                     The Hellenistic Age*, Cambridge: Cambridge University
                     Press, 614–56

Gager, J. G.
1972                 *Moses in Graeco-Roman Paganism*, Nashville/New York:
                     Abingdon Press
1983                 *The Origins of Anti-Semitism: Attitudes Towards Judaism
                     in Pagan and Christian Antiquity*, Oxford: Oxford
                     University Press

Gallas, S.
1990           '"Fünfmal vierzig weniger einen ..." Die an Paulus
              vollzogenen Synagogalstrafen nach 2Kor 11, 24', *ZNW*
              61, 178–91

Gauger, J.-D.
1977           *Beiträge zur jüdischen Apologetik. Untersuchungen zur
              Authentizität von Urkunden bei Flavius Josephus und im
              I. Makkabäerbuch*, Bonn: P. Hanstein

Geertz, C.
1979           'Suq: The Bazaar Economy in Sefrar', in C. Geertz,
              H. Geertz and L. Rosen, *Meaning and Order in
              Moroccan Society. Three Essays in Cultural Analysis*,
              Cambridge: Cambridge University Press, 123–313

Geffcken, J.
1902a          *Komposition und Entstehungszeit der Oracula Sibyllina*,
              Leipzig: J. C. Hinrichs
1902b          *Die Oracula Sibyllina*, Leipzig: J. C. Hinrichs

Georgi, D.
1980           *Weisheit Salomos*, JSHRZ III.4, Gütersloh: Gerd Mohn

Gilbert, M.
1973           *La critique des dieux dans le Livre de la Sagesse (Sg 13–
              15)*, Rome: Biblical Institute Press

Goldstein, J.
1981           'Jewish Acceptance and Rejection of Hellenism', in
              E. P. Sanders (ed.), *Jewish and Christian Self-Definition*,
              vol. 2, London: SCM Press, 64–87

Gooch, P. D.
1993           *Dangerous Food: 1 Corinthians 8–10 in Its Context*,
              Waterloo, Ontario: Wilfrid Laurier University Press

Goodenough, E. R.
1926           'Philo and Public Life', *Journal of Egyptian Archaeology*
              12, 77–79
1929           *The Jurisprudence of the Jewish Courts in Egypt*, New
              Haven: Yale University Press
1938           *The Politics of Philo Judaeus. Practice and Theory*, New
              Haven: Yale University Press
1953–68        *Jewish Symbols in the Graeco-Roman Period*, 13 vols., New
              York: Pantheon
1962           *An Introduction to Philo Judaeus*, second edition,
              revised, Oxford: Blackwell
1968           with A. T. Kraabel, 'Paul and the Hellenization of
              Christianity' in J. Neusner (ed.), *Religions in Antiquity*.

*Essays in Memory of E. R. Goodenough,* Leiden: Brill, 23–68

1969    *By Light, Light. The Mystic Gospel of Hellenistic Judaism,* Amsterdam: Philo Press (first published 1935)

Gooding, D. W.
1963    'Aristeas and Septuagint Origins: A Review of Recent Studies', *VT* 13, 357–79

Goodman, M.
1989    'Nerva, the *Fiscus Judaicus* and Jewish Identity', *JRS* 79, 40–44
1990a    'Identity and Authority in Ancient Judaism', *Judaism* 39, 192–201
1990b    'Kosher Olive Oil in Antiquity', in P. R. Davies and R. T. White (eds.), *A Tribute to Geza Vermes,* Sheffield: JSOT Press, 227–45
1994    *Mission and Conversion. Proselytizing in the Religious History of the Roman Empire,* Oxford: Clarendon Press

Goudriaan, K.
1988    *Ethnicity in Ptolemaic Egypt,* Amsterdam: J. C. Gieben
1992    'Ethnical Strategies in Graeco-Roman Egypt', in P. Bilde, T. Engberg-Pedersen et al. (eds.), *Ethnicity in Hellenistic Egypt,* Aarhus: Aarhus University Press, 74–99

Grabbe, L. L.
1977    'Orthodoxy in First Century Judaism: What are the Issues?', *JSJ* 8, 149–53
1992    *Judaism from Cyrus to Hadrian,* Minneapolis: Augsburg Fortress Press

Green, H. A.
1985    *The Economic and Social Origins of Gnosticism,* Atlanta: Scholars Press

Griffiths, J. G.
1987    'Egypt and the Rise of the Synagogue', *JTS* 38, 1–15

Griggs, C. W.
1990    *Early Egyptian Christianity From Its Origins to 451 C.E.,* Leiden: Brill

Grimm, C. L. W.
1853a    *Drittes Buch der Maccabäer,* Leipzig: S. Hirzel
1853b    *Viertes Buch der Maccabäer,* Leipzig: S. Hirzel
1860    *Das Buch des Weisheit,* Leipzig: S. Hirzel

Guterman, S. L.
1951    *Religious Toleration and Persecution in Ancient Rome,* London: Aiglon Press

Hadas, M.
1949        'Aristeas and III Maccabees', *HTR* 42, 175–84
1951        *Aristeas to Philocrates*, New York: Harper
1953        *The Third and Fourth Books of Maccabees*, New York: Harper

Hadas-Lebel, M.
1973        *De Providentia I et II*, Les Oeuvres de Philon d'Alexandrie, Paris: Cerf

Haenchen, E.
1971        *The Acts of the Apostles. A Commentary*, Oxford: Blackwell

Halbertal, M. and
   Margalit, A.
1992        *Idolatry*, Cambridge, Mass.: Harvard University Press

Harnack, A.
1908        *The Mission and Expansion of Christianity*, London: Williams & Norgate

Harris, H. A.
1976        *Greek Athletics and the Jews*, Cardiff: University of Wales Press

Harvey, A. E.
1985        'Forty Strokes Save One: Social Aspects of Judaizing and Apostasy', in A. E. Harvey (ed.), *Alternative Approaches to New Testament Study*, London: SPCK, 79–96

Hay, D. M.
1979–80    'Philo's References to Other Allegorists', *Studia Philonica* 6, 41–75

Hays, R. B.
1989        *Echoes of Scripture in the Letters of Paul*, New Haven: Yale University Press

Healy, J. F.
1957        'The Cyrene Half-Shekel', *Journal of Semitic Studies* 2, 377–79

Hegermann, H.
1989        'The Diaspora in the Hellenistic Age', in W. D. Davies and L. Finkelstein (eds.), *The Cambridge History of Judaism. Volume Two: The Hellenistic Age*, Cambridge: Cambridge University Press, 115–66

Heinemann, I.
1928        'Makkabäerbücher (IV)', in *PW* 14.1, 800–5
1931        'Antisemitismus', in *PW Supp* V, 3–43

1933        'Moses', in *PW* 16.1, 359–75

1962        *Philons griechische und jüdische Bildung*, Hildesheim: Georg Olms Buchhandlung (originally published in three parts, 1929–1932)

Heininger, B.

1989        'Der böse Antiochus. Eine Studie zur Erzähltechnik des 4. Makkabäerbuchs', *Biblische Zeitschrift* 33, 43–59

Hengel, M.

1971        'Proseuche und Synagoge', in G. Jeremias, H.-W. Kuhn and H. Stegemann (eds.), *Tradition und Glaube. Festschrift für K. G. Kuhn*, Göttingen: Vandenhoeck & Ruprecht, 157–84

1972        'Anonymität, Pseudepigraphie und "literarische Fälschung" in der jüdisch-hellenistischen Literatur', in *Pseudepigrapha I*; Fondation Hardt, Entretiens sur l'Antiquité Classique 18; Geneva: Vandœvres, 229–329

1974        *Judaism and Hellenism*, translated from 2nd German edition, London: SCM Press

1980        *Jews, Greeks and Barbarians*, London: SCM Press

1983        'Messianische Hoffnung und politischer "Radikalismus" in der "jüdisch-hellenistischen Diaspora"', in D. Hellholm (ed.), *Apocalypticism in the Mediterranean World and the Near East*, Tübingen: J. C. B. Mohr (Paul Siebeck), 655–86

1989        *The 'Hellenization' of Judaea in the First Century after Christ*, London: SCM Press

1991        *The Pre-Christian Paul*, London: SCM Press

Hennig, D.

1975        *L. Aelius Seianus*, Munich: C. H. Beck'sche Verlagsbuchhandlung

Herman, S. N.

1977        *Jewish Identity: A Social-Psychological Perspective*, Beverly Hills: Sage Publications

Highet, G.

1954        *Juvenal the Satirist*, Oxford: Oxford University Press

Hock, R. F.

1980        *The Social Context of Paul's Ministry: Tentmaking and Apostleship*, Philadelphia: Fortress Press

Holladay, C. R.

1976        'The Portrait of Moses in Ezekiel the Tragedian', in *Society of Biblical Literature 1976 Seminar Papers*, Missoula: Scholars Press, 447–52

1977          *THEIOS ANER in Hellenistic Judaism: A Critique of the Use of this Category in New Testament Christology*, Missoula: Scholars Press

1983          *Fragments from Hellenistic Jewish Authors. Volume 1: Historians*, Chico: Scholars Press

1989          *Fragments from Hellenistic Jewish Authors. Volume 2: Poets*, Atlanta: Scholars Press

Hollis, A. S.
1977          *Ovid: Ars Amatoria Book I*, Oxford: Clarendon Press

Holtz, T.
1967–68       'Christliche Interpolationen in "Joseph und Aseneth"', *NTS* 14, 482–97

Honigman, S.
1993          'The Birth of a Diaspora: The Emergence of a Jewish Self-Definition in Ptolemaic Egypt in the Light of Onomastics', in S. J. D. Cohen and E. S. Frerichs (eds.), *Diasporas in Antiquity*, Atlanta: Scholars Press, 93–127

Horbury, W.
1985          'Extirpation and Excommunication', *VT* 35, 13–38
1986          'Ezekiel Tragicus 106: δωρήματα', *VT* 36, 37–51
1991          'Herod's Temple and "Herod's Days"', in idem (ed.), *Templum Amicitiae. Essays on the Second Temple Presented to Ernst Bammel*, Sheffield: Sheffield Academic Press, 103–149

1994          'Jewish Inscriptions and Jewish Literature in Egypt, with Special Reference to Ecclesiasticus', in J. W. van Henten and P. W. van der Horst (eds.), *Studies in Early Jewish Epigraphy*, Leiden: Brill, 9–43

forthcoming   'The Jewish Revolts under Trajan and Hadrian', in *The Cambridge History of Judaism. Volume Four*, Cambridge: Cambridge University Press

Horbury, W. and
  Noy, D.
1992          *Jewish Inscriptions of Graeco-Roman Egypt*, Cambridge: Cambridge University Press

Horsley, G. H. R.
1981          *New Documents Illustrating Early Christianity 1*, Macquarie: Macquarie University
1987          *New Documents Illustrating Early Christianity 4*, Macquarie: Macquarie University

Hull, J. M.
1974          *Hellenistic Magic and the Synoptic Tradition*, London: SCM Press

Jacobson, H.
1981      'Two Studies on Ezekiel the Tragedian', *Greek, Roman and Byzantine Studies* 22, 167–78
1983      *The EXAGOGE of Ezekiel*, Cambridge: Cambridge University Press

Janne, H.
1934      'Impulsore Chresto', *Annuaire de l'Institut de Philologie et d'Histoire Orientales et Slaves* 2, 531–53

Jeremias, J.
1969      *Jerusalem in the Time of Jesus*, London: SCM Press

Jewett, R.
1979      *Dating Paul's Life*, London: SCM Press

Johnson, A. C.
1936      *Roman Egypt to the Reign of Diocletian*, An Economic Survey of Ancient Rome (ed. T. Frank), Volume 2; Baltimore: John Hopkins Press

Jones, A. H. M.
1971      *The Cities of the Eastern Roman Provinces*, 2nd edition, Oxford: Oxford University Press

Jones, H. S.
1926      'Claudius and the Jewish Question at Alexandria', *JRS* 16, 17–35

Juster, J.
1914      *Les Juifs dans l'Empire Romain*, 2 vols., Paris: P. Geuthner

Kamlah, E.
1974      'Frömmigkeit und Tugend. Die Gesetzesapologie des Josephus in cAp 2,145–295', in O. Betz et al. (eds.), *Josephus-Studien*, Göttingen: Vandenhoeck & Ruprecht, 220–32

Kasher, A.
1976      'A Comment on the Jewish Uprising in Egypt during the days of Trajan', *JJS* 27, 147–58
1985      *The Jews in Hellenistic and Roman Egypt. The Struggle for Equal Rights*, Tübingen: J. C. B. Mohr (Paul Siebeck)
1990      *Jews and Hellenistic Cities in Eretz-Israel*, Tübingen: J. C. B. Mohr (Paul Siebeck)

Kee, H. C.
1976      'The Socio-Religious Setting and Aims of "Joseph and Asenath"', in *Society of Biblical Literature 1976 Seminar Papers*, Missoula: Scholars Press, 183–92

1983       'The Socio-Cultural Setting of *Joseph and Aseneth*', *NTS* 29, 394–413

1986       *Medicine, Miracle and Magic in New Testament Times*, Cambridge: Cambridge University Press

Keresztes, P.
1973       'The Jews, the Christians, and Emperor Domitian', *VC* 27, 1–28

Klauck, H.-J.
1989       *4. Makkabäerbuch, JSHRZ* III.6, Gütersloh: Gerd Mohn

Kolarcik, M.
1991       *The Ambiguity of Death in the Book of Wisdom 1–6*, Rome: Pontifical Biblical Institute

Kraabel, A. T.
1979       'The Diaspora Synagogues: Archaeological and Epigraphic Evidence since Sukenik', in *ANRW* II.19.1, 477–510

1981       'The Disappearance of the "God-Fearers"', *Numen* 28, 113–26

1982       'The Roman Diaspora: Six Questionable Assumptions', *JJS* 33, 445–64

Kraeling, C. H.
1932       'The Jewish Community at Antioch', *JBL* 51, 130–60

1962       *Ptolemais. City of the Libyan Pentapolis*, Chicago: University of Chicago Press

Kraemer, R. S.
1986       'Hellenistic Jewish Women: The Epigraphical Evidence', in *SBL Seminar Papers 1986*, Atlanta: Scholars Press, 183–200

1989       'On the Meaning of the Term "Jew" in Graeco-Roman Inscriptions', *HTR* 82, 35–53

1991       'Jewish Tuna and Christian Fish: Identifying Religious Affiliation in Epigraphic Sources', *HTR* 84, 141–62

1992       *Her Share of the Blessings*, Oxford: Oxford University Press

Kraft, R. A. and Nickelsburg, G. W. E. (eds.)
1986       *Early Judaism and Its Modern Interpreters*, Philadelphia: Fortress Press; Atlanta: Scholars Press

Krauss, S.
1902       'Antioche', *REJ* 45, 27–49

Kroll, W.
1941       'Phocylides', in *PW* 20.1, 505–10

Küchler, M.
1979      *Frühjüdische Weisheitstraditionen*, Freiburg: Universitätsverlag; Göttingen: Vandenhoeck & Ruprecht

Kuhrt, A. and
  Sherwin-White,
  S. (eds.)
1987      *Hellenism in the East: The Interaction of Greek and non-Greek Civilizations from Syria to Central Asia after Alexander*, London: Duckworth

Kuiper, K.
1903      'Le Poète Juif Ezéchiel', *REJ* 46, 48–73, 161–77

Kümmel, W. G.
1966      *Introduction to the New Testament*, London: SCM Press
1973–      (ed.) *Jüdische Schriften aus hellenistisch-römischer Zeit (JSHRZ)*, Gütersloh: Gerd Mohn

La Piana, G.
1927      'Foreign Groups in Rome During the First Centuries of the Empire', *HTR* 20, 183–403

Lafargue, M.
1985      'Orphica', in *OTP* 2, 795–801

Lampe, P.
1987      *Die stadtrömischen Christen in den ersten beiden Jahrhunderten*, Tübingen: J. C. B. Mohr (Paul Siebeck)

Lane, E. N.
1979      'Sabazius and the Jews in Valerius Maximus: A Re-examination', *JRS* 69, 35–38

Lane Fox, R.
1986      *Pagans and Christians*, London: Penguin

Laqueur, R.
1970      *Der jüdische Historiker Flavius Josephus*, reprinted, Darmstadt: Wissenschaftliche Buchgesellschaft (originally published 1920)

Larcher, C.
1969      *Etudes sur le Livre de la Sagesse*, Paris: Gabalda
1983      *Le Livre de la Sagesse, ou, Le Sagesse de Salomon*, 3 vols., Paris: Gabalda

Lauer, S.
1955      'Eusebes Logismos in IV Macc.', *JJS* 6, 170–71

Lebram, J. C. H.
1974          'Die literarische Form des Vierten Makkabäerbuches',
              *VC* 28, 81–96

Lentz, J. C.
1993          *Luke's Portrait of Paul*, Cambridge: Cambridge
              University Press

Leon, H. J.
1960          *The Jews of Ancient Rome*, Philadelphia: The Jewish
              Publication Society of America

Levine, L. I.
1974          'The Jewish-Greek Conflict in First Century Caesarea',
              *JJS* 25, 381–97
1975          *Caesarea under Roman Rule*, Leiden: Brill

Levinskaya, I.
1996          *The Book of Acts in Its Diaspora Setting*, Grand Rapids:
              Eerdmans

Levy, I.
1950–51       'Ptoléméê Lathyre et les Juifs', *HUCA* 23.2, 127–36

Lewis, N.
1983          *Life in Egypt under Roman Rule*, Oxford: Clarendon Press
1986          *Greeks in Ptolemaic Egypt*, Oxford: Clarendon Press

Lieu, J., North, J.
and Rajak, T.
(eds.)
1992          *The Jews among Pagans and Christians in the Roman
              Empire*, London: Routledge

Lindner, H.
1972          *Die Geschichtsauffassung des Flavius Josephus im Bellum
              Judaicum*, Leiden: Brill

Litfin, D.
1994          *St. Paul's Theology of Proclamation*, Cambridge:
              Cambridge University Press

Llewelyn, S. R. (ed.)
1992          *New Documents Illustrating Early Christianity (1980–81)*,
              Macquarie: Macquarie University

Lloyd, J. (ed.)
1981          *Excavations at Sidi Khrebish Benghazi (Berenice)*, vol. 1,
              The People's Socialist Libyan Arab Jamahiriya:
              Department of Antiquities

Lüdemann, G.
1983    *Paulus der Heidenapostel, Band II: Antipaulinismus im frühen Christentum,* Göttingen: Vandenhoeck & Ruprecht
1984    *Paul: Apostle to the Gentiles. Studies in Chronology,* London: SCM Press

Lüdemann, H.
1872    *Die Anthropologie des Apostels Paulus und ihre Stellung innerhalb seiner Heilslehre,* Kiel: Universitäts Buchhandlung (Paul Toeche)

Lüderitz, G. (with Appendix by J. Reynolds)
1983    *Corpus jüdischer Zeugnisse aus der Cyrenaika,* Wiesbaden: Dr. Ludwig Reichert
1994    'What is the Politeuma?', in J. W. van Henten and P. W. van der Horst (eds.), *Studies in Early Jewish Epigraphy,* Leiden: Brill, 183–225

McEleney, N. J.
1973    'Orthodoxy in Judaism of the First Christian Century', *JSJ* 4, 19–42

McKay, H. A.
1994    *Sabbath and Synagogue: The Question of Sabbath Worship in Ancient Judaism,* Leiden: Brill

McKnight, S.
1991    *A Light among the Gentiles. Jewish Missionary Activity in the Second Temple Period,* Minneapolis: Fortress Press

MacMullen, R.
1966    *Enemies of the Roman Order: Treason, Unrest and Alienation in the Roman Empire,* Cambridge, Mass: Harvard University Press
1994    'The Unromanized in Rome', in S. J. D. Cohen and E. S. Frerichs (eds.), *Diasporas in Antiquity,* Atlanta: Scholars Press, 47–64

Maccoby, H.
1991    *Paul and Hellenism,* London: SCM Press

Magie, D.
1950    *Roman Rule in Asia Minor to the End of the Third Century After Christ,* 2 vols., Princeton: Princeton University Press

Malherbe, A. J.
1983    *Social Aspects of Early Christianity.* 2nd edition, Philadelphia: Fortress Press

1989            *Paul and the Popular Philosophers*, Minneapolis: Fortress Press

Marcus, J.
1989            'The Circumcision and the Uncircumcision in Rome', *NTS* 35, 67–81

Marcus, R.
1945            'Jewish and Greek Elements in the Septuagint', in *Louis Ginzberg Jubilee Volume I*, New York, 227–45

Marshall, A. J.
1975            'Flaccus and the Jews of Asia (Cicero *Pro Flacco* 28.67–69)', *Phoenix* 29, 139–54

Mason, S. N.
1989            'Was Josephus a Pharisee? A Re-examination of *Life* 10–12', *JJS* 40, 31–45
1992            *Josephus and the New Testament*, Peabody, Mass.: Hendrickson

Mattingly, H.
1936            *Coins of the Roman Empire in the British Museum*, vol. 3, London: British Museum

Meecham, H. G.
1932            *The Oldest Version of the Bible. 'Aristeas' On Its Traditional Origin*, London: Holborn

Meeks, W. A.
1967            *The Prophet-King. Moses Traditions and the Johannine Christology*, Leiden: Brill
1968            'Moses as God and King', in J. Neusner (ed.), *Religions in Antiquity: Essays in Memory of E. R. Goodenough*, Leiden: Brill, 354–71
1985            'Breaking Away: Three New Testament Pictures of Christianity's Separation from the Jewish Communities', in J. Neusner and E. S. Frerichs (eds.), *"To See Ourselves as Others See Us." Christians, Jews, "Others" in Late Antiquity*, Chico: Scholars Press, 93–115

Meeks, W. A. and Wilken, R. L.
1978            *Jews and Christians in Antioch in the First Four Centuries of the Common Era*, Missoula: Scholars Press

Meisner, N.
1977            'Aristeasbrief', in *JSHRZ* II.1, 35–85, Gütersloh: Gerd Mohn

Mendelson, A.
1982          *Secular Education in Philo of Alexandria*, Cincinnati: Hebrew Union College Press.

Merrill, E. T.
1919          'The Expulsion of Jews from Rome under Tiberius', *CP* 14, 365–72

Millar, F.
1983          'Empire and City, Augustus to Julian: Obligations, Excuses and Status', *JRS* 73, 76–96
1993          *The Roman Near East 31 BC - AD 337*, Cambridge, Mass.: Harvard University Press

Mitchell, S.
1993          *Anatolia: Land, Men, and Gods in Asia Minor*, 2 vols., Oxford: Clarendon Press

Modrzejewski, J. M.
1991          *Les Juifs d'Egypte, De Ramses II à Hadrien*, Paris: Editions Errance
1993          'How to be a Greek and Yet a Jew in Hellenistic Alexandria', in S. J. D. Cohen and E. S. Frerichs (eds.), *Diasporas in Antiquity*, Atlanta: Scholars Press, 65–92

Moehring, H. R.
1959          'The Persecution of the Jews and the Adherents of the Isis Cult at Rome A. D. 19', *NovT* 3, 293–304
1975          'The *Acta pro Judaeis* in the *Antiquities* of Flavius Josephus: A Study in Hellenistic and Modern Apologetic Historiography', in J. Neusner (ed.), *Christianity, Judaism and Other Greco-Roman Cults. Studies for Morton Smith at Sixty*, Part Three, Leiden: Brill, 124–58
1984          'Joseph ben Matthia and Flavius Josephus: The Jewish Prophet and Roman Historian', in *ANRW* II.21.2, 864–944

Momigliano, A.
1961          *The Emperor Claudius and His Achievement*, revised edition, Oxford: Oxford University Press
1975a         'La portata storica dei vaticini sul settimo re nel terzo libro degli Oracoli Sibillini', in *Forma Futuri. Studi in Onore del Cardinale Michele Pellegrino*, Turin: Bottega d'Erasmo, 1077–84. Reprinted in *Sesto Contributo Alla Storia degli Studi Classici e del Mondo Antico*, Rome: Storia e Letteratura, 1980, 2.551–59
1975b         *Alien Wisdom. The Limits of Hellenization*, Cambridge: Cambridge University Press

1982          Review of J.-D. Gauger, *Beiträge zur jüdischen Apologetik*, *CP* 77, 258–61

Mor, M. (ed.)
1992          *Jewish Assimilation, Acculturation and Accommodation: Past Traditions, Current Issues and Future Prospects*, New York: Lanham

Morgan, M. A.
1983          *Sepher Ha-Razim. The Book of the Mysteries*, Chico: Scholars Press

Morkholm, O.
1961          'Eulaios and Lenaios', *Classica et Mediaevalia* 22, 32–43

Morris, J.
1987          'The Jewish Philosopher Philo', in Schürer 3.809–89

Murray, O.
1967          'Aristeas and Ptolemaic Kingship', *JTS* 18, 337–71

Mussies, G.
1982          'The Interpretatio Iudaica of Thot-Hermes', in M. Heerma van Vos et al. (eds.), *Studies in Egyptian Religion dedicated to Professor Jan Zandee*, Leiden: Brill, 89–120

Musurillo, H. A.
1954          *The Acts of the Pagan Martyrs. Acta Alexandrinorum*, Oxford: Clarendon Press

Newbold, R. F.
1974          'Social Tension at Rome in the Early Years of Tiberius' Reign', *Athenaeum* 52, 110–43

Niebuhr, K.-W.
1987          *Gesetz und Paränese. Katechismusartige Weisungsreihen in der frühjüdischen Literatur*, Tübingen: J. C. B. Mohr (Paul Siebeck)
1992          *Heidenapostel aus Israel*, Tübingen: J. C. B. Mohr (Paul Siebeck)

Niehoff, M.
1992          *The Figure of Joseph in Post-Biblical Jewish Literature*, Leiden: Brill

Niese, B.
1876          'Bemerkungen über die Urkunden bei Josephus Archaeol. B. XIII. XIV. XVI.', *Hermes* 11, 466–88
1887–95       *Flavii Iosephi Opera*, Berlin: Weidmann

Nikiprowetzky, V.
1970          *La Troisième Sibylle*, Paris: La Haye

1977          *Le Commentaire de l'Écriture chez Philon d'Alexandrie*,
              Leiden: Brill

Nock, A. D.
1933          *Conversion: The Old and the New in Religion from
              Alexander the Great to Augustine of Hippo*, Oxford:
              Clarendon Press
1955          Review of E. R. Goodenough, *Jewish Symbols in the
              Greco-Roman Period*, vols. 1–4, *Gnomon* 27, 558–72.
1972          'Paul and the Magus', in *Essays on Religion and the
              Ancient World* (edited by Z. Stewart), Oxford:
              Clarendon Press, 308–30

Nolland, J.
1979a         '*Sib. Or.* III.265–94, An Early Maccabean Messianic
              Oracle', *JTS* 30, 158–66
1979b         'Proselytism or Politics in Horace *Satires* I,4,138–143?',
              *VC* 33, 347–55

Norden, E.
1909          *Die Antike Kunstprosa*, Berlin/Leipzig: Teubner

North, J.
1979          'Religious Toleration in Republican Rome', *Proceedings
              of the Cambridge Philological Society* 25, 85–103

Noy, D.
1993          *Jewish Inscriptions of Western Europe. Volume 1: Italy
              (excluding the City of Rome), Spain and Gaul*, Cambridge:
              Cambridge University Press

Parke, H. W.
1988          *Sibyls and Sibylline Prophecy in Classical Antiquity* (edited
              by B. C. McGing), London: Routledge

Paul, A.
1986          'Le Troisième Livre des Macchabées', in *ANRW*
              II.20.1, 298–336

Pearson, B. A.
1980          'Jewish Elements in Gnosticism and the Development
              of Gnostic Self-Definition', in E. P. Sanders (ed.),
              *Jewish and Christian Self-Definition*, vol. 1, London: SCM
              Press, 151–60
1986          'Earliest Christianity in Egypt: Some Observations',
              in *The Roots of Egyptian Christianity*, Philadelphia:
              Fortress Press, 132–60

Pelletier, A.
1962          *Lettre d'Aristée à Philocrate*, Paris: Cerf

Penna, R.
1982                'Les Juifs à Rome au temps de l'apôtre Paul', *NTS*
                    28, 321–47

Pfitzner, V. C.
1967                *Paul and the Agon Motif,* Leiden: Brill

Philonenko, M.
1968                *Joseph et Asénath. Introduction, Texte Critique et Notes,*
                    Leiden: Brill

Pohlenz, M.
1949                'Paulus und die Stoa', *ZNW* 42, 69–104

Porten, B.
1984                'The Jews in Egypt', in W. D. Davies and L. Finkelstein
                    (eds.), *The Cambridge History of Judaism. Volume One:
                    The Persian Period,* Cambridge: Cambridge University
                    Press, 372–400

Preisendanz, K.
1928, 1931          *Papyri Graecae Magicae. Die griechischen Zauberpapyri,* 2
                    vols., Berlin/Leipzig: Teubner

Pucci (ben
  Ze'ev), M.
1981                *La Rivolta Ebraica al Tempo di Traiano,* Pisa: Giardini
                    Editori e Stamatori
1989                'Greek Attacks Against Alexandrian Jews During
                    Emperor Trajan's Time', *JSJ* 20, 31–48
1993                'The Reliability of Josephus Flavius: The Case of
                    Hecataeus' and Manetho's Accounts of Jews and
                    Judaism: Fifteen Years of Contemporary Research
                    (1974–1990)', *JSJ* 24, 215–34

Radice, R. and
  Runia, D. T.
1988                *Philo of Alexandria: An Annotated Bibliography 1937–
                    1986,* Leiden: Brill

Radin, M.
1915                *The Jews Among the Greeks and Romans,* Philadelphia:
                    Jewish Publication Society of America
1925                Review of H. I. Bell, *Jews and Christians in Rome, CP*
                    20, 368–75

Räisänen, H.
1983                *Paul and the Law,* Tübingen: J. C. B. Mohr (Paul
                    Siebeck)

Rajak, T.
  1978    'Moses in Ethiopia', *JJS* 29, 111–22
  1979    Review of E. M. Smallwood, *The Jews under Roman Rule*, *JRS* 69, 192–94
  1982    'Josephus and the "Archaeology" of the Jews', *JJS* 33, 465–77
  1983    *Josephus. The Historian and his Society*, London: Duckworth
  1984    'Was there a Roman Charter for the Jews?', *JRS* 74, 107–23
  1985    'Jewish Rights in the Greek Cities under Roman Rule: A New Approach', in W. S. Green (ed.), *Approaches to Ancient Judaism*, vol. 5, Atlanta: Scholars Press, 19–35
  1994    'Inscription and Context: Reading the Jewish Catacombs of Rome', in J. W. van Henten and P. W. van der Horst (eds.), *Studies in Early Jewish Epigraphy*, Leiden: Brill, 226–41

Rappaport, U.
  1981    'Jewish-Pagan Relations and the Revolt against Rome in 66–70 C.E.', *Jerusalem Cathedra* 1, 81–95

Redditt, P. L.
  1983    'The Concept of *Nomos* in Fourth Maccabees', *CBQ* 45, 249–70

Reese, J. M.
  1965    'Plan and Structure in the Book of Wisdom', *CBQ* 27, 391–99
  1970    *Hellenistic Influence on the Book of Wisdom and its Consequences*, Rome: Biblical Institute Press

Reinach, T.
  1888    'Mithridate et les Juifs', *REJ* 16, 204–10
  1895    *Textes d'Auteurs Grecs et Romains relatifs au Judaisme*, Paris: Leroux

Rémondon, R.
  1960    'Les antisémites de Memphis (P.IFAO inv. 104 = CPJ 141)', *Chronique d'Égypte* 35, 244–61

Renehan, R.
  1972    'The Greek Philosophical Background of Fourth Maccabees', *Rheinisches Museum für Philologie* 115, 223–38

Rex, J,
  1986    *Race and Ethnicity*, Milton Keynes: Open University Press

Reynolds, J. M. and
  Tannenbaum, R.
  1987                *Jews and Godfearers at Aphrodisias*, Cambridge:
                     Cambridge Philological Society

Riaud, J.
  1986                'Les Thérapeutes d'Alexandrie dans la tradition et
                     dans la recherche critique jusqu'aux découvertes de
                     Qumran', in *ANRW* II.20.2, 1189–1295

Robert, L.
  1937                'Un Corpus des Inscriptions Juives', *REJ* 101, 73–86
  1940                *Les gladiateurs dans l'orient grec*, Limoges: A. Bontemps

Robertson, R. G.
  1985                'Ezekiel the Tragedian', in *OTP* 2, 803–19

Roddaz, J.-M.
  1984                *Marcus Agrippa*, Rome: École française de Rome

Rogers, G. M.
  1991                *The Sacred Identity of Ephesos*, London: Routledge

Romanelli, P.
  1971                *La Cirenaica Romana (96 a.C - 642 d.C)*, Rome:
                     'L'Erma' di Bretschneider

Rostovtzeff, M.
  1941                *The Social and Economic History of the Hellenistic World*,
                     3 vols., Oxford: Clarendon Press

Runia, D. T.
  1986                *Philo of Alexandria and the Timaeus of Plato*, Leiden: Brill

Rutgers, L. V.
  1990                'Überlegungen zu den jüdischen Katakomben Roms',
                     *JAC* 33, 140–57
  1992                'Archaeological Evidence for the Interaction of Jews
                     and Non-Jews in Late Antiquity', *American Journal of
                     Archaeology* 96, 101–18
  1995                *The Jews in Late Ancient Rome*, Leiden: Brill

Rzach, A.
  1923                'Sibyllinische Orakel', in *PW* 2A, 2103–83

Sacks, J.
  1993                *One People? Tradition, Modernity, and Jewish Unity*,
                     London: The Littman Library of Jewish Civilization

Safrai, S.
  1974                'Relations between the Diaspora and the Land of
                     Israel', in S. Safrai and M. Stern (eds.), *The Jewish*

| | *People in the First Century*, Compendia Rerum Iudaicarum ad Novum Testamentum I.1, Assen: Van Gorcum; Philadelphia: Fortress Press, 184–215 |
|---|---|
| 1976 | 'Education and the Study of the Torah', in S. Safrai and M. Stern (eds.), *The Jewish People in the First Century*, Compendia Rerum Iudaicarum ad Novum Testamentum I.2, Assen: Van Gorcum; Philadelphia: Fortress Press, 945–70 |

**Samuel, A. E.**

| 1983 | *From Athens to Alexandria: Hellenism and Social Goals in Ptolemaic Egypt*, Louvain |
|---|---|
| 1989 | *The Shifting Sands of History: Interpretations of Ptolemaic Egypt*, Lanham: University Press of America |

**Sandbach, F. H.**

| 1975 | *The Stoics*, 2nd edition, London: Chatto & Windus |
|---|---|

**Sanders, E. P.**

| 1976 | 'The Covenant as a Soteriological Category and the Nature of Salvation in Palestinian and Hellenistic Judaism', in R. Hammerton-Kelly and R. Scroggs (eds.), *Jews, Greeks and Christians. Religious Cultures in Late Antiquity. Essays in Honor of William David Davies*, Leiden: Brill, 11–44 |
|---|---|
| 1977 | *Paul and Palestinian Judaism: A Comparison of Patterns of Religion*, London: SCM Press |
| 1983 | *Paul, The Law, and the Jewish People*, Philadelphia: Fortress Press |
| 1990a | *Jewish Law from Jesus to the Mishnah. Five Studies*, London: SCM Press |
| 1990b | 'Jewish Association with Gentiles and Galatians 2.11–14', in R. T. Fortna and B. R. Gaventa (eds.), *The Conversation Continues: Studies in Paul and John in Honor of J. Louis Martyn*, Nashville: Abingdon Press, 170–88 |
| 1992 | *Judaism: Practice and Belief, 63 BCE - 66 CE*, London: SCM Press |

**Sanders, J. T.**

| 1993 | *Schismatics, Sectarians, Dissidents, Deviants. The First One Hundred Years of Jewish-Christian Relations*, London: SCM Press |
|---|---|

**Sandmel, S.**

| 1956 | *Philo's Place in Judaism: A Study of Conceptions of Abraham in Jewish Literature*, Cincinnati: Hebrew Union College Press |
|---|---|
| 1979a | *Philo of Alexandria: An Introduction*, Oxford: Oxford University Press |

|  |  |
|---|---|
| 1979b | *The Genius of Paul*, Philadelphia: Fortress Press |
| 1983 | 'Philo Judaeus: An Introduction to the Man, his Writings, and his Significance', in *ANRW* II.21.1, 3–46 |

Sänger, D.

|  |  |
|---|---|
| 1980 | *Antikes Judentum und die Mysterien. Religionsgeschichtliche Untersuchungen zu Joseph und Aseneth*, Tübingen: J. C. B. Mohr (Paul Siebeck) |
| 1985 | 'Erwägungen zur historischen Einordnung und zur Datierung von "Joseph und Aseneth" ', *ZNW* 76, 86–106 |

Saulnier, C.

|  |  |
|---|---|
| 1981 | 'Lois Romaines sur les Juifs selon Flavius Josèphe', *RB* 88, 161–98 |

Schalit, A.

|  |  |
|---|---|
| 1959–60 | 'The Letter of Antiochus III to Zeuxis Regarding the Establishment of Jewish Military Colonies in Phrygia and Lydia', *JQR* 50, 289–318 |

Schäublin, Ch.

|  |  |
|---|---|
| 1982 | 'Josephus und die Griechen', *Hermes* 110, 316–41 |

Schreckenberg, H.

|  |  |
|---|---|
| 1968/1979 | *Bibliographie zu Flavius Josephus*, Leiden: Brill; *Supplementband mit Gesamtregister*, 1979 |

Schürer, E.
(revised)

|  |  |
|---|---|
| 1973–1987 | *The History of the Jewish People in the Age of Jesus Christ (175 B.C. - A.D. 135)*, revised and edited by G. Vermes, F. Millar, M. Black and M. Goodman, 3 vols., Edinburgh: T & T Clark |

Schwartz, D.

|  |  |
|---|---|
| 1992 | *Studies in the Jewish Background of Christianity*, Tübingen: J. C. B. Mohr (Paul Siebeck) |

Schwartz, J.

|  |  |
|---|---|
| 1953 | 'Note sur la famille de Philon d'Alexandrie', *Annuaire de L'Institut de Philologie et d'Histoire Orientales et Slaves* 13, 591–602 |

Schwartz, S.

|  |  |
|---|---|
| 1990 | *Josephus and Judaean Politics*, Leiden: Brill |

Scramuzza, V. M.

|  |  |
|---|---|
| 1940 | *The Emperor Claudius*, Cambridge, Mass.; Harvard University Press |

Seager, A. R. and
  Kraabel, A. T.
1983            'The Synagogue and the Jewish Community', in G.
                M. A. Hanfmann (ed.), *Sardis from Prehistoric to Roman
                Times. Results of the Archaeological Exploration of Sardis
                1958–1975*, Cambridge, Mass.: Harvard University
                Press, 168–90

Segal, A. F.
1990            *Paul the Convert: The Apostolate and Apostasy of Saul the
                Pharisee*, New Haven: Yale University Press

Sevenster, J. N.
1961            *Paul and Seneca*, Leiden: Brill

Sharot, S.
1976            *Judaism: A Sociology*, New York: Holmes & Meier

Sherwin-White,
  A. N.
1967            *Racial Prejudice in Imperial Rome*, Cambridge: Cam-
                bridge University Press

Shutt, R. J. H.
1961            *Studies in Josephus*, London: SPCK
1985            'Letter of Aristeas', in *OTP* 2, 7–34

Siegel, B. J.
1955            *Acculturation: Critical Abstracts, North America*, Stanford:
                Stanford University Press

Siegert, F.
1973            'Gottesfürchtige und Sympathisanten', *JSJ* 4, 109–64

Silver, J. D.
1973–74         'Moses and the Hungry Birds', *JQR* 64, 123–53

Simon, M.
1976            'Jupiter-Yahve', *Numen* 23, 40–66
1983            'Sur quelques aspects des Oracles Sibyllins juifs', in
                D. Hellholm (ed.), *Apocalypticism in the Mediterranean
                World and the Near East*, Tübingen: J. C. B. Mohr (Paul
                Siebeck), 219–33
1986            *Verus Israel: A Study of the Relations between Christians
                and Jews in the Roman Empire (AD 135–425)*, The
                Littmann Library of Jewish Civilization, Oxford:
                Oxford University Press (French original, Paris 1948)

Slingerland, D.
1989            'Suetonius *Claudius* 25.4 and the Account in Cassius
                Dio', *JQR* 79, 305–22

Smallwood, E. M.
1956a        'Some notes on the Jews under Tiberius', *Latomus* 15, 314–29
1956b        'Domitian's Attitude toward the Jews and Judaism', *CP* 51, 1–13
1959         'The alleged Jewish sympathies of Poppaea Sabina', *JTS* 10, 329–35
1970         *Philonis Alexandrini Legatio ad Gaium*, 2nd edition, Leiden: Brill
1981         *The Jews under Roman Rule. From Pompey to Diocletian*, 2nd edition, Leiden: Brill

Smith, J. Z.
1980         'Fences and Neighbours: Some Contours of Early Judaism', in W. S. Green (ed.), *Approaches to Ancient Judaism II*, Chico: Scholars Press, 1–25

Smith M.
1967         'Goodenough's *Jewish Symbols* in Retrospect', *JBL* 86, 53–68
1987         *Palestinian Parties and Politics that Shaped the Old Testament*, London: SCM Press

Solin, H.
1983         'Juden und Syrer im westlichen Teil der römischen Welt', in *ANRW* II.29.2, 587–789

Stambaugh, J. E.
1988         *The Ancient Roman City*, Baltimore: John Hopkins University Press

Stein, E.
1929         *Die allegorische Exegese des Philo aus Alexandreia*, Giessen: Alfred Töpelmann

Sterling, G. E.
1992         *Historiography and Self-Definition. Josephos, Luke-Acts and Apologetic Historiography*, Leiden: Brill

Stern, M.
1974         'The Jewish Diaspora', in S. Safrai and M. Stern (eds.), *The Jewish People in the First Century*, Compendia Rerum Iudaicarum ad Novum Testamentum I.1, Assen: Van Gorcum; Philadelphia: Fortress Press, 117–83
1974–84      *Greek and Latin Authors on Jews and Judaism*, Jerusalem: The Israel Academy of Sciences and Humanities, 3 vols. (1974, 1981, 1984)

Sullivan, J. P.
1991         *Martial: The Unexpected Classic*, Cambridge: Cambridge University Press

Swete, H. B.
1914      *An Introduction to the Old Testament in Greek*, 2nd edition revised, Cambridge: Cambridge University Press

Tajra, H. W.
1989      *The Trial of St. Paul*, Tübingen: J. C. B. Mohr (Paul Siebeck)

Tarn, W. W. and
Griffith, G. T.
1959      *Hellenistic Civilisation*, 3rd edition, London: Arnold

Tatum, W. Barnes
1986      'The LXX Version of the Second Commandment (Ex. 20,3–6; Deut. 5,7–10): A Polemic against Idols, not Images', *JSJ* 17, 177–95

Tcherikover, V.
1956      'Jewish Apologetic Literature Reconsidered', *Eos* 48, 169–93
1958      'The Ideology of the Letter of Aristeas', *HTR* 51, 59–85
1961a      *Hellenistic Civilization and the Jews*, translated by S. Applebaum; Philadelphia: Jewish Publication Society of America; Jerusalem: Magnes Press
1961b      'The Third Book of Maccabees as a Historical Source of Augustus' Time', in A. Fuks and I. Halpern (eds.), *Scripta Hierosolymitana VII*, Jerusalem: Magnes Press, 1–26

Tcherikover, V.
and Fuks, A.
1957–64      *Corpus Papyrorum Judaicarum*, Jerusalem: Magnes Press; Cambridge, Mass.: Harvard University Press; 3 vols. (1957, 1960, 1963), 3rd vol. with M. Stern and D. M. Lewis

Terian, A.
1981      *Philonis Alexandrini De Animalibus*, Chico: Scholars Press

Thackeray, H. St. J.
1929      *Josephus. The Man and the Historian*, New York: Jewish Institute of Religion

Theissen, G.
1992      *The Gospels in Context. Social and Political History in the Synoptic Tradition*, Edinburgh: T & T Clark.

Thompson, D. J.
1988      *Memphis under the Ptolemies*, Princeton: Princeton University Press

Thompson, L. A.
1982            'Domitian and the Jewish Tax', *Historia* 31, 329–42

Thornton, J. C. G.
1989            'Jewish New Moon Festivals, Galatians 4. 3–11 and
                Colossians 2. 16', *JTS* 40, 97–100

Tiede, D. L.
1972            *The Charismatic Figure as Miracle Worker*, Missoula:
                Society of Biblical Literature

Tomson, P. J.
1990            *Paul and the Jewish Law*, Compendia Rerum Iudaicarum
                ad Novum Testamentum III.1, Assen: Van Gorcum

Tracey, S.
1928            'III Maccabees and Pseudo-Aristeas. A Study', *Yale
                Classical Studies* 1, 241–52

Trachtenberg, J.
1939            *Jewish Magic and Superstition: A Study in Folk-Religion*,
                New York: Behrman

Trebilco, P.
1991            *Jewish Communities in Asia Minor*, Cambridge:
                Cambridge University Press

Turner, E. G.
1954            'Tiberius Iulius Alexander', *JRS* 44, 54–64

Urbach, E. E.
1975            *The Sages, Their Concepts and Beliefs*, Jerusalem: Magnes
                Press

van der Horst, P. W.
1978            *The Sentences of Pseudo-Phocylides*, Leiden: Brill
1983            'Moses' Throne Vision in Ezekiel the Dramatist', *JJS*
                34, 21–29
1984            *Chaeremon: Egyptian Priest and Stoic Philosopher*, Leiden:
                Brill
1988            'Pseudo-Phocylides Revisited' *JSP* 3, 3–30
1991            *Ancient Jewish Epitaphs*, Kampen: Kok Pharos Publishing
                House
1994            'Jewish Poetical Tomb Inscriptions', in J. W. van
                Henten and P. W. van der Horst (eds.), *Studies in Early
                Jewish Epigraphy*, Leiden: Brill, 129–47

van Henten, J. W.
1986            'Datierung und Herkunft des Vierten
                Makkabäerbuches', in J. W. van Henten et al. (eds.),

Tradition and Re-Interpretation in Jewish and Early
Christian Literature. Essays in Honour of J. C. H. Lebram,
Leiden: Brill, 136–49

van Unnik, W. C.
1962      *Tarsus or Jerusalem: The City of Paul's Youth*, London:
          Epworth Press
1974      'Josephus' Account of the Story of Israel's Sin with
          Alien Women in the Country of Midian (Num. 25.
          1ff)', in M. S. H. G. Heerma von Voss (ed.), *Travels in*
          *the World of the Old Testament: Studies Presented to Professor*
          *M. A. Beek*, Assen: Van Gorcum, 241–61
1993      *Das Selbstverständnis der jüdischen Diaspora in der*
          *hellenistisch-römischen Zeit*, (edited by P. W. van der
          Horst), Leiden: Brill

Vermes, G.
1955      'La figure de Moïse au tournant des deux Testaments',
          in *Moïse, L'Homme de l'Alliance*, Paris: Cahiers Sioniens,
          66–74

Vielhauer, P.
1966      'On the "Paulinism" of Acts,' in L. E. Keck and J. L.
          Martyn (eds.), *Studies in Luke-Acts*, Nashville:
          Abingdon Press, 33–50

Vogelstein, H.
1940      *History of the Jews in Rome*, Philadephia: Jewish
          Publication Society

von Stauffenberg,
A. S.
1931      *Die römische Kaisergeschichte bei Malalas, Griech. Text der*
          *Bücher IX–XII und Untesuchungen*, Stuttgart

Walbank, F. W.
1981      *The Hellenistic World*, London: Fontana

Walsh, P.
1970      *The Roman Novel*, Cambridge: Cambridge University
          Press

Walter, N.
1964      *Der Thoraausleger Aristobulos*, Berlin: Akademie-
          Verlag
1980a     *Fragmente jüdisch-hellenistischer Historiker*, JSHRZ I.2,
          2nd edition, Gütersloh: Gerd Mohn
1980b     *Fragmente jüdisch-hellenistischer Exegeten*, JSHRZ III.2,
          2nd edition, Gütersloh: Gerd Mohn

1983                           *Pseudepigraphische jüdisch-hellenistische Dichtung,* JSHRZ IV.3, Gütersloh: Gerd Mohn

Wardman, A.
1982                           *Religion and Statecraft among the Romans,* London: Granada

Wardy, B.
1979                           'Jewish Religion in Pagan Literature during the Late Republic and Early Empire', in *ANRW* II.19.1, 592–644

Watson, F.
1986                           *Paul, Judaism and the Gentiles. A Sociological Approach,* Cambridge: Cambridge University Press

Wedderburn, A. J. M.
1987                           *Baptism and Resurrection,* Tübingen: J. C. B. Mohr (Paul Siebeck)

Weisengoff, J. P.
1949                           'The Impious of Wisdom 2', *CBQ* 11, 40–65

West, S.
1974                           '*Joseph and Asenath*: A Neglected Greek Romance', *CQ* 68, 70–81

Westerholm, S.
1988                           *Israel's Law and the Church's Faith,* Grand Rapids: Eerdmans

Westermann, W. L.
1938                           'Enslaved Persons who are Free', *AJPh* 59, 1–30

Whitman, J.
1987                           *Allegory. The Dynamics of an Ancient and Medieval Technique,* Oxford: Clarendon Press

Whittaker, M.
1984                           *Jews and Christians: Graeco-Roman Views,* Cambridge: Cambridge University Press

Wiefel, W.
1991                           'The Jewish Community in Ancient Rome and the Origins of Roman Christianity', in K. P. Donfried (ed.), *The Romans Debate,* revised and expanded edition, Edinburgh: T & T Clark, 85–101

Williams, M. H.
1988                           'θεοσεβὴς γὰρ ἦν – the Jewish tendencies of Poppaea Sabina', *JTS* 39, 97–111

| 1989 | 'The Expulsion of the Jews from Rome in A.D. 19', *Latomus* 48, 765–784 |
| 1990 | 'Domitian, the Jews and the 'Judaizers' – a simple matter of cupiditas and maiestas?', *Historia* 39, 196–211 |
| 1994a | 'The Organisation of Jewish Burials in Ancient Rome in the Light of Evidence from Palestine and the Diaspora', *ZPE* 101, 165–182 |
| 1994b | 'The Structure of Roman Jewry Re-considered', *ZPE* 104, 129–141 |

Willrich, H.
| 1900 | *Judaica: Forschungen zur hellenistisch-jüdischen Geschichte und Literatur*, Göttingen: Vandenhoeck & Ruprecht |
| 1903 | 'Caligula. Dritter Teil. VII, Die Juden', *Beiträge zur alten Geschichte* (=*Klio*) 3, 397–419 |
| 1904 | 'Der historische Kern des III. Makkabäerbuches', *Hermes* 39, 244–58 |
| 1925 | 'Zum Brief des Kaisers Claudius an die Alexandriner', *Hermes* 60, 482–89 |

Wilson, S. G.
| 1992 | 'Gentile Judaizers', *NTS* 38, 605–16 |

Wilson, W. T.
| 1994 | *The Mysteries of Righteousness. The Literary Composition and Genre of the* Sentences *of Pseudo-Phocylides*, Tübingen: J. C. B. Mohr (Paul Siebeck) |

Winston, D.
| 1979 | *The Wisdom of Solomon*, New York: Doubleday |

Wolfson, H. A.
| 1944 | 'Philo on Jewish Citizenship in Alexandria', *JBL* 63, 165–68 |
| 1948 | *Philo. Foundations of Religious Philosophy in Judaism, Christianity, and Islam*, 2 vols., Cambridge, Mass.: Harvard University Press |

Wright, A. G.
| 1967 | 'The Structure of the Book of Wisdom', *Biblica* 48, 165–84 |

Wright, N. T.
| 1992 | *The New Testament and the People of God*, London: SPCK |

Yarbrough, O. L.
| 1993 | 'Parents and Children in the Jewish Family of Antiquity', in S. J. D. Cohen (ed.), *The Jewish Family in Antiquity*, Atlanta: Scholars Press, 39–59 |

Yavetz, Z.

1983    *Julius Caesar and his Public Image*, London: Thames & Hudson

1993    'Judaeophobia in Classical Antiquity: A Different Approach', *JJS* 44, 1–22

Ziener, G.

1956    *Die theologische Begriffssprache im Buche der Weisheit*, Bonn: P. Hanstein

Zuckerman, C.

1988    'Hellenistic *politeumata* and the Jews. A Reconsideration', *Scripta Classica Israelica* 8–9, 171–85

Zuntz, G.

1959    'Aristeas Studies I: "The Seven Banquets"', *Journal of Semitic Studies* 4, 21–36

# Index of Main Subjects and Places

Bold type represents main discussions.

Accommodation 10, 13, 80, 82, **92–101**, 138, 147, 156, 159, 224, 354, 356, 375, 393, 405–6

Acculturation 3, 13, 31, 42, 68, 82, **92–101**, 133–34, 141, 146–47, 149, 181, 191, 224, 281, 336–37, 345, 347, 358, 368–70, 375, 379, 387, 393

Adramyttium 266, 275

Agrippa I 52–53, 72, 251–54, 294–95, 302–3, 308–9

Agrippa II 72, 308, 328, 349, 354–55

Alexander the Alabarch 56, 68, 76, 105, 113, 159, 303, 328, 419

Alexandria, Jews in 1–2, 14, 20, 22–23, **27–81**, 106–7, 113–14, 117–18, 159, 161, 178–79, 225–26, 302–3, 337, 366, 401, 434, 436

Allegorists, pure 68, 109–10, 177, 345, 386, 394, 420, 439

Allegory 110, 141, **145–46**, 150, **154–58**, **165–71**, 173, **177–79**, 191, 348, 358, 374, 385, 390, 391, 401, 406, 420, 425, 427, 436–37

Aniconic worship (*see also* Art, Imperial images) 33, 55, 149, 165, 174, 286, **433–34**

Animals, sacred 33–34, 45–46, 73, 112, 124, 129–32, 144, 146, 174, 182, 186–89, 226, 366, 430

Anti-Jewish acts / attitudes (*see also* 'Anti-Social' charges, 'Atheist'/ 'Impious' charges) 9, **33–34**, 38, 40–41, 45–46, **50–60**, **72–81**, 136, 196, 199, 201, 222, **247–58**, 287–89, 297–98, 301, 306–7, 310, **312–17**, 351–52, 358, 360–61, 409–10, 428, 444

'Anti-Social' charges 33–34, 45, 175–76, 199, 248, 272–73, 298, 315, 358, 365, 429, 436–37

Antioch (in Syria), Jews in **242–45**, **249–58**, 322, 327, 329, 355, 370, 379, 384, 442

Apamea (Asia) 266, 275

Aphrodisias 7, 9, 259, 279–80, 404

Apion 38, 56, 59, 61, 68–69, **72–74**, 272, 302, 362, 366, 431, 438–39

Apollonius Molon 272–73, 276, 278, 362, 437

Apologetic, Jewish 31, 132, 134, 137, **148–49**, 169, 172, 261–62, 282, 313, 339, 342, 349, 356, 358, **361–68**, 401, 405, 422

'Apostasy' 32, 63, 77, 84, 86, 99, 107, 192–94, 196, 199–201, 294, 311, 321, 333, 344, 394–95, 431

Aramaic 25, 29, 30–31, 53, 182, 348, 351, 382

Art (*see also* Aniconic worship, Imperial images) 87, 90, 188, 283, 329–30

Assimilation (*see also* Integration) 2, 13, 25, 27, 56, 72, 75, 82, 84, 87, **92–101**, **103–24**, 147, 149, 238, 302, **320–35**, 345, 379, 384, 387, 393, 399, 403, 411, 435–37, 444

Athletics (*see also* Gymnasium) 58–59, 87, 89, 93, 114, 161, 175, 439

'Atheist'/'Impious' charges 33–34, 79, 272, 312, 315, 431–32

Berenice 26, 232, 234, 236–38, 425

Caesarea 243, 248, 249, 250, 252–53, 254, 255, 257, 258, 275, 276, 282, 332

Catacombs 5, 283–84, 318, 325, 329–30, 332, 414

*Chora* 19, 20, 23–27, 38, 77, 78, 81, 111, 424

Christians / Christianity 107, 110,
120, 122, 179–80, 204, 211,
216–18, 244, 254, 256, 260, 279,
280, 283, 284, 303–6, 312, 317,
326, 381–95, 404, 416
Circumcision 41, 73, 87, 91, 94, 110,
136–37, 149, 172, 246, 296, 309,
311, 312, 314–15, 317, 323,
324–25, 343, 386, 394, 403–4, 409,
**411–12, 438–39**, 443
Citizenship (Greek) 28, 42, 49–51,
**57–71**, 161, 192, 194–95, 200,
234–35, 245, 256–57, 261, 271,
272, 276, 327–28, 382, 385
Citizenship (Roman) (*see also* Rome)
238, 270, 271, 276, 289–90, 292–93,
300, 324, 327–38, 351, 382
Civic rights 28, 49, 54–55, 58, **60–71**,
89, 191, 238, 245, 253, 261,
**269–277**, 292, 331, 346
Cleruchs 22–23, 24, 44, 115, 233
Community Organization 43, 65–66,
269, 270–71, 284, 316, 414
Cos 11, 266
Covenant/election 135, 149, 175,
188, 198, 221, 359, 443
Crete 294
Cyprus 11, 78, 332, 428
Cyrene 63, 70, **232–41**, 321, 327,
328, 331, 350, 416

Damascus 243, 253, 254
Day of Atonement 416
Delos 11, 263, 293, 416, 419
Demotic 25, 27, 111
Diaspora Revolt (116–117 CE) 11–12,
20, 38, 60, **78–81**, 118, 203,
**227–28**, 232, **240–42**, 258, 281,
319, 332, 421, 423
Districts, Jewish 25, 28–29, 53,
77–78, 81, 117–18, 274, 331, 414
Dora 249, 252
Dura Europos 5, 433

Education / *paideia* (*see also*
Gymnasium) 89–91, 92, 95, 109,
138–41, 147, 160, 176, 183, 185, 201,
235, 345, 347, 371, 382–83, 391

Elephantine 20, 26, 34, 36, 112, 415
Ephesus 263, 266, 268, 270, 271,
274, 332
Euhemerism 131, 144
Exodus, The 33–34, 73, **132–38**,
170, 182, **185–89**, 191, 219, 344,
366, 415, 428

Family 111, 214, 324–25, 374, **412–13**
Festivals, Jewish 30, 110, 172, 200,
202–3, 270, 274, 413, 415–16
Food laws 30, 90, 94, 199, 212,
268–69, 276, 290, 315, 317, 326,
343, 345, 372, 377–78, **434–37**
Jewish explanation of 145–47,
172, 202
Jews' non-observance of 106,
199, 246, 384–85, 435
oil 212, 245, 256–57, 435
pork 73, 149, 288, 294,
299, 307, 314
*Fiscus Iudaicus* **76–78, 310–13**, 323,
404, 407, 418, 419, 438

Gentile religion (*see also* Aniconic
Worship, Animals (sacred), images,
Monotheism, Polytheism,
Syncretism)
Jewish negativity towards, 30,
45, 70, 73, 79, 114, 143–45,
174, 182, 186–88, 196, 199,
202, 204, 205, 207–9, 212,
215, 219–20, 222, 226, 227,
241, 247, 269, 271–72, 274,
289, 293, 312, 341–44,
363–66, 385, 410, **429–34**,
435, 437
Jews' positive relations to,
32–33, 90, 94, 99–100,
**104–6**, 108, 111–12, 117,
123, 129–32, 250, 256, 280,
**321–23**, 325, 379
'God-fearers' (*see also*
Sympathisers) 7, 9, 210, 279, 280,
307–8, 403–4
Greek (language) 22, 24–25, 27,
30–31, 44, 88, 89, 94–95, 347–48

Gymnasium (*see also* Athletics,
Education/*paideia*) 42, 44–45, 49,
58–59, 68, 70–71, 94, 107, 114,
134, 160, 232, 234, 245, 250,
256–57, 271, 280, 327, 371, 383

Halicarnassus 263, 270, 276,
Hebrew (language) 30, 31, 77–78,
91, 120, 166, 170, 182, 382, 440
Heliopolis 127–28, 132
Hellenism/Hellenization 3, 6, 25,
27, 30, 44, 60, 81, 83, 87, **88–98**,
102, 149, 150, 173, 183, 184, 191,
232, 243, 244, 246, 248, 249,
345–47, 374, 384, 387, 390, 403, 410

Iasus 70, 271
Imperial images (*see also* Aniconic
worship) 53–54, 203, 251, 252,
301, 363, 366, 420, 434
Intermarriage 30, 44, 67, 87, 107–8,
138, 204, 215, 315, 324–25, 385,
**410–12**, 439
Integration (*see also* Assimilation)
24, 60, 80, 82, 94, 97, 235, 236,
240, 242, 281, 318, 326
Ionia 268, 271, 273, 277

Jerusalem / the temple,
contributions to 66, 76–77,
238–39, **266–69**, 271, 272,
286, 287, 290–92, 310, 386,
407, **417–18**
destruction of 76, 225–26,
309–10, 317, 350–56
Diaspora attitudes to 26, 33,
37, 76, 91, 113–14, 139, 149,
175, 198, 219–28, 239,
266–69, 290, 291, 293, 299,
345, 350–56, 386, **417–23**, 431
Gaius' threat to 55–56, 76,
179, 251–52, 302, 306, 420
Gentile attitudes to 141, 143–44,
192, 272, 293
pilgrimage to 36, 310, 386,
419, **421–23**, 443

Judaea (*see also* Jerusalem/the temple)
Diaspora relations with 35,
39–40, 56, 80, 130, 139,
198–99, 221, 223–24, 226,
233, 239, 241, 242–58, 264,
278, 290, 294–95, 302, 347,
359–60, **421–23**
emigration from 20–21,
25–26, 33, 35, 242, 289–90,
309–10, 333

Laodicea 263, 266, 270
Leontopolis 26, 32, 36, 40, 42, 46,
76, 113, 115, 132, 149, 225, 353,
401, 406, 420, 441
Liturgies (civic) 268–69, 272, 277, 328

Magic 87, 90, **119–23**, 129, 219, 332
Manetho 33–34, 72, 129–30, 132,
136, 356, 362, 428
Melos 295
Messianism 80, 227–28, 241, 355, 360
Miletus 268, 270, 276, 280, 328
Mission (*see also* Proselytes /
Conversion) 9, 215, 317, 342,
345, 384, 408
Monotheism (*see also* Gentile
religion) 132, 136, 145, 149, 157,
165, 214, 341, **429–32**
Moses
Gentile attitudes to 33–34, 73,
129–30, 136, 272, 314–15,
317, 426
Jewish identification with **127–
32, 133–38**, 150, **163–66**, 168,
173, 219, 387, **426–28**

New Moon 236, 296, 415
Nomenclature 25, 89–90, 104, 115,
123–24, 235, 236, 283
Numbers of Jews 4, 41, 294–95

'Orthodoxy' 8, 57, 62–63, **83–88**,
101, 124
Ostia **424**, 425

Passover   34, 133, 136, 138, 150, 155, 415–16, 419, 422

Pergamum   262, 263, 264, 266, 275, 277–78

Philosophy, Jewish use of   95–96, 128, 145, 149, **150–60, 167–78**, 201, 348, 358, **369–80**, 427

Platonism   126, 151, 164–67, 173, 175, 215, 371

Politeuma   25, 43–44, 50, 64–65, 71, 234, 236, 237, 245, 393, 414, 416

Polytheism (*see also* Gentile religion)   132, 144, 202, 207, 288, 341, 431–33

Proselytes / Conversion (*see also* Mission)   14, 173, 176, **205–16**, 222, 226, 236, 253, 286, 288, 296, 298–300, **314–18**, 324, 329, 403–4, **408–10**, 419, 439

Pythagoreanism   151, 164, 299


Rome (*see also* Citizenship (Roman))
  Jewish hostility to (*see also* Diaspora Revolt)   75, 225, 227, 241
  Jewish support for   40–41, 46–47, 262, 264, 350–56, 360, 366
  Jews in   10, 11, 13, 59, 77, 106, 278, **282–319**, 323, 326–29, 331, 333–34, 346–47, 350, 416, 417, 421, 423, 426


Sabbath   30, 73, 91, 94, 110, 149, 155, 157, 292, 312–13, 317, 326, 342–43, 385, 395, **440–42**
  disputes over   51, 256, 270–71, 291, 322, 324, 379, 407, 426
  instruction on   161, 176, 178, 273, 317, 417, 425, 427
  names derived from   123–24, 334
  rest on   68, 116, 172, 176, 290, 293, 296–97, 307, 314, 328–29, 343, **440–42**
  worship on   27, 416–17
Sardis   7, 9, 259, 260, 263, 268, 269, 271, 276, 280, 331

Septuagint   1, 12, 30–31, 33–34, 126, 128, 132–39, 149, 151, 165–66, 207, 338–40, 360, 424–25

Sexual mores   146, 175–76, 187, 219–20, 222, 227, 235, 324, 339, 344, 388

Slaves, Jews as   21–22, 92, 111, 201, 235, 244, 287, 289–90, 293, 300, 309–10, 325–26, 382, 421, 439

Soldiers, Jews as   20, 21–22, 23–24, 29, 34, 36–40, 113, 115, 233, 249, 256, 261, 291, 295, 298–300, 322, 325, 441

Stoicism   91, 153–55, 163–64, 340, 371, 373, 389–91

Sympathisers (*see also* 'God-fearers')   14, 253, 280, 294, 295, 307–8, 311–12, 317–18, 329, 360, 365, 403, 410

Synagogues/'Prayer-Houses' (*see also* Sabbath)
  and the community   26–27, 77, 117, 240, 290, 292
  as buildings   5, 7, 29, 32, 79, 100, 195, 236–37, 239, 251, 255, 259, 274, 280, 313, 329, 331, 414
  as meetings   52, 236, 271, 279, 305–6, 416–17
  Christians' relations with   283, 326, 385–86, 393–95
  dedication of   24, 26, 31–32, 39, 293
  images in   53–54, 56, 59, 66, 203, 251–52
  instruction in   176, 178, 412, 416–17, 427
  officers in   284, 299, 316, 414, 433
  theft from   268, 276
Syncretism (*see also* Gentile religion)   87, 119–24, 132, 138, 156, 224, 285, 333–34


Tabernacles   54, 416, 419

Tarsus   70, 272, 327, 381

Taxes   23, 24, 49–50, 191, 194, 202, 238, 265, 267, 268, 287

Teuchira   70, 232, 235–36, 327

Theatre, Jewish attitudes to   85, 87, 89, 93, 114, 161, 175, 179, 237, 280, 328

Therapeutae   118–19, 162, 167, 175,
    211, 331, 400, 417
Tiberius Julius Alexander   75, 82,
    **105–6**, 113, 119, 400
Tyre   246, 248, 250

Women, Jewish   117–18, 204–16,
    312, 411–12, 416, 419,

# Index of References

**Old Testament/**
**Septuagint**

*Genesis*

| | |
|---|---|
| 1 | 154, 165 |
| 1.1–2 | 165 |
| 2 | 154, 165 |
| 2.1–3 | 155, 440 |
| 2.3 | 440 |
| 2.7 | 165 |
| 4.16 | 168 |
| 5.23 | 185 |
| 9 | 108 |
| 9.25 | 167 |
| 15 | 359 |
| 15.18 | 171 |
| 17 | 359 |
| 22 | 108 |
| 34 | 410, 411 |
| 34.14–16 | 411–12 |
| 41.45 | 126, 128, 204, 210 |
| 41.50 | 128 |
| 43.32 | 34, 208 |
| 46.34 | 34 |

*Exodus*

| | |
|---|---|
| 1.11 | 126 |
| 1.12 | 34, 46 |
| 2.11–14 | 358 |
| 2.12 | 129 |
| 3.14 | 126, 165 |
| 4.6–7 | 358 |
| 7.1 | 163 |
| 7.20–24 | 129 |
| 8.22 | 34 |
| 16.22–30 | 440 |
| 20–23 | 339 |
| 20.4–6 | 433 |
| 20.8–11 | 440 |
| 22.18 | 121 |
| 22.26–27 | 160, 431 |
| 22.30 | 338 |
| 23–25 | 338 |
| 23.9 | 344 |
| 30.11–16 | 417 |

| | |
|---|---|
| 30.12 | 418 |
| 31.12–17 | 441 |
| 32 | 435 |
| 34.15–16 | 410 |
| 35.3 | 441 |

*Leviticus*

| | |
|---|---|
| 11 | 434 |
| 11.6 | 126 |
| 11.17 | 132 |
| 11.44–45 | 437 |
| 18 | 339 |
| 19 | 342 |
| 19.33–34 | 344 |
| 20 | 339 |
| 20.24–26 | 437 |
| 26.44 | 198 |

*Numbers*

| | |
|---|---|
| 15.32–36 | 440 |
| 23.9 | 1 |
| 24.17 | 360 |
| 25 | 108, 410, 411, 435 |

*Deuteronomy*

| | |
|---|---|
| 5.8–10 | 433 |
| 6.6–7 | 412 |
| 6.14 | 430 |
| 6.20–25 | 412 |
| 7.1–4 | 410 |
| 10.9 | 169 |
| 11.19 | 412 |
| 12.16 | 434 |
| 12.23–24 | 434 |
| 12.30–31 | 430 |
| 13 | 108 |
| 13.6–11 | 344 |
| 14 | 434 |
| 14.7 | 126 |
| 14.8 | 149 |
| 16.1–8 | 415 |
| 18.9–14 | 121 |
| 22.6–7 | 338 |
| 25.1–3 | 394 |
| 28.63–68 | 359 |

| | |
|---|---|
| 29.17 | 430 |
| 29.25 | 430 |
| 30.1–5 | 199 |
| 31.10–13 | 412 |

*Judges*

| | |
|---|---|
| 14.3 | 412 |

*I Kingdoms* (**LXX**)

| | |
|---|---|
| 2.10 | 338 |

*Proverbs*

| | |
|---|---|
| 3.27–28 | 339 |

*Ezra*

| | |
|---|---|
| 9–10 | 410 |

*Esther* (**LXX**)

| | |
|---|---|
| Colophon | 421 |
| 4.17u | 412 |
| 4.17x | 435 |

*Isaiah*

| | |
|---|---|
| 11 | 221 |
| 19.19 | 36 |
| 41.2 | 223 |
| 41.25 | 223 |
| 47 | 227 |

*Jeremiah*

| | |
|---|---|
| 9.22 | 338 |
| 44 | 20, 112 |

*Daniel*

| | |
|---|---|
| 1 | 435 |
| 7 | 223 |

*Joel*

| | |
|---|---|
| 3.5 | 388 |

*Obadiah*

| | |
|---|---|
| 20 | 260 |

*Judith*

| | |
|---|---|
| 12.1–4 | 435 |
| 12.19 | 435 |

*Tobit*
4.12–13        410

*Susannah*
3              412

*1 Maccabees*
3.24           248
5.1–68         246
5.66           248
5.68           247
10.15–23       246
10.74–89       247
10.82–85       247
11.41–51       249
11.51          249
11.54–62       247
12.2–31        246
12.33–34       247
12.53          246
13.11          247
13.43–48       247
13.47–48       247
14.5–7         247
14.24          285
14.34–36       247
15.15–21       35
15.15–24       264, 285

*2 Maccabees*
1.1–9          421
1.10           37, 42,
               113, 152,
               446
1.1–2.18       35, 233
2.19–32        233
2.21           88, 410
2.23–31        233
2.25           233
2.29           233
ch. 3          32
4.12–13        88
4.32–38        245
chs.6–7        369, 376
6.4            376
6.8–9          246, 376
6.12–16        376
6.24–28        377
8.1            88, 410
8.1–7          376

8.16–17        376
10.2–5         376
12.2–9         376
12.2–31        246
12.39–45       123
13.9–12        376
14.38          88, 410
16.39          233

*3 and 4 Maccabees* (see
Main Diaspora
Authors)

**Main Diaspora Authors**

**Aristeas**      30, 31, 76,
                  113, 138–
                  50, 199,
                  201–2,
                  210–11,
                  223, 263,
                  445
1                 138
1–8               139
2                 142
3                 141, 143,
                  149, 406
3–5               141
5–8               141
6                 149, 406
7–8               140
9–82              139
10                141
12–27             21, 142
13                21
14                142
15                143
15–16             142
15–18             142
16                87, 143,
                  152, 360,
                  432
16–17             142
16–19             142
17–20             142
18                141
19                143
22–25             21, 202
23                142

24                141, 142
26–28             142
30–31             141
31                143, 149
35–40             142
36                149, 406
37                140, 142,
                  143
38                142
42                142, 143,
                  144
43                140, 141
44                142, 149,
                  406
45                142
46                141
51–82             139
83–120            139, 140,
                  420, 445
99                141
116               149
121–22            140
122               141, 142
124–25            140
125               141
126               149, 406
128               148, 434
128–38            342
130               141, 144,
                  147
130–71            139, 145–
                  47
131               142, 145
131–41            145
132               144, 145
132–33            142
134               144
134–38            144
135               433
135–37            144
138               46, 144,
                  187
139               147, 430
139–42            437
140               141, 144
140–41            141
142               147
142–69            145
142–71            434
143               146

**Aristeas** (*cont.*)

| | |
|---|---|
| 144 | 145–46 |
| 144–49 | 141 |
| 145–50 | 146 |
| 148 | 146 |
| 150 | 146 |
| 150–52 | 146, 437 |
| 151 | 146 |
| 151–52 | 144 |
| 153 | 146 |
| 153–62 | 146, 149 |
| 161 | 146 |
| 163–69 | 146 |
| 166–67 | 142 |
| 168 | 146 |
| 168–69 | 141 |
| 170 | 144, 149 |
| 170–71 | 141 |
| 175 | 142 |
| 177 | 142, 143 |
| 181 | 435 |
| 181–85 | 70 |
| 181–86 | 147 |
| 184 | 143 |
| 184–85 | 435 |
| 187–300 | 139, 140 |
| 189 | 145 |
| 190 | 142 |
| 193 | 145 |
| 195 | 145 |
| 197 | 145 |
| 200 | 141, 142, 145 |
| 201 | 141, 142 |
| 205 | 145 |
| 207 | 141, 145 |
| 210 | 142 |
| 215 | 141, 142 |
| 222–23 | 141, 144 |
| 229 | 142 |
| 233 | 1442 |
| 234 | 144, 345 |
| 235 | 140, 141, 145 |
| 237 | 141 |
| 255 | 145 |
| 256 | 141 |
| 285 | 141 |
| 293–94 | 142 |
| 295–300 | 141 |

| | |
|---|---|
| 296 | 141 |
| 301–11 | 149 |
| 310 | 25, 43, 65 |
| 312 | 142 |
| 313–16 | 142 |
| 321 | 140, 141 |

**Aristobulus** 150–58, 445–46

*Fragment 1=*

| | |
|---|---|
| 7.32.16–18 | 155, 415 |

*Fragment 2 =*

| | |
|---|---|
| 8.10.1–17 | 425 |
| 10.1 | 153, 155 |
| 10.2 | 154 |
| 10.3 | 150, 153, 154 |
| 10.4 | 151, 154 |
| 10.5 | 154 |
| 10.6 | 156 |
| 10.7–9 | 154 |
| 10.8 | 150, 153 |
| 10.9 | 153, 154 |
| 10.9–12 | 154 |
| 10.10 | 153 |
| 10.12 | 152–53 |
| 10.12–17 | 155 |
| 10.15 | 153 |
| 10.16 | 153 |
| 10.17 | 153 |

*Fragment 3 =*

| | |
|---|---|
| 13.12.1–2 | 150, 151, 156, 405 |

*Fragment 4 =*

| | |
|---|---|
| 13.12.3–8 | 432 |
| 12.3 | 150, 153, 154 |
| 12.3–4 | 155 |
| 12.4 | 151, 153 |
| 12.4ff. | 151 |
| 12.5 | 153 |
| 12.6 | 153 |
| 12.7 | 152, 153 |
| 12.8 | 150, 152 |

*Fragment 5 =*

| | |
|---|---|
| 13.12.9–16 | 440 |
| 12.9 | 153, 154 |
| 12.10–11 | 152 |
| 12.11 | 156, 405 |
| 12.11–12 | 153 |
| 12.12 | 153, 155 |
| 12.13 | 151, 155 |
| 12.13–16 | 155 |
| 12.15 | 153, 155 |

**Artapanus** 127–32, 446

*Fragment 1 =*

| | |
|---|---|
| 9.18.1 | 128, 130 |

*Fragment 2 =*

| | |
|---|---|
| 9.23.1–4 | |
| 23.1 | 128 |
| 23.2 | 128, 130 |
| 23.3 | 128 |
| 23.4 | 128, 130 |

*Fragment 3 =*

| | |
|---|---|
| 9.27.1–37 | |
| 27.1 | 128 |
| 27.2 | 130 |
| 27.3–4 | 128 |
| 27.4 | 128, 130, 131 |
| 27.4–6 | 130 |
| 27.6 | 129, 130 |
| 27.7–10 | 129 |
| 27.8 | 128 |
| 27.9 | 131 |
| 27.11 | 130 |
| 27.12 | 130, 131 |
| 27.16 | 130 |
| 27.19 | 130 |
| 27.20 | 130 |
| 27.21 | 130, 422 |
| 27.22 | 132 |
| 27.22–37 | 129 |
| 27.28 | 129 |
| 27.32 | 129, 130, 131 |
| 27.33 | 130 |
| 27.35 | 128, 131 |

**Ezekiel** 132–38, 207, 446–47

| | |
|---|---|
| 1–6 | 136 |
| 1–13 | 136 |
| 1–59 | 133 |
| 4–13 | 135 |
| 7 | 134 |
| 12 | 134, 405 |
| 35 | 134, 135, 138, 405 |
| 37 | 138 |
| 43 | 134, 405 |
| 50 | 135 |
| 68–82 | 137 |
| 68–89 | 133, 428 |
| 70 | 137 |
| 83 | 136, 138 |
| 83–89 | 137 |
| 90–131 | 133 |
| 104–8 | 135, 405 |
| 106 | 135 |
| 107 | 405 |
| 112 | 135, 405 |
| 130 | 136 |
| 132–51 | 136 |
| 132–92 | 133 |
| 148 | 135 |
| 154 | 137 |
| 155 | 135 |
| 162–66 | 136 |
| 167 | 422 |
| 167–68 | 137 |
| 192 | 415 |
| 193–242 | 133 |
| 204–13 | 135 |
| 213 | 135, 405, 430 |
| 217 | 136 |
| 236 | 135 |
| 239 | 135, 136 |
| 240 | 135 |
| 243–60 | 133 |
| 254ff. | 447 |

**Joseph and Aseneth**
204–16, 409, 447

| | |
|---|---|
| 1 | 204 |
| 1.1 | 207 |
| 1.3 | 209 |
| 1.5 | 214 |
| 2 | 207 |
| 2–4 | 205 |
| 2.3 | 207 |
| 3.3 | 209 |
| 3.4 | 209 |
| 3.6 | 208 |
| 4.7 | 209, 210 |
| 4.9–10 | 213 |
| 4.10 | 208 |
| 5–6 | 208 |
| 5–8 | 205 |
| 5.4–7 | 212 |
| 6.2 | 212 |
| 7.1 | 208, 211, 435 |
| 7.2 | 208 |
| 7.5 | 208, 430 |
| 8.5 | 205–6, 208, 209, 211, 212, 434 |
| 8.6 | 209, 214 |
| 8.6–7 | 215 |
| 8.9 | 209, 211, 213–14 |
| 8.10–11 | 206 |
| 9–13 | 205 |
| 9.1–5 | 206 |
| 10–13 | 206 |
| 10.1 | 210 |
| 10.12 | 209 |
| 10.13 | 209 |
| 11–13 | 213, 216 |
| 11.4–5 | 213 |
| 11.7–8 | 207 |
| 11.7–10 | 215 |
| 11.7–11 | 209 |
| 11.8 | 209 |
| 11.10 | 213, 430 |
| 12.1–2 | 209 |
| 12.5 | 209 |
| 12.9 | 209 |
| 12.10–15 | 213 |
| 14–17 | 205, 206, 211 |
| 15.3–17.3 | 211 |
| 15.4 | 214 |
| 15.4–5 | 209 |
| 15.5 | 211 |
| 15.7 | 214, 216 |
| 16.8 | 209 |
| 16.14 | 209, 211 |
| 16.16 | 211 |
| 16.17–23 | 211 |
| 17.6 | 214 |
| 18–21 | 205 |
| 19.1–5 | 209 |
| 19.5 | 211, 216 |
| 19.8 | 214 |
| 19.10–20.1 | 205 |
| 19.11 | 209 |
| 20.7 | 209, 210, 213 |
| 21.2–7 | 210 |
| 21.8 | 210 |
| 21.10–21 | 206 |
| 21.21 | 215 |
| 22–29 | 205, 214, 447 |
| 22.7–9 | 213 |
| 23.9 | 216 |
| 23.14 | 207 |
| 24.1–5 | 207 |
| 27.10 | 209 |
| 28.5 | 216 |
| 28.14 | 216 |
| 29.3 | 216 |
| 29.9 | 210 |

**Josephus** 346–68
*Bellum*

| | |
|---|---|
| 1.2 | 309, 351 |
| 1.3 | 346 |
| 1.3–6 | 346, 351 |
| 1.5 | 420 |
| 1.7–8 | 351 |
| 1.9–12 | 352, 355 |
| 1.10 | 352, 353 |
| 1.13–15 | 356 |
| 1.13–16 | 354 |
| 1.17 | 405 |
| 1.27 | 352 |
| 1.27–28 | 353 |
| 1.88 | 248 |
| 1.156 | 247 |
| 1.156–57 | 249 |
| 1.165–66 | 250 |
| 1.175 | 39, 40 |
| 1.187–92 | 40 |
| 1.190 | 36 |
| 1.396 | 250 |
| 1.422–25 | 250 |

**Bellum** (*cont.*)

| | |
|---|---|
| 1.425 | 250 |
| 2.85 | 250 |
| 2.101–10 | 294 |
| 2.119–66 | 354 |
| 2.184–203 | 252 |
| 2.186 | 251 |
| 2.197 | 293 |
| 2.206–10 | 302 |
| 2.214–16 | 303 |
| 2.223–31 | 251 |
| 2.266 | 253 |
| 2.266–70 | 253 |
| 2.267 | 254 |
| 2.268 | 251 |
| 2.284 | 253, 275 |
| 2.284–92 | 255 |
| 2.285–86 | 276 |
| 2.287 | 254, 329 |
| 2.287–88 | 276 |
| 2.291 | 425 |
| 2.309 | 106 |
| 2.310–14 | 309 |
| 2.345–401 | 349 |
| 2.358–87 | 354 |
| 2.388 | 409 |
| 2.390 | 355 |
| 2.393 | 349 |
| 2.402–5 | 309 |
| 2.455 | 353 |
| 2.456 | 441 |
| 2.457 | 255 |
| 2.457–86 | 74 |
| 2.458–60 | 255 |
| 2.461 | 248 |
| 2.461–80 | 255 |
| 2.463 | 253, 329 |
| 2.466–76 | 255, 323 |
| 2.469 | 254 |
| 2.478 | 248 |
| 2.479 | 256 |
| 2.487–88 | 28 |
| 2.487–98 | 74 |
| 2.488 | 29 |
| 2.489 | 74 |
| 2.490–91 | 74 |
| 2.494–98 | 74 |
| 2.495 | 29 |
| 2.502 | 248, 251 |
| 2.517 | 441 |
| 2.520 | 409 |
| 2.559–61 | 253, 254, 255, 329 |
| 2.561 | 4, 255 |
| 2.591 | 435 |
| 2.595–613 | 349 |
| 3.10 | 248 |
| 3.70–109 | 354 |
| 3.108 | 351 |
| 3.136 | 349 |
| 3.137 | 349 |
| 3.351 | 349 |
| 3.354 | 350 |
| 3.399–408 | 350 |
| 3.400 | 349 |
| 3.438–42 | 350 |
| 3.484 | 355 |
| 4.180–84 | 352, 356 |
| 4.250 | 349 |
| 4.381–88 | 353 |
| 4.567 | 419 |
| 5.45–46 | 106 |
| 5.55 | 419 |
| 5.199 | 419 |
| 5.201–5 | 419 |
| 5.205 | 76, 114, 160 |
| 5.257 | 352 |
| 5.354 | 355 |
| 5.363 | 352, 356 |
| 5.363–419 | 353, 355 |
| 5.364–66 | 354 |
| 5.367 | 354 |
| 5.375 | 350 |
| 5.402–6 | 356 |
| 5.412 | 353 |
| 5.442–45 | 352 |
| 5.510 | 106 |
| 5.541–47 | 350 |
| 5.550–51 | 248 |
| 5.556 | 248 |
| 5.562–63 | 293 |
| 6.38–39 | 355 |
| 6.96–110 | 353 |
| 6.101 | 356 |
| 6.101–2 | 352 |
| 6.107 | 351, 368 |
| 6.109–10 | 353 |
| 6.110 | 354 |
| 6.111 | 352 |
| 6.114 | 240 |
| 6.123 | 356 |
| 6.124–28 | 353 |
| 6.236–70 | 353 |
| 6.237–42 | 106 |
| 6.312–15 | 355 |
| 6.324 | 353 |
| 6.333–34 | 356 |
| 6.344 | 353 |
| 6.356 | 409 |
| 6.420 | 310 |
| 7.20 | 257 |
| 7.36–40 | 257 |
| 7.41–62 | 308 |
| 7.43 | 242, 243 |
| 7.43–44 | 245 |
| 7.44 | 245, 249 |
| 7.45 | 253, 254 |
| 7.46–53 | 256, 322 |
| 7.47 | 322 |
| 7.50 | 256, 322, 430 |
| 7.50–53 | 379 |
| 7.51 | 256 |
| 7.51–53 | 322 |
| 7.52 | 322, 442 |
| 7.52–53 | 256 |
| 7.54–62 | 257 |
| 7.96 | 257 |
| 7.100–11 | 257, 355 |
| 7.109 | 258 |
| 7.110 | 245 |
| 7.118 | 310 |
| 7.123–57 | 355 |
| 7.123–62 | 309 |
| 7.150 | 425 |
| 7.218 | 76, 311 |
| 7.361–63 | 248 |
| 7.361–69 | 243, 255 |
| 7.367 | 248 |
| 7.368 | 4, 255 |
| 7.375 | 422 |
| 7.409–20 | 75 |
| 7.420–21 | 353 |
| 7.420–35 | 76 |
| 7.421–36 | 36 |
| 7.423 | 36 |
| 7.437–53 | 239 |
| 7.438 | 239 |
| 7.447–50 | 240, 350 |

| | | | | | |
|---|---|---|---|---|---|
| ***Antiquitates*** | | 12.11–118 | 361, 424 | 14.185–267 | 263, 360 |
| 1.5 | 346, 360 | 12.21–22 | 360 | 14.190–212 | 277, 291 |
| 1.7 | 348 | 12.108 | 65 | 14.213 | 276 |
| 1.9 | 346, 405 | 12.119 | 245, 261 | 14.213–16 | 268, 270, |
| 1.10–12 | 360 | 12.119–24 | 245 | | 274, 277, |
| 1.14 | 357, 359 | 12.120 | 256, 435 | | 291, 292, |
| 1.18–26 | 358, 427 | 12.121–24 | 75 | | 415 |
| 1.24–25 | 358 | 12.125–26 | 261, 262, | 14.216 | 274 |
| 1.33 | 440 | | 271, 327 | 14.223–27 | 268, 270, |
| 1.108 | 357 | 12.126 | 271, 431 | | 277 |
| 1.183–85 | 359 | 12.147–53 | 261 | 14.223–34 | 293 |
| 1.191–93 | 359 | 12.186–89 | 30, 107 | 14.226 | 436, 441 |
| 1.192 | 412, 439 | 12.187 | 411 | 14.228 | 441 |
| 1.240–42 | 360 | 12.274–77 | 441 | 14.228–40 | 262, 271, |
| 2.94 | 360 | 12.387 | 36 | | 328 |
| 2.238–53 | 129 | 13.62–73 | 36, 132 | 14.230 | 276 |
| 2.348 | 357 | 13.65 | 36 | 14.232 | 407, 441 |
| 3.179 | 431 | 13.67 | 32 | 14.234 | 324, 404, |
| 3.179–87 | 358 | 13.74–79 | 37, 419 | | 441 |
| 3.223 | 425 | 13.135–42 | 249 | 14.234–40 | 325 |
| 3.240–43 | 416 | 13.242 | 420 | 14.235 | 269, 271, |
| 3.245 | 422 | 13.245 | 248 | | 327, 407 |
| 3.313 | 359 | 13.257–58 | 439 | 14.236 | 67 |
| 4.114 | 3, 359 | 13.287 | 39 | 14.238–40 | 270 |
| 4.114–17 | 2 | 13.349 | 39 | 14.239 | 324 |
| 4.115–16 | 360, 423 | 13.352–55 | 39, 113 | 14.241–43 | 270 |
| 4.126–28 | 359 | 13.354 | 39 | 14.242 | 276 |
| 4.131–51 | 325, 411 | 13.356–64 | 247 | 14.244–46 | 268, 270 |
| 4.137 | 435 | 13.395–97 | 247 | 14.245 | 275, 276, |
| 4.137–38 | 430, 431, | 13.397 | 247 | | 417, 435 |
| | 437 | 14.63–64 | 441 | 14.247 | 361 |
| 4.145–49 | 385 | 14.70–71 | 289 | 14.247–55 | 262, 264, |
| 4.176–95 | 359 | 14.75–76 | 249 | | 277 |
| 4.180 | 359 | 14.79 | 289 | 14.252–54 | 264 |
| 4.181–83 | 359 | 14.85 | 289 | 14.256 | 276 |
| 4.190–91 | 359 | 14.98–99 | 40 | 14.256–58 | 270 |
| 4.191–93 | 359 | 14.110–13 | 264 | 14.257 | 361 |
| 4.196–98 | 366 | 14.114 | 234 | 14.257–58 | 415 |
| 4.203–4 | 423 | 14.115–16 | 10, 234, | 14.258 | 274, 276, |
| 4.207 | 365, 431 | | 331, 407 | | 324, 407, |
| 4.326 | 426 | 14.117 | 43, 49, | | 417 |
| 4.327–31 | 358 | | 66, 406 | 14.259 | 271, 327 |
| 8.45–48 | 120 | 14.118 | 28, 49, | 14.259–61 | 269, 331 |
| 8.116–17 | 358 | | 67, 70, | 14.260 | 276, 407, |
| 8.191 | 411 | | 232 | | 415 |
| 10.210 | 360 | 14.119–20 | 289 | 14.261 | 274, 276, |
| 12.3–7 | 22 | 14.123–25 | 291 | | 435 |
| 12.8 | 28 | 14.127–32 | 40, 291 | 14.262–64 | 270, 328, |
| 12.9 | 22 | 14.131 | 36 | | 442 |
| 12.11–33 | 21 | 14.185–89 | 262, 360 | 14.263 | 407 |

*Antiquitates* (*cont.*)
14.265–67    262, 276, 360
14.306–23    250
14.314    250
14.323    262
14.381–89    294
14.394    250
15.267–91    250
15.342–43    294
15.351–58    250
16.18    266
16.27    270, 275, 328, 415, 442
16.27–65    271, 277
16.28    268, 272, 327, 328
16.31–57    262, 263, 268, 273, 277, 361
16.35–38    277
16.41    268, 273
16.42    273
16.43–44    273, 417
16.45    268, 270, 275, 328, 415
16.46    361
16.48–54    277
16.50    277
16.50–56    277
16.55    277
16.57    277
16.59    273
16.60    274, 298
16.86–87    294
16.148    250
16.160    238, 261
16.160–61    238, 274
16.160–78    360
16.162    277
16.162–65    268, 270, 292
16.162–68    417
16.163    270, 442
16.164    274, 415
16.167–68    268, 442
16.168    270, 276
16.169–70    238, 417

16.171    263, 268
16.171–73    417
16.172–73    268
16.174    346, 360
16.174–78    262, 361
16.177–78    15
17.20–21    294
17.52–53    294
17.134–41    326
17.138–41    293
17.149–63    433
17.300    295, 421
17.300–3    294
17.324–38    421, 294
18.82    419
18.18    295, 300
18.65–84    298
18.81–84    299, 329
18.84    293
18.139–42    294, 323
18.141    323, 350
18.143–44    294
18.143–60    302
18.143–239    53
18.151–60    53
18.159–60    105, 159
18.161–223    302
18.224–39    302
18.164–65    294
18.224–39    302
18.238–39    53
18.257–60    55, 56, 73
18.259    68, 159, 347
18.261–309    252
18.289–309    302
18.312–13    418, 419
18.340–52    411
19.236–47    302
19.276    56, 303
19.276–77    68, 105, 160
19.278    56
19.278–79    56
19.279    251
19.279–85    303
19.280–85    57, 61, 71, 263
19.281    28
19.283    49

19.283–84    66, 408
19.283–85    58, 434
19.286–91    303
19.290    408, 431
19.300–11    252
19.309    252
19.328–30    252
19.349    252
19.356–58    252
19.360–62    308
19.364–66    251
20.1–5    252
20.10–12    308
20.17–96    409
20.38    403, 439
20.38–39    409
20.49–50    419
20.49–53    409
20.100    106
20.100–3    105
20.134–36    308
20.139    411
20.141–44    309, 325, 411
20.142    332
20.143    325
20.145–46    309, 324, 411
20.147    68
20.173    253
20.173–78    253
20.178    254
20.182–84    253
20.183    253
20.195    308
20.263    347, 348
20.264    347
20.265    347
20.266    448
20.267    448
20.268    307, 358

*Vita*
7–9    347
10–12    348
12    348
13–16    348
14    348, 435
16    308, 321
24–27    255

| | | | | | |
|---|---|---|---|---|---|
| 26 | 255, 323 | 1.215–18 | 348 | 2.79–96 | 272 |
| 63–69 | 349 | 1.219–2.144 | 362 | 2.79–144 | 73 |
| 65 | 433 | 1.224–25 | 46 | 2.80–82 | 366 |
| 66–67 | 255 | 1.223–26 | 366 | 2.82 | 367, 426, |
| 74 | 435 | 1.225 | 366 | | 431 |
| 140 | 349 | 1.228–52 | 33 | 2.85 | 366 |
| 290–95 | 416, 417 | 1.229 | 34 | 2.85–86 | 46 |
| 359 | 448 | 1.237–50 | 130 | 2.89–96 | 248, 272 |
| 361–63 | 351 | 1.309 | 46, 431 | 2.89–111 | 365 |
| 410 | 255 | 1.315 | 347 | 2.90 | 272 |
| 416 | 350 | 2.3–7 | 366 | 2.102–9 | 421 |
| 418 | 350 | 2.8–32 | 73 | 2.117 | 431 |
| 422–29 | 310 | 2.28–32 | 74, 366 | 2.121–24 | 74 |
| 423 | 327 | 2.33–36 | 29 | 2.123–24 | 324, 365 |
| 424 | 239 | 2.33–44 | 28 | 2.125–26 | 366 |
| 424–25 | 350 | 2.33–64 | 28 | 2.130 | 365 |
| 428–29 | 350 | 2.33–78 | 73 | 2.137 | 439 |
| 429 | 313, 359, | 2.35 | 28 | 2.141 | 438 |
| | 361 | 2.37 | 28, 49, 66 | 2.142–44 | 438 |
| 430 | 448 | 2.37–72 | 67 | 2.144 | 365 |
| | | 2.38 | 69 | 2.145 | 272 |
| ***Contra Apionem*** | | 2.38–39 | 245 | 2.145ff. | 439 |
| 1.1 | 317, 347 | 2.38–42 | 70 | 2.145–286 | 362, 367 |
| 1.1–2 | 362 | 2.38–72 | 69 | 2.148 | 272, 365, |
| 1.1–218 | 362 | 2.39 | 245, 261 | | 367, 432, |
| 1.2 | 363 | 2.41 | 68, 366 | | 437 |
| 1.2–3 | 313 | 2.41–42 | 366 | 2.149 | 426 |
| 1.4 | 365 | 2.44 | 232 | 2.149–50 | 367 |
| 1.7–46 | 363 | 2.49 | 37 | 2.150 | 365 |
| 1.8 | 364 | 2.49–56 | 37, 38 | 2.151ff | 427 |
| 1.32–33 | 421 | 2.51–55 | 194 | 2.158 | 437 |
| 1.42 | 368 | 2.55 | 194, 415 | 2.160 | 367 |
| 1.42–43 | 367 | 2.60 | 41 | 2.165 | 367 |
| 1.47–56 | 362 | 2.61 | 49 | 2.166 | 367 |
| 1.50 | 348 | 2.61–67 | 70 | 2.168–74 | 367 |
| 1.50–52 | 351 | 2.63–64 | 51 | 2.168–89 | 367 |
| 1.60 | 413 | 2.64 | 39 | 2.171–78 | 425 |
| 1.60–61 | 367 | 2.65 | 59, 69, | 2.173–74 | 413, 436, |
| 1.60–68 | 366 | | 114, 272 | | 437 |
| 1.70 | 248 | 2.65–67 | 74, 431 | 2.175 | 417 |
| 1.73–91 | 33 | 2.66 | 46, 366 | 2.176–78 | 426 |
| 1.103 | 347 | 2.67 | 59 | 2.178 | 413 |
| 1.132 | 347 | 2.68–70 | 197 | 2.182–89 | 367 |
| 1.161–218 | 364 | 2.69 | 411 | 2.190–91 | 342 |
| 1.166 | 365 | 2.73 | 434 | 2.190–92 | 433 |
| 1.177–82 | 260 | 2.73–75 | 363 | 2.190–219 | 339, 366, |
| 1.180 | 91 | 2.73–78 | 366, 433 | | 367 |
| 1.186 | 22 | 2.74 | 366 | 2.193 | 419, 431 |
| 1.186–89 | 28 | 2.77 | 293 | 2.193–98 | 421 |
| 1.209 | 441 | 2.79 | 272, 431 | 2.202 | 429 |

**Contra Apionem** (*cont.*)

| Reference | Page |
|---|---|
| 2.204 | 344, 413 |
| 2.209–10 | 365, 385, 404 |
| 2.209–13 | 365 |
| 2.210 | 317, 404 |
| 2.211 | 314 |
| 2.213 | 339 |
| 2.218–19 | 367 |
| 2.220–35 | 364 |
| 2.220–86 | 364 |
| 2.225–31 | 367 |
| 2.226 | 365 |
| 2.232–35 | 367 |
| 2.234 | 436 |
| 2.236–54 | 363 |
| 2.237 | 365, 431 |
| 2.238–39 | 364 |
| 2.236–54 | 432 |
| 2.242 | 364 |
| 2.251 | 365 |
| 2.253 | 364 |
| 2.255–70 | 365 |
| 2.256–57 | 364 |
| 2.257–61 | 365 |
| 2.258 | 272 |
| 2.261 | 317, 365 |
| 2.263–64 | 365 |
| 2.271–78 | 364, 426 |
| 2.276–77 | 364 |
| 2.277 | 347 |
| 2.280–86 | 365 |
| 2.282 | 307, 317, 416, 436 |
| 2.287 | 365 |
| 2.291 | 365 |
| 2.293–94 | 368 |

**3 Maccabees** 32–33, 38, 57, 63, 69, 76, 192–203, 393, 448

| Reference | Page |
|---|---|
| 1.1–7 | 192 |
| 1.3 | 32, 104, 194, 197, 200, 403 |
| 1.8 | 195 |
| 1.8–29 | 192 |
| 1.11 | 197 |
| 1.22 | 197 |
| 1.23 | 197 |
| 2.1–8 | 195 |
| 2.1–20 | 192, 193 |
| 2.6 | 198 |
| 2.9 | 198 |
| 2.10 | 198 |
| 2.12 | 197 |
| 2.16 | 198 |
| 2.18 | 202 |
| 2.21 | 195 |
| 2.21–24 | 192 |
| 2.22 | 192 |
| 2.24 | 195 |
| 2.25–26 | 196 |
| 2.25–33 | 105, 192 |
| 2.26–27 | 199 |
| 2.27 | 197 |
| 2.28 | 194, 195, 448 |
| 2.28–33 | 194, 195 |
| 2.30 | 195 |
| 2.30–31 | 200 |
| 2.31 | 105, 195, 199 |
| 2.31–33 | 192, 201 |
| 2.32 | 195 |
| 2.33 | 196, 197, 394 |
| 3.1 | 192, 195 |
| 3.2 | 196, 197 |
| 3.2–10 | 193 |
| 3.3–7 | 199, 201 |
| 3.4 | 197, 437 |
| 3.6 | 197 |
| 3.7 | 199 |
| 3.8 | 196 |
| 3.8–10 | 196 |
| 3.10 | 43, 116 |
| 3.11 | 196 |
| 3.11–30 | 193 |
| 3.12–29 | 196 |
| 3.21 | 197, 198, 199 |
| 3.23 | 394 |
| 3.24 | 197, 200 |
| 3.25 | 200 |
| 4.1 | 193, 196, 197 |
| 4.1–11 | 193 |
| 4.6 | 197 |
| 4.10 | 200 |
| 4.12 | 197 |
| 4.12–21 | 193 |
| 4.13 | 195 |
| 4.14 | 195, 197 |
| 4.16 | 196 |
| 4.21 | 198 |
| 5.1 | 195 |
| 5.1–2 | 193 |
| 5.1–17 | 193 |
| 5.1–35 | 196 |
| 5.3 | 196 |
| 5.5 | 196, 197 |
| 5.6 | 197 |
| 5.13 | 197, 198, 430 |
| 5.16–17 | 196 |
| 5.18–35 | 193 |
| 5.20 | 196 |
| 5.21–22 | 196 |
| 5.24 | 196 |
| 5.30 | 195, 198 |
| 5.31 | 199 |
| 5.35 | 198 |
| 5.36 | 196 |
| 5.36–47 | 193 |
| 5.42 | 196 |
| 5.43 | 198 |
| 6.1–15 | 193 |
| 6.3 | 197, 198, 423 |
| 6.4 | 197 |
| 6.5 | 198 |
| 6.9 | 197 |
| 6.10 | 423 |
| 6.11 | 198, 202 |
| 6.12 | 200 |
| 6.13 | 197, 198 |
| 6.15 | 197, 198, 423 |
| 6.16–20 | 193 |
| 6.19 | 196 |
| 6.20 | 196 |
| 6.21–7.9 | 193 |
| 6.22 | 196 |
| 6.24 | 196 |
| 6.25–26 | 199 |
| 6.28 | 200 |
| 6.29 | 198 |
| 6.30 | 202 |

| | | | | | |
|---|---|---|---|---|---|
| 6.30–36 | 415 | 2.22–23 | 372 | 7.18–19 | 373 |
| 6.30–40 | 200 | 2.24–3.5 | 370 | 7.21 | 371 |
| 6.32 | 197, 198 | 3.5 | 371, 375 | 7.21–22 | 373 |
| 6.33 | 202 | 3.19 | 370 | 8.2 | 375 |
| 6.34 | 196 | 3.19–4.26 | 369 | 8.4–11 | 375 |
| 6.36 | 198, 423 | 3.19–17.6 | 369 | 8.5 | 377 |
| 6.38–40 | 194, 202 | 3.21–4.1 | 375 | 8.7 | 374, 379 |
| 6.40 | 202 | 4.2 | 449 | 8.7–8 | 379 |
| 7.2 | 200 | 4.19–20 | 379 | 8.14 | 377 |
| 7.3 | 200 | 4.19–21 | 375 | 8.19 | 378 |
| 7.4 | 197, 200 | 4.20 | 371 | 8.22 | 377 |
| 7.5 | 196, 200 | 4.23 | 374 | 8.24 | 378 |
| 7.6 | 198, 200 | 4.26 | 88, 379, | 8.25 | 377 |
| 7.7 | 199 | | 410 | 9.1 | 374 |
| 7.9 | 200, 201, | 5.1–2 | 375 | 9.2 | 374 |
| | 202, 203 | 5.6–15 | 375, 377 | 9.7 | 372 |
| 7.10 | 197 | 5.6–38 | 377 | 9.9 | 375 |
| 7.10–11 | 436 | 5.7 | 377 | 9.11 | 376 |
| 7.10–16 | 200 | 5.8–9 | 377 | 9.16 | 376 |
| 7.10–22 | 193 | 5.10 | 377, 378 | 9.18 | 375 |
| 7.11 | 199 | 5.11 | 377 | 9.21 | 374 |
| 7.14 | 197 | 5.13 | 377 | 9.23 | 374 |
| 7.16 | 197, 198, | 5.14–38 | 373 | 9.24 | 374, 375 |
| | 430 | 5.16–18 | 377 | 9.28 | 376 |
| 7.17–20 | 202 | 5.16–38 | 377 | 10.2–3 | 374 |
| 7.19 | 198, 423 | 5.19–21 | 377 | 10.13 | 377 |
| 7.21 | 196 | 5.22 | 371 | 10.17 | 375 |
| 7.22 | 195 | 5.22–24 | 378 | 11.4 | 375 |
| 7.23 | 194, 198 | 5.25 | 377, 378 | 12.2–5 | 375 |
| | | 5.25–26 | 378 | 12.5 | 379 |
| | | 5.26 | 374 | 12.11 | 374 |
| | | 5.29 | 373, 378 | 12.16–17 | 374 |
| **4 Maccabees** | 324, 369– | 5.33 | 374, 378 | 12.17 | 374, 430 |
| 80, 389, 448–49 | | 5.35 | 371 | 13.1 | 370 |
| 1.1 | 369, 370, | 5.37 | 373, 378 | 13.1–14.10 | 370 |
| | 373 | 5.38 | 373 | 13.9 | 372 |
| 1.1–12 | 369 | 6.1 | 376 | 13.12 | 374 |
| 1.1–3.18 | 369, 371 | 6.8 | 376 | 13.17 | 373 |
| 1.7 | 372 | 6.11–15 | 376 | 13.19–27 | 374 |
| 1.8 | 372 | 6.16–23 | 377 | 13.22–24 | 374 |
| 1.8–9 | 369 | 6.17 | 374 | 14.9 | 378 |
| 1.10 | 370, 372 | 6.18 | 378 | 15.20 | 375 |
| 1.11 | 375 | 6.19 | 378 | 16.1 | 370 |
| 1.16 | 370, 372 | 6.22 | 374 | 16.1–17.6 | 370 |
| 1.17 | 372 | 6.31 | 370 | 16.16 | 374, 375 |
| 1.18 | 370 | 6.31–7.23 | 370 | 16.19 | 372 |
| 1.20–28 | 370 | 7.7 | 371 | 17.7–18.24 | 369 |
| 1.30–35 | 374 | 7.9 | 371, 378 | 17.11–16 | 375 |
| 1.32–35 | 372 | 7.16 | 370, 373 | 17.14 | 375 |
| 2.4–6 | 372 | 7.16–23 | 373 | 17.20 | 376 |
| 2.15 | 379 | | | | |

**4 Maccabees** (*cont.*)

| | |
|---|---|
| 17.22 | 374 |
| 17.23–24 | 379 |
| 18 | 369 |
| 18.1 | 370, 372, 374 |
| 18.2 | 372 |
| 18.4 | 376 |
| 18.5 | 379 |
| 18.10–19 | 374, 412 |
| 18.20 | 375, 376 |
| 18.23 | 373 |

**Paul** (see Early Christian Writings)

**Philo**

*De Abrahamo*

| | |
|---|---|
| 20–25 | 162 |
| 52 | 170 |
| 52–55 | 170 |
| 68 | 166 |
| 85–87 | 162 |
| 98 | 174, 175 |
| 135–37 | 176 |
| 147 | 166, 170 |
| 178–93 | 108, 169 |
| 184 | 109 |
| 217 | 166 |
| 236 | 167 |

*De Aeternitate Mundi*

| | |
|---|---|
| 10 | 429 |
| 19 | 163 |
| 20 | 429 |
| 46–47 | 429 |

*De Agricultura*

| | |
|---|---|
| 23–25 | 171 |
| 35 | 175 |
| 64–65 | 171 |
| 95 | 166 |
| 103–4 | 171 |
| 113–19 | 175 |

*De Animalibus* 105, 179

| | |
|---|---|
| 2 | 179 |
| 54 | 179 |

*De Cherubim*

| | |
|---|---|
| 48 | 167 |
| 91–97 | 172, 175 |
| 98–101 | 172 |
| 119ff. | 171 |

*De Confusione Linguarum*

| | |
|---|---|
| 2 | 109, 169, 173 |
| 2–3 | 109 |
| 2–13 | 108 |
| 9–15 | 169 |
| 62 | 163 |
| 141 | 173 |
| 168–73 | 431 |
| 190 | 169 |

*De Congressu*  160

| | |
|---|---|
| 44 | 170 |
| 54 | 170 |
| 74–76 | 160 |
| 174 | 162 |
| 177 | 163, 166 |
| 180 | 170 |

*De Decalogo*

| | |
|---|---|
| 2–13 | 162 |
| 52–57 | 432 |
| 52–65 | 429, 432 |
| 52–81 | 174, 186 |
| 53–55 | 186 |
| 58 | 174 |
| 66–76 | 433 |
| 96–105 | 172, 176 |
| 102–5 | 440 |

*Quod Deterius*

| | |
|---|---|
| 13 | 169 |
| 19–21 | 172 |
| 146–48 | 176 |

*Quod Deus*

| | |
|---|---|
| 8–9 | 172 |
| 60–69 | 168 |
| 133 | 167 |

*De Ebrietate*

| | |
|---|---|
| 20 | 114 |
| 20–23 | 175 |

| | |
|---|---|
| 26 | 162, 171 |
| 65 | 167 |
| 80–87 | 178 |
| 108–10 | 433 |
| 109 | 173 |
| 144 | 170 |
| 170–202 | 164 |
| 177 | 161 |
| 217–19 | 161 |

*In Flaccum*

| | |
|---|---|
| 1 | 301 |
| 1–5 | 52 |
| 4 | 175 |
| 6–24 | 52 |
| 17 | 74, 175 |
| 23 | 52 |
| 27–28 | 52 |
| 29 | 52, 74, 175, 197 |
| 30 | 52 |
| 30–32 | 52 |
| 33–34 | 74 |
| 41 | 74 |
| 43 | 4, 41 |
| 45–56 | 422 |
| 47 | 62 |
| 48 | 54 |
| 48–49 | 74 |
| 53 | 55, 62 |
| 54 | 54, 65 |
| 55 | 29 |
| 56 | 118 |
| 57 | 43, 51, 116 |
| 62 | 179 |
| 64 | 51 |
| 72 | 54 |
| 73–77 | 179 |
| 73–85 | 43, 54 |
| 74 | 43, 49 |
| 78–80 | 51, 69 |
| 79 | 69 |
| 80 | 69 |
| 84–85 | 179 |
| 86–94 | 54, 74 |
| 89 | 118 |
| 95–96 | 179 |
| 96 | 53, 436 |
| 97–98 | 74, 178 |

| | |
|---|---|
| 103 | 52, 178 |
| 104 | 341 |
| 116–18 | 416 |
| 121 | 179 |
| 121–24 | 417 |
| 125–27 | 55 |
| 135–39 | 48 |
| 135–45 | 52 |
| 136 | 175 |
| 170 | 179 |
| 172 | 54, 55, 64, 65 |
| 191 | 179 |

**De Fuga et Inventione**

| | |
|---|---|
| 14 | 162 |
| 25–38 | 178 |
| 121 | 169 |
| 179 | 169 |

**De Gigantibus**

| | |
|---|---|
| 59 | 173 |

**Quis Heres**

| | |
|---|---|
| 81 | 108 |
| 82 | 171 |
| 168–70 | 433 |
| 169 | 173 |
| 293 | 422 |

**Hypothetica** 339, 367

| | |
|---|---|
| 7.9 | 339 |
| 7.10–14 | 176 |
| 7.10–20 | 343 |
| 7.11–12 | 417 |
| 7.14 | 412, 416 |

**De Iosepho**

| | |
|---|---|
| 28 | 166 |
| 42–45 | 176 |
| 254 | 111, 175 |

**Legum Allegoriae**

| | |
|---|---|
| 1.34 | 172 |
| 2.85 | 162 |
| 3.27 | 212 |
| 3.36 | 433 |
| 3.71 | 212 |
| 3.97–101 | 163 |
| 3.136–37 | 165 |
| 3.143 | 161 |

| | |
|---|---|
| 3.147 | 166 |
| 3.156 | 160 |
| 3.204–6 | 108, 169 |
| 3.219 | 212 |

**Legatio**

| | |
|---|---|
| 1 | 159 |
| 3 | 179 |
| 3–4 | 4, 175 |
| 14–25 | 74 |
| 72 | 412 |
| 115 | 161, 413 |
| 118 | 55 |
| 120 | 74, 179 |
| 129 | 43, 51, 116 |
| 132 | 29, 74 |
| 132–54 | 55 |
| 133 | 74 |
| 134 | 29, 54 |
| 141–54 | 74 |
| 150 | 422 |
| 155 | 289, 290, 325 |
| 155–57 | 292 |
| 156 | 290, 317 |
| 156–57 | 307, 417 |
| 157 | 62, 290, 293, 304–5, 418, 420, 422 |
| 158 | 290, 293, 327, 442 |
| 159 | 293 |
| 159–61 | 298, 301 |
| 162–65 | 179 |
| 166 | 74 |
| 166–70 | 197 |
| 170 | 74 |
| 178–79 | 178 |
| 184 | 179 |
| 184–94 | 179 |
| 184ff. | 56, 302, 420 |
| 191 | 55 |
| 193 | 62 |
| 193–94 | 420 |
| 194 | 62, 67, 71, 179 |
| 195 | 413 |

| | |
|---|---|
| 196 | 179 |
| 198 | 420 |
| 199–206 | 55 |
| 200 | 251 |
| 200–5 | 251 |
| 202 | 251, 422 |
| 205 | 248, 422 |
| 210 | 161, 413, 425, 426 |
| 211 | 426 |
| 212 | 420 |
| 214 | 41 |
| 216 | 418 |
| 220 | 179 |
| 226 | 41 |
| 230 | 74 |
| 231–32 | 74 |
| 261–338 | 302 |
| 261ff. | 423 |
| 279–80 | 74 |
| 280 | 74 |
| 281 | 260 |
| 281–82 | 10 |
| 281–83 | 422 |
| 281–84 | 179 |
| 291 | 418 |
| 306 | 175 |
| 311 | 26 |
| 311–12 | 270 |
| 311–13 | 268 |
| 311–16 | 52, 263 |
| 312 | 74 |
| 312–13 | 417, 418 |
| 315 | 268 |
| 317 | 293 |
| 318 | 174 |
| 319 | 293 |
| 330 | 179, 422 |
| 336–37 | 179 |
| 346 | 56 |
| 347 | 431 |
| 349 | 62 |
| 353–57 | 55 |
| 355–56 | 74 |
| 361–62 | 434, 436 |
| 370 | 179 |

**De Migratione Abrahami**

| | |
|---|---|
| 9–11 | 177 |

*De Migratione*
*Abrahami* (*cont.*)
44–45       169
89          109
89–93       91, 109,
            177, 345,
            386, 436,
            439, 440
90          110, 177
91          68
92          420
93          110, 177
106–8       177
113–14      174

*De Vita Mosis*
book 1      138, 428
1.1–3       163
1.3         176
1.4         161, 427
1.18–29     163
1.21        68
1.27        428
1.31        107
1.31–33     413
1.35        67
1.149       41, 175
1.254       419
1.278       1
1.295–305   108
book 2      138, 428
2.1–7       163
2.17        172
2.17–44     172
2.23–24     175
2.25ff.     424
2.29        30
2.32        160
2.37        425
2.37–41     166
2.38        166
2.41        424
2.41–43     31, 415,
            416
2.43        422
2.43–44     406
2.44        176, 408
2.45–52     172
2.51–52     427
2.107–8     172, 420

2.117–30    358
2.159       41
2.189       174
2.193       108
2.193–96    175
2.205       431
2.209–11    172
2.209–16    176
2.209–20    440
2.216       417
2.219       441
2.211       173, 441
2.290       163
2.290–91    426

*De Mutatione*
*Nominum*
27–28       172
213         162, 171
223         163
229         171

*De Opificio Mundi*
1–3         427
3           172
27          341
53          163
72          172
78          172
89          172
89–128      172
90–127      440
105         159
169         172
170–72      164, 429

*De Plantatione*
36          167
39          163
55–60       174, 175
69–72       108, 169

*De Posteritate Caini*
1–7         168
78          166
165         176
165–69      433

*De Praemiis et Poenis*
40–46       165

66          41
152         108, 404
162         413
162–72      176, 422
165–67      173
166         406

*Quod Omnis Probus*
*Liber sit* 171
6           67
26          161
57          163
72          171
81          26
81–82       417
141         48, 161

*De Providentia* 105
2.44–46     68, 160
2.58        161
2.64        419

*Quaestiones ... in*
*Genesin*
3.3         109
3.43        108
3.48        438
3.53        108
3.61        412
4.137       170
4.168       108

*Quaestiones ... in*
*Exodum*
2.2         409
2.5         431
2.76        176, 422

*De Sacrificiis*
8–10        163
9–10        428

*De Sobrietate*
31–33       167–68
62–63       172

*De Somniis*
1.52        170
1.92–101    160

| | | | | | |
|---|---|---|---|---|---|
| 1.102 | 167 | 1.314 | 161, 413 | 34–44 | 108 |
| 1.228–38 | 168 | 1.315–18 | 108, 173 | 64–65 | 174 |
| book 2 | 107 | 2.44–48 | 171 | 65 | 430 |
| 2.82–84 | 57 | 2.60–64 | 161 | 87 | 173 |
| 2.98 | 169 | 2.61–63 | 176, 417 | 102–4 | 176, 213 |
| 2.123 | 442 | 2.73 | 172, 173 | 103 | 409 |
| 2.123–24 | 441 | 2.88 | 161, 413 | 108 | 173, 408 |
| 2.123–32 | 51, 178, | 2.140–44 | 415 | 141 | 161, 176 |
| | 426, 442 | 2.145 | 415 | 147 | 173 |
| 2.124–29 | 178 | 2.145–49 | 415 | 175 | 408 |
| 2.126 | 442 | 2.150 | 172 | 175–86 | 176 |
| 2.127 | 26, 417 | 2.162 | 172 | 178 | 212, 408 |
| 2.189 | 163 | 2.163 | 175 | 180–86 | 409 |
| 2.255 | 171 | 2.164–67 | 174 | 182 | 106 |
| 2.301–2 | 167 | 2.165 | 430 | 187–227 | 404 |
| | | 2.165–66 | 431 | 206–10 | 173 |
| | | 2.167 | 175 | 212–22 | 176 |

**De Specialibus Legibus**

| | | | | | |
|---|---|---|---|---|---|
| 1.1–11 | 172, 439 | 2.188 | 172 | | |
| 1.2 | 41, 91, | 2.193–203 | 416 | **De Vita Contemplativa** | |
| | 137, 438, | 2.228 | 413 | | 118–19 |
| | 439 | 2.229–30 | 68 | 18–21 | 162 |
| 1.7 | 41 | 2.230 | 160 | 19–20 | 162 |
| 1.8 | 158 | 2.249–51 | 440 | 21–23 | 118 |
| 1.12–20 | 432 | 3.1–6 | 162, 178 | 30 | 442 |
| 1.12–31 | 174 | 3.3 | 162, 179 | 30–33 | 417 |
| 1.28–31 | 176, 433 | 3.7–82 | 176 | 40–63 | 175 |
| 1.51 | 408 | 3.29 | 108, 411 | 59–62 | 176 |
| 1.51–53 | 176, 409 | 3.37–42 | 176 | 72–74 | 119 |
| 1.52 | 213, 408, | 3.93–103 | 121 | 78 | 167 |
| | 409 | 3.101–3 | 121 | | |
| 1.53 | 176, 431 | 3.155 | 172, 173 | | |
| 1.54–58 | 108 | 3.169 | 117 | **Pseudo-Phocylides** | |
| 1.59–65 | 121 | 4.16 | 173 | | 336–46, |
| 1.61 | 121 | 4.48–52 | 121 | | 450 |
| 1.67 | 419, 431 | 4.50 | 121, 123 | 1–2 | 337, 344 |
| 1.69–70 | 423 | 4.55 | 173 | 3 | 339 |
| 1.76–78 | 418 | 4.95–131 | 434 | 3–8 | 339, 342 |
| 1.77–78 | 76, 418 | 4.100–25 | 172 | 8 | 340 |
| 1.78 | 41 | 4.122–23 | 434 | 9–41 | 338, 342 |
| 1.97 | 175 | 4.149 | 413 | 9–131 | 338 |
| 1.102 | 408 | 4.149–50 | 161, 413 | 10 | 338 |
| 1.133 | 41 | 4.159 | 173 | 22–23 | 339 |
| 1.153–54 | 419 | 4.178–213 | 408 | 29 | 340 |
| 1.168–69 | 175 | 4.179–80 | 4 | 39–41 | 344 |
| 1.186 | 416 | 4.179–81 | 176 | 48 | 340 |
| 1.190 | 175 | 4.180–81 | 175 | 53 | 338 |
| 1.192–93 | 175 | 4.180–82 | 173 | 54 | 340 |
| 1.211–22 | 408 | | | 59–60 | 340 |
| 1.212–14 | 168 | **De Virtutibus** | | 63–67 | 340 |
| 1.309 | 176, 408 | 34 | 176 | 71 | 341 |

**Pseudo-Phocylides**
(*cont.*)

| | |
|---|---|
| 71–75 | 341 |
| 75 | 341 |
| 76 | 340 |
| 77 | 341 |
| 84–85 | 338, 339 |
| 95–96 | 344 |
| 98 | 341 |
| 101 | 341 |
| 102 | 337 |
| 103–15 | 340 |
| 104 | 341 |
| 106 | 340 |
| 132–34 | 344 |
| 137 | 340 |
| 140 | 338 |
| 147–48 | 338, 343 |
| 153–74 | 338, 343 |
| 163 | 341 |
| 175–206 | 338 |
| 175–227 | 339 |
| 179–83 | 339 |
| 181 | 339 |
| 184–85 | 339 |
| 188 | 339 |
| 190–92 | 339 |
| 192 | 339 |
| 194 | 341 |
| 195–97 | 340 |
| 199–204 | 340 |
| 206–17 | 344 |
| 207–27 | 338 |
| 228 | 345 |
| 229 | 344, 346 |

**Sibylline Oracles** 80,
216–28, 241, 450–51

| | |
|---|---|
| books 1 and 2 | 259 |
| 1.196–98 | 259 |
| 1.261–67 | 259 |
| 2.56–114 | 342 |
| 2.59 | 342 |
| 2.96 | 342 |
| book 3 | 218–25 |
| 3.1–96 | 218, 225 |
| 3.8–45 | 222, 433 |
| 3.49–51 | 225 |
| 3.110–55 | 224 |
| 3.162–294 | 219 |

| | |
|---|---|
| 3.167 | 219 |
| 3.171–74 | 222 |
| 3.171–95 | 219 |
| 3.185–86 | 222 |
| 3.191–95 | 222 |
| 3.192–93 | 218, 222, 450 |
| 3.192–95 | 219 |
| 3.194–95 | 223 |
| 3.213–15 | 219 |
| 3.214 | 221 |
| 3.220–33 | 219, 222 |
| 3.234–47 | 219 |
| 3.234–64 | 221 |
| 3.248–58 | 219 |
| 3.259–81 | 219 |
| 3.265–94 | 221 |
| 3.272 | 222 |
| 3.275–76 | 221 |
| 3.282–83 | 220 |
| 3.282–94 | 220 |
| 3.284 | 219, 221 |
| 3.286 | 222 |
| 3.301–2 | 222 |
| 3.302 | 221 |
| 3.313–14 | 222 |
| 3.314–19 | 222 |
| 3.318 | 218, 222, 450 |
| 3.348–49 | 228 |
| 3.350–80 | 225, 278 |
| 3.381–83 | 223 |
| 3.396–97 | 223 |
| 3.401–88 | 224 |
| 3.489–544 | 220 |
| 3.489–600 | 220 |
| 3.544–45 | 222 |
| 3.545–49 | 223 |
| 3.545–72 | 220 |
| 3.545–600 | 433 |
| 3.550 | 220 |
| 3.556–72 | 220 |
| 3.556–79 | 221 |
| 3.573 | 221 |
| 3.573–75 | 220 |
| 3.580 | 220, 221 |
| 3.584–85 | 221 |
| 3.586–90 | 222 |
| 3.594–95 | 220 |
| 3.594–600 | 222 |

| | |
|---|---|
| 3.596–600 | 220 |
| 3.600 | 221 |
| 3.601–18 | 223 |
| 3.604–6 | 222 |
| 3.608–9 | 218, 222, 450 |
| 3.611–15 | 223 |
| 3.624–31 | 220 |
| 3.652–56 | 222, 223 |
| 3.657–68 | 220 |
| 3.657–808 | 220 |
| 3.665 | 221 |
| 3.669–709 | 221 |
| 3.686–87 | 221 |
| 3.703 | 221 |
| 3.711–12 | 221 |
| 3.718 | 221 |
| 3.718–19 | 221 |
| 3.719 | 221 |
| 3.720–23 | 222 |
| 3.725 | 221 |
| 3.734–35 | 221 |
| 3.758 | 221 |
| 3.764–66 | 222 |
| 3.767–68 | 221 |
| 3.768–69 | 221 |
| 3.772–75 | 221 |
| 3.809–29 | 218 |
| 3.813–18 | 224 |
| 4.145–51 | 278 |
| book 5 | 80, 225–28 |
| 5.1–51 | 451 |
| 5.48 | 451 |
| 5.52–74 | 226 |
| 5.68–70 | 226 |
| 5.75–85 | 226, 433 |
| 5.93–110 | 226 |
| 5.104–10 | 226 |
| 5.108–9 | 227 |
| 5.137–54 | 226 |
| 5.150–54 | 226 |
| 5.159–61 | 226 |
| 5.168–78 | 227 |
| 5.179–99 | 226 |
| 5.195–99 | 241 |
| 5.200–5 | 226 |
| 5.214–27 | 226 |
| 5.225–27 | 226 |
| 5.247–85 | 226 |

| | | | | | |
|---|---|---|---|---|---|
| 5.249 | 226 | 4.18–5.14 | 185 | 12.15 | 190 |
| 5.260–85 | 423 | 5.1 | 185 | 12.19 | 188 |
| 5.264 | 226 | 5.5 | 185 | 12.19–21 | 189 |
| 5.276–80 | 226 | 5.15–16 | 185 | 12.20 | 189, 190 |
| 5.281 | 422 | 5.17–23 | 185 | 12.20–22 | 190 |
| 5.328–32 | 226, 422 | 6 | 182 | 12.21 | 188 |
| 5.351–60 | 226, 433 | 6–10 | 392 | 12.22 | 189 |
| 5.361–85 | 226 | 6.3 | 451 | 12.23 | 188 |
| 5.362 | 227 | 6.4–11 | 185 | 12.23–27 | 186, 187 |
| 5.386–96 | 227 | 6.7 | 184, 185 | 12.24–25 | 188 |
| 5.398–401 | 225 | 6.12 | 183 | 12.26 | 190 |
| 5.403–5 | 226 | 6.12–9.18 | 182, 183, | 13–15 | 174, 182, |
| 5.408–13 | 226 | | 186, 190 | | 186, 191, |
| 5.414–33 | 227 | 6.21–23 | 183 | | 392 |
| 5.418–33 | 226 | 6.24 | 183 | 13.1 | 187 |
| 5.462 | 227 | 7.17–22 | 183 | 13.1–9 | 186, 432 |
| 5.484–91 | 226 | 7.22ff. | 191 | 13.6 | 187 |
| 5.492–503 | 226 | 7.27 | 183 | 13.8–9 | 187 |
| 5.492–511 | 226 | 7.28 | 190 | 13.10 | 187 |
| 5.494 | 226 | 8.1 | 183 | 13.10–15.17 | 187, 433 |
| 5.531 | 228 | 9.1–3 | 184 | 13.11–14.7 | 187 |
| | | 9.6 | 190 | 14.8–9 | 187 |
| **Wisdom of Solomon** | | 9.7–8 | 183 | 14.11 | 189 |
| 181–91, 364, 451–52 | | 10 | 182 | 14.12 | 187 |
| 1.1–2 | 183 | 10.1–2 | 392 | 14.12–21 | 187 |
| 1.1–6.11 | 182, 184 | 10.1–21 | 182, 183, | 14.17–20 | 451 |
| 1.2 | 184 | | 186, 191 | 14.22–31 | 187 |
| 1.3 | 184 | 10.15 | 188, 189 | 14.27 | 187 |
| 1.6 | 184 | 10.17 | 189 | 15.1–4 | 188, 190 |
| 1.6–11 | 184 | 10.20 | 188, 189 | 15.1–6 | 188 |
| 1.12–16 | 184 | 11–19 | 182, 186, | 15.2 | 189 |
| 1.13–14 | 184 | | 188, 189 | 15.7–17 | 187 |
| 1.16 | 190 | 11.1–14 | 189 | 15.14 | 189 |
| 2–5 | 109 | 11.3 | 189 | 15.15 | 189 |
| 2.1–11 | 185 | 11.5 | 189 | 15.18–19 | 187 |
| 2.10 | 185 | 11.8 | 189 | 15.18–16.15 | 46 |
| 2.12 | 109, 185 | 11.14 | 189 | 15.19 | 188 |
| 2.13 | 185 | 11.15–20 | 187, 189 | 16.1 | 190 |
| 2.15–16 | 186 | 11.16 | 190 | 16.1–4 | 189 |
| 2.16 | 185 | 11.20 | 190 | 16.2 | 188 |
| 2.18 | 185 | 11.21–12.22 | 190 | 16.5–14 | 189, 190 |
| 2.19–21 | 185 | 11.22–12.27 | 182 | 16.7 | 190 |
| 2.21–3.4 | 185 | 11.23 | 190 | 16.9 | 190 |
| 2.24 | 392 | 11.23–12.1 | 184 | 16.10 | 189 |
| 3.1–9 | 185 | 12.3 | 422 | 16.15–29 | 189 |
| 3.9 | 185 | 12.3–11 | 190 | 16.20 | 188 |
| 3.10 | 109 | 12.6 | 188 | 16.21 | 189 |
| 3.13–4.15 | 185 | 12.7 | 422 | 16.24–25 | 189 |
| 4.7–15 | 185 | 12.9 | 189 | 17.1–18.4 | 189 |
| 4.15 | 185 | 12.12 | 189 | 17.2 | 188, 189 |

**Wisdom of Solomon**
(*cont.*)
17.3–20    183
18.1    189
18.2    189
18.4    189, 191
18.5    189
18.5–25    189
18.6    188
18.7    188
18.9    189, 415
18.22    188
19.1    190
19.1–12    189
19.6    189
19.13–16    189, 191,
    451
19.16    191
19.22    189

**Other Jewish Writings**

**Cleodemus**    12, 360

**Demetrius**    12, 31,
    126, 138,
    411

**Eupolemus**    128, 151

**Ps-Eupolemus**    12, 129,
    151

**Ps-Hecataeus**    12, 342

*Qumran Literature*
CD 14.4    215
4QFlor 1.4    215
4Q504    417

*Rabbinic Literature*
b Pesahim 57a    240
b Sukkah 51b    29
b Yoma 38a    419
j Sanhedrin 10.6    249
j Sukkah 5.1    79
T Kethuboth 3.1    43

**Sepher Ha-Razim**    119
1.28ff.    122

1.125ff.    122
1.176ff.    122
4.60ff.    122

**Testament of**
    **Abraham**    12

**Testament of Job**    12

**Theodotus**    12,
    411

**Papyri**

*BGU*
1211    32
1764.12–13    46

*CAP*
21    415
22    112
24    112
30–31    34

*CPJ*
7    22, 111
9    21, 24,
    115, 124
10    116, 442
12    24, 116
13    24, 116
14    24, 116
15    116
18    116, 117
18–24    115
18–32    23
19    116, 117
20    116
22–24    117
23    85
24    23, 85
25    24, 116
28    25
29    116
31    115
33    25
36    24
37    24, 116
38    24, 115,
    124

39    24, 112,
    116
42    116
43    116
44    116
46    24, 111,
    112, 124
90    116
100–2    116
126    111
127    33, 104,
    194
132    36
133    24, 111,
    116
138    26, 117
139    117, 415
141    46
142    116
142–49    116–17
143    43
144    67, 116
146–49    51
148    111
150    49, 50,
    64, 67,
    69
151    50, 61,
    67, 422
152    56, 116
153    41, 51,
    56, 57,
    58–59,
    61, 63,
    64, 71,
    74, 78,
    263, 304,
    408, 424
154–59    72
156    72, 308
157    72
158    72, 78, 79
160–408    78
240    78, 116
282    116362
    116
375–403    81
404    116
405    116
409–34    78
411    116, 117

| | | | | | |
|---|---|---|---|---|---|
| 412 | 115 | 111 | 317 | 1532a | 26 |
| 413 | 116 | 113 | 317 | 1536 | 124 |
| 414 | 116 | 132 | 317 | 1537 | 100 |
| 417 | 116 | 146 | 407 | 1538 | 100 |
| 418 | 106 | 201 | 317 | | |
| 421 | 77 | 202 | 317 | **Horbury & Noy** | |
| 422 | 116 | 203 | 316, 407 | 1–8 | 29 |
| 423 | 25 | 222 | 317 | 9 | 26, 27, |
| 427 | 117 | 256 | 317 | | 29, 32 |
| 428 | 78 | 284 | 293 | 13 | 26, 29 |
| 435 | 78 | 287 | 330 | 20 | 26, 27 |
| 435–50 | 79 | 333 | 317 | 22 | 26 |
| 436–44 | 80 | 365 | 293 | 23 | 42 |
| 437 | 79 | 425 | 293 | 24 | 26, 27, 39 |
| 438 | 80, 432 | 462 | 317 | 24–25 | 26 |
| 445 | 81 | 464 | 330 | 25 | 39 |
| 448 | 81 | 476 | 316 | 27 | 24, 32 |
| 450 | 81 | 503 | 293 | 27–28 | 26 |
| 452 | 416 | 508 | 317 | 28 | 27 |
| 454 | 25 | 509 | 317 | 29–40 | 42 |
| 460 | 81 | 523 | 317, 409 | 29–105 | 36 |
| 468 | 25 | 524 | 330 | 39 | 406 |
| 489 | 123 | 531 | 330 | 114 | 42 |
| | | 537 | 317, 410 | 115 | 23 |
| **PGM** | | 556 | 326 | 117 | 26 |
| IV 1169–1226 | 122 | 643 | 325 | 121 | 100 |
| IV 3009–3085 | 122 | 678 | 330 | 122 | 100 |
| IV 3020–3021 | 122 | 694 | 410 | 123 | 100 |
| V 96–172 | 122 | 725 | 416 | 124 | 100 |
| XIII 335–340 | 122 | 742 | 333 | 125 | 32 |
| XXIIa 17–27 | 122 | 743 | 332 | 125–27 | 26 |
| XXIIb 1–26 | 122 | 748 | 237, 280, | 126 | 27 |
| XXV 1–42 | 122 | | 328 | 127 | 27 |
| | | 749 | 322 | 129 | 39 |
| | | 755 | 280, 327 | 133 | 124 |
| **Inscriptions** | | 766 | 280 | 154–56 | 111 |
| | | 770 | 271 | | |
| **CIG** | | 777 | 415 | **IGRR** | |
| 2924 | 280 | 1424–31 | 29 | 1.1024 | 236 |
| | | 1432 | 29 | | |
| **CIJ** | | 1433 | 27, 29, 32 | **Lüderitz** | |
| 21 | 317 | 1435 | 27 | 6–7 | 234 |
| 63 | 124, 334 | 1440 | 26 | 8 | 235, 321, |
| 68 | 124, 317, | 1441 | 26, 27, 39 | | 328 |
| | 334 | 1442 | 39 | 12 | 235, 409 |
| 69 | 334 | 1443 | 24, 32 | 27 | 239 |
| 71 | 124, 334 | 1444 | 27 | 35 | 239 |
| 72 | 317 | 1447 | 26, 27 | 36 | 328 |
| 73 | 334 | 1449 | 32 | 41 | 235 |
| 79 | 325 | 1451–1530 | 36 | 43–69 | 235 |
| 109 | 330 | 1531 | 23 | | |

**Lüderitz** (*cont.*)
70      236, 415,
        425
71      236, 415,
        416, 425
72      26, 236

**MAMA**
6.264   271, 280

**Noy**
22–24   425
26      326
159     332

**OGIS**
663     106
669     106

**SEG**
9.8     238
16.931  236
17.823  236

**Greek and Roman Authors**

**Aeschylus,**
  *Persae*    135

**Appian,**
  *Civil Wars*
2.90    79
  *Mithridatic Wars*
12.21–23  265

**Apuleius,**
  *Metamorphoses*  206
  book 11    207, 212
11.2    207
11.5    207
11.15   207
11.27–29  207

**Aratus,**
  *Phaenomena*  153

**Aristotle,** *Ars Poetica*
13.5    137

**Chariton,** *Chaereas and*
  *Callirhoe*   206

**Cicero,** *De Provinciis*
  *Consularibus*
5.10    287, 407
  *Pro Cluentio*
139     288
  *Pro Flacco*
8.19    278
28.59–61  265
28.66   286, 287,
        331, 423
28.66–69  260, 286,
        417
28.67   287, 290
28.68   266
28.69   287, 351

**Dio Cassius**
37.16–19  297
37.17.1  306
37.17.1–2  407
52.36.1–14  292
57.18.5a  298, 299
59.24.1  302
60.6.6  304
60.8.2–3  303
66.7.2  76, 311
66.15.3–4  309
66.18.1  309
67.14.1–2  312
68.1.2  312
68.32   79, 241
69.8    79

**Dio Chrysostom,**
  *Oratio* 32  48

**Diodorus**
  book 1    45
1.17–18  129
1.53–58  129
1.55    129
1.83.8  46
2.14    129
17.52.5  30
17.52.6  66
19.85.3–4  22

34.1.1–5  248
34.1.2  436
34.1.3  427
40.3.4  33, 434,
        437

**Epictetus,** *Dissertations*
2.9.19–20  317

**Erotianus,** *fragment*
        434

**Herodotus**
  book 2    45
2.104   137, 438
3.17–25  129
7.6     217

**Homer,** *Iliad*
9.312—13  340
  *Odyssey*
6.182–85  340

**Horace,** *Sermones*
1.4.140–43  295–96
1.5.100–1  297
1.9.60–78  296

**Historia Augusta,**
  *Vita Hadriani*
5       79

**Isocrates,** *Panegyricus*
50      89

**Jordanes,** *Romana*
81      40

**Juvenal,** *Satires*
3       313
3.10–18  313
3.296   314
6.153–60  294, 314
6.157–60  436
6.160   146, 436
6.542   313
6.542–48  120, 314
14.96–106  307, 314
14.97   434
14.98–99  436

14.100–1    410, 425
14.100–2    314
14.101–2    427
14.103–4    314

**Macrobius,** *Saturnalia*
2.4.11    294, 436

**Malalas**
244.18–245.21 251
260.21–261.14 257

**Martial,** *Epigrams*
4.4    312
7.30.5    312
7.35.3–4    312, 324
7.55.7–8    310
7.82    313, 324
7.82.5–6    312
11.94    312, 318,
         324
12.57.13    314

**Ovid,** *Ars Amatoria*
1.75–76    296
1.76    417
1.413–16    296
1.415    296
1.416    417
*Remedia Amoris*
219–20    296
220    440

**Persius,** *Satire*
5.179–84    294
5.180–84    307

**Petronius,** *Satyricon*
102.14    438
fragment
37    307, 434,
      436

**Philostratus,**
*Vita Apollonii*
33    437

**Plato,** *Timaeus* 164

**Pliny**  13.46    431

**Plutarch,** *Cicero*
7.6    288
*De Superstitione*
8    441
*Lucullus*
2.3    234
7.6    265
*Moralia*
397a    216
*Isis and Osiris*
380f–381a    146
*Quaestiones Conviviales*
4.5    307, 436
4.6.2    416

**Polybius**
5.86.10    31
13.2.1    38

**Pompeius Trogus**
36.2.14    296, 440

**Quintilian,**
*Institutio Oratoria*
3.7.21    312

**Seneca,** *De Superstitione*
300, 307, 407
*Dialogues*
12.19.6    48
*Letter*
108.22    299

**Strabo**  *(apud Josephus)*
10, 39, 43, 49, 66,
232, 234, 407
*Geographica*
16.2.37    248
16.35    434

**Suetonius,**
*Iulius*
42.3    270, 291
84.5    291
*Augustus*
32.1    292
76.2    296
*Tiberius*
36    298
*Claudius*
25.4    303–4

**Nero**
16.2    304
40.2    226
*Vespasian*
6.3    106
*Domitian*
12.2    77, 311,
        323, 407,
        438

**Tacitus,** *Annals*
2.85.4    295, 298,
          323
12.54    302
13.32    307
15.28    106
15.44    283, 308
*Histories*
1.1    106
2.2.1    309
2.74    106
2.79    106
5.1–13    314, 362
5.3    363
5.4    307
5.4.1    314–15,
         407
5.4.2    46, 315,
         363
5.4.3    363, 416
5.4.4    297
5.5    363
5.5.1    315, 419
5.5.1–2    410
5.5.2    315, 411,
         436, 438
5.5.3    315, 339,
         363
5.5.3–4    363
5.5.4    434
5.5.5    316
5.12.2    315

**Theocritus,** *Idyll*
17    30

**Theognis**
183–90    340

**Tibullus**
1.3.15–18    297

**Valerius Maximus**

| | |
|---|---|
| 1.3.3 | 285, 333–4 |

**Early Christian Writings**

**New Testament**

*Matthew*

| | |
|---|---|
| 6.5 | 417 |

*Mark*

| | |
|---|---|
| 1.21–22 | 417 |
| 15.21 | 239 |

*Luke*

| | |
|---|---|
| 4.16ff. | 417 |

*Acts*

| | |
|---|---|
| 2.5–11 | 419 |
| 2.9–11 | 10, 260 |
| 2.10 | 239 |
| 4.36–37 | 254 |
| 6.5 | 253 |
| 6.9 | 239, 290, 419 |
| 6.9–11 | 279 |
| 9.1–22 | 384 |
| 10–11 | 326, 436 |
| 10.1–2 | 254 |
| 10.19–26 | 254 |
| 11.20 | 239 |
| 13.1 | 239, 254 |
| 13.6–12 | 332 |
| 13.16 | 279 |
| 13.42 | 417 |
| 13.48–50 | 279 |
| 13.50 | 279 |
| 14.1 | 279 |
| 14.2 | 279 |
| 15 | 326, 436 |
| 15.20 | 434 |
| 15.21 | 417, 427 |
| 15.29 | 434 |
| 16.1–3 | 324 |
| 16.14 | 279 |
| 16.37 | 328 |
| 17 | 391 |
| 17.2 | 417 |
| 17.4 | 279 |

| | |
|---|---|
| 17.12 | 279 |
| 17.28 | 391 |
| 18.2 | 283, 303, 306 |
| 18.2–3 | 423 |
| 18.3 | 383 |
| 18.4 | 417 |
| 18.24 | 383 |
| 19.8–10 | 279 |
| 19.11–17 | 332 |
| 19.13 | 122 |
| 19.23–41 | 274 |
| 19.33–34 | 279 |
| 21.17–36 | 279 |
| 21.21 | 395 |
| 21.39 | 70, 272, 327, 381, 382 |
| 22.2 | 382 |
| 22.3 | 381, 383, 384 |
| 22.3–21 | 384 |
| 26.2–23 | 384 |
| 28.17–28 | 283 |

*Romans*

| | |
|---|---|
| 1 | 391 |
| 1–2 | 391, 392 |
| 1–3 | 392 |
| 1.15 | 384 |
| 1.18–22 | 391 |
| 1.18–32 | 385, 388, 392, 433 |
| 1.23 | 391 |
| 2 | 392 |
| 2.12–16 | 391 |
| 2.17–24 | 387 |
| 2.20 | 413 |
| 2.25–29 | 386, 388 |
| 2.27 | 392 |
| 2.29 | 386 |
| 3.29 | 388 |
| 4 | 387, 389 |
| 4.1 | 389 |
| 4.17–20 | 210 |
| 5.12–21 | 392 |
| 5.18 | 392 |
| 7.1–6 | 387 |
| 7.7–8.4 | 387 |
| 7.12 | 387 |
| 7.14 | 387 |

| | |
|---|---|
| 9–11 | 386, 389, 395 |
| 9.1–5 | 283, 382, 406 |
| 9.24 | 388 |
| 10.4 | 387 |
| 11 | 394 |
| 11.1 | 394, 406 |
| 11.13 | 384, 388 |
| 11.17–24 | 283, 389 |
| 11.28 | 406 |
| 11.32 | 392 |
| 14–15 | 283, 317, 326, 385, 435, 436 |
| 14 | 385, 387 |
| 14.1–2 | 283, 386, 435 |
| 14.5–6 | 283, 386 |
| 14.14 | 384 |
| 14.17 | 386 |
| 15.25–33 | 386 |
| 15.27 | 388 |
| 16.3 | 283, 306 |
| 16.3–16 | 283 |
| 16.4 | 388 |
| 16.7 | 283 |
| 16.11 | 283 |
| 16.16 | 385 |

*1 Corinthians*

| | |
|---|---|
| 1–2 | 383 |
| 1–4 | 390 |
| 1.2 | 388 |
| 1.18 | 391 |
| 1.18–25 | 391 |
| 1.23 | 388 |
| 2.6–16 | 391 |
| 2.9 | 388 |
| 3.9–17 | 389 |
| 3.16–17 | 386 |
| 4.12 | 383 |
| 5.1 | 388 |
| 5.5 | 391 |
| 6.19 | 389 |
| 6.19–20 | 386 |
| 7.18–19 | 386, 388 |
| 7.25–31 | 390 |
| 7.39 | 385 |
| 8–10 | 385 |
| 8.9 | 385 |

| 9 | 390 |
| 9.9–11 | 391 |
| 9.19–23 | 384 |
| 9.21 | 384 |
| 10.1 | 389 |
| 10.14–22 | 385 |
| 10.18 | 386 |
| 10.23–33 | 385 |
| 10.32 | 386 |
| 12.2 | 388, 391 |
| 15.20–22 | 392 |
| 15.20–28 | 390 |
| 15.33 | 383 |
| 15.35–58 | 390 |
| 16.2 | 395 |
| 16.8 | 395 |
| 16.20 | 385 |

*2 Corinthians*
| 3.13–16 | 386 |
| 3.15 | 386 |
| 4.4 | 391 |
| 6.16 | 386 |
| 8–9 | 386 |
| 10–13 | 383 |
| 11.6 | 383 |
| 11.22 | 382, 394 |
| 11.24 | 394 |
| 11.26 | 388, 394 |

*Galatians*
| 1.10 | 384 |
| 1.13 | 384 |
| 1.13–14 | 394, 410 |
| 1.14 | 383, 410 |
| 1.15–17 | 384 |
| 1.16 | 384 |
| 2.1–3 | 385 |
| 2.7–9 | 388 |
| 2.10 | 386 |
| 2.11–14 | 254, 326, 384, 436 |
| 2.11–21 | 436 |
| 2.12 | 388 |
| 2.14 | 386, 388 |
| 2.15 | 388 |
| 3 | 387 |
| 3.6–29 | 389 |
| 3.28 | 385 |
| 4.1–8 | 389 |
| 4.8–10 | 391 |

| 4.10 | 415, 416 |
| 4.21–31 | 389, 391 |
| 4.21–5.12 | 382 |
| 4.29 | 394 |
| 5.2–12 | 386 |
| 5.3 | 439 |
| 5.11 | 394 |
| 6.10 | 386 |
| 6.12 | 394 |
| 6.16 | 389 |

*Philippians*
| 1.28 | 393 |
| 2.15 | 388, 389 |
| 3.2–11 | 382, 394 |
| 3.3 | 386, 389 |
| 3.5 | 382, 383 |
| 3.6 | 384 |
| 3.20 | 393 |
| 4.8 | 391 |
| 4.10–19 | 390 |
| 4.11–12 | 383 |

*Colossians*
| 2.16 | 415, 416 |

*1 Thessalonians*
| 2.15–16 | 394 |
| 4.5 | 388 |
| 4.13–5.10 | 390 |

*Philemon*
| 10–12 | 385 |

*Revelation*
| 2.9 | 279 |
| 3.9 | 279 |
| 18 | 227 |

**Other Christian Writings**

Augustine,
*De Civitate Dei*
| 6.11 | 300, 307, 407, 426 |

Clement, *Stromata*
| 5.14.113.2 | 342 |

*1 Clement* 283

*Epistle to Diognetus*
| 4.5 | 415 |
| 4.12 | 415 |

Eusebius,
*Hist Eccles*
| 4.2 | 79, 80, 81, 241 |
| 4.2–3 | 79 |
| 7.32.16–18 | 445 |
| 32.16–18 | 150 |
*Praep Evang*
| 8.7.1–9 | 339 |
| 8.10.1–17 | 150, 445 |
| book 9 | 126 |
| 9.17 | 151 |
| 9.18.1 | 446 |
| 9.19.1–13 | 272 |
| 9.22.1–11 | 411 |
| 9.23.1–4 | 446 |
| 9.26.1 | 151 |
| 9.27.1–37 | 446 |
| 9.28 | 446 |
| 9.28.1 | 133 |
| 9.29 | 446 |
| 9.29.1 | 138, 411 |
| 13.12.1–2 | 150, 445 |
| 13.12.3–8 | 150, 445 |
| 13.12.9–16 | 150, 445 |

Ignatius, *Magnesians*
| 8.1 | 280 |
| 9.1–2 | 280 |
| 10.3 | 280 |
*Philadephians*
| 6.1 | 280 |
| 6.2 | 280 |

Jerome, *De Viris Illustribus*
| 11 | 165 |

Origen, *Contra Celsum*
| 1.26 | 120 |

Orosius, *Adversus Paganos*
| 7.6.15–16 | 304 |
| 7.12 | 79 |

# Index of Modern Authors

Abel, E. L. 21, 300
Albright, W. F. 31
Alessandri, S. 286
Alexander, P. S. 119, 122, 332
Amaru, B. H. 359
Amir, Y. 88, 107, 410, 426
Anderson, H. 195, 198, 370, 375, 378, 448, 449
Applebaum, S. 7, 78, 79, 232, 233, 234, 235, 237, 239, 241, 316, 414
Aptowitzer, V. 204, 447
Attridge, H. 157, 351, 356, 357, 359
Aune, D. E. 86, 120
Aziza, C. 34

Baldwin Bowsky, M. W. 238
Balsdon, J. P. V. D. 54, 297
Barclay, J. M. G. 85, 86, 106, 129, 283, 385, 389, 390, 393, 439
Barnes, T. D. 78, 80
Barraclough, R. 67
Barrett, C. K. 382
Barth, F. 92
Bartlett, J. R. 148
Bassler, J. 107, 171
Battifol, P. 447
Bauckham, R. 401
Becker, H. S. 85
Bell, H. I. 58, 63
Benko, S. 304
Bernays, J. 5, 337, 341-42, 343, 344
Betz, H. D. 119
Bevan, E. 38
Bickerman, E. 6, 23, 24, 25, 30, 35, 49, 98, 126, 152, 246, 247, 248, 249, 261, 263, 432, 445, 448, 449
Bilde, P. 349
Blau, L. 119, 122
Boccaccini, G. 9, 144, 145, 148
Bohak, G. 46
Bonner, C. 122
Bonz, M. P. 280
Borgen, P. 114, 178
Bornkamm, G. 382
Bousset, W. 158
Bowman, A. K. 44, 45, 112

Box, H. 43, 48, 54, 60, 63, 67, 69
Boyarin, D. 14, 390
Braun, H. 34, 129, 130
Braund, D. 234
Breitenstein, U. 369, 370, 371, 373, 449
Brooten, B. J. 416
Brown, P. 121
Bruce, F. F. 305
Bruce, I. A. F. 311
Burchard, C. 204, 205, 206, 211, 212, 447
Burr, V. 105, 106

Chadwick, H. 164, 165
Charlesworth, J. H. 7
Chesnutt, R. D. 204, 211, 215, 447
Classen, C. J. 383
Cohen, J. 448
Cohen, S. J. D. 9, 62, 89, 308, 313, 324, 329, 333, 349, 360, 403, 410, 412, 414, 429, 438, 448
Collins, A. Y. 154, 446
Collins, J. J. 8, 126, 128, 129, 130, 131, 132, 137, 138, 148, 149, 156, 157, 183, 184, 190, 197, 200, 203, 210, 214, 218, 219, 222, 223, 224, 225, 226, 259, 341, 381, 401, 439, 443, 445, 446, 447, 448, 449, 450, 451
Colson, F. H. 62, 105, 297
Courtney, E. 313, 314
Cowley, A. E. 34
Crook, J. 309
Crouch, J. E. 340
Cumont, F. 285, 333

Dalbert, P. 137, 148
Daniélou, J. 109
Davies, W. D. 381
Davis, S. 59, 64
Dawson, D. 154, 156, 173, 178
de Jonge, M. 354
Deissmann, A. 122, 280
Delia, D. 50, 62, 68
Delling, G. 207, 429

518

Derron, P.   337, 338, 346, 450
Dibelius, M.   391
Dillon, J.   164
Doran, R.   233
Douglas, R. C.   214
Downey, G.   245, 250, 251, 257
Droge, A. J.   128
Dunn, J. D. G.   384, 387, 389, 402
Dupont-Sommer, A.   369, 370, 371, 373, 449

Ellman, Y.   411
Engberg-Pedersen, T.   391
Engers, M.   63
Esler, P. F.   436
Ewald, H.   203, 448

Fascher, E.   432
Fasola, U. M.   284
Feldman, L. H.   9, 57, 84-87, 90, 114, 122, 294, 329, 353, 358, 408, 428, 448
Fischer, U.   340, 341, 374
Focke, F.   109, 191
Frankfurter, D.   80, 81
Fraser, P. M.   28, 29, 31, 32, 34, 40, 42, 45, 127, 218, 222, 445, 446
Frerichs, E. S.   9
Freudenthal, J.   126, 127, 132, 298, 369, 370
Frey, J. -B.   5, 7, 100, 283, 284, 316, 318, 330, 333
Friedländer, M.   110, 145, 148
Fuchs, H.   227
Fuks, A.   5, 19, 25, 68, 77, 79, 106, 241
Fuks, G.   290

Gabba, E.   33, 248
Gager, J. G.   9, 33, 120, 426, 427, 428
Gallas, S.   394
Gauger, J. -D.   261
Geertz, C.   91
Geffcken, J.   5, 217, 218, 219, 225, 259, 450
Georgi, D.   182, 451
Gilbert, M.   186
Goldstein, J.   89
Gooch, P. D.   435

Goodenough, E. R.   5, 6, 43, 83, 120, 122, 123, 138, 162, 163, 165, 174, 178, 330, 381, 413
Gooding, D. W.   139
Goodman, M.   9, 77, 257, 286, 318, 404, 408, 418, 435
Goudriaan, K.   9, 44, 72, 92, 175
Grabbe, L. L.   6, 86, 88, 98, 246
Green, H. A.   107
Griffith, G. T.   88
Griffiths, J. G.   25, 26
Griggs, C. W.   107
Grimm, C. L. W.   109, 182, 191, 198, 203, 369, 370, 379, 448
Guterman, S. L.   292

Hadas, M.   148, 194, 198, 201, 370, 371, 375, 378, 445, 448, 449
Hadas-Lebel, M.   105, 450
Haenchen, E.   279
Halbertal, M.   430
Harnack, A.   4
Harris, H. A.   59, 160, 161
Harvey, A. E.   394
Hay, D. M.   110, 158
Hays, R. B.   389
Healy, J. F.   239
Hegermann, H.   420
Heinemann, I.   5, 35, 132, 375
Heininger, B.   375
Hengel, M.   6, 26, 80, 83, 89, 132, 153, 156, 227, 233, 241, 244, 260, 272, 285, 341, 381, 382, 383, 384, 446
Hennig, D.   301
Herman, S. N.   400
Highet, G.   313
Hock, R. F.   383
Holladay, C. R.   7, 128, 130, 131, 132, 136, 137, 446, 447
Hollis, A. S.   297
Holtz, T.   204
Honigman, S.   24
Horbury, W.   7, 19, 23, 24, 26, 27, 29, 31, 32, 36, 39, 42, 78, 79, 80, 100, 111, 124, 135, 294, 394, 407, 423
Horsley, G. H. R.   100, 237, 284
Hull, J. M.   119

Jacobson, H.   7, 133, 134, 135, 136, 137, 138, 446, 447

Jacoby, F.   33
Janne, H.   305
Jeremias, J.   419
Jewett, R.   303, 381, 449
Johnson, A. C.   77
Jones, A. H. M.   249
Jones, H. S.   59
Juster, J.   4, 5, 63, 261, 264, 268, 278, 292, 295, 414

Kamlah, E.   367
Kasher, A.   8, 23, 25, 36, 37, 41, 50, 58, 59, 62, 63, 64, 65, 69, 71, 80, 195, 200, 245, 246, 247, 255, 256
Kee, H. C.   120, 212, 214, 215
Keresztes, P.   312
Klauck, H. -J.   369, 370, 371, 374, 378-79, 449
Kolarcik, M.   182, 185
Knox, W. L.   156
Kraabel, A. T.   7, 9, 259, 279, 280, 284, 333
Kraeling, C. H.   233, 239, 245, 250, 251, 257, 258
Kraemer, R. S.   100, 204, 325, 330, 335, 403, 416
Kraft, R. A.   5
Krauss, S.   245
Kroll, W.   341
Küchler, M.   340
Kuhrt, A.   88
Kuiper, K.   134
Kümmel, W. G.   7, 449

La Piana, G.   290
Lafargue, M.   157
Lampe, P.   283, 303, 312, 316
Lane, E. N.   285
Lane Fox, R.   120, 274
Laqueur, R.   351
Larcher, C.   109, 182, 183, 186, 191, 451, 452
Lauer, S.   373
Lebram, J. C. H.   371
Lentz, J. C.   382
Leon, H. J.   8, 283, 286, 287, 290, 293, 295, 303, 305, 306, 316, 318, 325, 330
Levine, L. I.   250, 252, 253, 258
Levinskaya, I.   8, 259

Levy, I.   40
Lewis, D. M.   25, 77
Lewis, N.   25, 44, 45, 77
Lieu, J.   9
Lindner, H.   354
Litfin, D.   383
Llewelyn, S. R.   23
Lloyd, J.   234, 236, 237
Lüdemann, G.   303, 305, 395, 449
Lüderitz, G.   7, 8, 25, 26, 44, 64, 65, 232, 234, 235, 236, 237, 238, 239, 328, 407, 409, 414, 415, 416, 425

McEleney, N. J.   86
McKay, H. A.   416-17
McKnight, S.   9, 408
MacMullen, R.   121, 226, 290
Maccoby, H.   390
Magie, D.   260, 265, 267, 269, 274, 279
Malherbe, A. J.   383, 390, 391
Marcus, J.   317
Marcus, R.   126, 245, 261
Margalioth, M.   119
Margalit, A.   430
Marshall, A. J.   266, 267, 286
Mason, S.   21, 348, 350
Mattingly, H.   311
Meecham, H. G.   148, 445
Meeks, W. A.   137, 245, 254, 258, 386, 428
Meisner, N.   144, 145
Mendelson, A.   114, 160
Merkelbach, R.   206
Merrill, E. T.   300
Millar, F.   249, 269
Mitchell, S.   266, 273, 279, 280
Modrzejewski, J. M.   8, 19, 20, 21, 25, 30, 32, 36, 46, 72, 81, 85, 104, 116
Moehring, H. R.   261, 262, 263, 299, 360
Momigliano, A.   6, 57, 59, 219, 223, 261, 304, 305, 306
Mor, M   96
Morgan, M. A.   119
Morkholm, O.   104
Morris, J.   160
Murray, O.   140, 445
Mussies, G.   129
Musurillo, H. A.   72

Newbold, R. F.   298
Nickelsburg, G. W. E.   5
Niebuhr, K. -W.   339, 340, 345, 394
Niehoff, M.   358
Niese, B.   234, 262, 355, 447
Nikiprowetzky, V.   164, 218, 219, 224, 450
Nock, A. D.   120, 122, 207
Nolland, J.   220, 223, 296
Norden, E.   383
North, J.   9, 286
Noy, D.   7, 19, 23, 24, 26, 27, 29, 32, 36, 42, 100, 111, 124, 282, 284, 326, 332, 407

Parke, H. W.   216, 217, 224
Paul, A.   194, 202
Pearson, B. A.   107
Pelletier, A.   145
Penna, R.   284, 295
Pfitzner, V. C.   375
Philonenko, M.   204, 210, 212, 215, 447
Pohlenz, M.   391
Porten, B.   20, 34
Preisendanz, K.   119
Pucci (ben Ze'ev), M.   33, 78

Radice, R.   450
Radin, M.   59, 300, 304
Rahlfs, A.   448
Räisänen, H.   345, 387
Rajak, T.   9, 129, 262, 263, 274, 276, 278, 284, 312, 334, 347, 348, 349, 350, 351, 353, 356, 362, 408, 448
Rappaport, U.   255
Redditt, P. L.   378, 379
Reese, J. M.   182, 183, 184, 186, 191
Reinach, T.   7, 266
Rémondon, R.   46
Renehan, R.   371
Rex, J.   402
Reynolds, J. M.   7, 232, 234, 236, 237, 259, 279, 403
Riaud, J.   118
Robert, L.   237, 271
Robertson, R. G.   446
Roddaz, J-M.   277
Rogers, G. M.   274
Romanelli, P.   234, 239

Rostovtzeff, M.   32
Runia, D. T.   164, 450
Rutgers, L. V.   8, 284, 318, 330, 331
Rzach, A.   218, 225

Sacks, J.   444
Safrai, S.   412, 420
Samuel, A. E.   44, 45
Sandbach, F. H.   153
Sanders, E. P.   6, 237, 268, 381, 384, 387, 392, 394, 395, 401, 402, 415, 419, 420, 434, 435, 443
Sanders, J. T.   279, 312, 333
Sandmel, S.   6, 91, 170, 177, 382
Sänger, D.   210, 211, 447
Saulnier, C.   263, 268
Scaliger, J. J.   337
Schalit, A.   261
Schäublin, Ch.   365, 366
Schreckenberg, H.   448
Schürer, E.   5, 6, 11, 29, 33, 36, 63, 65, 68, 73, 118, 119, 122, 131, 157, 160, 218, 233, 235, 247, 250, 251, 259, 260, 261, 264, 271, 279, 280, 288, 295, 305, 316, 321, 322, 328, 332, 337, 375, 414, 445, 446, 448, 449, 450, 451, 452
Schwartz, D.   177, 403
Schwartz, J.   160
Schwartz, S.   358, 448
Scramuzza, V. M.   306
Seager, A. R.   7, 259
Sebestyén, K.   344
Seeberg, A.   345
Segal, A. F.   9, 381, 384, 395
Sevenster, J. N.   391
Sharot, S.   92
Sherwin-White, A. N.   314, 316
Sherwin-White, S.   88
Shutt, R. J. H.   143, 356, 445
Siegel, B. J.   92
Siegert, F.   403
Silver, J. D.   132
Simon, M.   6, 120, 122, 222, 280, 285
Slingerland, D.   305, 306
Smallwood, E. M.   6, 25, 43, 49, 52, 54, 55, 60, 62, 63, 64, 65, 67, 68, 69, 76, 77, 78, 113, 241, 251, 256, 258, 262, 263, 267, 271, 272, 275, 278, 286, 289, 290, 292, 300, 301,

305, 306, 308, 309, 311, 312, 313, 321, 323, 333
Smith, J. Z.　4
Smith, M.　89
Solin, M.　284, 295, 300, 301, 304, 316, 318, 333
Stambaugh, J. E.　287, 295
Stein, E.　154, 157, 158
Sterling, G. E.　126, 128, 129, 130, 356, 446
Stern, M.　4, 7, 29, 72, 73, 248, 254, 260, 286, 296, 297, 298, 300, 305, 307, 438
Sullivan, J. P.　313
Swete, H. B.　445

Tajra, H. W.　292, 382
Tannenbaum, R.　7, 259, 279, 403
Tarn, W. W.　88, 271
Tatum, W. B.　433
Tcherikover, V.　4, 5, 19, 20, 22, 23, 24, 25, 26, 27, 28, 29, 30, 31, 33, 34, 35, 36, 37, 38, 40, 42, 43, 49, 50, 51, 57, 59, 60, 62, 64, 65, 67, 68, 69, 72, 74, 76, 77, 78, 79, 81, 89, 113, 115, 116, 123-24, 147, 148, 149, 150, 194, 195, 198, 200, 201, 202, 233, 245, 256, 260, 261, 264, 308, 322, 448
Terian, A.　105, 179, 450
Thackeray, H. St. J.　348, 351, 445, 447
Theissen, G.　248
Thompson, D. J.　25, 29, 77, 112
Thompson, L. A.　77, 311, 312
Thornton, J. C. G.　415
Tiede, D. L.　129, 131
Tomson, P. J.　9
Tracey, R.　237
Tracey, S.　201
Trachtenberg, J.　119
Trebilco, P.　9, 70, 259, 261, 264, 267, 271, 279, 280, 281, 285, 326, 327, 328, 332, 333
Turner, E. G.　106

Urbach, E. E.　121

van der Horst, P. W.　7, 42, 73, 137, 236, 337, 338, 339, 340, 341, 344, 345-46, 450

van Henten, J. W.　7, 370, 371, 449
van Unnik, W. C.　325, 384, 422, 437
Vermes, G.　132
Vielhauer, P.　382
Vogelstein, H.　286, 290, 295, 313
von Stauffenberg, A. S.　251

Walbank, F. W.　32, 44, 45, 88
Walsh, P.　206, 215
Walter, N.　128, 131, 151, 152, 153, 154, 155, 157, 345, 446, 450
Wardman, A.　289, 292
Wardy, B.　288, 316
Watson, F.　386
Wedderburn, A. J. M.　390
Weisengoff, J. P.　109
Wendland, P.　340, 345, 445, 449
West, S.　205, 215, 447
Westerholm, S.　21, 387
Westermann, W. L.　21
Whitman, J.　154
Whittaker, M.　436, 439, 440
Wiefel, W.　284
Wilcken, U.　63
Wilken, R. L.　245, 254, 258
Williams, M. H.　284, 298, 300, 308, 311, 312, 316
Willrich, H.　5, 38, 40, 48, 52, 54, 57, 63, 203, 266, 448
Wilson, S. G.　416
Wilson, W. T.　337, 338, 341, 344, 345, 450
Winston, D.　182, 186, 190, 191, 451, 452
Wolfson, H. A.　6, 67, 84, 107, 110, 160, 164, 173
Wright, A. G.　182
Wright, N. T.　7, 402

Yarbrough, O. L.　412
Yavetz, Z.　292, 410
Young, D.　450

Ziegler, J.　451
Ziener, G.　190
Zuckerman, C.　64, 65
Zuntz, G.　140